Handbook of
Alternative Assets

Second Edition

THE FRANK J. FABOZZI SERIES

Fixed Income Securities, Second Edition by Frank J. Fabozzi
Focus on Value: A Corporate and Investor Guide to Wealth Creation by James L. Grant and James A. Abate
Handbook of Global Fixed Income Calculations by Dragomir Krgin
Managing a Corporate Bond Portfolio by Leland E. Crabbe and Frank J. Fabozzi
Real Options and Option-Embedded Securities by William T. Moore
Capital Budgeting: Theory and Practice by Pamela P. Peterson and Frank J. Fabozzi
The Exchange-Traded Funds Manual by Gary L. Gastineau
Professional Perspectives on Fixed Income Portfolio Management, Volume 3 edited by Frank J. Fabozzi
Investing in Emerging Fixed Income Markets edited by Frank J. Fabozzi and Efstathia Pilarinu
Handbook of Alternative Assets by Mark J. P. Anson
The Exchange-Traded Funds Manual by Gary L. Gastineau
The Global Money Markets by Frank J. Fabozzi, Steven V. Mann, and Moorad Choudhry
The Handbook of Financial Instruments edited by Frank J. Fabozzi
Collateralized Debt Obligations: Structures and Analysis by Laurie S. Goodman and Frank J. Fabozzi
Interest Rate, Term Structure, and Valuation Modeling edited by Frank J. Fabozzi
Investment Performance Measurement by Bruce J. Feibel
The Handbook of Equity Style Management edited by T. Daniel Coggin and Frank J. Fabozzi
The Theory and Practice of Investment Management edited by Frank J. Fabozzi and Harry M. Markowitz
Foundations of Economic Value Added: Second Edition by James L. Grant
Financial Management and Analysis: Second Edition by Frank J. Fabozzi and Pamela P. Peterson
Measuring and Controlling Interest Rate and Credit Risk: Second Edition by Frank J. Fabozzi, Steven V. Mann, and Moorad Choudhry
Professional Perspectives on Fixed Income Portfolio Management, Volume 4 edited by Frank J. Fabozzi
The Handbook of European Fixed Income Securities edited by Frank J. Fabozzi and Moorad Choudhry
The Handbook of European Structured Financial Products edited by Frank J. Fabozzi and Moorad Choudhry
The Mathematics of Financial Modeling and Investment Management by Sergio M. Focardi and Frank J. Fabozzi
Short Selling: Strategies, Risks, and Rewards edited by Frank J. Fabozzi
The Real Estate Investment Handbook by G. Timothy Haight and Daniel Singer
Market Neutral Strategies edited by Bruce I. Jacobs and Kenneth N. Levy
Securities Finance: Securities Lending and Repurchase Agreements edited by Frank J. Fabozzi and Steven V. Mann
Fat-Tailed and Skewed Asset Return Distributions by Svetlozar T. Rachev, Christian Menn, and Frank J. Fabozzi
Financial Modeling of the Equity Market: From CAPM to Cointegration by Frank J. Fabozzi, Sergio M. Focardi, and Petter N. Kolm
Advanced Bond Portfolio Management: Best Practices in Modeling and Strategies edited by Frank J. Fabozzi, Lionel Martellini, and Philippe Priaulet
Analysis of Financial Statements, Second Edition by Pamela P. Peterson and Frank J. Fabozzi
Collateralized Debt Obligations: Structures and Analysis, Second Edition by Douglas J. Lucas, Laurie S. Goodman, and Frank J. Fabozzi

Handbook of
Alternative Assets

Second Edition

MARK J. P. ANSON

WILEY
John Wiley & Sons, Inc.

ISBN-13: 978-0-471-98020-9
ISBN-10: 0-471-98020-X

Printed in the United States of America.

10 9 8 7 6

Contents

Preface ix

About the Author xi

PART ONE

Overview of Alternative Assets 1

CHAPTER 1
What Is an Alternative Asset Class? 3

CHAPTER 2
Why Alternative Assets Are Important: Beta Drivers and Alpha Drivers 15

PART TWO

Hedge Funds 29

CHAPTER 3
Introduction to Hedge Funds 31

CHAPTER 4
Establishing a Hedge Fund Investment Program 71

CHAPTER 5
Due Diligence for Hedge Fund Managers 97

CHAPTER 6
Risk Management Part I: Hedge Fund Return Distributions 135

CHAPTER 7
Risk Management Part II: Additional Hedge Fund Risks 169

CHAPTER 8
Regulation of Hedge Funds   **203**

CHAPTER 9
Hedge Fund Benchmarks and Asset Allocation   **229**

CHAPTER 10
Hedge Fund Incentive Fees and the "Free Option"   **251**

CHAPTER 11
Top Ten Hedge Fund Quotes   **265**

PART THREE

Commodities and Managed Futures   **275**

CHAPTER 12
Introduction to Commodities   **277**

CHAPTER 13
Investing in Commodity Futures   **305**

CHAPTER 14
Commodity Futures in a Portfolio Context   **333**

CHAPTER 15
Managed Futures   **353**

PART FOUR

Private Equity   **377**

CHAPTER 16
Introduction to Venture Capital   **379**

CHAPTER 17
Introduction to Leveraged Buyouts   **419**

CHAPTER 18
Debt as Private Equity Part I: Mezzanine Debt   **455**

CHAPTER 19
Debt as Private Equity Part II: Distressed Debt 477

CHAPTER 20
The Economics of Private Equity 501

CHAPTER 21
Performance Measurement for Private Equity 523

CHAPTER 22
Trends in Private Equity 553

PART FIVE

Credit Derivatives 577

CHAPTER 23
Introduction to Credit Derivatives 579

CHAPTER 24
Collateralized Debt Obligations 609

CHAPTER 25
Collateralized Fund Obligations: Intersection of
Credit Derivative Market and Hedge Fund World 653

PART SIX

Corporate Governance 667

CHAPTER 26
Corporate Governance as an Alternative Investment Strategy 669

INDEX 695

Preface

When my editor, Frank Fabozzi, suggested that it was time to write a new edition of *The Handbook of Alternative Assets*, I wondered: Has it really been that long since the first edition? Then, I realized that it had been four years since the first edition had been released. The intervening time period from 2002 to 2006 was one filled with different macroeconomic effects compared to the first edition of this book. Most of my data analysis in the first edition had been conducted during a period of robust economic growth—through calendar year 2000. However, the second edition allowed me to analyze the merits of alternative assets during a different part of the economic cycle. During this time period, a worldwide economic recession reigned from 2001 to 2002, the technology bubble burst, massive accounting scandals rocked the U.S. financial markets, and a three-year bear market depressed equity prices around the globe.

Furthermore, in those intervening four years there have been significant changes in the world of alternative assets, as inflows into alternative investments initially shrunk from 2001 to 2003 and then roared back to life in 2004 and 2005, leading to massive inflows into hedge funds, private equity, credit derivatives, corporate governance, and commodities. As a result, my exposure to, and my knowledge base associated with, alternative investments have increased significantly. Enough so that a second book on the subject was indeed timely.

So, for the reader, you will find that I wrote every chapter from a fresh start, with all new tables, charts, data analysis, equations, explanations and the like. New chapters were added, different data sources were accessed, and new conclusions were reached. The results of these efforts are reflected in the length of this book. At 700 pages, this book is more than 200 pages longer than the first edition. This reflects not only my effort to start anew on the subject but also the growth of the alternative asset universe.

As in the first edition, my goal is to educate the reader and not dazzle him or her with my grasp of technical and arcane alternative asset jargon. This book is designed both to introduce the reader to the alternative asset universe as well to be used as a reference for the active investor in alternative assets. To that effect the reader will find that some chapters are more descriptive in nature to provide introductory material while other chapters are more empirical in nature to provide concrete examples and conclusions about the risks and benefits of using alternative assets.

As before, I hope that this book will stimulate readers to think critically about alternative assets, to question my conclusions, and to pose questions of their own. If so, I will count this book as a great success.

Last, this book reflects my individual insights and opinions and not those of my current employers, the British Telecom Pension Scheme and Hermes Pensions Management Ltd., or my former employer, the California Public Employees' Retirement System.

About the Author

Mark Anson has the unusual role of being both the Chief Executive Officer of the British Telecommunications Pension Scheme (BTPS) as well as the Chief Executive Officer of Hermes Pensions Management Ltd. At over £34 billion (approximately $61 billion), the BTPS is the largest pension fund in the United Kingdom, and at £65 billion (approximately $117 billion) assets under management, Hermes is one of the largest asset managers in the City of London. By wearing two very different hats, Mark has the perspective of both an end user of investment products as well as a product developer for the asset management industry.

At BTPS, Mark has full authority for every asset class in which the pension fund invests, including domestic and international equity, net zero equity products, Gilts, inflation linked bonds, high-yield bonds, credit default swaps, CDOs, real estate, corporate governance, commodities, securities lending, venture capital, leveraged buyouts, and hedge funds. At Hermes, Mark oversees a staff of 300 with annual revenues of over £75 million.

As the Chief Investment Officer at CalPERS, Mark had full responsibility for all asset classes in which CalPERS invested as well as the strategic plan for CalPERS' Investment Office including tactical asset allocation, risk management, business development, budget authority, new investment programs, trading technology, staffing, and back office operations. His responsibilities included an operating budget of $410 million and the generation of $7 billion in annual benefit payments. While at CalPERS, Mark oversaw the increase in fund value from $127 billion to $205 billion. In addition, he implemented the concept of separating beta from alpha and he was directly responsible for the generation of over $9 billion of excess returns.

Mark received a scholarship to attend the Northwestern University School of Law in Chicago where he received his law degree and graduated with honors as the Executive/Production Editor of the *Northwestern University Law Review*. Mark also received a scholarship to attend the Columbia University Graduate School of Business in New York City where he received both his Ph.D. and Masters in Finance, again with honors, as *Beta Gamma Sigma*. Mark graduated *With Distinction* from

St. Olaf College in Minnesota with a double major in Economics and Chemistry. Mark has also been honored with the *Distinguished Scholar Award* from the Institute of International Education and the Fulbright Foundation as well as the 2004 *Best Paper* award from the *Journal of Portfolio Management.*

Mark is a member of the New York and Illinois State Bar Associations. He has also earned the Chartered Financial Analyst, Chartered Alternative Investment Analyst, Certified Public Accountant, Certified Management Accountant, and Certified Internal Auditor professional degrees. Last, Mark has received the Series 3, 4, 7, 8, 24, and 63 NASD securities industry licenses.

In addition to the *Handbook of Alternative Assets*, Mark has published three other financial textbooks as well as over 80 research articles on the topics of separating beta from alpha, business models for the asset management industry, corporate governance, hedge funds, real estate, currency overlay, credit risk, private equity, risk management, and asset allocation. Mark is often the keynote speaker at investment conferences around the world on these topics. Furthermore, Mark sits on editorial and advisory boards for *The Journal of Portfolio Management, The Journal of Alternative Investments, The Journal of Private Equity, The Journal of Investment Consulting,* and *The Journal of Derivatives Accounting.*

Mark has served on Advisory and Executive Committees for the New York Stock Exchange, Euronext, MSCI-Barra International Indexes, the International Association of Financial Engineers, The International Corporate Governance Network, The CFA Institute's Task Force on Corporate Governance, The CFA Institute's Committee on Global Investment Performance Standards, The Chartered Alternative Investment Analyst Education Committee, The Professional Risk Managers' International Association Education Committee, The Conference Board Commission on Public Trust, The Center for Excellence in Accounting and Security Analysis at Columbia University, and the National Association of State Investment Officers.

Overview of
Alternative Assets

What Is an Alternative Asset Class?

Part of the difficulty of working with alternative asset classes is defining them. Are they a separate asset class or a subset of an existing asset class? Do they hedge the investment opportunity set or expand it? Are they listed on an exchange or do they trade in the over the counter market?

In most cases, alternative assets are a subset of an existing asset class. This may run contrary to the popular view that alternative assets are separate asset classes.[1] However, we take the view that what many consider separate "classes" are really just different investment strategies within an existing asset class.

In most cases, they expand the investment opportunity set, rather than hedge it. Finally, alternative assets are generally purchased in the private markets, outside of any exchange. While hedge funds, private equity, and credit derivatives meet these criteria, we will see that commodity futures prove to be the exception to these general rules.

Alternative assets, then, are just alternative investments within an existing asset class. Specifically, most alternative assets derive their value from either the debt or equity markets. For instance, most hedge fund strategies involve the purchase and sale of either equity or debt securities. Additionally, hedge fund managers may invest in derivative instruments whose value is derived from the equity or debt markets.

In this book, we classify five types of alternative assets: hedge funds, commodity and managed futures, private equity, credit derivatives, and corporate governance. Hedge funds and private equity are the best

---

[1] See, for example, Chapter 8 in David Swensen, *Pioneering Portfolio Management* (New York: The Free Press, 2000).

known of the alternative asset world. Typically these investments are accomplished through the purchase of limited partner units in a private limited partnership. Commodity futures can be either passive investing tied to a commodity futures index, or active investing through a commodity pool or advisory account. Private equity is the investment strategy of investing in companies before they issue their securities publicly, or taking a public company private. Credit derivatives can be purchased through limited partnership units, as a tranche of a special purpose vehicle, or directly through the purchase of credit default swaps or credit options. Corporate governance is also a form of shareholder activism designed to improve the internal controls of a public company.

We will explore each one of these alternative asset classes in detail, providing practical advice along with useful research. We begin this chapter with a review of *super* asset classes.

SUPER ASSET CLASSES

There are three *super* asset classes: capital assets, assets that are used as inputs to creating economic value, and assets that are a store of value.[2]

Capital Assets

Capital assets are defined by their claim on the future cash flows of an enterprise. They provide a source of ongoing value. As a result, capital assets may be valued based on the net present value of their expected returns.

Under the classic theory of Modigliani and Miller, a corporation cannot change its value (in the absence of tax benefits) by changing the method of its financing.[3] Modigliani and Miller demonstrated that the value of the firm is dependent upon its cash flows. How those cash flows are divided up between shareholders and bondholders is irrelevant to firm value.

Capital assets, then, are distinguished not by their possession of physical assets, but rather, by their claim on the cash flows of an underlying enterprise. Hedge funds, private equity funds, credit derivatives, and corporate governance funds all fall within the super asset class of capital assets because the value of their funds are all determined by the present value of expected future cash flows from the securities in which they invest.

---

[2] See Robert Greer, "What is an Asset Class Anyway?" *Journal of Portfolio Management* 23 (1997), pp. 83–91.

[3] Franco Modigliani and Merton Miller, "The Cost of Capital, Corporation Finance, and the Theory of Investment," *American Economic Review* (June 1958), pp. 433–443.

As a result, we can conclude that it is not the types of securities in which they invest that distinguishes hedge funds, private equity funds, credit derivatives, or corporate governance funds from traditional asset classes. Rather, it is the alternative investment strategies that they pursue that distinguishes them from traditional stock-and-bond investments.

Assets that Can be Used as Economic Inputs

Certain assets can be consumed as part of the production cycle. Consumable or transformable assets can be converted into another asset. Generally, this class of asset consists of the physical commodities: grains, metals, energy products, and livestock. These assets are used as economic inputs into the production cycle to produce other assets, such as automobiles, skyscrapers, new homes, and appliances.

These assets generally cannot be valued using a net present value analysis. For example, a pound of copper, by itself, does not yield an economic stream of revenues. Nor does it have much value for capital appreciation. However, the copper can be transformed into copper piping that is used in an office building, or as part of the circuitry of an electronic appliance.

While consumable assets cannot produce a stream of cash flows, we demonstrate in our section on commodities that this asset class has excellent diversification properties for an investment portfolio. In fact, the lack of dependency on future cash flows to generate value is one of the reasons why commodities have important diversification potential vis à vis capital assets.

Assets that Are a Store of Value

Art is considered the classic asset that stores value. It is not a capital asset because there are no cash flows associated with owning a painting or a sculpture. Consequently, art cannot be valued in a discounted cash flow analysis. It is also not an asset that is used as an economic input because it is a finished product.

Art requires ownership and possession. Its value can only be realized through its sale and transfer of possession. In the meantime, the owner retains the artwork with the expectation that it will yield a price at least equal to that which the owner paid for it.

There is no rational way to gauge whether the price of art will increase or decrease because its value is derived purely from the subjective (and private) visual enjoyment that the right of ownership conveys. Therefore, to an owner, art is a store of value. It conveys neither economic benefits nor is used as an economic input, but retains the value paid for it.

Gold and precious metals are another example of a store of value asset. In the emerging parts of the world, gold and silver are a significant means of maintaining wealth. In these countries, residents do not have access to the same range of financial products that are available to residents of more developed nations. Consequently, they accumulate their wealth through a tangible asset as opposed to a capital asset.

However, the lines between the three super classes of assets can become blurred. For example, gold can be leased to jewelry and other metal manufacturers. Jewelry makers lease gold during periods of seasonal demand, expecting to purchase the gold on the open market and return it to the lessor before the lease term ends. The gold lease provides a stream of cash flows that can be valued using net present value analysis. In May 2006, at a lease rate of 1.5% and a gold price of $700/ounce, the lease rate was only $10.5.

Precious metals can also be used as a transformable/consumable asset because they have the highest level of thermal and electrical conductivity among the metals. Silver, for example is used in the circuitry for most telephones and light switches. Gold is used in the circuitry for TVs, cars, airplanes, computers, and rocketships.

Real Estate

We provide a brief digression to consider where real estate belongs in our classification scheme. Real estate is a distinct asset class, but is it an alternative one? For purposes of this book, we do not consider real estate to be an alternative asset class. The reasons are several.

First, real estate was an asset class long before stocks and bonds became the investment of choice. In fact, In times past, land was the single most important asset class. Kings, queens, lords and nobles measured their wealth by the amount of property that they owned. "Land barons" were aptly named. Ownership of land was reserved only for the most wealthy of society.

However, over the past 200 years, our economic society changed from one based on the ownership of property to the ownership of legal entities. This transformation occurred as society moved from the agricultural age to the industrial age. Production of goods and services became the new source of wealth and power.

Stocks and bonds were born to support the financing needs of new enterprises that manufactured material goods and services. In fact, stocks and bonds became the "alternatives" to real estate instead of vice versa. With the advent of stock-and-bond exchanges, and the general acceptance of owning equity or debt stakes in companies, it is sometimes forgotten that real estate was the original and primary asset class of society.

In fact, it was only 25 years ago in the United States that real estate was the major asset class of most individual investors. This exposure was the result of owning a primary residence. It was not until the long bull market started in 1983 that investors began to diversify their wealth into the "alternative" assets of stocks and bonds.

Second, given the long-term presence of real estate as an asset class, several treatises have been written concerning its valuation.[4] These treatises provide a much more extensive examination of the real estate market than can be covered within the scope of this book.

Finally, we do not consider real estate to be an alternative asset class as much as we consider it to be an additional asset class. Real estate is not an alternative to stocks and bonds—it is a fundamental asset class that should be included within every diversified portfolio. The alternative assets that we consider in this book are meant to diversify the stock-and-bond holdings within a portfolio context.

ASSET ALLOCATION

Asset allocation is generally defined as the allocation of an investor's portfolio across a number of asset classes.[5] Asset allocation, by its very nature shifts the emphasis from the security level to the portfolio level. It is an investment profile that provides a framework for constructing a portfolio based on measures of risk and return. In this sense, asset allocation can trace its roots to Modern Portfolio Theory and the work of Harry Markowitz.[6]

Asset Classes and Asset Allocation

Initially, asset allocation involved four asset classes: equity, fixed income, cash, and real estate. Within each class, the assets could be further divided into subclasses. For example, stocks can be divided into large capitalized stocks, small-capitalized stocks, and foreign stocks. Similarly,

---

[4] See, for example, Howard Gelbtuch, David MacKmin, and Michael Milgrim (eds.), *Real Estate Valuation in Global Markets* (Chicago: Appraisal Institute, 1997); James Boykin and Alfred Ring, *The Valuation of Real Estate*, 4th ed. (Englewood Cliffs, NJ: Prentice Hall, 1993); Austin Jaffe and C.F. Sirmans, *Fundamentals of Real Estate Investment*, 3d ed. (Englewood Cliffs, NJ: Prentice Hall, 1994); and Jack Cummings, *Real Estate Finance & Investment Manual* (Englewood Cliffs, NJ: Prentice Hall, 1997).

[5] See William Sharpe, "Asset Allocation: Management Style and Performance Measurement," *Journal of Portfolio Management* 18, no. 2 (1992), pp. 7–19.

[6] See Harry Markowitz, *Portfolio Selection*, Cowles Foundation (New Haven, CT: Yale University Press, 1959).

fixed income can be broken down into U.S. Treasury notes and bonds, investment-grade bonds, high-yield bonds, and sovereign bonds.

The expansion of newly defined "alternative assets" may cause investors to become confused about their diversification properties and how they fit into an overall diversified portfolio. Investors need to understand the background of asset allocation as a concept for improving return while reducing risk.

For example, in the 1980s the biggest private equity game was taking public companies private. Does the fact that a corporation that once had publicly traded stock but now has privately traded stock mean that it has jumped into a new asset class? Furthermore, public offerings are the primary exit strategy for private equity; public ownership begins where private equity ends.[7] Therefore, it might be argued that private equity is just an extension of the equity markets where the dividing boundary is based on liquidity.

Similarly, credit derivatives expand the fixed income asset class, rather than hedge it. Hedge funds also invest in the stock-and-bond markets but pursue trading strategies very different from a traditional buy and hold strategy. Commodities fall into a different class of assets than equity, fixed income or cash, and will be treated separately in this book.

Last, corporate governance is a strategy for investing in public companies. It seems the least likely to be an alternative investment strategy. However, we will demonstrate that a corporate governance program bears many of the same characteristics as other alternative investment strategies.

Strategic versus Tactical Allocations

Alternative assets should be used in a tactical rather than strategic allocation. Strategic allocation of resources is applied to fundamental asset classes such as equity, fixed income, cash, and real estate. These are the basic asset classes that must be held within a diversified portfolio.

Strategic asset allocation is concerned with the long-term asset mix. The strategic mix of assets is designed to accomplish a long-term goal such as funding pension benefits or matching long-term liabilities. Risk aversion is considered when deciding the strategic asset allocation, but current market conditions are not. In general, policy targets are set for strategic asset classes with allowable ranges around those targets. Allowable ranges are established to allow flexibility in the management of the investment portfolio.

---

[7] See Jeffery Horvitz, "Asset Classes and Asset Allocation: Problems of Classification," *Journal of Private Portfolio Management* 2, no. 4 (2000), pp. 27–32.

Tactical asset allocation is short-term in nature. This strategy is used to take advantage of current market conditions that may be more favorable to one asset class over another. The goal of funding long-term liabilities has been satisfied by the target ranges established by the strategic asset allocation. The goal of tactical asset allocation is to maximize return.

Tactical allocation of resources depends on the ability to diversify within an asset class. This is where alternative assets have the greatest ability to add value. Their purpose is not to hedge the fundamental asset classes, but rather to expand them. Consequently, alternative assets should be considered as part of a broader asset class.

An example is credit derivatives. These are investments that expand the frontier of credit risk investing. The fixed income world can be classified simply as a choice between U.S. Treasury securities that are considered to be default free, and spread products that contain an element of default risk. Spread products include any fixed income investment that does not have a credit rating on par with the U.S. government. Consequently, spread products trade at a credit spread relative to U.S. Treasury securities that reflects their risk of default.

Credit derivatives are a way to diversify and expand the universe for investing in spread products. Traditionally, fixed income managers attempted to establish their ideal credit risk and return profile by buying and selling traditional bonds. However, the bond market can be inefficient and it may be difficult to pinpoint the exact credit profile to match the risk profile of the investor. Credit derivatives can help to plug the gaps in a fixed income portfolio, and expand the fixed income universe by accessing credit exposure in more efficient formats.

Efficient versus Inefficient Asset Classes

Another way to distinguish alternative asset classes is based on the efficiency of the market place. The U.S. public stock-and-bond markets are generally considered to be the most efficient marketplaces in the world. Often, these markets are referred to as "Semi-Strong Efficient." This means that all publicly available information regarding a publicly traded corporation, both past information and present, is fully digested in that company's traded securities.

Yet inefficiencies exist in all markets, both public and private. If there were no informational inefficiencies in the public equity market, there would be no case for active management. Nonetheless, whatever inefficiencies do exist, they are small and fleeting. The reason is that information is easy to acquire and disseminate in the publicly traded securities markets. Top quartile active managers in the public equity market earn excess returns (over their benchmarks) of approximately 1% a year.

In contrast, with respect to alternative assets, information is very difficult to acquire. Most alternative assets (with the exception of commodities) are privately traded. This includes private equity, hedge funds, and credit derivatives. The difference between top quartile and bottom quartile performance in private equity can be as much as 25%.

Consider venture capital, one subset of the private equity market. Investments in startup companies require intense research into the product niche the company intends to fulfill, the background of the management of the company, projections about future cash flows, exit strategies, potential competition, beta testing schedules, and so forth. This information is not readily available to the investing public. It is time consuming and expensive to accumulate. Furthermore, most investors do not have the time or the talent to acquire and filter through the rough data regarding a private company. One reason why alternative asset managers charge large management and incentive fees is to recoup the cost of information collection.

This leads to another distinguishing factor between alternative investments and the traditional asset classes: the investment intermediary. Continuing with our venture capital example, most investments in venture capital are made through limited partnerships, limited liability companies, or special purpose vehicles. It is estimated that 80% of all private equity investments in the United States are funneled through a financial intermediary.

Investments in alternative assets are less liquid than their public markets counterparts. Investments are closely held and liquidity is minimal. Furthermore, without a publicly traded security, the value of private securities cannot be determined by market trading. The value of the private securities must be estimated by book value, appraisal, or determined by a cash flow model.

Constrained versus Unconstrained Investing

During the great bull market from 1981 to 2000 the asset management industry only had to invest in the stock market to enjoy consistent, high, double-digit returns. During this heyday, investment management shops and institutional investors divided their assets between the traditional asset classes of stocks and bonds. As the markets turned sour at the beginning of the new millennium, asset management firms and institutional investors found themselves "boxed in" by these traditional asset class distinctions. They found that their investment teams were organized along traditional asset class lines and their investment portfolios were constrained by efficient benchmarks that reflected this "asset box" approach.

Consequently, traditional asset management shops have been slow to reorganize their investment structures. This has allowed hedge funds and other alternative investment vehicles to flourish because they are not bounded by traditional asset class lines—they can invest outside the benchmark. These alternative assets are free to exploit the investment opportunities that fall in between the traditional benchmark boxes. The lack of constraints allows alternative asset managers a degree of freedom that is not allowed the traditional asset class shops. Furthermore, traditional asset management shops remain caught up in an organizational structure that is bounded by traditional asset class lines. This provides another constraint because it inhibits the flow of information and investment ideas across the organization.

Asset Location versus Trading Strategy

One of the first and best papers on hedge funds by William Fung and David Hsieh show a distinct difference between how mutual funds and hedge funds operate. They show that the economic exposure associated with mutual funds is defined primarily by *where* the mutual fund invests. In other words, mutual funds gain their primary economic and risk exposures by the location of the asset classes in which they invest. Thus we get large-cap active equity funds, small-cap growth funds, Treasury bond funds, and the like.

Conversely, Fung and Hsieh show that hedge funds' economic exposures are defined more by *how* they trade. That is, a hedge fund's risk and return exposure is defined more by a trading strategy within an asset class than it is defined by the location of the asset class. As a result, hedge fund managers tend to have much greater turnover in their portfolios than mutual funds.

Asset Class Risk Premiums versus Trading Strategy Risk Premiums

Related to the idea of trading strategy versus investment location is the notion of risk premiums. You cannot earn a return without incurring risk. Traditional investment managers earn risk premiums for investing in the large-cap value equity market, small-cap growth equity market, high-yield bond market; in other words, based on the location of the asset markets in which they invest.

Conversely, alternative asset managers also earn returns for taking risk, but the risk is defined more by a trading strategy than it is an economic exposure associated with the systematic risk contained within broad financial classes. For example, hedge fund strategies such as convertible arbitrage, statistical arbitrage, and equity market neutral can earn a "complexity" risk premium.[8]

These strategies buy and sell similar securities expecting the securities to converge in value overtime. The complexity of implementing these strategies results in inefficient pricing in the market. Additionally, many investors are constrained by the *long-only* constraint—their inability to short securities. This perpetuates inefficient pricing in the marketplace which enables hedge funds to earn a return.

OVERVIEW OF THIS BOOK

This book is organized into six parts. The first part provides a framework to consider alternative assets within a broader portfolio context. Specifically, in Chapter 2 we expand on the concept of strategic versus tactical asset allocation and the use of beta drivers versus alpha drivers to achieve these goals.

The second part of this book reviews hedge funds. Chapter 3 begins with a brief history on the birth of hedge funds and an introduction to the types of hedge fund investment strategies. Chapter 4 provides some practical guidance as to how to build a hedge fund investment program. Chapter 5 is devoted to conducting due diligence, including both a qualitative and quantitative review. In Chapter 6 we analyze the return distributions hedge funds and begin to consider some risk management issues. In Chapter 7 we expand the discussion of hedge fund risks and highlight some specific examples of hedge fund underperformance. In Chapter 8 we review the regulatory framework in which hedge funds operate. Chapter 9 provides an introduction to hedge fund benchmarks and how these benchmarks can impact the asset allocation decision to hedge funds. In Chapter 10, we consider the fees charged by hedge fund managers—a key point of contention between hedge fund managers and their clients. Last, in Chapter 11 we conclude on a humorous note as we go through a top ten list of hedge fund quotes and accompanying anecdotes.

Part Three is devoted to commodity and managed futures. We begin with a brief review in Chapter 12 of the economic value inherent in commodity futures contracts. Chapter 13 describes how an individual or institution may invest in commodity futures, including an introduction to commodity future benchmarks. Chapter 14 considers commodity futures within a portfolio framework, while Chapter 15 examines the managed futures industry.

---

[8] See Lars Jaeger, *Managing Risk in Alternative Investment Strategies* (London: Financial Times/Prentice Hall, 2002).

Part Four covers the spectrum of private equity. In Chapter 16 we provide an introduction to venture capital, while Chapter 17 is devoted to leveraged buyouts. In Chapters 18 and 19 we show how two different forms of debt may be a component of the private equity marketplace. In Chapter 20 we review the economics associated with private equity investments, and in Chapter 21 we consider some issues with respect to private equity benchmarks. In Chapter 22, we review some new trends in the private equity market place.

Part Five is devoted to credit derivatives. In Chapter 23 we review the importance of credit risk, and provide examples of how credit derivatives are used in portfolio management. In Chapter 24 we review the collateralized debt obligation market. Specifically, we review the design, structure and economics of collateralized bond obligations and collateralized loan obligations. In Chapter 25 we consider a new form of asset backed security—the collateralized fund obligation.

Finally, we devote Chapter 26 to corporate governance as an alternative investment strategy.

Throughout this book we attempt to provide descriptive material as well as empirical examples. In each chapter you will find charts, tables, graphs, and calculations that serve to highlight a specific point. Our goal is both to educate the reader with respect to these alternative investment strategies as well as provide a reference book for data and research. Along the way we also try to provide a few anecdotes about alternative investing that, while providing some humor, also demonstrate some of the pitfalls of the alternative asset universe.

CHAPTER 2

Why Alternative Assets are Important: Beta Drivers and Alpha Drivers

The 1980s and 1990s experienced an unprecedented equity market expansion that provided an average annual total return to the S&P 500 of over 17% per year. It was hard to ignore the premium that the equity market delivered over U.S. Treasury Bonds during this time. Over the same time period the average total return for the 10-year U.S. Treasury Bond was 9.83%, and even that was an historically high number.

The long-term implied equity risk premium (over 10-year U.S. Treasury Bonds) has been estimated at 3.8%.[1] This is the risk premium implied by stock market valuations and forecasts of earnings in relation to current market value. Another way to state this is that it is the expected risk premium that a long-term investor must earn to entice her to hold equities over government bonds. However, throughout the

---

[1] See Henry Dickson and Charles Reinhard, "Weekly Earnings Comment," *Lehman Brothers Research*, July 21, 2004. The long-term ERP is measured for U.S. stocks, but the risk premium is remarkably consistent across international borders. Of interest, there are two time periods when the equity risk premium approached zero. The first was in the autumn of 1987, before the stock market undertook a massive correction in October of 1987. At that time, portfolio insurance was all the rage. Of course, this turned out to be a fallacy, but at the time, the ERP was driven close to zero because investors believed that they could "insure" against losses so that investing in the stock market was associated with a zero-risk premium. The second time was at the height of the tech bubble. Then, investors so overvalued stocks based on the technology hype that the ERP also approached zero.

15

1980s and 1990s, the *realized* risk premium frequently exceeded that implied by investors' expectations.

Exhibit 2.1 plots the realized equity risk premium compared to the long-term expected risk premium. It also graphs the cumulative equity risk premium earned over this period. Initially, in the early to mid 1980s, the realized equity risk premium was inconsistent—sometimes greater than the expected long-term risk premium, sometimes less. However, from the late 1980s through the end of the 1990s, the realized risk premium for holding equities consistently exceeded the expected premium. Investors were continually rewarded with equity market returns that exceeded their expectations.

This led large institutional investors to rely exclusively on asset allocation models where asset classes were defined by strict lines or "benchmark boxes."[2] For 20 years, this type of investing worked for large institutional investors. However, the global bear equity market of 2000 to 2002 demonstrated that mean reversion is a powerful force in finance.

EXHIBIT 2.1   Expected and Realized Equity Risk Premium

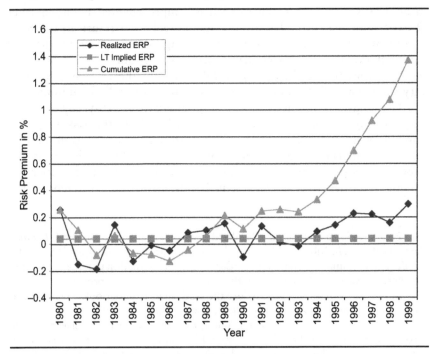

<hr>

[2] See Mark Anson, "Thinking Outside the Benchmark," *Journal of Portfolio Management*, 30th Anniversary Issue, 2004, pp. 8–22.

Throughout the 20-year period of 1981 to 2000, investors needed only to consider return—a traditional approach to asset allocation earned strong returns for many years. In addition, consultants encouraged such an approach because it made for convenient asset allocation, benchmarking of performance, and style classification. However, looking forward, traditional asset class definitions may not be sufficient to deliver the kind of portfolio performance that investors have come to expect and demand.

This leads to the focus of this book. Alternative investments have the ability to generate greater yield, reduce risk, and provide return streams that are less than perfectly correlated with the traditional stock-and-bond market. Throughout the course of this chapter we refer to *beta drivers* and *alpha drivers*. Beta drivers capture financial market risk premiums in an efficient manner while alpha drivers seek pockets of excess return often without regard to benchmarks. Alternative assets fall squarely into the category of alpha drivers. However, to understand how alternative assets might be used in an institutional portfolio, we first must review the asset allocation process of large institutional investors.

STRATEGIC VERSUS TACTICAL ASSET ALLOCATION

Generally, the board of trustees of a pension fund, endowment, or foundation establishes the strategic allocation among the major asset classes. Strategic asset allocation is the translation of an institutional investor's investment policy. This process identifies strategic benchmarks tied to broad asset classes that establish the *policy risk* for the fund. This is also known as the *beta* or *market risk* for the fund.

Strategic asset allocation is not designed to "beat the market." Instead, it is designed to meet the long-term funding goals of the organization such as paying retirement benefits, supplementing a university budget, or providing for philanthropic donations. It is the process by which long-term assets are matched against long-term pension fund liabilities, university budgets, foundation donation schedules, or high-net-worth wealth generation.

In contrast, tactical asset allocation facilitates an institutional investor's long-term funding goals by seeking extra return. It does this by taking advantage of opportunities in the financial markets when those markets appear to be out of line with fundamental economic valuations. As a result, tactical asset allocation requires more frequent trading than strategic asset allocation. This process uses actively managed investment products as alternatives to passive benchmark risk.

Boards of trustees engage in strategic asset allocation (SAA). SAA provides the pension fund with its target allocation among the major asset classes. Typically, percentage targets or ranges are set up to allocate a fund's investment capital across asset classes such as stocks, bonds, cash, and real estate. This type of allocation establishes the "beta" for the fund, that is, the fund's overall exposure to broad asset classes. After the broad allocations are made, active returns, or "alpha," is sought within each asset class.

Beta Drivers are Linear in their Performance

Under the traditional paradigm of asset management, active management or alpha is pursued within an asset class. The beta of the asset class and the alpha are not separated or pursued independently. This is most apparent in the search for alpha in traditional long-only active equity managers.

Exhibit 2.2 plots the weekly returns of a large-cap active equity manager to those of the S&P 500. The result is a straight line. With a beta of 1.00 and a correlation coefficient of 0.99, this large-cap active equity manager essentially replicates the S&P 500.

Exhibit 2.2 demonstrates that the returns generated by this active equity manager are perfectly consistent with the up and down movement of the S&P 500. Beta drivers are linear in their performance compared to a financial index. Despite this manager's claim of "active"

EXHIBIT 2.2   A Large-Cap Active Equity Manager

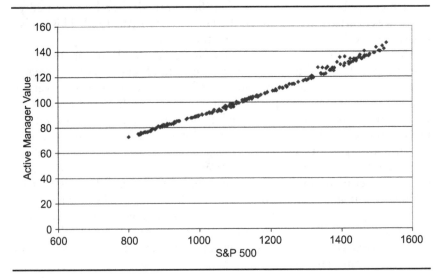

status, it is a beta driver, not an alpha driver—its returns are derived exclusively from the broad stock market.[3]

For comparison, we provide Exhibit 2.3, which shows the performance of a passive S&P 500 Index manager. Again, we see a straight line where the performance of this investment manager is in precise lock step with the up-and-down movement of the S&P 500. The only differences between this manager and the one in Exhibit 2.2 is the claim to "active" status by the manager in Exhibit 2.2 and the level of fees charged. The manager in Exhibit 2.2 charges 65 basis points a year to deliver the S&P 500 while the manager in Exhibit 2.3 charges only 4 basis points.

SEPARATING ALPHA FROM BETA

There must be a shift in the thought process of asset management. Investors need to break away from the traditional asset allocation model of trying to extract alpha from beta. A simple way to manage a total portfolio is to divide it into two classes of economic drivers: beta drivers and alpha drivers.

EXHIBIT 2.3   An Index Manager Benchmarked to the S&P 500

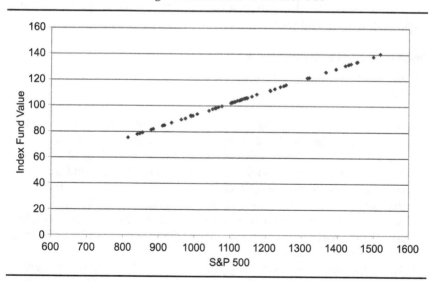

---

[3] In fact, over the five year time period studied, 2000 to 2004, this large-cap active equity manager under performed the S&P 500 by 276 basis points.

Beta drivers are designed to provide efficient economic exposure to establish the policy or market risk for an investor. This book does not seek to discredit beta drivers; they are an essential building block in institutional portfolios. They help to accomplish the primary funding/spending obligations of the investor.

In the traditional model, institutional portfolios find alpha but only when it is attached to beta. Institutional investors first make the allocation to strategic benchmarks to establish the policy risk of the institutional portfolio and then the investment staff try to squeeze alpha out of these policy benchmarks. This means that the investment staff is often hampered by investing in the traditional asset classes of stocks and bonds to seek excess return. As a consequence, alpha budgets are often misspent on the most efficient markets—those represented by the strategic benchmarks.

In the new investment model, alpha is sought independently of beta. Beta drivers remain important to implement the strategic asset allocation established by the investor. However, the professional investment staff can seek alpha from investment products that are "outside the benchmark."[4] This is where alternative assets are most useful.

More to the point, alpha risk budgets should not be spent on strategic benchmarks. Strategic benchmarks are designed to offer efficient beta exposure—the last place to look for extra value. Alpha risk budgets should be spent in less efficient markets—those markets described in this book—hedge funds, managed futures, commodities, private equity, credit derivatives, and corporate governance.

Broad Categories of Alpha Drivers

Alpha drivers are expected to out perform the market and fall into four general categories:

- *Absolute return strategies.* These are primarily hedge fund strategies where the hedge fund manager is unchained from a stock-and-bond index so she can pursue value added strategies regardless of size, market direction, or benchmark restrictions. Many hedge fund managers simultaneously pursue long and short investment strategies to extract the greatest value associated with their financial market insights. A diversified portfolio of such strategies would be expected to have a low correlation with broad financial market indexes, especially when measured over a full market cycle.
- *Market segmentation.* Often investors deselect themselves from certain markets. Consider the collateralized debt market. Many investors avoid this market because of the default risk associated with the lower

---

[4] See Anson, "Thinking Outside the Benchmark."

rated tranches of securities in this market. In fact some institutional investors are prohibited from investing in below investment grade bonds, while others eschew this market because it is less liquid than investment grade securities. Commodities are another example of market segmentation. Commodities are less well understood than even hedge funds and so many investors avoid what they do not have the time to understand.

■ *Concentrated portfolios.* Most traditional active managers tend to hug their benchmark and maintain well diversified portfolios (see Exhibit 2.2). Diversification, is a way to minimize the risk of under performance but, at the same time, it *minimizes the probability of out performance.* In contrast, concentrated portfolios frequently have significant tracking error to an established benchmark, but offer a greater opportunity for excess return. Corporate governance funds and private equity funds fall into this category because they typically have only a few very concentrated positions in their portfolio.

■ *Nonlinear return distributions.* Nonlinear return functions exhibit option-like payoffs with a "kinked" distribution. These alternative investments can be explicitly linked to an option like convertible bonds, or may replicate a option payoff structure by virtue of their trading strategy. Examples of the latter include merger arbitrage, event driven, fixed income arbitrage, and managed futures. This type of return distribution can be particularly useful when combined with a linear beta driver.

The alternative assets discussed in the following chapters of this book all fall into one of these four broad categories of alternative investments. A key point regarding the four categories discussed above is that they are not defined by asset class. Rather, they are defined by economic exposure or trading strategy.

The Separation of Alpha and Beta

Exhibit 2.4 provides a graphical depiction of the separation of alpha and beta. This graph defines products by their contribution to active risk and active return. At the zero axis, we find index products. These are the ultimate beta drivers; these products take no active risk, extract no added value, and are devoid of information (in fact, they toss any information aside). All they do is capture passively the risk premium associated with a risky asset class. Slightly above index products we find enhanced index products—products designed to take small amounts of risk within tightly controlled parameters and offer a little extra return, usually on a large pool of capital. Small, but consistent alpha is their game. Next, just

EXHIBIT 2.4   Separating Alpha Drivers from Beta Drivers

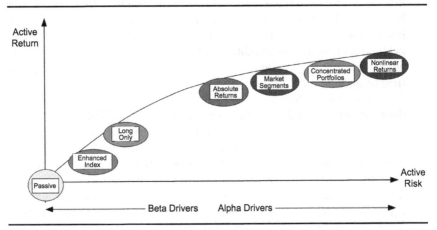

slightly above the enhanced indexes, we find the traditional "active" manager. A word of caution: as Exhibit 2.2 demonstrates, these products are often beta drivers dressed up in alpha driver clothing.

Collectively, these three products form the strategic core for the institutional portfolio to achieve the cost-effective implementation of the policy risk for the institutional portfolio. Although, sometimes a traditional active manager will charge large fees for delivering a product that has considerable beta risk and only a smidgen of alpha risk.

Exhibit 2.4 then has a large gap between the beta drivers at the lower end of the active risk/return scale and the alpha drivers presented at the higher end of the risk and return scale. Note that this gap does not necessarily need to be as large as depicted in Exhibit 2.4. Well-designed alpha drivers can be "delevered" to match their tracking error along the active risk spectrum. We draw Exhibit 2.4 with a gap to highlight the difference between alpha and beta drivers in their natural state of active risk taking.

Alpha is not static. Over time, alpha can migrate and become beta. A number of recent articles provide examples of investment strategies that had once been considered manager skill, that is, alpha, but are now regarded as a systematic capturing of existing risk premiums, that is, beta.[5] In addition, alpha strategies go through cycles of profitability,

---

[5] See Clifford Asness, "An Alternative Future," *Journal of Portfolio Management*, (30th Anniversary Issue 2004), pp. 94–103; Lars Jaeger, *Managing Risk in Alternative Investment Strategies* (Englewood Cliffs, NJ: Financial Times/Prentice Hall, 2002); Greg Jensen and Jason Rotenberg, "Hedge Funds Selling Beta as Alpha," *Bridgewater Daily Observations*, June 17, 2004.

sometimes in favor, sometimes out of favor. This is most appealing to those who pursue a tactical asset allocation among alpha drivers.

RETHINKING ASSET ALLOCATION

Asset allocation must allow for alpha drivers and beta drivers. Beta drivers will still play an important role in the construction of the pension portfolio, but the strict allocation lines to fixed income, real estate, public equity and private equity will break down. Investors are migrating to subasset classes with inefficient markets and trading strategies that have high alpha content.

Japanese pension funds have already moved in this direction. A 13-year bear market combined with near-zero interest rates have forced Japan to turn to alpha drivers. As of 2005, Japanese pension funds have allocated 8.1% of their assets to hedge funds, compared to 3% for U.S. corporate pension plans and 2% for U.S. public pension plans.[6]

Rather than draw bright lines across asset classes, the strategic allocation should allow for broad ranges or "tilts" in the portfolio.[7] Tilts recognize that asset class lines can become blurred. An investor should commit assets to beta drivers within an asset class when it believes it has the least amount of talent or insight to extract alpha. This approach has two implications.

First, investors should reduce their reliance on beta drivers for excess return generation and rely more on alternative assets that have the highest alpha content. Second, an institutional investor should commit its investment staff resources towards those alternative assets and trading strategies where it believes that it can add value. One of the greatest sources of alpha is derived from investments that fall "between the cracks" of traditional asset allocation. This means building teams of investment staff that bridge asset classes.

Exhibit 2.5 demonstrates a new way to allocate assets for an institutional portfolio. Four broad asset classes are identified: equity, fixed income, real estate, and inflation protection.[8] Within each asset class,

---

[6] See Russell Investment Group, *The 2005–2006 Russell Survey on Alternative Investing*, 2005.

[7] Joanne Hill and Meric Koksal, "The New Pension Paradigm: Implications for Investment Strategy, Managers and Markets," Goldman Sachs & Co., January 30, 2004.

[8] Hill and Koksal ("The New Pension Paradigm: Implications for Investment Strategy, Managers and Markets") identify six portfolio tilts: equity tilt, debt tilt, alpha-only strategies, low-liquidity strategies, cross-market and overlay, and flexible absolute return. We provide a more simplified approach that retains some of the traditional asset allocation themes of most pension funds.

EXHIBIT 2.5   A Different Strategic Asset Allocation

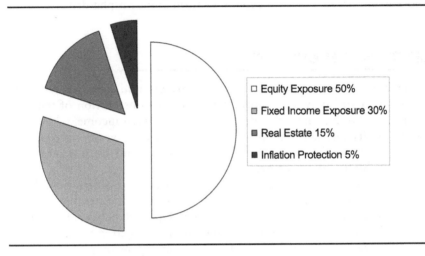

☐ Equity Exposure 50%

▨ Fixed Income Exposure 30%

▩ Real Estate 15%

■ Inflation Protection 5%

EXHIBIT 2.6   Equity Beta and Alpha Drivers

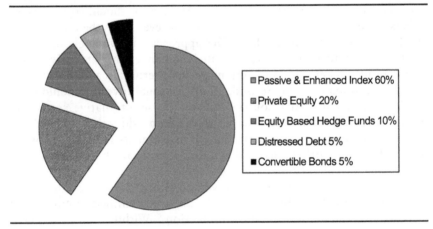

▨ Passive & Enhanced Index 60%

▨ Private Equity 20%

▨ Equity Based Hedge Funds 10%

▨ Distressed Debt 5%

■ Convertible Bonds 5%

there will be a blend of beta drivers that provide efficient asset class exposure and alpha drivers that are designed to extract greater value. For example, the strategic allocation to equity could be broken into the following subclasses as displayed in Exhibit 2.6:

■ Beta drivers—60%
    Passive equity
    Enhanced indexed equity

- Alpha drivers—40%
  Private equity
  Distressed debt
  Equity-based hedge fund strategies: merger arbitrage, equity long/short, short-selling hedge funds
  Convertible bonds

Notice that two fixed income instruments are classified as equity alpha drivers: convertible bonds and distressed debt. This highlights the fact that alpha drivers are not necessarily defined by neat benchmark boxes. Alpha drivers need to be sought out wherever they can be found. Similarly, the fixed income portfolio can be broken down into alpha and beta drivers as displayed in Exhibit 2.7:

- Beta drivers—75%
  U.S. Treasury bonds
  Investment-grade corporate bonds
  Agency mortgage-backed securities
- Alpha Drivers—25%
  Convertible bonds
  Mezzanine debt
  Collateralized debt obligations (CDOs)
  Fixed income-based hedge fund strategies: fixed income arbitrage, relative value, distressed debt

EXHIBIT 2.7   Fixed Income Beta and Alpha Drivers

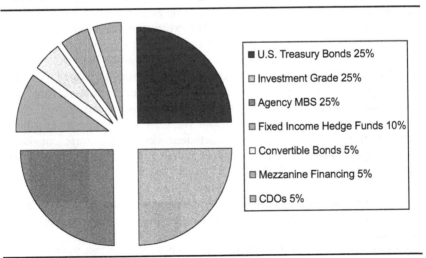

- U.S. Treasury Bonds 25%
- Investment Grade 25%
- Agency MBS 25%
- Fixed Income Hedge Funds 10%
- Convertible Bonds 5%
- Mezzanine Financing 5%
- CDOs 5%

Convertible bonds can be included in either the fixed income portfolio or the equity portfolio. This subasset class contains both equity and debt components, and highlights the point that pension plans should not adhere to strict asset allocation lines. Pension plans should acknowledge that certain subasset classes blur the distinction across traditional asset class lines.

SUMMARY

1. *Think outside the benchmark.* Institutional investors need to remove the artificial restrictions associated with strategic asset allocation models. Traditional asset allocation models partition the financial markets into neat benchmark "boxes." While this is useful for planning purposes, it can inhibit alpha extraction.

For example, active mandates should be sought throughout the equity spectrum, and not be tied to an investor's equity benchmark. Active equity management can be extended to long/short investing, convertible bonds, distressed debt, and other equity-based alpha drivers. The equity asset class must be considered on a global basis rather than being segmented into benchmark boxes. This leads back to the concept of portfolio "tilts."[9] Tilts recognize that asset class boundaries are not etched into stone, but rather, are flexible and even, dynamic.

There is, however, a cautionary note: thinking outside the benchmark is a useful alpha-generating exercise, but it might meet with some resistance. In the asset management industry consultants and institutional investors have long classified money managers into convenient style categories. The reasons are simple: it makes external manager searches easier (targeting a large-cap value manager search); it provides consistent style analysis (large cap versus small, growth versus value), and it allows for simpler recommendations (this manager out performs its peer group of other large-cap managers). Also, putting money managers into neat benchmark boxes makes the hiring and firing decisions easier.

Investors should worry less about the style of a manager and more about whether the manager has sufficient skill to generate consistent alpha. Alpha need not be captive to beta. Find skill first, and then worry about the systematic risk that may be attached to that alpha.

2. *Recognize that alpha can be generated across asset class boundaries.* A good example is convertible arbitrage. Because convertible bonds

---

[9] Hill and Koksal (2004) extend their analysis to consider both risk and return drivers within asset class tilts.

contain both equity and fixed income characteristics they fall outside the traditional boundaries of asset allocation. As a result, this strategy can capture a risk premium simply because the traditional market place is segmented into benchmark boxes. Market segmentation is an inherent inefficiency that can be exploited if the investor can look across asset class boundaries. Alpha drivers should be sought out wherever they lie; and market partitioning is great place to find them. Examples include convertible arbitrage, distressed debt, mezzanine debt, and credit derivatives, to name a few.

In a similar vein, institutional investors should deemphasize their organization structure along traditional asset class lines. Most pension funds build their investment teams by partitions: public equity, fixed income, real estate, private equity. This is the standard way to structure an institutional investor. Yet strict adherence to asset class divisions inhibits the ability of the investment team to seek alpha-driven returns across asset boundaries.

3. *Consider the risk of failing to out perform a peer group.* There is safety in numbers and "running with the pack." Institutional investors that hug their benchmarks will resemble more their peer group. This is a conservative investment strategy designed to minimize the under performance of the investor compared to a group of similar investors. Beta drivers reduce the risk of peer group under performance. This behavioral phenomenon is most often observed among pension funds.

This will leave alternative investments to other investors in the marketplace, traditionally endowments and foundations. For example, endowments have an average allocation to hedge funds of almost 13% compared to 6.5% for corporate pension plans and 6.1% for public pension plans.[10] In order to effectively access alpha drivers, investors must be willing to accept the risk that their fund performance will differ significantly from their peer group. Strict asset allocation reduces the risk of under performance but it *increases* the risk that the institutional investor will not generate superior performance.

4. *Pursue alternative assets where you have the greatest informational advantage.* It may not be possible to purse every alternative asset discussed in this book. Every investor should figure out where it can apply its resources to develop an informational advantage. For example, most institutional investors would not consider corporate governance (Chapter 25) to be an alpha driver. However, consider the California Public

---

[10] See Russell Investment Company, 2005, supra. Part of this difference is also related to the size of pension funds compared to endowment and foundation funds.

Employees' Retirement System (CalPERS) which has actively pursued shareowner rights for the past 20 years.[11] It has developed a competitive edge over other institutional investors through its corporate governance expertise over. The insights gained from its program give CalPERS an informational advantage over other investors, which it has translated into significant added value.

Conversely, it is not easy for an institutional investor to admit that it has no informational advantage in a particular market. As markets become more efficient, investors will recognize that they lack a competitive edge that can be translated into added value. When an institutional investor realizes that it has no advantage in active management (or in selecting active managers), cost control becomes the most important value added tool. Without an informational edge, institutional investors should exit the alternative asset arena and focus on reducing costs through indexation.

In summary, an investor should spend its alpha budget where it has the greatest ability to translate its competitive edge into added value. An informational advantage can be developed in external manager selection, superior risk control, extensive knowledge about an alternative asset class, better manager monitoring, or enhanced flexibility to practice tactical asset allocation.

---

[11] CalPERS calls itself a "Shareowner" instead of a "Shareholder" to emphasis its rights and obligations as an owner of a public corporation.

Hedge Funds

Introduction to Hedge Funds

There is a joke in the hedge fund industry that goes like this. Question: "What is a hedge fund?" Answer: "Anything that charges you 2 and 20!"

The joke refers to the fact that hedge funds are not well defined as an investment vehicle and, in fact, are often defined by the fees they charge where "2 and 20" refers to a 2% management fee and a 20% incentive fee. An anecdote can help hammer home this point.

Recently, a new startup hedge fund passed through the CalPERS Investment Office. I asked the managers of the fund—who were brand new to the hedge fund game—what their fee structure was. They promptly responded: "2 and 20." When I inquired why they thought they should charge 2 and 20 given that they had never managed a hedge fund before, they replied: "If we don't charge 2 and 20, no one will think we are serious." Ah, yes.

Therefore, it must be understood that the phrase "hedge fund" is a term of art. It is not defined in Securities Act of 1933 or the Securities Exchange Act of 1934. Additionally, "hedge fund" is not defined by the Investment Company Act of 1940, the Investment Advisers Act of 1940, the Commodity Exchange Act, or, finally, the Bank Holding Company Act. In fact the SEC has not attempted to define the term "hedge fund" and has stated that there is no regulatory or statutory definition of a hedge fund.[1]

So what is this investment vehicle that every investor seems to know but for which there is scant regulatory guidance?

---

[1] See Securities and Exchange Commission, "Registration Under the Advisers Act of Certain Hedge Fund Advisers," 17 CFR parts 275 and 279, 69 Federal Register 72054, December 10, 2004.

31

As a starting point, we turn to the American Heritage Dictionary, 3rd ed., which defines a hedge fund as:

> An investment company that uses high-risk techniques, such as borrowing money and selling short, in an effort to make extraordinary capital gains.

Not a bad start, but we note that hedge funds are not investment companies, for they would be regulated by the Securities and Exchange Commission under the Investment Company Act of 1940.[2] Additionally, as we will soon see, many hedge fund strategies produce consistent but conservative rates of return and do not "swing for the fences" to earn extraordinary gains.

We define hedge funds as:

> A privately organized investment vehicle that manages a concentrated portfolio of public and private securities and derivative instruments on those securities, that can invest both long and short, and can apply leverage.

Within this definition there are six key elements of hedge funds that distinguish them from their more traditional counterpart, the mutual fund.

First, hedge funds are private investment vehicles that pool the resources of sophisticated investors. One of the ways that hedge funds avoid the regulatory scrutiny of the SEC or the CFTC is that they are available only for high-net-worth investors. Under SEC rules, hedge funds cannot have more than 100 accredited investors in the fund. An accredited investor is defined as an individual that has a minimum net worth in excess or $1,000,000, or income in each of the past two years of $200,000 ($300,000 for a married couple) with an expectation of earning at least that amount in the current year. Additionally, hedge funds may accept no more than 500 "qualified purchasers" in the fund. These are individuals or institutions that have a net worth in excess of $5,000,000.

There is a penalty, however, for the privacy of hedge funds. They cannot raise funds from investors via a public offering. Additionally, hedge funds may not advertise broadly or engage in a general solicitation for new funds. Instead, their marketing and fundraising efforts must be tar-

---

[2] In fact, hedge funds take great pains to avoid being regulated by the SEC as an investment company. The National Securities Markets Improvement Act of 1996 greatly relieved hedge funds of any regulatory burden by increasing the number of "qualified purchasers" that hedge funds may have to 500.

geted to a narrow niche of very wealthy individuals and institutions. As a result, the predominant investors in hedge funds are family offices, foundations, endowments, and, to a lesser extent, pension funds.

Second, hedge funds tend to have portfolios that are much more concentrated than their mutual fund brethren. Most hedge funds do not have broad securities benchmarks. One reason is that most hedge fund managers claim that their style of investing is "skill based" and cannot be measured by a market return. Consequently, hedge fund managers are not forced to maintain security holdings relative to a benchmark; they do not need to worry about "benchmark" risk. This allows them to concentrate their portfolio only on those securities that they believe will add value to the portfolio.

Another reason for the concentrated portfolio is that hedge fund managers tend to have narrow investment strategies. These strategies tend to focus on only one sector of the economy or one segment of the market. They can tailor their portfolio to extract the most value from their smaller investment sector or segment. Furthermore, the concentrated portfolios of hedge fund managers generally are not dependent on the direction of the financial markets, in contrast to long-only managers.

Third, hedge funds tend to use derivative strategies much more predominately than mutual funds. Indeed, in some strategies, such as convertible arbitrage, the ability to sell or buy options is a key component of executing the arbitrage. The use of derivative strategies may result in nonlinear cash flows that may require more sophisticated risk management techniques to control these risks.

Fourth, hedge funds may go both long and short securities. The ability to short public securities and derivative instruments is one of the key distinctions between hedge funds and traditional money managers. Hedge fund manages incorporate their ability to short securities explicitly into their investment strategies. For example, equity long/short hedge funds tend to buy and sell securities within the same industry to maximize their return but also to control their risk. This is very different from traditional money managers that are tied to a long-only securities benchmark.

Fifth, many hedge fund strategies invest in nonpublic securities, that is, securities that have been issued to investors without the support of a prospectus and a public offering. Many bonds, both convertible and high yield, are issued as what are known as "144A securities." These are securities issued to institutional investors in a private transaction instead of a public offering. These securities may be offered with a private placement memorandum (ppm), but not a public prospectus. In addition, these securities are offered without the benefit of an SEC review as would be conducted for a public offering. Bottom line: with

144A securities it is buyer beware. The SEC allows this because, presumably, large institutional investors are more sophisticated than that average, small investor.

Finally, hedge funds use leverage, sometimes, large amounts. In fact, a lesson in leverage is described in this chapter with respect to Long-Term Capital Management. Mutual funds, for example, are limited in the amount of leverage they can employ; they may borrow up to 33% of their net asset base. Hedge funds do not have this restriction. Consequently, it is not unusual to see some hedge fund strategies that employ leverage up to 10 time their net asset base.

We can see that hedge funds are different than traditional long-only investment managers. We next discuss the history of the hedge fund development.

CATEGORIES OF HEDGE FUNDS

It seems like everyone has their own classification scheme for hedge funds.[3] This merely reflects the fact that hedge funds are a bit difficult to "box in"—a topic we will address further we examine a number of the hedge fund index providers. For purposes of this book, we try to break down hedge funds into broad categories as depicted in Exhibit 3.1.

We classify hedge funds into four broad buckets: market directional, corporate restructuring, convergence trading, and opportunistic. *Market directional* hedge funds are those that retain some amount of systematic risk exposure. For example, equity long/short (or, as it is sometime called, *equity hedge*) are hedge funds that typically contain some amount of net long market exposure. For example, they may leverage up the hedge fund to go 150% long on stocks that they like while simultaneously shorting 80% of the fund value with stocks that they think will decline in value. The remaining net long market exposure is 70%. Thus they retain some amount of systematic risk exposure that will be affected by the direction of the stock market.

Corporate restructuring hedge funds take advantage of significant corporate transactions like a merger, acquisition, or bankruptcy. These funds earn their living by concentrating their portfolios in a handful of companies where it is more important to understand the likelihood that the corporate transaction will be completed than it is to determine whether the corporation is under or over valued.

---

[3] See, for example, Francois-Serge Lhabitant, *Hedge Funds: Quantitative Insights*, (West Sussex, England: John Wiley & Sons, Inc. 2004); and Joseph G. Nicholas, *Market Neutral Investing* (Princeton, NJ: Bloomberg Press, 2000).

EXHIBIT 3.1   Categories of Hedge Funds

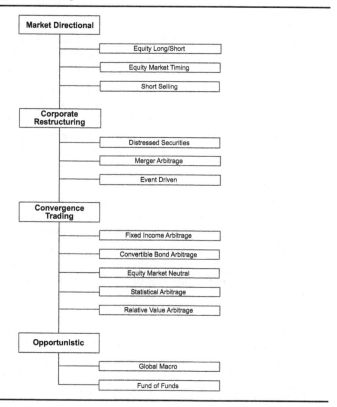

Convergence trading hedge funds are the hedge funds that practice the art of arbitrage. In fact the specialized subcategories within this bucket typically contain the work "arbitrage" in their description such as *statistical arbitrage, fixed income arbitrage,* or *convertible arbitrage.* In general these hedge funds make bets that two similar securities but with dissimilar prices will converge to the same value over the investment holding period.

Last, we have the *Opportunistic* category. We include *global macro-hedge* funds as well as *fund of funds* (FOF) in this category. These funds are designed to take advantage of whatever opportunities present themselves. Hence the term "opportunistic." For example, FOF often practice tactical asset allocation among the hedge funds contained in the FOF based on the FOF manager's view as to which hedge fund strategies are currently poised to earn the best results. This shifting of the assets around is based on the FOF manager's assessment of the opportunity for each hedge fund contained in the FOF to earn a significant return.

A BRIEF HISTORY OF HEDGE FUNDS

The first hedge fund was established in 1949, the Jones Hedge Fund. Alfred Winslow Jones established a fund that invested in U.S. stocks, both long and short. The intent was to limit market risk while focusing on stock selection. Consequently, this fund was not tied to a securities benchmark and may be properly classified as an equity long/short fund.

Jones operated in relative obscurity until an article was published in *Fortune* magazine that spotlighted the Jones Hedge Fund.[4] The interest in Jones' product was large, and within two years a survey conducted by the SEC established that the number of hedge funds had grown from one to 140.

Unfortunately, many hedge funds were liquidated during the bear market of the early 1970s, and the industry did not regain any interest until the end of the 1980s. The appeal of hedge funds has increased tremendously in the 1990s. By 1998, the President's Working Group on Financial Markets estimated that there were up to 3,500 hedge funds with more than $300 billion in capital and up to $1 trillion in total assets.[5] Compare this size to mutual funds, where the amount of total assets was $5 trillion in 1998.

Therefore, the hedge fund industry is about 1/5 the size of the mutual fund industry. Still the interest in hedge funds is growing. And despite the start of the Jones Hedge Fund five decades ago, the industry is still relatively new. Another estimate of the hedge fund industry is that it has grown from $50 billion in capital in 1990 to $362 billion in 1999. However, the hedge fund market is highly fragmented, with less than 20 funds managing $3 billion or more.[6] The fragmented nature of the hedge fund industry is indicative of its nascent beginning.

Long-Term Capital Management

The hedge fund market hit another speed bump in 1998 when Long-Term Capital Management (LTCM) of Greenwich, Connecticut had to be rescued by a consortium of banks and brokerage firms. At the time LTCM was considered to be one of the largest and best of the hedge fund managers.

LTCM was founded in 1994 by several executives from Salomon Brothers Inc. as well as well-known academics in the field of finance.

---

[4] See Carol Loomis, "The Jones Nobody Keeps Up With," *Fortune* (April 1966), pp. 237–247.
[5] See The President's Working Group on Financial Markets, "Hedge Funds, Leverage, and the Lessons of Long-Term Capital Management," April 1999.
[6] See Chip Cummins, "Hedge Funds Not Worried about Pending U.S. Regulations," Dow Jones International News (March 28, 2000); and the *New York Times*, "Hedge Fund Industry Creates a Dinosaur: The Macro Manager," May 6, 2000, Section B.

The reputation of the founding principals of LTCM were such that the fund enjoyed instant prestige within the hedge fund community.

LTCM implemented a variety of strategies best known as Relative Value trades. It earned returns, net of fees of approximately 40% in 1995 and 1996, and about 20% in 1997.[7] At the end of 1997, LTCM returned $2.7 billion to its investors, but did not noticeably reduce its investment positions. At the start of 1998, its capital base was $4.8 billion, with assets on its balance sheet of $125 billion. This was a leverage ration greater than 25 to 1.

In addition, the fund had over 60,000 trades on its books. The gross notional amount of the fund's futures contracts totaled $500 billion, the notional amount of its swap positions totaled $750 billion, and its options and other over the counter derivative positions totaled $150 billion.[8] The leverage ratio implied by these derivative positions was a whopping 291.67 to 1.

The troubles for LTCM began in May and June in 1998 with losses in its mortgage-backed arbitrage portfolio. By August 1998, LTCM's balance sheet still showed $125 billion in assets but its capital base had shrunk to about $2.3 billion.[9] This was a leverage ratio of about 54 to 1. LTCM suffered further losses in August and September, losing approximately 42% and 83%, respectively. By the end of September, LTCM's capital base had declined to just $400 million.[10]

Unfortunately, LTCM's positions were directly impacted by the Russian Bond default in the summer of 1998. In August 1998, the Russian government defaulted on the payment of its outstanding bonds. This caused a worldwide liquidity crisis with credit spreads expanding rapidly around the globe. The Federal Reserve Bank stepped in and acted quickly with three rate reductions within six months, but this action could not salvage LTCM.

The basis for most of LTCM's relative value trades is that the spread in prices between two similar securities would converge over time. LTCM would buy the cheaper security and short the more expensive security and wait for the spread between the two similar securities to narrow to lock in its profit. However, as a result of the Russian bond default, there was a sudden and drastic liquidity crisis, and spreads widened across a whole range of markets. The result was that instead of contracting as LTCM's pricing models had predicted, pricing spreads

---

[7] The President's Working Group on Financial Markets, p. 16.

[8] The President's Working Group on Financial Markets, p. 17.

[9] See Philippe Jorion, "Risk Management Lessons from Long Term Capital Management," working paper, January 2000.

[10] Id. at p. 7.

dramatically increased in most markets. LTCM quickly accumulated very large paper losses. The lost value of their paper positions led to a margin call from LTCM's prime broker. LTCM was forced to liquidate some of its positions in illiquid markets that were temporarily out of balance. This caused more losses, which led to more margin calls, and LTCM's financial positions began to spiral downward.

The situation for LTCM was bleak, and large financial institutions feared that if LTCM were forced to liquidate the majority of its portfolio there would be a negative impact in the financial markets. Finally, on September 23, at the neutral site of the Federal Reserve Bank of New York, 14 banks and brokerage firms met and agreed to provide a capital infusion of $3.6 billion to LTCM. In return the consortium of banks and brokerage firms received 90% ownership of LTCM.

While the cause of LTCM's demise was clear, the real questions is how did LTCM achieve such a huge amount of credit such that it could leverage its cash positions at a 25 to 1 ratio, and its derivative positions at almost a 300 to 1 ratio? It was simple: LTCM did not reveal its full trading positions to any of its counterparties. Each counterparty was kept in the dark about the size of LTCM's total credit exposure with all other counterparties. As a result, LTCM was able to amass tremendous credit and nearly sent a shock wave of epic proportions through the financial markets.[11]

It should be noted that LTCM's spread trades would have worked if it had had more time to work its way out of the liquidity crisis that gripped the markets. It was not that LTCM had poor trade ideas. On the contrary, its valuation models were robust. Instead, it was a significant imbalance of liquidity brought on by the Russian bond default that caused a flight to quality. When this happened, LTCM's relative value positions diverged instead of converging, and this punished LTCM's capital position. The liquidity crisis coupled with very large amounts of leverage only spelled trouble for LTCM.

Growth of the Hedge Fund Industry

By any stretch of the imagination, the growth of the hedge fund industry has been explosive. Because the hedge fund industry is by and large a private industry based on private limited partnerships, the growth of the hedge fund industry cannot be precisely tracked. However, Exhibit 3.2 provides a reasonable estimate of the growth of hedge funds in the United States. By most estimates, the hedge fund industry now has $1.5 trillion committed to it, a significant increase from just $500 billion in year 2000.

---

[11] As it was, the near demise of LTCM had an impact on the hedge fund industry. We examine this point more closely in our chapters on risk management.

EXHIBIT 3.2   Growth of the Hedge Fund Industry

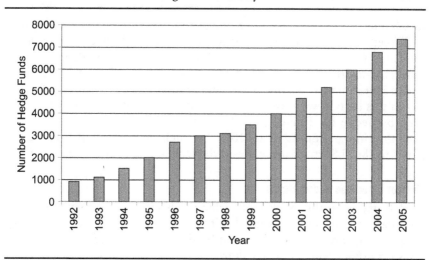

There are many reasons for the huge interest in hedge funds. First, a global three year bear market of 2000 to 2002 fueled the interest of those investors who saw their traditional stock-and-bond portfolios decline in value. Second, many investors recognize the advantage that hedge funds have to go both long and short to maximize the value of their information about stocks, bonds, and other securities. Third, in the current economic environment of 2005, many investors are forecasting single digit equity and bond returns. This has encouraged investors all the more to seek the potential double digit returns of the hedge fund industry.

Finally, there has been a consistent brain drain of investment talent drawn to the hedge fund industry. The ability to earn 2-and-20 fees is far greater than what a portfolio manager can earn running a mutual fund. The exodus of talent to the hedge fund industry continues to drive the growth of assets to this brand of investing as well as set the stage for some amazing compensation.

The best hedge fund managers can earn hundreds of millions of dollars in a single year. In 2004, the best paid hedge fund manager was Eddie Lampert of ESL. He took control of Kmart Holding Corp. and merged it with Sears Roebuck. For his efforts, he earned over $1 billion in incentive and management fees. All told, the top 10 hedge fund managers in the United States earned almost $4.4 billion in fees in 2004.[12]

---

[12] See David Clark, "Lampert is Top-Paid Hedge Fund Manager in 2004 Survey," *Bloomberg News*, May 27, 2005.

HEDGE FUND STRATEGIES

In Chapter 1 we indicated that hedge funds invest in the same equity and fixed income securities as traditional long-only managers. Therefore, it is not the alternative "assets" in which hedge funds invest that differentiates them from long-only managers, but rather, it is the alternative investment strategies that they pursue.

In this section we provide more detail on the types of strategies pursued by hedge fund managers. We also provide a performance history over the time period 1990 to 2005 for each hedge fund strategy compared to the U.S. stock market and the U.S. Treasury bond market.

Market Direction Hedge Funds

The strategies in this bucket of hedge funds either retain some systematic market exposure associated with the stock market such as *equity long/short* or are specifically driven by the movements of the stock market such are *market timing* or *short selling*.

Equity Long/Short

Equity long/short managers build their portfolios by combining a core group of long stock positions with short sales of stock or stock index options/futures. Their net market exposure of long positions minus short positions tends to have a positive bias. That is, equity long/short managers tend to be long market exposure. The length of their exposure depends on current market conditions. For instance, during the great stock market surge of 1996 to 1999, these managers tended to be mostly long their equity exposure. However, as the stock market turned into a bear market in 2000 to 2002, these managers decreased their market exposure as they sold more stock short or sold stock index options and futures.

For example, consider a hedge fund manager in 2005 who had a 150% long exposure to tobacco industry stocks and had a 50% short exposure to computer technology. The portfolio is net long at 100%. The beta of the Russell tobacco index is 0.85, and for the computer index it is 1.4. The weighted average beta of the portfolio is

$$[1.5 \times 0.85] + [-0.5 \times 1.4] = 0.58$$

Beta is a well-known measure of market exposure (or systematic risk). A portfolio with a beta of 1.0 is considered to have the same stock market exposure or risk as a broad-based stock index such as the S&P 500.

According to the *Capital Asset Pricing Model* (CAPM), the hedge fund manager has a conservative portfolio. The expected return of this portfolio according the model is[13]

$$4\% + 0.58 \times (3.4\% - 4\%) = 3.65\%$$

However, in 2005, the total return on the S&P Tobacco Index was 30.5% while for the computer technology it was –4.0%. This "conservative" hedge fund portfolio would have earned the following return in 2005:

$$[1.5 \times 30.5\%] + [-0.50 \times -4\%] = 47.75\%$$

This is a much higher return than that predicted by the CAPM. This example serves to highlight two points. First, the ability to go both long and short in the market is a powerful tool for earning excess returns. The ability to fully implement a strategy not only about stocks and sectors that are expected to increase in value but also stocks and sectors that are expected to decrease in value allows the hedge fund manager to maximize the value of her market insights.

Second, the long/short nature of the portfolio can be misleading with respect to the risk exposure. This manager is 100% net long. Additionally, the beta of the combined portfolio is only 0.58. From this an investor might conclude that the hedge fund manager is pursuing a low risk strategy. However, this is not true. What the hedge fund manager has done is to make two explicit bets: that tobacco stocks will appreciate in value and that computer stocks will decline in value.

The CAPM assumes that investors hold a well-diversified portfolio. That is not the case with this hedge fund manager. Most hedge fund managers build concentrated rather than broad portfolios. Consequently, traditional metrics such as the CAPM may not apply to hedge fund managers.

Equity long/short hedge funds essentially come in two flavors: fundamental or quantitative. Fundamental long/short hedge funds conduct traditional economic analysis on a company's business prospects compared to its competitors and the current economic environment. These shops will visit with management, talk with Wall Street analysts, contact customers and competitors and essentially conduct bottom-up analysis.

---

[13] The CAPM is expressed as:

E(Return on portfolio)

= Risk-free rate + Beta × (Return on the market – Risk-free rate)

In 2005, the return on the market, represented by the S&P 500 was 3.4%, while the one-year risk-free rate was about 4%.

The difference between these hedge funds and long-only managers is that they will short the stocks that they consider to be poor performers and buy those stocks that are expected to outperform the market. In addition, they may leverage their long and short positions.

Fundamental long/short equity hedge funds tend to invest in one economic sector or market segment. For instance, they may specialize in buying and selling internet companies (sector focus) or buying and selling small market capitalization companies (segment focus).

In contrast, quantitative equity long/short hedge fund managers tend not to be sector or segment specialists. In fact, quite the reverse, quantitative hedge fund managers like to cast as broad a net as possible in their analysis. These managers are often referred to as statistical arbitrage because they base their trade selection on the use of quantitative statistics instead of fundamental stock selection.

In Exhibit 3.3, we provide a graph of a hypothetical investment of $1,000 in an equity long/short fund of funds compared to the S&P 500 and 10-year U.S. Treasury Bonds. The time period is 1990 through 2004. The dashed line represents the hedge fund strategy, the dotted line represents the S&P 500, and the solid line represents the U.S. Treasury bond return. As can be seen, the returns to this strategy were quite favorable compared to the stock market and bond market.

EXHIBIT 3.3   Equity Long/Short Hedge Funds

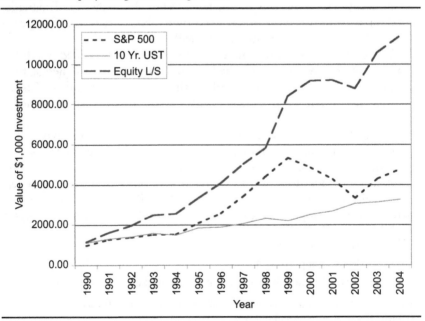

Market Timers

Market timers, as their name suggest, attempt to time the most propitious moments to be in the market, and invest in cash otherwise. More specifically, they attempt to time the market so that they are fully invested during bull markets, and strictly in cash during bear markets.

Unlike equity long/short strategies, market timers use a top-down approach as opposed to a bottom-up approach. Market-timing hedge fund managers are not stock pickers. They analyze fiscal and monetary policy as well as key macroeconomic indicators to determine whether the economy is gathering or running out of steam.

Macroeconomic variables they may analyze are labor productivity, business investment, purchasing managers' surveys, commodity prices, consumer confidence, housing starts, retail sales, industrial production, balance of payments, current account deficits/surpluses, and durable good orders.

They use this macroeconomic data to forecast the expected *gross domestic product* (GDP) for the next quarter. Forecasting models typically are based on multifactor linear regressions, taking into account whether a variable is a leading or lagging indicator and whether the variable experiences any seasonal effects.

Once market timers have their forecast for the next quarter(s) they position their investment portfolio in the market according to their forecast. Construction of their portfolio is quite simple. They do not need to purchase individual stocks. Instead, they buy or sell stock index futures and options to increase or decrease their exposure to the market as necessary. At all times, contributed capital from investors in kept in short-term, risk-free, interest bearing accounts. Treasury bills are often purchased which not only yield a current risk-free interest rate, but also can be used as margin for the purchase of stock index futures.

When a market timer's forecast is bullish, he may purchase stock index futures with an economic exposure equivalent to the contributed capital. He may apply leverage by purchasing futures contracts that provide an economic exposure to the stock market greater than that of the underlying capital. However, market timers generally do not borrow investment capital.

When the hedge fund manager is bearish, he will trim his market exposure by selling futures contracts. If he is completely bearish, he will sell all of his stock index futures and call options and just sit on his cash portfolio. Some market timers may be more aggressive and short stock index futures and buy stock index put options to take advantage of bear markets.

In general though, market timers tend to have long exposure to the market at all times, making them market directional. However, they attempt to trim this exposure when markets appear bearish. This is demonstrated during the bear market years of 2000 to 2002. Consequently, we find that market timers have a similar, but slightly more

EXHIBIT 3.4   Equity Market Timing

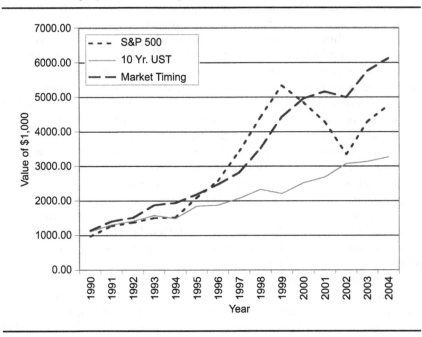

conservative risk profile than the stock market. Exhibit 3.4 presents the profile for market-timing hedge funds.

Short Selling

Short selling hedge funds have the opposite exposure of traditional long-only managers. In that sense, their return distribution should be the mirror image of long-only managers: they make money when the stock market is declining and lose money when the stock market is gaining.

These hedge fund managers may be distinguished from equity long/short managers in that they generally maintain a net short exposure to the stock market. However, short selling hedge funds tend to use some form of market timing. That is, they trim their short positions when the stock market is increasing and go fully short when the stock market is declining. When the stock market is gaining, short sellers maintain that portion of their investment capital not committed to short selling in short-term interest rate bearing accounts.

Exhibit 3.5 demonstrates the return to short selling hedge funds compared to the S&P 500 and U.S. Treasury bonds. In general short sellers do very well during a bear market. From Exhibit 3.4, short sellers provided

EXHIBIT 3.5   Short Selling

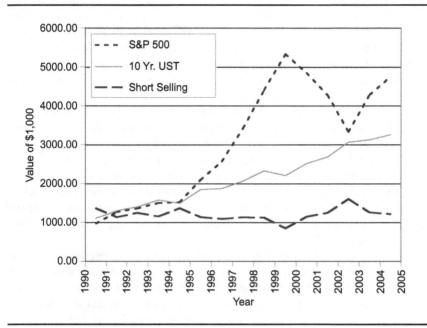

strong positive performance during the bear market of 2000 to 2002, but otherwise the returns to this strategy are not generally favorable because there was a significant bull market from 1990 through 1999. Short selling strategies, therefore, provide good downside protection for bear markets, but otherwise do not add positive value to a portfolio. They should be included in a hedge fund of funds for their protective ability, but should not be the focal point for generating excess returns.

Corporate Restructuring Hedge Funds

Many hedge fund articles call these strategies "event driven" or "risk arbitrage" but that does not really describe what is at the heart of each of these type of strategies. The focal point is some form of corporate restructuring such a merger, acquisition, or bankruptcy. Companies that are undergoing a significant transformation generally provide an opportunity for trading around that event. These strategies are driven by the deal, not by the market.

Distressed Securities

Distressed debt hedge funds invest in the securities of a corporation that it is in bankruptcy, or is likely to fall into bankruptcy. Companies can become distressed for any number of reasons such as too much leverage on their balance sheet, poor operating performance, accounting irregularities, even competitive pressure. Some of these strategies can overlap with private equity strategies that we will discuss in Part Four of this book. The key difference here is that hedge funds are less concerned with the fundamental value of a distressed corporation and, instead, concentrate on trading opportunities surrounding the company's outstanding stock-and-bond securities.

There are many different variations on how to play a distressed situation but most fall into three categories. In its simplest form, the easiest way to profit from a distressed corporation is to sell its stock short. This requires the hedge fund manager to borrow stock from its prime broker and sell in the market place stock that it does not own with the expectation that hedge fund manager will be able to purchase the stock back at a later date and at a cheaper price as the company continues to spiral downward in its distressed situation. This is nothing more than "sell high and buy low."

However, the short selling of a distressed company exposes the hedge fund manager to significant risk if the company's fortunes should suddenly turnaround. Therefore, most hedge fund managers in this space typically use a hedging strategy within a company's capital structure.

A second form of distressed securities investing is called *capital structure arbitrage*. Consider Company A that has four levels of outstanding capital: senior secured debt, junior subordinated debt, preferred stock, and common stock. A standard distressed security investment strategy would be to:

1. Buy the senior secured debt and short the junior subordinated debt.
2. Buy the preferred stock and short the common stock.

In a bankruptcy situation, the senior secured debt stands in line in front of the junior subordinated debt for any bankruptcy determined payouts. The same is true for the preferred stock compared to Company A's common stock. Both the senior secured debt and the preferred stock enjoy a higher standing in the bankruptcy process than either junior debt or common equity. Therefore, when the distressed situation occurs or progresses, senior secured debt should appreciate in value relative to the junior subordinated debt. In addition, there should be an increase in the spread of prices between preferred stock and common stock. When this happens, the hedge fund manager closes out her positions and locks in the profit that occurs from the increase in the spread.

Last, distressed securities hedge funds can become involved in the bankruptcy process to find significantly undervalued securities. This is

EXHIBIT 3.6   Distressed Debt

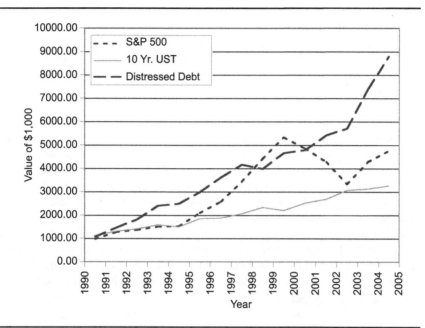

where an overlap with private equity firms can occur. To the extent that a distressed securities hedge fund is willing to learn the arcane workings of the bankruptcy process and to sit on creditor committees, significant value can be accrued if a distressed company can restructure and regain its footing. In a similar fashion, hedge fund managers do purchase the securities of a distressed company shortly before it announces a its reorganization plan to the bankruptcy court with the expectation that there will be a positive resolution with the company's creditors.

Exhibit 3.6 presents the value of distressed securities hedge funds compared to the U.S. stock-and-bond market. It shows a reasonably steady growth over the time 1990 through 2001, but significant growth from 2002 through 2005. This is indicative of distressed securities hedge funds capitalizing on the recovering of the U.S. credit markets and the U.S. economy after the three year bear market of 2000 to 2002. It appears that many distressed securities hedge funds followed the third strategy during this timeframe and enjoyed the benefits of successful reorganization of companies coming out of bankruptcy during a bull market.

Merger Arbitrage

Merger arbitrage is perhaps the best-known corporate restructuring investment among investors and hedge fund managers. *Merger arbitrage* generally entails the buying the stock of the firm that is to be acquired and selling the stock of the firm that is the acquirer. Merger arbitrage managers seek to capture the price spread between the current market prices of the merger partners and the value of those companies upon the successful completion of the merger.

The stock of the target company usually trades at a discount to the announced merger price. The discount reflects the risk inherent in the deal; other market participants are unwilling to take on the full exposure of the transaction-based risk. Merger arbitrage is then subject to event risk. There is the risk that the two companies will fail to come to terms and call off the deal. There is the risk that another company will enter into the bidding contest, ruining the initial dynamics of the arbitrage. There is finally regulatory risk. Various U.S. and foreign regulatory agencies may not allow the merger to take place for antitrust reasons. Merger arbitrageurs specialize in assessing event risk and building a diversified portfolio to spread out this risk.

Merger arbitrageurs conduct significant research on the companies involved in the merger. They will review current and prior financial statements, SEC EDGAR filings, proxy statements, management structures, cost savings from redundant operations, strategic reasons for the merger, regulatory issues, press releases, and competitive position of the combined company within the industries it competes. Merger arbitrageurs will calculate the rate of return that is implicit in the current spread and compare it to the event risk associated with the deal. If the spread is sufficient to compensate for the expected event risk, they will execute the arbitrage.

Once again, the term "arbitrage" is used loosely. As discussed above, there is plenty of event risk associated with a merger announcement. The profits earned from merger arbitrage are not riskless. Consider the saga of the purchase of MCI Corporation by Verizon Communications. Throughout 2005, Verizon was in a bidding war against Qwest Communications for the purchase of MCI. On February 3, 2005, Qwest announced a $6.3 billion merger offer for MCI. This bid was quickly countered by Verizon on February 10 that matched the $6.3 billion bid established by Qwest. The bidding war raged back and forth for several months before Verizon finally won the day in October of 2005 with an ultimate purchase price of $8.44 billion.

To see the vicissitudes of merger arbitrage at work, we follow both the successful Verizon bid for MCI as well as the unsuccessful bid by Qwest.

Starting with Verizon: at the announcement of its bid for MCI, its stock was trading at $36.00, while MCI was trading at $20. Therefore the merger arbitrage trade was:

Sell 1,000 shares of Verizon at $36 (short proceeds of $36,000).
Buy 1,000 shares of MCI at $20 (cash outflow of $20,000).

While for the Qwest bid, the trade was:

Sell 1,000 shares of Qwest at $4.20 (short proceeds of $4,200).
Buy 1,000 shares of MCI at $20 (cash outflow of $20,000).

Throughout the spring and summer of 2005, Qwest and Verizon battled it out for MCI with Verizon ultimately winning in October 2005. At that time, MCI's stock had increased in value to $25.50, while Verizon's stock had lost value and was trading at $30, and finally Qwest was trading unchanged at $4.20.

Total return for the MCI/Verizon Merger Arbitrage trade:

Gain on MCI long position:	$1,000 \times (\$25.50 - \$20)$	= $5,500
Gain on Verizon short position:	$1,000 \times (\$36 - \$30)$	= $6,000
Interest on short rebate:	$4\% \times 1,000 \times \$36 \times 240/360$ =	$960
Total		$12,460

The return on invested capital is: $12,460 ÷ $20,000 = 62.3%.

If the merger arbitrage manager had applied 50% leverage to this deal and borrowed half of the net outflow the return would have been (ignoring financing costs):

$$\$12,460 \div \$10,000 = 124.6\% \text{ total return}$$

Turning to the MCI/Qwest merger arbitrage trade, the total return was:

Gain on MCI long position	$1,000 \times (\$25.50 - \$20)$	= $5,500
Gain on Qwest short position:	$1,000 \times (\$4.20 - \$4.20)$	= $0
Gain on short rebate:	$4\% \times 1,000 \times \$4.20 \times 240/360$ =	$112
Total		$5,612

The return on invested capital is: $5,612 ÷ $20,000 = 28.06%. With 50% leverage the return would be: $5,612 ÷ $10,000 = 56.12%.

While both merger arbitrage trades made money, clearly, it made sense to bet on the Verizon/MCI merger than the Qwest/MCI merger. This is where merger arbitrage managers make their money, by assessing the likelihood of one bid over another. Also, in a situation where there are two bidders for a company, there is a very high probability that there will be a successful merger with one of the bidders. Consequently, many merger arbitrage hedge fund managers will play both bids. This is exactly what happened in the MCI deal—many merger arbitrage managers bet on both the MCI/Verizon deal as well as the MCI/Qwest deal, expecting that one of the two suitors would be successful in winning the hand of MCI.

Some merger arbitrage managers only invest in announced deals. However, other hedge fund managers will put on positions on the basis of rumor or speculation. The deal risk is much greater with this type of strategy, but so too, is the merger spread (the premium that can be captured).

To control for risk, most merger arbitrage hedge fund managers have some risk of loss limit at which they will exit positions. Some hedge fund managers concentrate only in one or two industries, applying their specialized knowledge regarding an economic sector to their advantage. Other merger arbitrage managers maintain a diversified portfolio across several industries to spread out the event risk.

Merger arbitrage is deal driven rather than market driven. Merger arbitrage derives its return from the relative value of the stock prices between two companies as opposed to the status of the current market conditions. Consequently, merger arbitrage returns should not be highly correlated with the general stock market.

Exhibit 3.7 highlights this point. We see steady consistent returns year after year. There are no years of extraordinary gains, and no years of extraordinary losses. Merger arbitrage is not driven by the systematic risk of the market; rather it is driven by the economics of the individual deals.

EXHIBIT 3.7 Merger Arbitrage

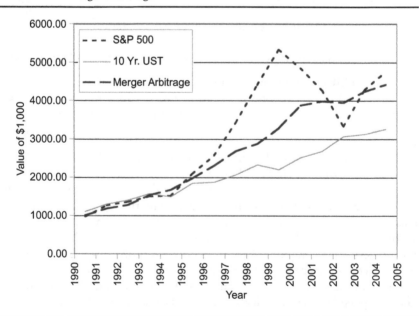

Event Driven

Event-driven hedge funds are very similar in their approach to investing as distressed securities and merger arbitrage. The only difference is that their mandate is broader than the other two corporate-restructuring strategies. Event-driven transactions include mergers and acquisitions, spin-offs, tracking stocks, accounting write-offs, reorganizations, bankruptcies, share buy-backs, special dividends, and any other significant market event. Event-driven managers are nondiscriminatory in their transaction selection.

By their very nature, these special events are nonrecurring. Therefore, the financial markets typically do not digest the information associated with these transactions in a timely manner. The financial markets are simply less efficient when it comes to large, isolated transactions. This provides an opportunity for event-driven managers to act quickly and capture a premium in the market. Additionally, most of these events may be subject to certain conditions such as shareholder or regulatory approval. Therefore, there is significant deal risk associated with this strategy for which a savvy hedge fund manager can earn a return premium. The profitability of this type of strategy is dependent upon the successful completion of the corporate transaction within the expected timeframe.

We would expect event-driven strategies to be less influenced by the general stock market, since the returns are driven by company specific events, not market-driven events. However, in Exhibit 3.8 we do see that the value of event-driven strategies does closely parallel that value of the S&P 500 from 1990 to 1999 and then significantly outperforms the stock market from 2000 to 2005. This may reflect the fact that event-driven hedge fund managers participated in the many positive corporate mergers and acquisitions that occurred during the bull market, but then, were also able to participate in the many corporate reorganizations that occurred during the bear market years of 2000 to 2002.

Convergence Trading Hedge Funds

Hedge fund managers tend to use the term "arbitrage" somewhat loosely. Arbitrage is defined simply as riskless profits. It is the purchase of a security for cash at one price and the immediate resale for cash of the same security at a higher price. Alternatively, it may be defined as the simultaneous purchase of security A for cash at one price and the selling of identical security B for cash at a higher price. In both cases, the arbitrageur has no risk. There is no market risk because the holding of the securities is instantaneous. There is no basis risk because the securities are identical, and there is no credit risk because the transaction is conducted in cash.

EXHIBIT 3.8   Event Driven

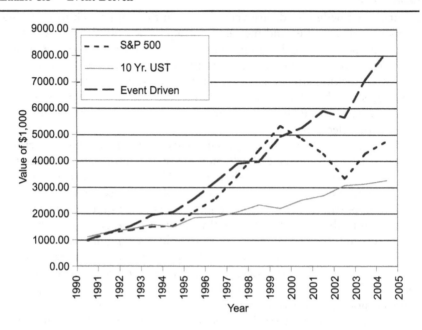

Instead of riskless profits, in the hedge fund world, arbitrage is generally used to mean low-risk investments. Instead of the purchase and sale of identical instruments, there is the purchase and sale of similar instruments. The securities also may not be sold for cash, so there may be credit risk during the collection period. Finally, the purchase and sale may not be instantaneous. The arbitrageur may need to hold onto its positions for a period of time, exposing him to market risk.

Fixed Income Arbitrage

Fixed income arbitrage involves purchasing one fixed income security and simultaneously selling a similar fixed income security with the expectation that over the investment holding period, the two security prices will converge to a similar value. Hedge fund managers search continuously for these pricing inefficiencies across all fixed income markets. This is nothing more than buying low and selling high and waiting for the undervalued security to increase in value or the overvalued security to decline in value, or wait for both to occur.

The sale of the second security is done to hedge the underlying market risk contained in the first security. Typically, the two securities are related

related either mathematically or economically such that they move similarly with respect to market developments. Generally, the difference in pricing between the two securities is small, and this is what the fixed income arbitrageur hopes to gain. By buying and selling two fixed income securities that are tied together, the hedge fund manager hopes to capture a pricing discrepancy that will cause the prices of the two securities to converge overtime.

However, because the price discrepancies can be small, the way hedge fund managers add more value is to leverage their portfolio through direct borrowings from their prime broker, or by creating leverage through swaps and other derivative securities. Bottom line, they find pricing anomalies then "crank up the volume" through leverage.

Fixed income arbitrage does not need to use exotic securities. For example, it can be nothing more than buying and selling U.S. Treasury bonds. In the bond market, the most liquid securities are the *on-the-run* Treasury bonds. These are the most currently issued bonds issued by the U.S. Treasury Department. However, there are other U.S. Treasury bonds outstanding that have very similar characteristics to the on-the-run Treasury bonds. The difference is that *off-the-run* bonds were issued at an earlier date, and are now less liquid as the on-the-run bonds. As a result, price discrepancies occur. The difference in price may be no more than one-half or one quarter of a point ($25) but can increase in times of uncertainty when investor money shifts to the most liquid U.S. Treasury bond. During the Russian Bond Default crisis, for example, on-the-run U.S. Treasuries were valued as much as $100 more than similar, off-the-run U.S. Treasury bonds of the same maturity.

Nonetheless, when held to maturity, the prices of these two bonds will converge to the same value. Any difference will be eliminated by the time they mature, and any price discrepancy may be captured by the hedge fund manager.

Fixed income arbitrage is not limited to the U.S. Treasury market. It can be used with corporate bonds, municipal bonds, sovereign debt, or mortgage backed securities.

Another form of fixed income arbitrage involves trading among fixed income securities that are close in maturity. This is a form of yield curve arbitrage. These types of trades are driven by temporary imbalances in the term structure of interest rates.

Consider an example where there are "kinks" in the term structure between the three-month and five-year time horizon. Kinks in the yield curve can happen at any maturity and usually reflect an increase (or decrease) in liquidity demand around the focal point. These kinks provide an opportunity to profit by purchasing and selling Treasury securities that are similar in maturity.

For example, suppose that there is a kink that peaks at the two-year maturity. The holder of the two-year Treasury bond profits by rolling down the yield curve. In other words, if interest rates remain static, the two-year Treasury note will age into a lower yielding part of the yield curve. Moving down the yield curve will mean positive price appreciation. Conversely, Treasury bonds maturing in the three to five year range will roll up the yield curve to higher yields. This means that their prices are expected to depreciate.

An arbitrage trade would be to purchase the two-year Treasury bond and short a three-year bond. As the three-year bond rolls up the yield curve, its value should decline while the two-year Treasury bond should increase in value as it rolls down the yield curve. This arbitrage trade will work as long as the kinks remain in place.

However, this trade does have its risks. First, shifts in the yield curve up or down can affect the profitability of the trade because the two securities have different maturities and duration. To counter this problem, the hedge fund manager would need to purchase and sell securities in proper proportion to neutralize the differences in duration. Also, liquidity preferences of investors could change and the kink could reverse itself, or flatten out. In either case, the hedge fund manager will lose money. Conversely, should liquidity preferences increase, the trade will become even more profitable.

Still another subset of fixed income arbitrage uses *mortgage-backed securities* (MBS). MBS represent an ownership interest in an underlying pool of individual mortgages loaned by banks and other financial institutions. Therefore, an MBS is a fixed income security with underlying prepayment options. MBS hedge funds seek to capture pricing inefficiencies in the U.S. mortgage backed market.

MBS arbitrage can be between fixed income markets such as buying MBS and selling U.S. Treasuries. This investment strategy is designed to capture credit spread inefficiencies between U.S. Treasuries and MBS. MBS trade at a credit spread over U.S. Treasuries to reflect the uncertainty of cash flows associated with MBS compared the lack of credit risk associated with U.S. Treasury bonds.

As noted above, during a flight to quality, investors tend to seek out the most liquid markets such as the on-the-run U.S. Treasury market. This may cause credit spreads to temporarily increase beyond what is historically or economically justified. In this case the MBS market will be priced "cheap" to U.S. Treasuries. The arbitrage strategy would be to buy MBS and sell U.S. Treasury, where the interest rate exposure of both instruments is sufficiently similar so as to eliminate most (if not all) of the market risk between the two securities. The expectation is that the credit spread between MBS and U.S. Treasuries will decline and MBS bonds will increase in value relative to U.S. Treasuries.

MBS arbitrage can be quite sophisticated. MBS hedge fund managers use proprietary models to rank the value of MBS by their option-adjusted spread (OAS). The hedge fund manager evaluates the present value of an MBS by explicitly incorporating assumptions about the probability of prepayment options being exercised. In effect, the hedge fund manager calculates the option-adjusted price of the MBS and compares it to its current market price. The OAS reflects the MBS' average spread over U.S. Treasury bonds of a similar maturity, taking into account the fact that the MBS may be liquidated early from the exercise of the prepayment option by the underlying mortgagors.

The MBS that have the best OAS compared to U.S. Treasuries are purchased, and then their interest rate exposure is hedged to zero. Interest rate exposure is neutralized using Treasury bonds, options, swaps, futures and caps. MBS hedge fund managers seek to maintain a duration of zero. This allows them to concentrate on selecting the MBS that yield the highest OAS.

There are many risks associated with MBS arbitrage. Chief among them are duration, convexity, yield curve rotation, prepayment risk, credit risk, and liquidity risk. Hedging these risks may require the purchase of sale of other MBS products such as interest-only strips and principal-only strips, U.S. Treasuries, interest rate futures, swaps, and options.

What should be noted about fixed income arbitrage strategies is that they do not depend on the direction of the general financial markets. Arbitrageurs seek out pricing inefficiencies between two securities instead of making bets on market direction.

This is clear from Exhibit 3.9. Fixed income arbitrage earns a steady consistent rate year after year, regardless of the movement of the stock market. The one exception is 1998 and the dual crisis of the Russian bond default and the LTCM bailout. Otherwise, the hypothetical value of $1,000 invested in fixed income arbitrage is almost a straight line, matching that of the 10 year U.S. Treasury bond.

Convertible Bond Arbitrage

Convertible bonds combine elements of both stock and bonds in one package. A convertible bond is a bond that contains an embedded option to convert the bond into the underlying company's stock.

Convertible arbitrage funds build long positions of convertible bonds and then hedge the equity component of the bond by selling the underlying stock or options on that stock. Equity risk can be hedged by selling the appropriate ratio of stock underlying the convertible option. This hedge ratio is known as the "delta" and is designed to measure the sensitivity of the convertible bond value to movements in the underlying stock.

EXHIBIT 3.9 Fixed Income Arbitrage

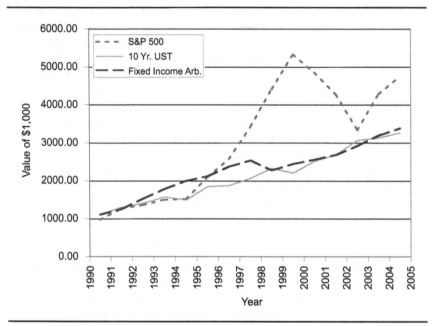

Convertible bonds that trade at a low premium to their conversion value tend to be more correlated with the movement of the underlying stock. These convertibles then trade more like stock than they do a bond. Consequently, a high hedge ratio, or delta, is required to hedge the equity risk contained in the convertible bond. Convertible bonds that trade at a premium to their conversion value are highly valued for their bond-like protection. Therefore, a lower delta hedge ratio is necessary.

However, convertible bonds that trade at a high conversion act more like fixed income securities and therefore have more interest rate exposure than those with more equity exposure. This risk must be managed by selling interest rate futures, interest rate swaps or other bonds. Furthermore, it should be noted that the hedging ratios for equity and interest rate risk are not static, they change as the value of the underlying equity changes and as interest rates change. Therefore, the hedge fund manager must continually adjust his hedge ratios to ensure that the arbitrage remains intact.

If this all sounds complicated, it is, but that is how hedge fund managers make money. They use sophisticated option pricing models and interest rate models to keep track of the all of moving parts associated with convertible bonds. Hedge fund managers make arbitrage profits by identifying pricing discrepancies between the convertible bond and its component parts, and then continually monitoring these component parts for any change in their relationship.

Consider the following example. A hedge fund manager purchases 10 convertible bonds with a par value of $1,000, a coupon of 7.5%, and a market price of $900. The conversion ratio for the bonds is 20. The conversion ratio is based on the current price of the underlying stock, $45, and the current price of the convertible bond. The delta, or hedge ratio for the bonds is 0.5. Therefore, to hedge the equity exposure in the convertible bond, the hedge fund manager must short the following shares of underlying stock:

10 Bonds × 20 Conversion ratio × 0.5 Hedge ratio = 100 Shares of stock

To establish the arbitrage, the hedge fund manager purchases 10 convertible bonds and sells 100 shares of stock. With the equity exposure hedged, the convertible bond is transformed into a traditional fixed income instrument with a 7.5% coupon.

Additionally, the hedge fund manager earns interest on the cash proceeds received from the short sale of stock. This is known as the "short rebate." The cash proceeds remain with the hedge fund manager's prime broker, but the hedge fund manager is entitled to the interest earned on the cash balance from the short sale (a rebate).[14] We assume that the hedge fund manager receives a short rebate of 4.5%. Therefore, if the hedge fund manager holds the convertible arbitrage position for one year, he expects to earn interest not only from his long bond position, but also from his short stock position.

The catch to this arbitrage is that the price of the underlying stock may change as well as the price of the bond. Assume the price of the stock increases to $47 and the price of the convertible bond increases to $920. If the hedge fund manager does not adjust the hedge ratio during the holding period, the total return for this arbitrage will be:

Appreciation of bond price:	10 × ($920 − $900)	=	$200
Appreciation of stock price:	100 × ($45 − $47)	=	−$200
Interest on bonds:	10 × $1,000 × 7.5%	=	$750
Short rebate:	100 × $45 × 4.5%	=	$202.50
Total:			$952.50

---

[14] The short rebate is negotiated between the hedge fund manager and the prime broker. Typically, large, well-established hedge fund managers receive a larger short rebate.

If the hedge fund manager paid for the 10 bonds without using any leverage, the holding period return is

$$\$952.50 \div \$9000 = 10.58\%$$

Suppose the underlying stock price declined from \$45 to \$43, and the convertible bonds declined in value from \$900 to \$880. The hedge fund manager would then earn:

Depreciation of bond price:	10 × (\$880 – \$900)	=	–\$200
Depreciation of stock price:	100 × (\$45 – \$43)	=	\$200
Interest on bonds:	10 × \$1,000 × 7.5%	=	\$750
Short rebate:	100 × \$45 × 4.5%	=	\$202.50
Total			\$952.50

What this example demonstrates is that with the proper delta or hedge ratio in place, the convertible arbitrage manager should be insulated from movements in the underlying stock price so that the expected return should be the same regardless of whether the stock price goes up or goes down.

However, suppose that the hedge fund manager purchased the convertible bonds with \$4,500 of initial capital and \$4,500 of borrowed money. We further assume that the hedge fund manager borrows the additional investment capital from his prime broker at a prime rate of 6%.

Our analysis of the total return is then:

Appreciation of bond price:	10 × (\$920 – \$900)	=	\$200
Appreciation of stock price:	100 × (\$47 – \$45)	=	–\$200
Interest on bonds:	10 × \$1,000 × 7.5%	=	\$750
Short rebate:	100 × \$45 × 4.5%	=	\$202.5
Interest on borrowing:	6% × \$4,500	=	–\$270
Total:			\$682.5

And the total return on capital is

$$\$682.5 \div \$4,500 = 15.17\%$$

The amount of leverage used in convertible arbitrage will vary with the size of the long positions and the objectives of the portfolio. Yet, in the above example, we can see how using a conservative leverage ratio of 2:1 in the purchase of the convertible bonds added almost 500 basis points of return to the strategy and earned a total return equal to twice that of the convertible bond coupon rate.

It is easy to see why hedge fund managers are tempted to use leverage. Hedge fund managers earn incentive fees on every additional basis point of return they earn. Furthermore, even though leverage is a two-edged sword—it can magnify losses as well as gains—hedge fund managers bear no loss if the use of leverage turns against them. In other words, hedge fund manages have everything to gain by applying leverage, but nothing to lose.

Leverage is also inherent in the shorting strategy because the underlying short equity position must be borrowed. Convertible arbitrage leverage can range from two to six times the amount of invested capital. This may seem significant, but it is lower than other forms of arbitrage.

Convertible bonds earn returns for taking on exposure to a number of risks such as (1) liquidity (convertible bonds are typically issued as private securities); (2) credit risk (convertible bonds are usually issued by less than investment grade companies); (3) event risk (the company may be downgraded or declare bankruptcy); (4) interest rate risk (as a bond it is exposed to interest rate risk); (5) negative convexity (most convertible bonds are callable); and (6) model risk (it is complex to model all of the moving parts associated with a convertible bond). These events are only magnified when leverage is applied.

Since convertible bond managers hedge away the equity risk through delta neutral hedging we should see little impact from the U.S. stock market. In addition for undertaking all of the risks listed above, convertible bond arbitrage managers should earn a return premium to U.S. Treasury bonds. Exhibit 3.10 confirms these expectations.

EXHIBIT 3.10 Convertible Bond Arbitrage

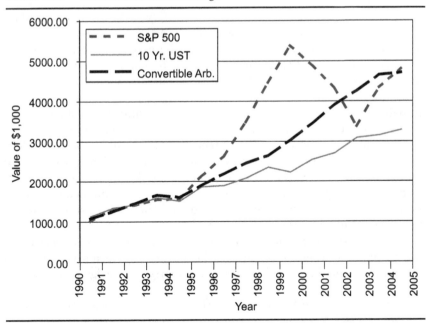

Market Neutral

Market-neutral hedge funds also go long and short the market. The difference, is that they maintain integrated portfolios, which are designed to neutralize market risk. This means being neutral to the general stock market as well as having neutral risk exposures across industries. Security selection is all that matters.

Market-neutral hedge fund managers generally apply the rule of one alpha.[15] This means that they build an integrated portfolio designed to produce only one source of alpha. This is distinct from equity long/short manages that build two separate portfolios: one long and one short, with two sources of alpha. The idea of integrated portfolio construction is to neutralize market and industry risk and concentrate purely on stock selection. In other words, there is no beta risk in the portfolio either with respect to the broad stock market or with respect to any industry. Only stock selection, or alpha, should remain.

Market-neutral hedge fund managers generally hold equal positions of long and short stock positions. Therefore, the manager is dollar neutral; there is no net exposure to the market either on the long side or on the short side. Additionally, market-neutral managers generally apply no leverage because there is no market exposure to leverage. However, some leverage is always inherent when stocks are borrowed and shorted. Nonetheless, the nature of this strategy is that it does not have credit risk.

Generally, market-neutral managers follow a three-step procedure in their strategy. The first step is to build an initial screen of "investable" stocks. These are stocks traded on the manager's local exchange, with sufficient liquidity so as to be able to enter and exit positions quickly, and with sufficient float so that the stock may be borrowed from the hedge fund manager's prime broker for short positions. Additionally, the hedge fund manager may limit his universe to a capitalization segment of the equity universe such as the midcap range.

Second, the hedge fund manager typically builds factor models. These models are often known as "alpha engines." Their purpose is to find those financial variables that influence stock prices. These are bottom-up models that concentrate solely on corporate financial information as opposed to macroeconomic data. This is the source of the manager's skill—his stock selection ability.

The last step is portfolio construction. The hedge fund manager will use a computer program to construct his portfolio in such a way that it is neutral to the market as well as across industries. The hedge fund manager

---

[15] See Bruce Jacobs and Kenneth Levy, "The Law of One Alpha," *The Journal of Portfolio Management* (Summer 1995).

EXHIBIT 9.11   Equity Market Neutral

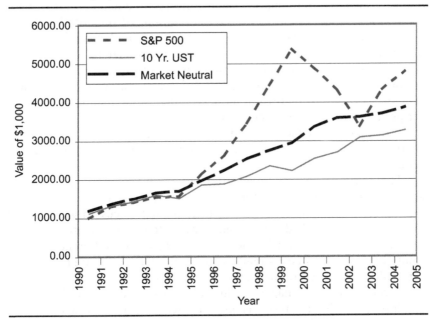

EXHIBIT 9.11   Equity Market Neutral

may use a commercial "optimizer"—computer software designed to measure exposure to the market and produce a trade list for execution based on a manager's desired exposure to the market—or he may use his own computer algorithms to measure and neutralize risk.

Most market-neutral managers use optimizers to neutralize market and industry exposure. However, more sophisticated optimizers attempt to keep the portfolio neutral to several risk factors. These include size, book to value, price/earnings ratios, and market price to book value ratios. The idea is to have no intended or unintended risk exposures that might compromise the portfolio's neutrality.

We have more to say about transparency in our chapters regarding the selection of hedge fund managers and whether the hedge fund industry should be institutionalized. For now, it is sufficient to point out that black boxes tend to be problematic for investors.

We would expect market-neutral managers to produce returns independent of the general market (they are neutral to the market). Exhibit 3.11 confirms this expectation. We see a steady linear progression of market-neutral values compared to the S&P 500.

Statistical Arbitrage

A close cousin to equity market-neutral hedge fund managers is statistical arbitrage. The key difference is the amount of quantitative input. While equity market-neutral is based more on fundamental research, statistical arbitrage is driven purely by quantitative factor models.

These managers use mathematical analysis to review past company performance in light of several quantitative factors. For instance, these managers may build regression models to determine the impact of market price to book value (price/book ratio) on companies across the universe of stocks as well as different market segments or economic sectors. Or they may analyze changes in dividend yields on stock price performance.

These are linear and quadratic regression equations designed to identify those economic factors that consistently have an impact on share prices. This process is very similar to that discussed with respect to equity long/short hedge fund manages. Indeed, the two strategies are very similar in their stock selection methods. The difference is that equity long/short managers tend to have a net long exposure to the market while market-neutral managers have no exposure.

Typically, these managers build multifactor models, both linear and quadratic, to identify those economic factors that have a consistent impact on share prices. One key part of building their alpha engines is to apply the quantitative model on prior stock price performance to see if there is any predictive power in determining whether the stock of a particular company will rise or fall. If the model proves successful on historical data, the hedge fund manager will then conduct an "out of sample" test of the model. This involves testing the model on a subset of historical data that was not included in the model building phase.

If a hedge fund manager identifies a successful quantitative strategy, it will apply its model mechanically. Buy and sell orders will be generated by the model and submitted to the order desk. In practice, the hedge fund manager will put limits on its model such as the maximum short exposure allowed or the maximum amount of capital that may be committed to any one stock position. In addition, quantitative hedge fund managers usually build in some qualitative oversight to ensure that the model is operating consistently.

Statistical arbitrage programs tend to be labeled "black boxes." This is a term for sophisticated computer algorithms that lack transparency. The lack of transparency associated with these investment strategies comes in two forms. First, hedge fund managers, by nature, are secretive. They are reluctant to reveal their proprietary trading programs. Second, even if a hedge fund manager were to reveal his propri-

EXHIBIT 9.12   Statistical Arbitrage

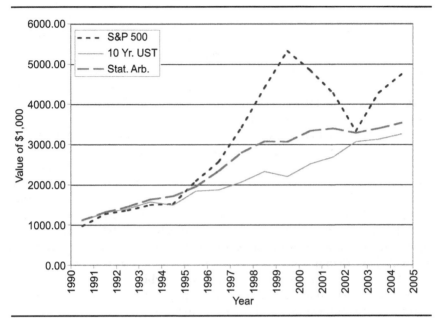

etary computer algorithms, these algorithms are often so sophisticated and complicated that they are difficult to comprehend.

Exhibit 3.12 displays the returns to statistical arbitrage. Note that this strategy does not share in the large up and down cycles of the stock market. It earns a steady return, not as great as the stock market, but in excess of U.S. Treasuries. Remember the goal of this strategy is to neutralize market risk and to profit on small price discrepancies between stocks in the same industry or sector. Consistent profits are the key; large bets are avoided.

Relative Value Arbitrage

Relative value arbitrage might be better named the *smorgasbord* of arbitrage. This is because relative value hedge fund managers are catholic in their investment strategies; they invest across the universe of arbitrage strategies. The best known of these managers was Long-Term Capital Management. Once the story of LTCM unfolded, it was clear that their trading strategies involved merger arbitrage, fixed income arbitrage, volatility arbitrage, stub trading, and convertible arbitrage.

In general, the strategy of relative value managers is to invest in spread trades: the simultaneous purchase of one security and the sale of another when the economic relationship between the two securities (the "spread") has become mispriced. The mispricing may be based on historical averages or mathematical equations. In either case, the relative arbitrage manager purchases the security that is "cheap" and sells the security that is "rich." It is called relative value arbitrage because the cheapness or richness of a security is determined *relative* to a second security. Consequently, relative value managers do not take directional bets on the financial markets. Instead, they take focused bets on the pricing relationship between two securities.

Relative value managers attempt to remove the influence of the financial markets from their investment strategies. This is made easy by the fact that they simultaneously buy and sell similar securities. Therefore, the market risk embedded in each security should cancel out. Any residual risk can be neutralized through the use of options or futures. What is left is pure security selection: the purchase of those securities that are relatively cheap and the sale of those securities that are relatively rich. Relative value managers earn a profit when the spread between the two securities returns to normal. They then unwind their positions and collect their profit.

We have already discussed fixed income arbitrage, convertible arbitrage and statistical arbitrage. Two other popular forms of relative value arbitrage are stub trading and volatility arbitrage.

Stub trading is an equity based strategy. Frequently, companies acquire a majority stake in another company, but their stock price does not fully reflect their interest in the acquired company. As an example, consider Company A whose stock is trading at $50. Company A owns a majority stake in Company B, whose remaining outstanding stock, or stub, is trading at $40. The value of Company A should be the combination of its own operations, estimated at $45 a share, plus its majority stake in Company B's operations, estimated at $8 a share. Therefore, Company A's share price is undervalued relative to the value that Company B should contribute to Company A's share price. The share price of Company A should be about $53, but instead, it is trading at $50. The investment strategy would be to purchase Company A's stock and sell the appropriate ratio of Company B's stock.

Let us assume that Company A's ownership in Company B contributes to 20% of Company A's consolidated operating income. Therefore, the operations of Company B should contribute one fifth to Company A's share price. A proper hedging ratio would be four shares of Company A's stock to one share of Company B's stock.

The arbitrage strategy is:

Buy four shares of Company A stock at 4 × $50 = $200
Sell one share of Company B stock at 1 × $40 = $40

The relative value manager is now long Company A stock and hedged against the fluctuation of Company B's stock. Let us assume that over three months, the share price of Company B increases to $42 a share, the value of Company A's operations remains constant at $45, but now the shares of Company A correctly reflect the contribution of Company B's operations. The value of the position will be:

Value of Company A's operations:	$4 \times \$45$	= $180
Value of Company B's operations	$4 \times \$42 \times 20\%$	= $33.6
Loss on short of Company B stock	$1 \times (\$40 - \$42)$	= –$2
Short rebate on Company B stock	$1 \times \$40 \times 4.5\% \times 3/12$ =	$0.45
Total:		$212.05

The initial invested capital was $200 for a gain of $12.05 or 6.02% over three months. Suppose the stock of Company B had declined to $30, but Company B's operations were properly valued in Company A's share price. The position value would be:

Value of Company A's operations:	$4 \times \$45$	= $180
Value of Company B's operations:	$4 \times \$30 \times 20\%$	= $24
Gain on short of Company B's stock:	$1 \times (\$40 - \$30)$	= $10
Short rebate on Company B's stock:	$1 \times \$40 \times 4.5\% \times 3/12$ =	$0.045
Total:		= $214.45

The initial invested capital was $200 for a gain of $14.45 or 7.22% over three months. Stub trading is not arbitrage. Although the value of Company B's stock has been hedged, the hedge fund manager must still hold its position in Company A's stock until the market recognizes its proper value.

Volatility arbitrage involves options and warrant trading. Option prices contain an *implied* number for volatility. That is, it is possible to observe the market price of an option and back out the value of volatility implied in the current price using various option pricing models. The arbitrageur can then compare options on the same underlying stock to determine if the volatility implied by their prices are the same.

The implied volatility derived from option pricing models should represent the expected volatility of the underlying stock that will be realized over the life of the option. Therefore, two options on the same underlying stock should have the same implied volatility. If they do not, an arbitrage opportunity may be available. Additionally, if the implied volatility is significantly different from the historical volatility of the underlying stock, then relative value arbitrageurs expect the implied volatility will revert back to its historical average.

Volatility arbitrage generally is applied in one of two models. The first is a mean reversion model. This model compares the implied volatility from current option prices to the historical volatility of the underlying security with the expectation that the volatility reflected in the current option price will revert to its historical average and the option price will adjust accordingly.

A second volatility arbitrage model applies a statistical technique called Generalized Autoregressive Conditional Heteroscedasticity (GARCH). GARCH models use prior data points of realized volatility to forecast future volatility. The GARCH forecast is then compared to the volatility implied in current option prices.

Both models are designed to allow hedge fund managers to determine which options are priced "cheap" versus "rich." Once again, relative value managers sell those options that are rich based on the implied volatility *relative* to the historical volatility and buy those options with cheap volatility relative to historical volatility.

Exhibit 3.13 presents the value of relative arbitrage compared to the S&P 500 and U.S. Treasury bonds. Once again, we see steady returns, without much influence from the direction of the stock or bond market.

EXHIBIT 3.13   Relative Value Arbitrage

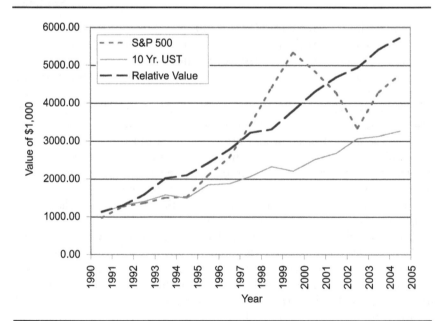

Opportunistic Hedge Fund Strategies

Along the lines of the *smorgasbord* comment for relative value hedge funds, these strategies have the broadest mandate across the financial, commodity and futures markets. These all encompassing mandates can lead to specific bets on currencies or stocks as well as a well diversified portfolio.

Global Macro

As their name implies, global macrohedge funds take a macroeconomic approach on a global basis in their investment strategy. These are top-down managers who invest opportunistically across financial markets, currencies, national borders, and commodities. They take large positions depending upon the hedge fund manager's forecast of changes in interest rates, currency movements, monetary policies, and macroeconomic indicators.

Global macro managers have the broadest investment universe. They are not limited by market segment or industry sector, nor by geographic region, financial market, or currency. Global macro also may invest in commodities. In fact, a fund of global macrohedge funds offers the greatest diversification of investment strategies.

Global macrohedge funds tend to have large amounts of investor capital. This is necessary to execute their macroeconomic strategies. In addition, they may apply leverage to increase the size of their macro bets. As a result, global macrohedge funds tend to receive the greatest attention and publicity in the financial markets.

The best known of these hedge funds was the Quantum Hedge Fund managed by George Soros. It is well documented, that this fund made significant gains in 1992 by betting that the British pound would devalue (which it did). This fund was also accused of contributing to the "Asian Contagion" in the fall of 1997 when the government of Thailand devalued its currency, the *baht*, triggering a domino effect in currency movements throughout southeast Asia.

In recent times, however, global macrohedge funds have fallen on hard times.[16] One reason is that many global macrohedge funds were hurt by the Russian bond default in August 1998 and the bursting of the technology bubble in March 2000. These two events caused large losses for the global macrohedge funds.

A second reason, as indicated above, is that global macrohedge funds had the broadest investment mandate of any hedge fund strategy. The ability to invest widely across currencies, commodities, financial markets, geographic borders, and time zones is a two-edged sword. On the one hand, it

---

[16] See *The New York Times*, "The Hedge Fund Industry Creates a Dinosaur: The Macro Manager," May 6, 2000.

EXHIBIT 3.14   Global Macro

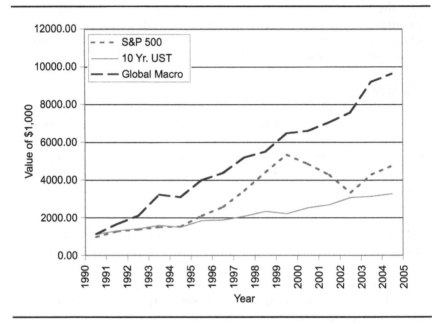

allows global macrohedge funds the widest universe in which to implement their strategies. On the other hand, it lacks focus. As more institutional investors have moved into the hedge fund market place, they have demanded greater investment focus as opposed to free investment reign.

Exhibit 3.14 is a comparison of global macrohedge funds to the S&P 500 and Treasury bonds over the period 1990 to 2005. During this time, Global macrohedge funds earned steady, favorable returns. Also, global macrohedge funds significantly outperformed the U.S. stock market without the fluctuations that affected the stock market.

Fund of Funds

Finally, we come to hedge fund of funds. These are hedge fund managers that invest their capital in other hedge funds. These managers practice tactical asset allocation; reallocating capital across hedge fund strategies when they believe that certain hedge fund strategies will do better than others. For example, during the bear market of 2000 to 2002, short-selling strategies performed the best of all hedge fund categories. Not surprisingly, fund of fund managers allocated a significant portion of their portfolios to short sellers during the recent bear market. Other strategies that are popular in fund of funds are global macro, fixed income

EXHIBIT 3.15   Hedge Fund of Funds

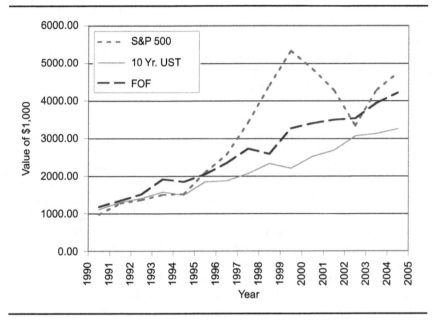

arbitrage, convertible arbitrage, statistical arbitrage, equity long/short, and event driven.

One drawback on fund of funds is the double layer of fees. Investors in hedge fund of funds typically pay a management plus profit sharing fees to the hedge fund of funds managers in addition to the management and incentive fees that must be absorbed from the underlying hedge fund managers. This double layer of fees makes it difficult for fund of fund managers to outperform some of the more aggressive individual hedge fund strategies. However, the tradeoff is better risk control from a diversified portfolio.

Exhibit 3.15 shows the returns for hedge fund of funds. Not surprisingly, hedge fund of funds did not earn as good a return as the U.S. equity market over the period 1990 to 2005 but, at the same time, did not demonstrate the excessive volatility associated with the stock market.

CONCLUSION

This chapter was intended to provide an overview of the hedge fund market; it was not intended to draw any conclusions about the value of hedge funds as an investment vehicle. The issues associated with hedge fund investing will be addressed in the following chapters. In the meantime, there are three key points that the reader should take from this chapter.

First, the hedge fund industry has grown dramatically over the past decade. Although invested capital is approximately 15% of the size of the mutual fund industry (which is about $10 trillion), in terms of investment assets its growth potential is much higher. New managers enter the hedge fund industry on a daily basis drawn by the tremendous fees that can be earned, and new capital, particularly from pension funds, is being drawn to the industry.

Second, the hedge fund strategies discussed above invest in the same securities as traditional long-only managers. This is a point that we made in Chapter 1, but it bears repeating. Hedge fund managers use the same securities as long-only managers. However, the distinguishing feature of hedge fund managers is the strategies in which they employ those securities. Therefore, hedge fund managers do not employ alternative assets, but rather, alternative strategies.

Last, there are many different hedge fund strategies. Which is best for the investor? That will really depend upon the strategic approach that the investor wishes to take. Some investors may be more focussed on equity based strategies. For them, equity long/short funds or market timing might be appropriate. For an investor with a fixed income bias, convertible arbitrage, fixed income arbitrage, or relative value arbitrage may be appropriate. Suffice it to say that there is sufficient variety in the hedge fund market place to suit most investors.

CHAPTER 4

Establishing a Hedge Fund Investment Program

The hedge fund market has grown tremendously over the past six years. From approximately $500 billion in 2000 to $1.5 trillion by the end of 2005, the assets under management have tripled. The reasons are as easy to see as a three-year bear market in 2000 to 2002 crushed equity market returns and drove investors to seek alternative sources of return. Yet before investors enter the hedge fund world they should have a plan of action to ensure the greatest opportunity for success.

This chapter addresses the opportunities associated with hedge funds. We will discuss the hazards in later chapters. We begin with a review of the research on hedge funds where we address questions regarding the benefits of hedge funds within an investment portfolio, whether their performance is persistent, and whether hedge funds undermine the financial markets. We then consider the investment strategies that may be applicable to hedge funds.

SHOULD HEDGE FUNDS BE PART OF AN INVESTMENT PROGRAM?

Before considering hedged funds as part of a strategic investment program, we must first ask the question: Are they worth it? Initially, we must consider the return potential of hedge funds. Second, we must determine whether hedge funds have a place within a diversified portfolio that includes stocks and bonds.

Goldman, Sachs & Co. and Financial Risk Management Ltd. in two reports study the returns to hedge funds over two time periods, 1993 to

1997 and 1994 to 1998.[1] Over the first time period, they find the return to four categories of hedge funds, market neutral, event driven, equity long/short, and tactical trading, to earn average annual returns of 13.37%, 17.25%, 19.29%, and 19.48%, respectively. This compared to an average annual return for the S&P 500 of 20.25% over the same time period. However, the volatility for each class of hedge funds was significantly lower than that for the S&P 500.

Furthermore, the correlation with the S&P 500 ranged from 0.06 (market neutral) to 0.6 (equity L/S). A portfolio of 60% S&P 500, 30% Lehman Aggregate Bond Index, and 10% absolute return hedge fund index outperformed the Pension Plan Index of 60/40 stocks/bonds by 78 basis points per year with a reduction in portfolio standard deviation of 31 basis points.

Over the second time period, which included the bailout of the Long-Term Capital Management hedge fund group, the four hedge fund groups earned an average annual return of 11.9% for market neutral, 12.7% for event driven, 15.15% for equity long/short, and 16.98% for tactical trading. The average annual return for the S&P 500 was 24.06% during this time period. Correlation of returns with the S&P 500 increased during this period ranged from 0.38 (market neutral) to 0.77 (equity long/short). A portfolio of 60% S&P 500, 30% Lehman Aggregate Bond Index, and 10% hedge funds increased the total return by 48 basis points per year over the 60/40 Pension Plan Index, but portfolio volatility also increased by 14 basis points.

For the time period 1991 to 1995, Schneeweis and Spurgin document a range of hedge fund average annual returns of 7.8% for short selling funds to 27.9% for global macro funds.[2] Average annual standard deviation calculations ranged from 3.1% for market-neutral funds to 18.4% for emerging market hedge funds. Correlation coefficients of the Hedge Fund Research hedge fund indexes with the S&P 500 ranged from −0.60 for short selling hedge funds to 0.74 to hedge funds focussing on growth sectors.

Separately, Schneeweis finds that a portfolio consisting of 80% that is equally weighted with U.S. stocks and U.S. bonds and 20% hedge funds outperforms the standalone stock-and-bond portfolio in terms or

---

[1] See Goldman, Sachs & Co. and Financial Risk Management Ltd., "The Hedge Fund 'Industry' and Absolute Return Funds," *The Journal of Alternative Investments* (Spring 1999), pp. 11–27; and "Hedge Funds Revisited," *Pension and Endowment Forum* (January 2000).

[2] See Thomas Schneeweis and Richard Spurgin, "Multifactor Analysis of Hedge Fund, Managed Futures, and Mutual Fund Return and Risk Characteristics," *The Journal of Alternative Investments* (Fall 1998), pp. 1–24.

expected return, standard deviation, Sharpe ratio, and *drawdown*.[3] (Drawdown is a measure of the decline in net asset value of an investment portfolio.) A similar test using international stocks yields the same results.

Liang finds for the time period 1990 to 1996 that an equally weighted portfolio of 921 hedge funds earned a total return of 208% compared to 156% for the S&P 500.[4] Monthly standard deviation for the hedge fund group was 4.04% compared to 3.37% for the S&P 500. Liang regressed the returns from 16 different hedge fund styles on the returns to stocks, bonds, currencies, and commodities. He found R-squares that ranged from 0.20 for currency based hedge funds to 0.77 for emerging market hedge funds, with the composite R-square for all hedge funds to be 0.23. Liang also compared his sample of hedge funds to a sample of mutual funds. He found that the average Sharpe ratio for hedge funds to be 0.44, while for mutual funds it was 0.26.

Peskin, Urias, Anjilvel, and Boudreau find that over the time period of January 1990 through June 2000, the average annual return for all hedge funds in their sample was 18.9%, with a volatility of 5.5% and a Sharpe ratio of 2.5.[5] This compares quite favorably to the return for the S&P 500 of 17.2%, volatility of 13.7%, and a Sharpe ratio of 0.9.

Edwards and Liew find that over the time period 1989 to 1996, an equally weighted fund of hedge funds earned an average annual return of 11.2% with a correlation coefficient with the S&P 500 of 0.37.[6] An unconstrained optimization including stocks, bonds, and fund of funds, selected an allocation of 84% to an equally weighted fund of hedge funds, 7% to the S&P 500, and 10% to long-term corporate bonds.

Brown, Goetzmann, and Ibbotson study the period 1989 to 1995.[7] They find that an equally weighted portfolio of offshore hedge funds earned an average return of 13.26%. Average annual standard deviations ranged from 6.16% for commodity pools to 22.15% for event-driven hedge funds. Correlation coefficients with the S&P 500 ranged

---

[3] See Thomas Schneeweis, "The Benefits of Hedge Funds: Asset Allocation for the Institutional Investor," Center for International Securities and Derivatives Markets (September 2000).
[4] See Bing Liang, "On the Performance of Hedge Funds," *Financial Analysts Journal* (July/August 1999), pp. 72–83.
[5] See Michael Peskin, Michael Urias, Satish Anjilvel, and Bryan Boudreau, "Why Hedge Funds Make Sense," Morgan Stanley Dean Witter Quantitative Strategies (November 2000).
[6] See Franklin Edwards and Jimmy Liew, "Hedge Funds versus Managed Futures as an Asset Class," *The Journal of Derivatives* (Summer 1999), pp. 45–62.
[7] See Stephen J. Brown, William N. Goetzmann, and Roger G. Ibbotson, "Offshore Hedge Funds: Survival and Performance, 1989–1995," *The Journal of Business* 72 (1999), pp. 91–117.

from −0.70 for short selling funds to 0.83 for opportunistic funds investing in the U.S. markets.

Ackermann, McEnally, and Ravenscraft review hedge funds within a portfolio context.[8] They find that over the period 1988 to 1995 the addition of hedge funds to either a stock, bond, or balanced portfolio results in an improved Sharpe ratio.

Fung and Hsieh[9] conduct a hedge fund performance attribution analysis similar to that performed by Sharpe for mutual funds.[10] They find low R-squares between the returns to hedge funds and those of traditional asset classes. Almost half (48%) of the hedge fund regression equations had an R-square below 25%. Furthermore, they found that 25% of the hedge funds were negatively correlated with the standard asset classes.

In a subsequent study, Fung and Hshieh regress the HFRI composite Index and the CSFB/Tremont Hedge Fund Index on nine financial market indexes including, stocks, bonds and currencies. They find that the R-square measure of overall regression fit to be 0.76 for the HFRI index and 0.55 for the CSFB/Tremont index.[11] This further demonstrates that hedge fund returns cannot be fully explained by market factors.

The body of research on hedge funds demonstrates two key qualifications for hedge funds. First, that over the time period of 1989 to 2000, the returns to hedge funds were positive. The highest returns were achieved by global macrohedge funds, and the lowest returns were achieved by short selling hedge funds. Not all categories of hedge funds beat the S&P 500. However, in many cases, the volatility associated with hedge fund returns was lower than that of the S&P 500.[12]

In Exhibit 4.1 we update the prior research by examining the returns to hedge funds over the period 1990 to 2005 for the HFRI Hedge Fund Composite Index as well as the HFRI FOF index compared to large-cap stocks, small-cap stocks, U.S. Treasury bonds, EAFE, and cash. The returns for the HFRI Composite index compare favorably with large-cap stocks but with much less volatility. The FOF index earns

---

[8] See Carl Ackermann, Richard McEnally, and David Ravenscraft, "The Performance of Hedge Funds: Risk, Return, and Incentives," *The Journal of Finance* (June 1999), pp. 833–873.

[9] See William Fung and David Hsieh, "Empirical Characteristics of Dynamic Trading Strategies: The Case of Hedge Funds," *The Review of Financial Studies* (Summer 1997), pp. 275–302.

[10] William Sharpe, "Asset Allocation: Management Style and Performance Measurement," *The Journal of Portfolio Management* (Winter 1992), pp. 7–19.

[11] See William Fung and David Hsieh, "Hedge Fund Benchmarks: Information Content and Biases," *Financial Analysts Journal* (January/February 2002), pp. 22–34.

[12] See Goldman, Sachs & Co. and Financial Risk Management Ltd., "The Hedge Fund 'Industry' and Absolute Return Funds" and "Hedge Funds Revisited."

EXHIBIT 4.1   Expected Return, Standard Deviations, and Sharpe Ratios,
1990–2005

Asset Class	Expected Return	Standard Deviation	Sharpe Ratio
S&P 500	12.43%	18.42%	0.43
10 Year UST	8.48%	8.13%	0.49
NASDAQ	16.38%	35.08%	0.34
EAFE	4.87%	19.91%	0.02
HFRI Composite	14.94%	11.42%	0.92
HFRI FOF	10.43%	9.51%	0.62
Cash	4.49%	1.93%	n/a

less than large-cap and small-cap stocks but significantly more than
EAFE, and has significantly less volatility than any of the stock categories. Both the HFRI Composite and FOF index earn premiums significantly in excess of a cash rate. Also, the HFRI FOF index has a volatility
that is not much greater than U.S. Treasury bonds. These findings are
consistent with the prior research cited above.

Of equal interest is what will be the returns to hedge funds looking
forward. A recent study by the Russell Investment Group indicates that
most investors believe hedge fund returns will be 9% over the next three
years.[13] This is a significant reduction in returns from those earned over
the prior 15 years.

Another benefit of hedge funds is that they provide good diversification benefits. In other words, hedge funds do, in fact, hedge other financial assets. Correlation coefficients with the S&P 500 range from –0.7
for short selling hedge funds to 0.83 for opportunistic hedge funds
investing in the U.S. markets.[14] The less than perfect positive correlation
with financial assets indicates that hedge funds can expand the efficient
frontier for asset managers.

Exhibit 4.4 presents the correlation of the HFRI Composite Index
and HFRI Fund of Funds Index with large-cap stocks, Treasury bonds,
small-cap stocks and international stocks over the time period 1990 to
2005. The low correlation coefficients reinforces the conclusion that
hedge funds provide good diversification benefits.

---

[13] Russell Investment Group, "The Russell Investment Group 2005–2006 Survey on
Alternative Assets," 2005.
[14] See Brown, Goetzmann, and Ibbotson, "Offshore Hedge Funds: Survival and Performance, 1989–1995," and Schneeweis and Spurgin, "Multifactor Analysis of
Hedge Fund, Managed Futures, and Mutual Fund Return and Risk Characteristics."

In summary, the recent research on hedge funds indicates consistent, positive performance with low correlation with traditional asset classes. The conclusion is that hedge funds can expand the investment opportunity set for institutions, offering both return enhancement as well as diversification benefits.

Nonetheless, there are several caveats to keep in mind with respect to the documented results for hedge funds. First, recent research provides clear evidence that shocks to one segment of the hedge fund industry can be felt across many different hedge fund strategies.[15] We will analyze this issue in more detail in a later chapter. Additionally, the recent roller-coaster ride in the U.S. stock markets has forced at least one large hedge fund shop to close its doors and has severely humbled another hedge fund giant.[16]

Second, most of the research to date on hedge funds has not factored in the tremendous growth of this industry over the past five years. Essentially, the hedge fund industry has tripled over the last five years, and the impact on returns has yet to be fully documented.

Perhaps the best way to measure the growth rate of hedge funds and their impact on returns is to measure investors' expectations regarding the future return potential of hedge funds. As noted above, the survey by the Russell Investment Group indicates that the return expectations for hedge funds are lower than that previously earned—in the range of 9% to 10%.

Third, some form of bias (survivorship bias, self-selection bias, and catastrophe bias) exist in the empirical studies. All of the cited studies make use of a hedge fund database. The building of these databases results in certain biases becoming embedded in the data. These biases, if not corrected, can unintentionally inflate the documented returns to hedge funds. It has been estimated that these three biases can add from 100 to 400 basis points to the estimated total return of hedge funds. We address this issue in greater detail in Chapters 6 and 7 that cover risk management.

IS HEDGE FUND PERFORMANCE PERSISTENT?

This is the age-old question with respect to all asset managers, not just hedge funds: Can the manager repeat her good performance? This issue, though, is particularly acute for the hedge fund marketplace because hedge

---

[15] See Goldman, Sachs & Co. and Financial Risk Management Ltd., "The Hedge Fund "Industry" and Absolute Return Funds" and "Hedge Funds Revisited;" and Mark Anson, "Financial Market Dislocations and Hedge Fund Returns," *The Journal of Alternative Assets* (Winter 2002), pp. 78–88.

[16] See "Hedge Fund Industry Creates a Dinosaur: The Macro Manager," *The New York Times*, 6 May 2000, 1C.

fund managers often claim that the source of their returns is "skill based" rather than dependent upon general financial market conditions. Unfortunately, the existing evidence is mixed, and there is no clear conclusion.

Brown, Goetzmann, and Ibbotson present a year-by-year cross-sectional regression (parametric analysis) of past hedge fund returns on current hedge fund returns.[17] Over the six years studied, they find that three of the years have positive slopes (indicating persistent positive performance) and three years have negative slopes (indicating no persistence). In other words, it is only a 50–50 chance that good performance in one year will be followed by good performance in the following year. They conclude that there is no evidence of performance persistence in their hedge fund sample.

Park and Staum measure skill by the ratio of excess return as measured by the Capital Asset Pricing model divided by the standard deviation of the hedge fund manager's returns.[18] They use this skill statistic to rank hedge fund managers on a year-by year basis and then compare this ranking to the following year's skill ranking. Using a nonparametric test, they find strong evidence that hedge fund manager skill persists from year to year.

Agarwal and Naik use both a parametric (regression) test and a nonparametric (ranking) test to measure the persistence of hedge fund performance.[19] They find that under both tests a considerable amount of performance persistence exists at the quarterly horizon. However, the persistence is reduced as one moves to yearly returns, indicating that performance persistence among hedge fund managers is primarily short term in nature.

Peskin, Urias, Anjilvel, and Boudreau find results similar to Agarwal and Naik.[20] They find that performance among hedge fund managers persists on a monthly basis, but it is much less so on an annual basis.

A different approach to performance persistence looks at the persistence of volatility in hedge fund returns. Specifically, other researchers have noted that the volatility of returns is more persistent over time than the size or direction of the return itself. Schneeweis[21] and Park and Staum[22] demon-

---

[17] See Brown, Goetzmann, and Ibbotson, "Offshore Hedge Funds: Survival and Performance, 1989–1995."
[18] See James Park and Jeremy Staum, "Performance Persistence in the Alternative Investment Industry," working paper (1999).
[19] See Vikas Agarwal and Narayan Naik, "Multi-Period Performance Persistence Analysis of Hedge Funds," *The Journal of Financial and Quantitative Analysis* (September 2000), pp. 327–342.
[20] See Peskin, Urias, Anjilvel, and Boudreau, "Why Hedge Funds Make Sense."
[21] See Thomas Schneeweis, "Evidence of Superior Performance Persistence in Hedge Funds: An Empirical Comment," *The Journal of Alternative Investments* (Fall 1998), pp. 76–80.
[22] See Park and Staum, "Performance Persistence in the Alternative Investment Industry."

strate that the best forecast of future returns is one that is consistent with prior volatility, instead of a forecast that is based upon prior returns.

Another way to look at the performance persistence of hedge funds is to measure the serial correlation among the returns to hedge funds. Serial correlation measures the correlation of the return in the current year to the return performance of the previous year. If performance persistence is present, we should expect to see positive serial correlation; that is good years followed by more good years. Exhibit 4.2 shows the serial correlation for large-cap stocks, small-cap stocks, EAFE, U.S. Treasury bonds, the cash return, and various hedge fund strategies.

EXHIBIT 4.2 Serial Correlation of Hedge Fund Returns

Asset Class	Serial Correlation
S&P 500	0.20
10-year UST	−0.59
NASDAQ	−0.11
EAFE	0.02
Cash	0.74
HFRI Composite	−0.21
Market Directional	
Equity Long/Short	−0.03
Market Timing	−0.04
Short Selling	−0.43
Corporate Restructuring	
Distressed Debt	−0.08
Merger Arbitrage	−0.01
Event Driven	−0.35
Convergence Trading	
Fixed Income Arbitrage	0.36
Convertible Arbitrage	−0.28
Market Neutral	0.33
Statistical Arbitrage	0.52
Relative Value	0.05
Opportunistic	
Global Macro	−0.14
HFRI FOF	−0.38

As can be seen both the HFRI Hedge Fund Composite Index and the FOF index have negative serial correlation. This means that a good year tended to be followed by a year with lower returns, and a lower returning year tended to be followed by a year with better returns. In other words, past performance was no indication of future results. The two asset classes that had positive serial correlation were large-cap stocks and cash. Here good years tended to be followed by even better years and past performance was a reasonable indication of future performance.

Examining the performance of the different categories of hedge funds, we can see that the Convergence Trading strategies consistently generated positive serial correlation, with the exception of convertible arbitrage hedge fund managers. That is, these managers demonstrated the greatest affinity for performance persistence. All of the other strategies—market directional, corporate restructuring, and opportunistic—did not demonstrate a high level of serial correlation.

Yet, the debate continues. For example, using multifactor models, Amenc, El Bied, and Martellini, in another study of hedge funds find strong evidence of predictability in hedge fund returns.[23] So do Edwards and Caglayan, who test for performance persistence using a nonparametric cross product ratio of winners versus losers. They find significant performance persistence.[24] Compare these results with those of Harry Kat who used a similar technique to measure hedge fund serial correlation over the time period 1994 to 2001, and found no performance persistence among hedge fund strategies.[25]

It is difficult to reconcile the varying conclusions regarding hedge fund performance persistence. The different conclusions could be due to different databases used or different time periods tested. This emphasizes all the more the need to conduct individual due diligence on each hedge fund manager.

DO HEDGE FUNDS UNDERMINE THE FINANCIAL MARKETS?

Hedge funds have often been made scapegoats for whatever ails the financial markets. This can be traced back to George Soros's currency attack on the British Pound Sterling. In 1992, George Soros bet heavily

---

[23] See Noel Amenc, Sina el Bied, and Lionel Martellini, "Predictability in Hedge Fund Returns," *Financial Analysts Journal* (September/October 2003), pp. 32–46.
[24] See Franklin Edwards and Mustafa Onur Caglayan, "Hedge Fund Performance and Manager Skill," *Journal of Futures Markets* 21 (2001), pp. 1003–1028.
[25] See Harry Kat, "10 Things that Investors Should Know about Hedge Funds," *Journal of Wealth Management* (Spring 2003), pp. 74–75.

and correctly that the British government would not be able to support the pound and that the pound would devalue.

In 1997, Soros was once again blamed for a currency crisis by the Malaysian Prime Minister Mahathir bin Mohammad. The Prime Minister attributed the crash in the Malaysian ringgit to speculation in the currency markets by hedge fund managers, including George Soros.

Brown, Goetzmann, and Park test specifically whether hedge funds caused the crash of the Malaysian *ringgit*.[26] They regress the monthly percentage change in the exchange rate on the currency exposure maintained by hedge funds. Reviewing the currency exposures of 11 large global macrohedge funds, they conclude that there is no evidence that the Malaysian ringgit was affected by hedge fund manager currency exposures. Additionally, they test the hypothesis that global hedge funds precipitated the slide of a basket of Asian currencies (the "Asian Contagion") in 1997. They find no evidence that hedge funds contributed to the decline of the several Asian currencies in the fall of 1997.

Fung and Hsieh measure the market impact of hedge fund positions on several financial market events from the October 1987 stock market crash to the Asian Contagion of 1997.[27] They found that there were certain instances where hedge funds did have an impact on the market, most notably with the devaluation of the pound sterling in 1992. However, in no case was there evidence that hedge funds were able to manipulate the financial markets away from their natural paths driven by economic fundamentals. For instance, the Sterling came under pressure in 1992 due to large-capital outflows from the United Kingdom. The conclusion is that, for instance, George Soros bet correctly against the Sterling and exacerbated its decline, but he did not trigger the devaluation.

HEDGE FUND INVESTMENT STRATEGIES

The above discussion demonstrates that hedge funds can expand the investment opportunity set for investors. The question now becomes: What is to be accomplished by the hedge fund investment program? The strategy may be simply a search for an additional source of return. Conversely, it may be for risk management purposes. Whatever its purpose, an investment plan for hedge funds may consider one of four strategies.

---

[26] See Stephen Brown, William Goetzmann, and James Park, "Hedge Funds and the Asian Currency Crisis," *The Journal of Portfolio Management* (Summer 2000), pp. 95–101.

[27] See William Fung and David Hsieh, "Measuring the Market Impact of Hedge Funds," *The Journal of Empirical Finance* 7 (2000), pp. 1–36.

Hedge funds may be selected on an opportunistic basis, as a hedge fund of funds, as part of a joint venture, or as an absolute return strategy.

Opportunistic Hedge Fund Investing

The term "hedge fund" can be misleading. Hedge funds do not necessarily have to hedge an investment portfolio. Rather, they can be used to expand the investment opportunity set. This is the opportunistic nature of hedge funds—they can provide an investor with new investment opportunities that she cannot otherwise obtain through traditional long only investments.

There are several ways hedge funds can be opportunistic. First, many hedge fund managers can add value to an existing investment portfolio through specialization in a sector or in a market strategy. These managers do not contribute portable alpha. Instead, they contribute above market returns through the application of superior skill or knowledge to a narrow market or strategy.

Consider a portfolio manager whose particular expertise is the biotechnology industry. She has followed this industry for years and has developed a superior information set to identify winners and losers. On the long only side the manager purchases those stocks that she believes will increase in value, and avoids those biotech stocks she believes will decline in value. However, this strategy does not utilize her superior information set to its fullest advantage. The ability to go both long and short biotech stocks in a hedge fund is the only way to maximize the value of the manager's information set. Therefore, a biotech hedge fund provides a new opportunity: the ability to extract value on both the long side and the short side of the biotech market.

The goal of this strategy is to identify the best managers in a specific economic sector or specific market segment that complements the existing investment portfolio. These managers are used to enhance the risk and return profile of an existing portfolio, rather than hedge it.

Opportunistic hedge funds tend to have a benchmark. Take the example of the biotech long/short hedge fund. An appropriate benchmark would be the AMEX Biotech Index that contains 17 biotechnology companies. Alternatively, if the investor believed that the biotech sector will outperform the general stock market, she could use a broad-based stock index such as the S&P 500 for the benchmark. The point is that opportunistic hedge funds are not absolute return vehicles (discussed below). Their performance can be measured relative to a benchmark.

All traditional long-only managers are benchmarked to some passive index. The nature of benchmarking is such that it forces the manager to focus on his benchmark and his tracking error associated with that benchmark. This focus on benchmarking leads traditional active managers to commit a large portion their portfolios to tracking their benchmark. The necessity to consider the impact of every trade on the portfolio's tracking error relative to its assigned benchmark reduces the flexibility of the investment manager.

In addition, long-only active managers are constrained in their ability to short securities. They may only "go short" a security up to its weight in the benchmark index. If the security is only a small part of the index, the manager's efforts to short the stock will be further constrained. The inability to short a security beyond its benchmark weight deprives an active manager of the opportunity to take full advantage of the mispricing in the marketplace. Furthermore, not only are long-only managers unable to take advantage of overpriced securities, but they also cannot fully take advantage of underpriced securities because they cannot generate the necessary short positions to balance the overweights with respect to underpriced securities. The "long-only" constraint is a well-known limitation on the ability of traditional active management to earn excess returns.[28]

Furthermore, when short sales are disallowed, the most a manager can reduce his holding of an overvalued security is to zero. For example, consider a manager for whom his most pessimistic forecast for a stock is one where it has only a small weight in the benchmark. The manager will only be able to sell a small amount of the company because of its relatively low weight in the benchmark even though the manager believes that this company has the most egregious valuation.

In addition, with a long-only constraint the only way to support you positive overweights is to underweight large-cap stocks that have a higher weight in the benchmark. Yet, this can introduce a size bias into the portfolio.

In summary, opportunistic hedge fund investing does not have to hedge the portfolio. Instead, in can lead to more efficient investing, a broader investment universe, and the freedom to allow managers to trade on an expanded information set. More to the point, opportunistic hedge fund managers can build a long/short market-neutral portfolio based on biotech stocks if that is where they have the expertise to add value.

As another example, most institutional investors have a broad equity portfolio. This portfolio may include an index fund, external value and growth managers, and possibly, private equity investments. However, along the spectrum of this equity portfolio, there may be gaps in its investment line-up. For instance, many hedge funds combine late stage private investments with public securities. These hybrid funds are

---

[28] See Richard Grinold and Ronald Kahn, *Active Portfolio Management* (New York: McGraw Hill, 2000).

a natural extension of an institution's investment portfolio because they bridge the gap between private equity and index funds. Therefore a new opportunity is identified: the ability to blend private equity and public securities within one investment strategy. We will discuss this strategy further in our section on private equity.

Again, we come back to one of our main themes: that alternative "assets" are really alternative investment strategies, and these alternative strategies are used to expand the investment opportunity set rather than hedge it. In summary, hedge funds may be selected not necessarily to reduce the risk of an existing investment portfolio, but to complement its risk-and-return profile. Opportunistic investing is designed to select hedge fund managers that can enhance certain portions of a broader portfolio.

Another way to consider opportunistic hedge fund investments is that they are finished products because their investment strategy or market segment complements an institutional investor's existing asset allocation. No further work is necessary on the part of the institution because the investment opportunity set has been expanded by the addition of the hybrid product. These "gaps" may be in domestic equity, fixed income, or international investments. Additionally, because opportunistic hedge funds are finished products, it makes it easier to establish performance benchmarks.

Constructing an opportunistic portfolio of hedge funds will depend upon the constraints under which such a program operates. For example, if an investor's hedge fund program is not limited in scope or style, then diversification across a broad range of hedge fund styles would be appropriate. If, however, the hedge fund program is limited in scope to, for instance, expanding the equity investment opportunity set, the choices will be less diversified across strategies. Exhibit 4.3 demonstrates these two choices.

EXHIBIT 4.3   Designing a Hedge Fund Investment Program

Diversified Hedge Fund Portfolio	Equity-Based Hedge Fund Portfolio
Equity long/short	Equity long/short
Short selling	Market timing
Market neutral	Distressed securities
Merger arbitrage	Event driven
Distressed securities	Convertible arbitrage
Convertible arbitrage	
Fixed income arbitrage	
Relative value arbitrage	
Global macro	

Hedge Fund of Funds

A *hedge fund of funds* (FOF) is an investment in a group of hedge funds, from five to more than 20. The purpose of a hedge fund of funds is to reduce the idiosyncratic risk of any one hedge fund manager. In other words, there is safety in numbers.

This is simply *modern portfolio theory* (MPT) applied to the hedge fund marketplace. Diversification is one of the founding principles of MPT, and it is as applicable to hedge funds as it is to stocks and bonds.

Henker reviews the diversification benefits for three styles of hedge funds: equity long/short, event driven, and relative value.[29] Using random sampling within each hedge fund style, he finds that a portfolio of about five funds captures most of the diversification benefits that can be achieved within each style. The reduction of risk is achieved because of the heterogeneous return characteristics of hedge funds comprising the fund of funds portfolio. The fact that hedge funds within the same style have different return patterns is consistent with the findings of Fung and Hsieh.[30] They found no evidence of "herding" among hedge funds that pursued currency investment strategies.

Park and Staum consider the optimal diversification for a random pool of hedge funds selected from a database of 1,230 hedge funds of all different styles.[31] Consistent with Henker, they demonstrate that a fund of funds portfolio of five hedge funds can eliminate approximately 80% of the idiosyncratic risk of the individual hedge fund managers. After five hedge funds, the diversification benefits decline significantly. They find that a fund of funds portfolio of 20 hedge funds can diversify away about 95% of the idiosyncratic risk.

What, then, is left in terms of return with a hedge fund of funds? Along with the diversification of risk, fund of funds also provide diversification of return. That is, the return on a fund of funds product is generally below that of individual hedge fund styles. Generally, the return is cash-plus with cash defined as LIBOR or T-bills and the plus equal to 200 to 600 basis points. Exhibit 4.1 shows that the HFRI FOF earns 500 basis points over cash.

This low volatility, cash-plus product may be applied in one of three ways: risk budgeting, portable alpha, or as a bond substitute.

---

[29] See Thomas Henker, "Naive Diversification for Hedge Funds," *The Journal of Alternative Assets* (Winter 1998), pp. 33–38.

[30] See Fung and Hsieh, "Measuring the Market Impact of Hedge Funds."

[31] See James Park and Jeremy Staum, "Fund of Funds Diversification: How Much is Enough?" *The Journal of Alternative Investments* (Winter 1998), pp. 39–42.

Risk Budgeting

It seems odd to think of hedge funds as a risk budgeting tool. However, the empirical studies cited above demonstrate that fund of funds have a low standard deviation and a low correlation with traditional asset classes. Therefore, they are excellent candidates for risk budgeting.

We digress for a moment to discuss risk budgeting. Risk budgeting is a subset of the risk management process. It is the process of measuring the risk that an investor is actually taking, assessing the investor's appetite for risk, quantifying how much risk the investor is willing to take, and then deciding how to allocate that risk across a diversified portfolio. The process of allocating risk across a portfolio is what is known as risk budgeting. Risk budgeting allows a manager to set risk target levels throughout her portfolio.

Consider Exhibit 4.1. In this exhibit, we present the monthly expected return, standard deviation, and Sharpe ratios for the S&P 500, the 10-year U.S. Treasury Bond, the NASDAQ index, Morgan Stanley Capital's Europe, Australia and Far East (EAFE) index, two hedge fund indexes, and one year cash investment. The period covered is January 1990 through 2005.

From Exhibit 4.1, we can see that hedge fund indexes have higher Sharpe ratios compared to that for stocks and bonds. But hedge funds should not be considered in isolation. To asses their true value to a diversified portfolio, we need to see how hedge fund returns are correlated with the returns to stocks and bonds.

Suppose an investor has an annual risk budget of 15% for her overall portfolio and she wishes to invest in small-capitalized stocks. From Exhibit 4.1 we can see that small-cap stocks have the highest expected return. Unfortunately, the monthly expected volatility for the NASDAQ stocks is 35%, which exceeds her risk budget.

The investor can solve her problem by combining a hedge fund of funds investment with small-cap stocks to meet her risk budget of 15%. Consider Exhibit 4.4. This exhibit is a correlation matrix that demonstrates that the returns received from hedge funds are less than perfectly correlated with stocks and bonds. For example, we can see that the correlation of the returns to the HFR FOF index with the returns to small-cap stocks is 0.46. Using the information in Exhibits 4.1 and 4.4 we can determine the optimal allocation to hedge fund of funds and small-cap stocks such that the investor can stay within her risk budget. The calculation is

$$0.15 = \text{square root of } \{[w(\text{FOF})]^2 \times 0.095^2 + [1 - w(\text{FOF})]^2 \times 0.35^2 + 2 \times [w(\text{FOF})] \times [1 - w(\text{FOF})] \times 0.095 \times 0.35 \times 0.46\}$$

where

EXHIBIT 4.4   Correlation Matrix

	S&P 500	10 yr UST	NASDAQ	EAFE	HFRI Comp.	HFRI FOF
S&P 500	1.00	0.10	0.84	0.64	0.62	0.33
10-year UST	0.10	1.00	–0.18	–0.24	–0.01	–0.06
NASDAQ	0.84	–0.18	1.00	0.73	0.74	0.46
EAFE	0.64	–0.24	0.73	1.00	0.53	0.29
HFRI Composite	0.62	–0.01	0.74	0.53	1.00	0.81
HFRI FOF	0.33	–0.06	0.46	0.29	0.81	1.00

w(FOF) is the weight in the portfolio allocated to a hedge fund of funds. $1 - w$(FOF) is the weight in the portfolio allocated to small-cap stocks.

Solving the equation for w(FOF) yields a value of 0.70. That is, the investor needs to invest at least 70% of her portfolio in a hedge fund of funds and no more than 30% in small-cap stocks to remain within her risk budget of 15% annual volatility.

Consider the power of a hedge fund of funds in this example. Without hedge funds, the investor could not allocate any of her portfolio to small-cap stocks because the annual standard deviation of small-cap stocks of 35% exceeded her risk budget of 15%. However, when combined with a fund of funds product, the investor can allocate up to 30% of her portfolio to small-cap stocks.

Simply put, the investor uses hedge funds to "buy" units of risk that can then be allocated to other portions of her portfolio. This may run counter to intuition because hedge funds are perceived to be risky investments; yet, in Exhibit 4.1 we can see that the risk associated with a portfolio of hedge funds, as measured by the annual standard deviation, is lower than large-cap stocks, small-cap stocks, and foreign stocks. Additionally, hedge fund returns have less than perfect correlation with stock returns. This less than perfect correlation only enhances the risk budgeting power of hedge funds.

Risk budgeting can change portfolio asset allocations by highlighting the less than perfect correlation between two investment strategies. In the risk budgeting world, different asset classes or investment strategies are assigned different hurdle rates. These hurdle rates quantify an asset's correlation with the overall portfolio.

For example, most portfolios have a large exposure to large-cap stocks. But from Exhibit 4.4, we can see that hedge fund of funds have the lowest correlation with large-cap stocks. As a result, the hurdle rate for hedge fund of funds would be lower than other asset classes or strategies.

Elton, Gruber, and Retnzler provide the calculation for determining the hurdle rate for hedge fund of funds vis-à-vis large-cap stocks.[32] In a study of commodity pools within a portfolio context, they show that a commodity pool should be added to an existing portfolio if the following equation is satisfied:

$$(R_c - R_f)/\sigma_c > (R_p - R_f) \times \rho_{c,p}/\sigma_p \qquad (4.1)$$

where

R_c is the expected return to the commodity pool.
R_p is the expected return to the portfolio.
R_f is the risk-free rate.
$\rho_{c,p}$ is the correlation between the returns to the commodity pool and the portfolio.
σ_c is the volatility of returns to the commodity pool.
σ_p is the volatility of returns to the portfolio.

We can take Equation (1) and transform it into a hurdle rate calculation for hedge fund of funds:

$$R_h = (R_p - R_f) \times \rho_{h,p} \times \sigma_h/\sigma_p + R_f \qquad (4.2)$$

Defining the S&P 500 as the portfolio, the hurdle rate for hedge fund of funds is

Hurdle rate = $(0.1243 - 0.045) \times 0.33 \times 0.095/0.184 + 0.045 = 0.0585$

In other words, hedge fund of funds must earn a rate of at least 5.85% per year to be a valuable addition for risk budgeting purposes. Given that the expected return for hedge fund of funds is 10.43% per year, the hurdle rate is met, and a hedge fund of funds is a valuable risk budgeting tool.

Compare this result to that obtained for international stocks. Using the EAFE stock index, we perform the same risk budgeting calculation for international stocks vis-à-vis large-cap stocks. The question is whether international stocks are appropriate risk budgeting tools versus large-cap stocks. Plugging in data from Exhibits 4.1 and 4.4 into equation (4.2) we get

Hurdle Rate = $(0.1243 - 0.045) \times 0.64 \times 0.199/0.184 + 0.045 = 0.10$

---

[32] See Edwin Elton, Martin Gruber, and Joel Rentzler, "Professionally Managed, Publicly Traded Commodity Funds," *The Journal of Business* (1987), pp. 175–199.

The hurdle rate for international stocks is 10% per year. From Exhibit 4.1, we can see that the expected return is only 4.87% per year. Therefore, international stocks are not suitable risk-budgeting tools with respect to large-cap stocks.

Portable Alpha

Portable alpha can be obtained from a diversified pool of hybrid managers with low correlation to traditional asset classes. This is a combination strategy of investing with multiple managers to achieve a portable alpha.

The idea is to invest with several hedge fund managers to achieve a distribution of returns that are uncorrelated with either stocks or bonds. Generally, this product yields a return equal to a cash rate of return plus a premium. The premium is the portable alpha. It represents the extra return that can be achieved with a hedge fund of funds above that which can be earned from investing in short-term cash instruments such as Treasury bills or high-grade commercial paper. The portable alpha is then applied to the equity or fixed income portion of the portfolio with futures contracts.

For example, Exhibit 4.4 demonstrates that the HFR fund of funds index has a very low correlation with the returns to the S&P 500. Furthermore, Exhibit 4.1 shows that hedge fund of funds earn an annual return of 10.43%, almost 2% greater than that for U.S. Treasury bonds. This extra return may be considered the "alpha." It is the return earned above that of a fixed income rate of return while providing an alternative investment that has a very low correlation with large-cap U.S. stocks.

Consider an investor who has $1 billion to invest in large-cap U.S. stocks. The expected return for large-cap stocks is 12.43% per year. Instead of investing the full $1 billion in the S&P 500, she invests $500 million in the S&P 500, and $500 million in hedge fund of funds. In addition, the investor purchases S&P 500 equity futures contracts such that the combination of hedge fund of funds plus equity futures contracts will be equivalent to an economic exposure of $500 million invested in the S&P 500. This process is known as "equitization," and the investor does it to equitize her hedge fund of funds investment.

We digress for a moment to discuss the embedded financing cost associated with a portable alpha strategy. To prevent arbitrage in the financial markets, the S&P 500 futures contract reflects a short-term risk-free rate of financing. That is, the difference in the futures price and the current spot price of the S&P 500 reflects the relevant risk-free rate. This is because speculators who buy or sell the S&P 500 futures contracts must hedge their position by selling or buying the underlying stocks. To purchase or borrow the underlying stocks, the speculator must borrow, and this cost of short-term financing is reflected in the pricing of the S&P 500 futures contract.[33] Therefore, any portable alpha strategy must earn at least the cost of the cost of short-term financing embedded within the futures contract. Otherwise, the alpha will be negative, not positive.

For our example, we use the return of the cash rate from Exhibit 4.1 as the financing rate reflected in the S&P 500 futures contracts. Over the period 1990 through 2005, this rate was 4.5% per year. Therefore, the hedge fund of funds strategy must earn at least 4.5% per year to provide an excess return, or alpha.

In building the portable alpha strategy, we note that the systematic, or market, risk of hedge fund of funds is not zero. Therefore, we will need to take into account that our portable alpha strategy already contains a component of systematic or market risk. From Exhibits 4.1 and 4.4 we can calculate the beta of the hedge fund of funds, using the S&P 500 as the proxy for the market:[34]

$$beta = [0.33 \times 0.184 \times 0.095]/[0.184 \times 0.184] = 0.17$$

The low beta value of the hedge fund of funds strategy demonstrates that it has minimal market risk. Our goal is to add equity futures contracts to our $500 million investment in the hedge fund of funds until the combination of futures contracts and our hedge fund of funds investment matches the systematic risk of $500 million invested in the S&P 500. We then determine how much extra return we receive from this portable alpha strategy compared to what we could earn by purchasing large-cap stocks.

By definition, we establish the S&P 500 as the market portfolio. Therefore, its beta, or measure of systematic risk is 1.0. We know that the beta of the hedge fund of funds strategy is 0.17. We need to add suf-

---

[33] Suppose this were not the case. Suppose that the futures contract was priced "rich" compared to the underlying S&P 500 stocks. Then the arbitrage would be to borrow cash to finance the purchase of the S&P 500 stocks and sell the futures contract to lock in an arbitrage profit. To prevent a risk-free arbitrage, therefore, futures contracts must reflect the cost of financing.

[34] The beta of an asset relative to the market portfolio is defined as

$$beta = \rho(a,m) \times \sigma(a) \times \sigma(m)/\sigma(m)^2$$

where

$\rho(a, m)$ is the correlation coefficient between the asset return and the market return.

$\sigma(a)$ is the standard deviation of the asset's returns.

$\sigma(m)$ is the standard deviation of the market's returns.

ficient S&P 500 futures contracts so that combination of hedge fund of funds and equity futures contracts matches the systematic risk of $500 million invested in the S&P 500. This means that the equity futures contracts must contribute 1 – 0.17 = 0.83, or 83%, of the systematic risk of the portable alpha strategy.

Since our goal is to match the systematic, or beta, risk of an investment of $500 million in the S&P 500, we must purchase equity futures contracts such that they contribute 83% of the beta risk of the portable alpha strategy. This amount is

$$83\% \times \$500 \text{ million} = \$415 \text{ million of equity futures contracts}$$

Given an S&P 500 market value of about 1,300, this would translate into $415,000,000 ÷ [$250 × 1300] = 1,277 S&P 500 futures contracts.[35]

Finally, we now come to the amount of portable alpha we achieve with this strategy. The $500 million invested in the hedge fund of funds earns an expected annual return of 10.4%. Plus we have an investment in S&P 500 futures contracts that provides a return that is equivalent to 83% of that earned by an investment of $500 million in the S&P 500. In total, this portable alpha strategy is expected to earn a monthly return of

$$9.43\% + 0.83 \times 12.43\% = 19.75\%$$

To summarize, the portable alpha strategy requires a cash investment in the hedge fund of funds of $500 million. Equity futures contracts are added so that the combination of hedge fund of funds and equity futures contracts matches the systematic, or beta, risk of an investment of $500 million in the S&P 500. The portable alpha strategy earns the combination return from the hedge fund of funds and equity futures contracts.

The last piece that we must account for is the embedded financing cost in the S&P 500 futures contracts. We assumed that this was 4.5% per year. Therefore, our portable alpha strategy earns a net return of 19.75% – 4.5% = 15.25%. Compare this to the expected return of 12.43% of investing only in the S&P 500. The portable alpha strategy outperforms the S&P 500 by 2.82% per year. On a $500 million dollar investment, this is an additional $14.1 million above that earned by investing in large-cap stocks.

This portable alpha strategy demonstrates part of the allure of hedge funds. The ability to use low market risk strategies to build porta-

---

[35] Every point of the S&P 500 index is worth $250 dollars under the S&P 500 futures contract. Therefore, one S&P 500 contract represents $250 × 1,300 = $325,000 of economic exposure to the S&P 500.

ble alpha strategies that can outperform traditional investment strategies can add significant value to an investment portfolio.

Portable alpha strategies are beta driven because the purpose is to add an excess return component while maintaining a similar systematic risk as the overall asset class. Equity futures or fixed income futures are added to "equitize" or "fixed incometize" the generated alpha, matching the beta or market risk of the asset class, but at the same time, adding the portable alpha. The investor receives the market return plus the alpha.

Bond Substitute

Exhibit 4.1 demonstrates that hedge fund of funds have significantly lower risk than large-cap, small-cap, or foreign stocks. In fact, the HFRI FOF index generates a risk profile that is just slightly greater than U.S. Treasury bonds while generating greater return.

This has led some researchers to consider whether hedge funds can replace bonds in an efficient portfolio. Lamm studies the issue of hedge funds as a cash substitute.[36] He combines hedge funds with stocks and bonds in an efficient frontier analysis. He finds that hedge funds enter efficient frontiers across all risk levels because of their superior risk-adjusted returns. More importantly, Lamm finds that hedge funds enter efficient portfolios largely at the expense of bonds. That is, hedge funds primarily displace cash and bonds in efficient portfolios. This suggests that hedge funds may be used as a cash substitute.

We note that in Exhibit 4.1 the FOF index has a superior Sharpe ratio compared to U.S. Treasury bonds. While the volatility associated with hedge funds is greater than Treasury bonds, it is marginally so. Conversely, the volatility of hedge fund returns is considerably less than that for the three categories of stock investments. Additionally, hedge funds earn higher returns than bonds.

Exhibit 4.4 demonstrates that hedge fund returns have a low correlation with the returns to large-cap, small-cap, and foreign stocks. Therefore, hedge funds have a risk profile similar to bonds in terms of risk and correlation with stock returns. Yet hedge funds earn a better return than Treasury bonds. This makes hedge funds a potential substitute for bonds in an efficient portfolio.

Absolute Return

Hedge funds are often described as "absolute return" products. This term comes from the skill-based nature of the industry. Hedge fund

---

[36] See R. McFall Lamm, Jr., "Portfolios of Alternative Assets: Why Not 100% Hedge Funds?" *The Journal of Investing* (Winter 1999), pp. 87–97.

managers generally claim that their investment returns are derived from their skill at security selection rather than that of broad asset classes. This is due to the fact that most hedge fund managers build concentrated portfolios of relatively few investment positions and do not attempt to track a stock or bond index. The work of Fung and Hsieh, discussed earlier, shows that hedge funds generate a return distribution that is very different from mutual funds.[37]

Furthermore, given the generally unregulated waters in which hedge fund managers operate, they have greater flexibility in their trading style and execution than traditional long-only managers. This flexibility provides a greater probability that a hedge fund manager will reach his return targets. As a result, hedge funds have often been described as absolute return vehicles that target a specific annual return regardless of what performance might be found among market indexes. In other words, hedge fund managers target an absolute return rather than determine their performance relative to an index.

The flexibility of hedge fund managers allows them to go both long and short without benchmark constraints. This allows them to set a target rate of return or an "absolute return."

Specific parameters must be set for an absolute return program. These parameters will direct how the hedge fund program is constructed and operated and should include risk and return targets as well as the type of hedge fund strategies that may be selected. Absolute return parameters should operate at two levels: that of the individual hedge fund manager and for the overall hedge fund program. The investor sets target return ranges for each hedge fund manager but sets a specific target return level for the absolute return program. The parameters for the individual managers may be different than that for the program. For example, acceptable levels of volatility for individual hedge fund managers may be greater than that for the program.

The program parameters for the hedge fund managers may be based on such factors as volatility, expected return, types of instruments traded, leverage, and historical drawdown. Other qualitative factors may be included such as length of track record, periodic liquidity, minimum investment, and assets under management. Liquidity is particularly important because an investor needs to know with certainty her timeframe for cashing out of an absolute return program if hedge fund returns turn sour.

Exhibit 4.5 demonstrates an absolute return program strategy. Notice that the return for the portfolio has a specific target rate of 10%,

---

[37] See Fung and Hsieh, "Empirical Characteristics of Dynamic Trading Strategies: The Case of Hedge Funds."

EXHIBIT 4.5   Absolute Return Portfolio of Hedge Funds

Absolute Return Portfolio	Individual Hedge Fund Strategies
Target return: 10%	Target returns: 8% to 15%
Target volatility: 7%	Target volatility 10% to 15%
Largest acceptable drawdown: 10%	Largest acceptable drawdown: 15%
Liquidity: semiannual	Liquidity: semiannual
Correlation to U.S. stocks: 0	Maximum correlation to stocks: 0.5
Correlation to U.S. bonds: 0	Maximum correlation to bonds: 0.5
Hedge fund style: diversfied	Hedge fund styles: convergence
	Trading, corporate restructuring, and market directional

while for the individual hedge funds, the return range is 8% to 15%. Also, the absolute return portfolio has a target level for risk and drawdowns, while for the individual hedge funds, a range is acceptable.

However, certain parameters are synchronized. Liquidity, for instance, must be the same for both the absolute return portfolio and that of the individual hedge fund managers. The reason is that a range of liquidity is not acceptable if the investor wishes to liquidate her portfolio. She must be able to cash out of each hedge fund within the same timeframe as that established for the portfolio.

As an example of an absolute return program, consider Exhibits 4.6 and 4.7. These exhibits demonstrate CalPERS' Risk Managed Absolute Return Strategies program. The monthly RMARS returns are plotted against the U.S. stock market returns in Exhibit 4.6 and against the U.S. investment grade bond market in Exhibit 4.7. Both Exhibits 4.6 and 4.7 indicate a random scatter plot between the returns to the RMARS program and the stock-and-bond market. The beta of the RMARS program with respect to the stock market in Exhibit 4.6 is 0.125 with an R-square measure of 0.18. For the bond market in Exhibit 4.7, the beta is −0.12 and the R-square is 0.013. This is what is meant by an Absolute return strategy—a strategy that has limited or no correlation to the broader financial markets—effectively a zero beta to stocks and bonds.

Exhibit 4.8 shows the breakdown with respect to the strategies in the RMARS. Although there is an overweight to equity long/short managers (which accounts for the small beta of 0.125 with respect to the U.S. stock market) the program is well diversified with respect to several hedge fund strategies. Again, portfolio diversification works. In this case, it is used to drive down the beta or systematic risk exposures to the traditional financial markets.

EXHIBIT 4.6   CalPERS' Absolute Return Program versus S&P 500

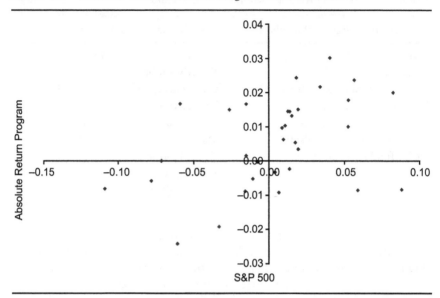

EXHIBIT 4.7   CalPERS' Absolute Return Program versus Lehman Aggregate

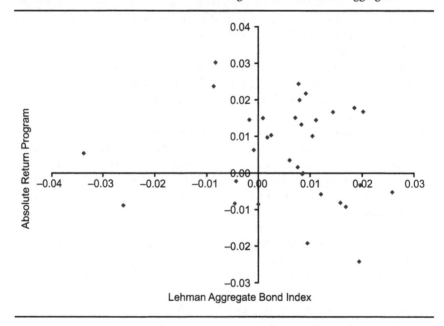

EXHIBIT 4.8   An Absolute Return Strategies Program

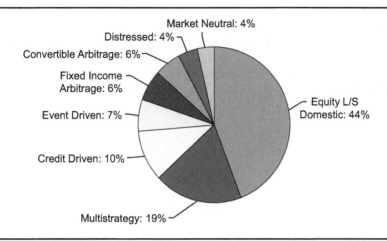

Market Neutral: 4%
Distressed: 4%
Convertible Arbitrage: 6%
Fixed Income Arbitrage: 6%
Event Driven: 7%
Credit Driven: 10%
Multistrategy: 19%
Equity L/S Domestic: 44%

CONCLUSION

Recent research indicates that hedge fund investments can expand the investment opportunity set for investors. The returns to hedge funds are generally positive, have lower volatility than the S&P 500, and have less than perfect correlation with traditional asset classes. Consequently, hedged funds provide a good opportunity to diversify a portfolio and are an excellent risk budgeting tool.

The issue of performance persistence will continue to dog hedge fund managers. Our study of the serial correlation associated with the returns to hedge funds found that convergence trading strategies have the greatest positive serial correlation. In other words, these hedge fund strategies generate the most consistent returns; a positive return in one year is followed by a positive return in the following year.

An investor must decide what is the best strategy for investing in hedge funds. Hedge funds may be invested in as part of an opportunistic strategy, as part of a fund of funds strategy, as part of a private equity investment strategy, or as an absolute return strategy. In each case, hedge funds can add value to an existing portfolio.

Opportunistic hedge fund investing runs counter to the name "hedge funds." This strategy uses hedge funds to expand the investment opportunity set, not hedge it. Typically, opportunistic hedge funds will have a benchmark associated with their performance.

Hedge fund of funds strategies may have one of three purposes. Fund of funds products may be used for risk budgeting, portable alpha, or as a fixed income substitute. In each case, the fixed income-like volatility associated with a fund of funds product makes it an excellent portfolio diversifier.

Finally, absolute return strategies target a specific risk and return profile. The goal is to produce a consistent return no matter in which part of the economic cycle the investor may find herself.

CHAPTER 5

Due Diligence for Hedge Fund Managers

In the previous chapters, we addressed the questions of what (What are hedge funds?), why (Why should hedge funds be included in an investment portfolio?), and how (How should a hedge fund program be constructed?). We now turn to the question of who. Who should be selected as your hedge fund manager depends on due diligence.

At the outset, we realize that this is one of the longer chapters in the Handbook. This reflects the time it takes to perform proper due diligence on a hedge fund manager. Unfortunately, there is no substitute for detailed diligence on a hedge fund manager; this takes time and effort.

Due diligence starts the initial process of building a relationship with a hedge fund manager. It is an unavoidable task that investors must follow in order to choose a manager. Due diligence is the process of identifying the best and the brightest of the hedge fund managers. This is where the investor must roll up her sleeves and get into the devilish details that can prove to be so elusive with hedge fund managers.

Due diligence consists of seven parts: structure, strategy, performance, risk, administrative, legal, and references. This chapter reviews each part of the due diligence procedure. In the appendix to the chapter, we provide a due diligence checklist.

We start this chapter with three fundamental questions that every investor should ask a hedge fund manager. Although these questions seem simplistic, they should be part of the initial meeting with the hedge fund manager and should be addressed before an investor decides to put the hedge fund manager through a full blown due diligence review.

THREE FUNDAMENTAL QUESTIONS

Although the first hedge fund was introduced more than 50 years ago,[1] the hedge fund industry is still relatively new because it has attracted attention only within the past decade. In fact, most of the academic research on hedge funds was conducted during the 1990s. As a result, for most hedge fund managers, a two- to three-year track record is considered long term. In fact, Park, Brown, and Goetzmann find that the attrition rate in the hedge fund industry is about 15% per year and that the half-life for hedge funds is about 2.5 years. Liang documents an attrition rate of 8.54% per year for hedge funds. Weisman indicates that relying on a hedge fund manager's past performance history can lead to disappointing investment results.[2] Consequently, performance history, while useful, cannot be relied upon solely in selecting a hedge fund manager.

Beyond performance numbers, there are three fundamental questions that every hedge fund manager should answer during the initial screening process. The answers to these three questions are critical to understanding the nature of the hedge fund manager's investment program. The three questions are:

1. What is the investment objective of the hedge fund?
2. What is the investment process of the hedge fund manager?
3. What makes the hedge fund manager so smart?

A hedge fund manager should have a clear and concise statement of its investment objective. Second, the hedge fund manager should identify its investment process. For instance, is it quantitatively or qualitatively based? Last, the hedge fund manager must demonstrate that he or she is smarter than other money managers.

The questions presented in this chapter are threshold issues. These questions are screening tools designed to reduce an initial universe of hedge fund managers down to a select pool of potential investments. They are not, however, a substitute for a thorough due diligence review. Instead, these questions can identify potential hedge fund candidates for which due diligence is appropriate.

---

[1] Alfred W. Jones introduced the first hedge fund in 1949. See David Purcell and Paul Crowley, "The Reality of Hedge Funds," *The Journal of Investing* (Fall 1999), pp. 26–44.
[2] See James Park, Stephen J. Brown, and William N. Goetzmann, "The Performance Benchmarks and Survivorship Bias of Hedge Funds and Commodity Trading Advisors," *Hedge Fund News* (August 1999); Bing Liang "Hedge Fund Performance: 1990–1999," *Financial Analysts Journal* (January/February 2001), pp. 11–18; and Andrew Weisman, "The Dangers of Historical Hedge Fund Data," working paper (2000).

Investment Objective

The question of a hedge fund manager's investment objective can be broken down into three additional questions:

1. In which markets does the hedge fund manager invest?
2. What is the hedge fund manager's general investment strategy?
3. What is the hedge fund manager's benchmark, if any?

Although these questions may seem straightforward, they are often surprisingly difficult to answer. Consider the following language from a hedge fund disclosure document:

> The principal objective of the Fund is capital appreciation, primarily through the purchase and sale of securities, commodities, and other financial instruments including without limitation, stocks, bonds, notes, debentures, and bills issued by corporations, municipalities, sovereign nations or other entities; options, rights, warrants, convertible securities, exchangeable securities, synthetic and/or structured convertible or exchangeable products, participation interests, investment contracts, mortgages, mortgage and asset-backed securities, real estate and interests therein; currencies, other futures, commodity options, forward contracts, money market instruments, bank notes, bank guarantees, letters of credit, other forms of bank obligations; other swaps and other derivative instruments; limited partnership interests and other limited partnership securities or instruments; and contracts relating to the foregoing; in each case whether now existing or created in the future.

Let us analyze the above statement in light of our three investment objective questions.

Question 1: In which markets does the hedge fund manager invest?
Answer: In every market known to exist.

By listing every possible financial, commodity, or investment contract currently in existence (or to exist in the future), the hedge fund manager has covered all of his bases, but has left the investor uninformed. Unfortunately, the unlimited nature of the hedge fund manager's potential investment universe does not help to narrow the scope of the manager's investment objective.

Question 2: What is the hedge fund manager's general strategy?
Answer: Capital appreciation.

This answer, too, is uninformative. Rarely does any investor invest in a hedge fund for capital *depreciation*. Generally, hedge funds are not used as tax shelters. Furthermore, many institutional investors are tax-exempt so that taxes are not a consideration. Capital appreciation is assumed for most investments, including hedge funds. The above language is far too general to be informative.

Question 3: What is the manager's benchmark, if any?
Answer: There is no effective benchmark. The manager's investment universe is so widespread as to make any benchmark useless.

Unfortunately, the above disclosure language, while very detailed, discloses very little. It does cover all of the manager's legal bases, but it does not inform the investor.

By contrast, consider the following language from a second hedge fund disclosure document.

> The Fund's investment objective is to make investments in public securities that generate a long-term return in excess of that generated by the overall U.S. public equity market while reducing the market risk of the portfolio through selective short positions.

This one sentence answers all three investment objective questions. First, the manager identifies that it invests in the U.S. public equity market. Second, the manager discloses that it uses a long/short investment strategy. Lastly, the manager states that its objective is to outperform the overall U.S. equity market. Therefore, a suitable benchmark might be the S&P500, the Russell 1000, or a sector index.

In summary, long-winded disclosure statements are not necessary. A well-thought out investment strategy can be summarized in one sentence.

Investment Process

Most investors prefer a well-defined investment process that describes how an investment manager makes its investments. The articulation and documentation of the process can be just as important as the investment results generated by the process. Consider the following language from another hedge fund disclosure document:

> The manager makes extensive use of computer technology in both the formulation and execution of many investment decisions. Buy and sell decisions will, in many cases, be made and executed algorithmically according to quantitative trading strategies embodied in analytical computer software running the manager's computer facilities or on other computers used to support the Fund's trading activities.

This is a "black box." A black box is the algorithmic extension of the hedge fund manager's brain power. Computer algorithms are developed to quantify the manager's skill or investment insight. For black box managers, the black box itself is the investment process. It is not that the black boxes are bad investments. In fact, the hedge fund research indicates that proprietary quantitative trading strategies can be quite successful.[3] Rather, the issue is whether good performance results justify the lack of a clear investment process.

Black box programs tend to be used in arbitrage or relative value hedge fund programs Hedge fund managers use quantitative computer algorithms to seek out pricing discrepancies between similar securities or investment contracts. They then sell the investment that appears to be "expensive" and buy the investment that appears to be "cheap." The very nature of arbitrage programs is to minimize market risk. Leverage is then applied to extract the most value from their small net exposure to market risk.

A black box is just one example of process versus investment results. The hedge fund industry considers itself to be "skill based." However, it is very difficult to translate manager skill into a process. This is particularly true when the performance of the hedge fund is dependent upon the skill of a specific individual.

Let's consider another, well publicized skill-based investment process. In the spring of 2000, the hedge funds headed by George Soros stumbled, leading to the departure of Stanley Druckenmiller, the chief investment strategist for Soros Fund Management. The *Wall Street Journal* documented the concentrated skill-based investment style of this hedge fund group:

> For years, [Soros Fund Management] fostered an entrepreneurial culture, with a cadre of employees battling wits to persuade Mr. Druckenmiller to invest.

> "[Mr. Druckenmiller] didn't scream, but he could be very tough. It could be three days or three weeks of battling it out until he's convinced, or you're defeated."[4]

---

[3] See CrossBorder Capital, "Choosing Investment Styles to Reduce Risk," *Hedge Fund Research* (October 1999); Goldman, Sachs & Co. and Financial Risk Management Ltd., "The Hedge Fund "Industry" and Absolute Return Funds," *The Journal of Alternative Investments* (Spring 1999), and "Hedge Funds Revisited," *Pension and Endowment Forum* (January 2000).

[4] "Shake-Up Continues at Soros's Hedge-Fund Empire," *The Wall Street Journal*, May 1, 2000, page C1.

The above statement does not describe an investment process. It is a description of an individual. The hedge fund manager's investment analysis and decision-making is concentrated in one person. This is a pure example of "skill-based" investing. There is no discernible process. Instead, all information is filtered through the brain of one individual. In essence, the institutional investor must trust the judgment of one person.

Mr. Druckenmiller compiled an exceptional track record as the manager of the Soros Quantum Fund. However, the concentration of decision-making authority is not an economic risk, it is a process risk.

Investors are generally unwilling to bear risks that are not fundamental to their tactical and strategic asset allocations. Process risk is not a fundamental risk. It is an idiosyncratic risk of the hedge fund manager's structure and operations.

Generally, process risk is not a risk that investors wish to bear. Nor is it a risk for which they expect to be compensated. Furthermore, how would an investor go about pricing the process risk of a hedge fund manager? It can't be quantified, and it can't be calibrated. Therefore, there is no way to tell whether an institutional investor is being properly compensated for this risk.[5]

Process risk also raises the ancillary issue of lack of transparency. Skill-based investing usually is opaque. Are the decisions of the key individual quantitatively based? Qualitatively based? There is no way to really tell. This is similar to the problems discussed earlier with respect to black boxes.

To summarize, process risk cannot be quantified and it is not a risk that investors are willing to bear. Process risk also raises issues of transparency. Investors want clarity and definition, not opaqueness and amorphousness.

What Makes the Hedge Fund Manager so Smart?

Before investing money with a hedge fund manager, an investor must determine one of the following. The hedge fund manager must be able to demonstrate that he or she is smarter than the next manager. One way to be smarter than another hedge fund manager is to have superior skill in filtering information. That is, the hedge fund manager must be able to look at the same information set as another manager but be able to glean more investment insight from that data set.

---

[5] See James Park and Jeremy Staum, "Fund of Funds Diversification: How Much is Enough?" *The Journal of Alternative Investments* (Winter 1998), pp. 39–42. They demonstrate that idiosyncratic process risks can largely be eliminated through a diversified fund of funds program. They indicate that a portfolio of 15 to 20 hedge funds can eliminate much of the idiosyncratic risk associated with hedge fund investments.

Alternatively, if the hedge fund manager is not smarter than the next manager, he must demonstrate that he has a better information set; his competitive advantage is not filtering information, but gathering it. To be successful, a hedge fund manager must demonstrate one or both of these competitive advantages.

Generally speaking, quantitative, computer-driven managers satisfy the first criteria. That is, hedge fund managers that run computer models access the same information set as everyone else, but have better (smarter) algorithms to extract more value per information unit than the next manager. These managers tend to be relative value managers.

Relative value managers extract value by simultaneously comparing the prices of two securities and buying and selling accordingly. This information is available to all investors in the marketplace. However, it is the relative value managers that are able to process the information quickly enough to capture mispricings in the market.

Alternatively, hedge fund managers that confine themselves to a particular market segment or sector generally satisfy the second criteria. They have a larger information set that allows them to gain a competitive edge in their chosen market. Their advantage is a proprietary information set accumulated over time rather than a proprietary data filtering system.

Consider the following statement from a hedge fund disclosure document:

> The Adviser hopes to achieve consistently high returns by focusing on small- and mid-cap companies in the biotechnology market.

The competitive advantage of this type of manager is his or her knowledge not only about a particular economic sector (biotechnology), but also about a particular market segment of that sector (small- and mid-cap). This type of manger tends to take more market risk exposure than credit risk exposure and generally applies equity long/short programs.

Identifying the competitive advantage of the hedge fund manager is the key to determining whether the hedge fund manager can sustain performance results, although we note that the issue of performance persistence is undecided. Therefore, an investor cannot rely on historical hedge fund performance data as a means of selecting good managers from bad managers. Furthermore, every hedge fund disclosure document contains some variation of the following language:

> Past performance is no indication of future results.

Essentially, this statement directs the investor to ignore the hedge fund manager's performance history.

To asses the likelihood of performance persistence, the investor must then determine whether the hedge fund manager is an information gatherer or an information filterer. Consider the following language from a hedge fund disclosure document.

> The General Partner will utilize its industry expertise, contacts, and databases developed over the past 11 years to identify ____ company investment ideas outside traditional sources and will analyze these investment opportunities using, among other techniques, many aspects of its proven methodology in determining value.

This hedge fund manager has a superior information set that has been developed over 11 years. It is an information gatherer. This manager applies an equity long/short program within a specific market sector.

Finally, consider the following disclosure language from a merger arbitrage hedge fund manager:

> [The] research group [is] staffed by experienced M&A lawyers with detailed knowledge of deal lifecycle, with extensive experience with corporate law of multiple U.S. states, U.S. and foreign securities laws regarding proxy contests, and antitrust laws (both of the U.S. and EU), and who have made relevant filings before regulators and have closed a wide variety of M&A transactions.

This hedge fund manager is an information filterer. Its expertise is sifting through the outstanding legal and regulatory issues associated with a merger and determining the likelihood that the deal will be completed.

To summarize, a good lesson is that successful hedge fund managers know the exact nature of their competitive advantage, and how to exploit it.

STRUCTURAL REVIEW

The structural review defines the organization of the hedge fund manager. We start with the basics: How is the fund organized? It is important to remember that the hedge fund manager and the hedge fund are separate legal entities with different legal structures and identities. We then consider the structure of the hedge fund manager, any regulatory registrations, and key personnel.

Fund Organization

The hedge fund manager may invest the hedge fund's assets through an offshore master trust account or fund. An offshore master trust account is often used to take into account the various tax domiciles of the hedge fund's investors. Often, a hedge fund manager will set up two hedge funds, one onshore (U.S.-based) and one offshore. Master trusts are typically established in tax-neutral sites such as Bermuda or the Cayman Islands.

The purpose of the master trust is to invest the assets of the both the onshore hedge fund and the offshore hedge fund in a consistent (if not, identical) manner so that both hedge funds share the benefit of the hedge fund manager's insights. Investors in either fund are not disadvantaged by this structure. Instead, it allows the tax consequences to flow down to the tax code of each investor's domicile country.

Master trusts/funds are often viewed suspiciously as tax evasion vehicles. This is not their purpose. Their purpose is tax neutrality, not evasion. In Bermuda, for example, master trust funds do not pay any corporate income tax. They only pay a corporate licensing fee. Therefore, there are no adverse tax consequences to the hedge fund investors at the master trust level.

Instead, the tax consequences for the investors will depend upon their domicile. Investors in the onshore U.S.-based hedge fund are subject to the U.S. Internal Revenue Code. Investors in the offshore fund are subject to the tax code of their respective domicile. Therefore, master trust vehicles are used to accommodate the different tax domiciles of foreign and domestic investors.

Consider a hedge fund manager who has two investors: one based in the United States and one in France. Where should she locate her hedge fund? If she locates the hedge fund in the United States, the U.S. investor will be happy, but the French investor may have to pay double the income taxes: both in the United States and in France. The best way to resolve this problem is to set up two hedge funds, one onshore and one offshore. In addition, a master trust account is established in a tax-neutral site. The hedge fund manager can then invest the assets of both hedge funds through the master trust account and each investor will be liable only for the taxes imposed by the revenue code of their respective countries.[6] Exhibit 5.1 demonstrates the master trust structure.

Hedge fund structures do not have to be as complicated as that presented in Exhibit 5.1. The majority of hedge fund managers in the

---

[6] In reality, the United States and France have a tax treaty so the threat of double taxation is minimal. However there are many countries that do not have tax treaties, and the potential for double taxation is a reality.

EXHIBIT 5.1   Master Trust Account

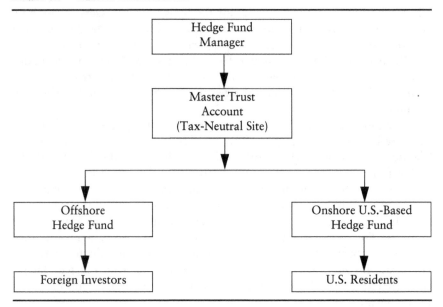

United States operate only within the United States, have only an onshore hedge fund, and accept only U.S. investors. Nonetheless, the popularity of hedge fund investing has resulted in operating structures that are sometimes as creative as the hedge fund strategies themselves.

In addition to a Master Feeder structure, the hedge fund manager may also have separate accounts. These are single client asset management accounts. An investor in a hedge fund should ascertain whether these separate accounts are managed in the same strategy as the hedge fund. If so, fee economics should be similar. In addition, these separate accounts must also be allocated trade ideas by the hedge fund manager. The investor should determine that there is a fair and equitable allocation of the hedge fund manager's trade ideas to the hedge fund as well as the separate accounts. This is a critical piece of the due diligence process because it is unlikely that the hedge fund manager's prime brokers or custodians will monitor whether the trade allocation was done in a fair and impartial manner.

Hedge Fund Manager Organization

First, the basics: Where is the hedge fund manager located, are there any satellite offices, and where is the nearest office to the investor? These questions can be very important if the hedge fund manager operates overseas and there are significant time differences between the manager's business hours and that of the investor.

Second, an organization chart is mandatory. Who is the Chief Executive Officer, the Chief Investment Officer, and Chief Operating Officer? A warning: It is not a good business plan if they are all the same person. Hedge fund managers should do what they do best: invest money and leave the operating details to someone else.

Of special importance is the Chief Financial Officer. The CFO will be the investor's most important link with the hedge fund manager after an investment is made because the CFO will be responsible for reporting the hedge fund manager's performance numbers. Consequently, the investor should make certain that the CFO has strong background in accounting, preferably a Certified Public Accountant, a Chartered Accountant, or another professional accounting designation. Finally, the investor must determine who are the senior managers in charge of trading, information systems, marketing, and research and development.

The educational and professional background of all principals should be documented. It should be determined whether they have graduate degrees, whether there are any Chartered Financial Analysts, and what was their prior investment experience before starting a hedge fund.

Another warning: Many equity long/short hedge fund managers were former long-only managers. Yet, shorting stocks is very different than going long stocks. The ability to locate and borrow stock, limit losses in a bull market, and short on the uptick rule are special talents that cannot be developed overnight.

Before investing money with a long/short hedge fund manager, an investor should find out where the hedge fund manager learned to short stocks. If it is a hedge fund manager that previously managed a long-only portfolio, chances are that she might not have much experience with respect to shorting stocks and will therefore be learning to short stocks with your money.

Ownership

Ownership of the hedge fund manager must be documented. It is important to know who owns the company that advises the hedge fund. This is important for "key person" provisions of the contractual documentation.

Ownership is also important for ensuring that there is a proper alignment of interests with the hedge fund manager's employees as well as retention of employment. By sharing the ownership of the hedge fund management company with key employees, the hedge fund manager can ensure proper alignment of interests as well as retention of key personnel.

Registrations

The investor should document the regulatory registrations of the hedge fund manager. The hedge fund manager might be registered with the Securities and Exchange Commission as an Investment Adviser under the Investment Adviser's Act of 1940. If so, the hedge fund manager must file annually Form ADV with the SEC that contains important financial and structural information regarding the hedge fund manager.

Alternatively, the hedge fund manager might be registered with the National Futures Association (NFA) and the Commodity Futures Trading Commission (CFTC) as either a Commodity Trading Advisor (CTA) or a Commodity Pool Operator (CPO). The NFA is the self-regulatory organization for the managed futures industry. It is approved by the CFTC to handle all registrations for CTAs and CPOs. Also, the hedge fund manager might be registered with the NFA as an introducing broker or futures commission merchant. If the hedge fund manager is registered as either a CTA, CPO, introducing broker, or futures commission merchant, it must obey the rules and regulations of the NFA and the CFTC.

If the hedge fund manager is registered with either the SEC or the CFTC, the investor should ascertain the date of the original registration and whether there are any civil, criminal, or administrative actions outstanding against the hedge fund manager. This information must be filed with either the NFA (for the managed futures industry) or the SEC (for investment advisers).

Outside Service Providers

The investor must document who is the hedge fund manager's outside auditors, prime broker, and legal counsel. Each of these service providers must be contacted.

First, the investor should receive the hedge fund manager's last annual audited financial statement as well as the most current statement. Any questions regarding the financial statements should be directed to the CFO and the outside auditors. Any opinion from the auditors other than an unqualified opinion must be explained by the outside auditors. Additionally, outside auditors are a good source of information regarding the hedge fund manager's accounting system and operations.

The hedge fund manager's prime broker is responsible for executing the hedge fund manager's trades, lending securities to short, and providing short-term financing for leverage. It is essential that the investor contact the prime broker because the prime broker is in the best position to observe the hedge fund manager's trading positions.

There was an incident on President's Day in 1997 where a prime broker contacted one of its hedge fund manager clients and demanded a margin call. In a margin call the prime broker demands that the hedge fund manager post more cash or collateral to cover either her short positions or her borrowing from the manager.

Margin calls can happen for several reasons. First and foremost, a short position can move against a hedge fund manager creating a large negative balance with the hedge fund manager's prime broker. To protect itself from the credit exposure to the hedge fund manager, the prime broker will make a margin call, in effect, demanding that the hedge fund manager either put up cash or more securities as collateral to cover the prime broker's credit exposure to the hedge fund manager.

On this particular President's Day, a prime broker made a margin call on a hedge fund manager that invested in the mortgage-backed securities market. The essence of the margin call is that the prime broker was skeptical of the market value of positions that the hedge fund manager claimed. The prime broker demanded that the hedge fund manager either confirm the market value of her positions by soliciting bids in the mortgage-backed securities market to buy some of the hedge fund manager's portfolio, or post more collateral.

Unfortunately, President's Day is a national holiday when banks and insurance companies, two key investors in the mortgage-backed securities market, are closed. As a result the market for mortgage-backed securities was very thin that day and the hedge fund manager had no choice but to be a price taker. Additionally, the hedge fund manager's marking to market values proved to be optimistic. The resulting fire sale had a significant impact on the hedge fund manager's performance.

This unfortunate example demonstrates the important relationship between the prime broker community and the hedge fund community. Every hedge fund manager has at least one prime broker, and these prime brokers monitor the hedge fund manager's portfolio.

Finally, the investor should speak with the hedge fund manager's outside counsel. This is important for two reasons. First, outside counsel is typically responsible for keeping current all regulatory registrations of the hedge fund manager. Second, outside counsel can inform the investor of any criminal, civil, or administrative actions that might be pending against the hedge fund manager. Outside counsel is also responsible for preparing the hedge fund manager's offering document. This is with whom the investor will negotiate should an investment be made with the hedge fund manager.

STRATEGIC REVIEW

The second phase of due diligence is a review of the hedge fund manager's investment strategy. This should include a clear statement of the hedge fund manager's style, the markets in which she invests, what competitive advantage the hedge fund manager brings to the table, the source of her investment ideas, and what benchmark, if any, is appropriate for the hedge fund.

Investment Style

In Chapter 3, we listed several styles of hedge fund managers. While these are the major hedge fund styles, they are by no means exhaustive. The creativity of hedge fund managers is such that there are as many styles as there are colors of the rainbow.

For instance, convergence trading is a hedge fund style frequently seen. Recall that convergence trading compares two similar securities and buys the security that is "cheap" relative to the other security while selling the security that is relatively "rich." Convergence trading can be subdivided into economic arbitrage and statistical arbitrage. Economic arbitrage compares the pricing fundamentals of two similar securities to determine if the prices set by the market are inconsistent with the fundamentals. If an inconsistency is identified, the "cheap" security is purchased and the "rich" security is sold. The hedge fund manager will hold on to these positions until the market corrects itself and the two security prices are in proper balance. This holding period may be a day, week, or several months. In some cases, it may be necessary to hold the two securities to maturity (in the case of bonds).

Conversely, "stat arb" is another form of convergence trading where the trading is based not on economic fundamentals, but rather, on statistical anomalies that temporarily occur in the market. Typically, these anomalies occur only for a moment or for a day at most. Consequently, statistical arbitrage is a very short-term relative value trading program with positions entered and exited within the same trading day.

Additionally, economic relative value or statistical arbitrage can occur in the fixed income, equity, or convertible bond markets. Exhibit 5.2 diagrams how an investment strategy should be documented.

Investment Markets

Next, the investor should document in which markets the hedge fund manager invests. Recall that this was one of our basic questions we previously discussed. We provided an example of a well-defined equity long/short manager.

EXHIBIT 5.2   Documenting a Hedge Fund Investment Strategy

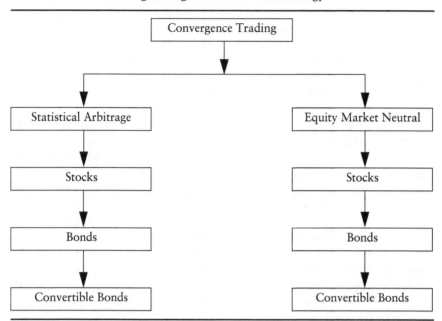

For other hedge fund managers, however, the answer is not so obvious. For instance, global macro managers typically have the broadest investment mandate possible. They can invest across the world equity, bond, commodity, and currency markets. Pinning down a global macro manager may be akin to picking up mercury. Nonetheless, the investor should document as best she can in what markets the hedge fund manager invests. If the hedge fund manager is a global macro manager, the investor may have to accept that the manager can and will invest in whatever market it deems fit.

The investor should also determine the extent to which the hedge fund manager invests in derivative securities. Derivatives are a two-edged sword. On the one hand, they can hedge an investment portfolio and reduce risk. On the other hand, they can increase the leverage of the hedge fund and magnify the risks taken by the hedge fund manager.

Investment Securities

Closely related to the investment markets are the types of securities in which the hedge fund manager invests. For some strategies, it will be straightforward. For instance, the sample language provided above indicates that the hedge fund manager will invest in the stock of U.S. companies.

However, other strategies will not be so clear. Recall the language from above where one hedge fund manager listed every security, futures contract, option, and derivative contract "in each case whether now existing or created in the future." This manager needs to be pinned down, and the due diligence checklist is the place to do it.

Oftentimes, hedge fund disclosure documents are drafted in very broad and expansive terms. The reason is that the hedge fund manager does not want to be legally bound into an investment corner. The purpose of due diligence is not to legally bind the hedge fund manager but to document the types of securities necessary to effect her investment strategy.

It is very important that the investor determine the hedge fund manager's strategy for using derivatives, the type of derivatives used, and in which markets will derivatives be purchased. Of particular concern is the extent to which hedge fund manager may "short volatility."

Shorting volatility is a strategy where hedge fund managers sell out of the money call or put options against their investment portfolio. If the options expire unexercised, the hedge fund manager receives the option premiums and this increases the return for the hedge fund. However, if the options are exercised against the hedge fund manager, significant negative results may occur. In Chapter 7 on risk management, we demonstrate the dangers of shorting volatility.

Benchmark

Establishing a benchmark for hedge fund managers is one of the thorniest issues facing the industry. We will have quite a bit to say about this in Chapter 9. For now, suffice it to say that hedge fund managers eschew benchmarks.

One reason is the skill-based nature of their investment styles. Manager skill cannot be captured by a passive securities benchmark. Skill, in fact, is orthogonal to passive investing.

Second, most hedge fund managers apply investment strategies that cannot be captured by a passive securities index. For instance, it can be argued that a long-only passive equity index is not an appropriate benchmark for an equity long/short hedge fund. Additionally, hedge fund managers also use derivative instruments, such as options, that have nonlinear payout functions. Passive securities indexes do not reflect nonlinear payout strategies.

Last, hedge fund managers tend to maintain concentrated portfolios. The nature of this concentration makes the investment strategy of the hedge fund manager distinct from a broad-based securities index.

Nonetheless, some performance measure must be established for the hedge fund manager. For instance, if the hedge fund manager runs a long/short equity fund concentrating on the semi-conductor sector of the technology industry, a good benchmark would be the SOX/semi-conductor index maintained by the Philadelphia Stock Exchange.

If the hedge fund manager does not believe that any index is appropriate for his strategy, then a *hurdle rate* must be established. Hurdle rates are most appropriate for absolute return hedge fund managers whose rate of return is not dependent upon the general economic prospects of a sector or a broad-based market index.

Competitive Advantage

Recall the three fundamental questions at the beginning of this chapter. One of the key factors that must be uncovered during the due diligence process is the competitive advantage of the hedge fund manager. What does this manager do that is different/special from other hedge fund managers? What is her insight? Is it better fundamental analysis, good risk control, better quantitative models? Furthermore, how does she exploit this in the financial markets? This advantage must be documented as part of the due diligence process.

Another way to ask this question is: What makes the hedge fund manager different from the other managers? For instance, there are many merger arbitrage managers. However, some invest only in announced deals while some speculate on potential deals. Some merger arbitrage funds invest in cross-border deals while others stay strictly within the boundaries of their domicile. Some participate in deals only of a certain market capitalization range while others are across the board. And finally, some merger arbitrage funds use options and convertible securities to capture the merger premium while others invest only in the underlying equity.

As we demonstrated above another competitive advantage, some merger arbitrage experts develop large in-house legal staffs to review the regulatory (antitrust) implications of the announced deals. These managers rely on their expert legal analysis to determine whether the existing merger premium is rich or cheap. They exploit the legal issues associated with the merger instead of the economic issues.

Current Portfolio Position

This part of the due diligence is meant to provide a current snapshot of the hedge fund. First, the investor should ascertain the fund's current long versus short exposure. Additionally, the investor should determine the amount of cash that the hedge fund manager is keeping and why. Too much cash indicates an investment strategy that may be stuck in neutral.

The investor should also ascertain how many investments the hedge fund manager currently maintains in the fund. As we have previously discussed, hedge fund managers typically run concentrated exposure. Therefore, the investor is exposed to more stock specific risk than market risk. Again, this is the essence of hedge fund management: Hedge fund managers do not take market risk, they take security specific risk. This stock or security specific risk is the source of the hedge fund manager's returns.

Last, the investor should ask the hedge fund manager how she has positioned the hedge fund portfolio in light of current market conditions. This should provide insight not only as to how the hedge fund manager views the current financial markets, but also her investment strategy going forward.

Source of Investment Ideas

What is the source of the hedge fund manager's investment ideas? Does she wait until "it just hits her?" Conversely, is there a rigorous process for sourcing investment ideas? Idea generation is what hedge fund investing is all about. This is the source of the manager's skill.

The source of investment ideas is closely tied in with the nature of competitive advantage. The hedge fund manager's competitive advantage could be her research department that generates investment ideas better or faster than other hedge fund managers. Conversely, some hedge fund managers, such as merger arbitrage managers, wait for deals to be announced in the market.

In addition, the investor should determine in which type of market the hedge fund manager's ideas work best. Do they work best in bear markets, bull markets, flat markets, volatile markets, or none at all? For instance, an absolute return hedge fund manager (a manager with a hurdle rate for a benchmark) should be agnostic with respect to the direction of the market. Otherwise, an argument could be made that the hedge fund manager's performance should be compared to a market index.

Capacity

A frequent issue with hedge fund managers is the capacity of their investment strategy. Hedge fund manager's have investment strategies that are more narrowly focused than traditional long-only managers. As a consequence, their investment strategies frequently have limited capacity. This is more the case for hedge fund managers that target small sectors of the economy or segments of the financial markets.

For instance, the convertible bond market is much smaller than the U.S. equity market. Consequently, a convertible bond hedge fund manager may have more limited capacity than an equity long/short manager.

Global macrohedge fund managers, with their global investment mandate, have the largest capacity. This large capacity is derived from their unlimited ability to invest across financial instruments, currencies, borders, and commodities.

Capacity is an important issue for the investor because the hedge fund manager might dilute her skill by allowing a greater number of investors into the hedge fund than is optimal from an investment standpoint. This may result in too much money chasing too few deals.

PERFORMANCE REVIEW

List of Funds and Assets Under Management

First, the investor should document how many hedge funds the hedge fund manager advises and the assets under management for each fund. The investor should know the size of the hedge fund manager's empire. This is important not only for the collection of performance data, but also it may give the investor some sense of the hedge fund manager's investment capacity.

Verifying the assets of the hedge fund manager may not be as easy as it sounds. First, the hedge fund manager may have onshore and offshore accounts or hedge funds. Second, the hedge fund manager may use multiple prime brokers and custodians to keep and trade its assets. The investor should ask how many custodians and prime brokers the hedge fund manager uses and get the latest monthly statement of each. Then the investor can piece together the total size of the hedge fund manager's empire.

There are three important questions to ask. How long has the hedge fund manager been actively managing a hedge fund? Have her performance results been consistent over time? Are the investment strategies the same or different for each hedge fund?

Previously, we noted that the attrition rate in the hedge fund is very high, up to 15% a year according to one study. Successful hedge fund managers have a long-term track record with consistent results. However, "long-term" in the hedge fund industry is a relative term. For hedge funds, five years is generally sufficient to qualify as long-term.

Additionally, if a hedge fund manager manages more than one hedge fund, the investment strategy and style should be documented for both. If the hedge funds follow the same style, then the issue of trade allocation must be resolved. The investor should determine how the hedge fund manager decides which trades go into which hedge fund.

Drawdowns

Drawdowns are a common phenomenon in the hedge fund industry. Simply defined, a drawdown is a decline in the net asset value of the hedge fund. Drawdowns are not unique to the hedge fund industry; they also occur in the mutual fund industry. However, in the long-only world of mutual funds, drawdowns are often motivated by declines in market indexes. This reflects the market risk associated with mutual funds.

The difference with hedge funds is that they eschew market risk in favor of security specific risk. The amount of security specific risk in the hedge fund is reflective of the hedge fund manager's skill level of finding overpriced and underpriced securities regardless of the condition of the general financial markets. Therefore, drawdowns in the hedge fund world indicate a lapse of hedge fund manager skill.

Hedge fund managers often claim that their industry is skill based. This claim is a two-edged sword. On the one hand, it protects hedge fund managers from being compared to a passive long-only index as a benchmark. On the other hand, it also means that when the hedge fund declines in value, the blame rests solely with the hedge fund manager and not with the condition of the financial markets.

Therefore, it is important to measure how much a lapse of hedge fund manager skill cost the fund, and how long it took for the hedge fund manager to regain her skill and recoup the losses. Last, the hedge fund manager should explain her temporary loss of skill.

Statistical Data

This section covers the basic summary information that is expected of all active managers: the average return over the life of the fund as well as the standard deviation (volatility) or returns and the Sharpe ratio.

As an aside, Sharpe ratios can be misleading statistics when measuring hedge fund performance because of the nonlinear strategies that hedge fund managers can pursue. We provide an example of this danger in our chapter on risk management.

Additionally, if a benchmark can be identified for the hedge fund, then the systematic risk of the hedge fund with that benchmark should be measured. This statistic is known as the beta of the hedge fund and it measures the extent by which the hedge fund returns move in tandem with the benchmark.

Also, if a benchmark is identified, then an Information Ratio (IR) statistic can be calculated. This is the excess return of the hedge fund (the returns to the hedge fund minus the returns to the benchmark) divided by the standard deviation of the excess returns. The IR measures the amount of active return that is earned for each unit of active risk exposure. As a rule of thumb, successful long-only managers generally earn an IR between 0.25 to 0.50. With respect to hedge funds, an investor should expect to receive an IR between 1 and 1.5.

Withdrawals

Withdrawals can be detrimental to fund performance. If a hedge fund manager is fully invested at the time of a redemption request, fund performance will suffer. First, the hedge fund manager must sell securities to fund the withdrawal. This means transaction costs that would not otherwise be incurred will be charged to the fund and will be borne by all investors. Additionally, to the extent that a hedge fund manager cannot liquidate a portion of her investment strategy on a pro rata basis to fund the withdrawal, there may be a loss to the hedge fund from foregone investment opportunities.

Finally, the less liquid the securities in which the hedge fund manager invests, the greater will be these costs. Equity long/short hedge funds usually have the lowest cost associated with a withdrawal because the equity markets are typically the most liquid markets in which to transact. However, more arcane investment strategies and securities such as mortgage-backed arbitrage can have significant costs associated with a withdrawal.

Recall the incident discussed above with respect to a prime broker executing a margin call on President's Day to a mortgage-backed hedge fund manager. The timing of the margin call had severe implications for fund performance. A withdrawal request is similar to a margin call in that a hedge fund investor demands that the hedge fund manager liquidate some of her positions to fund the redemption request. The results, if unexpected, can have a negative impact of fund performance.

Pricing

One of the biggest issues with hedge fund performance is how does the hedge fund manager value the securities in her portfolio in order to create performance records. This issue is particularly acute for hedge fund managers that invest in esoteric and illiquid securities such as collateralized debt obligations, distressed debt, or convertible bonds. One of the reasons that hedge fund managers can earn significant excess returns is because the lack of liquidity in these markets provides the hedge fund manager with two sources of return: (1) a liquidity premium for simply buying and holding securities that trade infrequently, and (2) the ability to earn excess returns in a less efficient market.

For publicly traded securities such as stocks and bonds, the issue is less acute, but still has the potential for unscrupulous behavior. For example, every publicly traded stock has both a bid and offer price. For a stock like IBM where the bid is $83.85 and the offer is $83.86, the issue is non existent, because the difference between the bid and the offer price is only 1 penny.

However, consider the stock of Digitas Inc., an Internet professional services firm with a less than $1 billion market capitalization. Its bid price is $10.60 while its offer is $10.66, a spread of 6 cents. Depending on whether the hedge fund manager is long or short this stock, marking her positions to the bid or offer can create an instant 6 cent swing in the value of her position.

The best hedge fund managers take a conservative approach to pricing their positions. For example for a long position in Digitas, the hedge fund manager could mark to the bid price of $10.60 while a hedge fund manager that is short could mark her position to the offer of $10.66. A common practice in the hedge fund industry is to take the mid-market price in between the bid and offer prices, or $10.63, and use this for both short and long positions with respect to Digitas. Also, many hedge fund managers (or their administrators) use outside pricing services for their portfolio positions.

For stocks and bonds that are not publicly traded, the solution to marking the portfolio becomes especially problematic. Many hedge fund managers "Mark to Model." That is, they use their own internal valuation models to determine the price of illiquid securities. However, this pricing is neither independent nor objective. Furthermore, as the lessons of LTCM show us, even if the pricing models are theoretically correct, there can be periods of illiquidity where the price of less liquid securities declines significantly.

The bottom line is that every investor must document how the hedge fund manager marks to market her portfolio. The issue of illiquid securities must be especially detailed. If the hedge fund manager uses a Mark to Model methodology for less liquid securities, then the investor should determine how the hedge fund manager's model works under periods of market stress. This is all the more important because investors tend to flee hedge funds during periods of market stress and therefore, this might be a scenario when hedge fund manager will have to sell a significant portion of her portfolio.

RISK REVIEW

Risk Management

There are four important questions that must be answered to understand the risk profile of the hedge fund:

- What is the level of risk involved in the hedge fund manager's strategy?
- What risks are managed?
- How is risk measured?
- How is risk managed?

First, investors need to understand whether the hedge fund manager pursues a conservative or aggressive strategy. For example, the hedge fund manager may pursue an equity long/short strategy. The investor should asses whether the manager attempts to hedge away unwanted market risk and just focuses on his stock calls. Additionally, does the hedge fund manager borrow to leverage up the long/short positions? Or, does the hedge fund manager concentrate in small market-cap stocks where liquidity is less available and the underlying stocks are more volatile? In sum, the investor should insure that his level of risk tolerance/aversion is consistent with that of the hedge fund manager's investment strategy.

Second, it is important to determine what risks the hedge fund manager monitors. Does she have limits on the percentage of the portfolio that may be invested in any one company or security? Additionally, does the manager monitor her gross long exposure, gross short exposure, and net market exposure? To what extent can the manager be long and to what extent can she be short the market? What is the minimum or maximum market exposure that the hedge fund manager will take? Does the hedge fund manager hedge against currency risk, interest rate risk, credit risk, or market risk?

Third, risk can be monitored through measures of standard deviation, semivariance, Sortino measures, by value-at-risk, and by style analysis. The investor must document what type of risk measurement system the hedge fund manager applies.

Last, the investor must determine how the hedge fund manager manages the risk of her positions. As indicated above, one way to control risk is by setting limits on the size of any investment position. This is particularly important because of the concentrated nature of most hedge fund portfolios.

Another way to manage risk is to set an upper boundary on the standard deviation of the hedge fund's returns. Alternatively, the hedge fund manager could set a limit on the amount of *active risk* (the standard deviation of excess returns) in the hedge fund.

Two additional risks that must be discussed are *short volatility risk* and *counterparty risk*. As already mentioned, hedge fund managers can sell options as part of their investment strategy. When a hedge fund manager sells an option, she collects the option premium at the time of the sale. If the option expires unexercised, the hedge fund manager keeps the option premium and the hedge fund's returns will be increased by the amount of the option premium. However, if the option is exercised against the manager, this may have a negative impact on the hedge fund performance.

Additionally, hedge fund managers frequently trade in over-the-counter derivative instruments. These are essentially private contracts between two parties: the hedge fund manager and her counterparty. The counterparty to such trades is often a large Wall Street investment house or large money center bank. Nonetheless, when a hedge fund manager negotiates these custom derivative contracts with a counterparty, the hedge fund manager takes on the credit risk that her counterparty will fulfill its obligations under the derivative contract.

Exchange-traded derivative contracts such as listed futures and options contracts do not have this counterparty risk because the clearinghouse for the exchange will make good on any defaulted contract. However, in the over-the-counter world of derivatives, the hedge fund manager must rely on its counterparty's good faith and credit to perform its obligations under the derivative contract.

In sum, the investor must determine how the hedge fund manager looks at risk, what are the most important risk exposures in the portfolio, and how the hedge fund manager reacts to excess risk.

Leverage

Some hedge fund managers specifically limit the leverage they will employ. This limit is typically set in the limited partnership agreement so that the hedge fund manager is legally bound to stay within a leverage limit. Nonetheless, within the leverage limit, the hedge fund manager has considerable flexibility. Also, many hedge fund managers never set a limit on the amount of leverage that they may apply.

If leverage is applied, the investor should document the highest amount of leverage used by the hedge fund manager as well as the average leverage of the fund since inception. As we indicated in Chapter 3, one of the reasons for the demise of Long-Term Capital Management was the massive amount of leverage employed in its strategy. While leverage can be a successful tool if employed correctly, it will have a significantly detrimental impact on hedge fund performance during periods of minimal liquidity.

Risk Officer

Last and most important, who monitors risk? The chief investment officer and the chief risk officer should not be the same person. If so, there is a conflict in risk control because risk management should function separately from investment management. Without this independence, there can be no assurance that risk will be properly identified and managed.

Often the chief financial officer serves as the risk officer. This is a good solution as long as the CFO is not also the chief investment officer (rarely is this the case). In the smaller hedge fund shops, this is the usual procedure. However, larger hedge funds have established a chief risk officer who monitors the hedge fund manager's positions across all hedge funds and separate accounts.

If the amount of leverage is not contractually specified in the limited partnership agreement, then the risk manager must set the limit. Even if there is a limit on leverage, the risk manager must monitor the leverage in each hedge fund to ensure that it is consistent with that fund's investment strategy. Finally, the risk manager should establish the position limits for any one investment within a hedge fund portfolio.

ADMINISTRATIVE REVIEW

Civil, Criminal, and Regulatory Actions

The hedge fund manager should fully disclose all civil, criminal, and regulatory actions against the hedge fund manager or any of its principals over the past five years. Normally a three-year history is asked for, but five years is also common.

The hedge fund manager may balk at listing civil or criminal actions previously or currently pending against its principals. However, in addition to the expected red flags that legal actions raise, this is necessary information for two more reasons.

First, a history of civil or criminal actions filed against one of the hedge fund manager's principals is a valuable insight into that principal's character. Given the litigious nature of current society, it would not be unusual for a principal to be involved in a civil lawsuit outside the operating business of the hedge fund. However, a pattern of such lawsuits might indicate trouble.

Second, lawsuits are distracting. They take a toll in terms of time, money, and emotions. Such a distraction could impede a principal's performance with respect to the hedge fund.

Employee Turnover

Given the skill-based nature (or claim, thereof) of the hedge fund industry, a hedge fund manager's personnel is its most valuable resource. This is where the skill resides.

A complete list of hired and departing employees is important for three reasons. First, as previously discussed, a good hedge fund manager knows her competitive advantage and how to exploit it. One type of competitive advantage is the people employed by the hedge fund manager. Preserving this workforce may be one of the keys to maintaining her advantage.

Second, similar to lawsuits, turnover is distracting. It takes time, money, and sometimes emotions to recruit new talent. Additionally, new employees take time to come up the learning curve and comprehend all of the nuances of a hedge fund manager's investment strategy.

Last, high employee turnover may be indicative of a volatile Chief Executive Officer. If the employees do not have faith enough in the CEO to remain with the hedge fund manager, why should the investor?

Account Representative

This is very simple. A primary contact person should be designated. This representative will handle issues regarding performance, withdrawals, increased investment, distributions, and meetings. Ideally it should be someone other than the Chief Executive Officer, whose job it is to keep the hedge fund manager on course rather than take client phone calls.

Disaster Planning

Disaster planning has become commonplace in the aftermath of the terrorist attacks of 9/11. Hedge fund managers employ sophisticated trading models that require considerable computing power. This is especially true for those hedge fund managers that employ quantitative arbitrage models. The loss of trading time can severely hurt a hedge fund managers's performance.

The hedge fund manager should have a recovery plan if a natural or other disaster shuts down its trading and investment operations. This plan could be leasing space at a disaster recovery site owned by a computer service provider, a back-up trading desk at another remote location, or the sharing of facilities with other trading desks.

Consider the case of Hurricane Rita in 2005 and the total evacuation of New Orleans. How would a hedge fund manager located in Louisiana monitor its investment positions and its risk exposures? How would it trade without the use of its analytical computer programs? How would the hedge fund manager maintain connectivity with its employees if they cannot get to the recovery site?

LEGAL REVIEW

Type of Investment

Most hedge fund investments are structured as limited partnerships. Limited partnership units are purchased by the investor where the number of units that the investor owns entitles her to a pro rata share of the returns earned by the hedge fund.

Some hedge fund managers offer separate accounts for their investors. These are individual investment accounts that are dedicated solely to one investor. There are pros and cons of both types of investments.

In a limited partnership structure, the hedge fund manager acts as the general partner, and invests a portion of her own capital in the hedge fund side by side with that of the limited partners. This ensures an alignment of interests between the hedge fund manager and her investors.

Also, a limited partnership provides a "financial firewall" for the investor. Limited partnership laws protect the limited partners so that they are at risk only to the extent of their capital committed. Therefore, the limited partner's maximum downside is known with certainty. Any excess risk is borne by the hedge fund manager as the general partner.

Separate accounts do not have the advantages of alignment of interests or financial firewalls. There is more risk associated with this type of investment. However, there are two advantages of a separate account.

First, the investor need only worry about her own motivations. In our section on Performance Review, we discussed how withdrawals of capital from a hedge fund can be detrimental to the fund's performance. Therefore, the withdrawal of capital by one limited partner could disadvantage the remaining investors in the hedge fund. With a separate account, this issue does not exist because there is only one investor per account.

Second, separate accounts facilitate reporting and risk management. In a limited partnership, the investor receives her pro rata share of the fund's return and owns a pro rata share of each individual investment. Reporting these pro rata shares, or aggregating them for risk management purposes, can be cumbersome. However, with a separate account, all gains, losses, and investments are owned 100% by the investor. This simplifies any reporting or risk management requirements.

Fees

The standard in the hedge fund industry as explained earlier, is "2 and 20." This means a 2% management fee and a 20% profit sharing or incentive fee. However, this structure is by no means uniform. Some of the larger hedge funds charge up to a 3% management fee and a 30%

incentive fee, while some newer hedge funds may charge less than the standard "2 and 20."

In addition to the fee structure, the investor should determine how frequently fees are collected. Typically, management fees are collected on a quarterly basis, but they may also be structured semiannually or annually. Incentive fees are usually collected on an annual basis.

The investor should also determine if there is a "high watermark" or a "clawback" with respect to the incentive fees. A high watermark means that a hedge fund manager cannot collect any incentive fee until she exceeds the highest previous net asset value.

This is particularly important because of the nature of drawdowns. If a hedge fund manager suffers a drawdown, she should not collect any incentive fees while she recoups this lost value. Incentive fees should begin only after the manager has regained the lost fund value and produced new value for her investors. Most hedge funds have high watermarks.

Clawbacks are rare in the hedge fund world. They are much more common in the private equity marketplace. As its name implies, a clawback provision allows the investors in the fund to "claw back" incentive fees previously received by the hedge fund manager. Clawback arrangements generally apply if, over the life of the fund, the hedge fund manager has failed to produce an agreed upon hurdle rate.

Lock-Ups and Redemptions

While lock-up periods are the standard in the private equity world, they are less common in hedge funds. However, more and more hedge funds are requiring lock-up periods for their investors. A lock-up period is just that: The investor's capital is "locked-up" for a designated period. During this time, the investor cannot redeem any part of her investment.

Lock-up periods provide two benefits. First, they give the hedge fund manager time to implement her investment strategy. Imagine how difficult it might be to implement a sophisticated investment strategy while at the same time worrying about how to fund redemption requests.

Second, we have already pointed out that ill-timed withdrawals of capital by one limited partner in a hedge fund can disadvantage the remaining investors. During the lock-up period, this is not an issue. Nervous investors have no choice but to have their capital committed for a specified period of time. Confident investors can be assured that their investment will not be undermined by a fickle limited partner.

Third, with the advent of SEC regulation requiring hedge fund managers to register as investment advisers, longer lock-up periods should be expected. The reason is that the SEC allowed an exemption from registration for investment funds that have lock-up periods exceeding two years. We will discuss this more in our chapter on hedge fund regulation.

The investor should also determine whether there is a redemption fee. Hedge fund managers may charge a fee to redeem shares in the hedge fund. This redemption fee serves two purposes. First, it discourages investors from leaving the fund and maintains a larger pool of funds for the hedge fund manager and, second, it allows the hedge fund manager to recoup some of the costs associated with liquidating a portion of the hedge fund portfolio to redeem shares (or to make up for the drag on performance from a cash balance that hedge fund manager maintains to fund investor redemptions.)

Withdrawals and redemptions are specified in the limited partnership agreement. Some hedge funds provide monthly liquidity, but the norm is quarterly or semiannual redemption rights. Also, limited partners typically must give notice to the hedge fund manager that they intend to redeem. This notice period can be from 30 to 90 days in advance of the redemption. The purpose of the notice is to give the hedge fund manager the ability to position the hedge fund's portfolio to finance the redemption request.

A last risk to consider is whether the liquidity provisions provided by the hedge fund manager match the liquidity of the underlying securities in which the hedge fund manager invests. For example, the distressed debt market is one of the least liquid of securities markets. Liquidity is nonexistent and typically comes only with the private negotiation between two parties. It can take several months to find a willing seller and buyer. Now, if the hedge fund manager were to allow monthly redemptions, there would be a liquidity mismatch that could cause a run on the hedge fund's assets when there is no ready market to buy the assets the hedge fund manager needs to sell to fund the redemptions of its investors.

Subscription Amount

All hedge funds have a minimum subscription amount. Generally, this amount is quite high for two reasons. First, the hedge fund manager needs sufficient investment capital to implement his investment strategy. Second, higher capital commitments ensure that only sophisticated investors with a large net worth will subscribe in the hedge fund. Hedge fund investing is not for the average investor. Rather, they are designed for sophisticated investors who can appreciate and accept the risks associated with hedge funds.

Some hedge funds may also have a maximum subscription amount. This is done so that no single investor becomes too large relative to other investors in the fund. Also, the hedge fund manager may have capacity issues that require limits on an investor's capital contribution.

Advisory Committee

Advisory committees serve as a source of objective input for the hedge fund manager. They are comprised of representatives from the hedge fund manager and investors in the hedge fund.

Advisory committees may provide advice on the valuation of certain investments, particularly illiquid investments. The committee may advise the hedge fund manager when it is time to mark down or mark up an illiquid security where objective market prices are not available.

The advisory committee may also advise the hedge fund manager as to whether she should open up the hedge fund for new investors, and how much more capacity the hedge fund manager should take. Before, allowing new investors into the fund, the hedge fund manager may wish to seek the counsel of the advisory committee to see if the existing investors have concerns about capacity or the types of additional investors that may be allowed to invest.

While advisory committees are a useful device for control by the hedge fund limited partners, they are more common in the private equity world than with hedge funds.

REFERENCE CHECKS

Service Providers

We indicated previously, in the Structural Review section of this chapter, the importance of speaking with a hedge fund manager's primary service providers. For instance, with respect to the outside auditors, the investor should ask when the last audit was conducted and whether the auditors issued an unqualified opinion. Additionally, the investor should inquire about any issues that outside auditors have raised with the hedge fund manager over the course of their engagement.

With respect to the prime broker, the investor should inquire how frequently margin calls have been made, the size of the calls, and whether any calls have not been met. Remember that the prime broker is in the best position to evaluate the market value of the hedge fund manager's investments. A discussion with the prime broker should give the investor a reality check whether or not the hedge fund manager is recognizing the proper value of the hedge fund's portfolio.

Legal counsel is important to check on the veracity of any civil, criminal, or regulatory actions against the hedge fund manager or its principals. This conversation should confirm those actions listed by the hedge fund manager under the administrative review. Last, the legal counsel can confirm the status of any regulatory registrations under which the hedge fund manager operates.

Existing Clients

Talking to existing clients is a necessary step to check the veracity of the hedge fund manager's statements and to measure his "client responsiveness."

Typical questions to ask are: Have the financial reports been timely? Have the reports been easy to understand? Has the hedge fund manager responded positively to questions about financial performance? Has the hedge fund manager done what she said she would do (maintain her investment strategy)? What concerns does the current investor have regarding the hedge fund manager of the hedge fund's performance? Would the existing client invest more money with the hedge fund manager?

In sum, this is a chance for a prospective investor to ask current investors for their candid opinion of the hedge fund manager. If the prospective investor has any doubts regarding the hedge fund manager, these doubts should be either confirmed or dispelled.

CONCLUSION

Is this chapter we addressed the question of who. We provided a comprehensive discussion on due diligence with respect to selecting a hedge fund manager. This process is not a simple exercise. A thorough investor should expect to spend 75 to 100 hours of their time reviewing a hedge fund manager.[7]

In the Appendix to this chapter, we provide an easy to follow due diligence checklist. In developing this checklist, we attempted to err on the side of being overly inclusive. An investor may choose to use all of this checklist, expand it, or edit it to suit his or her purposes. We believe, however, that the attached checklist is a good starting point for the best practices with respect to hedge fund due diligence.

---

[7] We know of at least one hedge fund of funds manager that spends between 75 and 100 hours of due diligence with each hedge fund manager.

APPENDIX:
DUE DILIGENCE EXECUTIVE SUMMARY

Name of Hedge Fund _____

Hedge Fund Manager_____

Address_____

Phone Number_____

Facsimile Number_____

Chief Executive Officer_____

Key Contact Person_____

Hedge Fund Style_____

Assets under Management_____

Years of Operation_____

DUE DILIGENCE CHECKLIST

I. STRUCTURAL REVIEW

Type of Investment

    Hedge Fund (name)_____

    Separate Account_____

    Other (specify)_____

    Onshore Account or Fund?   ____Yes ____No

    Master Trust Account?   ____Yes ____No

Hedge Fund Manager

    Main Business Office_____

    Nearest Satellite Office_____

    Telephone Number_____

    Facsimile Number_____

    Type of Legal Entity_____

    Ownership Structure_____

Key Personnel

    Chief Executive Officer_____

    Chief Operating Officer_____

    Chief Investment Officer_____

Chief Financial Officer_____

Head of Trading_____

Attach biographies of key principals: include education, work experience, and professional degrees (this may be taken from the offering memorandum).

Regulatory Registrations (please check)

Commodity Pool Operator_____

Commodity Trading Advisor_____

Investment Adviser_____

Investment Company_____

Broker-Dealer_____

Futures Commission Merchant_____

Introducing Broker_____

Other_____

If any of the above were checked, please indicate the regulatory authority with whom the hedge fund manager is registered, and the date of the registration.

Outside Service Providers

Independent Auditor_____

Legal Counsel_____

Prime Broker_____

II. STRATEGIC REVIEW

Hedge Fund Style (e.g., Market Neutral, Global Macro, etc.)

_____

_____

Description of investment strategy

_____

_____

_____

Description of instruments used to implement strategy

_____

_____

_____

What is your benchmark or hurdle rate?

_____

_____

What is your competitive advantage?/What makes your strategy different from other hedge fund managers?

_____

_____

_____

How many investments are in your current portfolio?

_____

_____

_____

What is your current long/short/cash position?

_____

_____

_____

What is your current strategy given the current market conditions?

_____

_____

_____

What is the source of your investment ideas?

_____

_____

_____

In which markets do your strategies perform best?

_____

_____

_____

What is the maximum capacity of your strategy?

_____

_____

_____

III. PERFORMANCE DATA

List all funds managed, assets under management for each fund, and date of performance inception.

_____

_____

_____

List the maximum drawdown for each fund, including: % of drawdown, recovery period, and reason for drawdown.

_____
_____
_____

Provide the average return, standard deviation, Sharpe ratio, and number of positive versus negative months of performance for each fund since inception. Also please attach a track record for each fund.

_____
_____
_____

List the largest withdrawal from each fund including: the date, percentage of equity, and reason for the withdrawal.

_____
_____
_____

If there is a benchmark for each fund, provide each fund's beta relative to the benchmark and information ratio.

_____
_____
_____

What pricing services does the hedge fund manager use for its portfolio?

_____
_____
_____

How does the hedge fund manager mark his long positions and his short positions?

_____
_____
_____

Does the hedge fund manager use midmarket quotes for publicly traded securities?

_____

How does the hedge fund manager mark to market his illiquid securities?

_____
_____
_____

If the hedge fund manager uses a "Mark to Model" methodology for its illiquid securities, has this model been tested for periods of market stress?

_____

IV. RISK

Risk Management

What risks are measured?_____

How is risk measured?_____

How is risk managed?_____

What level of risk is associated with the hedge fund manager's investment program?
_____
_____

Are position limits used?_____

What is your gross long exposure, your gross short exposure, and your net market exposure?_____
_____

What types of derivatives do you use in your investment strategy, and how do you monitor the risks associated with these instruments?_____
_____
_____
_____

How do you monitor counterparty credit risk?_____
_____
_____
_____

Do you hedge market, interest rate, credit, or currency risk?
_____

How do you decide which of these economic exposures to hedge or maintain?
_____

Leverage

What is the current level of leverage?_____

What is the maximum amount of leverage that may be employed in your strategy?
_____

Historically, what is the maximum amount of leverage that you have employed?

_____

Historically, what is the average leverage amount employed?_____

Risk Officer

Who is responsible for monitoring risk?_____

If the person responsible for risk is also the Chief Investment Officer or another investment person, please explain how the risk function can remain independent.

_____

_____

_____

V. ADMINISTRATION

Have there been any civil, criminal, or regulatory actions against the hedge fund manager or any of its principals within the last three years?

_____

_____

_____

Has there been any significant turnover or personnel within the last three years?

_____

_____

_____

Who will be the primary account representative for our investment?

_____

_____

_____

What is your disaster recovery plan?

_____

_____

_____

VI. LEGAL REVIEW

What type of investment product is being offered?

_____

_____

_____

What is the management fee?

___

What is the incentive fee?

___

Is there any fee recapture or "high watermark"?

___

Is there a lock-up period?

___

How frequently can an investor redeem its investment?

___

Is there a redemption fee?

___

What is the minimum and maximum subscription?

___

Is there an advisory committee?

___

VII. REFERENCES

Accounting firm contact

___

Prime broker contact

___

Legal counsel contact

___

Existing investors (please provide at least two)

___

___

___

CHAPTER 6

Risk Management Part I: Hedge Fund Return Distributions

Most of the prior studies of hedge funds have generally examined hedge funds within a mean-variance efficient frontier. Generally, Sharpe ratios are used to compare hedge fund returns to those of stock-and-bond indexes. However, hedge funds may pursue investment strategies that have nonlinear payoffs or are exposed to significant event risk, both of which may not be apparent from a Sharpe ratio analysis. Consequently, the distributions associated with hedge funds may demonstrate properties that cannot be fully captured by the mean and variance.

The purpose of this chapter is to take some of the "mystery" out of hedge funds by examining their return distributions. Analyzing these return distributions will provide us with necessary insight to understand and manage the risks associated with hedge fund investing. Additionally, we should be able to determine whether there is, in fact, skill at work.

We start with a brief review of the hedge fund literature on mapping the distribution of returns to hedge funds. We then expand on our prior description of hedge funds versus traditional long-only investors. We use this graphical description to classify and examine the type of return distributions we might expect from hedge funds. Finally, we discuss the risk management implications for hedge funds.

A REVIEW OF HEDGE FUND STUDIES

In Chapter 4, we provided an extensive review of the research literature regarding hedge fund returns. A growing body of empirical research demonstrates that hedge funds can be a valuable addition to a diversified portfolio of stocks and bonds. These portfolio optimization studies demonstrate that the low correlation between the returns to hedge funds and those of traditional asset classes make hedge funds a valuable portfolio addition.

In summary, the prior research indicates that hedge funds are a valuable addition to a diversified portfolio within a mean-variance efficient frontier. Yet, hedge fund returns may exhibit properties that cannot be described by the first two moments of a distribution.

The moments of a distribution are statistics that describe the shape of the distribution. When an investor invests capital in a security, a hedge fund, or some other asset, she receives a distribution of returns from that investment. This distribution of returns can be described by certain statistics called "moments." Everyone is familiar with the first moment of a distribution, this is the mean, or average return, and it is denoted by $E(R)$. The second moment of the distribution is denoted by $E(R^2)$, and it is used to determine the variance and the standard deviation of the distribution.

The normal, or bell-shaped, distribution can be completely described by its first two moments. Often in finance, the returns to most securities are assumed to follow a normal distribution. However, several studies have demonstrated that hedge funds generate returns that differ significantly from those generated by traditional financial asset classes.

Fung and Hsieh attempt to analyze the returns to hedge funds by applying the factor or style analysis conducted by William Sharpe with respect to mutual funds.[1] In his 1992 study, Sharpe compared the returns of mutual funds to the returns from financial asset class indexes to determine the amount of variation in mutual fund returns explained by asset class returns. His results indicated that up to 90% of mutual fund returns are explained by asset class returns.

Fung and Hsieh find that the amount of variation of hedge fund returns that is explained by financial asset class returns is low; R-square measures were less than 25% for almost half of the hedge funds studied. They then apply a principal components analysis based on a hedge fund's trading style. They find that five different trading styles (systems/opportunistic, glo-

---

[1] See William Fung and David Hsieh, "Empirical Characteristics of Dynamic Trading Strategies: The Case of Hedge Funds," *Review of Financial Studies* 10 (1997), pp. 275–302; and William Sharpe, "Asset Allocation: Management Style and Performance Measure," *Journal of Portfolio Management* (Winter 1992), pp. 7–19.

bal/macro, value, systems/trend following, and distressed) explain about 45% of the cross-sectional variation in hedge fund returns. In a second study of asset based style factors, Fung and Hsieh find that mapping hedge fund returns onto traditional long-only indexes results in R-square measures from 0.17 (equity market neutral) to 0.82 (equity long/short). Again, the lack of uniformity of hedge fund styles when mapped onto traditional financial market indexes demonstrates that traditional mean-variance analysis does not fully capture the return patterns of hedge funds.[2]

Liang conducts a style analysis similar to Sharpe and finds R-squares in the range of 20% for hedge funds that invest in foreign exchange to 77% for hedge funds that invest in emerging markets.[3] Schneeweis and Spurgin conduct a regression analysis of the returns to various hedge fund categories to the returns of stocks, bonds, commodities, and currency returns.[4] They find R-square measures that range from near zero for relative value hedge funds to 0.67 for hedge funds that pursue primarily a long equity investment strategy.

These studies indicate that hedge fund return patterns do not map as well on to financial assets as do mutual fund returns. It is possible that hedge funds generate return distributions that are very different from traditional financial assets. In this chapter, we consider some common characteristics shared between hedge fund returns and those of financial asset classes and their impact on the shape of hedge fund return distributions.

Recall from Chapter 3 that we defined four broad categories of hedge funds: market directional, corporate restructuring, convergence trading, and opportunistic. These four categories present different exposures to the financial markets as well as corporate events and macroeconomic trends.

Equity long/short, short selling, and equity market-timing hedge funds have exposure to stock market risk. Long/short equity hedge funds are exposed to the stock market, but this exposure varies depending on the ratio of long positions to short positions. Equity long/short managers have some amount net long stock market exposure so their predominant risk is that of the broader stock market. Short sellers also have market exposure. They take the opposite position of long-only mangers. Equity market timers jump in and out of the stock market depending on when they see good performance opportunities. Their risk exposure is primarily that of the stock market.

---

[2] See William Fung and David Hsieh, "Asset-Based Style Factors for Hedge Funds," *Financial Analysts Journal* (September/October 2002), pp. 16–27.
[3] Bing Liang, "On the Performance of Hedge Funds," *Financial Analysts Journal* (July/August 1999), pp. 72–85.
[4] Thomas Schneeweis and Richard Spurgin, "Multifactor Analysis of Hedge Fund, Managed Futures, and Mutual Fund Return and Risk Characteristics," *The Journal of Alternative Investments* (Fall 1998), pp. 1–24.

Corporate restructuring involves investing in the securities of companies that are about to undergo a significant transaction such as a merger, acquisition, spin-off, or bankruptcy. The key risk associated with these hedge fund strategies is the risk that the proposed transaction will fail to come to fruition. The transaction can fail because of lack of shareholder approval, lack of regulatory approval, squabbling parties, or a significant drop in the share price of the concerned company. These strategies bet on the completion of the corporate transaction, and underwrite the risk that the transaction will, in fact, proceed as planned.

In this sense, corporate restructuring hedge fund strategies provide financial market insurance against the completion of the transaction. If the corporate event is successful, the hedge fund manager reaps the rewards. However, if the corporate transaction fails, the hedge fund manager is on the hook for the losses—very similar to an insurance contract. In return for insuring against the loss from a failed corporate transaction, the hedge fund manager collects an "insurance premium" for willing to bear the risk of loss should the corporate event fail to come to fruition.

It is important to understand this insurance analogy because insurance contracts are essentially the sale of a put option. For example, in a homeowner's policy, if a house burns down, the homeowner can "put" his losses back to the insurance company. If the house doesn't burn down, the insurance company collects the insurance premium (put option premium), and records a profit.

The sale of put options is also known as a "short volatility" exposure. Short volatility trading strategies are exposed to event risk. Under normal market conditions, a short volatility exposure will make a profit through the collection of premiums, but in rare cases, it will incur a significant loss when the unexpected happens. Consequently, if a merger breaks down, or a company fails to exit bankruptcy proceedings, or the corporate spin-off fails to happen, corporate restructuring hedge fund managers are liable for the loss associated with the failure of the expected event.

Convergence trading strategies are also subject to the same type of event risk as corporate restructuring hedge fund strategies. Convergence trading strategies bet that the prices of two similar securities will converge to the same price over the investment holding period. These strategies earn a return premium for holding the less liquid or lower credit quality security while going short the more liquid or credit worthy security. At maturity, the two securities are expected to converge in price and the hedge fund manager earns the spread, or premium, that once existed between the two securities.

This is similar to selling financial market insurance. Under normal market conditions, the two securities are expected to converge in price.

If so, the hedge fund manager earns an (insurance) premium for betting correctly that the spread between the two securities will decline by maturity of the holding period. However, if there is an unusual or unexpected event in the financial markets, then the two securities will likely diverge in price and the hedge fund manager will lose on the trade. Again, this is similar to the sale of an insurance contract. Convergence trading strategies are essentially short volatility strategies, much like corporate restructuring hedge fund strategies.

Last, opportunistic hedge fund strategies like global macro can place bets across a wide spectrum of financial, commodity, and currency markets. Their ability to seek profits across such a wide range of investment opportunities provides the ability for excellent diversification. As a consequence, we would expect these strategies to reflect close to a normal distribution.

Exhibit 6.1 provides a brief summary of the major risks affecting these four categories of hedge fund returns.

EXHIBIT 6.1 Major Risks of Hedge Fund Strategies

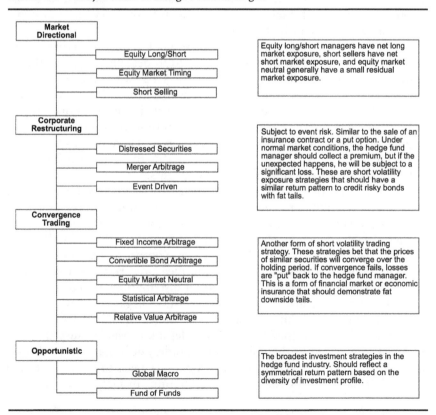

With respect to corporate restructuring and convergence trading hedge funds, these strategies bear similarities to investing in credit risky securities such as high-yield bonds. Credit risk distributions are generally exposed to significant downside risk. This risk is embodied in the form of credit events such as downgrades, defaults, and bankruptcies.

Consequently, credit risky investments are also similar to insurance contracts or the sale of put options. An investment in high-yield bonds is essentially the sale of an insurance contract that says that the investor will be on the hook for any credit events that may occur (downgrades, defaults, bankruptcies). Under normal market conditions, a credit event is not expected, and the investor collects the high coupons (insurance premiums) associated with the high-yield bond. But if an unexpected event occurs such as a default, downgrade of credit ranking, or a bankruptcy filing, the high-yield investor is on the hook for the losses.

We use the example of credit risky securities because their return distributions should be similar to that of corporate restructuring hedge funds and convergence trading hedge funds. This is because both are exposed to event risk that can result in significant downside risk exposure if an unexpected event occurs.

This downside return distribution can be described in terms of *kurtosis* and *skewness*. Kurtosis is a term used to describe the general condition that the probability mass associated with the tails of a distribution, or outlier events, is different from that of a normal distribution. The condition of large tails in the distribution is known as *leptokurtosis*. This term describes a distribution of returns that has significant mass concentrated in outlier events. Therefore, to say a distribution of returns is leptokurtic is to mean that the distribution of returns has a greater exposure to outlier events.

The converse of leptokurtosis is *platykurtosis*—the condition where the tails of a distribution are thinner than that expected by a normal distribution.[5] A platykurtic distribution has less probability mass concentrated in outlier events. Generally, platykurtic distributions are less risky than leptokurtic distributions because they have less exposure to extreme events.

The skew of a distribution is again measured relative to a normal (i.e., bell-shaped) distribution. A normal distribution has no skew, it is perfectly symmetrical. Distributions with a negative skew indicate downside exposure, while a positive skew indicates an upward bias.

Credit risky investments experience leptokurtosis because they are exposed to event risk: the risk of downgrades, defaults, and bankruptcies. These events cause more of the probability mass to be concentrated in the left hand tail of the return distribution. In fact, credit risk is a

---

[5] My wife Mary calls this "scrunching the bell curve."

general way to describe the several types of event risk affecting the return distribution of credit risky investments. In addition, credit risky investments also tend to have a negative skew. The combination of leptokurtosis and negative skew results in large downside tails associated with the return distribution. This translates into considerable downside risk. This downside risk is sometimes referred to as "fat-tail" risk because it reflects that credit risky investments have a large probability mass built up in the downside tail of their return distributions. We will demonstrate this fat-tail effect in just a moment.

We expect that convergence trading and corporate restructuring hedge funds should demonstrate similar distributions to credit risky securities, that is, fat downside tails with a distribution skewed to the left. The fat downside tails and the skewed distribution reflect the event risk inherent in arbitrage investment strategies.

Conversely, those hedge funds that have more market exposure should exhibit symmetrical distributions. This should be consistent with the findings of Fama[6] and Blume[7] who found that the returns to stocks to have no skew. However, they also observed that equity market returns exhibit the condition of leptokurtosis, or fat tails in the distribution. Consequently, we expect hedge funds with market exposure to also exhibit leptokurtosis.

Finally, there are the hedge funds that minimize credit risk and market risk. This would be the market-neutral and market timing hedge funds. We would expect these hedge funds to have a small skew or none at all and exhibit low values of leptokurtosis, or even, *platykurtosis*— where the tails of the distribution are thinner than a normal distribution.

HEDGE FUND RETURN DISTRIBUTIONS

We use data from Hedge Fund Research Inc. We examine the monthly returns to hedge fund strategies over the time period of 1990 through 2005.[8]

---

[6] See Eugene Fama, *Foundations of Finance* (New York: Basic Books, 1976).

[7] Marshall Blume, "Portfolio Theory: A Step Toward its Practical Application," *The Journal of Business* 43 (April 1970), pp. 152–173.

[8] One significant caveat must be mentioned with respect to using hedge fund indexes for economic analysis. Hedge funds are not as accessible to all investors as are stocks and bonds. Normally, the hedge fund managers impose minimum net worth or earning power requirements on an investment in their fund. Additionally, there are issues of capacity when pursuing alternative investment as well as regulatory restrictions as to the number of investors in a hedge fund. Consequently, an index of hedge funds is not investable compared to a stock or bond index.

EXHIBIT 6.2　Summary Statistics for Hedge Fund Returns, the S&P 500 and High-Yield Bonds

	Expected Return	Standard Deviation	Skewness	Kurtosis	Sharpe Ratio
S&P 500	1.01%	4.40%	−0.63	0.58	0.14
SB High Yield Index	0.75%	2.05%	−0.81	4.16	0.17
HFRI Composite Index	1.13%	1.98%	−0.61	2.90	0.37
Equity long/short	1.36%	2.55%	0.19	1.41	0.38
Short sellers	0.32%	6.10%	0.14	1.55	−0.01
Market timers	1.03%	1.95%	0.09	−0.52	0.32
Distressed securities	1.21%	1.75%	−0.67	5.69	0.47
Merger arbitrage	0.82%	1.22%	−2.63	11.64	0.34
Event driven	1.17%	1.89%	−1.32	4.83	0.41
Fixed income arbitrage	0.68%	1.23%	−1.72	10.60	0.23
Convertible arbitrage	0.81%	1.03%	−1.12	1.96	0.39
Equity market neutral	0.74%	0.91%	0.17	0.38	0.38
Statistical arbitrage	0.69%	1.13%	−0.06	0.50	0.26
Relative value	0.95%	1.04%	−0.83	10.51	0.53
Global macro	1.25%	2.40%	0.36	0.57	0.35
Fund of funds	0.80%	1.61%	−0.24	4.34	0.25

Exhibit 6.2 presents the monthly expected returns, standard deviations, and Sharpe ratios for the asset classes and the different hedge fund styles. Except for short selling hedge funds, the Sharpe ratios of the hedge fund indexes are higher than those for stocks and bonds. However, as alluded to earlier, Sharpe ratios may not fully capture the risks associated with hedge fund return distributions. For this reason we also include two additional distribution statistics, the skew and kurtosis.

Skewness and kurtosis are defined by the third and fourth moments of the distribution, respectively. Normal distributions can be defined by the first two moments of the distribution—the mean and the variance. Therefore, for a normal distribution, a Sharpe ratio is an appropriate measure for risk and return. However, if higher moments of the distribution are present, a Sharpe ratio may not capture the complete risk and return profile. As we examine each hedge fund return distribution, we will refer back to the values of skew and kurtosis in Exhibit 6.2.

EXHIBIT 6.3 Frequency Distribution for the U.S. Stock Market

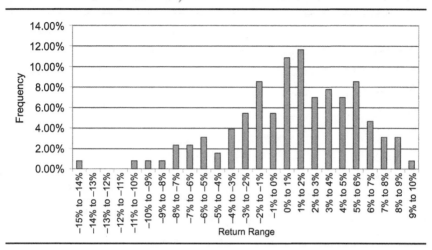

For comparison, we include two financial asset classes that demonstrate market risk and credit risk. For market risk, we use large-capitalization stocks represented by the S&P 500 Index. For credit risk, we use high-yield bonds represented by the Salomon Brothers High Yield Cash Pay Index. These two asset classes provide us with distribution benchmarks for analyzing hedge fund returns. We analyze the returns to these two financial asset classes over the same time period as for hedge funds.

We take the raw data contained in the HFRI database, and recalibrate it to plot a frequency distribution of the returns associated with each hedge fund investment style. Such a distribution provides a graphical depiction of the range and likelihood of returns associated with a hedge fund return. We calculate the mean, standard deviation, skew, and kurtosis associated with the returns to each hedge fund strategy.

We begin by graphing the frequency distribution for large-cap stocks and high-yield grade bonds. We use these two asset classes to capture market risk and credit risk, respectively. In Exhibit 6.3 we can see that the S&P 500 has a distribution with a negative skew of −0.63 and a low but positive value of kurtosis of 0.58. We measure kurtosis relative to a normal distribution so that a positive value of kurtosis indicates more mass is built up in the tails of the return distribution than a normal distribution while a negative value of kurtosis indicates thinner tails than a normal distribution.

The positive value of kurtosis indicates that the return distribution of the S&P 500 has greater probability mass in the tail of the distribution than would be expected compared to a normal distribution. This

EXHIBIT 6.4   Frequency Distribution for High-Yield Bonds

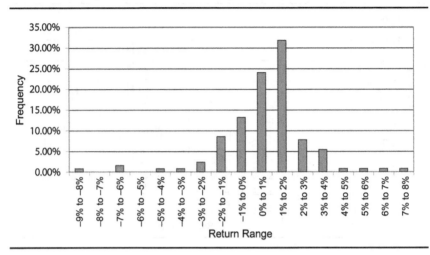

means that there are more outlier events associated with the distribution of returns to the S&P 500 than would be predicted by a normal distribution. A negative value for kurtosis would indicate the reverse—that there is less probability mass in the tails (fewer outlier events) than a normal distribution. However, the value of kurtosis is small, at 0.58, indicating that the tails of the return distribution for the stock market are very close to a normal, bell curve distribution.

The negative skew found in the returns to stocks is contrary to the findings of both Fama and Blume discussed earlier. This could be due to the different time period examined in this study compared to earlier research rather than indicating a fundamental change in the distribution of equity returns.

A negative skew indicates that the mean of the distribution is to the left of (less than) the median of the distribution. This means that there are more frequent large return observations to the left of the distribution (negative returns) and there are more small- and midrange positive return observations to the right of the distribution. In other words, large negative outlying returns occur more frequently than large positive outlying returns, indicating a bias to the downside.

A positive skew indicates the reverse of a negative skew. It indicates that the mean of the distribution is to the right of the median and that there are more frequent large positive returns than there are large negative returns. A positive skew demonstrates a bias to the upside.

For high-yield bonds, the return distribution is distinctly nonnormal. In Exhibit 6.4 we see a negative skew value of −0.81 as well as a large

EXHIBIT 6.5   Frequency Distribution for HFRI Composite Index

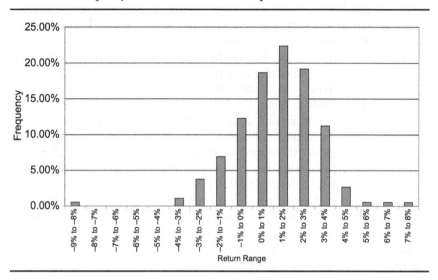

positive value of kurtosis of 4.16. This distribution demonstrates significant leptokurtosis. Specifically, the distribution of returns to high-yield
bonds demonstrates a significant downside tail. This "fat" tail reflects the
event risk of downgrades, defaults, and bankruptcies. We note again that
credit risk is simply another way to describe event risk. For example, the
downgrade of General Motors debt to below investment grade (junk status) by Moody's Investor Services in 2005 caused a significant one day
decline in the value of GM debt from 87 to 78—an 11% decline.

We also include for comparison the HFRI Composite Index of all
hedge fund styles as Exhibit 6.5. We can see from Exhibit 6.2 that this
index has a higher Sharpe ratio that either stocks or high-yield bonds.
However, it also has a negative skew, and a value of kurtosis between
stocks and high-yield bonds.

Hedge Funds that Exhibit Market Risk

We begin with those hedge funds that are exposed to stock market risk:
equity long/short, short sellers, and market timers. These hedge funds
invest primarily in equity securities and always retain some stock market exposure.

Equity Long/Short Hedge Funds

This type of investing focuses on stock selection. This is the source of
what many hedge fund mangers claim is "skill-based" investing. Rather

than mimic an equity benchmark, these managers focus their skill on a particular market segment or industry sector to generate their returns.

Equity long/short strategies tend to have a long bias. That is, equity long/short managers tend to be more on the long side of the market than they are on the short side. Partly this is because it is more difficult to borrow stocks to short, and partly it is because many long/short equity managers came from the traditional long-only investment world and thereby have a built-in long bias. Therefore, we would expect equity long/short hedge fund return distributions to also demonstrate the leptokurtic properties of the S&P 500.

Yet the ability to short stocks at appropriate times should reduce some of the outlier events associated with the stock market. Therefore, while we still expect a positive value of kurtosis, we also expect it to be less than the broad stock market. Furthermore, the ability to go both long and short in the stock market should give equity long/short hedge fund managers an advantage over long-only passive investing. This added dimension to their strategy should reduce the negative skew associated with long-only investing.

Exhibit 6.6 presents the distribution for the HFRI Equity Long/Short Hedge Index. This distribution has a positive skew of 0.19. This is particularly noteworthy given the negative skew observed with respect to the S&P 500 returns over the same time period.

EXHIBIT 6.6   Frequency Distribution of Equity Long/Short

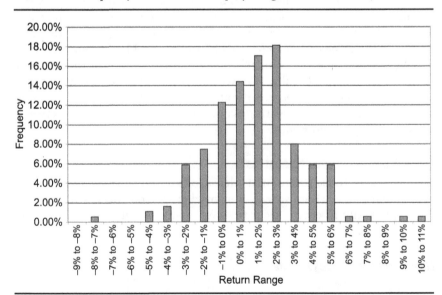

The positive skew to the equity long/short distribution is a demonstration of hedge fund manager skill. The ability to shift the distribution of stock returns from a negative skew to a positive skew is a concrete example of skill-based investing for which the hedge fund industry is so often associated.

Additionally, the distribution of returns for equity long/short investing has a positive kurtosis value of 1.41, consistent with that of the stock market. However, the value of kurtosis is slightly greater than that for the S&P 500, instead of less which is what we had predicted.

One explanation might be that these hedge fund managers attempt to generate a "double-alpha" strategy. That is, they attempt to add value by investing long in those companies that they expect to increase in value and short those companies that they expect to decrease in value. This is a double-alpha strategy in that the short sales are not generated to reduce exposure to market risk, but instead, to provide additional value through stock selection. The double-alpha strategy would also be consistent with a positive skew if manager skill can indeed select both winners and losers. However, it is possible that the pursuit of a double-alpha strategy increases the hedge fund's exposure to outlier events, resulting in a larger value of kurtosis for the distribution than would be predicted by observing the returns to the broad stock market.

Short-Selling Hedge Funds

Short-selling hedge funds perform well in down markets and poorly in up markets. Short-selling hedge funds should be the mirror image of long-only investments. However, they may attempt to limit their short positions in up markets, thus timing their positions to limit their losses when the financial markets are improving. Consequently, we might expect a slight positive skew to their return distribution.

With respect to fat tails, we would expect to see a value of kurtosis similar to that for long-only stocks. This is because they have the reverse position from a traditional long-only manager. Short-selling hedge funds are down when long-only managers are up and vice versa. Consequently, their returns should reflect the same type of kurtosis as that for a long-only equity benchmark.

Exhibit 6.7 presents the frequency distribution for the HFRI Short Selling Index. We can see that this distribution has a slight positive skew of 0.14 and with a kurtosis of 1.55 similar to that of the general stock market. We note that this distribution is centered slightly above zero. However, short selling hedge funds, on average, earn a positive return of about 0.32% per month and have a negative Sharpe ratio.

EXHIBIT 6.7 Frequency Distribution for Short Selling

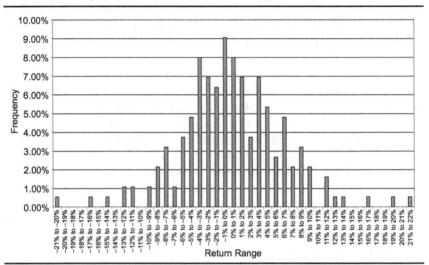

Also, short sellers have the largest standard deviation of any hedge fund style or of the traditional asset classes. This is the most volatile hedge fund strategy which further contributes to its poor Sharpe ratio.

Given the positive returns associated with the stock market over the time period 1990 to 2000, the positive return to short-selling hedge funds indicates a bias to market timing. This bias allowed them to produce a positive skew to their return distribution. Unfortunately, this positive bias was not sufficient to produce a favorable Sharpe ratio compared to stocks or high-yield bonds.

Market-Timing Hedge Funds

Market-timing hedge funds use either macroeconomic forecasts of market returns, or technical trend following models based on momentum factors to determine whether the stock market will continue to go up or down. These hedge funds jump in and out of the market using cash, mutual funds, and stock index futures and options to capture the trend of the market.

In this sense, some investors might classify equity market timers as opportunistic managers. We classify them as *market directional* because the main source of their returns is the general direction of the stock market.

Given their ability to jump in and out of the stock market, we would expect equity market timers to have a positive skew to demonstrate their skill level as well as a lower level of kurtosis to reflect a more opportunistic exposure to the stock market where significant negative stock market movements are avoided.

EXHIBIT 6.8   Frequency Distribution for Market Timing

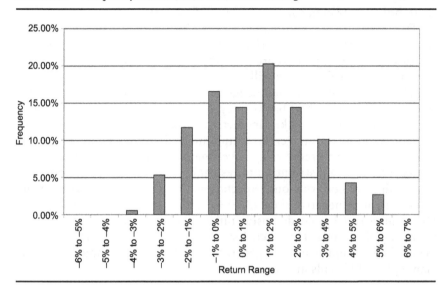

Exhibit 6.8 fulfills our expectations. There is a positive skew associated with this return distribution of 0.09 as well as a negative value of kurtosis of –0.52. This demonstrates a positive upward bias of returns with exposure to outlier events less than the broad stock market and, in fact, thinner tails than that of a normal distribution. The thinner tails indicates less exposure to outlier events as we expected.

Corporate Restructuring Hedge Funds

The investment strategies of these funds involve taking less market exposure and a lot of company specific risk. Note carefully, that these strategies do not offer a diversified portfolio. Quite the reverse, their investment strategies may be concentrated in only a handful of significant corporate transactions. Consequently, these funds are exposed to event risk: the risk that the corporate transaction will fail to be completed. Their exposure to event risk should be demonstrated with a large, downside tail in their return distributions. In other words, they should exhibit distributions with a large value of kurtosis and a negative skew.

Distressed Securities

Distressed securities hedge fund managers can pursue a number of strategies regarding a company that is in financial distress, in bankruptcy, or about to enter bankruptcy. A company can become distressed because of liquidity problems, a credit downgrade, the need to reorganize, or simply to hold off its creditors until its cash flows improve.

Distressed hedge fund managers can short the securities of companies that they expect to experience financial stress, or can go long the securities of companies that are in financial distress with the expectation that the companies fortunes will improve.

The key is that distressed hedge fund managers are exposed to significant event risk such as bankruptcy, liquidation, foreclosure, creditors seizing assets, and the like. In fact, distressed hedge fund managers invest in the lowest of the credit rating categories. They might be viewed as the ultimate in credit risky investments. Consequently, we would expect their return distribution to resemble that for high-yield bonds.

Exhibit 6.9 confirms our expectations. Distressed hedge fund managers generate a negative skew of –0.67 with a value of kurtosis of 5.69. This demonstrates a fat downside tail similar to the return distribution for high-yield bonds. However, for taking on this additional risk, distressed hedge fund managers generate a larger average monthly return than high-yield bonds and a larger Sharpe ratio.

Merger Arbitrage Hedge Funds

Merger arbitrage hedge funds seek to capture the spread between the market prices of two companies engaged in a merger and the value of those securities upon successful completion of the merger or takeover.

EXHIBIT 6.9 Frequency Distribution for HFRI Distressed Debt

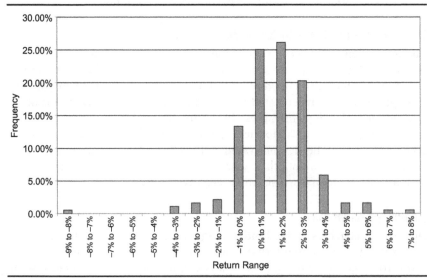

The spread in the market reflects the unwillingness of other market participants to take on the risk that the transaction will not be completed. Mergers collapse because the two firms may fail to come to complete agreement on terms, government agencies may intervene (e.g., review of possible monopolies), or because a third party may bid on the target firm.

Some hedge fund managers transact only in announced deals, while others will take on more transaction risk based on speculation or rumors of mergers. In either case, the transaction risk is large. If a deal craters, merger arbitrage funds stand to lose a considerable portion of their investment. Consequently, we expect the distribution of returns to demonstrate a large downside tail. This is similar to what we find with credit risk—the risk of bankruptcy has the ability to wipe out an investment in that company.

In addition to the event risk of a collapsed deal, merger arbitrage funds also apply leverage. Leverage exposes merger arbitrage funds to additional event risk that should magnify the tails of the distribution.

The upside potential for merger arbitrage is limited. Once the terms of a merger deal are announced, the amount of value to be gained is known with precision. There is no upside beyond what is offered in the spread between the price of the target company and the price of the acquiring company. The greater the transaction risk, the larger the spread, but the spread represents all the merger arbitrage manager can expect to earn. Because the upside to a merger deal is limited, and the downside can be considerable, we expect to see a distribution with a negative skew.

Exhibit 6.10 presents the HFRI Merger Arbitrage Index. This distribution is consistent with our expectations. A very large kurtosis value of 11.64 indicates a significant exposure to outlier events such as failed merger deals. Additionally, we observe a negative skew of −2.63 to the distribution that further reflects the transaction or "deal" risk associated with merger arbitrage. Together, these two statistics indicate a large, negative, fat tail.

Despite the large downside tail associated with merger arbitrage, Exhibit 6.10 also demonstrates very consistent positive returns. Notice how the probability mass of the distribution is concentrated in the 1% to 2% range. About 76% of the time merger arbitrage funds deliver 1% to 2% returns per month. In other words, most of the mass of the return distribution associated with merger arbitrage hedge funds is concentrated in the return range of positive 1% to 2%. This is consistent with our analysis above with respect to the amount of premium that merger arbitrage managers can earn. The premium is known with precision at the time of the merger announcement. If all goes according to plan, the hedge fund manager knows exactly how much premium he will earn as the spread between the stock prices of the target company compared to

EXHIBIT 6.10   Frequency Distribution for Merger Arbitrage

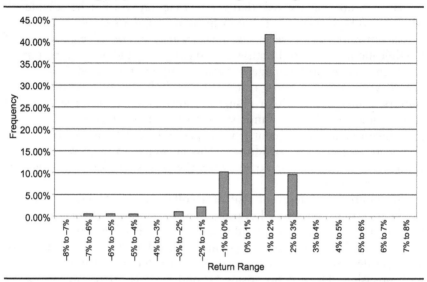

the acquiring company. This produces very consistent returns with the occasional "hiccup" when the merger fails to come to fruition. Therefore, when merger deals go "bad," merger arbitrage managers experience significant losses. The tradeoff is that the overwhelming majority of the time, they generate positive monthly returns in the 1% to 2% range with a long-term expected return of 0.82% per month.

Event-Driven Hedge Funds

Event-driven hedge funds follow the same pattern of investing as merger arbitrage managers but their investment mandate is broader. In addition to mergers and acquisitions, these hedge fund managers can invest in spin-offs, liquidations, reorganizations, recapitalizations, share buy-backs, and other events. The very nature of the investing exposes this type of hedge fund to event risk: The risk that the anticipated event will not come to fruition. Additionally, these hedge funds may apply leverage to amplify their investment bets. Consequently, we would expect to see large/fat tails in the distribution and a negative skew to the distribution to reflect the event risk associated with this strategy. However, given their broader mandate than merger arbitrage hedge funds, we would expect to see more diversification compared to merger arbitrage hedge funds and a less obese downside tail to their return distribution.

Exhibit 6.11 confirms this analysis. Event-driven hedge funds have a large negative skew value of −1.32 and a large positive kurtosis value of

EXHIBIT 6.11   Frequency Distribution for Event Driven

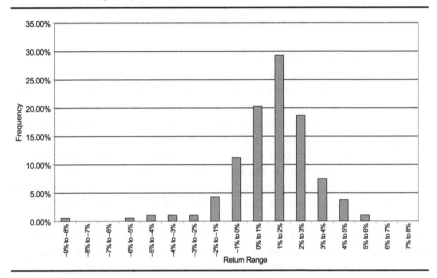

4.83. This is consistent with the exposure to event risk but also, is consistent with the expectation that event-driven hedge fund managers should have a "less fat" tail to their return distribution than merger arbitrage managers.

Also, notice that the probability mass for event-driven hedge funds is less concentrated than it is for merger arbitrage managers. Only 50% of the probability mass is concentrated in the 1% to 2% range. Therefore, there is a tradeoff compared to merger arbitrage hedge funds: a smaller downside tail, but less consistency of returns.

Convergence Trading Hedge Funds

Convergence trading strategies are often called arbitrage strategies. The reason is that hedge fund managers go long and short securities that reflect similar economic characteristics to "arbitrage" any pricing differential that may exist at the time of the purchase and sale. Over time, any price difference between two securities with similar economic characteristics should dissipate as the securities converge to the same price. When this happens, the hedge fund manager captures the spread between the two securities.

However, if the two securities do not converge in price, the hedge fund manager will lose money. As we described above, this is similar to selling financial market insurance. Convergence trading hedge fund managers underwrite the risk that two securities will converge in price over time. Under normal market conditions convergence is expected and the hedge fund manager collects a premium. However, if an unusual market event occurs, then the hedge fund manager will bear the loss.

Fixed Income Arbitrage Hedge Funds

Fixed income arbitrage, as its name suggests, involves the buying and selling of similar types of fixed income securities to capitalize on mispricing opportunities. For example, fixed income arbitrage funds may combine an interest only mortgage-backed strip and a principal only mortgage-backed strip to form a traditional mortgage passthrough certificate and then sell a similar passthrough certificate to take advantage of any differences in price. Or the hedge fund manager may short the more liquid on-the-run U.S. Treasury bond and purchase an off-the-run U.S. Treasury bond with similar duration and convexity characteristics. The key to all of these trades is that the hedge fund manager expects the two securities to converge in value over the investment holding period. Leverage is applied to extract the most value from any difference in price.

Fixed income arbitrage is dependent upon the prices of the two similar securities converging. However, there are many events that might prevent this conversion. For instance, the Federal Reserve Bank may decide to cut interest rates, encouraging mortgage refinancing, and thereby speeding up the rate by which mortgage holders prepay their mortgage debt. The change in prepayment rates is a considerable risk for a mortgage-backed fixed income hedge fund manger. This type of event risk should manifest itself in a large downside tail to the return distribution.

Exhibit 6.12 presents a distribution consistent with this conclusion: a large positive value of kurtosis of 10.60 and a negative skew of –1.72. In sum, a large downside tail indicates significant exposure to event risk. However, like merger arbitrage, fixed income arbitrage produces consistent monthly returns. The probability mass of the return distribution is concentrated in the 1% to 2% range. Seventy-two percent of the time, fixed income arbitrage produces a return in the range of 1% to 2% per month. This is much more consistent than either the stock market or the high-yield market, and reflects the consistent "insurance premium" that can be earned through convergence trading.

Convertible Arbitrage

Convertible bonds combine the holding of a bond with a call option on the issuing company's stock. Because the call option associated with the convertible bond does not trade separately, mispricing opportunities can occur. Convertible arbitrage funds seek to buy undervalued convertible

EXHIBIT 6.12   Frequency Distribution for Fixed Income Arbitrage

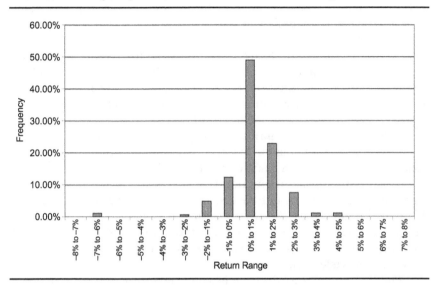

bonds and then hedge out the systematic risk associated with them. For convertible bonds that trade more like equity, the hedge fund manager shorts an appropriate ratio of stock (the delta) to neutralize the equity position. For convertible bonds that trade more like fixed income instruments, the hedge fund manager may short interest rate futures to hedge the interest rate risk. In either case the investor is betting that the option to exchange the bond for stock is mispriced by the market.

More specifically, convertible bond arbitrage is often the search for "cheap volatility." That is, convertible arbitrage managers seek to buy convertible bonds where the embedded call option is not priced at its full value. This is known as buying cheap volatility because one the most important inputs into the Black-Scholes option pricing model is the underlying volatility of the issuing company's stock price. A higher volatility translates into higher option prices. So an option that is undervalued, usually has a lower volatility associated with its value than the market would predict. Hedge fund managers search for this cheap volatility in the embedded stock options contained within a convertible bond.

The upside potential of the trade is typically known with precision—it is usually based on an option pricing model. However, the downside cannot be determined with the same certainty. Convertible arbitrage can fail because of redemption risk—the risk that the company may redeem the convertible bonds and the option value will be lost. In addition there is the credit risk associated with distressed security investing. If the company goes bankrupt, the bonds and any equity option attached to them may be worthless. In sum, convertible arbitrage is exposed to event risk.

In addition, convertible arbitrage funds employ leverage. This leverage is implicit in the margin account used to borrow stock or bonds for the short position. In addition, these funds may borrow additional capital to boost their returns. For these reasons, we expect a large downside tail and a negative skew to the distribution.

Exhibit 6.13 partly confirms these expectations. We observe a negative skew of −1.12 but a value for kurtosis of 1.96 which indicates some tail risk, but not as great as that for high-yield bonds. These observations are consistent with the redemption risk and event risk faced by convertible arbitrage managers, but the downside risk is not as great as that for high-yield bonds. With the advent of the credit derivatives market, convertible arb manages have more tools today to hedge credit event risk than they did in the past. This is demonstrated by the thinner tails than that for high-yield bonds.

Our last issue is to determine whether there is any skill at work. From Exhibit 6.13 we can see that 78% of the time an investor should expect to receive a return of 1% to 2% a month from convertible arbitrage. This consistency of return is a good indication of manager skill and is much more consistent that what an investor might expect to earn from the stock market or high-yield bonds.

EXHIBIT 6.13 Frequency Distribution of HFRI Convertible Arbitrage

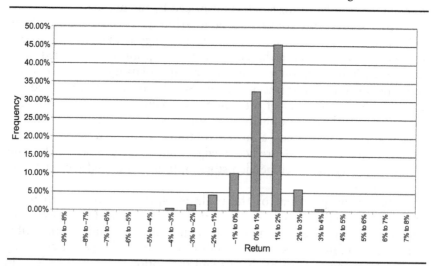

Market Neutral

Market-neutral hedge funds go long and short the market. These funds seek to maintain neutral exposure to the general stock market as well as having neutral risk exposures across industries, countries, currencies, market capitalization ranges, and style (value versus growth) ranges. The hedge fund manager builds an integrated portfolio so that market, industry, and other factor exposures cancel out. Security selection is all that matters. There is no "beta," or market risk in the portfolio either with respect to the broad stock market or with respect to any industry. Only the alpha associated with stock selection should remain.

With risk factors all balanced to zero, convergence trading might seem like a strange category in which to place these managers. However, the underlying fundamental strategy of these managers is that two similar securities are mispriced and will converge to a similar price over the investment holding period. Market-neutral managers simply take this strategy one step further and ensure that all extraneous risk factors are neutralized—sounds sinister doesn't it?

All kidding aside, with minimal market and credit risk exposure, we would expect a distribution that does not have a negative skew (either from market or credit risk) or large tails. In fact, if a market-neutral hedge fund manager is successful in removing credit risk and market risk from his portfolio, we would expect to see the statistical biases of skewness and leptokurtosis disappear.

Exhibit 6.14 confirms our expectations. The values for skewness and kurtosis are very low with a positive 0.17 for the skew and the value of kurtosis is 0.38. This is as close to a normal distribution as we have seen with any hedge fund investment strategy. Furthermore, equity market-neutral managers produce consistent returns. Seventy-one percent of the return distribution mass is concentrated in the range of 1% to 2% return per month.

In summary, market-neutral hedge funds exhibit the properties of minimal credit and market risk, consistent with their intended strategy.

Statistical Arbitrage

Statistical arbitrage is a first cousin of equity market-neutral hedge funds. Both strategies go long and short stocks in equal dollar off-setting amounts. A net dollar-zero exposure is common to both strategies. In addition to neutralizing stock market exposure other risks are typically zeroed out such as small- versus large-cap bias, growth versus value, and any momentum factors such as winners versus losers.

The difference between the two strategies is defined by the level of fundamental analysis done by equity market-neutral managers versus

EXHIBIT 6.14 Frequency Distribution for Equity Market Neutral

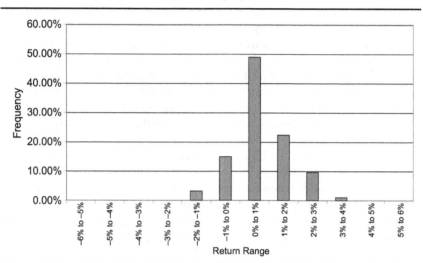

quantitatively driven models employed by stat arb managers. More typically, equity market-neutral managers tend to have more discretion in their stock selection and in whether they maintain any residual exposures to the stock market, cap ranges, sector exposures, and the like. Conversely, stat arb plays are purely model driven. They have almost no discretion in the selection of stocks or the zeroing out of other risk exposures—this is all driven by the quantitative models that they employ.

As a result, we would expect stat arb manager to have a similar distribution profile as equity market neutral—consistent returns with very low dispersion of results. Exhibit 6.15 confirms our expectations. About 65% of the time, stat arb managers earn 1% to 2% per month. In addition, stat arb managers have a very low volatility, although not as low as equity market neutral. Still, if an investor is looking for consistent results, with very little dispersion of performance, statistical arbitrage hedge fund managers fit the bill. Last, stat arb has virtually no skew and a very low value of kurtosis—very similar to its cousin, equity market neutral.

Relative Value Arbitrage

Relative value strategies are short volatility strategies. These funds seek out arbitrage pricing opportunities wherever they exist: merger arbitrage, convertible arbitrage, fixed income arbitrage, mortgage-backed securities arbitrage, and options arbitrage. As we stated earlier, relative

EXHIBIT 6.15   Statistical Arbitrage

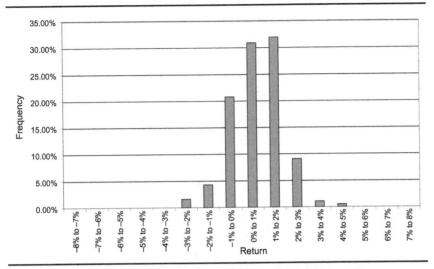

value hedge fund managers are the smorgasbord of convergence trading. They do not limit the scope of their arbitrage opportunities. Often, they apply considerable leverage in their investment strategies. Long-Term Capital Management is the best example of a relative value hedge fund.

Exhibit 6.16 presents the results for the relative value hedge fund managers. Similar to the other arbitrage funds, we find a large ("fat") downside tail and a large, negative skew to the distribution. Relative value funds have a large positive value of kurtosis equal to 10.51, indicating large fat tails. Additionally, relative value hedge funds also have a large negative skew value of –0.83. This is consistent with event risk expected of this investment strategy.

Relative arbitrage managers also produce consistent results. Seventy-six percent of the distribution mass is concentrated in the 1% to 2% range, with a long-term average just under 1% per month. As previously noted, consistency of performance results is an indication of manager skill.

Opportunistic Hedge Funds

Opportunistic hedge fund managers have the greatest ability to diversify their portfolios. They are not constrained to any hedge fund strategy or market and have a mandate that allows them to be nimble and quick as they move across financial markets (global macro players) or hedge fund strategies (fund of fund managers).

EXHIBIT 6.16   Frequency Distribution for Relative Value Arbitrage

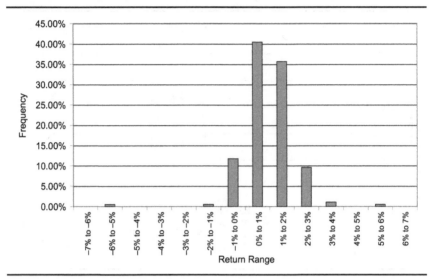

Global Macrohedge Funds

Exhibit 6.17 presents the distribution for global macrohedge funds. This distribution more closely resembles a normal distribution than that demonstrated by large-cap stocks or high-yield bonds. Global macro funds exhibit a slightly positive skew of 0.36 with a low value of leptokurtosis of 0.57. This is consistent with our expectations for global macro. Given their broad investment mandate across all financial markets, we are not surprised to find a return pattern that most closely resembles a normal distribution.

By definition, global macrohedge funds invest across the currency, stock, bond, and commodity markets. They are not limited either by geographic scope or by asset class. Their broad investment mandate allows them to achieve the most widely diversified portfolio where the idiosyncratic distribution properties of specific markets are diversified away. Indeed global macrohedge funds invest across financial, commodity, and currency markets around the world. This breadth of investment strategies provides the best opportunity to achieve a diversified portfolio of returns, minimize the impact of outlier events, and to approximate a normal distribution.

In any event, the ability to produce a positive skew to their return distribution while providing less exposure to outliers (a lower value of kurtosis) than the general stock market indicates that global macrohedge fund managers have provided a positive level of skill.

EXHIBIT 6.17   Frequency Distribution for Global Macro

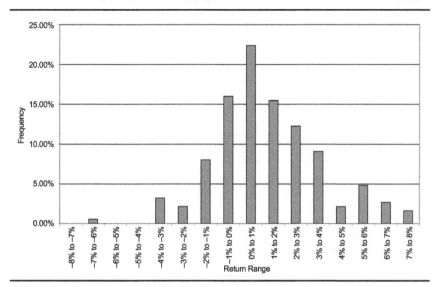

Hedge Fund of Funds

Hedge *fund of funds* (FOF) have the mandate to pick and choose hedge fund strategies depending upon which strategies have the greatest current profitability expectation. This is the definition of opportunistic investing—allocating capital across strategies based on the FOF manager's expectation about which hedge fund strategies will produce the greatest return.

Similar to what we saw for global macrohedge funds, we would expect the diversification potential of this strategy to produce a return distribution consistent with a normal distribution of returns. Presumably, FOF managers have the ability to diversify the risks of the individual hedge funds in which they invest. However, Exhibit 6.18 does not confirm our expectations. We find a negative skew of –0.24 and a large value of kurtosis of 4.34—very similar to that for credit risk investments and indicative of a large downside tail.

This is somewhat surprising since one of the skills a FOF manager is presumed to have is the ability to limit the exposure to large downside events. Yet Exhibit 6.18 demonstrates otherwise. However, returns are reasonably consistent with 56% of the return mass concentrated in the 1% to 2% return range.

EXHIBIT 6.18   Frequency Distribution for Fund of Funds

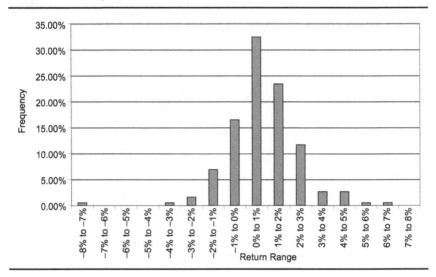

IMPLICATIONS FOR RISK MANAGEMENT

Before risk management of hedge funds can be applied, the risks of the several hedge fund strategies must be understood. Specifically, the distribution of returns of each hedge fund strategy must be analyzed to determine its shape and properties. In this chapter we found that many hedge fund return distributions exhibit properties that are distinctly nonnormal. The issue before us is how to apply this information when constructing a hedge fund program. We offer some practical observations and suggestions.

One observation is: Do not construct a hedge fund program based on only one type of hedge fund strategy. As indicated in Exhibits 6.6 through 6.18, the different hedge fund styles exhibit different return distributions. Therefore, benefits can be obtained by diversifying across hedge fund strategies. This is plain old portfolio theory: Do not put all of your eggs into one hedge fund basket.

Hedge Funds that Exhibit Market Risk

The good news here is that three types of market risk hedge funds—equity long/short, equity market timers, and short selling—exhibit risk profiles that all have a positive skew—a bias to the upside.

Consider equity long/short hedge funds. These hedge funds demonstrate a value of leptokurtosis of 1.41 and a skew factor of 0.19. First, the value of kurtosis is slightly larger compared to that of the S&P 500. Therefore, this type of hedge fund strategy exposes the investor to outlier events at a slightly greater rate as investing in the S&P 500 but less than that for credit risky bonds.

In addition, equity long/short strategies, provide a positive skew factor compared to the negative skew for the S&P 500. This means that equity long/short hedge fund managers have been able to shift the distribution of returns from the left, or downside, of the distribution, to the right, or upside, of the distribution. In other words, there are more positive observations to the right of the median of the distribution for long/short managers than there are negative observations to the left of the median. Therefore, equity long/short managers demonstrate a positive upward bias to their returns, compared to the S&P 500 with about the same exposure to outlier events.

In summary, there is a shift in the skew of the stock return distribution from negative to positive with only a slight increase in leptokurtosis. In addition, there is a considerable increase in the Sharpe ratio. On the whole, it appears the equity long/short hedge fund managers offer a better return versus total risk profile than the stock market.

The simplest way to reduce the impact of outlier events is to diversify. Therefore, equity long/short programs should be diversified across industry sector and market capitalization. Additionally, equity long/short strategies should be combined with other hedge fund strategies to diversify the sources of return and risk.

Short sellers also produce a positive skew with a value of kurtosis similar to that for equity long/short managers. However, the biggest detraction for short sellers is the volatility of returns. At a 6.1% volatility for monthly returns, short sellers were the most volatile of any hedge fund strategy and more volatile than stocks or high-yield bonds. Furthermore, short sellers have a negative Sharpe ratio, indicating a poor risk versus return tradeoff.

Last, market timers produce a positive skew with a negative value of kurtosis. This indicates a bias towards positive returns and a smaller exposure to outlier returns than a normal distribution—an excellent combination for risk averse investors.

Hedge Funds that Exhibit Insurance Risk

The return distributions both for corporate restructuring and convergence trading hedge funds demonstrate properties similar to a credit risk distribution: they have large (fat) downside risk exposures. These large downside tail exposures reflect the event risk inherent in arbitrage and event-driven strategies.

Consider merger arbitrage. As Exhibit 6.10 demonstrates, about 76% of the time you should expect monthly returns in the 1% to 2% range. These results are very favorable compared to the S&P 500 where the frequency of returns are much more dispersed. Therefore, the consistency with which merger arbitrage funds deliver performance is less risky than that for the S&P 500. Furthermore, the standard deviation of merger arbitrage returns is one third that for the S&P 500.

However, merger arbitrage is exposed to significant event risk. Exhibit 6.10 shows that merger arbitrage has the largest negative skew and the largest value of leptokurtosis. This means that when deals break down, significant losses will be incurred. The reason is that merger arbitrage is similar to selling a put option or selling insurance. In effect, merger arbitrage managers underwrite the risk of loss associated with a failed merger or acquisition.

With a short put option, the hedge fund manager sells the put and collects a cash premium from the sale. If the put expires unexercised (the merger is completed), the hedge fund manager keeps the premium and adds it to the total return. However, if the merger fails to be completed and the stock prices of the two companies diverge instead of converging, the put option will be exercised against the hedge fund manager. The manager must either purchase the underlying asset at the strike price (which is above the market price), or settle the option in cash. In both cases, the hedge fund manager incurs a loss.

The payoff for a short put option is presented in Exhibit 6.19. Notice that the short put option earns a consistent payout until the strike price is reached, and then declines in value. This is similar to the payout expected from merger arbitrage: a consistent payout, but a loss of value if the merger is not completed. Therefore, the distribution of returns associated with a short put option strategy will also be skewed to the left, because a short put option holder is exposed to downside risk.

Another way to consider this risk is that it is similar to the sale of an insurance contract. Insurers sell insurance policies and collect premiums. In return for collecting the insurance premium, they take on the risk that there will be no unfortunate economic events.

Therefore, an insurance contract is like the sale of a put option. If nothing happens, the insurance company gets to keep the insurance/option premium. However, if there is an event, the insurance policy holder can "put" his policy back to the insurance company for a payout. The insurance company must then pay the face value (the strike price) of the insurance contract and accept a loss. Insurers make money by spreading these insurance contracts across many different types of

EXHIBIT 6.19 Payoff to a Short Put Option

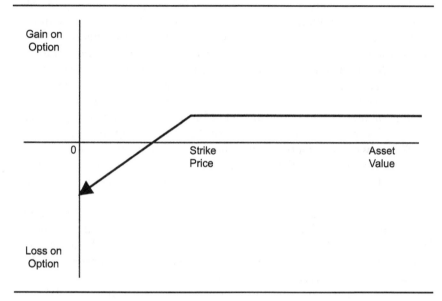

policyholders and thereby diversifying the risk of loss on any one economic event.

What is most important to note about this type of risk is that it is *off-balance sheet risk*. If you were to look at the balance sheet of a merger arbitrage hedge fund manager you would see off-setting long and short equity positions reflecting the purchase of the target company's stock and the sale of the acquiring company's stock. From this, an investor might conclude that the hedge fund manager has a hedged portfolio with long positions in stock balanced against short positions in stock.

Yet, the balance sheet positions mask what is really the true risk of merger arbitrage: financial market insurance against the possibility that the deal will break down. This short volatility strategy will not show up from just an observation of the hedge fund manager's investment statement. Therefore, it is vital that investors understand a hedge fund manager's *risk exposure* and not just its trading positions.

Merger arbitrage hedge funds can then be viewed as insurance agents. What they are insuring is the risk of loss should the deal collapse. By purchasing the stock of the target company and selling the stock of the acquiring company stock from investors who do not have as much confidence in the merger deal, merger arbitrage hedge funds accept/insure against the risk of the deal collapsing. If the merger fails, they are on the hook for the loss instead of the shareholders from whom they purchased or sold shares.

When viewed as insurance agents, three risk management suggestions can be made for merger arbitrage funds. First, apply the same principles as insurance companies: Diversify the risks. It is better to invest with two or three merger arbitrage funds than with one, because this will spread the insurance risk among three different funds. In the insurance industry, this is called reinsurance. Second, do not invest in merger arbitrage funds that concentrate in the same industry, or market capitalization range. This will concentrate and compound the insurance risk. Last, limit the amount of leverage that the merger arbitrage manager may apply. The more the leverage, the larger the size of the short put option risk.

While we used merger arbitrage to highlight the downside risk exposure, this risk is similar for every arbitrage or event-driven strategy. Each of these strategies have a similar short put option exposure. They are all at risk to outlier events.

For instance, recall our discussion of the demise of Long-Term Capital Management in Chapter 3. LTCM was a relative value arbitrage hedge fund manager. LTCM's strategy was simple: securities with similar economic profiles should converge in price by maturity. This strategy worked well as long as a severe economic event did not occur. Year in and year out LTCM was able to collect option-like premiums in the financial markets for insuring that the prices of similar securities would converge.

However, a disastrous economic event eventually occurred: the default by the Russian government on its bonds in the summer of 1998. There was an instantaneous flight to quality in the financial markets as investors sought the security of the most liquid and credit worth instruments. Instead of converging as LTCM had bet they would, prices of similar securities diverged. LTCM's short put option profile worked against it, and it lost massive amounts of capital.[9] Those investors that had sold their positions to LTCM benefited, and just like an insurance company, LTCM was forced to accept the losses. Additionally, the huge leverage LTCM employed only exacerbated its short put option exposure.

In summary, convergence trading and corporate restructuring hedge funds act like insurance companies: If there is a disastrous financial event, they bear the loss. This is consistent with the ideas of Fung and Hsieh.[10] This exposure is exacerbated to the extent arbitrage funds apply leverage. Therefore, a simple risk management tool is to invest with those hedge funds that employ limited leverage. A two-to-one ratio should be sufficient for these funds to effect their strategies.

---

[9] See Philippe Jorion, "Risk Management Lessons Learned from Long-Term Capital Management," working paper (2000).

[10] William Fung and David Hsieh, "A Primer on Hedge Funds," *Journal of Empirical Finance* 6, no. 3 (September 1999), pp. 309–331.

Hedge Funds that Have Low Market and Insurance Risk

We found two hedge fund strategies, equity market neutral and equity market timing to have the most conservative risk profiles. Both had positive skew indicating a bias to larger positive returns than negative returns and each had a low value of kurtosis. In fact, market timing hedge funds demonstrated a negative value of kurtosis—indicating thinner tails in the patter of returns than a normal distribution.

For risk averse investors, these would be the ideal investment. Also, both earn Sharpe ratios significantly greater than the stock market. However, these two strategies diverge with respect to the concentration of return mass. Market-neutral managers had 71% of their distribution mass concentrated in the 1% to 2% range while for market timers this was only 35%. Market timing hedge funds have a much greater dispersion of returns than equity market-neutral managers.

CONCLUSION

This chapter explored the different nature of hedge fund strategies by providing a frequency distribution of their returns. We found that the return patterns for hedge funds are very different, reflecting different trading strategies, different levels of exposure to the financial markets, and different levels of off-balance sheet risk. This emphasizes the point of diversifying across the hedge fund strategies to ensure the best complementary risk exposure. However, we note that the risk exposure of Fund of Funds was not much better than that for high-yield bonds—there was still considerable exposure to downside risk events. Consequently, it does not appear that FOF managers used diversification techniques to full advantage.

Finally, we find considerable evidence of hedge fund manager skill throughout the hedge fund manager strategies examined. This skill manifested itself in one of three ways: the ability to shift the distribution of returns from a negative skew to a positive skew; the ability to shrink the tails of the return distribution (reduce exposure to outlier events); and last, the ability to produce consistent returns with greater frequency than observed in the stock-and-bond markets.

CHAPTER 7

Risk Management Part II: Additional Hedge Fund Risks

In Chapter 6 we focused on drawing a picture of risk through frequency distributions of hedge fund returns. We showed that hedge fund managers generate return distributions that are often distinctly nonnormal. Most of these distributions displayed return patterns very different from the traditional bell curve often assumed in the financial markets.

In this chapter we explore a number of additional risks that are peculiar to hedge funds. Some of these risks are described qualitatively, while others can be documented in an empirical fashion. The purpose of this discussion is not to scare off the reader from hedge funds but rather to illuminate some of the less obvious issues associated with hedge fund managers.

PROCESS RISK

Most investors prefer a well-defined investment process that describes how an investment manager makes its investments. In Chapter 5 we highlighted the investment process as one of the three basic questions that must be documented as part of the due diligence process. Yet documenting a hedge fund manager's investment process is not always a straightforward task. Consider the following language from a hedge fund disclosure document:

> The General Partner makes extensive use of computer technology in both the formulation and execution of many investment decisions. Buy and sell decisions will, in many cases, be made and executed algorithmically according to quantitative trading strategies embodied in analytical computer software running the General

Partner's computer facilities or on other computers used to support the Fund's trading activities.

Hedge fund processes that depend primarily on computer algorithms generally lack transparency. This is what is meant by a "black box." Hedge fund managers that can be classified as information filterers rely on sophisticated computer programs to sift through current market data to find securities that appear to be mispriced. Yet to describe a hedge fund manager's investment process as "computer programs" is insufficient documentation. The problem is that for black box managers, the black box itself is the investment process.

The lack of transparency in the investment process is what we describe as "process risk." There are two ways to manage this risk. The first is quite direct: Don't invest in what you cannot document. This is a blunt risk management policy, but if an investor cannot understand the investment process, chances are, he may not be able to comprehend the risks associated with the process. This is especially true for a hedge fund manager that will not let an investor examine its investment algorithms.

The second way to manage this risk is to "pop the hood" of the hedge fund manager's black box. It is not necessary to read the underlying computer code behind every computer algorithm. Instead, the investor must understand the structure of the algorithms.

First, the investor should determine that different computer algorithms are used to evaluate different financial instruments. As an example, mortgage-backed securities and convertible bonds are affected by different economic variables and pricing dynamics. One computer algorithm size does not fit all of the financial markets.

Second, the investor should determine that the computer algorithm includes all relevant variables. For instance, with respect to convertible bond arbitrage, appropriate economic inputs might be the underlying stock price, the historical volatility, the implied volatility, the current term structure of interest rates, the credit rating of the instrument, the duration of the bond, the convertible strike price, and any call provisions in the bond indenture.

Third, the investor should determine what the computer algorithms attempt to accomplish. Convertible arbitrage funds, for example, build long positions of convertible bonds and then hedge the equity component of the bond by selling the underlying stock or options on that stock. Equity risk can be hedged by selling the appropriate ratio, or "delta," of stock underlying the convertible option. The delta is a measure of the sensitivity of the convertible bond value to movements in the underlying stock, and it changes as the price of the underlying stock changes. Therefore, convertible bond arbitrage algorithms must be designed to measure and track the delta hedge ratio and to provide a signal as to when an existing hedge ratio must be adjusted.

Black boxes are an example of a sophisticated process risk. However, process risk need not be embedded in a computer program, it can also exist with an individual.

Consider another example of the hedge funds run by George Soros. Mr. Soros had long ago ceded day-to-day investment management of his hedge funds to Stanley Druckenmiller. The *Wall Street Journal* documented the concentrated skill-based investment style of this hedge fund group:

> For years, [Soros Fund Management] fostered an entrepreneurial culture, with a cadre of employees battling wits to persuade Mr. Druckenmiller to invest.
>
> "[Mr. Druckenmiller] didn't scream, but he could be very tough. It could be three days or three weeks of battling it out until he's convinced, or you're defeated."[1]

This is another example of process risk. There is no documented investment process. Instead, there is one person. An investor may be able to document the existence of a person, but not the thought process of that individual. Filtering all information through the brain of one individual raises two issues.

First, the investment process is dependent upon a single person. Should that person leave the hedge fund, the investment process will leave with him. Hedge fund documents often contain a "key person" provision for this reason. If a key investment person leaves or dies, then the investors have the right to withdraw from the hedge fund.

Second, hedge fund investment strategies that are dependent upon one person also lack of transparency. Skill-based investing usually is opaque. There is no way to really tell whether the decisions of the key investment person are quantitatively or qualitatively based.

Investors should accept the fundamental economic risks of the asset classes in which they invest. However, investors are generally unwilling to bear risks that are not fundamental to their tactical and strategic asset allocations.

Process risk is not a fundamental risk. It is an idiosyncratic risk of the hedge fund manager's structure and operations. Generally, it is not a risk that investors wish to bear. Unfortunately, process risk is peculiar to the hedge fund industry because of the industry's "skill-based" nature.

The solution to this problem is diversification. *Modern portfolio theory* (MPT) teaches us that a diversified basket of stocks will elimi-

---

[1] "Shake-Up Continues at Soros's Hedge-Fund Empire," *Wall Street Journal*, May 1, 2000, page C1.

nate most, if not all, of the idiosyncratic risk of the individual companies, leaving only market risk to be compensated. Similarly, MPT can be applied to hedge fund investing. Park and Staum[2] and Henker[3] indicate that a portfolio of 15 to 20 hedge fund managers can eliminate up to 95% of the idiosyncratic/process risk associated with hedge fund managers.

MAPPING RISK

Another issue with hedge fund risk management is that there is no standard platform for measuring risk and no standard format for reporting risk. Different hedge funds map risk differently. For example, hedge fund managers may use different time periods and different confidence levels to measure the value at risk of their portfolios. Consequently, it is difficult to combine the risks of several hedge funds.

A good example of the mapping problem is the work done by Fung and Hsieh[4] and Liang.[5] Both studies attempt to analyze the returns to hedge funds by applying the factor or style analysis conducted by William Sharpe with respect to mutual funds.[6] In his 1992 study, Sharpe compared the returns of mutual funds to the returns from financial asset class indexes to determine the amount of variation in mutual fund returns explained by asset class returns. His results indicated that up to 90% of mutual fund returns are explained by asset class returns.

Fung and Hsieh apply Sharpe's style analysis to hedge funds. They find that the amount of variation of hedge fund returns that is explained by financial asset class returns is low; R-square measures were less than 25% for almost half of the hedge funds studied. Fung and Hsieh then apply a principal components analysis based on a hedge fund's trading style. They find that five different trading styles (systems/opportunistic, global/macro, value, systems/trend following, and distressed) explain about 45% of the cross sectional variation in hedge fund returns.

[2] James Park and Jeremy Staum, "Fund of Funds Diversification: How Much is Enough?" *The Journal of Alternative Investments* (Winter 1998), pp. 39–43.
[3] Thomas Henker, "Naive Diversification for Hedge Funds," *The Journal of Alternative Investments* (Winter 1998), pp. 23–39.
[4] William Fung and David Hsieh, "Empirical Characteristics of Dynamic Trading Strategies: The Case of Hedge Funds," *Review of Financial Studies* 10 (1997), pp. 275–302.
[5] Bing Liang, "On the Performance of Hedge Funds," *Financial Analysts Journal* (July/August 1999), pp. 72–85.
[6] William Sharpe, "Asset Allocation: Management Style and Performance Measure, *Journal of Portfolio Management* (Winter 1992), pp. 7–19.

In a subsequent study, Fung and Hsieh regress the returns to the HFRI Composite Index and the CSFB/Tremont Hedge Fund Index on nine financial indexes including large- and small-cap stocks, international stocks, bond indexes, currencies and commodities. They find an R-square measure for the HFRI Composite to be only 70% while for the CSFB/Tremont Index it was only 52%.

Liang conducts a style analysis similar to Sharpe and finds R-squares in the range of 20% for hedge funds that invest in foreign exchange to 77% for hedge funds that invest in emerging markets.

The point of these studies is that hedge fund returns do not map as well onto standard asset classes as do mutual funds. One reason is the skill-based nature of the hedge fund industry; hedge fund managers tend to hold concentrated portfolios that do not resemble passive indexes. Another reason is that hedge funds often invest in derivative instruments that have nonlinear payoffs, and nonlinear derivative instruments map poorly onto linear (financial) asset classes.

To demonstrate the difficulty of mapping hedge fund returns onto financial asset returns, consider Exhibit 7.1. In this exhibit we map the returns to convertible bond arbitrage managers onto four financial indexes.

A convertible bond has four economic drivers:

- It is a bond so it has interest rate/duration risk.
- It is convertible into stock so it has stock market risk.
- It is usually issued by companies with less than stellar credit ratings.
- It has an embedded option which increases or decreases in value with the level of stock market volatility.

To capture these four economic drivers we regress the returns to the HFRI Convertible Bond Arbitrage Index against the S&P 500 (stock market risk), U.S. Treasury bonds (duration risk), the Salomon Brothers High Yield Cash Pay Index (credit risk), and the VIX volatility index (implied volatility for stock options on the S&P 500).

EXHIBIT 7.1   Regression Results for Convertible Bond Arbitrage

	Alpha	Treasury Bonds	S&P 500	SBHY Cash Pay	VIX	R-Square
Value	–0.07%	0.001	–0.018	0.16	0.057	0.37
T-statistic	–1.75[a]	0.028	–0.55	3.41[b]	3.1*	

[a] Significant at the 10% level.
[b] Significant at the 1% level.

Exhibit 7.1 provides our results. We can see that the beta for both stock market risk and duration/bond risk are zero. This indicates that hedge fund managers hedge out (put on a delta neutral) hedge with respect to stock market risk and interest rate risk. What remains is credit exposure and volatility exposure, both with significant betas. This is not unexpected. Convertible arbitrage is often classified as the search for cheap volatility—that is embedded options in a convertible bond, which are not fully priced by the market. In addition, convertible arb managers typically take some level of credit risk. That is they also do fundamental analysis on individual companies and are willing to take on credit risk, particularly in strong economic environments.

However, note that the R-square measure is still only 0.37. Despite breaking down convertible bonds into their four primary economic drivers, a considerable amount of the variation of hedge fund manager returns are left unexplained. This unexplained variation is embedded in the intercept or alpha for convertible arb managers which, disappointingly, is negative.

Second, different hedge fund managers have different types of concentrated risk exposure that cannot simply be added to give a total exposure. For instance, equity long/short hedge funds have considerable market risk. Conversely, merger arbitrage hedge funds are exposed to significant event risk but little market risk. Even if they all measured risk in a consistent manner, their risk exposures are sufficiently different such that combining them into one risk statistic would be misleading.

Two solutions to the mapping problem are possible. First, institutions can act as global risk managers. It is the hedge fund manager's responsibility to generate the excess returns, and the investor's job to manage the risks that arise from that investment. This is a macro approach to risk management.

Under this solution, the investor loads each hedge fund manager's risk exposures into her risk management system and determines the risk of her overall portfolio. This solution has the advantage that the investor controls the mapping of the risk exposures rather than the individual hedge fund managers. The difficulty is getting sufficient performance data from the hedge fund manager to be able to measure the manager's exposures accurately.

As a second solution, the investor could ask for each hedge fund manager's investment positions. This is a microapproach.

Unfortunately, this is problematic for two reasons. First, hedge fund managers are reluctant to reveal their individual investment positions. Hedge fund managers, in general, do not like to disclose their investment positions because these tend to be the manager's proprietary data. The concern is that the distribution of such detailed information might erode the hedge fund manager's competitive edge should this informa-tion be inadvertently disclosed. However, this reluctance is changing. As more institutional investors have entered the hedge fund investment world, more hedge fund managers have become comfortable with pro-viding full transparency.

As a result, a more important problem is that the investor must aggregate all of the individual positions across the several hedge fund programs within its risk management system. This requires a very sophisticated internal risk management system to collect individual hedge fund positions and combine them into reportable risk exposures, not to mention the pragmatic difficulties of having the hedge fund man-agers transmit their daily positions to the investor.

One possibility is that the hedge fund managers could report this information to a central agent such as a prime broker or a hedge fund administrator who could use its risk platform to prepare the risk analy-sis. In fact, more and more hedge fund administrators have begun to offer their position reporting and risk management services to investors. While hedge funds have long been their exclusive clientele, hedge fund administrators have realized that their services are equally valuable to investors in hedge funds.

TRANSPARENCY RISK

We alluded to transparency risk as an ancillary issue associated with process risk. Transparency is a continuing issue with hedge fund manag-ers because of their mostly unregulated nature. The new SEC registra-tion rules for hedge funds becomes effective in 2006. Still this only requires hedge funds to file an annual Form ADV with the SEC. This form provides basic information regarding the hedge fund manager's place of business, products offered, key individuals, etc. but does not require performance data. Hedge fund managers that operate outside the regulatory jurisdiction of the SEC or the CFTC typically do not pro-vide as complete disclosure as their regulated counterparts.

Hedge funds generally provide an annual financial statement and performance review. However, hedge funds rarely disclose their existing portfolio positions. Without an accounting of their trading and portfo-lio positions, three issues arise for the investor.

The first is the authenticity of the hedge fund manager's perfor-mance. For instance, did an equity long/short manager really earn 10% in the current quarter from stock selection, or did she make market tim-ing bets on the S&P 500 using SPX futures contracts? Without a position report, there is no way to establish the provenance of the hedge fund manager's performance results.

Second, without disclosure of trading and portfolio positions, an investor cannot appropriately monitor and measure the risks of the hedge fund manager. Again, using the example of an equity long/short manager, did the manager earn 10% in the quarter from long/short stock selections in the media sector of the economy as described in the manager's offering memorandum, or did she stray into other sectors?

Third, without transparency, investors cannot aggregate risks across their entire investment program to understand the implications at the portfolio level. It will be difficult for an investor to verify whether the hedge fund managers in her program are making stock selections in the same economic sector and therefore compounding their collective risk positions instead of diversifying them.

Hedge fund managers are reluctant to disclose their trading and portfolio positions for several reasons. First, hedge fund managers contend that if they were to disclose their investment positions, other managers might be able to reverse engineer the hedge fund manager's investment strategy. In effect, a snapshot of the hedge fund manager's portfolio might reveal useful investment information to other market participants.

A second concern for hedge fund managers is that if they disclose to the financial markets their investment intentions, they will not be able to execute their trades as advantageously as possible. Essentially, this contention is that other market participants might line up in an attempt to "pick off" the hedge fund manager as she attempts to either establish or unwind her investment portfolio.

In an effort to resolve the competing needs and concerns of investors and hedge fund managers, the International Association of Financial Engineers and the Global Association of Risk Professionals jointly sponsored a steering committee on "Hedge Fund Risk Disclosure." This industry committee consists of hedge fund managers, investors, risk management professionals, and prime brokers. The purpose of the steering committee is to establish transparency guidelines that will satisfy hedge fund managers and investors alike.

The steering committee reached the conclusion that full, daily position reporting by hedge fund managers is not the solution. First, daily position reporting may compromise the hedge fund manager's investment strategy. Second, the vast quantity of position data generated by a hedge fund manager may overwhelm an investor's risk monitoring system.

The steering committee concluded that exposure reporting combined with delayed position reporting was sufficient for risk monitoring and management purposes. Exposure reporting is the practice of reporting the risk exposures of the hedge fund manager instead of her individual trading positions. These exposures are known as "risk buckets." It is much more practical to manage risk buckets than it is to manage individual trading positions. In fact, the practice of risk management is to measure and manage the aggregate risk exposures across a diversified portfolio. Risk buckets accomplish this task by identifying the factors that most impact the value of an investment portfolio.

For instance, exposure reporting might indicate the total dollar exposure to each industry or sector in which the hedge fund manager invests. It might also report the top ten investment positions, as well as net market exposure, total long exposure and total short exposure. Exposure reporting might also indicate the amount of leverage in the portfolio as well as the duration and convexity (for a bond portfolio), or beta exposure (for a stock portfolio). Last, exposure reporting might indicate the extent to which the hedge fund manager is exposed to market events (short volatility).

Second, the Steering Committee concluded that position reporting could be reported with a sufficient lag to protect the hedge fund manager's investment strategy. Ninety days, for example, might be a sufficient delay between when a hedge fund manager executes a trade and when the manager reports its positions to an investor. The investor can satisfy itself that the hedge fund manager has not incurred any style drift, while the hedge fund manager is secure in the secrecy of her positions.

RISK MANAGEMENT RISK

Value at risk (VaR) is a statistical method of quantifying a potential risk of loss. VaR can be defined as the maximum loss that can be expected under normal market conditions over a specified time horizon and at a specified level of confidence. For instance, a VaR calculation might determine that, with a 95% level of confidence, the worst loss that a hedge fund manager might incur over one month's trading horizon is $10 million.

VaR calculations are based on several statistical inputs: the level of confidence, the time horizon, the volatility of the underlying asset, and the expected return of the underlying asset. The level of confidence is chosen by the hedge fund manager. For example, a 95% confidence level translates into a 1 in 20 chance of the loss exceeding $10 million. The manager also chooses the time horizon. This might be daily if the risk being monitored is a trading desk, monthly if the risk is a hedge fund performance, or annually for long-only managers.

The volatility and expected return of the underlying asset are determined by historical data. Hedge fund managers might wish to look only at the most recent data, possibly the last 90 trading days, to ensure the most current information regarding the hedge fund manager's return distribution. Alternatively, a hedge fund manager might wish to look at a longer period of time such as a year or more to capture the long-term volatility and expected return associated with her performance.

This short discussion highlights the first risk in VaR. The hedge fund manager has control over three critical variables that underlie the VaR calculation: confidence level, time horizon, and time period over which to measure volatility and expected return. Hedge fund managers will have different time horizons, confidence levels, and measuring periods. VaR is not applied consistently across hedge fund managers and therefore cannot be properly compared from hedge fund manager to manager.

A second risk is that VaR measures are not additive. VaR is a statistic that measures the likelihood of a loss exceeding a certain threshold dollar amount over a specified period of time. It is a measure of probability that is dependent upon a manager's time horizon, specified confidence level, and asset mix. Given that hedge fund managers may have different time horizons, confidence levels, and asset mixes, VaR measures will vary widely across hedge fund managers. Additionally, different types of hedge fund strategies will have different types of risk exposures.

Third, VaR is often based on the assumption that the returns to an underlying asset, such as a hedge fund investment, are normally distributed. Under this assumption, VaR considers only the mean and standard deviation of a distribution of returns. However, as we indicated in Chapter 6, the return distributions to hedge fund managers are distinctly nonnormal. In particular, most of the hedge fund strategies examined in Chapter 6 demonstrated either considerable kurtosis or skewness, or both. VaR analysis based on the assumption of normality will not capture these additional risk factors.

Fourth, VaR is based on "normal" market conditions (i.e., that market outliers occur infrequently). In fact, outlier events occur more frequently than predicted by a normal distribution of returns. Consequently, VaR calculations based on the assumption may lead to unfortunate surprises.

Exhibit 7.2 demonstrates the summary statistics and VaR analysis for the monthly return to the S&P 500 over the past 11 years. The expected monthly return was 1.01% and the standard deviation of S&P 500 returns was 4.40%. Under the assumption of normally distributed returns, VaR analysis would say that, with a 97.5% level of confidence, the monthly returns on the S&P 500 should not exceed 1.96 standard deviations from the expected return. Therefore, a VaR of 97.5% confidence interval would predict that the return to the S&P 500 in any given

EXHIBIT 7.2   VaR Calcuation for the S&P 500

Expected Return	1.01%
Standard Deviation	4.40%
$E(R) + 1.96*SD$	9.63%
$E(R) - 1.96*SD$	-7.61%

EXHIBIT 7.3   Monthly Returns to the S&P 500 2000 & 2001

Jan-00	-5.05%	Jan-01	3.55%
Feb-00	-1.88%	Feb-01	-9.12%
Mar-00	9.77%	Mar-01	-6.34%
Apr-00	-3.00%	Apr-01	7.77%
May-00	-2.04%	May-01	0.67%
Jun-00	2.44%	Jun-01	-2.43%
Jul-00	-1.54%	Jul-01	-0.98%
Aug-00	6.21%	Aug-01	-6.26%
Sep-00	-5.28%	Sep-01	-8.08%
Oct-00	-0.45%	Oct-01	1.91%
Nov-00	-7.86%	Nov-01	7.67%
Dec-00	0.51%	Dec-01	0.88%

month should not exceed 9.63% or be less than -7.61%. In other words, there is a 1 in 40 chance that the monthly return to the S&P 500 will exceed 9.63% or be less than -7.61%.

Despite the 97.5% confidence level from the VaR analysis, consider the monthly returns to the S&P 500 over the period 2000 and 2001. Exhibit 7.3 demonstrates that in these two years, there were four months that exceeded the VaR confidence interval. Therefore, the "1 in 40" event that should occur only once in every 40 months occurred four times within a space of 24 months. This example simply highlights that the financial markets are uncertain and descriptive statistics such as VaR can only describe, they cannot predict.

Therefore, if VaR is to be used in hedge fund risk management, it must be used with care. First, the VaR calculations of hedge fund managers must be synchronized. An investor should ask its hedge fund managers to use consistent time horizons, confidence levels, and measuring periods.

Second, the VaR calculations of the hedge fund managers cannot be added together to achieve a total VaR for a hedge fund program. However, this is good news because the total VaR for a hedge fund program will be less than the sum of the individual VaR calculations for each hedge fund manager. The reason is that the returns to each hedge fund manager will be less than perfectly correlated with the returns to other hedge fund managers.[7]

The hedge fund managers should be selected so that their investment programs are different from one another. This means that there will be offsetting risks among the hedge fund managers. As a result, the VaR for a hedge fund program will be less than the sum of the VaR calculations for the individual hedge fund managers.

Third, VaR may not capture the complete risk profile of a hedge fund manager. Additional information might be necessary. In particular, the extent to which a hedge fund manager is short volatility must be determined. In Chapter 6 we demonstrated how corporate restructuring hedge fund managers mimic a strategy of selling put options. This is a short volatility strategy, and the expected loss from this strategy should be calculated.

Last, the financial markets are anything but normal. Financial events have a way of occurring with greater frequency than expected. One way to compensate for this in a VaR calculation is to increase the confidence level. By specifying a 1 in 100 probability (99% level of confidence) in the VaR calculation, an investor can project a more realistic expectation of the worst loss that might occur. For instance, using our example of the S&P 500, if we had used a 99% confidence level for assessing VaR, only one month—February 2001—would have exceeded the confidence range.

DATA RISK

Much of the desire to invest in hedge funds stems from the academic research regarding the performance of this asset class. The empirical studies with respect to hedge funds demonstrate convincingly that hedge funds are a valuable addition to a diversified portfolio. In summary, these studies demonstrate that an allocation to hedge funds can increase the overall return to the portfolio while reducing its risk.[8] However, there are several caveats with respect to these studies.

First, almost all of these studies were conducted during the same, and relatively brief, period of the early to mid-1990s. Given that these studies examined the return behavior of hedge funds during the same

---

[7] In fact, the individual VaR calculations would be additive only if the returns to each hedge fund were perfectly correlated.

[8] For a more detailed summary of these studies, see our discussion in Chapter 3.

time period, it is not surprising that they find consistent performance. Additionally, the fact that they also find consistently positive performance is a tribute to the lack of financial market turmoil during most of the 1990s.

However, the dual punch of the Russian bond crisis and the Long-Term Capital Management disaster in 1998 were sufficient to send ripple effects throughout the hedge fund industry. Therefore, prior empirical studies must be taken with a grain of salt. In the last section of this chapter we examine instances of market turmoil to determine how hedge funds operate during troubled times.

A second reason to be skeptical of hedge fund performance data is the inherent biases found in hedge fund databases used in most of the research regarding hedge funds.[9] As a reminder, hedge funds are generally organized as private investment vehicles and do not generally disclose their investment activities to the public. Therefore, many hedge funds do not disclose their performance record to a reporting service in the same way that mutual funds do. A complete performance record of every hedge fund is simply unobtainable.

For example, Liang found that across 16 different hedge fund styles, the highest Sharpe ratio achieved was 1.11 (for merger arbitrage) and the average Sharpe ratio across all hedge funds was 0.36.[10] However, another recent study across 21 hedge funds styles found Sharpe ratios as high as 3.63 (for relative value) with an average Sharpe ratio across all hedge funds of 2.23.[11]

These are large differences. Part of the difference might be explained by time periods that overlapped but were not synchronized (but this would then indicate the time sensitivity of hedge fund returns). However, the more likely explanation is the fact that the two studies used different databases. Therefore, the different results indicate that some portion of performance depends on the database used in the study. Most of the databases that track hedge fund performance did not come into existence until the early 1990s, the starting period for most of the hedge fund research to date. Consequently, the performance of hedge funds prior to 1990 may be lost forever. We have more to say about this in our chapter on hedge fund indexes. For now, the key issue is to discuss the risks associated with using hedge fund indexes.

---

[9] For a thorough discussion on the subject of data biases, see William Fung and David Hsieh, "Hedge Fund Performance Benchmarks: Information Content and Measurement Biases," *Financial Analysts Journal* (January/February 2002), pp. 22–34.

[10] See Liang, "On the Performance of Hedge Funds."

[11] See Andrew Lo, "Risk Management for Hedge Funds: An Introduction and Overview," *Financial Analysts Journal* (November/Decmber 2001), pp. 16–33.

Within this imperfect framework there are three data biases that can affect the reported performance of hedge funds. The first is survivorship bias. Survivorship bias arises when a database of hedge funds includes only surviving hedge funds. Those hedge funds that have ceased operations may be excluded from the database. This leads to an upward bias in performance reporting because presumably, those hedge funds that ceased operations performed poorly. In other words, only the good hedge funds survive, and their positive performance adds an upward bias to the reported financial returns.

In addition, the database may be biased downwards in risk relative to the universe of all hedge funds because those hedge funds that ceased operations may have had more volatile returns (the cause for their demise). Survivorship bias is a natural result of the way the hedge fund industry (or any new financial industry) evolved. Databases were not developed until sufficient interest by the academic and institutional community rendered such a service necessary. By that time, many hedge funds that had started and failed were never recorded.

Survivorship bias has been documented in the mutual fund industry. One way to measure this bias is to obtain the population of all funds that operated during a certain period. The average return of all funds operating during that period is compared to the average return generated by the funds in existence at the end of the period. The difference is the amount of survivorship bias.[12]

The amount of survivorship bias in the hedge fund industry has been estimated at 2% to 3% per year.[13] This is the amount of upward bias reflected in the returns reported to a hedge fund database if not corrected for hedge funds that ceased operations. Clearly, this is a very large bias that, if not corrected, can provide misleading conclusions about the investment benefits of hedge funds.

Survivorship bias is all the more important in the hedge fund industry compared to the mutual fund industry because of the high turnover rate. It has been estimated that the average life of a hedge fund is about three years and that the yearly attrition rate is greater than 15%.[14] Con-

---

[12] See Burton Malkiel, "Returns from Investing in Equity Mutual Funds 1971 to 1991," *Journal of Finance* 50, no. 2 (1995), pp. 549–572.

[13] See William Fung and David Hsieh, "Performance Characteristics of Hedge Funds and Commodity Funds: Natural versus Spurious Biases," *The Journal of Financial and Quantitative Analysis* 25 (2000), pp. 291–307; Stephen Brown, William Goetzmann, and Roger Ibbotson, "Offshore Hedge Funds: Survival and Performance, 1989–1995," *The Journal of Business* (1999), pp. 91–118; and Bing Liang, "Hedge Funds: The Living and the Dead," *The Journal of Financial and Quantitative Analysis* 25 (2000), pp. 309–336.

sequently, hedge funds cease operations with great frequency, and this should be expected to exacerbate the survivorship problem.

Ackermann, McEnally, and Ravenscraft, however, find no systematic bias in their study of hedge funds.[15] Specifically, they find that there are competing forces in survivorship bias: termination bias and self-selection bias. Some funds stop reporting their information because they terminate their operations while other funds stop reporting their performance because they have become so successful that it is no longer in their best interests to publicly report their performance.

A second bias affecting hedge fund performance results is selection bias. Generally, those hedge funds that are performing well have an incentive to report their results to a database in order to attract new investors into the fund. This would result in hedge funds included in the database having better performance than those that are excluded because of their (presumably) poor performance.

A process known as "backfilling" further magnifies this selection bias. When a database adds a hedge fund's historical performance to its pool of funds, it "backfills" the hedge fund's performance to the date it began operations. This creates an instant history of hedge fund returns. Because a hedge fund manager holds the option of when to reveal her historical performance, it is reasonable to expect that she will disclose the performance when her results look most favorable. This leads to an upward bias in performance results within the hedge fund database. To eliminate a backfill bias, it has been estimated that the first 12 to 24 months of reported data should be eliminated from a hedge fund manager's performance history. Barry finds that this instant history bias adds up to 40 basis points per year.[16]

There is a converse to the selection bias. It is also possible that those hedge funds that are very successful have no incentive to report their performance to a database because they have already attracted a sufficient number of investors to their fund. This would lead to a downward bias of hedge fund performance reported by the databases. Ackermann, McEnally, and Ravenscraft find that selection bias is offset with no

---

[14] See Franklin Edwards and Jimmy Liew, "Hedge Funds versus Managed Futures as Asset Classes," *The Journal of Derivatives* (Summer 1999), pp. 45–64; and James Park, Stephen Brown, and William Goetzmann, "Performance Benchmarks and Survivorship Bias for Hedge Funds and Commodity Trading Advisors," *Hedge Fund News* (August 1999).

[15] See Carl Ackermann, Richard McEnally, and David Ravenscraft, "The Performance of Hedge Funds: Risk, Return, and Incentives," *The Journal of Finance* (June 1999), pp. 833–874.

[16] See Ross Barry, *Hedge Funds: a Walk Through the Graveyard*, MFAC Research Paper No. 25, September 20, 2002.

impact on hedge fund reported performance, while Fung and Hsieh find that selection bias adds approximately 1.4% to reported hedge fund returns.[17]

Finally, a third bias is called "catastrophe" or "liquidation" bias. This bias arises from the fact that hedge funds that are performing poorly and likely to cease operations stop reporting their performance before they actually close shop. A hedge fund that is performing poorly and likely to go out of business has no incentive to continue to report its performance. Indeed, the hedge fund probably has greater issues to deal with such as liquidating positions to fund customer redemptions than reporting its performance.

Catastrophe bias results in an upward bias in returns and a downward bias in risk because poor performance history is excluded from the data bias. Ackermann, McEnally, and Ravenscraft attempted to measure this bias by contacting hedge fund managers directly to determine their return performance subsequent to the termination of reporting. Their study measures the impact of liquidation bias to be approximately 70 basis points.

As Exhibit 7.4 demonstrates, the combination of survivorship and selection bias can add up to 450 basis points in hedge fund returns before the impact of catastrophe bias is considered. As a consequence, it is safe to say that studies of hedge funds, if not properly discounted for inherent data biases, will inflate the returns to hedge funds.

Every hedge fund disclosure document contains the language: "Past Performance is no indication of future results." This is all the more apparent when considering the data biases associated with historical hedge fund performance.

PERFORMANCE MEASUREMENT RISK

The Sharpe ratio is the statistic most often used to compare the performance of two investment managers. It is a measure of risk-adjusted returns. It divides the performance of an investment manager in excess of the risk-free rate by the standard deviation of that manager's performance results. Its purpose is to provide a basis to compare the performance of different managers that may invest in different financial assets.

However, there are some practical difficulties with using a Sharpe ratio analysis to compare hedge fund returns. As previously indicated,

---

[17] See Fung and Hsieh, "Performance Characteristics of Hedge Funds and Commodity Funds: Natural versus Spurious Biases," and Ackermann, McEnally, and Ravenscraft, "The Performance of Hedge Funds: Risk, Return, and Incentives."

EXHIBIT 7.4 Biases Associated with Hedge Fund Data

Bias	Park, Brown, and Goetzmann, 1999	Brown, Goetzmann, and Ibbotson, 1999	Fung and Hsieh, 2000	Ackermann, McEnally, and Ravenscraft, 1999	Barry, 2003
Survivorship	2.60%	3%	3%	0.01%	3.70%
Selection	1.90%	Not estimated	Not estimated	No impact	Not estimated
Instant history	Not estimated	Not estimated	1.40%	No impact	0.40%
Liquidation	Not estimated	Not estimated	Not estimated	0.70%	Not estimated
Total	4.50%	3%	4.40%	0.71%	4.10%

Sources: James Park, Stephen Brown, and William Goetzmann, "Performance Benchmarks and Survivorship Bias for Hedge Funds and Commodity Trading Advisors," *Hedge Fund News* (August 1999); Stephen Brown, William Goetzmann, and Roger Ibbotson, "Offshore Hedge Funds: Survival and Performance, 1989–1995," *The Journal of Business* (1999), pp. 91–118; William Fung and David Hsieh, "Performance Characteristics of Hedge Funds and Commodity Funds: Natural versus Spurious Biases," *The Journal of Financial and Quantitative Analysis* 25 (2000), pp. 291–307; Carl Ackermann, Richard McEnally, and David Ravenscraft, "The Performance of Hedge Funds: Risk, Return, and Incentives," *The Journal of Finance* (June 1999), pp. 833–874; and, Ross Barry, *Hedge Funds: a Walk Through the Graveyard*, MFAC Research Paper No. 25, September 20, 2002.

many hedge funds use derivatives with nonlinear payoff structures as part of their investment plan. These nonlinear instruments can lead to misleading Sharpe ratio conclusions.

In Chapter 6, we demonstrated that many hedge fund managers have investment styles that contain a short option exposure. When a hedge fund manager shorts/sells an option, she collects the option premium. If the option expires worthless, the hedge fund manager pockets the option premium at no cost and can thereby increase her total return.

Selling options results in an asymmetric payoff profile. The upside potential is limited to the option premium collected, while the downside can be quite large depending on the size of the market event. As we indicated in Chapter 6, this type of strategy is similar to selling insurance contracts against a decline in the financial markets.

Short options exposure also helps to boost a manager's Sharpe ratio because the hedge fund manager collects the option premium and deposits it in a cash account with low volatility. The result is high total return with low (apparent) risk. Portfolio optimization techniques will tend to overallocate to these hedge fund managers because of their high total return and Sharpe ratio and the fact that the risk inherent in short option positions did not manifest itself during the hedge fund manager's short operating history.

This overallocation process is sometimes referred to as a "short volatility bias," and it is a dangerous trap for unaware investors.[18] Hedge fund managers using a short volatility strategy can pump up their returns with low risk in the short run by collecting option premiums. Selling options is just like selling insurance: Premiums continue to be collected and invested in short-term cash instruments until some catastrophe hits the financial markets and the options are exercised just like an insurance policy. This strategy will work until a hedge fund manager experiences a "volatility event."

To the extent that risk-adjusted returns are inflated through the short selling of options, portfolio optimizers tend to overallocate to those strategies. Yet allocating to these hedge fund managers will increase portfolio risk rather than reduce it because the portfolio has now increased its exposure to a financial market catastrophe event.

The trap is that hedge fund managers can boost their short-term risk-adjusted performance through a short volatility strategy only to increase their exposure to a volatility event. Portfolio optimizers base their selections only on patent risk, the volatility of the hedge fund man-

---

[18] See Andrew Weisman and Jerome Abernathy, "The Danger of Historical Hedge Fund Data," working paper, 1999.

ager's returns to date. However, optimizers do not incorporate latent risk (i.e., the risk of a volatility event).

To highlight this problem, consider the following example. A hedge fund manager accepts a $1,000,000 investment from a pension fund and invests this money in six-month U.S. Treasury bills. In addition, at the beginning of every month, the hedge fund manager sells fairly priced out-of-the-money call options and out-of-the-money put options on the S&P 500 that will expire at the end of the month. (This type of option strategy is known as a "strangle.") The strike prices are chosen to be 2.5 standard deviations away from the current market price. The hedge fund manager invests the option premiums received in U.S. Treasury bills. The hedge fund manager writes enough of these options to generate a return equal to 1.5 times that of the risk-free rate.

Since a 2.5 standard deviation event occurs only about 1% of the time, the manager has a 99% chance of outperforming the risk-free rate in any one month. In other words, it would take a "one in one hundred" type market event to trigger the exercise of the options in any given month. This means that a volatility event is expected once about every eight years (100 months divided by 12). A volatility event occurs when the S&P 500 trades outside the 2.5 standard deviation range of the put/call option strangle.

In the meantime, the manager collects the option premiums and produces impressive Sharpe ratios. In addition, a sufficient track record is established that can be fed into an optimizer resulting in the selection of the hedge fund manager. This hedge fund house of cards will come tumbling down, however, when the market turns against this short volatility investment strategy. The large short option exposure will result in a large negative cumulative return for the hedge fund manager that will wipe out most of the hedge fund manager's prior gains.

Let's put some actual numbers on this. For simplicity, we will assume that the U.S. Treasury bill rate stays constant is 6% a year. Using monthly data from 1990 through 2005, we find that the monthly standard deviation of the S&P 500 Index is about 4%. Therefore, a 2.5 standard deviation move up or down means that the S&P 500 would have to increase or decrease by more than 10% for the put/call option strangle to be exercised against the hedge fund manager.

Option pricing simulation shows that a 10% out-of-the-money option strangle on the S&P 500 would cost about $7.50 per strangle. The goal of the hedge fund manager is to collect enough option premiums each month to generate a rate of return that is 150% greater than the Treasury-bill rate. Therefore, each month, the hedge fund manager must leverage her invested capital by selling enough strangles so that her return on invested capital is 9% or 1.5 times the Treasury bill rate of 6%.

As an example, assume that in the first month the hedge fund manager receives $1,000,000 from her client which she invests for 1 month at 9%. This would generate an end of period total of ($1,000,000) × (1.0075) = $1,007,500. The catch is that the manager invests the money in U.S. Treasury bills earning 6%. Therefore, the hedge fund manager must sell enough put/call strangles and take in enough option premium so as to generate a total return equal to $1,007,500. The calculation is:

$$(\$1,000,000 + \text{Option premiums}) \times (1 + 0.06/12) = \$1,007,500$$

The amount of option premiums is $2,487. At an expected cost of $7.50, the hedge fund manager must sell 331 put/call strangles to generate a return of 9%.

This strategy will work until a volatility event occurs and the expected loss of capital results. At that point, the S&P 500 will move by more than the 10% limit (2.5 standard deviations) so that the strangle will be exercised. Also, as the size of the investment increases, the hedge fund manager must sell more and more options to maintain the 9% return.

We performed a Monte Carlo Simulation to determine how long it would take for a volatility event to occur. Running 5,000 simulations, our model estimated that it would take 80 months (almost seven years) for the options to be exercised against the hedge fund manager. This is a little less than we predicted initially for our "1 in 100" event. Our simulation indicated that a volatility event could occur as early as the first month and take as long as 237 months. Additionally, we used a conservative estimate that the option is in the money by 10 S&P 500 points when exercised.

Exhibit 7.5 demonstrates what happens when the manager employs this strategy. It works fine for the first almost seven years. Then a volatility event occurs and the options are exercised against the portfolio manager. The exercise of the options does not wipe out all of the manager's gains, but it does eliminate a good portion. In the end, the manager is left with an effective annual return of 2.85%, well below that of U.S. Treasury bills.

Exhibit 7.6 shows the returns and Sharpe ratios generated by the hedge fund manager before the volatility event and after the volatility event. As can be seen, the hedge fund manager looks like a star before the volatility event, but is unmasked once the event occurs. Unfortunately, before the volatility event is reached, the hedge fund manager can achieve a stellar track record. The low volatility associated with Treasury bill returns allows the hedge fund manager to achieve a large, positive Sharpe ratio before the volatility event occurs.

EXHIBIT 7.5   Short Volatility Investment Strategy

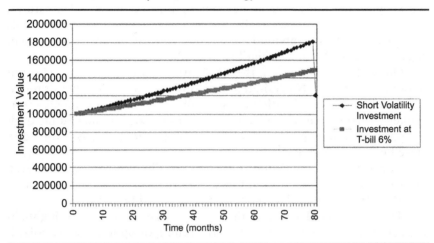

EXHIBIT 7.6   Performance Statistics for Short Volatility Investment Strategy

	Prevolatility Event	Postvolatility Event
Average annual return	9%	2.85%
Excess return	3%	−3.15%
Standard deviation	0.42%	3.71%
Sharpe ratio	7.14	−0.85

The volatility event, however, not only decreases the total return of the investment strategy, it also increases the volatility of the hedge fund manager's returns. In the month that the options are exercised against the hedge fund manager, the hedge fund earns a −33% return. This severe decline in one month causes the volatility of the hedge fund manager's returns to jump from 0.42% to 3.71%. Therefore, the volatility event reveals the latent risk associated with the hedge fund manager's strategy.

The above example may seem extreme, but at least one well-known hedge fund manager employed this strategy (and lost). Victor Niederhoffer was a well-known trader and author of a successful book: *The Education of a Speculator*. Dr. Niederhoffer, generally considered to be an excellent investor and savvy trader, earned a doctorate from the University of Chicago Graduate School of Business. He built trading programs based on statistical analysis. After analyzing stock market returns over many prior years, Dr. Niederhoffer believed that the stock market would never fall by more than 5% on any given day. He put this idea to work by selling out-of-the-money put options on stock index futures. His strategy worked successfully for several years. In fact, he was able to generate a 20% compound annual return.[19] However, his investment strategy eventually hit a "volatility event."

On October 27, 1997, the S&P 500 declined by 7%. The put options that Victor Niederhoffer had sold increased in value dramatically, and he was faced with a margin call of $50 million from his prime brokers. Unable to meet the margin call, his brokers liquidated his trading positions and wiped out his hedge fund portfolio. He was forced to close his hedge fund door.

Curiously, Mr. Niederhoffer's analysis did not include (or, even more curious, chose to ignore) the history of the market crash on October 19, 1987. On that day, the S&P 500 declined by 20%.[20]

The above simulation and the history of Dr. Niederhoffer highlight the problems associated with the short selling of options. Short volatility positions can increase performance of the hedge fund manager, but they expose the hedge fund to large downside risk should a volatility event occur.

Unfortunately, there is no simple solution for this problem but there are some practical suggestions. First, hedge fund managers with short track records and high Sharpe ratios should be scrutinized carefully. They may not have experienced a volatility event sufficient to damage their performance history. It is possible that selecting managers based on their history of risk-adjusted returns may in fact be a negative selection process if their trading history is too short.

Second, this gets to the age-old issue with respect to the hedge fund industry: transparency. Just what is the hedge fund manager doing? How is she generating her excess performance? To what extent does she use options (particularly, short options) in her trading strategies? In Chapter 5 we included these questions as part of our due diligence process.

Last, new analytical tools are needed. Risk-adjusted ratios were developed for the linear investment world of traditional long-only investment managers and mutual funds. Additional analysis is needed to account for the nonlinear investment strategies employed by many hedge funds.

---

[19] See David Segal, "Market's Crash Destroys Trader: A Risky Bet Brings Down a Millionaire Money Manager," *The Washington Post* (November 17, 1997), p. A1.
[20] The history of Victor Niederhoffer's trading strategy is documented in Philippe Jorion, "Risk Management Lessons Learned from Long-Term Capital Management," working paper, University of California at Irvine (2000).

EVENT RISK

Hedge funds, by their very name are supposed to hedge the risk and return profile of a diversified portfolio. Indeed many, if not most, hedge fund managers claim that their return distributions are "skill based;" that is, returns are not readily identifiable with the returns to financial asset classes. This argument is the source for the additional claim that hedge funds are "total return" or "absolute return" investments, for which no benchmark is appropriate. The lack of an identifiable benchmark for a hedge fund would indicate that hedge fund returns are independent of financial market returns.

In addition, we would also expect the returns to hedge funds to be independent of each other. Again, this stems from the skill-based, absolute return claim of hedge fund managers. If hedge fund returns are truly skill based, not only should they be independent of the returns in the financial markets, but also their returns should be uncorrelated with each other. Benchmarks would be inappropriate.

We put these claims to the test by conducting an event analysis. The third quarter of 1998 saw two serious financial events that added considerable turmoil to the financial markets. First, in August 1998, The Russian government defaulted on its outstanding treasury bonds. Credit spreads on all types of debt widened significantly relative to U.S. Treasury bonds, and liquidity in many debt markets was reduced. It is this type of financial turmoil that hedge funds are expected to hedge. If hedge fund managers truly generate returns through pure skill, such economic events should have very little impact on the distribution of returns from hedge funds.

Second, in September of 1998, Long-Term Capital Management (LTCM) of Greenwich, Connecticut, one of the best known and largest of the hedge fund managers, almost collapsed. A consortium of commercial and investment banks, acting in consultation with the Federal Reserve Bank of New York, fearing the possible reverberations in the financial markets, injected $3.6 billion of fresh capital into LTCM. Again, if hedge fund managers derive their returns from pure skill, their returns should be independent of each other, and events such as LTCM, should have very little impact on their return distribution.

First, we examine the returns to hedge funds in the month of August 1998. Again, if hedge funds returns are generated independent of the financial markets, we would expect to see their returns unaffected by the Russian bond crisis during this time. Second, we examine the returns to hedge funds in the month of September 1998. If hedge funds offer skill-based returns independent of each other, we should expect to see no impact on their performance from the near demise of LTCM.

We use the data from the Hedge Fund Research Inc. hedge fund indexes. Using data from 1990 through 1998 we conducted an event analysis.

Economists and other financial researchers often ask the question, What is the impact of an economic event on the value of a financial asset? Under the principle of efficient capital markets, the effect of the event should be reflected immediately in the asset value. Therefore, the economic impact of the event can be measured using asset prices over a short interval of time.

The objective of an event study is to measure the difference between the actual returns observed with respect to an investment and the returns that are expected to occur in the absence of the observed event. The difference between the actual returns observed and those expected is called the "abnormal" or "excess" return. The excess returns are observed around the event date, and conclusions are drawn as to whether the event had a significant impact on an asset class.[21]

We focus on two event months, August and September 1998. These two months should capture much of the turmoil caused by the Russian bond default and the LTCM near-collapse. We acknowledge that these two events are intertwined. For instance, the Russian bond debacle resulted in widening credit spreads that caused spillover effects on LTCM's positions even though this hedge fund did not own any Russian Bonds. To capture the interconnected nature of these two events, we also measure the combined excess return of August and September 1998.

Exhibit 7.7 presents the results of our analysis.[22] For each hedge fund style, we present the excess returns for August and September 1998. We also present the t-statistics associated with these two event months. Student t-statistics greater than or equal to, in absolute value, 1.68, 1.97, and 2.3 are significant at the 10%, 5%, and 1% level of confidence, respectively. We also present the cumulative excess return for the two-month event period of August and September 1998 combined.

For comparison, in Exhibit 7.7 we also present the excess returns associated with large-cap stocks, high-yield bonds, and U.S. Treasury bonds. We include these traditional asset classes to determine how they reacted to the Russian bond default and the LTCM crisis.

As might be expected, both large-cap stocks and high-yield bonds were significantly negatively impacted by the Russian bond default. Also, there was a flight to quality as indicated by the positive excess returns earned by U.S. Treasury bonds during this time period. In addition, large-cap stocks quickly recovered in September while high-yield bonds suffered only a one-month decline in August. Last, the two-month event period is significantly negative for large-cap

[21] For a review of event studies and their application to hedge funds, see Mark Anson, "Financial Market Dislocations and Hedge Fund Returns," working paper (2001).

[22] For each hedge fund style we use the 102 months of data prior to August 1998 to calculate the mean and standard deviation of the index.

EXHIBIT 7.7   Hedge Fund Excess Returns

Strategy	Aug-98	t-Stat	Sep-98	t-Stat	Aug-Sept	t-Stat
Equity L/S	-9.37%	-4.37	1.44%	0.67	-7.93%	-2.62
Global macro	-5.46%	-2.00	-2.26%	-0.83	-7.73%	-2.00
Short selling	18.98%	3.54	-4.60%	-0.86	14.38%	1.90
Convertible arb	-4.11%	-4.37	-1.99%	-2.11	-6.10%	-4.58
Merger arbitrage	-6.73%	-5.33	0.70%	0.56	-6.03%	-3.38
Fixed income arb	-2.16%	-1.93	-7.43%	-6.63	-9.59%	-6.05
Relative value	-7.03%	-6.82	-1.04%	-1.01	-8.06%	-5.53
Event driven	-10.34%	-6.08	-2.06%	-1.21	-12.40%	-5.16
Market neutral	-2.63%	-3.30	-0.15%	-0.19	-2.78%	-2.47
Market timing	-0.44%	-0.25	-1.49%	-0.87	-1.92%	-0.79
S&P 500	-15.70%	-4.46	5.12%	1.45	-10.58%	-2.13
High Yield	-8.31%	-4.22	0.53%	0.27	-7.78%	-2.79
U.S. Treasury	2.00%	1.60	2.10%	1.68	4.11%	2.32

stocks and high-yield bonds, but significantly positive for U.S. Treasury bonds. This reflects the flight to safety of a significant amount of capital during this time period. Many investors sought the safe haven of U.S. Treasury bonds during this period of uncertainty.

In Exhibit 7.7 the t-statistic for all hedge fund styles is statistically negative at the 1% level for August 1998 except for short sellers and market timers. Short sellers earned significantly positive excess returns during this time period, while market timers show no demonstrable impact. Our first conclusion is that, except for short sellers and market timers, hedge funds did not offer significant diversification benefits during this market event, and were, in fact, affected by the same turmoil that impacted the traditional financial markets. Even market-neutral hedge funds demonstrated significantly negative excess returns.

When we examine the two-month event period around LTCM, we find the cumulative excess returns to be significantly negative for all hedge fund strategies except for short sellers and market timers.

Several lessons can be gleaned from this analysis. First, many of the mispricing (arbitrage) opportunities that hedge funds attempt to capture can require an investment horizon of several months or greater. Additionally, arbitrage strategies generally make the assumption of normal liquidity. However, when that liquidity dried up as a result of the Russian bond default, many of mispricing relationships increased instead of decreasing, thus creating large, temporary paper losses. This situation was further exacerbated by margin calls from prime brokers which forced some hedge fund managers to liquidate their positions and turned paper losses into realized losses.

Second, many lending institutions that provided liquidity to hedge funds were themselves invested in the same markets and under pressure to manage their own risk exposures. These institutions were unable to provide liquidity to the market at the time hedge fund managers needed it the most. Third, many hedge fund strategies are premised on the convergence in pricing of similar securities. At times of market crisis, prices often diverge instead of converging. This temporary imbalance can lead to large short-term losses.

Finally, hedge fund manager received redemption calls from their investors during this period. This forced hedge fund managers to liquidate positions to fund their customer's redemption requests. Hedge fund managers were faced with a liquidity mismatch between the investment horizon of their arbitrage strategies and the investment horizon of their investors. This is similar to a mismatch between the duration of an institution's liabilities and assets. Pension funds and banks long ago learned the lessons of immunization, but hedge fund managers were forced to learn this lesson the hard way in 1998.

In conclusion, what this event analysis demonstrates is that hedge fund returns are influenced by the same financial market dislocations as traditional asset classes. An absence of liquidity in the financial markets can have the same impact on hedge fund managers as it does for long-only managers. A hedge fund manager may have all of its economic risks appropriately balanced or hedged only to be caught in a liquidity crisis. This is all the more exacerbated to the extent that a hedge fund manager invests in less liquid financial markets or custom-tailored derivative transactions.

Beta Expansion Risk

Beta expansion is a phenomenon that can happen with respect to those hedge funds that short securities—which is virtually all hedge fund strategies. To short a security, a hedge fund manager must borrow the security from her prime broker. The prime broker lends the security to the hedge fund manager who then sells the security in the market with the intention to purchase the security back at a later date once the security has declined in value.

The problem is that hedge fund managers often short the same security in the collective belief/analysis that the value of that security will decline. This can lead to the condition known as "crowded shorts" (we will have more to say about crowded shorts in our Top Ten List in Chapter 11).

EXHIBIT 7.8 Beta Expansion Risk

Hedge Fund Strategy	Beta Up	R-Square Up	Beta Down	R-Square Down	Total Beta	R-Square Total
HFRI Composite Index	0.18	0.09	0.39	0.35	0.34	0.51
HFRI Event Driven	0.07	0.02	0.40	0.38	0.28	0.44
HFRI Equity Long/Short	0.29	0.07	0.39	0.24	0.41	0.45

When a short position in a security becomes crowded, there is extra selling pressure on that security. This can lead to a greater sensitivity of that security to downward changes in the financial markets than upward movements. In turn, this means that hedge fund managers' performance may have greater sensitivity to downward stock market movements instead of upward movements.

Exhibit 7.8 documents the phenomenon of beta expansion. We use the HFRI Composite Index as well as two strategies that specifically incorporate shorting stocks into their investment process: equity long/short and merger arbitrage. We can see that the beta of the hedge fund managers' returns is significantly larger for down markets than upward market movements—that is the hedge fund manager's performance is more sensitive to downward stock market movements.

What is the pragmatic conclusion from this example? Simply, that hedge fund managers are more sensitive and therefore provide less hedging in a down stock market. This is also confirmed by the R-square measures in Exhibit 7.8 which demonstrate that a greater percentage of a hedge fund manager's performance is explained by negative stock market movements than by positive stock market movements.

Short Volatility Risk

We discussed the situation in Chapter 6 that certain hedge fund strategies replicate a short put option position. These are know as short volatility positions because the trading strategy resembles the sale of (shorting) put options. Specifically, we discussed how the corporate restructuring hedge fund strategies most resemble a short put option strategy.

The reason is that these strategies bet on the completion of the corporate event whether that be a merger, spinoff, restructuring, or successful emergence from bankruptcy. These hedge fund managers underwrite the risk of a successful corporate transaction much the same way as typical insurance companies underwrite the risk of homeowner's insurance. If a home burns to the ground, the homeowner can "put" his losses back to the insurance company. Similarly, if a corporate event fails to reach fruition, financial market participants collectively put the losses back on the hedge fund manager. Under normal market conditions, no loss is expected, and the hedge fund manager collects a premium for underwriting the risk of the corporate transaction.

To demonstrate this exposure to short volatility, we regress the three corporate restructuring strategies—merger arbitrage, distressed debt, and event driven—on the VIX stock market volatility index. If these strategies have significant exposure to short volatility, we should expect to see a negative beta associated with stock market volatility. That is, these strategies should suffer when stock market volatility increases because they are short volatility strategies.

Exhibit 7.9 confirms our expectations. Each of the corporate restructuring strategies does indeed have a negative beta associated with stock market volatility indicating a significant relationship between increasing stock market volatility and negative hedge fund returns.

As we noted earlier an important point with respect to this risk is that is an off-balance sheet risk. If you were to look at the balance sheet of a corporate restructuring hedge fund manager you would see a series of long and short stock positions. From this you might conclude that the hedge fund manager maintains a low risk portfolio because his stock market exposure is minimized by the offsetting long and short security positions. True enough; corporate restructuring hedge fund managers have limited exposure to the broad securities markets. However, they have considerable exposure to event risk or short volatility risk, and this risk cannot be observed by looking at the hedge fund manager's trading positions.

Multimoment Optimization

The discussion of the prior sections with respect to short volatility strategies shows that hedge fund strategies are exposed to significant short volatility risk. This leads to return distributions that are distinctly nonnormal with negative skews and long downside, fat tails. Furthermore, short volatility risk is off the balance sheet of the hedge fund manager and is not apparent from reviewing the hedge fund manager's trading positions.

EXHIBIT 7.9 Corporate Restructuring and Short Volatility

Strategy	Beta	t-Stat
Distressed debt	−1.389696333	−2.65
Merger arbitrage	−1.366233836	−1.81
Event driven	−1.25326267	−2.99

To capture the off balance risk of hedge fund manager, higher moments of the return distribution must be incorporated into the optimization procedure. Specifically, the skew and kurtosis of each hedge fund manager must be considered in addition to the mean and volatility of their returns. This requires an optimization process more advanced than the standard mean-variance models used by most investors.

The assumption of normality in hedge fund returns is a weak link in portfolio construction. Anson, Ho, and Silberstein explore this issue and fashion a solution that rejects the assumption of a normal distribution of returns for hedge fund managers.[23] Following the work of Davies, Kat, and Lu, they incorporate higher moments of the return distribution to select a "live" portfolio of hedge fund managers.[24] They build an optimal portfolio of hedge funds based on the mean return, variance, skewness, and kurtosis. This type of optimization is known as a Multiple Objective Approach to portfolio selection.

The math for this solution is a bit technical and we apologize for the equations that follow, but this is not an easy solution to fashion. To solve this problem, the solution may be expressed as a series of optimized equations. This is called *polynomial goal programming*. The following notation is used:

$$\text{Mean} = X'E[R]$$

where

X = $(x_1, x_2, x_3...)$ and $x(i)$ is the percentage of wealth invested with hedge fund (i).

$E(R)$ = $(E[r_1], E[r_2], E[r_3]...)$ and $E[r(i)]$ is the expected return associated with hedge fund (i).

$$\text{Variance} = X'VX$$

where

V = the variance-covariance matrix of all of the returns (vector $E(R)$) associated with the hedge funds available for selection in the hedge fund portfolio.

$$\text{Skewness} = E[X'(R - E[R])/(X'VX)^{1/2}]^3$$

[23] See Mark Anson, Ho Ho and Kurt Silberstein, "Building a Hedge Fund Portfolio with Skewness and Kurtosis," working paper, CalPERS, 2005.

[24] See Ryan Davies, Harry Kat, and Sa Lu, "Fund of Hedge Funds Portfolio Selection: A Multiple Objective Approach," working paper, ISMA Centre, The Business School for Financial Markets, University of Reading, 2004.

where

$R = (r_1, r_2, r_3...)$ and $r(i)$ is the actual return associated with hedge fund (i).

Excess kurtosis $= E[X'(R - E[R])/(X'VX)^{1/2}]^4 - [3(t - 1)^2/(t - 2)(t - 3)]$

referred to henceforth as kurtosis.

With the four moments of the return distribution identified, the portfolio optimization problem may be expressed as:

$$\text{Maximize } X'E[R] \tag{4.1}$$

$$\text{Maximize } E[X'(R - E[R])/(X'VX)^{1/2}]^3 \tag{4.2}$$

$$\text{Minimize } E[X'(R - E[R])/(X'VX)^{1/2}]^4 - [3(t - 1)^2/(t - 2)(t - 3)] \tag{4.3}$$

$$\text{Subject to} X'VX = 1 \tag{4.4}$$

$$\Sigma x_i = 1$$

For all $x_i \geq 0$.

Our goal is to select an optimal amount of wealth to be allocated to each hedge fund in the portfolio, represented by the vector of weights $X = (x_1, x_2, x_3...)$. The vector of weights must sum to 1 (all money must be invested). Also, we constrain each investment (every x_i) to be positive; that is, the investor cannot go short a hedge fund manager. Last, since the purpose of this exercise is to select the relative percentage to be invested in any hedge fund, the vector of weights, X, can be rescaled so that the variance of the portfolio is restricted to the unit variance space: $X'VX = 1$.

It is unlikely that equations (4.1) through (4.4) can be satisfied simultaneously. To solve this problem, the PGP solution is typically expressed as:

$$\text{Minimize } Z = (1 + d_1)^a + (1 + d_3)^b + (1 - d_4)^c \tag{4.5}$$

Subject to

$$X'E[R] + d_1 = Z_1^* \tag{4.6}$$

$$[X'(R - E[R])/(X'VX)^{1/2}]^3 + d_3 = Z_3^* \tag{4.7}$$

$$E[X'(R - E[R])/(X'VX)^{1/2}]^4 - [3(t - 1)^2/(t - 2)(t - 3)] + d_4 = Z_4^* \quad (4.8)$$

$$\Sigma x_i = 1 \quad (4.9)$$

$$\text{For all } x_i \geq 0 \quad (4.10)$$

where

$$d_1, d_3 \geq 0$$
$$d_4 \leq 0$$

Z_1^*, Z_3^*, and Z_4^* represent the optimal values for equations (1), (2), and (3). The value d_1, represents the distance or deviation of the expected portfolio mean from the optimal value expressed in equation (1). Similarly, d_3 is the distance or deviation from the expected portfolio skewness and the optimal value represented by Z_3^*, and d_4 represents the distance or deviation from the expected portfolio kurtosis and the optimal portfolio kurtosis represented by Z_4^*.

The goal of equation (5) is to minimize the deviations associated with the mean return (d_1), skewness (d_3), and kurtosis (d_4) of the resulting portfolio from the optimal portfolio values of mean return, skewness and kurtosis. The parameters a, b, and c represent an investor's preferences for the values of mean return, skewness, and kurtosis. In a traditional, mean-variance optimization, the values of b and c are zero.

Exhibit 7.10 shows the distributional statistics for an existing portfolio of hedge fund managers. Note that all of these strategies have significant skewness and kurtosis and the assumption of normality is explicitly rejected. Exhibit 7.11 provides a demonstration of using multimoment optimization. The top line, marked by small triangles is the performance of the hedge fund portfolio incorporating skewness and kurtosis into the optimization process. The bottom line, marked by squares, is the standard mean-variance optimization. Clearly, the multimoment optimization provides superior performance.[25]

Headline Risk

What is it about hedge funds that seems to attract hucksters and charletons alike? Is it the, sometimes, outrageous fees generated? Their mostly unregulated nature? Or simply the irresistible urge to make a quick

---

[25] The mean-variance portfolio are the existing portfolio returns while the multimoment portfolio was constructed going back in time and building an optimal hedge fund portfolio as if skewness and kurtosis had been incorporated from the beginning.

EXHIBIT 7.10 Descriptive Statistics and Statistical Tests (equal weighted hedge fund strategy portfolio)

	Data Range	Normality Test at 5%	Auto-correlation Test at 5%	Max-imum	Min-imum	Mean	Monthly Std.	Mean/ Std.	Skew-ness	Kurtosis
Equity L/S	1/99–5/05	No	No	0.096	−0.029	0.012	0.021	0.572	1.093	5.916
Multistrategies	1/99–5/05	Yes	Yes	0.065	−0.049	0.011	0.020	0.549	−0.284	3.788
Statistical arbitrage	1/99–5/05	No	Yes	0.188	−0.065	0.011	0.038	0.278	1.722	9.085
Convertible arbitrage	1/99–5/05	Yes	Yes	0.073	−0.056	0.009	0.024	0.375	0.297	3.786
Global macro	1/99–5/05	Yes	No	0.044	−0.034	0.008	0.018	0.425	−0.095	2.567
Credit L/S	1/99–5/05	No	No	0.066	−0.034	0.011	0.016	0.693	0.059	4.733
Fixed income arbitrage	1/99–5/05	No	Yes	0.110	−0.040	0.007	0.023	0.316	1.473	8.336

EXHIBIT 7.11   Multimoment Optimization

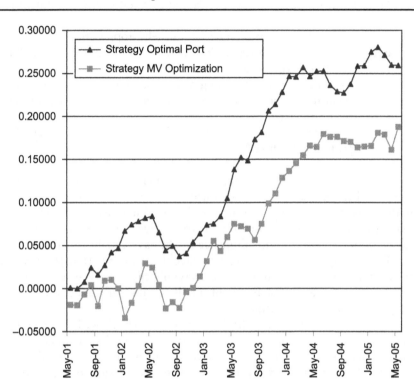

buck? Whatever—but hedge funds and the investors who invest in them are subject to headline risk.

The latest example in 2005 was Bayou Capital. The Bayou Funds were managed by Daniel Marino of Connecticut and Samuel Israel III of New York. According to SEC documents, between 1999 and 2005 Marino and Israel collected $450 million from investors and perpetrated a massive fraud.[26] Specifically the SEC charges that Marino and Israel:

■ Overstated the Funds' 2003 performance claiming a $43 million profit in four hedge funds while trading records show that the funds actually lost $49 million.

---

[26] See SEC v. Samuel Israel III; Daniel Marino and the Bayou Funds, SEC Litigation Release No. 19406, September 29, 2005.

- In 1999, Marino created a sham accounting firm to fabricate annual "independent" audits of the Funds and to attest to the fraudulent performance.
- By mid-2004 Marino and Israel had largely stopped trading securities and had transferred all remaining fund assets of approximately $150 million to non-Bayou related entities.
- Despite having suspended trading activities, Marino and Israel continued to send fraudulent statements to investors showing a high level of profitable trading strategies.
- And last, Marino and Israel continued to collect incentive fees from their "profitable trading."

Bayou was nothing more than a Ponzi scheme where current investors were used to pay back former investors. Eventually, the fraud caught up with Marino and Israel. Unfortunately, headline risk and hedge fund manager fraud are the most difficult to uncover. Some of the points we raised in our chapter on due diligence might have caught this fraud.

For example, our due diligence checklist requires that the investor speak with the outside auditors. In Bayou's case, there was no outside auditor—it was a complete phantom. Basic due diligence would have caught this sham accounting firm.

A second due diligence checklist item is to check with a hedge fund manager's prime brokers. Given that Bayou Capital suspended trading operations, a discussion with Bayou's prime brokers would have revealed no trading activity related to the generation of "profits" or incentive fees related to those profits.

Again, not to beat the horse into glue, but there is no substitute for thoughtful, thorough due diligence. Ask the right questions and you will not run afoul of the hucksters out there.

CONCLUSION

The hedge fund industry has received tremendous attention over the past decade as an alternative investment strategy to hedge traditional portfolio returns. However, as a new investment strategy, there are new risks that bear consideration. This chapter does not purport to cover every risk associated with hedge fund managers. Indeed, such a full discussion would require a whole separate treatise of several hundred pages. Instead, in this chapter we selected the essential risk factors that every investor must confront when investing in hedge funds. While not exhaustive, we believe an investor can structure a successful hedge fund program if she can successfully manage the risks outlined in this chapter.

CHAPTER 8

Regulation of Hedge Funds

In prior chapters we have mentioned briefly the mostly unregulated waters in which hedge funds operate. In this chapter we review the relevant regulatory authorities and consider what jurisdiction they have over hedge fund managers. While we will try to keep this chapter as brief as possible, brevity is not the hallmark of the laws that regulate the financial industry. The securities and commodities laws can be both arcane and tedious.[1]

We begin the chapter with a review of the federal securities laws and their application to hedge funds. Specifically, we examine how these laws apply to the sale of hedge fund limited partnership units as well as how hedge funds are classified within the securities law framework. We also consider the regulations of the Commodity Exchange Act and their application to hedge fund managers. We then review several initiatives that were born in the wake of the Long-Term Capital Management bailout.

THE SECURITIES ACT OF 1933

The Securities Act of 1933 (the "1933 Act") was born out of the Great Depression. With the collapse of the stock market in 1929 and the economic depression that followed, Congress sought to make the financial markets a safer place for investors. The 1933 Act was enacted to regulate the initial sale of securities to investors.

Prior to the 1933 Act, the initial sale of securities to investors was unregulated. Legitimate corporations and partnerships as well as scam artists could produce an offering document with misleading and material mis-

---

[1] This is one reason why hedge fund attorneys are well paid: They are trained to master the arcane and the tedious.

statements contained therein. Furthermore, there was no central authority to review offering documents before they were distributed to investors. As a consequence, investor sentiment in the stock market hit bottom.

Enacted more than 70 years ago, the Securities Act of 1933 continues to this day essentially in its original form. We highlight two key provisions of the 1933 Act that apply to hedge funds. First, the general law of the 1933 Act is that there can be no sale of any security without a registration statement filed with the Securities and Exchange Commission (SEC). Second, there are exceptions to the general rule, of which hedge fund managers may take advantage.

The Initial Sale of Securities

Section 5(a) of the 1933 Act states:

Unless a registration statement is in effect as to a security, it shall be unlawful for any person, directly or indirectly:

1. To make use of any means or instruments of transportation or communication in interstate commerce or of the mails to sell such security through the use or medium of any prospectus or otherwise; or
2. To carry or cause to be carried through the mails or in interstate commerce, by any means or instruments of transportation, any security for the purposes of sale or delivery after sale.

First, notice that the 1933 Act applies to the sale of a security. Hedge fund managers might argue that the offering of limited partnership units in a hedge fund is not a sale of a security. However, under Section 2(a)(1), the 1933 Act defined the term broadly:

The term "security" means any note, stock, treasury stock, bond, debenture, evidence of indebtedness, certificate of interest or participation in any profit-sharing agreement, collateral-trust certificate, preorganization certificate or subscription, transferable share, investment contract, voting-trust certificate, certificate of deposit for a security, fractional undivided interest in oil, gas or other mineral rights . . .

Clearly, the purchase of limited partnership units in a hedge fund may be classified as a "certificate of interest or participation in any profit-sharing agreement." Consequently, hedge fund managers fall within the jurisdiction of Section 5(a).

As an aside, notice how broad the regulatory language is. We provided only a portion of the language of Section 2(a)(1). The lengths to which Congress went to define a security indicates that they intended the term to be construed as broadly as possible, and the courts have implemented this intent. Additionally, in Section 5(a), the phrase "to make use of any means or instruments of transportation or communication in interstate commerce or of the mails" is just as applicable today to the Internet and Federal Express as it was to the telegraph and the U.S. Postal Service in 1933.

Section 5(a) sets out that before a public sale of securities can be made, a registration statement must be effective. This registration statement must be filed with the SEC for its review. The form and content of the registration statement is further spelled out in the 1933 Act.[2] The SEC will review the registration statement and return it with comments. The comments must be addressed in amendments ("preeffective" amendments) that are filed to the original registration statement. Depending upon the comments and questions raised by the SEC, several preeffective amendments might be required.

Finally, when all of the SEC's comments and questions are satisfied and all material information is properly disclosed, the SEC will declare a registration statement "effective." This is a key point. It is a violation of the 1933 Act to say that the SEC has "approved" the registration statement. This might mislead investors to believe that the SEC has approved the merits of the investment securities being offered. Consequently, the SEC never "approves" a registration statement; it merely informs the registrant that it has no further issues and that the registration statement is now "effective."

Once effective, a registration statement is called a prospectus, and it is good for one year. If a registrant wishes to sell securities after one year, it must file a posteffective amendment to update the current prospectus. The posteffective amendment will go through the same review process as the original registration statement.[3]

---

[2] The 1933 Act spells out several types of registration statements that may be submitted. For example, an S-1 registration statement must be filed with the SEC for an initial public offering of a security. Given the first time offering of the security, an S-1 registration statement requires the greatest disclosure. However, for secondary offerings, less disclosure is required, and short form registration statements may be filed.

[3] Mutual funds, for example, continually sell units in their fund year after year. Consequently, each year, every mutual fund must file a posteffective amendment to its original prospectus to keep the sale of its mutual fund units current.

As the above discussion indicates, the registration process can be long and legally intensive. Yet most hedge funds manage to avoid it. There are two ways.

The first is simple: Avoid the jurisdiction of the SEC. This is accomplished by operating an "offshore" hedge fund. Offshore hedge funds are organized in a jurisdiction outside of the United States in places such as Bermuda or the Cayman Islands. In addition, these offshore funds sell their limited partnership interests to non-U.S. investors. By operating outside of the borders of the United States, and by selling their limited partnership interests to non-U.S. investors, hedge funds can avoid the registration requirements of the SEC.

The second way to avoid the lengthy registration process is to find an exemption from registration within the 1933 Act. These "safe harbors" are listed in Section 4 of the 1933 Act. Specifically, Section 4(2) of the 1933 Act states that:

> The provisions of Section 5 shall not apply to: Transactions by an issuer not involving a public offering.

In summary, if a hedge fund manager can avoid a "public offering" of its limited partnership units, it may forego the lengthy registration process. This is what is meant by a "private offering." It is any sale of a security that is not done as part of a public offering where a registration statement must be filed.

Congress enacted Section 4(2) to provide relief from the lengthy registration process when the likelihood that the public would benefit from this process was remote. Issuers, like hedge funds, can rely on the Section 4(2) exemption if they make private offerings to investors who are either sophisticated investors or institutional investors. Generally these type of nonpublic offerings fall within Regulation D.

Regulation D

Under the 1933 Act, Congress has provided issuers with ready-made safe harbors from the registration requirements. The most often-used are "The Rules Governing the Limited Offer and Sale of Securities Without Registration under the Securities Act of 1933." These rules are universally known as "Regulation D."

Under Regulation D, a hedge fund must file a Notice of Sale with the SEC within 15 days of the first sale made of hedge fund units. Additionally, there are two important rules that must be followed: Rule 506 and Rule 501.

Rule 506 is titled "Exemption for Limited Offers and Sales Without Regard to Dollar Amount of the Offering." It states:

(a) *Exemption.* Offers and sales of securities by an issuer that satisfy the conditions in paragraph (b) of this rule shall be deemed to be transactions not involving any public offering within the meaning of Section 4(2) of the [1933] Act.

(b) *Conditions to be Met.* (1) *General Conditions.* To qualify for an exemption under this rule, offers and sales must satisfy all terms and conditions of Rules 501 and 502. (2) *Specific Conditions.* (i) *Limitation on the Number of Purchasers.* There are no more than, or the issuer reasonably believes that there are no more than 35 purchasers of securities from the issuer in any offering under this rule. (ii) *Nature of Purchasers.* Each purchaser who is not an accredited investor either alone or with his purchaser representative has such knowledge and experience in financial and business matters that he is reasonably capable of evaluating the merits and risks of the prospective investment, or the issuer reasonably believes immediately prior to making any sale that such purchaser comes within this description.

Rule 501 provides terms and definitions for the other rules contained in Regulation D (including Rule 506). Two key provisions apply. First, under Rule 501(e):

Calculation of Number of Investors. For purposes of calculating the number of purchasers under Rule 506(b), the following shall apply: (1) The following purchasers shall be excluded: (iv) any accredited investor.

Therefore, under Rule 506 (b) and Rule 501(e), a hedge fund manager can sell her limited partnership units to an unlimited number of accredited investors, and to no more than 35 nonaccredited investors.

The second important provision is Rule 501(a) that defines the term "accredited investor." This rule provides a laundry list of what constitutes an accredited investor. Essentially, the definition includes any large institutional investor or organization, provided that it was not formed for the specific purpose of acquiring the securities offered and that it has total assets in excess of $5,000,000. With respect to individuals, an accredited investor is defined as:

Any natural person whose individual net worth, or joint net worth with that person's spouse, at the time of his purchase exceeds $1,000,000; or
Any natural person who had an individual income in excess of $200,000 in each of the two most recent years or joint income with that person's spouse in excess of $300,000 in each of those years and has a reasonable expectation of reaching the same income level in the current year.

In summary, "high-net-worth" individuals under Rule 501 must have a net worth in excess of $1,000,000 or make $200,000 a year ($300,000 if they include their spouse). The high-net-worth test is particularly important for the hedge fund industry, because family offices and wealthy investors have been the mainstay investor of the hedge fund industry for years.

In Exhibit 8.1 we provide a flowchart for how hedge fund managers navigate the waters of the 1933 Act. A hedge fund manager has three choices. She can file a registration statement with the SEC to sell limited partnership interests in her hedge fund, she can take advantage of the ready-made safe harbors under Regulation D, or she can take her hedge fund offshore. Most hedge fund managers follow the second choice; they take advantage of the provisions of Regulation D and sell only to accredited investors. Other hedge fund managers simply move offshore and find non-U.S. clients. Very few hedge fund managers take the time to go through a full SEC registration process.

One last important point needs to be made with respect to the 1933 Act. Regulation D is explicit that it serves only as a safe harbor from the registration requirements of the 1933 Act, but it is not a safe harbor from the antifraud provisions of the 1933 Act. In fact, there is no safe harbor from the antifraud provisions of the 1933 Act. Section 17 of the 1933 Act states that:

(a) It shall be unlawful for any person in the offer or sale of any securities by the use of any means or instruments of transportation or communication in interstate commerce or by the use of the mails, directly or indirectly:

1. To employ any device, scheme, or artifice to defraud, or
2. To obtain money or property by means of any untrue statement of a material fact or omission to state a material fact necessary in order to make the statements made, in light of the circumstances under which they were made, not misleading, or

EXHIBIT 8.1   The Securities Act of 1933

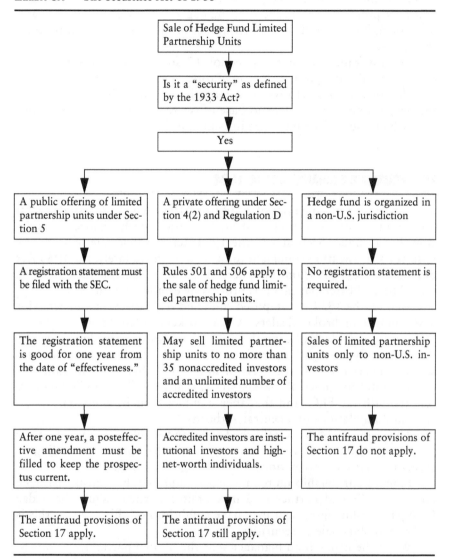

3. To engage in any transaction, practice, or course of business which operates or would operate as a fraud or deceit upon the purchaser.

Section 17 of the 1933 Act is applicable to a hedge fund manager whether she offers her limited partnership units for sale in a public or private offering. Even if the hedge fund manager avails herself of Regulation D, the SEC will have jurisdiction over the hedge fund manager, and may prosecute the hedge fund manager for any material misstatement or failure to disclose a material fact in the sale of limited partnership units.

The antifraud provisions of Section 17 do not apply, however, to an offshore fund selling to non-U.S. investors. The reason is that Section 17 was designed to protect investors domiciled in the United States. Also, the hedge fund manager has no base of operations in the United States over which the SEC could assert jurisdiction.

THE SECURITIES EXCHANGE ACT OF 1934

The Securities Exchange Act of 1934 (the "1934 Act") addressed several important issues. First, it created the Securities and Exchange Commission. Recall under Section 5 of the 1933 Act, a public sale of securities requires a registration statement to be filed. Unfortunately, the 1933 Act did not address to whom or where registration statements should be sent. The 1934 Act clarified this process by establishing the SEC.

Second, the 1934 Act imposed rules and regulations on the behavior and conduct of broker-dealers. Many brokers failed during the Great Depression from lack of capital, while others closed their doors because they were "fly-by-night" operations. The 1934 Act ensures that all broker-dealers are properly registered with the SEC, that they maintain adequate capital for times of market stress, that they file periodic financial reports with the SEC, and that they conduct their business within the rules and regulations of a central authority.[4]

Third, the 1934 Act established rules and regulations regarding the secondary trading of issued securities. It is the secondary trading of securities that has implications for the hedge fund industry.

Limited partnership units in a hedge fund may be transferred from an existing limited partner to a new limited partner. While the hedge fund partnership agreement may have conditions on this transfer, this is still a secondary sale of securities.

When the hedge fund manager sells the limited partnership units to the initial investors, this is considered a *primary offering* or *initial public offering* of securities. Primary offerings and IPOs are governed by the 1933 Act. However, the offer or sale of securities that were previously distributed in an IPO is covered by the 1934 Act.

---

[4] The SEC has delegated a portion of its authority to the National Association of Securities Dealers, Inc. to define the industry standard of conduct for broker-dealers.

Rule 10b-5

The 1934 Act applies to resales of limited partnership interests by the investors in the hedge fund, rather than the hedge fund manager. In particular, all secondary sales of limited partnership interests in a hedge fund are subject to Rule 10b-5: *Employment of Manipulative and Deceptive Devices*.

Rule 10b-5 states:

> It shall be unlawful for any person, directly or indirectly, by the use of any means or instrumentality of interstate commerce, or of the mails, or of any facility of any national securities exchange:
>
> 1. To employ any device, scheme, or artifice to defraud,
> 2. To make any untrue statement of a material fact or to omit to state a material fact necessary in order to make the statements made, in light of the circumstances under which they were made, not misleading, or
> 3. To engage in any act, practice, or course of business which operates or would operate as a fraud or deceit upon any persons,
>
> in connection with the purchase or sale of any security.

Notice that the language of Rule 10b-5 parallels the antifraud language in Section 17 of the 1933 Act. Congress ensured that the same antifraud standard applies for the secondary sale of securities as well as for initial public offerings.

Rule 10b-5 is sometimes known as the "Insider Trading Rule." One of its purposes is to prevent corporate insiders, people who know more about a corporation's prospects and business, from taking advantage of outsiders by way of their superior knowledge about the company in question. However, this rule is general enough to capture any secondary sale of securities where one party is in possession of material nonpublic information and uses this nonpublic information to its advantage.

For instance, a limited partner in a hedge fund might be aware that the hedge fund manager is about to be indicted on criminal charges, but this information has not been publicly announced. This is material nonpublic information, and the limited partner must disclose it to prospective buyers if he intends to sell his limited partnership interests. Conversely, the hedge fund manager would need to disclose this information only if she intends to sell new limited partnership interests to either existing or new limited partners.

THE INVESTMENT COMPANY ACT OF 1940

The Investment Company Act of 1940 (the "Company Act") was designed to regulate investment pools. Today, this act primarily regulates the mutual fund industry. Mutual funds are investment companies for purposes of the Company Act and the SEC.

Under Section 3(a) of the Company Act, an investment company:

> Means any issuer which is or holds itself out as being engaged primarily, or proposes to engage primarily, in the business of investing, reinvesting, or trading in securities.

While this definition clearly incorporates mutual funds, it is also broad enough to encompass hedge funds. Hedge funds are investment companies for purposes of the Company Act. Falling within the jurisdiction of the Company Act means that hedge funds must adhere to the same registration requirements under Section 8 of the Company Act as do mutual funds.[5] Fortunately, the Company Act also provides two ready-made safe harbors of which hedge fund managers may take advantage.

First, Section 3(c)(1) of the Company Act states, in part:

> Notwithstanding subsection 3(a), none of the following persons is an investment company within the meaning of this title:
>
> 1. Any issuer whose outstanding securities (other than short-term paper) are beneficially owned by not more than one hundred persons and which is not making and does not presently propose to make a public offering of its securities.

"3(c)(1) funds," as they are known, can be offered to any type of investor, sophisticated and unsophisticated, accredited and nonaccredited, provided that the hedge fund manager does not allow more than 100 investors into the fund. For smaller hedge fund managers, the 100 person limit should not be an issue. For larger hedge funds, however, that wish to attract additional capital, the 100 person limit may prove binding.

In 1996, Congress added a new paragraph 7 to Section 3(c) of the Company Act. This paragraph recognizes that an investment pool might contain many investors that are sophisticated, and consequently, might not

---

[5] Even if a hedge fund failed to register with the SEC as an investment company, it would still be subject to the SEC jurisdiction under Section 7, *Transactions by Unregistered Investment Companies*. This section of the Company Act allows the SEC to assert jurisdiction over an investment company even if it has not registered with the SEC.

need the oversight of the SEC. Section 3(c)(7) states, in part, that the following entity will not fall within the meaning of an investment company:

> Any issuer, the outstanding securities of which are owned exclusively by persons who, at the time of acquisition of such securities, are qualified purchasers, and which is not making and does not at that time propose to make a public offering of such securities.

This new type of fund is often referred to as a "3(c)(7) fund," and it is designed for sophisticated investors. Prior to the introduction of Section 3(c)(7), hedge funds were limited to accepting no more than 100 investors in their fund. Any more than that, and they would have to register with the SEC as an investment company.[6] Section 3(c)(7) removes this limit and provides more flexibility for hedge fund managers.

The term "qualified purchaser" was introduced in the 1996 amendment to the Company Act. This term means:

1. any natural person (including any person who holds a joint account, community property or other similar shared ownership interest in an issuer with that person's qualified spouse) who owns not less than $5,000,000 in investments;
2. any company that owns not less than $5,000,000 in investments and that is owned directly or indirectly by or for two or more natural persons who are not related as siblings or spouse (including former spouse), or direct lineal descendants by birth or adoption, spouses of such persons, the estates of such persons, or foundations, charitable organizations, or trusts established by or for the benefit of such persons;
3. any trust that is not covered by clause (2) and that was not formed for the specific purpose of acquiring the securities offered, as to which the trustee or other person authorized to make decisions with respect to the trust, and each settlor or other person who has contributed assets to the trust, is a person described in clause (1), (2), or (4); or
4. any person, acting for its own account or the accounts of other qualified purchasers, who in the aggregate owns and invests on a discretionary basis, not less than $25,000,000 in investments.

Therefore, 3(c)(7) funds cater only to the very wealthy (with investments — not net worth — of at least $5,000,000) as well as endowments, pension plans, trust companies, and other investment organizations.

---

[6] An existing 3(c)(1) fund can become a 3(c)(7) fund providing it notifies its existing investors that future investors will be limited to qualified purchasers, and that it provides existing investors in the fund with an opportunity to redeem their interests in the hedge fund. See Section 3(c)(7)(B)(ii)(I)&(II).

EXHIBIT 8.2   The Investment Company Act of 1940

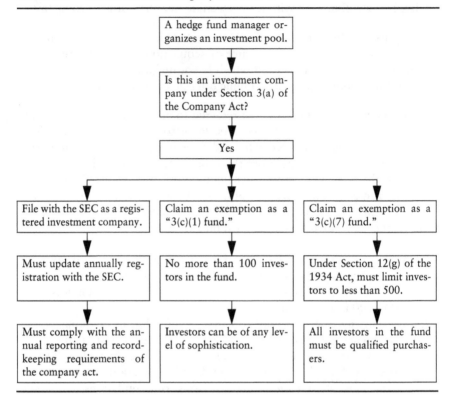

It is often stated that Section 3(c)(7) limits hedge funds to no more than 499 investors. This is not true; Section 3(c)(7) imposes no such limit. However, there is another practical limit established by Section 12 of the 1934 Act (Registration Requirements for Securities). Specifically, under Section 12(g)(1)(A)&(B) any issuer who is engaged in interstate commerce must register its securities with the SEC in a registration statement within a certain period of time after the issuer achieves $1,000,000 in total assets and has a class of equity security held of record by 500 or more persons.[7] Therefore, hedge fund managers that apply the Section 3(c)(7) safe harbor limit the number of investors in their fund to 499.

In Exhibit 8.2, we provide a review of the Company Act. We can see that a hedge fund manager has three choices. She can register the hedge fund as an investment company under Section 3(a) of the Company Act,

---

[7] This is another way attorneys earn their keep. There is no cross reference between Sections 3(c)(7) of the Company Act and Section 12(g) of the 1934 Act.

however, this will expose the hedge fund to the same reporting, disclosure, and record keeping requirements of a typical mutual fund.

Alternatively, the hedge fund manager can take advantage of the exemptions under Sections 3(c)(1) or 3(c)(7). Under 3(c)(1), the hedge fund manager cannot accept more than 100 investors in the hedge fund. The tradeoff is that investors can be of any level of sophistication. Under Section 3(c)(7), the hedge fund manager can have an unlimited number of investors in the hedge fund (practically limited to 499 persons by Section 12(g) of the 1934 Act). But, in return, 3(c)(7) investors must have large investment portfolios or be large institutional investors.

THE INVESTMENT ADVISERS ACT OF 1940

In the same breath that created the Company Act, Congress also established the Investment Advisers Act of 1940 (the "Advisers Act"). The purpose of the Advisers Act is to regulate those individuals that provide investment advice to investment companies, pension plans, endowments, and other individuals. Under the Advisers Act, an investment adviser is defined, in part, as:

> Investment adviser means any person who, for compensation, engages in the business of advising others, either directly or indirectly or through publications and writings, as to the value of securities or as to the advisability of investing in, purchasing, or selling securities, or who, for compensation as part of a regular business, issues or promulgates analyses or reports concerning securities...

This definition is broad enough to include hedge fund managers. For example, the Advisers Act does not address the issue of long or short investing. Instead, it addresses the business of giving advice on the value of securities, good or bad. Long or short investing is the investment adviser's strategy. Once again, this broad language is sufficient to include hedge fund managers within the federal securities laws. Section 203(a) of the Advisers Act requires investment advisers as defined above to register with the SEC.

Fortunately, Congress once again provided exceptions to the general rule. First, there is the small adviser exception. Section 203A (1) states:

> No investment adviser that is regulated or required to be regulated as an investment adviser in the state in which it maintains its principal office and place of business shall register under Section 203,

unless the investment adviser (A) has assets under management of not less than $25,000,000; or (B) is an adviser to an investment company registered under Title I of this Act.

In other words, if the investment adviser does not manage assets greater than $24,999,999 and is not an investment adviser to a mutual fund, then it does not need to register with the SEC.

Second, there is the limited client exception. Under Section 203(b)(3) of the Advisers Act, the registration requirements of Section 203(a) do not apply to:

Any investment adviser who during the course of the preceding 12 months has had fewer than 15 clients and who neither holds himself out generally to the public as an investment adviser nor acts as an investment adviser to any investment company registered under Title 1 of this Act.

Initially, under Section 203(b), for purposes of counting the number of people that an investment adviser advises, the SEC provided that each hedge fund counts as one client no matter how many investors there may be in the hedge fund.[8] Therefore, for a hedge fund manager that only advises one or a small group of hedge funds, it is easy to stay within this exception. However, a growing phenomenon in the hedge fund industry is the management of separate accounts.

A separate account is an investment account for a single investor. More and more investors are asking for separate accounts because of the transparency that it provides. While a hedge fund manager may be reluctant to provide all of her positions contained within a hedge fund for many investors, she may be more willing to provide full transparency for an individual account. The reason is that the damage to a separate account from a breach of confidentiality will lay solely at the investor's feet. Should an investor in a separate account reveal the hedge fund manager's positions to the market, the investor will be harming only himself.

The growth of separate accounts may force a hedge fund manager to register as an investment adviser. Each separate account counts as one full "person," equivalent in counting status to one hedge fund for purposes of the Advisers Act. Therefore, most hedge fund managers that accept separate accounts have registered as an investment adviser. Reg-

---

[8] The key to counting the hedge fund as only one client is to manage the hedge fund in accordance with the terms of the limited partnership agreement or other organization document. In this way, the hedge fund manager is advising only the hedge fund and not its individual investors.

istration as an investment adviser requires the hedge fund manager to file an annual disclosure form (Form ADV) with the SEC.

Finally, the antifraud provisions of Section 206 of the Advisers Act apply to all investment advisers whether registered or exempt. Essentially, it is illegal for any investment adviser to employ any scheme, to engage in any transaction, or to engage in any course of action which is fraudulent, deceptive, or manipulative.

New Regulations for Hedge Funds under the Advisers Act

The New Rule

In 2005, the SEC passed new regulations for hedge funds under the Advisers Act that will require hedge funds to register as Investment Advisers with the SEC. The new regulations become effective in 2006. We first review the requirements of the new rule, and then consider the implications and benefits of the regulation.

As noted above, previously, a hedge fund did not have to register as an investment adviser with the SEC as long as it had no more than 15 clients. This was knows as the "private adviser exemption." Furthermore, hedge fund managers counted each hedge fund as one client regardless of the number of investors that might have contributed capital to the hedge fund.

Under new Rule 203(b)(3)-2, a hedge fund must count each investor in each hedge fund as a client. In other words, the new rule requires hedge fund managers to "look through" each hedge fund that they manage to count the individual investors who have contributed capital to each hedge fund for purposes of determining whether the hedge fund manager advises more than 15 clients. For most hedge fund managers, effectively this means that they will have to register as investment advisers because most hedge funds have more than 15 investors.

However, the SEC still provided two escape hatches for hedge fund managers. First, new Rule 203(b)(3)-2 does not affect the general rule that an adviser must have at least $25,000,000 in gross assets under management in order to be eligible to register with the SEC. Therefore, small and emerging hedge fund managers can still remain off the SEC's radar screen.

Second, the SEC amended Rule 203(b)(3)-1 to make it clear that the private adviser exemption is withdrawn only for those private investment funds that permit their clients to redeem any portion of their ownership interests within two years of the purchase of such interests. In other words, the private adviser exemption still applies if the hedge fund manager requires a lock-up period for its investors greater than two years. This means that if there is a two-year or longer lock-up provision in the hedge fund, the hedge fund manager is not required to look through the hedge fund to count the individual investors.

This two year redemption/lock-up provision was put into the code so that Rule 203(b)(3)-2 would not apply to private equity funds. Most private equity funds (Leveraged Buyout Funds, Venture Capital Funds, Mezzanine Debt Funds) require a 10-year lock-up period, and the SEC's intent is to regulate hedge fund managers not private equity managers.

The Benefits of Hedge Fund Registration

The SEC noted that there would be several benefits to hedge fund registration. The first, is census information. No one really knows the true size of the hedge fund industry. Previously, with voluntary reporting to hedge fund databases and voluntary registration with the SEC, there has been no central repository of information on the size and growth of the industry.

Second, registration with the SEC should provide deterrence of fraud. While the SEC cannot prevent fraud—criminal conduct will always exist—it can put hedge fund managers on notice that they are now subject to formal SEC regulation and all the penalties that flow from the violation of securities laws.

Third, registration as an investment adviser will require hedge fund managers to adopt formal compliance procedures, and to appoint a Chief Compliance Officer. This will strengthen the internal controls of hedge fund managers and make it harder for a rogue trader to operate within a hedge fund.

Last, hedge fund managers will now have to file Form ADV with the SEC annually, this will provide both investors and the SEC with basic information regarding the hedge fund manager. For the SEC, it will allow the regulatory agency to track the growth of the hedge fund industry while for investors it will provide a starting point for due diligence.

Practical Issues Associated with Registration as an Investment Adviser

First, there will be a cost with establishing internal compliance controls and hiring a Chief Compliance Officer. However, given some of the very large fees that hedge fund managers earn, this cost is unlikely to be burdensome.

Second, given the two year lock-up escape hatch, it is likely that we will see more hedge funds adopt a two-year lock-up provision. This would be unfortunate for the SEC and investors. For the SEC, it will prevent the regulator from tracking the growth of that hedge fund industry, and for investors, they will end up with less liquidity and less regulation.

Exhibit 8.3 demonstrates the choices for a hedge fund manager under the Advisers Act.

EXHIBIT 8.3   The Investment Advisers Act of 1940

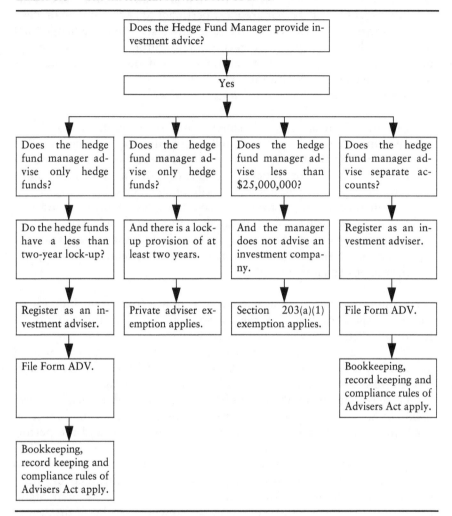

THE COMMODITY EXCHANGE ACT

The Commodity Exchange Act (the "CEA") was promulgated by Congress in 1974. The CEA accomplished two major goals. First, it established the Commodity Futures Trading Commission as the regulatory authority for the futures industry including the futures exchanges. Second, it established disclosure, record keeping, and reporting rules for *commodity pool operators* (CPOs), *commodity trading advisors* (CTAs), *futures commission merchants* (FCMs), and introducing brokers. It is the rules that regulate CPOs that are most pertinent to hedge fund managers.

CPOs are a subset of the hedge fund universe. These are hedge fund managers who invest primarily in commodity futures contracts. We will discuss their strategies in the section on commodities investing. For now, we are concerned with their regulation.

Section 1.3(cc) of the CEA defines a CPO as:

Any person engaged in a business which is of the nature of an investment trust, syndicate, or similar form of enterprise, and who, in connection therewith, solicits, accepts, or receives from others, funds, securities, or property, either directly or indirectly or through capital contributions, the sale of stock or other forms of securities, or otherwise, for the purpose of trading in any commodity for future delivery or commodity option on or subject to the rules of any contract market, but does not include such persons not within the intent of this definition as the Commission may specify by rule or regulation or order.

In summary, any person who collects money from other individuals for the purpose of investing the money collectively in the commodity futures markets is a commodity pool operator.

If a hedge fund manager is a CPO under the definition of Section 1.3(cc), she must register with the CFTC[9] and the National Futures Association under Sections 4(m) and 4(n) and Rule 3.10.

Once registered, a CPO must obey the disclosure document requirements of Sections 4.21 and 4.24, the reporting requirements of Section 4.22, the record keeping requirements of section 4.23, and the performance disclosures of Section 4.25 of the CEA. These sections collectively detail the type of information the CPO must disclose to prospective investors in its offering documents, the financial information that it must present to existing investors in their Account Statements, and the format for presenting performance results in disclosure documents and annual reports. Last, the CPO must keep detailed books and records for the CFTC to audit.

However, as we have seen with respect to the regulation of the financial markets, Congress provided several exemptions from registering as a CPO. The CEA provides three safe harbors for CPOs.

---

[9] All registrations for commodity pool operators as well as other business associated with the futures industry are filed with the National Futures Association. The NFA is the designated self-regulatory authority for the futures industry, and the CFTC has delegated the registration requirements to the NFA.

First, under Section 4.5 certain entities are excluded from the definition of the term CPO. These include investment companies registered
under the Investment Company Act of 1940, insurance companies, banks,
trust companies, ERISA plans, other pension plans, and employee welfare
plans. Section 4.5 is meant to exclude any entity that is regulated under
another federal law such as the federal securities laws, the Employee
Retirement Income Security Act, or federal banking laws. Unfortunately,
this exemption has limited application to most hedge funds because they
are not otherwise regulated by another federal agency.

To claim an exemption under Section 4.5, an entity must file a
notice of eligibility with the CFTC. As part of the notice, the entity must
represent that it will use commodity futures or commodity options contracts solely for bona fide hedging purposes.

Second, under Section 4.13, there are two safe harbors. First, Section 4.13(a) exempts a commodity pool operator from registration if:
(1) she receives no compensation from operating the pool, (2) she operates only one pool, (3) she does not advertise the pool, and (4) she is not
otherwise required to register with the CFTC. Second, section 4.13(b)
exempts a CPO from registration if: (1) the total capital contributions
received for all pools does not exceed $200,000; and (2) there are no
more than 15 participants in any pool. Section 4.13 is meant to apply to
the small CPO, most likely someone whose primary business is not managing a commodity pool. It is unlikely to apply to a hedge fund manager
whose livelihood depends on receiving income from the pool.

Last, there is Section 4.7. This is the section most applicable to
CPO/hedge fund managers. This section is directed at entities whose primary business is managing a commodity pool. Section 4.7 does not
exempt a CPO from registering with the CFTC and the NFA and filing
annual reports thereto. However, it does exempt the CPO from the disclosure, reporting, and record keeping requirements of Sections 4.21–
4.25. The catch is that the CPO must sell its pool interests only to *Qualified Eligible Participants* (QEPs). Additionally the CPO must file a
Claim for Exemption with the CFTC.

Section 4.7 provides a long laundry list of the standard types of
institutional investors that qualify as a QEPs. These include banks,
FCMs, broker-dealers, trusts, other CPOs and commodity trading advisors, insurance companies, investment companies, and pension plans. In
addition there is a test for individuals.

For individual investors, the CFTC chose to the use the same
requirements for an accredited investor (see Regulation D earlier in this
chapter) but with an extra kicker. The accredited investor must also
own securities with an aggregate market value of $2,000,000, or the
investor must have had on deposit with a futures commission merchant

within the last six months $200,000 in initial margin and option premiums for futures contracts and options thereon. Therefore, it is not enough for an accredited investor to have a high-net-worth or high-earning potential, he must also have an existing investment portfolio worth at least $2 million or be actively involved in the futures markets (as demonstrated by his futures account activity).

Despite these three registration exemptions, the antifraud provisions of the CEA still apply. Section 6 of the CEA states, in part:

> It shall be unlawful for a commodity trading advisor, associated person of a commodity trading advisor, commodity pool operator, or associated person of a commodity pool operator, by use of the mails or any means or instrumentality of interstate commerce, directly or indirectly (A) to employ any device, scheme, or artifice to defraud any client or participant or prospective client or participant; or (B) to engage in any transaction, practice, or course of business which operates as a fraud or deceit upon any client or participant or prospective client or participant.

In conclusion, there are several ways for hedge funds to avoid either registration as a CPO, or the disclosure, record keeping, and reporting requirements for CPOs. These paths are diagrammed in Exhibit 8.4. However, no matter which path a hedge fund manager might choose, she cannot avoid the antifraud section of the CEA.

THE PRESIDENT'S WORKING GROUP ON FINANCIAL MARKETS

In the wake of the Long-Term Capital Management (LTCM) bailout, a working group (the "Working Group") was appointed by President Clinton to review the circumstances that led up to the rescue of LTCM. The Working Group was spearheaded by Robert Rubin, Secretary of the Treasury; Arthur Levitt, Chairman of the SEC; Alan Greenspan, Chairman of the Federal Reserve System; and, Brooksley Born, Chairperson of the CFTC. This group produced a report titled "Hedge Funds, Leverage, and the Lessons of Long-Term Capital Management."[10]

---

[10] See the President's Working Group on Financial Markets, "Hedge Funds, Leverage, and the Lessons of Long-Term Capital Management," April 28, 1999. Other participants in the working group included the Council of Economic Advisers, the Federal Deposit Insurance Corporation, the National Economic Council, the Federal Reserve Bank of New York, the Office of the Comptroller of the Currency, and the Office of Thrift Supervision.

EXHIBIT 8.4   The Commodity Exchange Act and Rules

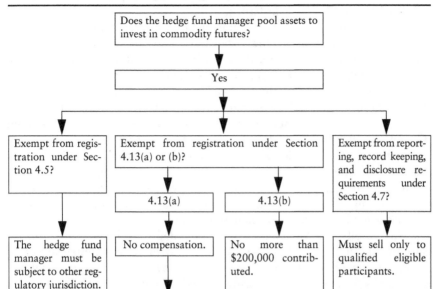

The principal policy arising out of the events surrounding the LTCM episode regards how to constrain excessive leverage. As we previously discussed in Chapter 2, LTCM used massive amounts of leverage and had a leverage ratio in excess of 100 to 1. The concern was that extreme amounts of leverage concentrated with one investor can increase the likelihood of a general breakdown in the functioning of the financial markets.

To put LTCM's leverage into perspective, at the end of 1998, it had $1.5 trillion in derivative positions. In contrast, the six largest commercial banks and two investment banks combined had over $1 trillion of notional derivative positions.[11] LTCM had approximately 50% greater

---

[11] President's Working Group on Financial Markets, "Hedge Funds, Leverage, and the Lessons of Long-Term Capital Management."

exposure to derivative instruments than the total exposure of eight large commercial and investment banks.

Yet, LTCM, and any hedge fund for that matter, cannot achieve significant leverage without the extension of credit by commercial and investment banks. Therefore, these financial institutions must take some of the blame/credit for helping to create the LTCM situation. The Working Group concluded that the financial institutions that extended credit to LTCM did not fully understand the extent to which LTCM was leveraged.

Consequently, one set of recommendations made by the Working Group was directed not at hedge funds but squarely at large financial institutions. The Working Group stated that financial institutions needed to implement improved standards for extending credit so that their own financial safety and soundness would be enhanced. In turn, the Working Group expected that financial institutions would then impose greater discipline on their borrowers.

Specifically, the Working Group concluded that financial institutions should establish procedures to measure and monitor counterparty risk exposure, set limits on credit exposure to any one institution, establish procedures for ongoing monitoring of credit quality, develop programs to mitigate credit risk through collateral calls, implement valuation practices for derivatives, and last, integrate credit risks and market risks.

In summary, the Working Group asked banks and other financial institutions to strengthen the risk management practices with respect to credit-based services provided to major counterparties in the derivatives and securities markets. This set of recommendations can be summarized into one rule: Know your customer.

Second, the Working Group concluded that the existing authority of the SEC, CFTC, and the Treasury Department should be expanded to monitor the risks posed by these market participants and the highly leveraged hedge fund counterparties that are their counterparties. The Working Group suggested that one method to enhance the regulatory overview would be to increase the SEC's and CFTC's risk assessment authority to include expanded reporting, record keeping, and examination of unregulated affiliates of broker dealers and future commission brokers. Many broker-dealers and FCMs form holding companies that are not registered either with the SEC or the CFTC, and these holding companies transact in swaps and other OTC derivatives with hedge funds. Because they are not registered with any regulatory authority, these holding companies can transact outside the radar screen of the SEC, CFTC, and the Treasury Department. In addition, the Working Group recommended that these three regulators be granted the authority to require broker-dealers, FCMs, and their unregulated affiliates to report credit risk information by counterparty.

Last, the Working Group made two recommendations with respect to hedge funds. First, the Working Group recommended more frequent and meaningful disclosures by hedge funds. Specifically, the Working Group indicated that there should be improved transparency for hedge fund reporting, and pointed to the reporting requirements for CPOs as a possible standard for hedge funds.[12]

Second, the Working Group recommended that a group of hedge funds should draft and publish a set of sound risk management practices. It suggested that such practices should address the measurement of market risk, liquidity risk, stress testing, collateral management, internal controls, identification of position concentration, and frequent marking to market of trading positions and collateral. Finally, the Working Group suggested that hedge funds should assess their performance against the sound practices for investors and counterparties.

THE GROUP OF FIVE HEDGE FUNDS

In February 2000, a group of five large hedge funds responded to the President's Working Group on Financial Markets.[13] Not surprisingly, this group of five of the largest hedge funds stopped short of endorsing any regulatory change to the hedge fund industry. However, it did conclude that hedge fund managers should work with regulators and counterparties to develop a broad consensus approach to public disclosure. Furthermore, the Group of Five made several recommendations regarding the management of market risk, credit risk, and liquidity risk.

With respect to market risk, the Group of Five recommended that hedge fund managers should measure their aggregate market risk for each hedge fund portfolio as well as the relevant subcomponents of the portfolio. These subcomponents could be monitored by geographic region, industry sector, investment strategy, asset class, or by type of instrument used.

Additionally, the Group of Five recommended that hedge fund managers should perform stress tests to determine how potential changes in market conditions could impact the market risk of the hedge fund portfolio. Last, the Group of Five recommended that hedge fund managers should validate their market risk models via regular back testing on historical data.

---

[12] See Mark Anson, "Performance Presentation Standards: Which Rules Apply When?" *Financial Analysts Journal* (March/April 2001), pp. 53–60.

[13] The Group of Five consisted of Caxton Corporation, Kingdon Capital Management, LLC, Moore Capital Management, Inc., Soros Fund Management LLC, and Tudor Investment Corporation.

With respect to credit risk, the Group of Five recommended that hedge fund managers should establish policies and procedures to manage the Fund's exposure to potential defaults by trading counterparties. Specifically, hedge fund managers should identify acceptable counterparties based on a reasonable analysis of their credit worthiness and then set appropriate exposure limits. In addition the Group of Five recommended that hedge fund managers should seek to establish appropriate collateral provisions and other forms of credit support in their counterparty agreements.

These recommendations on credit risk mirror those made by the President's Working Group. Perhaps the clearest lesson learned from LTCM is the need for monitoring, measuring, and managing counterparty credit exposure.

Finally, liquidity risk is critical to a hedge fund manager's ability to continue trading in times of stress. During periods of financial market dislocations, a hedge fund manager may be faced with both margin calls from its brokers as well as redemption requests from its investors. As LTCM demonstrated, liquidity risk can have a devastating impact on performance.

The Group of Five recommended that hedge fund managers perform a liquidity analysis of their hedge fund portfolios. This analysis should take into account the investment strategies employed, the terms governing the rights of investors to redeem their partnership interests, and the liquidity of the assets in the portfolio. The Group of Five also suggested that hedge fund managers assess their cash and borrowing capacity under the worst historical drawdown for the fund as well as for stressed market conditions (when margin calls are frequent). Last, the Group of Five recommended that hedge fund managers should forecast their liquidity requirements and potential changes to liquidity measures.

While this report provided a clear set of risk management guidelines for the hedge fund industry, it may not become an industry standard for two reasons. First, the recommendations made by the Group of Five were at "the high end of what a risk management program should be."[14] The Group of Five consisted of five of the largest hedge fund managers in existence. Their recommendations may not be adopted by smaller hedge funds in the industry.

Second, none of the five hedge funds that sponsored the report pledged to adopt the recommendations. Although many of the practices recommended had been adopted by at least one member of the Group of Five, not all of the recommendations have been adopted by all of the members. Therefore, consistency of risk disclosure and risk management, even among the largest in the hedge fund industry, remains an issue.

---

[14] See Mitchell Pacelle, "Five Hedge Funds' Report on Industry Stops Short of Call for New Regulation," *Wall Street Journal* (February 8, 2000), p. C21.

CONCLUSION

This brief overview on the regulation of the hedge fund industry is meant to demonstrate the regulatory quagmire through which a hedge fund manager must navigate. For example, under the 1933 Act, we have a class of investors called "Accredited Investors," while under the Company Act we have "qualified purchasers," and under the CEA we have "qualified eligible participants." Did we mention at the beginning of the chapter that the laws regulating the financial markets were arcane?

Nonetheless, there are several points to highlight. First, the laws of the financial markets can be confusing. Smart hedge fund legal counsel is an important component of a hedge fund's success. In fact, as we noted in our chapter on due diligence, speaking with the hedge fund manager's legal counsel is a crucial part of the due diligence process.

Second, within every piece of federal legislation are safe harbors that hedge fund managers have been quick to turn to their advantage. However, it is the use of these safe harbors that have led many pundits to claim that hedge funds are "unregulated." Yet these safe harbors generally provide that the hedge fund manager must contract only with sophisticated investors. The general public remains protected under the federal laws of the financial markets.

Third, even though hedge fund managers may take advantage of many of these safe harbors, the antifraud provisions of the federal laws still apply to hedge fund managers. Therefore, although they may avoid the registration, disclosure, record keeping, and reporting requirements of the securities and commodities laws, hedge fund managers are still on the hook for the most serious offenses: fraud, deceit, material misstatements, and failure to disclose material information.

Finally, with the advent of the new SEC registration rules for hedge fund managers, some regulatory oversight has been brought to the hedge fund industry. In fact, the hedge fund industry had been moving in this direction already. As an example, most of the hedge fund managers with whom CalPERS has invested captial had already registered as investment advisers with the SEC even before the new regulations under Rules 203(b)(3)-1&2 became effective.

CHAPTER 9

Hedge Fund Benchmarks and Asset Allocation

Initially, hedge funds were the domain of high-net-worth individuals. However, in the latter half of the 1990s, large institutional investors discovered the charms of these investments. Endowments and foundations were first, followed by corporate and public pension plans. As more and more institutional investors entered the hedge fund arena, they demanded many of the investment parameters that they had come to expect from their traditional long-only programs.

Generally, with respect to external investment managers, institutional investors demand three things:

1. A well-defined investment process
2. Transparency
3. Relative returns

It is the last requirement, relative returns, that we explore in this chapter. Relative returns are one of the primary reasons for index construction. We begin by reviewing issues regarding the construction of hedge fund indexes. Next we compare and contrast the hedge fund indexes in existence. Then we consider some issues regarding the selection of hedge fund indexes.

HEDGE FUNDS AS AN INVESTMENT

As Brown, Goetzmann, and Ibbotson note, the most interesting feature of the hedge fund industry is that an investment in a hedge fund is

229

almost a "pure bet" on the skill of a specific manager.[1] Hedge fund managers tend to seek out arbitrage or mispricing opportunities in the financial markets using a variety of cash and derivative instruments. They tend to take small amounts of market exposure to exploit mispricing opportunities, but employ large amounts of leverage to extract the greatest value. The key point is that hedge fund managers pursue investment strategies unfettered by conventional financial market benchmarks. Their investment styles are "alpha-driven" rather than "beta-driven."

In prior chapters we have shown that hedge funds have favorable risk/return benefits compared to traditional stocks and bonds and that hedge funds have demonstrated ability to add value to a traditional portfolio of stocks and bonds.

However, capturing this "pure skill" can be problematic. Still, hedge fund indexes serve two key purposes. First, they serve as a proxy for the hedge fund asset class. This is important for asset allocation studies. Second, hedge fund indexes can serve as performance benchmarks to judge the success or failure of hedge fund managers. However, as we demonstrate below, there are many differences among the several hedge fund index products offered. We begin with a discussion on index construction.

ISSUES WITH HEDGE FUND INDEX CONSTRUCTION

In this chapter we review the information on 12 hedge fund indexes. Each index is based on a different number of hedge funds, ranging from 60 to over 5,000. Most of these indexes use simple averages, while others use capital-weighted indexes. Also, some index providers collect the underlying data themselves, while others allow the hedge fund managers to enter the data. Still other hedge fund indexes include managed futures while some do not. In sum, there are many different construction techniques of hedge fund indexes. We discuss the challenges of implementing these methodologies below.

The Size of the Hedge Fund Universe

One of the problems with constructing a hedge fund index is that the size of the total universe of hedge funds is not known with certainty. Depending on which report you choose, there are 5,000, 6,000, or

---

[1] Stephen Brown, William Goetzmann, and Roger Ibbotson, "Offshore Hedge Funds: Survival and Performance, 1989–95," *The Journal of Business* 72, no. 1 (1999), pp. 91–117.

7,000 hedge funds in existence with assets ranging from $800 billion to $1.5 trillion.[2]

The uncertainty regarding the true size of the hedge fund industry stems from the fact that for most of its history, it was an unregulated industry. Recent rules from the Securities and Exchange Commission now require hedge funds to register as investment advisers under the Investment Advisers Act of 1940. Indeed, one of the reasons the SEC cited for pursuing this rulemaking was to provide census data on the number and size of hedge fund managers. These rules will apply for hedge fund managers beginning in 2006. Previously, hedge funds had no requirement to report their performance to an index provider. They enjoyed relative secrecy. This is in contrast to their mutual fund counterparts.

Mutual funds are regulated investment companies that are required to register with the SEC. In addition, investment advisers to mutual funds are also required to register with the SEC. In fact, mutual funds are considered public investment companies that issue public securities (mutual fund shares) on a continual basis. Therefore, they are required by law to report and publish their performance numbers to the SEC and the public.

A good example of the unknown size of the hedge fund universe was demonstrated by Liang.[3] He studied the composition of indexes constructed by two well-known providers: TASS and Hedge Fund Research Inc.[4] At the time of his study there were 1,162 hedge funds in the HFR index and 1,627 hedge funds in the TASS index. He found that only 465 hedge funds were common to both hedge fund indexes. Furthermore, of these 465 common hedge funds, only 154 had data covering the same time period.

Another problem with measuring the size of the hedge fund universe is that the attrition rate for hedge funds is quite high. Park, Brown, and Goetzmann[5] and Brown, Goetzmann, and Ibbotson[6] find that the aver-

---

[2] See Daniel Collins, "Alternative Vehicles Open to Retail," *Futures* (December 1, 2002); Robert Clow, "Investors Pile into Alternative Fund Strategies," *Financial Times* (April 30, 2002); Robert Clow, "Hedge Fund Data are no More than a Rough Guide," *Financial Times* (March 14, 2002); and Malcolm Shearmur, "Pension Plans Delay Hedge Fund Investments as Returns Slump," *Bloomberg News*, November 17, 2005.

[3] Bing Liang, "Hedge Funds: The Living and the Dead," *Journal of Financial and Quantitative Analysis* 35, no. 3 (September 2001), pp. 309–326.

[4] The Tass database is now used by the joint venture of CSFB/Tremont Advisors.

[5] Brown, Goetzmann, and Ibbotson, "Offshore Hedge Funds: Survival and Performance, 1989–95."

[6] James Park, Stephen Brown, and William Goetzmann, "Performance Benchmarks and Survivorship Bias for Hedge Fund and Commodity Trading Advisors," *Hedge Fund News* (August 1999).

age life of a hedge fund manager is two and a half to three years. The short half-life of the average hedge fund means that there will be considerable turnover on an annual basis with respect to hedge fund index construction. In conclusion, the hedge fund universe is not known with certainty, there is very little overlap between hedge fund index providers, and the high attrition rate for hedge funds results in constant turnover of the index construction.

Data Biases

There are several data biases associated with hedge fund indexes. The first, is the well-known *survivorship* bias. Survivorship bias arises when constructing a hedge fund index today based on hedge fund managers that have survived the time period of study and are available for index construction. Those hedge fund managers that have not survived are excluded from the index construction. This creates and upward bias to the performance of a hedge fund index because, presumably, the remaining hedge funds survived as a result of their superior performance. This bias is also common with mutual fund studies.

However, the lack of a regulatory environment for hedge funds creates the opportunity for other data biases that are unique to the hedge fund industry. In addition to survivorship bias, there are three other biases that may affect hedge fund index construction. First, there is *selection* bias.

Essentially, hedge fund managers have a free option to report their data. In fact, the new rules from the SEC require hedge fund managers to report annually basic operating data on SEC Form ADV, but do not require hedge fund managers to report their performance record to an index provider. Therefore, hedge fund managers can still pick and choose when and with whom to report their data. Selection bias also pushes hedge fund index returns upward because it is the better performing hedge fund manager who will choose to exercise his option and report his performance to an index provider.[7]

Closely related to selection bias is *instant history* or *backfill* bias. Instant history bias occurs because once a hedge fund manager begins to report his performance to an index provider, the index provider backfills the hedge fund manager's historical performance into the database. Again, because it is more likely that a hedge fund manager will begin reporting his performance after a period of good performance, this bias pushes index returns upward.

---

[7] A contrary argument can be made for selection bias: that is, good hedge fund managers choose not to report their data to hedge fund index providers because they have no need to attract additional assets.

Last, there is *liquidation* bias. Frequently, hedge fund managers go out of business or shut down an unsuccessful hedge fund. When this happens, these managers stop reporting their performance in advance of the cessation of operations. In other words, several months of poor performance is lost because hedge fund managers are more concerned with winding down their operations than they are in reporting their performance to an index provider.[8]

In Chapter 7, on risk management, we note that these biases can add up to 3% to 4.5% of annual performance enhancement to a hedge fund index. It is important to take note of these biases because they cannot be diversified away by constructing a portfolio of indexes because all indexes suffer from these biases. We reprint this table from Chapter 7 here as Exhibit 9.1 to refresh the reader's memory on the size of these biases and their impact on hedge fund returns.

Strategy Definition and Style Drift

Strategy definitions can be very difficult for index providers. An index must have enough strategies to capture the broad market for hedge fund returns. Index providers determine their own hedge fund strategy classification system, and this varies from index to index.

Consider a hedge fund manager who goes long the stock of a target company subject to a merger bid and short the stock of the acquiring company. The strategy of this hedge fund manager may be classified alternatively as merger arbitrage by one index provider (e.g., HFR), relative value by another index provider (e.g., MSCI), or event driven by still another index provider (e.g., CSFB/Tremont). In summary, there is no consistent definition of hedge fund styles among index providers. Indeed, the dynamic trading nature of hedge funds makes them difficult to classify—and this is part of the appeal of hedge fund managers.

Further complicating strategy definition is that most hedge fund managers are classified according to the disclosure language in their offering documents. However, consider the following language from an actual hedge fund private placement memorandum:

> Consistent with the General Partner's opportunistic approach, there are no fixed limitations as to specific asset classes invested in by the Partnership. The Partnership is not limited with respect to the types of investment strategies it may employ or the markets or instruments in which it may invest.

---

[8] The flipside to liquidation bias is *participation* bias. This bias may occur for a successful hedge fund manager who closes his fund and stops reporting his results because he no longer needs to attract new capital.

EXHIBIT 9.1 Biases Associated with Hedge Fund Data

Bias	Park, Brown, and Goetzmann, 1999	Brown, Goetzmann, and Ibbotson, 1999	Fung and Hsieh, 2000	Ackermann, McEnally, and Ravenscraft, 1999	Barry, 2003
Survivorship	2.60%	3%	3%	0.01%	3.70%
Selection	1.90%	Not estimated	Not estimated	No impact	Not estimated
Instant history	Not estimated	Not estimated	1.40%	No impact	0.40%
Liquidation	Not estimated	Not estimated	Not estimated	0.70%	Not estimated
Total	4.50%	3%	4.40%	0.71%	4.10%

234

Where to classify this manager? Relative value? Global macro? Market neutral? Unfortunately, with hedge funds this type of strategy description is commonplace. The lack of specificity may lead to guesswork on the part of index providers with respect to the manager's strategy. Alternatively, some index providers may leave out this manager because of lack of clarity (e.g., Zurich Hedge Fund Indices), but this adds another bias to the index by purposely excluding certain types of hedge fund managers. Essentially, there is no established format for classifying hedge funds. Each index provider develops its own scheme without concern for consistency with other hedge fund index providers, and this makes comparisons between hedge fund indexes difficult.

Even if an index provider can successfully classify a hedge fund manager's investment strategy, there is the additional problem of strategy drift. Again, because of the mostly unregulated nature of hedge fund managers, there is no requirement for a hedge fund manager to notify an index provider when his investment style has changed.

Let us continue with our example of merger arbitrage managers. With a sluggish U.S. economy during 2001 and 2002, the market for mergers and acquisitions declined significantly. There were simply too few deals to feed all of the merger arbitrage manager mouths. Consequently, many of these managers changed their investment style to invest in the rising tide of distressed debt deals which are countercyclical from mergers and acquisitions. In addition, many merger arbitrage managers expanded their investment portfolio to consider other corporate transactions such as spin-offs and recapitalizations. All too often, once a hedge fund manager has been classified as merger arbitrage, it will remain in that category despite significant changes in its investment focus.

Investability

A key issue is whether a hedge fund index can be or should be investable. This is an issue for hedge funds that is distinct and different from their mutual fund counterparts. Mutual funds are public companies. They can and do continually offer their shares to the public. Capacity issues are virtually nonexistent. However, hedge funds generally do have capacity issues as certain strategies only work well within certain limits of investment capital. This means that hedge fund managers often refuse further capital when they have achieved a maximum level of assets under management. Consequently, it is very difficult for hedge fund indexes to remain investable when the underlying hedge funds close their doors to new investors.

A related issue is whether hedge fund indexes should be investable. The argument is that an investable index will exclude hedge fund managers that are closed to new investors and therefore, exclude a large section of the hedge fund universe. Most index providers argue that to be a truly representative index that acts as a barometer for hedge fund performance, both open and closed funds should be included. The tradeoff, therefore, is between having as broad a representation as possible of hedge fund performance versus having a smaller pool of hedge fund managers that represent the performance that may be accessed through investment.

HEDGE FUND INDEXES

In this section, we provide summary information on 12 hedge fund index providers. These indexes vary as to number of hedge fund managers, types of strategies employed, and investability. Exhibit 9.2 summarizes the key attributes of the hedge fund indexes.

First, at a glance, these index providers have significant variation in the number of hedge funds they track, the number of subindexes that they offer, whether they are cap weighted or equal weighted, the date they were launched, and so on. Beyond the information presented, the key takeaway from this table is the distinct lack of consistency in hedge fund index construction. Each index is unique and very little overlap should be expected. We now discuss some of their key differences.

Fees

All of the hedge fund indexes listed in Exhibit 9.2 calculate hedge fund performance net of fees. However, there are two issues related to fees that can result in difference performance than portrayed by a hedge fund index. First, incentive fees, that portion of hedge fund remuneration that is tied to the performance of hedge funds, are normally calculated on an annual basis. However, all of these indexes provide month-by-month performance. Therefore, on a monthly basis, incentive fees must be estimated and subtracted from performance. The actual fees collected at yearend may be very different than the monthly estimates.

Second, hedge funds are a form of private investing. Indeed, virtually all hedge funds are structured as private limited partnerships. As a consequence, the terms of specific investments in hedge funds often may not be negotiated in a consistent manner among different investors or across different time periods. The lack of consistency means that the net-of-fees returns earned by one investor may not be what another investor can negotiate. In fact, the more successful the hedge fund manager, the greater the likelihood that he will increase his fee structure to take advantage of his

EXHIBIT 9.2 Summary of Hedge Fund Indexes

Index Provider	Provides a Single Index	Data History	Number of Sub-indexes	Number of Funds	Includes CTAs	Equal or Asset Wtd	Investable	Net of Fees	Website
Altvest/Investor Force	Yes	1993	13	2,500	No	Equal	No	Yes	investorforce.com
EACM	Yes	1996	12	100	No	Equal	Yes	Yes	eacm100@eacm.com
MAR/CISDM[a]	No	1990	15	3,100	Yes	Equal	No	Yes	cisdm.som.umass.edu
Hedge Fund Research	Yes	1990	33	5,000	No	Equal	No	Yes	hedgefundresearch.com
Zurich Capital	No	2001	5	60	No	Equal	No	Yes	zindex.com
CSFB/Tremont	Yes	1994	10	4,000	Yes	Asset	Yes	Yes	hedgeindex.com
Van Hedge	Yes	1995	19	6,000	No	Equal	No	Yes	hedgefund.com
Hennessee Group	Yes	1992	23	3,000	No	Equal	No	Yes	hedgefnd.com
Tuna Indices	Yes	1979	33	3,500	Yes	Equal	No	Yes	hedgefund.net
MSCI	Yes	2002	150	1,500	Yes	Equal & Asset	No	Yes	msci.com
Standard and Poor's	Yes	2002	9	30–40	Yes	Equal	Yes	Yes	standardandpoors.com
Barclays CTA Indexes	Yes	1980	6	400	Only	Equal	Yes	Yes	barclaygrp.com

[a] The data originally compiled by Managed Account Reports were sold to Zurich Capital Markets which, in turn, gifted the database to the Center for International Securities and Derivatives Markets

success. The end result is that index returns may overstate what a new investor can obtain in the hedge fund market place. We call this the *fee bias*.

At least one index provider has offered an investment product tied to the performance of the index. Credit Suisse First Boston (CSFB) in conjunction with the Tremont hedge fund index has offered an investable CSFB/Tremont product tied to the total return of the Tremont hedge fund composite. When first introduced, this product was initially offered for a fee of 1%, but competition may soon lower this fee.

Turnover

Most of the turnover with respect to hedge fund indexes tends to be one-sided. That is, the index composite grows as more hedge funds report their performance to the index provider. However, some hedge funds go out of business or close their fund to new investors and cease reporting their returns. This can lead to several of the data biases presented in Exhibit 9.2. In sum, turnover tends to be low, with more hedge fund returns added to the composite over time.

Inclusion of Managed Futures

Managed futures, or Commodity Trading Advisors are sometimes considered a subset of the hedge fund universe. These are investment manages who invest in the commodity futures markets using either fundamental economic analysis, or trend following models. CTAs may invest in financial futures, energy futures, agriculture futures, metals futures, livestock futures, or currency futures. Because of their different trading style from other hedge fund managers (mostly trend following models) and the markets in which they invest, CTAs and managed futures accounts are sometimes segregated from the hedge fund universe. In fact, we discuss managed futures in a separate section that follows our discussion of hedge funds. From Exhibit 9.2 we can see that the hedge fund index providers are split roughly 50-50 as to whether they include managed futures in their database or not.

Performance

Exhibit 9.3 demonstrates the historical performance of the 12 indexes.[9] The most striking observation is that the risk/return performance of the 12 indexes varies significantly. The highest return is associated with the Tuna funds (average annual return of 16.35%) and the lowest associ-

---

[9] In the case of Zurich Capital, we used the average performance across its five subindexes, and for MAR/CISDM we used the performance of its Fund of Funds index. Data for S&P and MSCI are based on pro-forma performance prior to 2002.

EXHIBIT 9.3   Risk and Return of Hedge Fund Indexes and Market Indexes

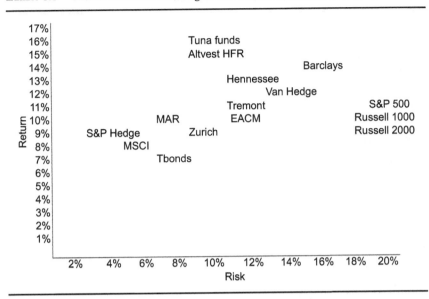

ated with MSCI (7.62%). Also the standard deviation of annual returns ranges from 14% (Van Hedge) to 3% for the S&P Hedge Fund index.

We also include as an additional reference, the risk and return of the S&P 500, the Russell 1000 and 2000 stock indexes, and 10-year U.S. Treasury Bonds. We include Treasury bonds to provide a low risk/low return alternative to stocks. All three of the stock indexes appear as outliers on this chart with average returns of 9% to 11%, but with volatility significantly higher than that for the hedge fund indexes, at 19% to 20%.

Exhibit 9.3 underscores our earlier comments regarding the diversity of index construction and the fact that the size of the hedge fund universe is not known with certainty. Furthermore, the wide range of historical risk/return performance carries over to the hedge fund subindexes. In Exhibit 9.4, we present the historical risk/return profile for equity long/short indexes.[10] There is just as much variability with an individual hedge fund style as there is with the composite indexes.

All of this means that when choosing a hedge fund composite index or subindex, an investor must use care to ensure that the chosen index is representative of her hedge fund investment program. For example

---

[10] Equity long/short hedge fund subindexes are also referred to as equity hedge (HFR and EACM), long/short hedged (Tuna funds), and market-neutral long/short (MAR and Van Hedge).

EXHIBIT 9.4   Long/Short Equity Hedge Fund Subindexes

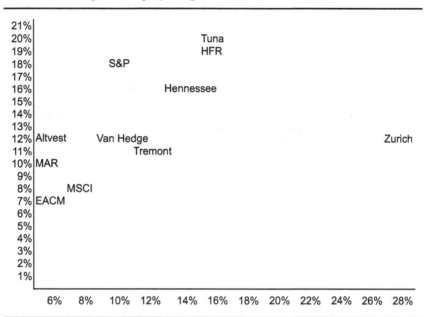

using the Zurich long/short equity hedge index to measure the performance of a program that resembles more the economic parameters of the MSCI long/short equity hedge index could lead to inaccurate conclusions regarding the performance of the program.

Correlation across Hedge Fund Indexes and Stock Indexes

Exhibit 9.5 presents a table of correlation measures between the hedge fund indexes and the stock indexes. We omit the S&P Hedge Fund Index and the MSCI Hedge Fund Index from this analysis because of their shorter, pro forma track records.

The variability of historical risk/return profiles is demonstrated in the correlation coefficients between the hedge fund indexes. The coefficients range from a high of 0.98 (Tuna funds/HFR) to a low of 0.67 (Tremont/Zurich). Most of the correlation coefficients are in the range of 0.8 to 0.9. Compared to equity stock indexes, these correlations are low; the correlation between the S&P 500 and the Russell 1000 stock indexes is 0.99, although the correlation between the S&P 500 and the Russell 2000 is only about 0.75. This simply underscores the fact that the hedge fund known universe is not known with certainty and while certain indexes

EXHIBIT 9.5 Correlation Coefficients between Hedge Fund Indexes and Stock Indexes

	Tuna Agg	Van Hedge	Hennessee	MAR	HFR	Zurich	Tremont	EACM	S&P 500	Russell 1000	Russell 2000	Barclays	Altvest
Tuna Agg	1.000												
Van Hedge	0.968	1.000											
Hennessee	0.983	0.986	1.000										
MAR	0.869	0.812	0.895	1.000									
HFR	0.980	0.982	0.992	0.882	1.000								
Zurich	0.935	0.952	0.959	0.818	0.919	1.000							
Tremont	0.842	0.777	0.842	0.927	0.877	0.673	1.000						
EACM	0.933	0.973	0.971	0.856	0.953	0.951	0.776	1.000					
S&P 500	0.681	0.520	0.542	0.455	0.578	0.454	0.575	0.383	1.000				
Russell 1000	0.695	0.532	0.556	0.477	0.591	0.470	0.589	0.401	0.999	1.000			
Russell 2000	0.883	0.793	0.858	0.861	0.873	0.765	0.870	0.717	0.744	0.753	1.000		
Barclays CTA	-0.501	-0.625	-0.575	-0.292	-0.549	-0.664	-0.174	-0.537	-0.099	-0.093	-0.454	1.000	
Altvest	0.989	0.979	0.986	0.859	0.996	0.916	0.862	0.934	0.644	0.655	0.888	-0.549	1.000

may capture similar parts of the universe, there is still a wider variation among hedge fund index returns than among equity index returns.

It is worthwhile to note that the Barclays CTA composite index is negatively correlated with both hedge fund and stock indexes. With respect to hedge fund indexes, a large component of these strategies include convergent, or arbitrage, type managers. That is, many hedge fund managers engage in arbitrage trades where they expect the prices of two securities to converge over time. These types of strategies are also known as short volatility (see the discussion in Chapter 6). However, managed futures strategies tend to be long volatility trades, or divergent trading. They thrive on higher volatility. As a result, managed futures provide good diversification benefits for other hedge fund styles.

It is interesting to note that the hedge fund indexes are much more highly correlated with small-cap stocks (represented by the Russell 2000) than with large-cap (S&P 500) or mid cap stocks (Russell 1000).[11] We offer two suggestions for this observation. First, the small-cap stock market is generally considered to be less efficient than large or mid cap stocks. To the extent that this market is driven by the similar pricing anomalies that drive hedge fund investment returns, a higher correlation of returns would be expected. Second, hedge fund managers may concentrate in small-cap stocks as a way to avoid the phenomenon of "crowded shorts." That is, hedge fund managers prefer to short stocks that do not already have a large short interest typically associated with larger capitalized companies.

Asset versus Equal Weighted

An asset-weighted index is susceptible to disproportionate representation from large funds that have a very large gain or loss in any given time period. Additionally, an asset-weighted index can be distorted by errors in reporting by larger funds. Furthermore, some of the largest funds choose not to report their data to public databases, and it may be difficult to interpret an asset weighted index return that does not include some of the larger hedge funds.

Equal weighting has the advantage of not favoring large funds or hedge fund strategies that attract a lot of capital (like global macro or relative value). Investors may be prone to chasing either returns or the latest hedge fund flavor of the year. This can distort a market capitalization index because the returns of a market cap index will be influenced by the flows of capital. Most hedge fund index providers argue that a hedge fund index should be equally-weighted to reflect fully all strategies.

---

[11] I am indebted to Matt Moran of the Chicago Board Options Exchange for pointing this out to me.

Yet there are two worthwhile arguments for an asset-weighted hedge fund index. First, smaller hedge funds can transact with a smaller market impact. An asset weighted index would more accurately reflect the full market impact from the hedge fund universe as it conducts its transactions. This is all the more important for hedge fund managers because of the nature of the high portfolio turnover associated with their frequent and opportunistic trading patterns.

Second, many other asset classes are benchmarked against capital weighted indexes. The S&P 500 and the Russell 1000, for example, are cap-weighted equity indexes. This is important because large institutional investors use these cap-weighted indexes in their asset allocation decision models. Therefore, to compare on an apples-to-apples basis, hedge fund indexes should also be cap-weighted when used for asset allocation decisions.

Index Diversification

The size of the 12 hedge fund indexes varies from 60 funds to over 5000. Most index providers have a single composite index with the exception of MAR and Zurich Capital. However, MAR provides a Fund of Funds median index that acts as a proxy for its total universe, while Zurich Capital does not. Each index provider constructs several sub-indexes so that the performance of specific hedge fund strategies can be tracked more closely.

But what is the right size of an index? For instance, does 60 funds offer sufficient diversification such that the idiosyncratic risk of individual managers are diversified away? Two studies have examined the issue of the proper diversification for hedge funds. Henker finds that the majority of idiosyncratic risk associated with equity long/short hedge funds can be diversified away with as little as 10 funds, while most of the risk is diversified away with about 20 funds.[12] Similarly, Park and Staum find that fund of funds about 95% of hedge fund idiosyncratic risk can be diversified away with 20 hedge funds.[13] Therefore, each hedge fund index listed in Exhibit 9.2 should provide a well-diversified benchmark of hedge fund performance.

However, another question that should be asked is how many hedge funds are necessary in an investment program to produce a correlation with a chosen hedge fund index that is sufficiently high? This is important since hedge fund indexes may be used for asset allocation purposes

---

[12] Thomas Henker, "Naïve Diversification for Hedge Funds," *Journal of Alternative Assets* (Winter 1998), pp. 33–38.

[13] James Park and Jeremy Staum, "Fund of Funds Diversification: How Much is Enough?" *Journal of Alternative Assets* (Winter 1998), pp. 39–42.

and the resulting hedge fund investment program should meet the expectations of the asset allocation study. L'habitant and Learned examine several hedge fund strategies, and find that an investment program of 20 hedge funds captures 80% to 90% of the correlation with the chosen hedge fund index.[14]

ASSET ALLOCATION WITH HEDGE FUND INDEXES

As we noted previously in this chapter, one of the benefits of a hedge fund index is that it can be used for asset allocation studies. Asset allocation studies are used to determine the target weights in a diversified portfolio to allocate across individual asset classes. In this example we seek to find the allocation that might be made to hedge funds using different hedge fund indexes. Asset allocation studies attempt to solve for the portfolio that provides the greatest utility to the investor.

When presented with various outcomes of portfolio return and volatility, an investor will choose the portfolio that provides the greatest expected utility. The issue we examine is whether the addition of hedge funds to a portfolio of stocks and bonds will increase an investor's expected utility beyond that obtained with only stocks and bonds.

The following equation has been used by many researchers to determine the target allocation level to be made across individual asset classes:[15]

$$E(U_i) = E(R_p) - A_i \sigma^2(R_p)$$

where

$E(U_i)$ is the expected utility of the i-th investor.
$E(R_p) = \Sigma_i w_i E(R_i)$ is the expected return of the portfolio.
$\sigma^2(R_p) = \Sigma_i \Sigma_j w_i w_j \sigma_i \sigma_j \rho_{ij}$ is the variance of the portfolio returns.
A_i is a measure of relative risk aversion for the i-th investor.
w_i and w_j are the portfolio weights of the i-th and j-th asset classes.

---

[14] Francois-Serge Lhabitant, and Michelle Learned, "Hedge Fund Diversification: How Much is Enough?" *Journal of Alternative Investments* (Winter 2002), pp. 23–49.
[15] See Philippe Jorion, "Risk Management Lessons Learned from Long Term Capital Management," working paper, University of California at Irvine, 2000; Richard Grinold and Ronald Kahn, *Active Portfolio Management* (New York: McGraw-Hill, 2000); William Sharpe, "Asset Allocation," in John Maginn and Donald Tuttle (eds.), *Managing Investment Portfolios: A Dynamic Process* (New York: Warren, Gorham and Lamont, 1990); and Mark Anson, "Maximizing Expected Utility with Commodity Futures," *Journal of Portfolio Management* (Summer 1999), pp. 86–94.

σ_i and σ_j are the volatilities of the i-th and j-th asset classes.
ρ_{ij} is the correlation coefficient between the I-th and j-th asset classes.

The expected utility in the equation may be viewed as the expected return on the investor's portfolio minus a risk penalty. The risk penalty is equal to the risk of the portfolio multiplied by the investor's relative risk aversion. This is another way to say that the equation is just a risk-adjusted expected rate of return for the portfolio, where the risk adjustment depends on the level of an investor's risk aversion.

It should be noted that the equation is based on the mean and variance and does not include the higher moments of the return distribution such as skew and kurtosis that we discussed in Chapter 6. Three comments are necessary. First, incorporating higher moments into a utility function can lead to the counter economic results of increasing marginal utility.[16] Second, the impact of skew or kurtosis for an asset class should have a lesser impact within a diversified portfolio. Finally, most investors apply a mean-variance analysis in their asset allocation models.

Whether we call the equation the expected utility or the risk-adjusted return, solving this function requires quadratic programming. This is because solving for $E(U)$ involves both squared terms (the individual asset variances) as well as multiplicative terms (the covariances of the various asset classes). The important point to realize is that quadratic solutions recognize that the risk of the portfolio depends upon the interactions among the asset classes.

There are two problems with determining the exact asset allocation for hedge funds. First, utility functions are hard to define in terms of all of the factors that affect investors' behavior. Second, even if a utility function could be specified for each investor, these functions would be as varied and as different as the investors they attempt to describe. Consequently, asset allocation and expected utility will be unique for each investor.

Instead of trying to describe the unique benefits of hedge funds for every investor, we develop a simple scale to measure risk aversion. An asset allocation study should consider how an investor's behavior is affected by his or her tolerance for risk. In this asset allocation example we specifically incorporate investors' risk preferences into their investment decisions by maximizing expected utility as the objective function, with the level of risk aversion incorporated in the equation.

---

[16] See Pierre-Yves Moix, "The Measurement of Market Risk," Ph.D. dissertation, University of St. Gallen, 2000. Increasing marginal utility would mean that the more an investor invests in hedge funds, the greater the utility. There is no point of saturation. This would lead to an even higher allocation to hedge funds than shown in the accompanying exhibit.

In this example, we consider three levels of investor risk aversion: low, moderate, and high. At low risk aversion, the investor is driven to maximize total return instead of reducing risk. At the moderate level of risk aversion, risk reduction becomes a more important factor. At a high level of risk aversion, reducing risk becomes more important than maximizing total return. As the level of risk aversion increases portfolio volatility becomes a greater concern in the investor's utility function, and the investor will seek greater diversification to manage her risk.

We use four hedge fund indexes that have data back to 1990: Tuna Aggregate, HFRI FOF index, Hennessee Index, and CISDM/MAR index. It is important have as a long a historical track record as possible when conducting asset allocation studies, because in any short time period (five years, for example) the relationships among asset classes can become distorted.[17] We include the S&P 500 to represent stock market exposure, 10-year Treasury bonds to represent bond market exposure, the High-Yield Bonds to represent credit exposure, and one-year Treasury bills to represent cash. Our objective is to mix these asset classes together with hedge funds according to the above equation, to see what is the optimal asset allocation to hedge funds.

A constrained optimization program is run to solve the equation at each level of risk aversion.[18] In Exhibit 9.6 we present the results for each hedge fund index.

At low levels of risk aversion, there is a very high allocation to hedge funds—as high as 87% for the low risk averse investor using the Tuna Aggregate index. However, as the investor's level of risk aversion increases, we see that the amount allocated to hedge funds declines. The reason is that these asset classes have less than perfect correlation with each other. By diversifying across a number of asset classes, the investor can reduce the volatility of her investment portfolio. This volatility dampening effect has greater utility as the level of risk aversion increases.

Similar results are found for HFRI, Hennessee, and the CISDM/MAR indexes. Smaller amounts are allocated to hedge funds as risk aversion grows. The reason that so much is allocated to hedge funds at low a low level of risk aversion is because the four hedge fund indexes have a very favorable risk and return tradeoff—high levels of return with low to moderate levels of volatility.

---

[17] For an example of this, see Mark Anson, "Maximizing Utility with Private Equity," *Journal of Investing* (Summer 2001), pp. 17–25.

[18] To solve the utility maximization equation, we program an optimization as follows:

$$\text{Maximize } E(U) = \Sigma_i w_i E(R_i) - A_i \Sigma_i \Sigma_j w_i w_j \sigma_i \sigma_j \rho_{ij}$$

Subject to the constraints $\Sigma w_i = 1$, and $0 \leq w_i \leq 1$.

EXHIBIT 9.6 Asset Allocation with Different Hedge Fund Indexes

Tuna Aggregate

Risk Aversion	Hedge Fund	10 yr. T-bond	S&P 500	1 yr. T-bill	High Yield	Expected Utility	Sharpe Ratio
Low	0.87	0.13	0	0	0	0.12	1.19
Moderate	0.66	0.34	0	0	0	0.095	1.25
High	0.46	0.24	0	0.3	0	0.079	1.2

HFRI FOF Index

Risk Aversion	Hedge Fund	10 yr. T-bond	S&P 500	1 yr. T-bill	High Yield	Expected Utility	Sharpe Ratio
Low	0.62	0.38	0	0	0	0.0944	0.88
Moderate	0.36	0.25	0	0.39	0	0.073	0.845
High	0.25	0.15	0	0.6	0	0.0648	0.781

Hennessee Index

Risk Aversion	Hedge Fund	10 yr. T-bond	S&P 500	1 yr. T-bill	High Yield	Expected Utility	Sharpe Ratio
Low	0.61	0.39	0	0	0	0.09	0.84
Moderate	0.38	0.3	0	0.32	0	0.07	0.789
High	0.25	0.18	0	0.57	0	0.0616	0.696

CISDM/MAR Index

Risk Aversion	Hedge Fund	10 yr. T-bond	S&P 500	1 yr. T-bill	High Yield	Expected Utility	Sharpe Ratio
Low	0.66	0.33	0.01	0	0	0.079	0.69
Moderate	0.46	0.24	0	0.3	0	0.066	0.659
High	0.32	0.14	0	0.54	0	0.06	0.59

Notice that there is a very large range of allocations to hedge funds depending upon the hedge fund index selected and the level of risk aversion of the investor. Allocation levels range from 25% to 87%. Such a wide range of results would not be expected for a homogenous asset class. This simply highlights our earlier point that the hedge fund universe is unknowable—each index has its own methods of construction that results in very little overlap with other available hedge fund indexes.

Therefore, should a hedge fund index be used for asset allocation purposes, the investor must take care to select an index that reflects the economic parameters of the hedge fund program that is expected to be implemented. Otherwise, unusual results may result from an asset allocation study.

As a final note, as a practical matter, most large institutional investors would not normally allocate more than 25% of their investment portfolio to hedge funds although some endowments and foundations do go as high as 50%. In fact, most public pension funds have a less than 5% allocation to hedge funds, and many place a specific asset allocation limit on hedge fund investing in the 1% to 10% range. Therefore, many of the allocation examples presented in Exhibit 9.6 might be beyond an explicit asset allocation constraint.

SUMMARY

Benchmarks serve two useful purposes. First, they provide a yardstick for measuring performance of an asset class or an individual external manager. Second, they can be used in asset allocation studies to determine how much to allocate among broad asset classes. Benchmarks are tools for building and monitoring portfolios.

With respect to hedge funds, investors have a wide variety to choose from. Unfortunately, there is a lack of consistency in the construction of hedge fund indexes. This lack of consistency was demonstrated in the wide range of risk and return measures in Exhibits 9.3 and 9.4 as well as the wide range of correlation coefficients in Exhibit 9.5.

This creates two distinct problems. First, given the large range of performance among the hedge fund indexes, an investment manager who invests in hedge funds can significantly outperform or underperform her bogey by the choice of hedge fund index. Second, asset allocation studies that are driven by the risk/return tradeoff of different asset classes may over or under allocate to hedge fund investments based on the simple choice of hedge fund index. Some variability among hedge fund indexes is good, but too much can result in misleading asset allocation decisions. Last, all of these indexes suffer from several data biases that can boost returns by 3% to 4%.

In summary, the world of hedge fund performance measurement is still maturing. Currently, there are many indexes to choose from, each with its own pros and cons. Also, the consistency among hedge fund indexes is considerably less than that than for equity indexes. Perhaps the best way to choose a hedge fund index is to first state clearly the risk and return objectives of the hedge fund investment program. With this as their guide, investors can then make an informed benchmark selection.

CHAPTER 10

Hedge Fund Incentive Fees and the "Free Option"

Hedge fund managers earn money from two sources: management fees and incentive fees. The management fee is a constant percentage applied to the amount of assets managed in the hedge fund while the incentive fee is a form of profit sharing. Incentive fees are received only if the hedge fund manager earns a profitable return for its investors.

While management fees are widely accepted throughout the money management industry, it is the incentive fees that draw the most scrutiny and publicity. The fact is that incentive fees may be considered as a "free option." In this chapter we review the nature of this incentive fee option, provide a way to value the option, and then consider some of the interesting ways this option can motivate hedge fund manager behavior.

HEDGE FUND INCENTIVE FEES

One attraction of the hedge fund market place for money managers is the ability to share in the profits earned for clients. Mutual fund managers, for example, are prohibited by law from accepting fees based on performance.[1] Mutual funds may only charge a management fee. In contrast, hedge fund managers may charge both a management fee and a profit-sharing fee.

The general rule of thumb in the hedge fund market is "2 and 20." That is, a 2% management fee and a 20% incentive fee. However, hedge

---

[1] See Section 205 of the Investment Advisers Act of 1940.

fund fees may range from 1% to 3% for management fees and up to 40% for incentive fees.

The management fee is collected whether or not the hedge fund manager earns a profit. The management fee may be collected on a quarterly, semiannual or annual basis while the incentive fee is collected annually. An incentive fee is collected by the hedge fund manager if the end-of-year net asset value of the hedge fund is greater than the beginning-of-year net asset value.

HEDGE FUND FEES AND OPTION THEORY

Hedge fund incentive fees can be considered a call option on a portion of the profits that the hedge fund manager earns for her investors. If the manager earns a profit, she collects an incentive fee. If the hedge fund manager does not earn a profit, she collects no fee. This binary type of payoff is the same as the payout for a call option and may be described as

$$\text{Payout on incentive fees} = \text{Max}\,[i(\text{ENAV} - \text{BNAV}),\, 0] \qquad (10.1)$$

where

> i is the incentive fee rate, e.g., 20%.
> ENAV is the ending net asset value of the hedge fund.
> BNAV is the strike price of the call option and is equal to the beginning net asset value of the hedge fund at the start of the period.

The option on incentive fees is "free" because the manager does not have to pay for it. If the option is out of the money at maturity—the end of the year—the hedge fund manager is not out of pocket any option premium. Conversely, if the option is in the money at the end of the year, the hedge fund manager exercises the option and collects her incentive fee.

The maturity of the incentive fee option is one year. That is at the beginning of every year, the hedge fund manager receives a new call option from investors to share in the increase in hedge fund value at yearend. If the hedge fund does not increase in value over the course of the year, the incentive fee call option expires worthless. If the hedge fund increases in value over the course of the year, the hedge fund manager exercises the option at yearend and collects an incentive fee.

Equation (10.1) describes the payout at maturity for a call option. Using risk neutral pricing, the current value of the incentive fee option may be expressed as[2]

$$\text{Call(incentive fee)} = e^{-r(T - t)} \times \text{Max}[i(\text{ENAV} - \text{BNAV}), 0] \qquad (10.2)$$

where

r is the risk-free rate.

$T - t$ is the time until maturity of the option.

e is the exponential operator.

If an investor could approximate the expected return for the hedge fund, $E(R)$, then equation (10.2) can be expressed as

$$\text{Call(incentive fee)} = e^{-r(T - t)} \times \text{Max}[i(e^{R(T - t)} \times \text{BNAV} - \text{BNAV}), 0] \qquad (10.3)$$

where

R is the expected return earned by the hedge fund manager.

Equation (10.3) says that the current value of the call option is equal to the discounted value of the expected future incentive fees col-

---

[2] One of the great insights of Black and Scholes is that an option can be combined with stock to form a portfolio that is precisely hedged from market risk. (See Fisher Black and Myron Scholes, "The Pricing of Options and Corporate Liabilities," *The Journal of Political Economy*, vol. 81 (1973), pp. 637–654.) With this insight, Black and Scholes concluded that an option can be priced using a risk-free discount rate.

Another way to infer the risk-neutral valuation property is to consider the Black-Scholes differential equation for pricing derivative securities:

$$\delta f / \delta t + rS \delta f / \delta S + (?^2/2)S^2 \delta^2 f / \delta S^2 = rf$$

where

S is the underlying stochastic variable, e.g., stock prices.

f is the price of the derivative security, a function of S and time, t.

r is the risk-free rate.

δ is the volatility of the underlying stochastic variable, e.g., the volatility of stock price.

The above equation does not involve any variable that is affected by the risk preferences of investors. Black and Scholes were able to conclude that if risk preferences do not enter into the above equation, they cannot affect its solution. Therefore, any set of risk preferences will satisfy the above equation, including the simplifying assumption of risk neutral preferences.

lected at the end of the reporting period. The expected future fees are dependent upon the hedge fund manager earning a rate of return of $E(R)$ over time period $(T - t)$.

We measure the value of the hedge fund manager's call option on incentive fees using the Black-Scholes option pricing model:

$$\text{Call(incentive fees)} = i \times (\text{NAV} \times N(d_1) - e^{-r(T-t)} \times \text{BNAV} \times N(d_2)) \quad (10.4)$$

where

NAV is the monthly NAV for the hedge fund.
BNAV is the beginning net asset value.
$N(d_1)$ and $N(d_2)$ are the cumulative probability distribution function for a standard unit normal variable.[3]

The other terms are defined as before.

The Black-Scholes option pricing model is dependent upon five inputs: the current value of the asset, the strike price, the time until maturity of the option, the risk-free rate, and the volatility of the underlying asset's returns. The call option on incentive fees is affected by these five variables, plus one more; the size of the profit sharing percentage, i:

$$\text{Call(incentive fees)} = f(\text{NAV, BNAV}, T - t, r, \sigma, i) \quad (10.5)$$

There are some issues with applying the Black-Scholes formula to hedge fund incentive fees. First, the Black-Scholes model assumes continuous trading and pricing. Unfortunately, hedge fund asset values are determined discretely, at monthly intervals.[4] In addition, the Black-Scholes model assumes that short selling of all securities is permitted, and hedge fund limited partnership units cannot be sold short. Last, each security is assumed to be perfectly divisible whereas limited partnership units are not divisible and may be denominated in large values of $1,000 or more.

---

[3] $d1 = [\ln(\text{NAV/BNAV}) + (r + \sigma^2/2) \times (T-t)]/(\sigma\sqrt{(T-t)})$ and $d2 = d1 - \sigma\sqrt{(T-t)}$.
[4] One solution to this problem might be a discrete time option-pricing model such as a binomial tree. (See John Cox, Stephen Ross, and Martin Rubinstein, "Options Pricing: A Simplified Approach," *Journal of Financial Economics* (September 1979), pp. 229–263 and Richard Rendleman and Clifford Smith, "Two-State Option Pricing," *Journal of Finance* (December 1979), pp. 1093–1110.) Alternatively, Goetzmann, Ingersoll, and Ross) provide a continuous-time diffusion process for hedge fund net asset values. (See William Goetzmann, Jonathan Ingersoll, Jr., and Stephen Ross, "High-Water Marks and Hedge Fund Management Contracts," working paper presented at the Berkeley Program in Finance (March 2001).)

Conversely, there are some distinct advantages to applying the Black-Scholes option pricing model with respect to hedge fund incentive fees. First, the Black-Scholes model was developed for European options—options that can be exercised only at maturity. This is consistent with the way hedge fund managers collect their incentive fees; they collect incentive fees only at yearend—at the expiration of the option. Second, the Black-Scholes model assumes that no dividends are paid during the life of the option. This is also consistent with the fact that hedge funds rarely make intermediate distributions to their investors.

DATA AND RESULTS

We use data from the Hedge Fund Research Inc. over the time period 1990 to 2005. We examine the returns for three of the most popular types of hedge fund strategies: equity long/short, convertible arbitrage, and merger arbitrage. These strategies provide a spectrum of return distributions and resulting call option values. Exhibit 10.1 provides summary statistics for these three strategies.

Exhibit 10.1 demonstrates that equity long/short hedge fund managers have the highest volatility associated with their strategy. The Black-Scholes model teaches us that the higher the volatility, the more valuable the option, other factors held equal. Consequently, equity long/short managers benefit from the higher volatility created by their trading strategies.

At the beginning of each calendar year the strike price for the call option on incentive fees is struck to the beginning of year net asset value, provided that the hedge fund manager earned a profit in the prior year. This is the same as setting the strike price for the incentive fee call option at the money each year.

However, should the hedge fund manager lose money in any calendar year, the strike price for the incentive fee call option is struck at the previous "High Watermark" for the hedge fund. The high watermark is the previous highest net asset value achieved by the hedge fund manager. Typically, a hedge fund manager may not collect incentive fees until it

EXHIBIT 10.1   Summary Performance Statistics

Trading Strategy	Expected Return	Standard Deviation	Sharpe Ratio
Equity Long/Short	17.74%	13.84%	0.92
Convertible Arbitrage	10.14%	7.28%	0.71
Merger Arbitrage	10.25%	7.02%	0.75

has exceeded the previous high watermark. The high watermark becomes the new strike price for the incentive fee call option. Consequently, if a hedge fund manager loses money in any calendar year, the strike price for the incentive fee call option will be struck at the previous high watermark. This is the same as setting the strike price "out of the money." Setting the strike price for the incentive fee call option out of the money means that the strike price is set at a net asset value that is greater than the current net asset value of the hedge fund. This is done because if the hedge fund manager loses money in any calendar year, the current net asset value of the hedge fund will be below the high watermark. Call options that have strike prices struck out of the money will be less valuable than call options struck at the money.

Most hedge fund managers collect the incentive fee annually. Therefore, we measure the value of the call option on incentive fees over the course of one year. From month to month, the value of the call option will increase or decrease depending whether the net asset value is higher or lower than the beginning net asset value.

Exhibit 10.2 provides the month by month return earned by equity long/short managers and the month by month incentive fee call option value.[5] In each of Exhibits 10.2, 10.3, and 10.4, we assume an incentive fee of 20% for purposes of valuing the call option.

Each month represents the value of the incentive fee call option to the hedge fund manager per $1,000,000 of assets managed. Notice how the value of the incentive fee call option increases with positive monthly returns and decreases with negative monthly returns. In January, February, and March of 2004, for example, the incentive fee option increased in value as positive returns were earned. However, the incentive fee option declined in value in April, May, July, and August as negative returns were recorded in those months.

At maturity, the value of the incentive fee call option reduces to the formula in equation (10.1). It is simply a percentage (20%) of the increase in net asset value in the hedge fund.

Exhibit 10.2 Panels A and B present the simple case where the incentive fee call option is struck at the money at the beginning of every calendar year, unless there was a negative return in the prior year. We can see that for equity long/short managers, there was only one negative year, 2002. Therefore, for year 2003, the hedge fund incentive fee for equity long/short managers was out of the money, and the strike price for the option was set at the prior high watermark. In all prior years

---

[5] HFRI databases provide hedge fund returns net of incentive and management fees. Therefore, the returns have been adjusted to provide returns before management and incentive fees have been deducted.

EXHIBIT 10.2 HFRI Equity Hedge
Panel A. Monthly Returns (in percent)

Year	Jan	Feb	Mar	Apr	May	Jun	Jul	Aug	Sep	Oct	Nov	Dec	YTD
2005	-0.58	2.13	-1.05	-2.23	1.55	1.96	2.95	0.73	2.32	-1.87	2.13	2.34	10.62
2004	1.95	1.11	0.36	-2.08	-0.19	1.07	-1.88	-0.37	1.99	0.48	3.37	1.76	7.68
2003	-0.01	-0.78	-0.07	2.43	4.08	1.52	2.41	2.38	0.78	3.12	1.14	1.93	20.54
2002	0.22	-0.89	2.03	0.17	0	-2.63	-3.93	0.28	-1.96	0.56	2.67	-1.14	-4.71
2001	2.88	-2.56	-2.3	2.27	0.9	-0.32	-1.06	-1.22	-3.73	1.85	1.97	1.99	0.4
2000	0.25	10	1.73	-4.19	-2.44	4.85	-1.58	5.35	-1.08	-2.01	-4.3	3.16	9.09
1999	4.98	-2.41	4.05	5.25	1.22	3.8	0.61	0.04	0.35	2.33	6.76	10.88	44.22
1998	-0.16	4.09	4.54	1.39	-1.27	0.5	-0.67	-7.65	3.16	2.47	3.84	5.39	15.98
1997	2.78	-0.24	-0.73	-0.27	5.04	1.97	5.05	1.35	5.69	0.39	-0.93	1.42	23.41
1996	1.06	2.82	1.9	5.34	3.7	-0.73	-2.87	2.63	2.18	1.56	1.66	0.83	21.75
1995	0.3	1.68	2.09	2.64	1.22	4.73	4.46	2.93	2.9	-1.44	3.43	2.56	31.04
1994	2.35	-0.4	-2.08	-0.37	0.41	-0.41	0.91	1.27	1.32	0.4	-1.48	0.74	2.61
1993	2.09	-0.57	3.26	1.3	2.72	3.01	2.12	3.84	2.52	3.11	-1.93	3.59	27.94
1992	2.49	2.9	-0.28	0.27	0.85	-0.92	2.76	-0.85	2.51	2.03	4.51	3.38	21.32
1991	4.9	5.2	7.22	0.47	3.2	0.59	1.41	2.17	4.3	1.16	-1.08	5.02	40.15
1990	-3.34	2.85	5.67	-0.87	5.92	2.52	2	-1.88	1.65	0.77	-2.29	1.02	14.43

EXHIBIT 10.2 HFRI Equity Hedge (Continued)
Panel B. Incentive Fee Call Option (per $1,000,000 of net assets)

Year	Jan	Feb	Mar	Apr	May	Jun	Jul	Aug	Sep	Oct	Nov	Dec
2005	$10,520	$13,407	$11,471	$7,936	$9,754	$12,583	$17,891	$19,323	$24,442	$21,532	$26,461	$21,420
2004	14,310	15,913	16,311	12,447	11,834	13,363	9,811	8,835	12,010	$12,793	$20,112	15,360
2003	10,754	9,731	9,637	13,269	21,072	24,906	31,330	38,151	41,074	49,521	53,018	41,080
2002	11,429	9,634	12,046	11,762	11,194	$6,715	2,009	1,681	145	-23	542	0
2001	15,568	10,963	7,301	9,767	10,555	9,480	7,295	5,009	883	1,510	2,542	800
2000	11,750	29,374	33,241	23,845	18,724	28,860	25,336	37,581	35,138	30,514	20,670	18,180
1999	20,764	17,482	26,670	40,000	44,812	55,974	59,493	61,583	64,483	72,614	93,050	88,440
1998	11,361	17,967	27,043	30,423	27,927	29,440	28,325	11,853	18,316	24,219	33,233	31,960
1997	16,194	16,110	15,166	15,016	25,261	30,338	42,822	46,932	61,637	63,520	61,970	46,820
1996	13,373	18,375	22,407	34,349	43,729	42,740	36,541	43,527	49,523	54,095	59,023	43,500
1995	12,507	15,726	20,203	26,449	30,185	42,231	54,208	62,812	71,634	69,123	79,644	62,080
1994	14,781	13,692	10,016	9,009	9,093	7,982	8,776	10,300	12,224	12,639	9,255	5,220
1993	15,214	14,716	21,143	24,530	31,346	39,331	45,485	55,892	63,346	72,588	68,560	55,880
1992	15,643	21,150	20,997	21,966	24,231	22,786	29,482	28,227	34,730	40,157	51,551	42,640
1991	20,468	32,251	50,365	53,296	63,068	66,415	71,940	79,627	93,459	98,929	97,872	80,300
1990	7,112	10,605	19,955	18,358	30,764	36,936	42,091	37,942	42,237	44,418	39,168	28,860

EXHIBIT 10.3 HFRI Convertible Arbitrage

Panel A. Index Returns (in percent)

Year	Jan	Feb	Mar	Apr	May	Jun	Jul	Aug	Sep	Oct	Nov	Dec	YTD
2005	-0.9	-0.44	-1.48	-2.64	-1.17	1.03	1.18	0.57	1.23	-0.07	0.04	0.77	-2.00
2004	1.01	0.18	0.68	0.25	-1.19	-1.04	0.46	0.27	-0.25	-0.48	0.88	0.43	1.18
2003	2.5	1.29	0.73	1.36	1.14	-0.57	-0.7	-0.69	1.41	1.4	0.81	0.88	9.93
2002	1.38	0.19	0.46	0.87	0.53	0.22	-1.28	0.35	1.59	1	2.02	1.42	9.05
2001	2.73	1.7	1.68	1.57	0.71	0.13	0.76	1.26	0.64	0.93	0.62	-0.08	13.37
2000	1.91	2.21	1.75	1.78	1.34	1.66	0.68	1.42	1.21	0.42	-0.71	-0.01	14.5
1999	2.11	0.25	1.53	2.66	1.4	1.09	1.05	0.42	0.66	0.33	0.99	1.08	14.41
1998	1.91	1.52	1.58	1.35	0.4	0.22	0.49	-3.19	-1.07	-0.48	3.33	1.6	7.77
1997	1.01	1.11	0.59	0.68	1.4	1.71	1.61	1.14	1.11	1.19	0.09	0.41	12.72
1996	1.82	1.06	1.17	1.88	1.73	0.44	-0.37	1.4	1.23	1.27	1.4	0.66	14.56
1995	0.55	0.98	1.83	1.9	1.88	2.32	2.13	0.96	1.55	1.25	1.58	1.33	19.85
1994	0.66	0.24	-2.11	-2.79	0.03	0.15	1.55	0.8	0.12	-0.09	-0.79	-1.48	-3.73
1993	0.93	0.86	2.19	1.5	1.24	1.04	1.41	1.4	1.03	1.29	0.6	0.77	15.22
1992	2.12	0.94	0.99	0.8	1.7	0.71	1.85	1.65	1.46	1.24	0.7	1.09	16.35
1991	0.44	1.61	1.39	1.49	0.94	0.98	1.57	2.09	1.31	1.22	1.66	1.63	17.6
1990	-1.47	-0.92	1.26	1.48	1.75	1.72	1.15	-0.18	-0.47	-1.56	-0.05	-0.49	2.16

EXHIBIT 10.3 HFRI Convertible Arbitrage (Continued)
Panel B. Incentive Fee Call Option (per $1,000,000 of net assets)

Year	Jan	Feb	Mar	Apr	May	Jun	Jul	Aug	Sep	Oct	Nov	Dec
2005	$9,979	$8,828	$6,391	$3,266	$2,029	$2,236	$2,583	$2,472	$2,930	$2,091	$1,231	$0
2004	12,938	12,736	13,376	13,300	10,723	8,492	8,621	8,451	7,385	5,875	6,712	6,950
2003	15,733	17,942	19,234	21,882	24,223	22,969	21,431	19,911	22,922	26,004	27,831	28,825
2002	13,809	13,917	14,508	15,900	16,741	17,017	14,302	14,816	17,972	20,047	24,405	26,625
2001	16,256	19,417	22,823	26,225	27,911	28,361	30,228	33,263	34,937	37,309	38,991	37,425
2000	14,886	18,923	22,487	26,368	29,485	33,418	35,226	38,772	41,904	43,207	41,796	40,250
1999	15,223	15,671	18,557	24,014	27,184	29,792	32,380	33,586	35,359	36,390	38,982	40,025
1998	14,649	17,118	19,941	22,510	23,208	23,548	24,491	17,420	15,004	13,819	20,726	23,425
1997	13,327	15,138	16,155	17,415	20,212	23,859	27,473	30,158	32,834	35,744	36,137	35,800
1996	14,736	16,629	18,897	22,785	26,623	27,796	27,196	30,542	33,583	36,779	40,348	40,400
1995	12,685	14,500	18,109	22,251	26,654	32,231	37,578	40,356	44,585	48,191	52,688	53,625
1994	12,340	12,187	8,433	4,542	4,049	3,651	4,659	4,965	4,396	3,475	1,614	0
1993	13,282	14,743	18,834	21,970	24,760	27,240	30,618	34,064	36,736	40,066	41,821	42,050
1992	15,309	17,089	19,108	20,883	24,648	26,458	30,843	34,914	38,649	41,950	44,023	44,875
1991	12,573	15,367	18,087	21,258	23,493	25,916	29,725	34,822	38,268	41,577	46,011	48,000
1990	9,235	7,555	8,735	10,428	12,851	15,567	17,417	16,619	15,214	11,533	10,981	9,400

EXHIBIT 10.4 HFRI Merger Arbitrage
Panel A. Monthly Returns (in percent)

Year	Jan	Feb	Mar	Apr	May	Jun	Jul	Aug	Sep	Oct	Nov	Dec	YTD
2005	-0.03	0.72	0.12	-1.42	1.62	1.14	1.12	0.74	0.69	-1.57	1.29	1.81	6.24
2004	1.02	0.59	0.07	-0.85	-0.14	0.32	-1.02	0.2	0.59	0.54	1.62	1.1	4.08
2003	0.15	-0.01	-0.1	1.29	1.76	0.43	0.71	0.69	0.63	0.72	0.29	0.69	7.47
2002	0.86	-0.36	0.56	-0.04	-0.25	-1.23	-1.9	0.5	-0.44	0.36	0.59	0.52	-0.87
2001	1.1	0.44	-0.75	0.23	1.69	-0.84	0.93	0.87	-2.72	0.84	0.23	0.78	2.76
2000	1.63	1.88	0.82	2.47	1.51	1.58	1.19	1.34	1.44	0.48	1.2	1.16	18.02
1999	0.71	0.25	1.05	1.31	2.04	1.61	1.38	0.52	1.25	0.69	2.23	0.46	14.34
1998	0.96	1.89	1.05	1.59	-0.6	0.5	-0.57	-5.69	1.74	2.14	2.33	1.94	7.23
1997	1.04	0.39	1.05	-0.7	1.92	2.13	1.6	1.04	2.13	0.84	2.02	1.9	16.44
1996	1.57	1.29	1.51	1.62	1.46	0.78	0.81	1.64	0.81	1.23	1.38	1.37	16.61
1995	0.86	1.45	1.49	0.35	1.26	2.47	1.35	1.35	1.63	0.91	2.13	1.31	17.86
1994	1.5	-0.41	1.37	-0.25	1.22	0.89	0.68	1.99	0.59	-0.26	-0.22	1.48	8.88
1993	2.12	1.64	0.49	1.3	1.17	2.25	1.54	1.67	1.85	2.05	0.86	1.65	20.24
1992	1.96	0.96	1.34	0.14	0	0.3	1.45	0.12	1.34	0.4	-2.22	1.91	7.9
1991	0.01	1.59	2.3	2.83	1.55	1.12	1.44	0.64	1.1	1.41	1.38	1.2	17.86
1990	-6.46	1.71	2.9	0.98	2.28	0.73	0.02	-0.82	-4.58	0.73	2.19	1.21	0.44

EXHIBIT 10.4 HFRI Merger Arbitrage (Continued)
Panel B. Incentive Fee Call Option (per $1,000,000 of net assets)

Year	Jan	Feb	Mar	Apr	May	Jun	Jul	Aug	Sep	Oct	Nov	Dec
2005	$11,418	$12,164	$11,972	$9,316	$11,461	$13,065	$14,814	$15,957	$17,087	$14,085	$16,606	$12,480
2004	13,049	13,636	13,358	11,500	10,830	10,919	8,730	8,547	9,058	9,581	$12,491	8,160
2003	11,785	11,441	10,975	12,803	15,734	16,337	17,556	18,815	20,011	21,446	21,963	14,940
2002	12,655	11,543	11,890	11,261	10,273	7,755	4,606	4,536	3,315	2,925	2,685	0
2001	13,134	13,425	11,724	11,634	14,114	12,111	13,350	14,602	8,819	9,853	9,847	5,520
2000	14,534	18,051	19,855	25,181	28,792	32,693	35,820	39,363	43,220	44,856	48,265	36,040
1999	12,894	13,263	15,063	17,533	21,712	25,285	28,509	29,898	32,963	34,801	40,257	28,680
1998	13,058	16,020	17,729	20,644	19,222	20,054	18,676	7,358	9,926	13,880	18,645	14,460
1997	13,500	14,205	16,155	14,954	18,758	23,374	27,122	29,751	34,905	37,216	42,345	32,880
1996	14,384	16,747	19,767	23,263	26,635	28,650	30,785	34,844	37,085	40,349	44,038	33,220
1995	13,255	15,849	18,810	19,732	22,586	28,205	31,595	35,072	39,277	41,882	47,465	35,720
1994	13,999	13,086	15,241	14,579	16,678	18,292	19,573	23,730	24,976	24,354	23,819	17,760
1993	15,445	18,691	19,963	22,966	25,867	31,260	35,256	39,658	44,600	50,163	52,934	40,480
1992	14,735	16,195	18,495	18,578	18,391	18,820	21,696	21,833	24,648	25,447	20,392	15,800
1991	11,902	14,591	18,979	24,974	28,658	31,524	35,188	37,094	40,104	43,910	47,730	35,720
1990	3,666	4,664	7,294	8,040	10,911	11,582	11,033	8,974	2,129	2,037	3,737	880

where a positive return was earned, the incentive fee option was in the money where the ending net asset value of the prior year became the strike price for the incentive fee option in the following year. As long as the hedge fund manager earns a positive return, a new high watermark will be established, and the incentive fee call option will be struck at the money in the following year.

Exhibits 10.3 Panels A and B and 10.4 Panels A and B demonstrate the same results for convertible arbitrage and merger arbitrage hedge fund managers. It is clear from these exhibits that the incentive fee option is quite valuable to hedge fund managers.

CONCLUSIONS AND IMPLICATIONS

This chapter examined the option-like payout accruing to hedge fund managers for incentive fees. Hedge fund managers share in the upside of the hedge fund net asset value, but not the downside. The binary nature of this payout is the same as the payout to a call option at maturity. We used the Black-Scholes option pricing model to determine an approximate value of this option for three hedge fund strategies, and found that the option had considerable value.

There are several implications for how this option analysis can affect hedge fund manager behavior. First, an important implication of this analysis is that hedge fund managers can increase the value of their incentive fee call option by increasing the volatility of hedge fund net asset values. The holder of a call option will always prefer more variance in the value of the underlying asset because, the greater the variance, the greater the probability that the asset value will exceed the strike price at maturity of the option.

This establishes a key distinction between investors in the hedge fund and the hedge fund manager. Investors in the hedge fund own the underlying partnership units, and receive payoffs offered by the entire distribution of return outcomes associated with the hedge fund net asset value. They are generally risk averse and dislike higher volatility.

In contrast, the hedge fund manager is the holder of a contingent claim (the incentive fee call option) on the value of the underlying partnership units. The hedge fund manager, as the owner of the option, receives payoffs only from the tails of the hedge fund return distribution. The contingent claim nature of the incentive fee call option makes higher volatility in the net asset value of the hedge fund desirable to the hedge fund manager.

The irony is that investors in the hedge fund actually provide the incentive to the hedge fund manager to increase the volatility of the return distribution for the hedge fund. Furthermore, the higher the percentage of profit sharing, such as, a 30% profit sharing fee versus a 20% profit sharing fee, the greater the incentive for the hedge fund manager to increase the variance of the hedge fund's returns.

A second important implication of hedge fund manager behavior is how hedge fund managers react when their incentive fee call option is significantly out of the money. This happens when the hedge fund net asset value has declined significantly below the high watermark. Then the strike price for the incentive fee option is significantly out of the money—the current net asset value of the hedge fund is significantly below the previous high net asset value of the hedge fund.

When an option is out of the money the hedge fund manager has two choices to increase the value of the option. The first is to increase the volatility of the underlying asset. As the Black Scholes model demonstrates, one way to increase the value of the option is to increase the volatility of the underlying asset—for example, increasing the volatility of the hedge fund net asset value. This means that the hedge fund manager is encouraged to increase the volatility of the hedge fund's trading strategy to increase the value of the incentive fee call option.

Another strategy for a hedge fund manager to pursue is to reprice the option when it is out of the money. However, it is unlikely that the hedge fund manager's current investors will allow the hedge fund manager to lower the high water mark for the hedge fund manager back to the current (below water) hedge fund value. Therefore, the only way to reprice the incentive fee call option back to being "at the money" is to start a new hedge fund. With a new hedge fund, the incentive fee call option is automatically priced at the money at the start of any new hedge fund.

This is a growing phenomenon in the hedge fund world. Hedge fund managers that have their incentive fee struck out of the money often start new hedge funds. This leaves the existing investors from the old hedge fund out of luck when the hedge fund manager starts a new hedge fund and diverts his time and attention to the new hedge fund where the incentive fee call option is more valuable than the old hedge fund.

CHAPTER 11

Top Ten Hedge Fund Quotes

We turn now to a little humor surrounding the hedge fund industry. Throughout the course of my career at CalPERS and Hermes, I have visited with and have spoken to hundreds of hedge fund managers. At these meetings, I have asked the questions that were laid out in our chapter on due diligence. The responses from the hedge fund managers are not always what you would expect. So, I decided to compile my own "Top Ten List" of quotes from hedge fund managers to provide a humorous insight to the hedge fund industry.

At the outset, it should be realized that these quotes are not indicative of the whole industry. Rather, they demonstrate some of the chaff out there that has to be separated from the wheat. However, should you ever run across one of these quotes in your due diligence, proceed with caution. With no further ado, here we go.

NUMBER 10: "IF WE DON'T CHARGE 2 AND 20, NOBODY WILL TAKE US SERIOUSLY."

A while back a brand new hedge fund manager passed through CalPERS' investment offices looking to raise money. They knocked on our door through a contact well-known to CalPERS. The two principals of the hedge fund had successful track records investing in traditional long only securities, but had never started a hedge fund before.

When I inquired as to where they learned to short, their response was that they had not previously shorted securities in their investment program. I then inquired why these two novice hedge fund managers with no prior hedge fund experience should be worthy of a 2% management fee and a 20% profit sharing fee. And the response that I received was the quote above.

Let us take a moment to analyze their response. These two startup hedge fund managers did not take the time to justify their fees based on their investment acumen. Rather, they responded that their fee structure was what the market would bear—indeed, what the market expected from a hedge fund manager. There was no attempt to justify their fee structure based on their investment skill set.

Well, that may be what the market will bear, but not what CalPERS will bear. As a well-known investor in the hedge fund community, CalPERS is sometimes a bellwether indicator of what the market will accept, and in this case, we decided that we would not pay a 2-and-20 fee structure for neophyte hedge fund managers. Beware of hedge fund managers trying to justify their fees based on what they think that the market will bear.

NUMBER 9: "WE CHARGE 3 AND 30 BECAUSE THAT IS THE ONLY WAY WE CAN KEEP OUR ASSETS BELOW SEVERAL BILLION DOLLARS."

Top Ten Quote #9 is the mirror imaging of Top Ten Quote #10. A few years back a very well-known and successful hedge fund manager visited CalPERS headquarters. In the middle of their presentation, I asked what his fee structure was. He initially responded "3 and 30," which was followed by dead silence for about one-half minute until he came back with the quote above.

Let's analyze this statement a bit more. First, this gets back to an argument about what the market will bear. The hedge fund manager did not attempt to justify his fee structure based on his skill, investment acumen, or financial market insights. Rather, he justified it in terms of market demand.

Second, this manager was all about fee generation, not wealth generation. There is nothing in his statement that indicates that he is earning/making value for his clients. Granted, his statement does indicate some attempt to limit the capacity of his fund and he should be given some credit for that. Still this is a statement more about making the hedge fund manager rich than it is making his clients wealthy. Beware of hedge fund managers that focus on fees first and client wealth second.

NUMBER 8: "WE ARE 75% CASH BECAUSE WE CANNOT FIND SUFFICIENT INVESTMENTS."

This statement is bad on so many levels, it is hard to decide where to begin. First, this hedge fund manager billed himself as an equity long/short investor. The keyword there is "Equity" not "cash." His job is to find long/short investment opportunities in the U.S. equities market. Furthermore, the cash he had in his account was not generated by short rebates held at the prime broker—it was capital that had not been put to work.

This manager sat on cash during 2001 and 2002. Why? Because he had changed his stripes from an equity long/short investor to a market timer. In 2001 and 2002, the best way to outperform the U.S. equity market when it declined by double digits was to sit on cash. It was easy to generate significant profits compared to the U.S. equity market during the three year bear period of 2000 to 2002 and in turn, to earn generous incentive fees.

Second, when CalPERS or Hermes hires a manager, we expect our investment capital to put to full use. Cash is our decision, and we manage our cash position at monthly asset allocation meetings. We expect our external managers to put to work fully the investment capital that they have been allocated. If an external manager decides to sit on cash in a Hermes account, it introduces an unintended bet into the portfolio. Managers that cannot find sufficient investments should return the capital to their investors.

Third, neither CalPERS or Hermes are willing to pay a 2% management fee for a manager to sit on cash. Hedge fund managers that sit on cash are the most expensive cash managers on the face of the earth. At the beginning of 2006, with overnight money earning 4.5% in the United States less a 2% hedge fund manager fee, cash balances held by hedge fund managers only earn investors 2.5%—you are better off putting this money to work in short-term U.S. Treasury bills.

NUMBER 7: "WE DON'T INVEST IN CROWDED SHORTS."

I cannot count the number of times that I have heard this statement from hedge fund managers. First, what does the term "crowded shorts" mean? This refers to a situation where a large group of hedge fund managers collectively short the same stock in expectation that it will decline in value. The shorting becomes crowded because all of the hedge fund managers rush to their prime brokers and request the same stock to borrow for their shorting strategies.

There are two problems with crowded short positions. First, crowded short positions can lead to the phenomenon of "beta expansion." This is the case where the stock price becomes even more sensitive to the movements of the stock market—its beta "expands" to reflect a greater covariance with the stock market than an investor would normally expect. We showed a demonstration of this in our chapter on risk management. This can contribute to additional volatility in the stock price as well as a covariance with the broader stock market that is temporarily out of balance.

The second issue is one of a "short squeeze." Short squeezes occur when hedge fund managers have to cover their short sales by purchasing in the market the underlying stock that they had previously shorted. This now puts upward pressure on the stock price, reducing the profits to the shorting strategy. The last few hedge fund managers to evacuate their short position as the stock price increases are "squeezed" and see their profits from the short position erode dramatically. This phenomenon is all the more exacerbated the more crowded the short position.

Yet all of this should not be a problem if hedge fund managers never invest in crowded shorts. In fact, based on the number of times that I have heard hedge fund managers claim that they do not invest in crowded shorts, this phenomenon does not exist at all. Therefore, the associated phenomena of beta expansion and short squeezes are really just figments of our overheated investor imaginations!

Come on, we all know that crowded shorts exist and we have all seen the phenomena of beta expansion and short squeezes. This top 10 quote demonstrates that you sometimes have to take with a large grain of salt that which hedge fund managers tell you.

NUMBER 6: "I HAVEN'T SHORTED BEFORE BUT I DO HAVE MY CFA."

Again we have the example of an inexperienced hedge fund manager who came from the world of traditional long-only investing. While it is commendable that this new hedge fund manager had his Chartered Financial Analyst (CFA) designation, this alone does not qualify him to be an expert in shorting stocks.

Shorting securities is very different than traditional long-only investing. First, there is unlimited downside with a shorted security. With a long position the maximum amount an investor can lose is the dollar amount invested as the long position can decline no further than zero. However, for a short position, in theory, the loss can be unlimited because the stock price has no bounds on how high it can go.

Second, as we just discussed above, the phenomena of beta expansion and short squeezes are new challenges to hedge fund managers that do not occur in the world of long only management.

Third, there is an additional skill set of knowing with which prime brokers to borrow general collateral (easy to borrow stocks) versus hard to borrow stocks, and how to negotiate with the prime broker the short rebate received from the short sales.

While the CFA program is indeed a respected and rigorous investment learning process, it is no substitute for developing short selling skills. Bottom line, an investor has to ask himself: does he want to pay 2-and-20 fees to a hedge fund manager to allow that hedge fund manager to get an education on shorting stock with the investor's capital?

NUMBER 5: "HEDGE FUNDS ARE BETTER INVESTMENTS THAN MANAGED FUTURES BECAUSE MANAGED FUTURES IS A ZERO-SUM GAME."

Excuse me? Aren't all alpha generating ideas a zero sum game? For every winner there has to be a loser. Regardless of whether the alpha generating idea makes a profit for a hedge fund manager or a managed futures manager, someone has to lose money on the other side.

Now there can be reasons why investors on the other side of the trade might be willing to lose money. For example, in the managed futures world, commodity trading advisors may be able to capture a return premium for providing risk transference services to commodity producers or commodity purchasers who wish to hedge the price risk of their commodity sales or purchases. Another example might be merger arbitrage where investors may be willing to forego the premium associated with a merger transaction because they do not wish to underwrite the risk of the deal collapsing. Still, for every gain there has to be a commensurate loss.

The fact that this hedge fund manager tried to promote his hedge fund over managed futures products by using this argument reflects a fundamental lack of understanding about the financial markets. This statement was all the more surprising because it was made at an alpha conference in front of a room of intelligent and sophisticated investors. Go figure.

NUMBER 4: "WHAT'S A MASTER TRUST?"

Several years ago a brand new hedge fund based in Texas passed through the doors of CalPERS. The group contained some well-known characters from the great state of Texas. They brought with them their top attorney, a partner from a well-known and respected Texas law firm. In the course of our discussions with this new hedge fund I asked them whether they intended to have an onshore hedge fund and an off-shore hedge fund. They assured me that given the success they antici-pated, they would have both types of funds.

When I then asked their top attorney how they would resolve the inevitable conflicts of interest for trade allocation between the onshore and offshore hedge funds, he responded with "That's a good question." This alone should have qualified for the top 10 list, but it gets better.

When I suggested to the lawyer that he might wish to consider a mas-ter trust and master feeder structure for the onshore and offshore hedge funds, his response was "What's a Master Trust?" But, it gets better.

As I began to explain how a master trust and feeder structure worked, the top lawyer from this well-known law firm opened up his briefcase, pulled out the classic lawyer's legal pad and began to take notes as I lectured.

Now what's wrong with this picture? First a hedge fund manager that intends to run both an onshore and offshore hedge fund better have his infrastructure in place before rushing forward. Even better, why should CalPERS pay fees of 2 and 20 to a hedge fund manager when we were the ones to give them an education about how onshore versus off-shore hedge funds work? In my mind, given the lessons learned that day by that hedge fund manager, they should have paid CalPERS 2 and 20, not the other way around.

NUMBER 3: "YOUR HEAD OF EQUITY DOESN'T UNDERSTAND OUR HEDGE FUND STRATEGY."

This is the same bunch of Texans as above in Quote #4. According to this group, in one hedge fund, they were going to demonstrate their expertise in (and I quote, here): convertible arbitrage, merger arbitrage, managed futures, equity long/short, and corporate governance.

Putting aside for the moment that this Texas group did not have a clue about a master trust account or how to resolve conflicts of interest between onshore and offshore accounts, their statement about their five areas of expertise does stretch one's credulity a bit.

First, each of their five purported areas of expertise requires just that: considerable experience and expertise to invest successfully. For example, convertible arbitrage and merger arbitrage are very different strategies. As we discussed previously, convertible arbitrage is the search for cheap beta exposure among four primary systematic risk exposure, while merger arbitrage is a form of financial market insurance sales such as the sale of put options. These are very different investment programs with very different risk profiles that require significantly different skill sets to perform well. Throw on top of these two strategies purported additional expertise in managed futures, equity long/short investing and corporate governance, and this begins to strain the levels of credibility.

Furthermore, consider that CalPERS itself is an expert in corporate governance, and the strategy suggested by this hedge fund manager group did not even begin to make sense to the CalPERS Investment Staff, and you begin to wonder.

Therefore, I turned down an investment in this hedge fund. At the time I was head of Global Equity for CalPERS. I explained to this group that I thought that their strategy lacked focus, that they needed to figure out their infrastructure between onshore and offshore hedge fund management, and last, I did not think that there corporate governance strategy really fitted in with a hedge fund. When I spoke with this group and told them politely that I had declined to invest in their hedge fund, they were shocked. In their minds, a check for $100 million was virtually in their pocket.

So shocked and disappointed were the Texans that they immediately drafted a letter to the Chief Investment Officer of CalPERS with the opening line of the letter stating: "Your Head of Equity does not understand our hedge fund strategy."

There was only one problem with this letter. Between the time they drafted their letter and mailed it to the CalPERS CIO, the former CIO for CalPERS had resigned and I had been promoted to be the new CIO of CalPERS, and therefore, I was the recipient of their letter. I wonder how those guys ever made out—I have not heard from them since.

NUMBER 2: "BASICALLY I LOOK AT SCREENS ALL DAY AND GO WITH MY GUT."

As part of the due diligence with any hedge fund manager, I follow the three basic questions that I outlined in my chapter on due diligence. Bottom line, I try to find out what makes the hedge fund manager so smart. How does he generate his trade ideas, what is his investment process, and where does he find good investments?

One day about three years ago, while visiting a hedge fund manager in London, I asked the basic question: How do you generate your trade ideas? I never expected to get the response that I received above.

Humor aside, how do you document such a process? What happens if the hedge fund manager decides to take a vacation? Who will watch the screens then? Whose gut will substitute for the hedge fund manager while he is away? What happens if the hedge fund manager's gut gets indigestion? The questions are endless. Bottom line there is no process other than the random thoughts and ideas that bounce around in the hedge fund manager's head and the intuition of his gut. While he may be a gutsy investor, there is simply too much process risk associated with this hedge fund manager to make a credible investment.

However, as a postscript, this hedge fund manager had about €250 million under management, so at least there was a sizeable portion of investors willing to trust his gut.

AND THE NUMBER 1 TOP TEN QUOTE: "HE WILL BE WITH YOU IN JUST A MINUTE SIR, HE'S STILL MEETING WITH HIS ARCHITECT."

Let me lay out the scene for you. Several years ago I went to visit a hedge fund manager on the East Coast. I had an appointment and showed up promptly at the agreed upon hour. However, I was kept waiting in the reception area for a while. Five minutes passed, then 10, 15, and finally 20 minutes passed our meeting date.

I began to wonder about the hedge fund manager—is he in the middle of a dynamic trade? Is he trying to negotiate an exotic swap agreement? Is he in the tied up in an important conference call? Finally, after 20 minutes, I went up to the receptionist and asked what the delay was and received the above quote.

This statement told me everything I needed to know about the hedge fund manager. He was more interested in building his new house than he was in meeting with a potential client.

Now it is indeed everyone's right to have a nice home to live in, but when the design of a hedge fund manager's new home supersedes his business, it is time to cash out. A good friend of mine, Mark Yusko of Morgan Creek Capital calls this the "Red Ferrari Syndrome." Simply, when a hedge fund manager begins to overly indulge in the pleasures of life, it is more than likely that the hedge fund manager has become risk averse and will now worry more about the preservation of his wealth than the generation of capital appreciation. This is a red flag (or Ferrari) and it is a good time to cash out of the hedge fund.

CONCLUSION

This chapter is not meant to discourage readers from pursuing hedge funds as a viable investment. Indeed, I am a committed investor to hedge funds; both CalPERS and Hermes have strong hedge fund programs. However, it does serve as a humorous reminder that hedge fund managers sometimes lose focus on generating wealth for their clients. This lack of focus may occur because of a shift in emphasis towards fee generation instead of wealth generation, or an over indulgence in the good things in life, or a lack of focus on their single best investment strategy.

My final thought is that I would never have developed a Top 10 list if I did not ask questions. Keep asking questions, and you will find some pretty interesting answers from hedge fund managers—some might even make your own personal Top 10 list.

Commodities and Managed Futures

CHAPTER 12

Introduction to Commodities

In Chapter 1 we discussed how most alternative "asset classes" are really alternative investment strategies within an existing asset class. This statement applies to hedge funds, and private equity, for example. However, it does not apply to commodities. Commodities are a separate asset class.

Capital assets such as stocks and bonds can be valued on the basis of the net present value of expected future cash flows. Expected cash flows and discount rates are a prime ingredient to determine the value of capital assets. Conversely, commodities do not provide a claim on an ongoing stream of revenue in the same fashion as stocks and bonds.[1] Consequently, they cannot be valued on the basis of net present value, and interest rates have only a small impact on their value.

Commodities generally fall into the category of consumable or transformable assets. You can consume a commodity such as corn as either feedstock or as food stock. Alternatively you can transform commodities like crude oil into gasoline and other petroleum products. Consequently, they have economic value, but they do not yield an ongoing stream of revenue.

Another distinction between capital assets and commodities is the global nature of commodity markets. Worldwide, commodities markets are all dollar-denominated. Furthermore, the value of a particular commodity is dependent upon global supply and demand imbalances rather than regional imbalances. Consequently, commodity prices are determined globally rather than regionally.

This is very different from the equity markets where, for instance, you have the U.S. stock market, foreign developed stock markets, and

---

[1] An exception to this rule are the precious metals such as gold, silver, and platinum which can be lent out at a market lease rate.

emerging markets. Foreign stock markets will reflect economic developments within their own regions compared to the United States.

Consider Exhibit 12.1. In this exhibit we provide the correlation coefficients between the S&P 500 and the FTSE 100 stock indexes for the past 15 years. We can see that the stock prices in the two countries are less than perfectly correlated with a correlation coefficient of 0.87.

Compare this to the correlation coefficient associated with the change in prices of crude oil listed on the New York Mercantile Exchange and the International Petroleum Exchange in London.[2] The correlation is 0.98. The change in crude oil prices in London and New York move in much closer lock step than stock prices in London and New York. This is because crude oil prices are determined by global economic factors while stock markets, despite the ease of moving capital around the globe, still retain some regional factors.

Note also, that the U.S. and U.K. stock markets are negatively correlated with the price of crude oil. This is not surprising given that energy products are the single most important input to any economy. We will come back to this point in the following chapters.

Finally, commodities do not conform to traditional asset pricing models such as the capital asset pricing model (CAPM). Under the CAPM, there are two components of risk: market or systematic risk and company specific or unsystematic risk. CAPM teaches us that investors should only be compensated for systematic risk or market risk because unsystematic risk (company specific risk) can be diversified away. CAPM uses a linear regression model to determine beta, a measure of an asset's exposure to systematic or market risk. The financial markets compensate for market risk by assigning a market risk premium above the risk-free rate.

EXHIBIT 12.1 Correlation Coefficients

	S&P 500	FTSE	NY Crude	London Crude
S&P 500	1.00	0.87	−0.24	−0.20
FTSE	0.87	1.00	−0.17	−0.15
NY Crude	−0.24	−0.17	1.00	0.98
London Crude	−0.20	−0.15	0.98	1.00

---

[2] In order to make a fair comparison of the correlation coefficients associated with the stock market returns of the United States and the United Kingdom and the crude oil markets in the United States and the United Kingdom, I converted FTSE prices into dollars. This removes any currency effects that might confound our analysis. Therefore, the correlation coefficients presented in Exhibit 12.1 are based on changes in dollar denominated prices. I am indebted to Peter Nguyen for pointing this out to me.

Bodie and Rosansky[3] and Dusak[4] find that commodity beta values are not consistent with the CAPM. The reason is twofold. First, under CAPM, the market portfolio is typically defined as a portfolio of financial assets such as stocks and bonds, and commodity returns map poorly onto financial market returns. Consequently, distinctions between market/systematic risk and unsystematic risk cannot be made. Second, commodity prices are dependent upon global supply and demand factors, not what the market perceives to be an adequate risk premium for this asset class.

This brief introduction is meant to establish commodities as a separate asset class from stocks, bonds, and real estate. However, like stocks and bonds, there are different investment strategies within this asset class. In this chapter we describe the physical commodities markets in more detail and provide an overview of their pricing and underlying economics.

EXPOSURE TO COMMODITIES

Most investors do not include commodities in their investment portfolio. Part of the reason is lack of familiarity with this asset class. Another issue is how to gain exposure to commodity assets. There are five ways to obtain economic exposure to commodity assets.

Purchase the Underlying Commodity

An investor can simply purchase the underlying commodity to gain economic exposure. Actual ownership of physical commodities can be problematic, however. For instance, on the New York Mercantile Exchange, crude oil contracts are denominated in 1,000 barrel lots. Therefore, if an investor wished to own crude oil, she would have to find a storage tank with a minimum storage capacity of 1,000 barrels of oil.

Similarly, wheat, traded on the Chicago Board of Trade, is denominated in units of 5,000 bushels. These bushels must be stored in a silo. Most investors are not familiar with the storage issues of physical commodities, let alone willing to bear the storage costs of ownership associated with physical commodities.

However, there are parts of the world where physical ownership of commodities is still the major form of economic wealth. India, for

---

[3] See Zvi Bodie and Victor Rosansky, "Risk and Return in Commodity Futures," *Financial Analysts Journal* (May/June 1980), pp. 27–39.
[4] K. Dusak, "Futures Trading and Investor Returns: An Investigation of Commodity Market Risk Premiums," *Journal of Political Economy* (November–December 1973), pp. 1387–1406.

example, is the second largest consumer of precious metals in the world after the United States. The reason is that many parts of India are geographically remote, far removed from the financial services and products that are commonplace in the United States. Stocks, bonds, mutual funds, and even bank savings accounts are the exception not the rule. Consequently, people in these remote regions denominate their wealth in gold, silver, and platinum.

Natural Resource Companies

Another way to gain exposure to commodities is to own the securities of a firm that derives a significant part of its revenues from the purchase and sale of physical commodities. For instance, purchasing shares of ExxonMobil might be considered a "pure play" on the price of oil since three-fourths of ExxonMobil's revenues are derived from the exploration, refining, and marketing of petroleum products.

However, there are several reasons why this "pure play" might not work. First, part of the value of the stock in ExxonMobil is dependent upon the movement of the general stock market. This is the CAPM, discussed above, and, as a result, an investment in the stock of any company will result in exposure to systematic, or market risk, as well as firm specific risk.

Systematic risk is measured by the beta of a stock. Beta measures the amount of market risk associated with a given security. A beta equal to one indicates the same level of systematic risk as the overall market, while a beta less than one indicates less risk than the market, and a beta greater than one indicates more risk than the market.

Consider Exhibit 12.2. In this exhibit, we list the correlation coefficients and the betas associated with the stock returns four large petroleum companies compared to the S&P 500 (the "market"). We also include correlation coefficients and betas for the stock returns of the four oil companies compared to the price of crude oil.

EXHIBIT 12.2   Beta Coefficients and Correlation Coefficients

	Stock Market Beta	Stock Market Correlation Coefficient	Crude Oil Beta	Crude Oil Correlation Coefficient
ExxonMobile	0.67	0.86	−0.04	−0.14
Chevron/Texaco	0.67	0.6	−0.08	−0.22
Royal Dutch Shell	0.85	0.78	0.38	0.02
BP Amoco	0.71	0.55	0.12	0.26

First, we can see that the oil companies all have large betas with respect to the S&P 500. This indicates that oil companies have significant stock market risk. Furthermore, the correlation coefficients between the stock returns of these four companies and the S&P 500 are very large. We can conclude that oil companies have considerable exposure to the general stock market.

The analysis changes when we examine the returns of these four companies to the prices of crude oil. Exhibit 12.2 indicates that the betas associated with crude oil prices are very low, and, in the case of ExxonMobil and Chevron, are slightly negative. In this case we define the market as the current price of crude oil traded in New York City. In addition, the correlation coefficients between the oil company stock prices and crude oil stock prices are all much lower than that of the correlation with the stock market. We can conclude the stock prices of oil companies are much more dependent upon the movement of the stock market than they are by the movement of crude oil prices. Therefore, investing in an oil company as a "pure play" on crude oil prices provides an investor with significant stock market exposure and very little crude oil exposure.

Second, when an investor invests with an oil company (or any company for that matter) the investor assumes all of the idiosyncratic risks associated with that company. Consider the example of Texaco when, in the 1980s it attempted an ill-fated merger with the Getty Oil Company even though the Getty Oil Company had an outstanding bid from Pennzoil. The result was massive litigation resulting in a several billion dollar verdict against Texaco, forcing the company to seek Chapter 11 bankruptcy protection. Furthermore, in the 1990s, Texaco was the subject of a race discrimination lawsuit by many of its workers. This litigation cost Texaco several hundred million dollars.

Neither of these lawsuits, however, had anything to do with the price of oil. They were part of the idiosyncratic risk associated with the management practices of Texaco. Most investors seeking a pure play on oil would be disappointed to receive instead lengthy and expensive lawsuit exposure.

Additionally, there are other operating risks associated with an investment in any company. A company's financing policies, for example, affect the price of its stock. ExxonMobil has a debt/equity ratio of about 1.22. This is a little above average for the oil industry. There is also operating leverage (i.e., the ratio of fixed to variable expenses). Oil companies tend to have high variable costs associated with their exploration, refining, and marketing programs. While financial and operating leverage affect the price of a stock, they have nothing to do with the price of oil.

Even if all of the other risks associated with an investment in an oil company are accepted, the investor might find that the oil company has hedged away its oil exposure. Most large oil and energy companies maintain their own trading desks. One main goal of these trading desks is to hedge the risk associated with the purchase and sale of petroleum products. The reason is that oil companies, like most companies, prefer to smooth their annual earnings rather than be subject to large swings due to the price of oil.

The proof is demonstrated in Exhibit 12.2, where oil companies have low betas with respect to the price of crude oil. This is consistent with the fact that oil companies hedge away a considerable amount of their exposure to fluctuating oil prices.

Commodity Futures Contracts

The easiest way to gain exposure to commodity prices is through commodity futures contracts. Futures contracts offer several advantages. First, these contracts are traded on an exchange. Therefore, they share the same advantages as stock exchanges: a central marketplace, transparent pricing, clearinghouse security, uniform contract size and terms, and daily liquidity.

Second, the purchase of a futures contract does not require automatic delivery of the underlying commodity. An offsetting futures position can be initiated that will close out the position of the initial futures contract. In this way an investor can gain exposure to commodity prices without worrying about physical delivery. In fact, only about 1% of all commodity futures contracts result in the actual delivery of the underlying commodity.

Third, futures contracts can be purchased without paying the full price for the commodity. When a futures contract is purchased, a down payment on the total futures price is required. This is called the *initial margin*. This margin requirement is a small percentage of the full purchase price of the underlying commodity, usually less than 10%. The initial margin is a good faith deposit to ensure full payment upon delivery of the underlying commodity. In the futures markets, the investor does not need to put up the total price for the underlying commodity unless she takes physical delivery of the commodity.

Futures accounts also have two other margin requirements. On a day by day basis, the value of the futures contract will fluctuate. Fluctuation of prices in the futures markets will cause the value of the investor's margin account to increase or decrease. This is called the *variation margin*. If the price of the futures contract increases, the holder of a long futures position will accrue positive variation margin. This adds to the equity in the futures margin account and may be withdrawn by the investor. Conversely, for an investor that has a short futures position, the increase in the price of the futures contract will result in a negative variation margin.

The *maintenance margin* is the minimum amount of equity that a futures margin account may have and is usually set at 75% to 80% of the initial margin. If subsequent variation margins reduce the equity in an investor's account down to the maintenance margin level, the investor will receive a *margin call* from the futures commission merchant. A margin call is a demand for additional cash to be contributed to the account to bring the equity in the account back over the maintenance margin level. If the investor cannot meet the margin call, the futures commission merchant has the right to liquidate the investor's positions in the account.

There can be some disadvantages to taking positions in futures contracts. First, if an investor wishes to maintain her exposure to commodity prices without taking physical delivery of the underlying contract, she will have to continually close out her existing futures position and reestablish a new position by entering into a new futures contract. This "rolling" of futures contracts can be costly depending on the term structure of the futures market. (We will discuss this more in detail below.)

Second, as we noted above, once a long futures position is established, there may be ongoing margin calls if the futures contract declines in value. Conversely, if an investor's futures contracts increase in value, she may withdraw the additional equity from her account. Nonetheless, managing the contributions and withdrawals from a futures account may require more activity than a traditional long-only security account. Futures accounts may only be opened with licensed futures commission merchants who are registered with the National Futures Association and the Commodity Futures Trading Commission.

Commodity Swaps and Forward Contracts

Close economic cousins to commodity futures contracts are commodity swaps and forward contracts. Commodity swap contracts and commodity forward contracts perform the same economic function as commodity futures contracts. However, there are some key structural differences.

■ Commodity swaps and forward contracts are custom made for the individual investor. While this provides precise tailoring of the commodity exposure desired by the investor, it also makes commodity swaps and forward contracts less liquid because what works for one investor will not work for all investors. Typically, if an investor wishes to terminate a commodity swap or forward contract prior to maturity, the investor will negotiate with the counterparty who sold the swap or forward contract to the investor.

■ Commodity swaps and forward contracts are not traded on an exchange. Again, this impacts liquidity. Exchange-traded products with standardized terms and public pricing provide a much greater liquidity than customized commodity swap or forward contracts.

■ A key advantage is that commodity swaps and forward contracts are private contracts; traded outside the public domain of an exchange. To the extent an investor wishes to be discreet about its investment strategy for commodities, commodity swaps, and forward contracts provide a degree of privacy not afforded by the public markets.

Commodity-Linked Notes

The last way an investor can gain exposure to the commodity markets is through a commodity-linked note. This is where financial engineering and the commodities markets intersect. In its simplest form, a commodity-linked note is an intermediate term debt instrument whose value at maturity will be a function of the value of an underlying commodity futures contract or basket of commodity futures contracts.

Commodity-linked notes are not a new invention. In 1863, the Confederacy of the South issued a 20-year bond denominated in both Pounds Sterling and French Francs. Also, at the option of the bondholder, the bond could be converted into bales of cotton. This was a dual currency, commodity-linked bond.[5]

Commodity-linked notes have several advantages. First, the investor does not have to worry about the rolling of the underlying futures contracts. This becomes the problem of the issuer of the note who must roll the futures contracts to hedge the commodity exposure embedded in the note.

Second, the note is, in fact, a debt instrument. Many investors may have restrictions on investing in the commodities markets. However, they can have access to commodity exposure through a debt instrument. The note is recorded as a liability on the balance sheet of the issuer, and as a bond investment on the balance sheet of the investor. In addition, the note can have a stated coupon rate and maturity just like any other debt instrument. The twist is that the investor accepts a lower coupon payment than it otherwise could receive in return for sharing in the upside of the commodity prices.

---

[5] See S. Warte Rawls III and Charles Smithson, "The Evolution of Risk Management Products," *The New Corporate Finance*, 2nd ed., Donald H. Chew, Jr. (ed.) (New York: Irwin/McGraw-Hill, 1999).

Last, the holder of the note does not have to worry about any tracking error issues with respect to the price of a single commodity or basket of commodities. Once again, this problem remains with the issuer.

In practice, commodity-linked notes are tied to the prices of commodity futures contracts or commodity options. Consider the following example. A pension fund is not allowed to trade commodity futures directly but wants to invest in the commodity markets as a hedge against inflation. To diversify its portfolio, it purchases at par value from an investment bank a $1,000,000 structured note tied to the value of the Goldman Sachs Commodity Index (GSCI). The GSCI is a diversified basket of physical commodity futures contracts.

The note has a maturity of one year and is principal guaranteed, at maturity, the pension fund will receive at least the face value of the note. However, if the GSCI exceeds a certain level at maturity of the note the pension fund will share in this appreciation. Principal repayment therefore depends upon the settlement price of the GSCI index at the note's maturity. The pension fund has, in fact, a call option embedded in the note. If the GSCI exceeds a predetermined level (the strike price) at the maturity date, the pension fund will participate in the price appreciation.

The embedded call option on the GSCI is costly. The pension fund will pay for this option by receiving a reduced coupon payment (or no coupon) on the note. The closer to the money the call option is set, the lower will be the coupon payment. Assume that the strike price for a GSCI call option is set at 10% out of the money and that the coupon on the note is 2%.

Under normal circumstances, a plain-vanilla note from the issuer would carry a coupon of 6%. Therefore, the pension fund is sacrificing 4% of coupon income for the price of the call option on the GSCI. Assume that at the time the note is issued, the GSCI is at the level of 1000. Therefore, the strike price on the call option (set 10% out of the money) is 1100. If, at maturity of the note, the value of the GSCI is above 1100, the investor will receive her 2% coupon plus the appreciation of the GSCI:

$$[1 + (GSCI_T - GSCI_x)/GSCI_x] \times \$1,000,000 + \$20,000$$

where

$GSCI_T$ is the value of the GSCI index at maturity of the note.
$GSCI_x$ is the strike price for the call option embedded in the note.
$20,000 = 2\%$ coupon $\times \$1,000,000$ face value note.

If the option expires out of the money (the GSCI is less than or equal to 1100 at maturity), then the investor receives the return of her principal plus a 2% coupon. Exhibit 12.3 presents the possible payoffs to the structured note.

From Exhibit 12.3 we can see that the pension fund shares in the upside but is protected on the downside. The tradeoff for principal protection is a lower coupon payment and only a partial sharing in the upside (above the call strike price).

With respect to the issuer of the note, it will go out and purchase a one-year call option on the GSCI index with a strike price equal to 1100. If the option matures in the money, the issuer will pass on the price appreciation to the pension fund. In this way, the issuer maintains the commodity call option on its balance sheet, not the pension fund, but the pension fund gets the benefit of the option's payout.

Structured notes do not have to be principal protected. The pension fund can share fully in the upside as well as the downside. Consider a second note also with a $1,000,000 face value. However, this note shares fully in the change in value of the GSCI from the date the note is purchased. The trick here is that the change in value can be positive or negative. This is a commodity note linked to a futures contract instead of an option contract.

The note will pay a 5% coupon at maturity. Recall that the pension could otherwise purchase a regular one-year note from the same issuer (without commodity exposure) with a 6% coupon. The difference in coupon payments of 1% reflects the issuer's transaction and administration costs associated with the commodity-linked note. Compared to the prior example, a commodity-linked note with an embedded futures contract is less costly to issue than a note with an embedded commodity option.

The terms of the note state that at maturity the issuer will pay to the investor

$$[1 + (GSCI_T - GSCI_0)/GSCI_0] \times \$1,000,000 + \$50,000$$

where

$GSCI_T$ is the value of the GSCI index at maturity of the note.
$GSCI_0$ is the value of the GSCI index at the purchase date of the note.

EXHIBIT 12.3   Structured Note with a GSCI Call Option

GSCI	900	1000	1100	1200	1300
Principal	$1,000,000	$1,000,000	$1,000,000	$1,000,000	$1,000,000
Option value	$0	$0	$0	$90,909	$181,818
Coupon	$20,000	$20,000	$20,000	$20,000	$20,000
Total payment	$1,020,000	$1,020,000	$1,020,000	$1,110,909	$1,201,818
Total return	2%	2%	2%	11.09%	20.18%

EXHIBIT 12.4   Structured Note with a GSCI Futures Contract

GSCI	900	1000	1100	1200	1300
Principal	$1,000,000	$1,000,000	$1,000,000	$1,000,000	$1,000,000
Futures value	-$100,000	$0	$100,000	$200,000	$300,000
Coupon	$50,000	$50,000	$50,000	$50,000	$50,000
Total payment	$950,000	$1,050,000	$1,150,000	$1,250,000	$1,350,000
Total return	-5%	5%	15%	25%	35%

The payout for this second note is presented in Exhibit 12.4.

Notice the difference between Exhibits 12.3 and 12.4. In Exhibit 12.4 we can see that the pension fund shares in a linear payout stream: if the GSCI increases in value, the pension gains; if the GSCI declines in value, the pension fund loses. However, in Exhibit 12.3, the pension fund shares only in the gains, it does not share in the losses. This is a demonstration of the nonlinear payout function associated with a commodity option. In contrast, a commodity note linked to a futures contract will provide an investor with a linear payout function—sharing in both the upside and downside of commodity price movement.

Last, note that the pension fund has the opportunity for a much greater gain with the commodity note linked to a futures contract. However, in return for this upside potential, the pension fund must bear the risk of loss of capital should the GSCI decline below its initial level of 1000.[6] Another way of stating this is that with a commodity note linked to an option, the pension fund sacrifices some upside potential for the preservation of capital.

The financial engineering demonstrated in Exhibits 12.3 and 12.4 would not be necessary if the pension fund could invest directly in commodity futures and options. Engineering becomes necessary because of the pension fund's prohibition against purchasing commodities directly.

Commodity-linked notes are completely transparent because these notes utilize exchange-traded commodity futures and options contracts with daily pricing and liquidity. Furthermore, the equation to calculate their value is specified as part of the note agreement. As a result, pension funds, insurance companies, endowments, and other institutional inves-

---

[6] With respect to the issuer of the note, it will go out and purchase one-year futures contracts on the GSCI sufficient to cover the face value of the note. If the futures contracts increase in value, the issuer passes on this value to the pension fund. If the futures contracts decline in value, the issuer will close out its position at a loss. However, the issuer will be reimbursed for these losses because it does not have to return the full principal value of the note to the pension fund.

tors may participate in viable securities that offer transparent exposure to a new asset class without a direct investment in that asset class.

In the above examples, it was assumed that the issuer was a large commercial bank that purchased the commodity futures or options and passed through either the gains or losses to the investor. However, commodity producers are also likely issuers of such notes.

Consider an oil producer who would like to reduce its cost of debt financing. One way to lower the coupon rate on its debt would be to issue calls on crude oil attached to its bonds. As we demonstrated in Exhibit 12.3, if a commodity-linked note is tied to a call option, the coupon payment will be lower than what the issuer would otherwise offer. From the oil producer's perspective, any cash outflows as a result of the call option being exercised should be offset by the lower cost of financing it receives. From the investor's perspective, it trades a lower coupon payment on the note for the potential to share in the price appreciation of crude oil.

THE RELATIONSHIP BETWEEN FUTURES PRICES AND SPOT PRICES

As we noted above, the easiest way to gain exposure to commodities is through commodity futures contracts. These contracts are transparent, are denominated in standard units, are exchange traded, have daily liquidity, and depend upon the spot prices of the underlying commodity. The last point, the relationship between spot and futures prices, must be developed to understand the dynamics of the commodity futures markets.

A futures contract obligates the seller of the futures contract to deliver the underlying asset at a set price at a specified time. Conversely, the buyer of a futures contract agrees to purchase the underlying asset at the set price and at a specified time. If the seller of the futures contract does not wish to deliver the underlying asset, she must close out her short futures position by purchasing an offsetting futures contract. Similarly, if the buyer of the futures contract does not wish to take delivery of the underlying asset, he must close out his long futures position by selling an offsetting futures contract. Only a very small percentage of futures contracts (usually less than 1%) result in delivery of the underlying asset.

There are three general types of futures contracts regulated by the Commodity Futures Trading Commission: financial futures, currency futures, and commodity futures. Commodity trading advisors and commodity pool operators invest in all three types of futures contracts.

Additionally, many hedge fund managers apply arbitrage strategies with respect to financial and currency futures. The following examples demonstrate these arbitrage opportunities. We begin with financial futures.

Financial Futures

Financial futures include U.S. Treasury bond futures, agency futures, Eurodollar CD futures, and stock index futures. In the United States, these contracts are traded on the Chicago Board of Trade, the Chicago Mercantile Exchange, and the FINEX division of the New York Cotton Exchange. Consider the example of a financial asset that pays no income.

In the simplest case, if the underlying asset pays no income, then the relationship between the futures contract and the spot price is

$$F = Se^{r(T-t)} \tag{12.1}$$

where

F = the price of the futures contract
S = the spot price of the underlying asset
e = the exponential operator, used to calculate continuous compounding
r = the risk-free rate
$T - t$ = the time until maturity of the futures contract

In words, the price of the futures contract depends upon the current price of the underlying financial asset, the risk-free rate and the time until maturity of the futures contract. Notice that the price of the futures contract depends upon the risk-free rate and not the required rate of return for the financial asset. The reason that this is the case is because of arbitrage opportunities that exist for speculators such as hedge funds.

Consider the situation where $F > Se^{r(T-t)}$. A hedge fund manager could make a profit by applying the following strategy:

1. Borrow cash at the risk-free rate, r, and purchase the underlying asset at current price S.
2. Sell the underlying asset for delivery at time T and at the futures price F.
3. At maturity, deliver the underlying asset, pay the interest and principal on the cash borrowed, and collect the futures price F.

Exhibit 12.5 demonstrates this arbitrage strategy.

EXHIBIT 12.5   Financial Asset Arbitrage when $F > Se^{r(T-t)}$

Time	Cash Inflow	Cash Outflow	Net Cash
t (initiate the arbitrage)	S (cash borrowed)	S (to purchase the asset)	$S - S = 0$
T (maturity of the futures contract)	F (price for future delivery of the asset)	$Se^{r(T-t)}$ (pay back principal and interest)	$F - Se^{r(T-t)}$

EXHIBIT 12.6   Financial Asset Arbitrage when $F < Se^{r(T-t)}$

Time	Cash Inflow	Cash Outflow	Net Cash
t (initiate the arbitrage)	S (the asset is sold short)	S (invested at interest rate r)	$S - S = 0$
T (maturity of the futures contract)	$Se^{r(T-t)}$ (receive principal and interest)	F (the price paid for the asset at maturity of the futures contract)	$Se^{r(T-t)} - F$

Two points about Exhibit 12.5 must be noted. First, to initiate the arbitrage strategy, no net cash is required. The cash outflow matches the cash inflow. This is one reason why arbitrage strategies are so popular.

Second, at maturity (time T), the hedge fund manager receives a positive net cash payout of $F - Se^{r(T-t)}$. How do we know that the net payout is positive? Simple, we know that at the initiation of the arbitrage strategy that $F > Se^{r(T-t)}$. Therefore, $F - Se^{r(T-t)}$ must be positive.

If the reverse situation were true at time t, $F < Se^{r(T-t)}$, then a reverse arbitrage strategy would make the same amount of profit: Buy the futures contract and sell short the underlying asset. This is demonstrated in Exhibit 12.6.

Exhibit 12.6 demonstrates the arbitrage profit $Se^{r(T-t)} - F$. How do we know this is a profit? Because we started with the condition that $Se^{r(T-t)} > F$. At maturity of the futures contract, the hedge fund manager will take delivery of the underlying asset at price F and use the delivery of the asset to cover her short position.

In general, futures contracts on financial assets are settled in cash, not by physical delivery of the underlying security.[7] However, this does not change the arbitrage dynamics demonstrated above. The hedge fund manager will simply close out her short asset position and long futures

---

[7] However, certain futures exchanges allow for a procedure known as "exchange for physicals" where a holder of a financial asset can exchange the financial asset at maturity of the futures contract instead of settling in cash.

position at the same time and net the gains and losses. The profit will be the same as that demonstrated in Exhibit 12.6.

Most financial assets pay some form of income. Consider stock index futures contracts. A stock index tracks the changes in the value of a portfolio of stocks. The percentage change in the value of a stock index over time is usually defined so that it equals the percentage change in the total value of all stocks comprising the index portfolio. However, stock indexes are usually not adjusted for dividends. In other words, any cash dividends received by an investor actually holding the stocks is not reflected in measuring the change in value of the stock index.

There are futures contracts on the S&P 500, the Nikkei 225 Stock Index, the NASDAQ 100 Index, the Russell 1000 Index, and the Dow Jones Industrials Stock Index. By far, the most popular contract is the S&P 500 futures contract (SPX) traded on the Chicago Mercantile Exchange.

Consider the S&P 500 futures contract. The pricing relationship as shown in equation (12.1) applies. However, equation (12.1) must be adjusted for the fact that the holder of the underlying stocks receives cash dividends, while the holder of the futures contract does not.

In Exhibit 12.5 we demonstrated how an arbitrage strategy may be accomplished by borrowing cash at the risk-free rate to purchase the underlying financial asset. With respect to stocks, the hedge fund manager receives the benefit of cash dividends from purchasing the stocks. The cash dividends received reduce the borrowing cost of the hedge fund manager. This must be factored into the futures pricing equation. We can express this relation as

$$F = Se^{(r - q)(T - t)} \qquad (12.2)$$

where the terms are the same as before, and q is equal to the dividend yield on the basket of stocks.

The dividend rate, q, is subtracted from the borrowing cost, r, to reflect the reduction in carrying costs from owning the basket of stocks. Consider the example of a three-month futures contract on the S&P 500. Assume that the index is currently at 1200, that the risk-free rate is 6%, and that the current dividend yield on the S&P 500 is 2%. Using equation (12.2), the fair price for a three-month futures contract on the S&P 500 is

$$F = 1200e^{(0.06 - 0.02)(0.25)} = 1212$$

Notice again that the futures price on stock index futures does not depend upon the expected return on stocks. Instead, it depends on the risk-free rate and the dividend yield. Expected asset returns do not affect the pricing relationship between the current asset price and the future asset price because any expected return that the underlying asset should earn will also be reflected in the futures price. Therefore, the difference between the futures price and the spot price should reflect only the time value of money, adjusted for any income earned by the financial asset over the term of the futures contract.

Suppose that instead of a price of 1212, the three-month futures contract for the S&P 500 was priced at 1215. Then a hedge fund could establish the following arbitrage: borrow cash at an interest rate of 6% and purchase a basket of S&P 500 stocks worth $300,000 ($250 × 1200, where each point of the S&P 500 is worth $250 in the underlying futures contract), and sell the S&P 500 futures at a price of 1215. At the end of three months, the hedge fund would earn the following arbitrage profit:

Futures price received for the S&P 500 stocks
$$= 1215 \times \$250 = \qquad\qquad \$303{,}750$$
Plus dividend yield on stocks
$$= \$300{,}00 \times (e^{(0.02) \times (0.25)} - 1) = \qquad \$1{,}504$$
Less repayment of the loan plus interest
$$= \$300{,}000 \times e^{(0.06) \times (0.25)} = \qquad \$304{,}534$$
Equals arbitrage profits $\qquad\qquad\qquad\qquad\qquad \$704$

Exhibit 12.7 demonstrates the stock index arbitrage flow chart. A reverse arbitrage similar to Exhibit 12.6 can be implemented when $F < Se^{(r-q)(T-t)}$. That is, short the stocks, invest the cash at the risk-free rate, and buy the futures contract.

Currencies

A foreign currency may be considered an income-producing asset. The reason is that the holder of the foreign currency can earn interest at the risk-free rate prevailing in the foreign country. We define this foreign risk-free rate as f. Considered in this context, the relationship between a

EXHIBIT 12.7   Stock Index Arbitrage when $F > Se^{(r-q)(T-t)}$

Time	Cash Inflow	Cash Outflow	Net Cash
t (initiate the arbitrage)	S (cash borrowed)	S (to purchase S&P 500 stocks)	$S - S = 0$
T (maturity of the futures contract)	F (price for future delivery of S&P 500 stocks)	$Se^{(r-q)(T-t)}$ (pay back principal and interest less dividends received)	$F - Se^{(r-q)(T-t)}$

futures contract on a foreign currency and the current spot exchange rate can be expressed as

$$F = Se^{(r - f)(T - t)} \tag{12.3}$$

where the terms are defined as before, and f is the risk free interest rate in the foreign country.

Equation (12.3) is similar to equation (12.2) because a foreign currency may be considered analogous to an income producing asset or a dividend paying stock. Equation (12.3) also expresses the well-known *interest rate parity theorem*. This theorem states that the exchange rate between two currencies will be dependent upon the differences in their interest rates.

Consider the exchange rate between the U.S. dollar and the Japanese yen. Assume that the current U.S. risk-free rate is 6% while that for the yen is approximately 1%. Also, assume that the current spot rate for yen to dollars is 120 yen per U.S. dollar, or 0.00833 dollars per yen. A three-month futures contract on the yen/dollar exchange rate would be

$$F = 0.00833e^{(0.06 - 0.01)(0.25)} = 0.0084382$$

The futures price on Japanese yen for three months is 0.0084382 dollars per yen, or 118.51 yen per dollar.

To demonstrate a currency arbitrage when $F > Se^{(r - f)(T - t)}$ consider a hedge fund manager who can borrow 12,000 yen for three months at a rate of 1%. In three months time, the hedge fund manager will have to repay $12,000e^{(0.01 \times 0.25)} = 12,030$ yen. The manager converts the yen into dollars at the spot exchange rate of 120 yen/\$1 = \$100. This \$100 can then be invested at the U.S. risk-free rate of interest for three months to earn $\$100e^{(0.060 \times 0.25)} = \$101.50$. If the three-month currency futures price on Japanese yen were the same as the spot exchange rate of 120 yen/\$1, the hedge fund manager would need to sell 12,030/120 = \$100.25 dollars to repay the yen loan. Since the manager receives \$101.50 back from her three-month investment in the United States, she will pocket the difference of \$101.50 – \$100.25 = \$1.25 in arbitrage profits.

Exhibit 12.8 demonstrates that 150 yen of arbitrage profits may be earned if the futures contract price does not take into account the differences in the interest rates between the foreign and domestic currencies. The 150 yen of arbitrage profit may be converted back to dollars: 150 yen/ 120 = \$1.25. Therefore, to prevent arbitrage, the currency futures price for Japanese yen must be 118.51 yen per U.S. dollar. Then the amount of cash inflow received will be exactly equal to the cash outflow necessary to pay back the Japanese yen loan: \$101.50 × 118.51 yen/USD = 12,030 yen.

EXHIBIT 12.8   Currency Arbitrage when $F > Se^{(r-f)(T-t)}$

Time	Cash Inflow	Cash Outflow	Net Cash
t (initiate the futures contract)	12,000 yen borrowed at 1%	12,000 yen/120 = $100 invested at 6%	0
T (maturity of the futures contract)	$101.50 from U.S. interest bearing account	12,030 yen to repay loan plus interest	($101.50 × 120) − 12,030 yen = 150 yen.

In practice, arbitrage opportunities do not occur as obviously as our example. Currency prices may be out of balance for only a short period of time. It is the nimble hedge fund manager that can take advantage of pricing discrepancies. Furthermore, more famous hedge fund managers engage in currency speculation as opposed to currency arbitrage. In currency speculation, the hedge fund manager takes an unhedged position on one side of the market. Cash is committed to establish the position. The best example of this is George Soros's bet against the British pound sterling in 1992.

Commodity Futures

Commodities are not financial assets. Nonetheless, the pricing dynamics between spot prices and futures prices are similar to those for financial assets. However, there are important distinctions that will affect the pricing relationship.

First, as we discussed above, there are storage costs associated with physical commodities. These storage costs must be factored into the pricing equation. Storage costs can be considered as negative income. In other words, there is a cash outflow associated with holding the physical commodity. This is in contrast to financial assets discussed above. With financial assets, we demonstrated that income earned on the underlying asset will defray the cost of purchasing that asset. With physical commodities, however, there is both the cost of financing the purchase of the physical commodity and the storage cost associated with its ownership. This relationship may be expressed as

$$F = Se^{(r+c)(T-t)} \qquad (12.4)$$

where the terms are as defined before, and c is the storage cost associated with ownership of the commodity.

In equation (12.4), the cost of storage, c, is added the cost of financing the purchase of the commodity. For example, consider a 1-year futures contract on crude oil. Assume that (1) it costs 2% of the price of crude oil to store a barrel of oil and the payment is made at the end of the year; (2) the current price of oil is \$50; and (3) the risk-free rate of interest is 6%.[8] Then the future value of a 1-year crude oil futures contract is

$$F = \$50e^{(0.06 + 0.02)(1)} = \$54.16$$

A second difference between commodity futures and financial futures is the *convenience yield*. Consumers of physical commodities feel that there are benefits from the ownership of the commodity that are not obtained by owning a futures contract; that it is convenient to own the physical commodity. This benefit might be the ability to profit from temporary or local supply and demand imbalances, or the ability to keep a production line in process. Alternatively, the convenience yield for certain metals can be measured in terms of *lease rates*. Gold, silver, and platinum can be leased (loaned) to jewelry and electronic manufacturers with the obligation to repay the precious metal at a later date.

Taking both the cost of storage and the convenience yield into account, the price of a futures contract may be stated as

$$F = Se^{(r + c - y)(T - t)} \qquad (12.5)$$

where the terms are defined as before and y is the convenience yield.

Notice that the convenience yield is subtracted from the risk-free rate, r, and the storage cost, c. Similar to financial assets, the convenience yield, y, reduces the cost of ownership of the asset.

Consider the following example. The current price of an ounce of gold is \$400, the risk-free rate is 6%, the cost of storage is 2% of the purchase price, and the lease rate to lend gold is 1%. A six-month futures contract on gold will be

$$F = \$400e^{(0.06 + 0.02 - 0.01)(0.5)} = \$429$$

Assume that $F > Se^{(r + c - y)(T - t)}$. Then an investor can earn an arbitrage profit by borrowing S to purchase the underlying commodity and selling the futures contract, F. This arbitrage is detailed in Exhibit 12.9.[9]

---

[8] If the storage costs are expressed as a dollar amount, then the appropriate equation is $F = (S + C)e^{r(T - t)}$ where C represents the present value of all storage costs incurred during the life of the futures contract.

[9] In practice, storage costs may be quoted in dollar terms rather than as a percentage of the commodity's value, while convenience yields are quoted as a percentage of the commodity's value. Consider the case where C is equal to the present value of the storage costs that must be paid over the life of the futures contract. Then equation (12.5) many be expressed as

$$F = Se^{(r - y)(T - t)} + Ce^{r(T - t)}$$

EXHIBIT 12.9 Commodity Futures Arbitrage when $F > Se^{(r + c - y)(T - t)}$

Time	Cash Inflow	Cash Outflow	Net Cash
t (initiate the arbitrage)	S (cash borrowed)	S (to purchase the asset)	$S - S = 0$
T (maturity of the futures contract)	$F + S(e^{y(T - t)} - 1)$ (price for future delivery of the asset plus lease income)	$Se^{(r + c)(T - t)}$ (pay back principal and interest on loan plus storage costs)	$F + S(e^{y(T - t)} - 1)$ $- Se^{(r + c)(T - t)}$

Exhibit 12.9 demonstrates the payment received from the arbitrage. At maturity of the futures contract, the investor receives a positive cash flow of $F + S(e^{y(T - t)} - 1) - Se^{(r + c)(T - t)}$. The amount $F + S(e^{y(T - t)} - 1)$ represents the futures price received at maturity of the contract plus any income from the lease of the commodity, and $Se^{(r + c)(T - t)}$ represents the cash that must be paid back for the loan, interest on the loan, and storage costs.

This arbitrage cannot work in reverse if the investor does not already own the commodity. Except for precious metals, commodities are difficult to borrow. Consequently, they cannot be shorted in the same fashion as financial assets. Furthermore, companies that own the underlying commodity do so for its consumption value rather than its investment value.

ECONOMICS OF THE COMMODITY MARKETS: NORMAL BACKWARDATION VERSUS CONTANGO

With this pricing framework in place, we turn to the economics of commodity consumption, production, and hedging. Commodity futures contracts exhibit a term structure similar to that of interest rates. This curve can be downward sloping or upward sloping. The reasons for the different curves will be determined by the actions of hedgers and speculators.

Consider a petroleum producer such as ExxonMobil. Through its exploration, developing, refining, and marketing operations, this company is naturally long crude oil exposure. This puts Exxon at risk to declining crude oil prices. To reduce this exposure, Exxon will sell crude oil futures contracts.[10]

---

[10] As we discussed before, oil producers have energy trading desks to hedge their long crude oil exposure. Another way that Exxon hedges this risk is through long-term delivery contracts where the price of crude oil is fixed in the contract.

From Exxon's perspective, by selling crude oil futures contracts it can separate its commodity price risk from its business risk (i.e., the ability to find crude oil, refine it and market it to consumers). By hedging, Exxon can better apply its capital to its business risks rather than holding a reserve of capital to protect against fluctuating crude oil prices. Simply stated, hedging allows for the more efficient use of ExxonMobil's invested capital. In fact, we demonstrated this very point in Exhibit 12.2 where we show that ExxonMobil's stock price has virtually no economic link to fluctuating oil prices. However, there must be someone on the other side of the trade to bear the price risk associated with buying the futures contract. This is the speculator.

If Exxon transfers its risk to the speculator, the speculator must be compensated for this risk. The speculator is compensated by purchasing the futures contract from the petroleum producer at less than the expected future spot price of crude oil. That is, the price established in the commodity futures contract will be below the expected future spot price of crude oil. The speculator will be compensated by the difference between the futures price and the expected spot price. This may be expressed as

$$E(S_T) > F_T \qquad\qquad (12.6)$$

where

$E(S_T)$ = the expected spot price of the underlying commodity at time T (the maturity of the futures contract)

F_T = the agreed upon price in the futures contract to be paid at time T

If the inequality of equation (12.6) remains true at the maturity of the futures contract, the speculator will earn a profit of $S_T - F_T$. However, nothing is certain, commodity prices can fluctuate. It might turn out that the price agreed upon in the futures contract exceeds the spot price at time T. Then the speculator will lose an amount equal to $F_T - S_T$.

This is the risk that the petroleum producer transferred from its income statement to that of the speculator's. Therefore, to ensure the speculator is compensated more often than not for bearing the commodity price risk, it must be the case that agreed upon futures price F_T is sufficiently discounted compared to the expected future spot price S_T. This condition of the futures markets is referred to as *normal backwardation*, or simply, *backwardation*.

The term backwardation comes from John Maynard Keynes. Keynes was the first to theorize that commodity producers were the natural hedgers in the commodity markets and therefore would need to offer a risk premium to speculators in order to induce them to bear the risk of fluctuating commodity prices. This risk premium is represented by the difference of $E(S_T) - F_T$. Conversely, hedgers, because they are reducing their risks, are willing to enter into contracts where the expected payoff is slightly negative.[11]

Backwardated commodity markets have downward sloping futures curves. The longer dated the futures contract the greater must be the discount compared to the expected future spot price to compensate the speculator for assuming the price risk of the underlying commodity for a longer period of time. Therefore, longer dated futures contracts are priced cheaper than shorter term futures contracts.

The reverse situation of a backwardated commodity market is a *contango market*. In a contango market, the inequality sign in equation (12.6) is reversed — the expected future spot price, S_T, is less than the current futures price, F_T.

A contango situation will occur when the most likely hedger of the commodity is naturally short the underlying commodity. Consider the aircraft manufacturer, Boeing. The single largest raw material input in the construction of any jet aircraft is aluminum for the superstructure of the plane. Boeing is a major consumer of aluminum, but it does not own any aluminum mining interests. Therefore, it is naturally short aluminum and must cover this short exposure by purchasing aluminum to meet its manufacturing needs.

This puts Boeing at risk to rising aluminum prices. To hedge this risk, Boeing can purchase aluminum futures contracts.[12] However, a speculator must be lured to the market to sell the futures contract to Boeing and to take on commodity price risk. To entice the speculator, Boeing must be willing to purchase the futures contract at a price F_T that is greater than the expected future spot price:

$$F_T > E(S_T) \tag{12.7}$$

Boeing is willing to purchase the futures contract at an expected loss in return for eliminating the uncertainty over aluminum prices. The speculator will sell the futures contract and expect to earn a profit of $F_T - E(S_T)$.

---

[11] Although the term backwardation is used to describe generally the condition where futures prices are lower than the current spot price, the term *normal backwardation* refers to the precise condition where the expected future spot price is greater than the current futures price. I am indebted to Ray Venner, Ph.D., of the CalPERS Investment Staff for this important distinction.

[12] This is but one way that Boeing hedges its short exposure to aluminum. It can enter into long-term contracts to purchase aluminum at fixed prices. These are essentially custom-tailored futures contracts, or forward contracts.

Of course, the speculator might earn more or less (or even lose money) depending upon the actual spot price of aluminum at maturity of the futures contract. If the inequality in equation (12.7) remains true at maturity of the aluminum futures contract, then the speculator will earn $F_T - S_T$.

The reader might ask why the speculator is necessary. Why doesn't Boeing negotiate directly with aluminum producers in fixed price contracts to lock in the price of aluminum and eliminate its commodity price exposure? To the extent it can, Boeing does. In fact, to the extent that commodity producers and commodity consumers can negotiate directly with one another, price risk can be eliminated without the need for speculators. However, the manufacture of aluminum does not always match Boeing's production cycle, and Boeing will have short-term demands for aluminum that will expose it to price risk. Speculators fill this gap.

Similarly, ExxonMobil has a nondiversified exposure to crude oil. It can reduce the price risk associated with oil by selling its production forward. Yet, in many cases there may not be a willing consumer to purchase the forward production of crude oil. Therefore, ExxoMobiln must sell its future production at a discount to entice the speculator/investor into the market.

Contango futures markets have an upward sloping price curve. That is, the longer dated the futures contract, the greater must be the futures price that the speculator receives from selling the futures contract to the hedger. Higher prices reflect the additional risk that the speculator accepts over the longer period of time.

Backwardated versus contango markets also depend upon global supply and demand of the underlying commodity. Consider the case of crude oil. In early 1999, the market was awash in crude oil. Additional production from Iraq, a slowdown in Asian economies from the Asian Contagion in 1998, and lack of agreement (read cheating) by OPEC members led to a glut of crude oil. As a result, crude oil futures contracts reflected a contango market.

However backwardated versus contango markets can also reflect who bears the most risk of commodity price changes at any given time. For example, in December 2005, most consumers of crude oil had experienced a significant period of prolonged crude oil price increases. The cost of a gallon of gasoline in the United States peaked at $3.25 a gallon in the late autumn of 2005. In addition, ongoing concern over the stability of Iraq—the second largest produce of oil in OPEC—led to instability of crude oil prices. Then the devastating impact of Hurricane Katrina (remember the complete evacuation of New Orleans) and other tropical storms in the autumn of 2005 disrupted oil supplies throughout the United States.

As a result, in late 2005, the risk of commodity price changes was felt squarely by oil consumers and not oil producers. Oil consumers are naturally short crude oil and they bore greater risk regarding the future price of crude oil than the oil producers because of all of the adverse supply shocks in the oil market during 2005. To hedge this risk, they purchased crude oil futures contracts to lock in with certainty the price of their oil consumption. The result is demonstrated by the contango crude oil market displayed in Exhibit 12.10. Consumers of oil were literally shocked by all of the price shocks associated with crude oil over the prior 18 months and naturally became cautious and risk averse concerning the direction of oil prices in the near future. As a result, the primary hedger of oil prices in late 2005 was not the oil producers but oil consumers. The result was a contango market where oil consumers had to compensate speculators by purchasing crude oil futures contracts at a futures price that was greater than the expected future spot price (see equation (12.7)).

In contrast, consider Exhibit 12.11. This is the futures market for crude oil as of the beginning of 2004. This market clearly demonstrates a backwardated crude oil price curve.

Why the difference? At the beginning of 2004, the crude oil market was functioning normally. There were no excessive price shocks, no drastic weather, and Iraq had been liberated from the oppressive regime of Sadaam Hussein. At this time, the price risk of crude oil rested upon the shoulders of crude oil produces. In order to hedge their risk, they had to entice speculators into the market by offering a futures price that

EXHIBIT 12.10   Contango Market for Crude Oil Futures, December 2005

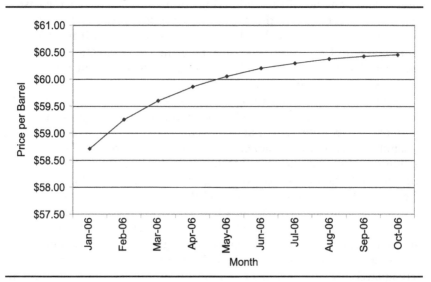

EXHIBIT 12.11   Backwardated Market for Crude Oil Futures, January 2004

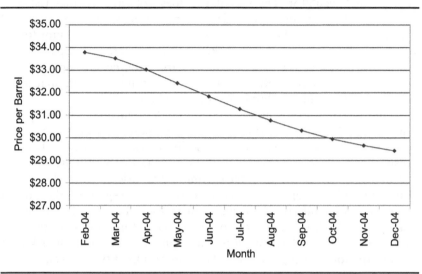

was sufficiently less than the expected future spot price. The result is the backwardated curve in Exhibit 12.11.

Commodity markets are backwardated most of the time. In fact the crude oil market is in backwardation approximately 70% of the time. The reason is that backwardated markets encourage commodity producers to produce. Consider Exhibit 12.11. In January 2004, ExxonMobil had a choice: It could produce crude oil immediately and sell it at a price of $33.78 per barrel or it could wait 12 months and sell it at an expected price of $29.42. The choice is easy; ExxonMobil would prefer to produce today and sell crude oil at a higher price rather than produce tomorrow and sell it a lower price. Therefore, backwardation is a necessary condition to encourage current production of the underlying commodity.

However, sometimes supply and demand become unbalanced as was the case with crude oil in 2005. When this occurs, commodity futures markets can reverse their natural course and flip between backwardation and contango. In addition, a contango market can develop when the risk bearing shifts from commodity producers to commodity consumers. This happened in December 2005. After several price shocks over the prior two years, commodity crude oil consumers became extremely risk averse. Their increased level of risk aversion led to a shift in the risk bearing for crude oil prices, and they became the dominant hedger in the crude oil market. This resulted in the contango market documented in Exhibit 12.10.

Exhibits 12.10 and 12.11 also highlight another useful point: the role of the speculator. The speculator does not care whether the commodity markets are in backwardation or contango; she is agnostic. All the speculator cares about is receiving an appropriate premium for the price risk she will bear. If the market is backwardated, the speculator is willing to purchase the futures contract from the hedger, but only at a discount. If the commodities market is in contango, the speculator will sell the futures contract, but only at a premium.

One last important point must be made regarding Exhibits 12.10 and 12.11. The speculator/investor in commodity futures can earn a profit no matter which way the commodity markets are acting. The conclusion is that the expected long-term returns to commodity investing are independent of the long-term commodity price trends. As we just demonstrated, the speculator is agnostic with respect to the current price trend of crude oil. Investment profits can be earned whether the market is in backwardation or contango. Therefore, profits in the commodity markets are determined by the supply and demand for risk capital, not the long-term pricing trends of the commodity markets.

COMMODITY PRICES COMPARED TO FINANCIAL ASSET PRICES

In this section, we compare commodity prices to financial asset prices. As we stated at the beginning of the chapter, financial asset prices reflect the long-term discounted value of a stream of expected future revenues. In the case of stock prices, this future revenue stream may be eternal. In the case of a bond, the time is finite but can be very long, 10 to 20 years of expected cash flows. Investors in financial assets are compensated for the risk of fluctuating cash flows, and this risk is reflected in the interest rate used to discount those cash flows.

Thus, long-term expectations and interest rates are critical for pricing financial assets. Conversely, speculators and investors in commodities earn returns for bearing short-term commodity price risk. By bearing the price risk for commodity producers and commodity consumers, commodity investors and speculators receive exposure to the hedger's short-term earnings instead of its long-term cash flows. This point is all the more illuminated by how quickly the commodity markets can flip flop between a contango market and a backwardated market. Exhibits 12.10 and 12.11 demonstrate that the nature of risk bearing can shift dramatically from producers to consumers of commodities.

This short-term exposure to a hedger's earnings illustrates that commodities will be priced very differently from financial assets. Long-term expectations and interest rates have only a minimal impact on commodity prices. Therefore, commodity prices can react very differently from financial asset prices when short-term expectations and long-term expectations diverge. This divergence occurs naturally as part of the course of the business cycle.

For instance, at the bottom of a recession, the short-term expectation of the economy's growth is negative. Commodity prices will decline to reflect this lower demand for raw inputs. However, it is at the bottom of a recession when discount rates are low and when long-term earnings expectations are revised upwards that stocks and bonds begin to perform well. The converse is true at the peak of an expansion. Commodity prices are high, but long-term earnings expectations decline.

The different reactions to different parts of the business cycle indicate that commodities tend to move in the opposite direction of stocks and bonds. This has important portfolio implications that we will discuss in the following chapters. Suffice for now to understand that commodity prices follow different pricing dynamics than that of financial assets.

CONCLUSION

We established commodity futures as a separate asset class distinct from financial assets. Commodity futures contracts are important tools not only for hedgers but also for speculators. Many hedge funds make use of the futures markets either for arbitrage opportunities or to earn risk premiums.

We also laid the groundwork in terms of pricing dynamics and discussed the economics of commodity futures markets. In the next two chapters we will demonstrate how commodity futures can be added to a diversified portfolio to improve the overall risk and return profile of that portfolio.

CHAPTER 13

Investing in Commodity Futures

I n Chapter 12 we presented an introduction to the commodity markets and the methods by which investors access those markets. In this chapter we expand the discussion to discuss the strategic reasons for investing in commodity futures.

We begin by developing the economic case for commodity futures. We then review the existing literature on the diversification benefits of commodity futures. Last, we examine several investable benchmarks that have been developed for the commodity futures markets.

Our discussion in this chapter focuses on the class of physical commodity futures. These commodity futures are sometimes referred to as "real assets"—assets that increase in value with inflation.[1] Real assets may also be defined by the tangible nature of their existence. A stock or a bond is represented by a piece of paper, but a real asset has a physical presence such as gold, oil, cattle, or wheat.[2]

ECONOMIC RATIONALE

We previously stated that commodities are an asset class distinct from stocks and bonds. In this section we clarify that distinction and demonstrate where and why commodity prices react differently than capital asset prices.

---

[1] See Kenneth Froot, "Hedging Portfolios with Real Assets," *The Journal of Portfolio Management* (Summer 1995), pp. 60–77.

[2] Under this definition, real estate also qualifies as a real asset because there is a tangible nature to the investment (i.e., a building, a shopping center, an apartment complex).

Commodities and the Business Cycle

In Chapter 12, we demonstrated that commodity prices are not as directly impacted by changes in discount rates as stocks and bonds. We also discussed how commodity prices are not determined by the discounted value of future cash flows. Instead, commodity prices are determined by the current supply and demand of the underlying commodity. Since commodity prices are driven by different economic fundamentals as stocks and bonds, they should be expected to have little correlation or even negative correlation with the prices of capital assets.

There are three arguments why commodity prices should be negatively correlated with the prices of stocks and bonds. The first is the relationship that commodity futures prices have with inflation. Inflation is well documented to have a detrimental impact on the values of stocks and bonds. However, inflation is expected to have a positive impact on commodity futures prices for two reasons.

First, physical commodity prices such as oil are an underlying source of inflation. As the cost of raw materials increases, so does the producers' price inflation and the consumer price inflation. In fact, commodity prices are a component of the producer price index and the consumer price index. Therefore, higher commodity prices mean higher inflation.

Also higher inflation means higher short-term interest rates. This is also has a beneficial impact on commodity futures investments because of their collateral yield. As we discussed in the prior chapter, commodity futures contracts can be purchased with a down payment known as the initial margin. The initial margin can be contributed in the form of cash or in U.S. Treasury bills. This means that one component of return from an investment in commodity futures is the interest that is earned on the margin deposit that supports the futures contract.[3] Higher inflation, therefore, means a higher interest rate on the margin on deposit, and a higher return from investing in commodity futures contracts.

Exhibit 13.1 documents the relationship between inflation, commodity futures, and stocks and bonds. This chart plots the correlation of monthly returns between large-cap stocks (the Russell 1000), small-cap stocks (the Russell 2000), international stocks (MSCI EAFE and the FTSE indexes) high-yield bonds (the Salomon Smith Barney High Yield Cash Pay Index) U.S. Treasury bonds, and commodities (as represented by the Goldman Sachs Commodity Index) with the rate of inflation. The time period is January 1990 through December 2005.[4]

---

[3] If the futures margin is deposited in cash, then the futures broker may pay a higher interest rate on that deposit. Alternatively, if the futures margin is deposited in Treasury bills, as the T-bills mature, newer, higher yielding T-bills may be used to replace them.

EXHIBIT 13.1   Correlation of Stocks, Bonds and Commodities with the U.S.
Inflation Rate

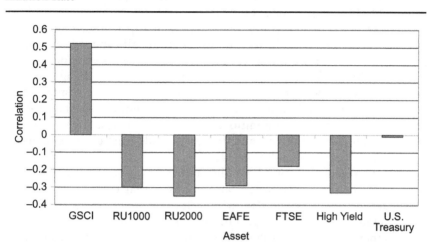

As can be seen, commodity futures prices are positively correlated with inflation. Conversely, capital assets such as stocks and bonds are negatively correlated with inflation. Therefore, throughout the course of the business cycle, as inflation increases, capital asset values decrease, but commodity futures values increase. The reverse is also true, as inflation decreases, capital asset prices increase, but commodity futures prices decrease.

Notice that the Financial Times Stock Index (FTSE) of the 100 largest stocks traded on the London Stock Exchange and the MSCI EAFE index (Europe, Australia and the Far East) are also negatively correlated with the U.S. inflation rate. This is important to note because an investor seeking international diversification as a means to escape the ravages of domestic inflation did not find it in foreign stocks.

Even more important, commodity futures prices are positively correlated with *the change* in the inflation rate while capital assets are negatively correlated with changes in the rate of inflation.[5] This is important because changes in the rate of inflation tend to reflect inflation shocks (i.e., unanticipated changes that force investors to revise their expectations about future inflation). A positive change in the inflation rate means

---

[4] We use the Goldman Sachs Commodity Index as our proxy for commodity prices. There are, in fact, several commodity indexes that we will discuss later in the chapter. Data for the GSCI was provided by Heather Shemilt at Goldman Sachs.

[5] See Philip Halpern and Randy Warsager, "The Performance of Energy and Non-Energy Based Commodity Investment Vehicles in Periods of Inflation," *The Journal of Alternative Assets* (Summer 1998), pp. 75–81.

that investor's expectations regarding future inflation rates will increase. Stocks and bond prices react negatively to such revised expectations while commodity futures prices react positively.

Exhibit 13.2 demonstrates the reaction of capital assets and commodity assets to changes in the rate of inflation. All capital assets (with the exception of MSCI EAFE—curious but we have no explanation for this) including U.S. Treasury bonds react negatively to changes in the inflation rate, while commodities react positively. In fact, commodities have a stronger correlation to changes in the inflation rate than to the absolute inflation rate. In addition, some capital assets, such as small-cap stocks, high-yield bonds, and Treasury bonds react even more negatively to changes in the inflation rate.

A second reason why commodity returns may be negatively correlated with the returns to stocks and bonds is that commodity futures prices are impacted by short-term expectations while stocks and bonds are affected by long-term expectations. For example, in a strong economy financial assets may decline over fears of increased inflation or sustainability of the economic growth. These are long-term concerns. Conversely, commodity prices will react favorably because they are influenced by the high demand for raw materials under the current market conditions. The result is that commodity futures prices and stock-and-bond prices can react very differently at different parts of the business cycle. Exhibit 13.3 diagrams these different cyclical price moves.

This counter-cyclical movement between commodity futures and stocks and bonds is demonstrated by research conducted by Goldman

EXHIBIT 13.2 Correlation of Stocks, Bonds, and Commodities with Changes in Inflation

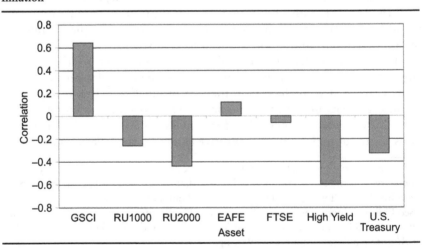

EXHIBIT 13.3   The Business Cycle and Stock, Bond, and Commodity Prices

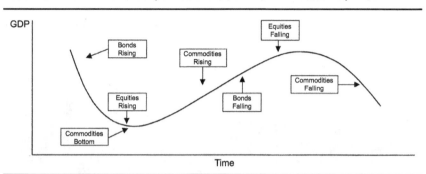

Sachs & Co.[6] When the economy is below capacity (as measured by long-run GDP), equity returns have been at their highest, but commodity prices have been at their lowest. This occurs at the bottom of an economic cycle. As economic growth accelerates, stock prices begin to decline but commodity prices increase. When the economy heats up and exceeds long-run GDP, the return to commodity futures exceeds that for stocks. In sum, commodity prices rise and fall coincident with the current state of the economic cycle while stocks and bonds are priced based on their future cash flows and not the current state of the economy.

The point of Exhibit 13.4 is that stocks and bonds are anticipatory in their pricing while commodities are priced based on the state of current economic conditions. The value of stocks and bonds is derived from expectations regarding long-term earnings and coupon payments. Consequently, they perform best when the economy appears the worst but the prospects for improvement are the highest.

Real assets, on the other hand, show the opposite pattern. Commodity prices are determined not so much by the future prospects of the economy, but by the level of current economic activity. Consequently commodity prices are at their lowest when economic activity is at its lowest, and vice versa.

A third argument for the negative correlation between commodity prices and capital assets is based on economic production.[7] Consider the three primary inputs to economic production: capital, labor, and raw materials. The returns to these three factors should equal the price of

---

[6] See Goldman Sachs & Co., "The Strategic Case for Using Commodities in Portfolio Diversification," Goldman Sachs Research Series on Commodities as an Asset Class (July 1996).
[7] See Robert Greer, "Institutional Use of Physical Commodity Indices," in *Commodity Derivatives and Finance* (London: Euromoney Books, 1999).

EXHIBIT 13.4   Commodity Returns are Coincident with the State of the Economic Cycle

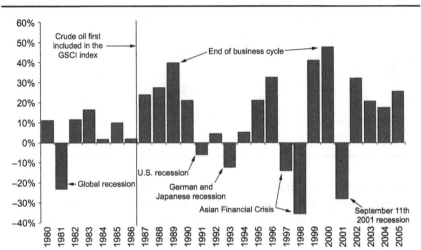

Reprinted with Permission from Goldman Sachs.

production. In the short to intermediate term, the cost of labor should remain stable. Therefore, for any given price level of production, an increase in the return to capital must mean a reduction in the return to raw materials, and vice versa. The result is a negative correlation between commodity prices and the prices of capital assets.

Commodity prices are expected to be at the very least uncorrelated with the returns to stocks and bonds. Additionally, there are three reasons to expect commodity prices to be negatively correlated with stocks and bonds. First, inflation has a positive effect on commodity prices but a negative impact on stocks and bonds. Second, commodity prices are impacted by a different set of expectations than that for stocks and bonds. Also, in the production process, there is a tradeoff between the returns to capital and the returns to raw materials.

Event Risk

In Chapters 6 and 7 we demonstrated how financial assets and hedge fund strategies are exposed to significant event risk. For example, our analysis of the returns to hedge funds around the financial turmoil of August and September 1998 indicated that most hedge fund strategies experienced significant negative returns. Additionally, we demonstrated that most arbitrage strategies have exposure to event risk, which can result in significant negative returns.

Commodities, by contrast, tend to have *positive* exposure to event risk. The reason is that the surprises that occur in the commodities markets tend to be those that unexpectedly reduce the supply of the commodity to the market. Events such as OPEC agreements to reduce the supply of crude oil, a cold snap in winter, war, or political instability can drive up energy prices. Similarly, events such as droughts, floods, and crop freezes all reduce the supply of agricultural products. Strikes and labor unrest can also drive up the prices of both precious and industrial metals.

These patterns of unexpected shocks to the commodity prices should provide a pattern of positively skewed returns. In Chapter 6 we demonstrated that many hedge fund strategies have positively skewed distributions—that is, more return observations to the right of the median (positive) than to the left of the median (negative). Positively skewed return distributions will have a beneficial impact to a diversified portfolio because they can provide an upward return bias to the portfolio.

We will examine the distribution of commodity futures returns later in this chapter. Suffice it for now, that these patterns of returns demonstrate a positive skew to commodity futures prices indicating a bias for upside returns, instead of downside returns.

Furthermore, these patterns of commodity shocks are expected to be uncorrelated. For example, OPEC agreements to cut oil production should be uncorrelated with droughts in the agricultural regions around the world or with labor strikes affecting metals mining. The point is that the global supply and demand factors for each individual commodity market that determine the price of each commodity are very different. The primary factors that determine the supply and demand for, and the price of, oil are very different from those that affect the price of wheat, gold or aluminum. Consequently, we would expect the price patterns of commodities to be uncorrelated with each other. This has important implications for commodity indexes.

Equally important is that shocks to the commodities markets are expected to be at the least, uncorrelated with the financial markets, and more likely, to be negatively correlated with the financial markets. The reason follows from our discussion above—most shocks to the commodity markets tend to reduce the supply of raw materials to the market. The sudden decrease of raw materials should have a positive impact on commodity prices, but a negative impact on financial asset prices, whose expected returns will be reduced by the higher cost of production inputs.

Consider Exhibit 13.5. This exhibit demonstrates several years where there were significant shocks to the supply and demand of physical commodities. Again, we use the GSCI as a benchmark for commodity returns. In the early and mid 1970s there were a series of oil price shocks. This was a boon for commodity prices, but disaster for financial asset prices. In contrast, 1981 was a year of severe recession for the

EXHIBIT 13.5   Annual Returns in Years of Market Stress

Year	S&P 500	Commodities
1973	–14.70%	74.96%
1974	–26.50%	39.50%
1977	–7.20%	10.40%
1981	–4.90%	–23.00%
1987	5.25%	23.80%
Oct. 1987	–21.50%	1.00%
1990	–3.10%	29.10%
1998	26.70%	–35.80%
2000	–10.10%	49.70%
2001	–11.80%	–31.90%
2002	–22.10%	32.10%

United States. Financial asset prices declined but so did commodities, as there was simply insufficient demand both for finished goods and raw materials to support either financial asset prices or commodity prices.

1990 was the year of the Iraqi invasion of Kuwait. This political instability had a negative impact on financial asset prices, but a positive impact on commodity prices. Then in 1998 there was a glut of cheap crude oil and petroleum products on in the market. In late 1997, OPEC voted to increase production just as the southeast Asian economies were slipping into a steep recession. In addition under the UN "food for oil" program, new oil production came on line from Iraq. Furthermore, an extremely mild winter (recall "El Niño") resulted in a build up of petroleum inventories around the world. The result, in 1998, was plenty of cheap raw materials, which in turn translated to strong stock market gains in the United States.

Then we had the three year equity bear market following the bursting of the technology bubble. Note that in 2001 when the economy slid into a brief recession, commodity prices and stock prices moved in the same direction. Otherwise, commodities were not correlated with the stock market movements during the bear market.

In conclusion, commodity price shocks tend to favor supply disruptions rather than sudden increases in supply. These disruptions provide positive returns for commodities at the same time that they provide negative returns for financial assets. Therefore, the event risk associated with commodities tends to favor investors in the commodity markets while detrimentally impacting investors in the financial markets. In the next section we discuss the empirical literature that supports the notion of commodities within a diversified portfolio.

THE EMPIRICAL EVIDENCE SUPPORTING COMMODITY FUTURES AS AN ASSET CLASS

While commodities within an investment portfolio are considered to be a new phenomenon, the fact is that organized commodity trading has been in existence far longer than stock-and-bond trading. The first commodity exchange was the Osaka rice exchange that began trading in Japan in the 1400s. By contrast, the New York Stock Exchange did not begin trading until the early 1800s. Nonetheless, commodity futures investing is relatively new compared to stock-and-bond investing.

In his seminal paper more than two decades ago, Greer introduced the idea of investing in commodity futures as a portfolio diversification tool.[8] In his article, he proposed an unleveraged index of commodity futures prices be used as an inflation hedge for a stock portfolio. He demonstrated that a combination of a commodity futures index and large-capitalized stocks provided a better risk and return profile than a portfolio constructed solely of stocks.

Five years later, Zvi Bodie examined how commodity futures contracts can supplement a portfolio of stocks and bonds to improve the risk and return tradeoff in an inflationary environment.[9] Studying the period of 1953 to 1981, he found that the inclusion of commodity futures shifts the efficient frontier up and to the left. He concluded that a portfolio of stocks, bonds, Treasury bills, and commodity futures improved the risk and return than an investment portfolio constructed without commodity futures.

In more recent research, Ankrim and Hensel,[10] Lummer and Scott,[11] Kaplan and Lummer,[12] Gibson,[13] and Anson[14] all examine adding com-

---

[8] See Robert Greer, "Conservative Commodities: A Key Inflation Hedge," *Journal of Portfolio Management* (Summer 1978), pp. 26–29.

[9] See Zvi Bodie, "Commodity Futures as a Hedge Against Inflation," *Journal of Portfolio Management* (Spring 1983), pp. 12–17.

[10] Ernest Ankrim and Chris Hensel, "Commodities in Asset Allocation: A Real Asset Alternative to Real Estate?" *Financial Analysts Journal* (May/June 1993), pp. 20–29.

[11] Scott Lummer and Laurence Siegel, "GSCI Collateralized Futures: A Hedging and Diversification Tool for Institutional Investors," *Journal of Investing* (Summer 1993), pp. 75–82.

[12] Paul Kaplan and Scott Lummer, "GSCI Collateralized Futures as a Hedging and Diversification Tool for Institutional Investors: An Update," working paper, Ibbotson Associates (November 1997).

[13] Roger Gibson, "The Rewards of Multiple Asset Class Investing," *Journal of Financial Planning* (March 1999), pp. 50–59.

[14] Mark Anson, "Spot Returns, Roll Yield, and Diversification with Commodity Futures," *Journal of Alternative Investments* (Winter 1998), pp. 16–32.

modity futures to an investment portfolio through an investment in a passive commodity futures index. All five studies conclude that an investment in a passive commodities futures index provides a good diversifier for stocks and bonds as well as an effective hedge against inflation.

Satyanarayan and Varagnis extend the investment analysis of commodity futures to an international portfolio.[15] They find that commodity futures returns are negatively correlated with the returns to all developed markets and with three of six emerging markets. One reason why all developed markets are negatively correlated with the returns to commodity futures is that developed markets are the primary consumers of commodity inputs. Conversely, emerging markets tend to be net suppliers of commodity inputs. Consequently, it is not surprising to find that some emerging markets are positively correlated with commodity futures prices.

Anson extends the analysis of commodity futures to utility theory. He finds that the marginal utility of commodity futures investing increases with an investor's level of risk aversion. That is, the more risk averse the investor, the greater the utility from investing in commodity futures.[16]

Froot compares three classes of real assets: real estate, commodity futures, and the stocks of companies that are commodity producers.[17] He finds that when commodity futures are the initial hedge in a portfolio, it renders the other real assets ineffective. Yet when commodity futures are added to the portfolio as a secondary hedge after other real assets have already been added, commodity futures still remain a significant portfolio diversifier. However, he concludes that the same cannot be said for real estate. Once commodity futures have been added to an investment portfolio, real estate does little to reduce portfolio volatility. The same conclusion is reached for commodity-based equity. In other words, commodity futures provide a more effective hedge against unexpected inflation than do either real estate or the stock of commodity producing companies.

In conclusion, prior empirical studies have found commodity futures to have significant diversification potential for financial assets. All of the studies to date have found that the addition of commodity futures to a portfolio of stocks and bonds has the ability to reduce the risk of the portfolio for a given level of return. Furthermore, each of these studies used an investable commodity futures index to reach their conclusions.

---

[15] See Sudhakar Satyanarayan and Panos Varangis, "Diversification Benefits of Commodity Assets in Global Portfolios," *The Journal of Investing* (Spring 1996), pp. 69–78.

[16] See Mark Anson, "Maximizing Utility with Commodity Futures," *The Journal of Portfolio Management* (Summer 1999), pp. 86–94.

[17] See Kenneth Froot, "Hedging Portfolios with Real Assets," *The Journal of Portfolio Management* (Summer 1995), pp. 60–77.

COMMODITY FUTURES INDEXES

In this section we review several investable commodity futures indexes, analyze their construction, and consider their application to a diversified portfolio.

Description of a Commodity Futures Index

The first commodity indexes were designed to reflect price changes either in the cash/spot markets or in the futures markets. However, these indexes did not reflect the total return that can be earned from commodity futures contracts. Therefore, they were not investable. An example of a price change index is the Commodity Research Bureau (CRB) Commodities Index.

A commodity futures index should represent the total return that would be earned from holding only long positions in unleveraged physical commodity futures. Financial futures should not be included because, as we demonstrated in Chapter 12, financial futures contracts are economically linked to the underlying financial assets. There is then no diversification benefit from adding long positions in financial futures to a portfolio of financial assets.

In Chapter 12, we also described how a futures contract may be purchased by paying only a small portion of the total price of the underlying commodity called the initial margin. The initial margin typically represents 5% to 10% of the futures price. Futures contracts are purchased with leverage. For example, a 10% initial margin requirement translates into a leverage ratio of 10 to 1. This means that for every dollar invested in a commodity futures contract, the investor would receive $10 of commodity price exposure. The application of leverage can enhance an investor's return, but at the same time can also exacerbate an investor's losses. Therefore, the leverage associated with a futures contract can increase the volatility of the investment.

In contrast, commodity futures indexes are constructed to be unleveraged. The face value of the futures contracts are fully supported (collateralized) either by cash or by Treasury bills. Futures contracts are purchased to provide economic exposure to commodities equal to the amount of cash dollars invested in the index. Thus every dollar of exposure to a commodity futures index represents one dollar of commodity price risk.

For example, the current initial margin for gold is $1,500. With gold selling at $500 and 100 ounces of gold being the size of the contract, one futures contract has economic exposure to gold of $50,000. A managed futures account would typically pay the initial margin of

$1,500 and receive economic exposure to gold equivalent to $50,000. The percentage of equity capital committed to the futures contract is equal to $1,500/$50,000 = 3%. In contrast, a commodity futures index will fully collateralize the gold futures contract. This means $50,000 of U.S. Treasury bills are held to fully support the face value of the gold futures contract. In fact, the face value of every futures contract included in a commodity index will be fully collateralized by an investment in U.S. Treasury bills.

In this way, an unleveraged commodity futures index represents the returns an investor could earn from continuously holding a passive long-only position in a basket of commodity futures contracts. The passive index must reflect all components of return from commodity futures contracts: price changes, collateral yield, and roll yield.

Finally, we note that a commodity futures index has several differences compared to a managed futures account. Managed futures accounts represent the returns that can be earned from the active investment style of a Commodity Trading Advisor (CTA) or a Commodity Pool Operator (CPO). In a managed futures account the CTA or CPO has discretion over the trading positions taken.

First, managed futures accounts are just that—actively managed accounts—while commodity futures indexes are designed to provide passive exposure to the commodity futures markets. Second, CTAs and CPOs tend to invest across the spectrum of the futures markets, including financial futures as well as commodity futures in their investment portfolio. Third, CTAs and CPOs may invest both long and short in futures contracts. Commodity futures indexes, in contrast, invest in long-only positions. Last, managed futures accounts tend to apply leverage in the purchase and sale of commodity futures contracts. We will have more to say about the managed futures industry in Chapter 15.

Sources of Index Return

The total return from an unleveraged commodity futures index comes from three primary sources: changes in spot prices of the underlying commodity, the interest earned from the Treasury bills used to collateralize the futures contracts, and the roll yield. Each component can be an important part of the return of a commodity index in any given year.

Spot Prices

As we indicated in Chapter 12, spot commodity prices are determined by the supply and demand characteristics of each commodity market as well as the current level of risk aversion between consumers and producers of commodities. We demonstrated, for example, how the price of crude oil plummeted in 1998 due to overproduction by OPEC members, extra production by Iraq, and the slow down in southeast Asia due to the Asian Contagion of late 1997. This supply imbalance drove crude oil prices down. However, in early 1999, OPEC members reached an agreement to cut production and restrict the supply of crude oil into the marketplace. This changed the supply and demand equilibrium from one of excess supply to one of excess demand, and crude oil prices rose significantly.

These price changes in the spot market are reflected directly in the commodity futures markets. Recall the following equation from Chapter 12:

$$F = Se^{(r + c - y)(T - t)} \tag{13.1}$$

where

F is the futures price.
S is the current spot/cash price of the underlying commodity.
r is the risk-free rate of return.
c is the cost of storage.
y is the convenience yield.
T − t is the time to maturity of the contract.

Other factors remaining equal (storage cost, risk-free rate, and convenience yield), when the spot price of the underlying commodity increases in value, so will the futures price. The reverse is also true, as spot prices decline, so will the futures price. So changes in the current cash price of a commodity flow right through to the futures price.

This is important to understand, because as we discussed above, most of the shocks with respect to physical commodities tend to be events that reduce the current supply. That is, physical commodities have positive event risk. Supply and demand shocks to the physical commodity markets result in positive price changes for both the spot market and the futures market.

Collateral Yield

As we discussed earlier, a commodity futures index is unleveraged. It is unleveraged because the economic exposure underlying the basket of futures contract is fully collateralized by the purchase of U.S. Treasury bills. Therefore, for every $1 invested in a commodity futures index, the investor receives $1 dollar of diversified commodity exposure plus interest on $1 dollar invested in U.S. Treasury bills.

The interest earned on the Treasury bills used as collateral is called the *collateral yield*, and it can be a significant part of the total return to a commodity futures index. Furthermore, changes in inflation rates will be reflected in the yield on Treasury bills. This is another way that a commodity futures index can hedge against inflation.

Roll Yield

Roll yield is the least obvious source of return for commodity futures. Roll yield is derived from the shape of the commodity futures term structure. Recall our discussion from Chapter 12 that commodity futures markets can either be in backwardation, where futures prices are below the spot price, or contango, where futures prices are above the current spot price for the underlying commodity.

When the futures markets are in backwardation, a positive return will be earned from a simple "buy and hold" strategy. The positive return is earned because as the futures contract gets closer to maturity, its price must converge to that of the spot price of the commodity. Since the spot price is greater than the futures price, this means that the futures price must increase in value. This convergence is known as "rolling up the yield curve," or simply, "roll yield." A demonstration should help.

Consider Exhibit 13.6. This exhibit demonstrates the term structure for crude oil futures contracts in June and July 2004. Notice that the futures prices decline the longer the maturity of the futures contract. The term structure is therefore downward sloping. This is a demonstra-

EXHIBIT 13.6   Term Structure for Crude Oil Futures

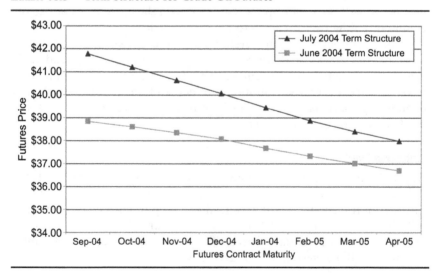

tion of backwardation—the futures prices are below the current spot price for crude oil.

Recall that a backwardated market indicates that producers of commodities are willing to hedge their commodity price risk by selling their future production at lower prices than the current spot price of the commodity. The farther out in time that they sell their future production, the greater the discount they must offer to investors to entice them to purchase the futures contracts. As a futures contract gets closer to maturity, less price risk remains, and an investor will harvest part of the price discount as profit by rolling up the futures yield curve. Rolling up the term structure results in profit harvesting.

In July 2004, the futures term structure is slightly above the crude oil term structure that existed in June, reflecting an increase in crude oil spot prices of about $1.50. The increase in spot prices shifted the whole term structure upwards. In addition to the price appreciation, the owner of a long crude oil can earn the roll yield.

Exhibit 13.7 calculates the roll yield associated with each futures contract over the one-month holding period of June to July 2004. As a futures contract approaches maturity, there is less price risk and therefore less of a discount is required to entice buyers into the market. Therefore, part of the price discount can be harvested by rolling up the yield curve.

For example, suppose an investor purchased at the beginning of June 2004 the crude oil futures contract maturing in September 2004. On June 1, 2004, the September futures contract was priced at $38.83. One month later, on July 1, 2004, the September crude oil futures contract was priced at $41.77. Of the $2.94 increase in price for the September futures contract, $1.50 was due to an increase in spot prices. The remainder, $1.44, was the roll yield earned from the buy-and-hold strategy.

EXHIBIT 13.7 Calculation of the Roll Yield for Crude Oil Futures

Contract Maturity	Price as of July 2004	Less Price at June 2004	Less Change in Spot Price	Equals Roll Yield
Sep-04	$41.77	$38.83	$1.50	$1.44
Oct-04	$41.20	$38.60	$1.50	$1.10
Nov-04	$40.62	$38.34	$1.50	$0.78
Dec-04	$40.05	$38.06	$1.50	$0.49
Jan-05	$39.43	$37.67	$1.50	$0.26
Feb-05	$38.87	$37.32	$1.50	$0.05
Mar-05	$38.39	$37.00	$1.50	–$0.11
Apr-05	$37.97	$36.69	$1.50	–$0.22

As can be seen, the roll yield is greater the closer the futures contract is to maturity. This is because a greater amount of uncertainty is reduced the closer the futures contract is to maturity. The farther out on the term structure an investor goes, the less uncertainty can be resolved as a futures contract rolls up the curve. Consequently, as an investor moves farther out on the term structure, the roll yield declines, and can even be negative.

How large can this roll yield be? A study of crude oil futures prices found that a long position in the first nearby futures contract (the contract closest to maturity) earned an average annual roll yield of 9% over the period 1987 to 1995.[18] Additionally, the study found that the roll yield was greatest for commodity futures contracts that were closer to maturity.

Notice that the roll yield can also be negative. In a contango market, when futures prices are greater than spot prices, the futures prices will roll down the term structure resulting in lost value as the futures price converges to the spot price. Recall from Chapter 12, in a contango market, commodity consumers are the natural hedgers, and they purchase futures contracts. Investors who sell short the futures contracts to the commodity consumers will collect the futures premium as the futures contract rolls down the term structure.

Comparing the Components of a Commodity Index

To give the reader some sense of how the different components of a commodity index work, Exhibit 13.8 presents the returns to the GSCI Excess Return Index and the GSCI Total Return Index. The GSCI Excess Return Index measures the return from investing in the nearby GSCI futures contract and rolling this contract forward each month. It captures the roll yield as well as the movement in the underlying commodity prices over the prior month. The GSCI Total Return Index captures the all the effects associated with investing in commodity futures— roll yield, collateral yield, and commodity price changes. Notice that the GSCI Total Return is always greater than the GSCI Excess Return. This reflects the additional yield associated with Treasury bills posted as collateral against the futures positions. Unfortunately, you cannot add the return to Treasury bills (the collateral yield) directly to the GSCI Excess Return to get the GSCI Total Return because this ignores the impact of the reinvestment of Treasury bill collateral yield gains back into commodity futures as well as gains/losses from commodity futures back out of or into Treasury bills. Therefore, the difference between the Total Return Index and the Excess Return index is only an estimate of what the collateral yield was in any given year.

---

[18] See Daniel Nash, "Relative Value Trading in Commodities," working paper (July 15, 1996).

EXHIBIT 13.8　　GSCI Total Return and Excess Return

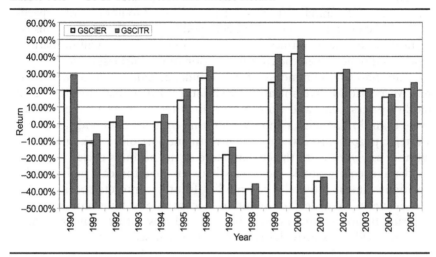

One last point to note about the returns to commodity indexes. Not only are commodity indexes excellent diversification tools vis a vis stocks and bonds, but they also have excellent diversification with respect to their sources of return. Commodity indexes earn returns from spot prices, roll yield, and collateral yield. This provides a diversification of return that enhances the probability of a positive return in any given month or year.

One last point to note about the returns to commodity indexes. Not only are commodity indexes excellent diversification tools vis a vis stocks and bonds, but they also have excellent diversification with respect to their sources of return. Commodity indexes earn returns from spot prices, roll yield, and collateral yield. This provides a diversification of return that enhances the probability of a positive return in any given month or year.

COMMODITY INDEXES

It may surprise investors that there are several commodity futures indexes in existence. These indexes have all the benefits of a stock index: They are transparent, they are liquid, you can trade in the underlying component parts of the index, and they are investable. Even if an investor, such as a pension plan, cannot invest directly into commodity futures indexes, it may still gain exposure through a commodity-linked note of the type described in Chapter 12.

An investment manager can use commodity futures indexes in two ways. First, a commodity futures index can be used to implement a specific view on the expected returns from commodities as an asset class. This is a tactical bet by the investment manager that commodities will outperform stocks and bonds given the current position of the business cycle.

Alternatively, commodity futures indexes can be used to provide passive portfolio diversification. Exhibit 13.3 demonstrated that commodity prices peak and bottom out at different parts of the business cycle than do financial assets. Within this context, commodities have a strategic purpose: to diversify the investment portfolio's risk and return, without any view as to the current state of the business cycle.

Unlike equity stock indexes, where an investor can maintain her positions almost infinitely, commodity futures contracts specify a date for delivery. In order to maintain a continuous long-only position, expiring futures contracts must be sold and new futures contracts must be purchased. This provides the roll yield discussed above.

The Goldman Sachs Commodity Index

The GSCI is designed to be a benchmark for investment in the commodity markets and as a measure of commodity market performance over time. It is also designed to be a tradable index that is readily accessible to market participants. It is a long-only index of physical commodity futures. Not only is the GSCI comprised of physical commodity futures contracts, a futures contract trades on the index itself. In other words, investors can purchase a futures contract tied to the future expected spot value of the GSCI.

The GSCI was introduced in 1991. Although the GSCI was not published prior to that time, Goldman Sachs has calculated the historical value of the GSCI and related indexes dating back to January 1970, based on historical prices of futures contracts and using the selection criteria and index construction established in 1991. The GSCI has been normalized to a value of 100 on December 31, 1969.

The GSCI is composed only of physical commodity futures. Financial futures contracts (on securities, currencies, or interest rates) are not included. The limitation to only physical commodity futures focuses the construction of the index on real assets that are the inputs to the global production process. Additionally, the GSCI is composed of the first nearby futures contract in each commodity (the futures contract that is closest to maturity).

The GSCI is a production-weighted index that is designed to reflect the relative significance of each of the constituent commodities to the world economy while preserving the tradability of the index by limiting eligible futures contracts to those with adequate liquidity. The use of production weighting is designed as an economic indicator. The GSCI assigns the appropriate weight to each commodity in proportion to the amount that commodity flows through the global economic engine. The GSCI is constructed using five-year averages of a particular commodity's contribution to world production. This is done to mitigate the effect of any aberrant year with respect to the production of a commodity.

The GSCI is constructed with 24 physical commodities across five main groups of real assets: precious metals, industrial metals, livestock, agriculture, and energy. Exhibit 13.9 presents the weights of these five commodity groups in the GSCI as of December 2005. Energy is the largest component of the index. This reflects the importance of energy products in the global production process as well as the global surge in energy prices throughout 2005. Clearly, at almost 76% of the total index as of the end of 2005, energy was the most dominant component of the worldwide production cycle. The next largest component to the index was agriculture—not surprising given the need to feed the growing worldwide population. Precious metals, on the other hand, represent the smallest component of the GSCI. While precious metals may be held as a store of value, they are a smaller input to global production.

The GSCI physical weights are set once a year (in January) and then the dollar percentage values are allowed to float for the remainder of the

EXHIBIT 13.9 GSCI Commodity Group Weights, December 2005

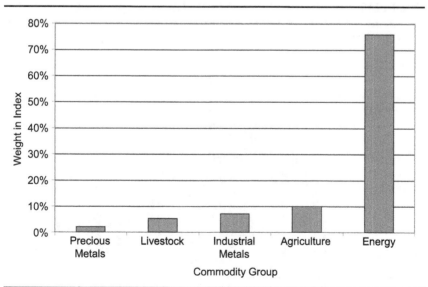

year. There is no limit to the weight any one commodity may become of the index and no minimum weight for any commodity. The GSCI is a (production) value-weighted index. Value-weighted indexes represent a momentum investment strategy because those commodity futures contracts that do well represent an increasing portion of the index.

Last, we consider the distribution of returns associated with the GSCI. In Exhibit 13.10 we plot the monthly return distribution for the GSCI over the period 1990 to 2005. First, note the wide dispersion of monthly returns to the GSCI. These returns vary from –15% at one end to +22% at the other end of the return distribution. In addition, the mass of the distribution is not concentrated to the same extent as hedge fund returns. For example, the mass of the GSCI return distribution in the 0% to 2% range is only 17%. This dispersion is further evidenced by the very high standard deviation of monthly returns of 5.67%. Compare this with the return mass associated with hedge funds. In Chapter 6 we showed how the return mass for hedge funds is frequently concentrated in the 0% to 2% range up to 77% of the time. Clearly, the GSCI generates much less consistent returns than certain hedge fund strategies.

The GSCI has a positive value of skew of 0.52 and a positive value of kurtosis of 1.28. From our discussion in Chapter 6, we know that this condition of leptokurtosis means that commodity returns experience large outlier returns more frequently than might be expected with a normal distribution. This indicates that commodity futures are exposed

EXHIBIT 13.10   Distribution of Returns for the GSCI[a]

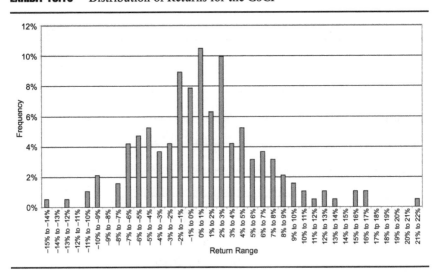

[a] Average = 0.79%, Std. Dev. = 5.67%, Slew = 0.52, Kurtosis = 1.28, Sharpe = 0.07.

to event risk: the risk of sudden shocks to the global supply and demand for physical commodities. From our discussion of commodity event risk being mostly shocks that reduce the supply of commodities, we expect that exposure to event risk to have a beneficial impact on commodity returns. The positive value of skew is consistent with this analysis.

Dow Jones-AIG Commodity Index

The Dow Jones-AIG Commodity Index (DJ-AIGCI) is designed to provide both liquidity and diversification with respect to physical commodities.[19] It is a long-only index composed of futures contracts on 19 physical commodity products. These products include energy (crude oil, heating oil, unleaded gasoline, and natural gas), precious metals (gold and silver), industrial metals (copper, aluminum, zinc, and nickel), grains (wheat, corn, soybeans, and soybean oil), livestock (live cattle and lean hogs), and the "soft" commodities (coffee, cotton, and sugar). The DJ-AIGCI is composed of commodities traded on U.S. commodity exchanges and also on the London Metals Exchange (LME). Contracts on the LME provide exposure to industrial metals such as aluminum, nickel, and zinc.

Unlike the GSCI, to determine the weightings of each commodity in the index, the DJ-AIGCI relies primarily on liquidity data. This index considers the relative amount of trading activity associated with a particular commodity to determine its weight in the index. Liquidity is an important indicator of the interest placed on a commodity by financial and physical market participants. The index also relies to a lesser extent on dollar-adjusted production data to determine index weights. Therefore, the index weights depend primarily on endogenous factors in the futures markets (liquidity), and secondarily, on exogenous factors to the futures markets (production).

The component weightings are also determined by several rules to ensure diversified commodity exposure. Disproportionate weighting to any particular commodity or sector could increase volatility and negate the concept of a broad-based commodity index. The DJ-AIGCI index also applies two important diversification rules:

1. No related group of commodities (e.g., energy products, precious metals, livestock, or grains) may constitute more than 33% of the index weights.
2. No single commodity may constitute less than 2% of the index.

---

[19] Information on the DJ-AIGCI can be found at the Dow Jones web site, www.dj.com, and using the dowjones web links to the DJ-AIGCI.

EXHIBIT 13.11   Dow Jones-AIG Commodity Index Weights, December 2005

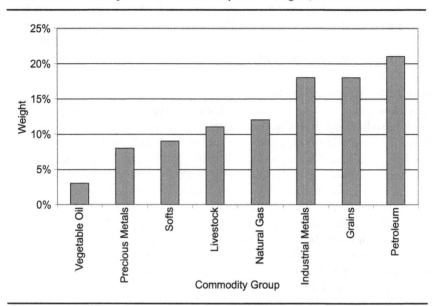

The DJ-AIGCI is reweighted and rebalanced every January. Rebalancing and reweighting are designed to reduce the exposure of the index to commodities that have appreciated in value and to increase the index's exposure to commodities that have underperformed. During the course of the year, commodity weights are free to increase or decrease as their values increase or decrease, subject to the two limits imposed above. This represents a momentum type of index.

Exhibit 13.11 presents the weights as of December 2005 associated with the DJ-AIGCI. Notice that the addition of natural gas at 12% plus petroleum products at 21% is at the 33% limit for any commodity sector (in this case, energy).

Exhibit 13.12 presents a frequency distribution of the monthly returns to the DJ-AIGCI Index over the time period 1991 to 2005.[20] Similar to the GSCI, this distribution of returns demonstrates a positive skew indicating that more positive returns are experienced more frequently than negative returns. However, the kurtosis is virtually zero indicating no greater exposure to outlier events than a normal distribution.

---

[20] The Dow Jones-AIG Index has been in operating existence only since 1998. Therefore, to calculate returns prior to 1998, Dow Jones and AIG had to calculate index returns back in time using the index construction rules currently in place. Also, the DJ-AIG only has returns calculated back to 1991.

EXHIBIT 13.12 Distribution of Returns for the DJ-AIG Index[a]

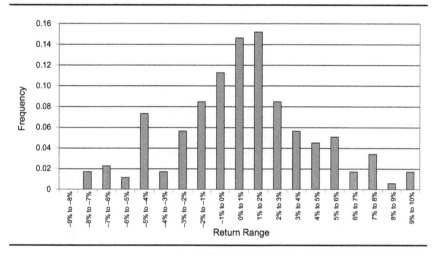

[a] Average = 0.70%, Std. Dev. = 3.54%, Skew = 0.13, Kurtosis = 0.03, Sharpe = 0.084.

Notice that the dispersion of returns to the DJ-AIG is much less than that for the GSCI. At 3.54%, the standard deviation of the DJ-AIG is about 40% less than the monthly standard deviation for the GSCI. This is due to the construction rules for the DJ-AIG index that expressly limit the exposure to any one commodity group at 33%. Compare this to the exposure of the GSCI to energy at 75%. This limitation ensures broader diversification among the different physical commodities—the index cannot become top heavy in any one commodity group.

But does this make a better commodity index? Like everything else in life, there are pros and cons. On the one hand, the DJ-AIG index is less volatile. On the other hand, the GSCI provides exposure to the very large price shocks (both positive and negative) that affect commodity prices. The choice of an index is really a matter of preference.

Commodity Research Bureau Commodity Index

The Reuters/Jefferies CRB Futures Pirce Index is an arithmetic average of 19 commodities with monthly rebalancing to keep the index equal weighted. It was not originally designed to be an investable index. We include it as part of our discussion because it is an often-cited index of commodity prices even though its investment merits have not been promoted.

Exhibit 13.13 provides the distribution of returns for the CRB index. This return distribution demonstrates much less dispersion as indicated by its low standard deviation of 2.51%. In addition, it indicates a posi-

EXHIBIT 13.13 Distribution of Returns for the CRB Index[a]

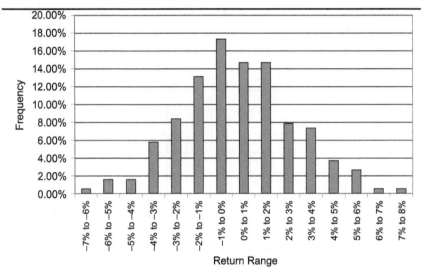

^a Average = 0.19%, Std. Dev. = 2.51%, Skew = 0.18, Kurtosis = –0.07, Sharpe = –0.08.

tive skew of 0.18 while providing a value of kurtosis of –0.07—indicating thinner tails than a normal distribution. However, you do not get something for nothing as evidenced by the low expected monthly return of 0.19%. Furthermore, the Sharpe ratio is negative. This highlights the lack of suitability of the CRB as an investment product.

MLM Index

Mount Lucas Management introduced the MLM Index (MLMI) in 1988.[21] It is a first passive index designed to capture the returns to active futures investing. The MLMI differs significantly from the previous futures indexes in three ways.

First, the MLMI is designed to be a trend following index. The MLMI uses a 12-month look back window for calculating the moving average unit asset value for each futures market in which it invests. Once a month, on the day prior to the last trading day, the algorithm examines the current unit asset value in each futures market compared to the average value for the prior 12 months. If the current unit asset value is above the 12-month moving average, the MLMI purchases the

---

[21] Information regarding the MLMI was provide by Karin Deutsch and Raymond Ix at Mount Lucas Management.

futures contract. If the current unit asset value is below the 12-month moving average, the MLMI takes a short position in the futures contract.

This highlights the second difference associated with the MLMI. This index can be both long and short futures contracts whereas the GSCI, DJ-AIGCI, and the CRB only take long positions in futures contracts.

The theory behind the MLMI is that the mismatch in commercial firms' futures positions is greatest, and investors can profit the most, when the underlying futures market is moving broadly from one price level to another, either up or down. The object of this index construction is to capture the potential profits represented by such broad market trends.

The last difference with respect to the MLMI is that it invests in physical commodity, financial, and currency futures. There are 22 commodity future contracts in the three categories. Exhibit 13.14 provides the details of the component parts of the MLMI.[22]

The MLMI is equal-weighted. The purpose of its construction is to capture the pricing trend of each commodity without regard to its production value or trading volume in the market. Therefore, the price trend for each futures contract in the index is given the same consideration. Given its trend following design, the MLMI rebalances every month based on the prior 12-month moving average.

EXHIBIT 13.14   Composition of the Mt. Lucas Management Index

Commodities: 25%	Currencies: 32.5%	Global Bonds: 42.5%
Crude oil	Australian dollar	Canadian government
Heating oil	British pound	Euro bund
Natural gas	Canadian dollar	Japanese government
Unleaded gas	Euro currency	Long gilt
Corn	Japanese yen	U.S. 10-year Treasury
Soybeans	Swiss franc	
Wheat		
Copper		
Gold		
Live cattle		
Sugar		

[22] There is one additional difference with respect to the MLMI. Two versions of the index are calculated. One version is unleveraged, and one version is three times levered.

EXHIBIT 13.15   Distribuiton of Returns for the MLMI[a]

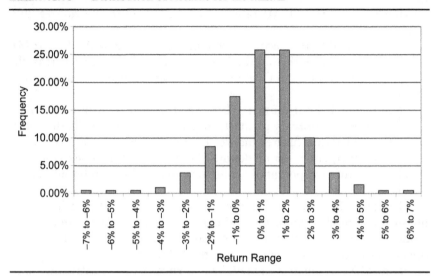

[a] Average = 0.57%, Std. Dev. = 1.74%, Skew = –0.257, Kurtosis = 1.93, Sharpe = 0.10.

In Exhibit 13.15, we present the probability distribution for the MLMI index. While the MLMI has a negative skew, indicating a slight bias towards downside returns, it has the highest Sharpe ratio of the four indexes as well as the lowest standard deviation and dispersion. Again, we have a tradeoff: a slight bias to the downside in return for lower volatility and a higher Sharpe ratio.

Comparison of Commodity Futures Indexes

It is worthwhile to summarize some of the differences between the commodity indexes discussed above. The GSCI, for example, is economically weighted. The weights in the index are determined solely by exogenous economic data (e.g., production values for the global economy). The argument for constructing such an index is analogous to that for the capitalization weighted S&P 500; the most economically important commodities should influence a portfolio tracking an index.[23]

In contrast, the DJ-AIGCI is primarily activity-weighted. Those commodities that are most actively traded determine its construction. This index relies upon endogenous variables (trading volume and liquidity) to determine its weights. This approach assures maximum liquidity for portfolios tracking the index.

---

[23] See Greer, "Institutional use of Physical Commodity Indices."

CRB is an equal-weighted index—it provides no weighting scheme either based on liquidity or productivity. It maintains a constant relationship between the quantities of the various physical commodity futures. For example, no matter whether the price of crude oil goes up or down, the index will maintain the same ratio of crude oil contracts to gold contracts, wheat contracts, orange juice contracts, and so on. Apparently, this does not produce a return advantage as the expected monthly return is significantly less than that for the GSCI or the DJ-AIG indexes.

We note that the GSCI and the DJ-AIGCI have a positive skew to the distribution. From our discussion of return distributions in Chapter 6, we recall that a positive skew indicates that the mean of the distribution is to the right of (greater than) the median of the distribution. This means that there are more frequent large return observations to the right of the distribution (positive returns) and there are more small and mid-range positive return observations to the left of the distribution. In other words, large positive outlying returns occur more frequently than large negative outlying returns, indicating a bias to the upside.

This is good news for investors. Any return distribution that demonstrates a positive skew (i.e., more frequent large positive returns than large negative returns) is a potentially valuable portfolio addition.

The positive skew is larger for the GSCI compared to the DJ-AIGCI. One explanation could be the production weighting of the GSCI versus the liquidity weighting of the DJ-AIGCI. It could be that greater exposure to the most economically important commodity futures provides the greatest source of positive upside potential.

The MLMI is the only futures index that has a negative skew associated with it. This value indicates a negative bias to event risk. There is, however, a tradeoff. The MLMI has much less dispersion in its returns than the other three indexes. The standard deviation of the MLMI returns is 70% less than that for the GSCI, 50% less than that for the DJ-AIGCI, and 30% less than that of the CRB. This should be expected given the construction of the MLMI. Its trend following strategy should reduce its exposure to extreme outlier events. In addition, the MLMI has the largest Sharpe ratio of the four commodity futures indexes. Therefore, the MLMI may have a bias towards downside exposure, but it does have the best reward-to-risk ratio.

The GSCI and the MLMI have similar positive values of kurtosis, indicating slightly overweight tails in the distribution of returns. For the GSCI, this could be due to the momentum style of the GSCI. Commodity prices are allowed to run up or down in the GSCI, changing the weights of the index dramatically. For the MLMI, the large value of kurtosis could be due to sudden changes in commodity price trends. Given a sudden price spike or trough in commodity prices, it may take time for the MLMI to apply its 12-month moving average to adjust for the trend. This could lead to fat tails.

Conversely, the DJ-AIGCI specifically limits the exposures of commodity sectors so that the index does not become "top heavy" with respect to any particular commodity or sector. This cap may reduce the exposure of outlier events within the DJ-AIGCI compared to the GSCI. This cap, in fact, acts like a short call option position that truncates the distribution of returns above the allowable percentage limit in the index. Truncating a return distribution will reduce an investor's exposure to large outlier returns. The result is a lower value of leptokurtosis. Similarly, the CRB specifically limits the exposure to any one commodity through its scheme of equal weighting. By rebalancing monthly, the CRB index always adjusts the commodities back to equal weights so that no one commodity drivers the performance of the index. This limitation on outlier returns leads to the slightly negative value of kurtosis.

CONCLUSION

This chapter introduced the reader to the economic rationale behind investing in commodity futures. It also introduced several commodity futures indexes that can be used for performance benchmarking.

In this sense, commodity futures investing has developed further than the hedge fund industry because several well-defined and transparent benchmarks have been invented to track the performance of commodity futures investing. However, investment capital committed to commodity futures is considerably smaller than that invested with hedge funds. Estimates are in the range of $100 to $150 billion, considerably less than the $1.5 trillion invested in hedge funds.

One reason is the lack of understanding of the product. Therefore, this chapter provided an introduction to commodity futures investing. A second reason is the perceived view that commodity futures are extremely risky investments best left for cowboy speculators and flamboyant floor traders. In the next chapter, we disarm this myth and consider whether commodity futures have a place within an investment portfolio.

Despite the resistance to investing in commodities, it is estimated that commodity futures investing will exceed $150 billion in the next few years. This has encouraged other brokerage houses to develop new commodity indexes to catch this wave of investor demand. For instance, in 2003, Deutsche Bank launched its Liquid Commodity Index and in January 2006, Lehman Brothers announced its plans to introduce a commodity index that year.

CHAPTER 14

Commodity Futures in a Portfolio Context

In the prior two chapters we first identified commodity futures as a distinct asset and we discussed the economics associated with the pricing of commodity futures. In addition, we indicated that commodity futures prices are influenced by factors different than those for financial assets. This led us to the conclusion that commodity futures have the potential to be excellent diversifying agents for a stock-and-bond portfolio.

In this chapter we consider commodity futures within a portfolio context. First, we compare the economic statistics of commodity futures to those for stocks and bonds. Next we build portfolios of commodity futures, stocks, and bonds and observe the risk and return of these portfolios compared to those constructed without commodity futures. Then we examine commodity futures as a defensive investment. Our analysis concludes that commodity futures are indeed valuable diversification tools.

ECONOMIC SUMMARY OF COMMODITY FUTURES

In this section we briefly review the inflation protection offered by commodity futures. We also compare the risk and return profile of commodity futures compared to stocks and bonds over a long period of time.

Inflation Protection

Bonds are a contingent claim on the earning power of a corporation. They have a senior claim on revenue earned by a corporation. However, bonds perform poorly when the purchasing power of money declines in an inflationary environment.

Conversely, stocks, as the residual claim on the physical assets of a corporation provide better purchasing power protection. Stocks also represent a claim on the future earning potential of the corporation. When this earning power is eroded due to inflationary concerns, stocks also decline in value.

Real assets such as commodity futures can hedge this decline in value due to inflation. In Chapter 13 we introduced three investable commodity futures indexes—the Goldman Sachs Commodity Index (GSCI), the Dow Jones-AIG Commodity Index (DJ-AIGCI), the Mount Lucas Management Index (MLMI), and the Commodity Research Bureau (CRB), a noninvestable commodity index.

Exhibit 14.1 presents the correlation of the four indexes with domestic U.S. inflation over the time period 1990 to 2005. We also include the S&P 500 for domestic stocks, EAFE (Europe, Australia, and the Far East) and FTSE (Financial Times Stock Index) for international stocks, and the 10-year U.S. Treasury Bond and high-yield bonds for fixed income exposure. Exhibit 14.1 demonstrates that every class of stocks and bonds are negatively correlated with the rate of inflation. Higher inflation means lower returns to stocks and bonds, and vice versa. Conversely, all of the commodity indexes are positively correlated with inflation. Higher inflation means higher returns to commodity futures and vice versa. Therefore, commodity futures offer good inflation protection for financial assets.

An argument might be made that an investor could purchase Treasury Inflation Protected Securities (TIPS) as a hedge against inflation. It is true that the cash flows accruing to TIPS are adjusted to maintain

EXHIBIT 14.1   Correlation with Inflation

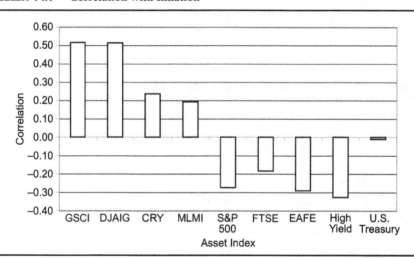

their value in an inflationary environment. However, TIPS do not offer inflation protection for other assets in the portfolio.

TIPS are designed to have the coupon rate increase so that the price of a TIPS does not decline when inflation increases. This preserves or *maintains* the value of the TIPS investment. However, the preservation of TIPS value does not offer relief for other assets in the portfolio. In contrast, commodity futures increase in value when inflation goes up. This increase in value can be used to shelter some of the decline in value suffered by financial assets in the portfolio.

Note that the returns earned by international stocks experience the same level of negative correlation with the U.S. inflation rate. One reason is that price increases of raw materials affect foreign economies just as much as the U.S. economy. Consequently, an investor seeking a hedge against domestic inflation did not find it by diversifying into foreign stocks.

Average Return and Volatility

Commodity futures are often perceived to be extremely volatile, with large price swings up and down. We expect commodity futures to be riskier than U.S. Treasury bonds, but we also expect the return to be greater to compensate for the additional risk.

We might also expect commodity futures to have greater volatility than that for large-capitalization stocks because futures prices are subject to short-term fluctuations based on supply-and-demand imbalances, but not significantly greater. In turn, we expect to earn an average rate of return greater than stocks for this additional volatility. These expectations are summarized in Exhibits 14.2 and 14.3.

EXHIBIT 14.2   Average Returns for Stocks, Bonds and Commodities, 1990–2005

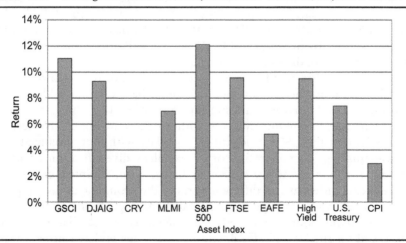

EXHIBIT 14.3   Volatility of Stocks, Bonds and Commodity Returns

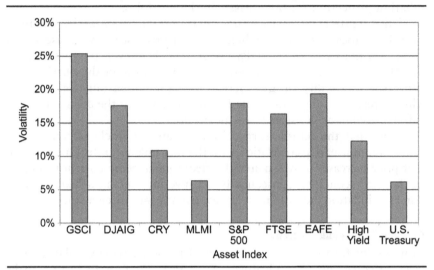

Exhibit 14.2 shows mixed results for commodity futures. For example, the GSCI and the DJ-AIG outperform bonds and foreign stocks but not the S&P 500 over this time period. Furthermore, the CRB and the MLMI earn returns less than high-yield bonds or Treasury bonds. On returns alone, commodities show mixed results, especially when compared to U.S. stocks or bonds.

Thus we examine the second part of the equation: risk. Exhibit 14.3 compares the volatility of the commodity indexes to those for domestic and foreign stocks and for bonds. We can see that the GSCI has considerably more volatility than stocks and bonds while the DJ-AIG has stock like volatility. The CRB and the MLMI, however, have volatility more like bonds. In fact, the MLMI has virtually the same volatility as U.S. Treasury bonds—an admirable quality.

With mixed results for return and risk, we turn to the third criteria for determining whether commodities might be a valuable addition to a stock-and-bond portfolio: diversification. Exhibit 14.4 shows the correlation of the commodity indexes with stocks and bonds. Notice, for example, that the GSCI is negatively correlate with every financial asset class—this is a demonstration of an excellent diversification agent for stocks and bonds. As we discussed in the prior chapter, commodity prices react differently at different parts of the economic cycle compared to financial assets. This provides an excellent opportunity to diversify a traditional portfolio comprised of financial assets. Similar results are observed for the DJ-AIG, CRB, and MLMI. They all have either a nega-

EXHIBIT 14.4 Correlation of Stocks, Bonds and Commodities with Inflation

	GSCI	DJAIG	CRY	MLMI	S&P 500	FTSE	EAFE	High Yield	U.S. Treasury	CPI
GSCI	1.00									
DJAIG	0.96	1.00								
CRY	0.68	0.80	1.00							
MLMI	−0.04	−0.12	−0.29	1.00						
S&P 500	−0.21	−0.21	−0.33	0.09	1.00					
FTSE	−0.18	−0.15	−0.12	−0.06	0.88	1.00				
EAFE	−0.07	0.06	0.21	−0.11	0.63	0.70	1.00			
High Yield	−0.29	−0.23	−0.17	−0.31	0.66	0.57	0.49	1.00		
U.S. Treasury	−0.13	−0.23	−0.10	0.22	0.07	0.00	−0.32	0.24	1.00	
CPI	0.52	0.51	0.24	0.19	−0.27	−0.18	−0.29	−0.33	−0.004	1.00

tive or very low positive correlation with stocks and bonds. Any asset that is less than perfectly correlated with stocks and bonds will provide diversification to a stock-and-bond portfolio, and commodities demonstrate distinctly favorable diversification properties.

Therefore, an investment in commodity futures should not be analyzed in a vacuum. Instead, commodity futures are best considered within a portfolio context, where their diversification potential can be achieved. In the next section, we consider commodity futures as part of a diversified portfolio.

On a final note, it is worthwhile to observe that each of the commodity futures indexes are positively correlated with inflation. Stocks and bonds, on the other hand, are negatively correlated with inflation. This is a demonstration of an excellent inflation hedge to provide protection to a traditional portfolio of stocks and bonds.

COMMODITY FUTURES AND THE EFFICIENT INVESTMENT FRONTIER

Having established commodity futures as a distinct new asset class in Chapters 12 and 13, we consider how this asset class performs when considered in a diversified portfolio of stocks and bonds. In this section, we construct efficient frontiers for stocks, bonds, and passive commodity futures.

The efficient frontier is a graphical depiction of the tradeoff between risk and return. It provides a range of the risk and return that can be achieved in a balanced portfolio of investable assets. First, we graph the efficient frontier using domestic stocks and bonds to provide a benchmark of risk and return data points that can be achieved without commodity futures. We then add commodity futures to the investment portfolio and observe how the efficient frontier changes with the addition of this new asset class.

Exhibit 14.5 presents the initial frontier using stocks and bonds. At the highest return point on the frontier, the portfolio consists of 100% stocks. At the lowest return point, the portfolio consists completely of U.S. Treasury bonds. In between the portfolio mix of assets ranges from 90% stocks and 10% bonds to 10% stocks and 90% bonds.

The efficient frontier in Exhibit 14.5 indicates that higher return may be achieved only at the cost of assuming more risk. Along the efficient frontier, there is no other combination of stocks and bonds that will yield a higher return for a given level of risk, or a lower level of risk for a given level of return. This is why the frontier is efficient; it provides a graphical description of the best portfolios that may be achieved using stocks and bonds.

EXHIBIT 14.5   Efficient Frontier for Stocks and Bonds

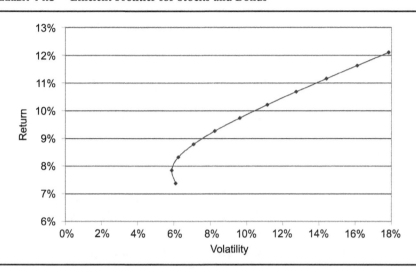

The efficient frontier changes when commodity futures are added to the mix. Exhibit 14.6 demonstrates the efficient frontier when commodity futures are added to the stock-and-bond portfolio. Initially, we use the GSCI to represent an asset allocation to commodity futures.

Again, the two endpoints of the graph are defined by 100% stocks at the highest return level and 100% bonds at the lowest return level. In between, the allocation to commodity futures remains constant at 10%, with a 5% less allocation to stocks and a 5% less allocation to bonds. For example, in Exhibit 14.5, we plot risk and return data points at 90% stocks and 10% bonds, 80% stocks and 20% bonds, etc. With commodity futures, in Exhibit 14.6, the data points become 85% stocks, 5% bonds, and 10% commodity futures, 75% stocks, 15% bonds, and 10% commodity futures, and so forth.

In Exhibit 14.6, the new efficient frontier including commodity futures is above and to the left of the original frontier plotted in Exhibit 14.5. We include the original frontier from Exhibit 14.5 in Exhibit 14.6 for comparison. The original efficient investment frontier without commodity futures clearly lies below the efficient frontier with commodity futures. In other words, the addition of commodity futures into the investment portfolio pushes the investment frontier up and to the left into a more efficient risk and return area of the graph. This demonstrates that commodity futures improve the risk-and-return tradeoff for the investment portfolio.

EXHIBIT 14.6   Efficient Frontier with the GSCI

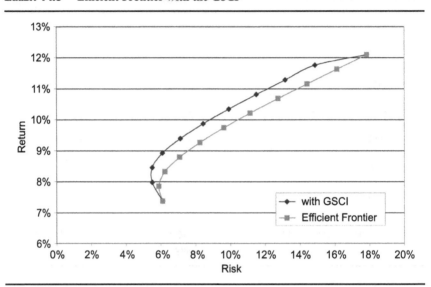

Reflect back for a moment to Exhibit 14.3. The GSCI had the highest volatility of returns of the major indexes presented. At first glance, an investor may discount the value of investing in commodity futures because of the higher volatility associated with the GSCI compared to the S&P 500. Such a comparison ignores the negative correlation of the returns to the GSCI with the returns to stocks and bonds. The impact of this negative correlation can only be achieved within a diversified portfolio. As a stand-alone investment, the diversification potential of commodity futures vis-à-vis stocks and bonds cannot be observed. It can only be appreciated within a portfolio context.

In Exhibit 14.7, we again present both the efficient frontier with the DJ-AIG and without commodity futures. The results are very similar to the GSCI. At every point along the efficient frontier, the addition of commodities represented by the DJ-AIG results in a better risk and return tradeoff. Exhibit 14.7 reinforces the results demonstrated in Exhibit 14.6. Another way to state these results is to say that a portfolio composed of stocks and bonds is *inefficient* compared to a portfolio comprised of stocks, bonds and commodities.

Efficient frontiers are a useful point from which to discuss utility theory. In modern portfolio theory it is assumed that investors are rational utility maximizers. This means that investors realize that life is full of tradeoffs: invest today to consume tomorrow or seek more return but only with the assumption of greater risk.

EXHIBIT 14.7 The Efficient Frontier with the DJ-AIG

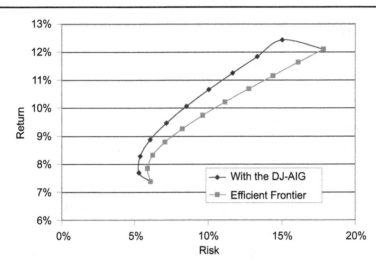

Maximizing utility with commodity futures is an important concept because the greater the risk aversion of the investor, the greater the benefit of investing in commodity futures. This point may seem counterintuitive because commodity futures are often perceived as risky investments. However, the returns to commodity futures are negatively correlated with the returns to financial assets. When considered within a portfolio context, commodity futures provide positive utility to a risk averse investor. In fact, Anson demonstrates that the greater the risk aversion of the investor, the greater will be the marginal utility of investing in commodity futures.[1]

Exhibit 14.8 plots the efficient frontier with a 10% constant allocation to commodity futures represented by the CRB. Here, the results of including commodity futures is much less impressive. The CRB has only a small beneficial impact on the risk and return of the diversified portfolio. Because even though the improvement is not as dramatic as the GSCI or the DJ-AIG, this is perhaps the best example of why the CRB is not an investable product for commodity futures exposure. Similar to Exhibit 14.6, the efficient frontier including the CRB lies above and to the left of the original efficient frontier with stocks and bonds. This means that there is a more efficient portfolio that can be achieved if

---

[1] See Mark Anson, "Maximizing Utility with Commodity Futures," *The Journal of Portfolio Management* (Summer 1999), pp. 86–94.

EXHIBIT 14.8   The Efficient Frontier with the CRB

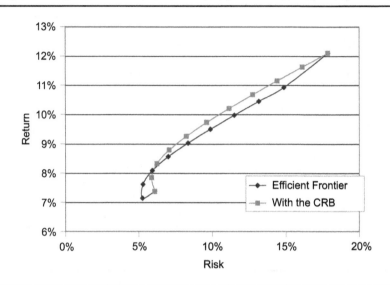

commodity futures are included in the portfolio—even in the case of the CRB which has a negative Sharpe ratio on a standalone basis.

Finally Exhibit 14.9 presents the efficient frontier for a portfolio of stocks, bonds and 10% futures as represented by the MLMI. Unfortunately, the MLMI does not appear to add much additional value to a stock-and-bond portfolio. In fact, the efficient frontier with the MLMI added to the stock-and-bond portfolio virtually overlaps that of our base stock-and-bond portfolio. There is a clear explanation for this result which we will discuss in the next chapter (and hope to entice the reader to stick with us for one more chapter).

It is important to note again that the GSCI, the DJ-AIG, and the MLMI are all *investable* commodity futures indexes. They were all designed with the investor in mind, and an investor can allocate a portion of her portfolio assets to any of these three indexes just as she might make an allocation to emerging market stocks, for instance. Therefore, each index is an appropriate proxy for investing in the commodity futures markets.

The above discussion was intended to demonstrate that commodity futures are best analyzed within a portfolio context. Only then can their full investment benefit be appreciated. The ability of commodity futures returns to move in the opposite direction of the returns to stocks and bonds provides a powerful tool for portfolio diversification. This is consistent with our discussion in Chapter 13 regarding how commodity futures

EXHIBIT 14.9 The Efficient Frontier with the MLMI

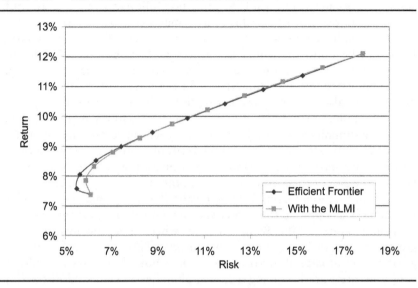

react differently than stocks and bonds to different parts of the economic cycle. Exhibits 14.6 through 14.9 translate this business cycle concept into portfolio construction. In the next section, we consider another useful element of commodity futures investing: downside risk protection.

COMMODITY FUTURES AS A DEFENSIVE INVESTMENT

It is an unfortunate fact of life that when things hit the fan, they tend to do it all at the same time. For example, a number of studies have examined the correlation of the U.S. domestic and international equity markets during periods of market stress or decline. The conclusion is that the equity markets around the world tend to be more highly correlated during periods of economic stress.[2] This means that international equity markets tend to decline at the same time as the U.S. stock market. Therefore, international equity diversification may not provide the requisite diversification when a U.S. domestic investor needs it most—during periods of economic turmoil or decline.

---

[2] See Claude Erb, Campbell Harvey, and Tadas Viskanta, "Forecasting International Equity Correlations," *Financial Analysts Journal* (November/December 1994), pp. 34–35; and Rex Sinquefield, "Where Are the Gains from International Diversification?" *Financial Analysts Journal* (January/February 1996), pp. 8–14.

One reason why international equity investments might not provide suitable diversification for a U.S. stock portfolio is that almost all traditional assets react in similar fashion to macroeconomic events. A spike in oil prices, for example, will be felt across all economies, and inflation fears will be uniform around the globe. In fact, Exhibit 14.1 demonstrates that both domestic and international equity markets are negatively impacted by the domestic inflation rate. International equity markets are also becoming increasing linked for four reasons.

First, policy makers from major industrial nations regularly attend economic summits where they attempt to synchronize fiscal and monetary policy. The Maastricht Treaty and the birth of "Euroland" is an example. Second, corporations are expanding their operations and revenue streams beyond the site of their domestic incorporation. Third, the increased volume of international capital flows means that economic shocks will be felt globally as opposed to country specific. Fourth, nations such as Japan have undergone a "Big Bang" episode where domestic investors have greater access to international investments. This provides for an even greater flow of capital across international boundaries. As a result, the equity markets are becoming a single, global asset class and distinctions between international and domestic stocks are beginning to fade.

This is one reason why "skill-based" investing has become so popular with investors. Hedge funds and other skill-based strategies might be expected to provide greater diversification than international equity investing because the returns are dependent upon the special skill of the manager rather than any broad macroeconomic events or trends.

Yet, diversification need not rely on active skill-based strategies. Diversification benefits can be achieved from the passive addition of a new asset class such as commodity futures.

The greatest concern for any investor is downside risk. If equity and bond markets are becoming increasingly synchronized, international diversification may not offer the protection sought by investors. The ability to protect the value of an investment portfolio in hostile or turbulent markets is the key to the value of any macroeconomic diversification.

Within this framework, an asset class distinct from financial assets has the potential to diversify and protect an investment portfolio from hostile markets. Commodity futures make a good choice for downside risk protection.

To demonstrate this downside risk protection, we start with a standard portfolio of stocks and bonds. We begin with a portfolio that is 60% the S&P 500 and 40% U.S. Treasury bonds. In Exhibit 14.10 we provide a frequency distribution of the monthly returns to this portfolio over the time period 1990 to 2005. This exhibit shows the return pattern for monthly returns to a 60%/40% stock/bond portfolio over this time period.

EXHIBIT 14.10   Distribution of Returns for 60/40 Stocks/Bonds

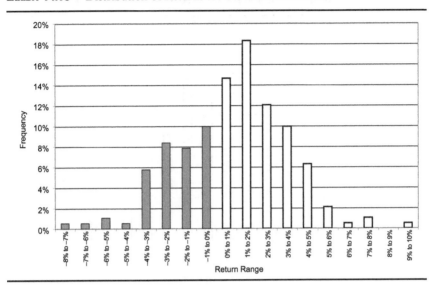

Our concern is the shaded part of the return distribution. This shows where the returns to the stock-and-bond portfolio were negative. That is, the shaded part of the distribution shows both the size and the frequency with which the combined portfolio of 60% S&P 500 plus 40% U.S. Treasury bonds earned a negative return in a particular month. It is this part of the return distribution that an investor attempts to avoid or limit.[3]

We find that the average monthly return to a 60/40 stock/bond portfolio in the shaded part of the distribution of Exhibit 14.10 is a negative 2.03%. In other words, when the standard stock/bond portfolio earned a negative return in any given month, on average the magnitude of that return was –2.03%. Sixty-six months experienced negative returns.

These negative returns are exactly the returns that investors want to reduce through diversification. We consider how this shaded part of the curve changes when we add in commodity futures.

In Exhibit 14.11 we change the standard stock/bond investment portfolio by providing a 10% allocation to commodity futures. The resulting portfolio is 55% S&P 500 stocks, 35% U.S. Treasury bonds, and 10% GSCI. Exhibit 14.11 plots the frequency distribution for this portfolio.

Once again, we are concerned with the shaded part of the frequency distribution of returns for this stock/bond/commodities portfolio. Although the distribution looks similar, it has in fact changed signifi-

---

[3] See Steve Strongin and Melanie Petsch, "Managing Risk in Hostile Markets," Goldman Sachs Commodities Research, April 24, 1996.

EXHIBIT 14.11   Return Distribution for 5535/10 Stocks/Bonds/GSCI

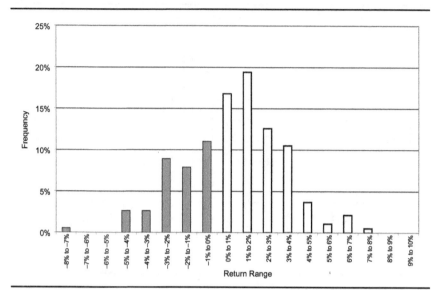

cantly from Exhibit 14.10. The average monthly return to the 55/35/10 stock/bond/commodities portfolio in the shaded part of Exhibit 14.11 is −1.88%. In other words, when the stock/bond/commodities portfolio earned a negative return in any given month, on average the magnitude of the return was −1.88%. In addition, there were only 64 months of negative returns, two less than in the stock/bond portfolio.

This is an improvement in return over Exhibit 14.10 of 15 basis points per month when the portfolio experiences a negative month of performance. That is, the addition of the commodity futures to the stock-and-bond portfolio provided on average 15 basis points per month of protection in hostile markets. Furthermore, notice that this reduction in risk came with a conservative allocation to commodity futures of 10%. Exhibit 14.16 summarizes the improvement in downside risk protection.

Exhibit 14.12 provides a frequency distribution for a portfolio that consists of 55% S&P 500, 35% U.S. Treasury bonds, and a 10% allocation to the DJ-AIGCI. Exhibit 14.12 provides a similar analysis to that of Exhibit 14.11. The average negative return in the shaded part of Exhibit 14.12 is −1.81%. This is an improvement over Exhibit 14.10 of 22 basis points per month, or about 0.90% (4.1 months × 0.22%) per year. Exhibit 14.16 shows that this is an improvement of almost 26% in downside risk protection over the sample period and there were only 60 months with negative returns.

EXHIBIT 14.12   Return Distribution for 55/35/10 Stocks/Bonds/DJ-AIG

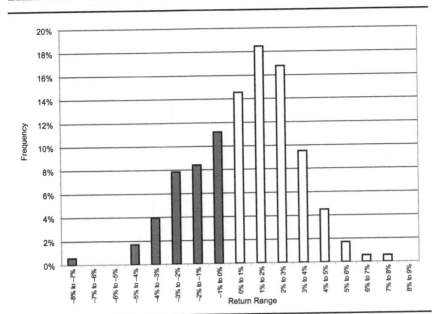

Exhibit 14.13 provides the same analysis for the CRB. This exhibit shows a plot of the frequency distribution for a 55/35/10 stock/bond/ CRB portfolio. The average return in the shaded part of the distribution is −1.93% and the number of negative months declines to 65.

Exhibit 14.14 plots the frequency distribution for a portfolio consisting of 55% S&P 500, 35% U.S. Treasury bonds, and 10% MLMI. Once again the shaded part of the distribution of portfolio returns improves significantly. The average return in the downside part of the return distribution is −1.89% and with only 62 months of negative returns.

Let us look at the impact of Exhibits 14.11 through 14.14. These graphs demonstrate that a small allocation of commodity futures benchmarked to a passive futures index can provide protection against downside exposure. This downside exposure is summarized in Exhibit 14.16. To put this in context, compare these results to the world of active equity investing where an annual alpha, or excess return, of 100 basis points is considered excellent performance. Yet, a 10% passive allocation to commodity futures can provide return protection on par with the excess return offered by the very best active managers.

Finally, we consider the downside protection of international stocks. We indicated above that the equity markets are becoming less distinct and resembling more of a global asset class. This reduces the diversification

EXHIBIT 14.13 Return Distribution for 55/35/10 Stocks/Bonds/CRB

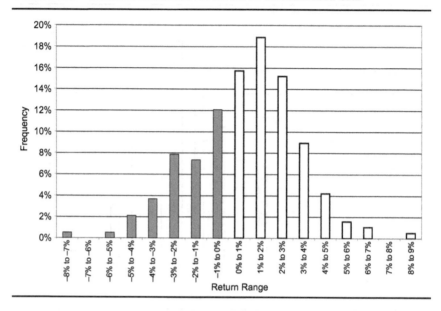

EXHIBIT 14.14 Return Distribution for 55/35/10 Stocks/Bonds/MLMI

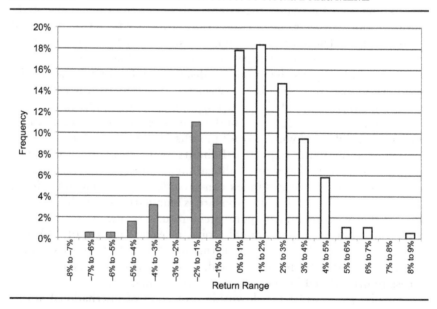

potential of international stocks. To demonstrate this idea, we build a portfolio consisting of U.S. stocks, U.S. bonds and foreign stocks. The exact allocation is 55% S&P 500, 35% U.S. Treasury bonds, and 10% EAFE.[4]

Exhibit 14.15 provides the frequency distribution for this portfolio. Again, we concentrate on the shaded part of the distribution. The average monthly return to the downside portion of this distribution is −2.23%. That is, a 10% allocation to international stocks provided an *additional* exposure to downside risk of −20 basis points. Therefore, an allocation to international stocks did not diversify an investment portfolio comprised of domestic stocks and bonds. In fact, a 10% allocation to international stocks *increased* the exposure to downside risk. We conclude that international stocks did not protect the standard 60/40 stock/bond portfolio from hostile markets.

We also consider what might be sacrificed to achieve this downside protection. It is possible that in protecting against some downside exposure, an investor must accept a reduction in positive returns in the non-shaded (positive) part of the return distributions. We examine this possibility in Exhibit 14.16.

The expected monthly return to the standard 60/40 stock portfolio over this period was 0.81%. Compare this to the expected monthly return to a 55/35/10 stock/bond/commodity futures portfolio in Exhibit

EXHIBIT 14.15   Return Distribution for 55/35/10 S&P 500/Bonds/EAFE

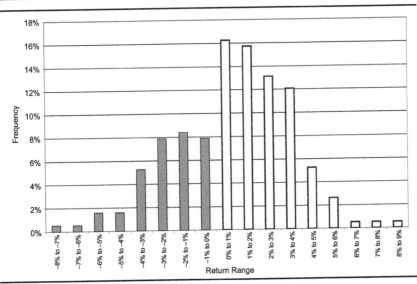

---

[4] EAFE is an international stock index developed and maintained by Morgan Stanley Capital International.

EXHIBIT 14.16 Summary of Downside Protection for Commodities

Portfolio	Average Return	Standard Deviation	Skew	Kurtosis	Sharpe	Number of Neg. Months	Average Return Negative Month	Downside Risk Protection
60/40 S&P 500/U.S. Treasury	0.81%	2.64%	−0.16	0.33	0.16	66	−2.03%	N/A
55/35/10 S&P500/Bonds/GSCI	0.81%	2.44%	−0.20	0.27	0.17	64	−1.88%	13.66%
55/35/10 S&P500/Bonds/DJ-AIG	0.84%	2.37%	−0.23	0.36	0.19	60	−1.80%	25.98%
55/35/10 S&P500/Bonds/CRB	0.75%	2.44%	−0.24	0.35	0.14	65	−1.93%	8.53%
55/35/10 S&P500/Bonds/MLMI	0.79%	2.38%	−0.12	0.26	0.16	62	−1.89%	16.80%
55/35/10 S&P 500/Bonds/EAFE	0.77%	2.72%	−0.30	0.37	0.14	63	−2.23%	−6.51%

14.16. The expected return for a portfolio with the GSCI is 0.81% per month, the same as the stock/bond portfolio. Therefore, a passive exposure to commodity futures represented by the GSCI resulted in significant downside protection without sacrificing any upside return. The other futures indexes had mixed results with the DJ-AIG increasing the average monthly return while the CRB and the MLMI resulted in a decline in the average monthly return.[5]

Finally, we compare the Sharpe ratios for the standard 60/40 stock/bond portfolio to those portfolios including commodity futures and international equity. In the case of the GSCI and the DJ-AIG indexes, the allocation to 10% commodity futures results in an improvement in the Sharpe ratio while the Sharpe ratio remains constant when the MLMI is added to the stock/bond portfolio and the CRB results in a decline in the Sharpe ratio. However, an allocation to 10% international equities results in a significant decline in the Sharpe ratio—international stocks are a poor diversifier compared to commodity futures.

CONCLUSION

Chapters 12 and 13 were concerned with the introduction to commodity futures as an asset class distinct from financial assets such as stocks and bonds. In this chapter we considered the diversification value of this new asset class.

The greatest value of commodity futures is achieved within a portfolio context. Analyzing commodity futures as a standalone investment ignores the fact that the returns to commodity futures tend to be negatively correlated with the returns to financial assets. We discussed in Chapter 13 that the returns to commodity futures tend to peak and trough at different parts of the economic cycle in contrast to stocks and bonds. This countercyclical effect provides the potential for portfolio diversification.

This diversification potential was revealed in two separate ways. First, we demonstrated how a 10% allocation of commodity futures provided an efficient investable frontier that dominated the efficient frontier that was achieved with stocks and bonds alone. Second, we demonstrated how a 10% allocation to commodity futures provided significant downside protection in hostile markets. In contrast, we found that international stocks provided no downside exposure and, in fact, increased the exposure to hostile markets for a standard 60/40 stock/bond portfolio.

---

[5] The DJ-AIG cannot be compared precisely to the GSCI, CRB or the MLMI because it has a shorter track record.

CHAPTER 15

Managed Futures

Managed futures refers to the active trading of futures contracts and forward contracts on physical commodities, financial assets, and currencies. The purpose of the managed futures industry is to enable investors to profit from changes in futures prices through active management by a trader. The goal here is not necessarily diversification, but instead, added value.

The managed futures industry is another skill-based style of investing. Investment managers attempt to use their special knowledge and insight in buying and selling futures and forward contracts to extract a positive return. These futures managers tend to argue that their superior skill is the key ingredient to derive profitable returns from the futures markets.

There are three ways to access the skill-based investing of the managed futures industry: (1) public commodity pools, (2) private commodity pools, and (3) individual managed accounts. *Commodity pools* are investment funds that pool the money of several investors for the purpose of investing in the futures markets. They are similar in structure to hedge funds and are considered a subset of the hedge fund marketplace.

Every commodity pool must be managed by a general partner. Typically, the general partner for the pool must register with the Commodity Futures Trading Commission and the National Futures Association as a *Commodity Pool Operator* (CPO). However, there are exceptions to the general rule, and these are discussed in detail in Chapter 8.

Public commodity pools are open to the general public for investment in much the same way a mutual fund sells its shares to the public. Public commodity pools must file a registration statement with the Securities and Exchange Commission before distributing shares in the pool to investors. An advantage of public commodity pools is the low minimum investment and the frequency of liquidity (the ability to cash out).

Private commodity pools are sold to high-net-worth investors and institutional investors to avoid the lengthy registration requirements of the SEC and sometimes to avoid the lengthy reporting requirements of the CFTC (see the discussion in Chapter 8). Otherwise, their investment objective is the same as a public commodity pool. An advantage of private commodity pools is usually lower brokerage commissions and greater flexibility to implement investment strategies and extract excess return from the futures markets.

Commodity pool operators (for either public or private pools) typically hire one or more *commodity trading advisors* (CTAs) to manage the money deposited with the pool. CTAs are professional money managers in the futures markets.

Like CPOs, CTAs must register with the *commodity futures trading commission* (CFTC) and the *National Futures Association* (NFA) before managing money for a commodity pool. In some cases a managed futures investment manager is registered as both a CPO and a CTA. In this case, the general partner for a commodity pool may also act as its investment adviser.

Last, wealthy and institutional investors can place their money directly with a CTA in an *individually managed account*. These separate accounts have the advantage of narrowly defined and specific investment objectives as well as full transparency to the investor.

CTAs may invest in both exchange-traded futures contracts and forward contracts. A forward contract has the same economic structure as a futures contract with one difference; it is traded over the counter. Forward contracts are private agreements that do not trade on a futures exchange. Therefore, they can have terms that vary considerably from the standard terms of an exchange listed futures contracts. Forward contracts accomplish the same economic goal as a futures contract but with the flexibility of custom tailored terms.

In this chapter, we examine the managed futures industry. First, we provide a brief history of the managed futures industry. We then review the prior empirical research regarding the benefits to investing in managed futures. Next, we examine the return distribution of managed futures returns. We then conduct an analysis of downside risk protection for managed futures within a portfolio context.

HISTORY OF MANAGED FUTURES

Organized futures trading began in the United States in the 1800s with the founding of the Chicago Board of Trade (CBOT) in 1848. It was founded by 82 grain merchants and the first exchange floor was above a flour store. Originally, it was a cash market where grain traders came to buy and sell supplies of flour, timothy seed, and hay.

In 1851, the earliest futures contract in the United States was recorded for the forward delivery of 3,000 bushels of corn, and two years later, the CBOT established the first standard futures contract in corn. Since then, the heart and soul of the CBOT has been its futures contracts on agricultural crops grown primarily in the midwestern states: corn, wheat, and soybeans. Thus commodity futures exchanges were founded initially by grain producers and buyers to hedge the price risk associated with the harvest and sale of crops.

Other futures exchanges were established for similar reasons. The *Chicago Mercantile Exchange* (CME), for example, lists futures contracts on livestock. Chicago was once famous for its stockyards where cattle and hogs were herded to the market. Ranchers and buyers came to the CME to hedge the price risk associated with the purchase and sale of cattle and hogs.

Other exchanges are the *New York Mercantile Exchange* (NYMEX) where futures contracts on energy products are traded. The *Commodity Exchange of New York* (now the COMEX division of the NYMEX) lists futures contracts on precious and industrial metals. The *New York Coffee, Sugar, and Cocoa Exchange* lists futures contracts on (what else?) coffee, sugar, and cocoa. The *New York Cotton Exchange* lists contracts on cotton and frozen concentrated orange juice.[1] The *Kansas City Board of Trade* lists futures contracts on wheat and financial products such as the Value Line stock index.

Over the years, certain commodities have risen in prominence while others have faded. For instance, the heating oil futures contract was at one time listed as inactive on the NYMEX for lack of interest. For years, heating oil prices remained stable, and there was little interest or need to hedge the price risk of heating oil. Then along came the Arab Oil Embargo of 1973, and this contract quickly took on a life of its own as did other energy futures contracts.

Conversely, other futures contracts have faded away because of minimal input into the economic engine of the United States. For instance, rye futures traded on the CBOT from 1869 to 1970, and barley futures traded from 1885 to 1940. However, the limited importance of barley and rye in finished food products led to the eventual demise of these futures contracts. For a while in the 1990s there was even a con-

---

[1] The New York Coffee, Sugar, and Cocoa Exchange and the New York Cotton Exchange have merged to form the New York Board of Trade, where each exchange exists as a separate subsidiary of the NYBOT.

tract on shrimp futures to hedge the prices of shrimp harvested from the Gulf of Mexico.

As the wealth of America grew, a new type of futures contract has gained importance: financial futures. The futures markets changed dramatically in 1975 when the CBOT introduced the first financial futures contract on Government National Mortgage Association mortgage-backed certificates. This was followed two years later in 1977 with the introduction of a futures contract on the U.S. Treasury Bond. Today this is the most actively traded futures contract in the world.

The creation of a futures contract that was designed to hedge financial risk as opposed to commodity price risk opened up a whole new avenue of asset management for traders, analysts, and portfolio managers. Now it is more likely that a financial investor will flock to the futures exchanges to hedge her investment portfolio than a grain purchaser will trade to hedge commodity price risk. Since 1975, more and more financial futures contracts have been listed on the futures exchanges. For instance, in 1997 stock index futures and options on the Dow Jones 30 Industrial Companies were first listed on the CBOT. The S&P 500 stock index futures and options (first listed in 1983) are the most heavily traded contracts on the CME. Additionally, currency futures were introduced on the CME in the 1970s (originally listed as part of the International Monetary Market).

With the advent of financial futures contracts more and more managed futures trading strategies were born. However, the history of managed futures products goes back more than 50 years.

The first public futures fund began trading in 1948 and was active until the 1960s. This fund was established before financial futures contracts were invented, and consequently, traded primarily in agricultural commodity futures contracts. The success of this fund spawned other managed futures vehicles, and a new industry was born.

The managed futures industry has grown from just $1 billion under management in 1985 to $70 billion of funds invested in managed futures products in 2005. The stock market's return to more rational pricing in 2000 helped fuel increased interest in managed futures products. Still, managed futures products are a fraction of the estimated size of the hedge fund marketplace of $1.5 trillion. Yet issues of capacity are virtually nonexistent in the managed futures industry compared to the hedge fund marketplace where the best hedge funds are closed to new investors.

Similar to hedge funds, CTAs and CPOs charge both management fees and performance fees. The standard "2 and 20" (2% management fee and 20% incentive fee) are equally applicable to the managed futures industry although management fees can range from 0% to 3% and incentive fees from 10% to 35%.

Unfortunately, until the early 1970s, the managed futures industry was largely unregulated. Anyone could advise an investor as the merits of investing in commodity futures or form a fund for the purpose of investing in the futures markets. Recognizing the growth of this industry, and the lack of regulation associated with it, in 1974 Congress promulgated the *Commodity Exchange Act* (CEA) and created the *Commodity Futures Trading Commission* (CFTC).

Under the CEA, Congress first defined the terms *Commodity Pool Operator* and *Commodity Trading Advisor*. Additionally, Congress established standards for financial reporting, offering memorandum disclosure, and bookkeeping. Furthermore, Congress required CTAs and CPOs to register with the CFTC. Last, upon the establishment of the *National Futures Association* (NFA) as the designated self-regulatory organization for the managed futures industry, Congress required CTAs and CPOs to undergo periodic educational training.

Today, there are four broad classes of managed futures trading; agricultural products, financial and metal products, currency products, and diversified trading strategies (across all futures markets). Before examining these categories we review the prior research on the managed futures industry.

PRIOR EMPIRICAL RESEARCH

There are two key questions with respect to managed futures: (1) Will an investment in managed futures improve the performance of an investment portfolio? (2) Can managed futures products produce consistent returns?

The case for managed futures products as a viable investment is mixed. Elton, Gruber, and Rentzler, in three separate studies examine the returns to public commodity pools.[2] In their first study, they conclude that publicly offered commodity funds are not attractive either as stand-alone investments or as additions to a portfolio containing stocks and/or bonds. In their second study, they find the historical return data

---

[2] See Edwin Elton, Martin Gruber, and Joel Rentzler, "Professionally Managed, Publicly Traded Commodity Funds," *Journal of Business* 60, no. 2 (1987), pp. 175–199; "New Public Offerings, Information, and Investor Rationality: The Case of Publicly Offered Commodity Funds," *Journal of Business* 62, no. 1 (1989), pp. 1–15; "The Performance of Publicly Offered Commodity Funds," *Financial Analysts Journal* (July–August 1990), pp. 23–30.

reported in the prospectuses of publicly offered commodity pools are not indicative of the returns that these funds actually earn once they go public. In fact, they conclude that the performance discrepancies are so large that the prospectus numbers are seriously misleading. In their last study, they did not find any evidence that would support the addition of commodity pools to a portfolio of stocks and bonds and that commodity funds did not provide an attractive hedge against inflation. Finally, they find that the distribution of returns to public commodity pools to be negatively skewed. The opportunity for very large negative returns is therefore greater than for large positive returns.

Irwin, Krukemeyer, and Zulauf,[3] Schneeweis, Savabyana, and McCarthy,[4] and Edwards and Park[5] also conclude that public commodity funds offer little value to investors as either standalone investments or as an addition to a stock-and-bond portfolio. However, Irwin and Brorsen find that public commodity funds provide an expanded efficient investment frontier.[6]

For private commodity pools, Edwards and Park[7] find that an equally weighted index of commodity pools have a sufficiently high Sharpe ratio to justify them as either a standalone investment or as part of a diversified portfolio. Conversely, Schneeweis, et al conclude that private commodity pools do not have value as standalone investments but they are worthwhile additions to a stock-and-bond portfolio.[8]

With respect to separate accounts managed by CTAs, McCarthy, Schneeweis, and Spurgin[9] find that an allocation to an equally weighted index of CTAs provides valuable diversification benefits to a portfolio of stocks and bonds. In a subsequent study, Schneeweis, Spurgin, and Potter find that a portfolio allocation to a dollar weighted index of CTAs

---

[3] See Scott Irwin, Terry Krukemyer, and Carl Zulauf, "Investment Performance of Public Commodity Pools: 1979–1990," *The Journal of Futures Markets* 13, no. 7 (1993), pp. 799–819.
[4] See Thomas Schneeweis, Uttama Savanayana, and David McCarthy, "Alternative Commodity Trading Vehicles: A Performance Analysis," *The Journal of Futures Markets* 11, no. 4 (1991), pp. 475–487.
[5] See Franklin Edwards and James Park, "Do Managed Futures Make Good Investments," *The Journal of Futures Markets* 16, no. 5 (1996), pp. 475–517.
[6] See Scott Irwin and B. Wade Brorsen, "Public Futures Funds," *The Journal of Futures Markets* 5, no. 3 (1985), pp. 463–485.
[7] See Edwards and Park, "Do Managed Futures Make Good Investments?"
[8] See Schneeweis, Savanayana, and McCarthy, "Alternative Commodity Trading Vehicles: A Performance Analysis."
[9] See David McCarthy, Thomas Schneeweis, and Richard Spurgin, "Investment Through CTAs: An Alternative Managed Futures Investment," *The Journal of Derivatives* (Summer 1996), pp. 36–47.

results in a higher portfolio Sharpe ratio.[10] Edwards and Park find that an index of equally weighted CTAs performs well as both a standalone investment and as an addition to a diversified portfolio.[11]

An important aspect of any investment is the predictability of returns over time. If returns are predictable, then an investor can select a commodity pool or a CTA with consistently superior performance. Considerable time and effort has been devoted to studying the managed futures industry to determine the predictability and consistency of returns. Unfortunately, the results are not encouraging.

For instance, Edwards and Ma find that once commodity funds go public through a registered public offering, their average returns are negative.[12] They conclude that prior prepublic trading performance for commodity pools is of little use to investors when selecting a public commodity fund as an investment. The lack of predictability in historical managed futures returns is supported by the research of McCarthy, Schneeweis, and Spurgin,[13] Irwin, Zulauf, and Ward,[14] and the three studies by Elton, Gruber, and Renzler.[15] In fact, Irwin, et al conclude that a strategy of selecting CTAs based on historical good performance is not likely to improve upon a naive strategy of selecting CTAs at random.

One measure of whether managed futures might have benefits in a diversified portfolio is whether they can hedge inflation. Exhibit 15.1 measures the correlation of various managed futures strategies (the full Barclay CTA Index, the Barclay Agriculture CTA Index, the Barclay Currency CTA Index, the Barclay Financial and Metals CTA Index, and the Barclay Diversified CTA Index) with U.S. inflation. As can be seen, each of the managed futures categories are positively correlated with inflation.

---

[10] See Thomas Schneeweis, Richard Spurgin, and Mark Potter, "Managed Futures and Hedge Fund Investment for Downside Equity Risk Management," in Carl C. Peters and Ben Warwick (eds.), *The Handbook of Managed Futures: Performance, Evaluation and Analysis* (New York: McGraw-Hill, 1997).

[11] Edwards and Park, "Do Managed Futures Make Good Investments?"

[12] See Franklin Edwards and Cindy Ma, "Commodity Pool Performance: Is the Information Contained in Pool Prospectuses Useful?" *The Journal of Futures Markets* 8, no. 5 (1988), pp. 589–616.

[13] McCarthy, Schneeweis, and Spurgin, "Investment Through CTAs: An Alternative Managed Futures Investment."

[14] Scott Irwin, Carl Zulauf, and Barry Ward, "The Predictability of Managed Futures Returns," *The Journal of Derivatives* (Winter 1994), pp. 20–27.

[15] Elton, Gruber, and Rentzler, "Professionally Managed, Publicly Traded Commodity Funds," "New Public Offerings, Information, and Investor Rationality: The Case of Publicly Offered Commodity Funds," and "The Performance of Publicly Offered Commodity Funds."

EXHIBIT 15.1 Managed Futures Correlation with Inflation

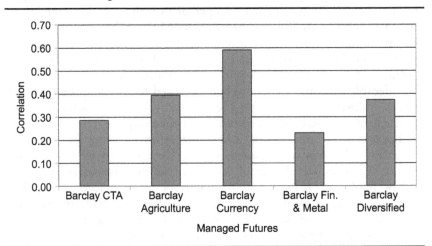

In summary, the prior research regarding managed futures is unsettled. There is no evidence that public commodity pools provide any benefits either as a standalone investment or as part of a diversified portfolio. However, the evidence does indicate that private commodity pools and CTA managed accounts can be a valuable addition to a diversified portfolio. Nonetheless, the issue of performance persistence in the managed futures industry is unresolved. Currently, there is more evidence against performance persistence than there is to support this conclusion.

In the next section, we begin to analyze the performance in the managed futures industry by examining the return distributions for different CTA investment styles. We then consider the potential for downside risk protection from managed futures.

RETURN DISTRIBUTIONS OF MANAGED FUTURES

Similar to our analysis for hedge funds and passive commodity futures, we examine the distribution of returns for managed futures. We use the Barclays Managed Futures Index to determine the pattern of returns associated with several styles of futures investing.

Managed futures products may be good investments if the pattern of their returns is positively skewed. One way to consider this concept is that it is similar to owning a Treasury bill plus a lottery ticket. The investor consistently receives low, but positive returns. However, every now and then an extreme event occurs and the CTA is able to profit from the movement of futures prices. This would result in a positive skew.

In Chapter 13, we saw that this was the case for passive commodity futures. They earned consistent positive returns, and every once in a while there is a commodity price shock that tends to push prices upward. As a result, the distribution of returns for passive commodity futures tend to be positively skewed.

To analyze the distribution of returns associated with managed futures investing, we use the Barclays CTA managed futures indexes that divide the CTA universe into four actively traded strategies: (1) CTAs that actively trade in the agricultural commodity futures; (2) CTAs that actively trade in currency futures; (3) CTAs that actively trade in financial and metal futures; and, (4) CTAs that actively trade a diversified basket of commodity futures.

Managed futures traders have one goal in mind: to capitalize on price trends. Most CTAs are considered to be trend followers. Typically, they look at various moving averages of commodity prices and attempt to determine whether the price will continue to trend up or down, and then trade accordingly. Therefore, it is not the investment strategy that is the distinguishing factor in the managed futures industry, but rather, the markets in which CTAs and CPOs apply their trend following strategies.[16]

In this chapter we use the Mount Lucas Management Index (MLMI) as a benchmark by which to judge CTA performance. Recall from our discussion in Chapter 13 that the MLMI is a passive futures index. It applies a mechanical and transparent rule for capitalizing on price trends in the futures markets. It does not represent active trading. Instead, it applies a consistent rule for buying or selling futures contracts depending upon the current price trend in any particular commodity futures market. In addition, the MLMI invests across agricultural, currency, financial, energy, and metal futures contracts. It provides a good benchmark by which to examine the four managed futures strategies.

Exhibit 13.15 in Chapter 13 demonstrates that the MLMI has a negative skew of −0.257. Therefore, a simple or naive trend following strategy will produce a distribution of returns that has more negative return observations below the median than positive observations above the median. In reviewing the distribution of returns for manage futures strategies, we keep in mind that the returns are generated from active management. As we indicated in our discussion of hedge funds in Chapter 6, one demonstration of skill is the ability to shift a distribution of

---

[16] In fact, one article has noted that the managed futures industry suffers because too many CTAs are following similar trend following strategies. See Daniel Collins, "A New Life for Managed Futures," *Futures* (April 1, 2001).

returns from a negative skew to a positive skew. Therefore, if CTAs do in fact have skill, we would expect to see distribution of returns with a positive skew.

Furthermore, the passive MLMI strategy produces a distribution of returns with mild leptokurtosis; the value of kurtosis for the MLMI is 1.93. This indicates that the tails of the distribution that have greater probability mass than a normal, bell-shaped distribution. Thus a passive trend following strategy has significant exposure to outlier events. Consequently, we would expect to observe similar leptokurtosis associated with managed futures.

Finally, the average return for the MLMI strategy was 0.57% per month. If managed futures strategies can add value, we would expect them to outperform the average monthly return earned by the naive MLMI strategy.

The Barclay Commodity Trading Advisor Index

In Exhibit 15.2 we provide the return distribution for the full Barclay Managed Futures CTA Index over the time period 1990 to 2005. This index contains 400 actively traded commodity futures programs across currencies, financials, metals, agriculture, and diversified strategies.

EXHIBIT 15.2 Return Distribuiton for Barclay CTA Index[a]

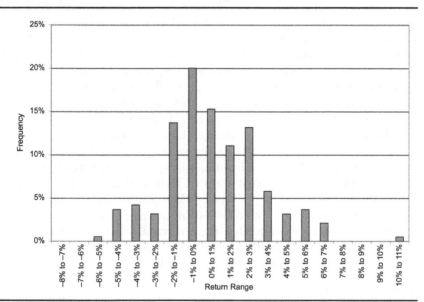

[a] E(Return) = 0.59%, Std. Dev. = 2.59%, Skew = 0.40, Kurtosis = 0.47, Sharpe = 0.06.

We note first that the expect return for the Barclay CTA Index is almost identical to that for the MLMI index—0.59% versus 0.57%. However, the Barclay CTA Index has a positive value of skew of 0.40 compared to a negative value for the MLMI. Actively traded managed futures therefore provide a bias towards large positive returns as compared to large negative returns. As we discussed in our prior chapters on hedge funds, the ability to shift the distribution of returns from a negative skew to a positive skew is a demonstration of skill. If we use the MLMI as our "market" indicator for actively managed futures trading, Exhibit 14.2 demonstrates a skill level where large positive returns are produced with greater frequency than large negative returns.

There is, however, a tradeoff for this demonstration of skill. The Barclay CTA Index has a higher volatility compared to the MLMI—2.59% versus 1.74%. In other words, there are no free lunches. While actively managed futures provides a bias to the upside that is not witnessed with the MLMI, it does so with higher volatility that results in a lower Sharpe ratio than the MLMI.

Managed Futures in Agricultural Commodities

In our prior discussion of commodity futures, we indicated that commodity prices are more likely to be susceptible to positive price surprises. The reason is that most of the news associated with agricultural products is usually negative. Droughts, floods, storms, and crop freezes are the main news stories. So new information to the agricultural market tends to result in positive price shocks instead of negative price shocks. (There is not much price reaction to the news that "the crop cycle is progressing normally.") We would expect the CTAs to capture the advantage of these price surprises and any trends that develop from them.

Exhibit 15.3 presents the return distribution for Barclays Agricultural CTA index. We use data over the period 1990 to 2005. From a quick review of this distribution, it closely resembles a bell curve type of distribution with a skew of almost zero and a very small value of kurtosis. Thus compared to the negative skew and moderate level of kurtosis observed for the passive MLMI, we can conclude that agricultural managed futures programs provided a return distribution that was symmetrical in nature with almost no greater exposure to outlier events than a normal distribution.

There is, however, a tradeoff for this normality. The average return to the Barclays Agricultural CTA index of 0.40% per month is less than that for the MLMI index of 0.57%. Additionally, the Sharpe ratio for the managed futures strategy is lower than that for the MLMI (in fact, it is zero). Consequently, the results for managed futures trading in the

EXHIBIT 15.3   Return Distribution for Barclay Agriculture CTAs[a]

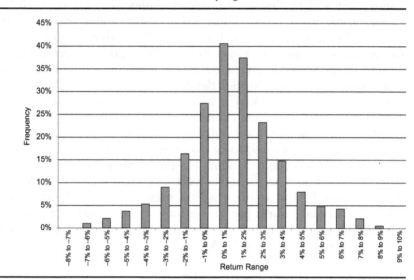

[a] E(Return) = 0.40%, Std. Dev. = 2.43%, Skew = 0.03, Kurtosis = 0.74, Sharpe = 0.00.

agriculture markets is mixed. On the one hand, we observe a positive shift to the normally distributed model distribution of returns, but a reduction in the risk and return tradeoff as measured by the Sharpe ratio. Again, there is no free lunch.

Managed Futures In Currency Markets

The currency markets are the most liquid and efficient markets in the world. The reason is simple, every other commodity, financial asset, household good, cheeseburger, and so on must be denominated in a currency. As the numeraire, currency is the commodity in which all other commodities and assets are denominated.

Daily trading volume in exchange listed and forward markets for currency contracts is in the hundreds of billions of dollars. Given the liquidity, depth, and efficiency of the currency markets, we would expect the ability of managed futures traders to derive value to be small.

Exhibit 15.4 provides the distribution of returns for actively managed currency futures. We can see from this graph that currency CTAs produced a distribution of returns with a very large positive skew of 1.53. This is considerably greater than that for the MLMI, and presents a strong case for skill. In addition, the average monthly return for CTAs trading in currency futures is 0.67% per month, an improvement of the average monthly return for the MLMI.

EXHIBIT 15.4   Return Distribution for Barclay Currency CTAs[a]

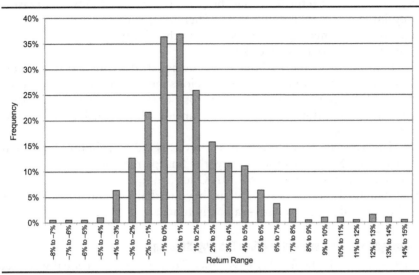

[a] E(Return) = 0.67%, Std. Dev. = 3.16%, Skew = 1.53, Kurtosis = 4.25, Sharpe = 0.08.

This strategy also provides a higher value of kurtosis, 4.25, indicating significant exposure to outlier events. However, a positive skew combined with a large value of kurtosis indicates a bias to positive instead of negative outlier events. Still this higher exposure to outlier events translates into a higher standard deviation of returns for managed currency futures, and a lower Sharpe ratio. Again, there are no free lunches.

The evidence for skill-based investing in managed currency futures is mixed. On the one hand, CTAs demonstrated an ability to shift the distribution of returns compared to a naive trend following strategy from negative to positive. On the other hand, more risk was incurred through greater exposure to outlier events resulting in a lower Sharpe ratio than that for the MLMI.

Managed Futures in the Financials and Metals Markets

As we discussed above, with the advent of the GNMA futures contract in the 1970s, financial futures contracts have enjoyed greater prominence than traditional physical commodity futures. However, considerable liquidity exists in the precious metals markets because gold, silver, and platinum are still purchased and sold primarily as a store of value rather than for any productive input into a manufacturing process. In this fashion, precious metal futures resemble financial assets.

In Chapter 6 we demonstrated how financial assets tend to have a negative skew of returns during the period 1990 to 2005 with a reasonably large value of leptokurtosis. Therefore, a demonstration of skill with respect to managed futures is again the ability to shift the distribution of returns to a positive skew.

Exhibit 15.3 and Exhibit 15.5 demonstrates this positive skew. Managed futures in financial and precious metal futures have a positive skew of 0.53 and a small positive kurtosis of 0.46. So CTAs were able to shift the distribution of returns to the upside while reducing exposure to outlier returns.

The average monthly return, however, is 0.59%, slightly more than that for the MLMI. Unfortunately, the Sharpe ratio for this CTA strategy is less than that for the MLMI. Once again, we find mixed evidence that managed futures can add value beyond that presented in a mechanical trend following strategy—a costly lunch.

Managed Futures in a Diversified Trading Strategy

Last we examine the Barclay Diversified Traders Index, an equal weighted composite of managed futures programs that trade a diversified portfolio of agriculture, currency, financials and metal futures contracts. We examine the period 1990 to 2005.

EXHIBIT 15.5   Return Distribution for Barclay Financial and Metal CTAs[a]

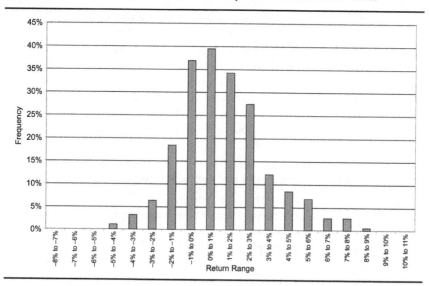

[a] E(Return) = 0.59%, Std. Dev. = 2.15%, Skew = 0.53, Kurtosis = 0.46, Sharpe = 0.09.

EXHIBIT 15.6   Return Distribuiton for Barclay Diversified CTAs[a]

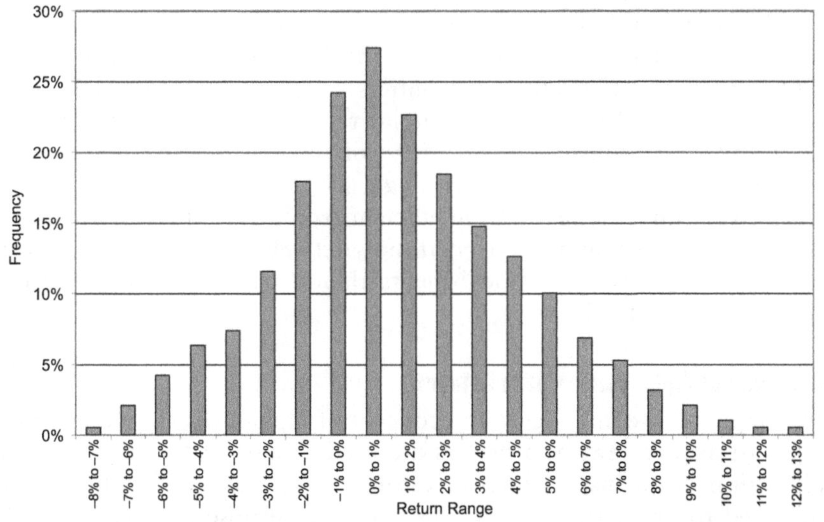

[a] E(Return) = 0.74%, Std. Dev. = 3.53%, Skew = 0.35, Kurtosis = 0.11, Sharpe = 0.1.

Exhibit 15.6 presents the return distribution for diversified managed futures programs. Again, we see a positive skew. This is a consistent theme with all of the managed futures programs. Using the MLMI as a base case for a passive or "naive" trading strategy, every managed futures strategy demonstrates the ability to shift the distribution of returns associated with futures trading programs from a negative skew to a positive skew, indicating a bias to upside returns. The return is also large compared to the MLMI at 0.74%. Although the standard deviation is also larger, the Sharpe ratio is the same as the MLMI at 0.10. In sum, diversified trading programs, provide a bias to the upside with low exposure to outlier returns (kurtosis is only 0.11) while maintaining a Sharpe ratio on par with the MLMI.

MANAGED FUTURES IN A PORTFOLIO CONTEXT

Similar to the analysis that we conducted in Chapter 14 on commodity futures and the efficient frontier, we add managed futures to a stock-and-bond portfolio to see if their are diversification benefits. Just as in Chapter 14, we blend in a 10% allocation to managed futures to our stock-and-bond portfolio, and then observe whether there is any improvement along the efficient frontier. The results of our analysis are presented in Exhibits 15.7 through 15.11.

Starting with Exhibit 15.7, we can see that there is no improvement in the efficient frontier from adding the Barclay CTA Index to stocks and bonds. The two efficient frontiers overlap one another. Looking back in Chapter 14, we can see similar results for the MLMI in Exhibit 14.9. In fact, Exhibits 15.7 and 14.9 look virtually identical.

Examining Exhibits 15.8 through 15.11, we find similar results. There is no improvement in the efficient frontier from adding managed futures to a stock-and-bond portfolio. Actively, managed futures provide no better diversification benefits than a naive trading rule represented by the MLMI.

A Review of Alpha versus Beta Drivers

In Chapter 2, we introduced the concept of alpha drivers and beta drivers. Just as a review, beta drivers are used as part of the strategic asset allocation of an institutional investor. Strategic asset allocation is not designed to "beat the market." Instead, its purpose is to establish the long-term funding goals of an organization such as paying retirement benefits (a pension fund), funding new research facilities (an endowment fund), or meeting a long-term philanthropic schedule (a foundation).

EXHIBIT 15.7 Efficient Frontier with the Barclay CTA Index

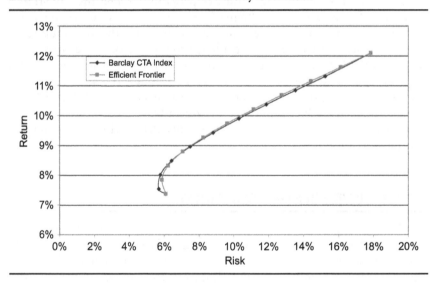

EXHIBIT 15.8   Efficient Frontier with Barclay Agriculture CTAs

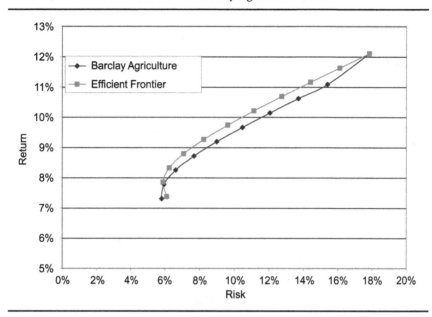

EXHIBIT 15.9   Efficient Frontier with Barclay Currency CTAs

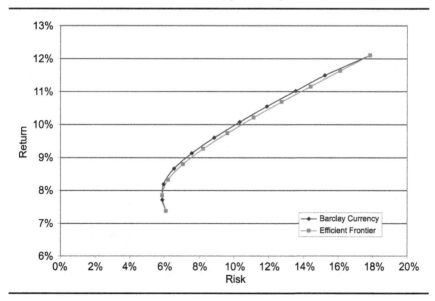

EXHIBIT 15.10 Efficient Frontier with Barclay Fin & Metal

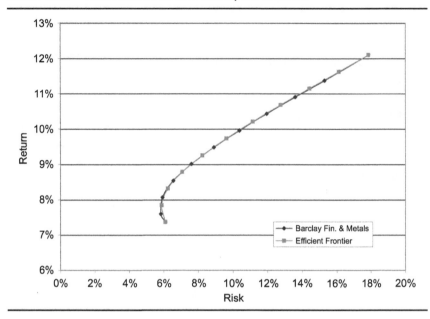

EXHIBIT 15.11 Efficient Frontier with Barclay Diversified

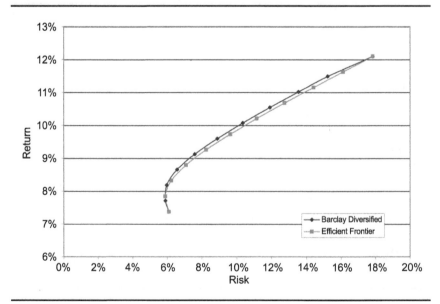

To accomplish this, the Board of Trustees of an institutional investor divide up the assets of the fund according to their long-term funding requirements and diversify across different asset classes. This establishes the policy risk, or beta risk, for the fund.

In contrast, alpha drivers are used as part of tactical asset allocation which facilitates an institutional investor's long-term funding goals by seeking extra return. The investment staff of an organization attempt to take advantage of opportunities in the financial markets when the markets appear to be out of line with fundamental economic valuations. In addition, active trading strategies may be pursued to extract excess returns. In sum, alpha drivers are not added to a portfolio for strategic reasons, they are added when excess returns can be generated.

It is not surprising that Exhibits 15.7 through 15.11 show no minimal improvement in the efficient frontier. The one exception is the Barclays Agriculture CTA index, where there may be some real commodities diversification. The reason is that alpha drivers are used for excess return (tactical) instead of portfolio diversification (strategic). Managed futures should not be used for strategic asset allocation because they are not a separate asset class, they are trading strategies. Active trading strategies add excess return but do not have the ability to diversify the portfolio. The same is true for Exhibit 14.9. The MLMI is designed to replicate a managed futures trading strategy. It is not designed to introduce a new class of assets to the portfolio and therefore, it does not provide diversification value.

Compare the results in Exhibits 15.7 through 15.11 with those in Exhibits 14.6 and 14.7. Exhibits 14.6 and 14.7 show how the efficient frontier is expanded when commodity futures are added to stocks and bonds. The reason why the efficient frontier expands is that the GSCI and the DJ-AIG provide strategic diversification into a new asset class: commodity futures. Neither the Goldman Sachs Commodity Index (GSCI) nor the Dow Jones-AIG Commodity Index (DJ-AIGCI) provide exposure to an actively traded strategy. These are passive indexes that are designed to diversify the strategic portfolio, not provide tactical trading opportunities.

MANAGED FUTURES AS DOWNSIDE RISK PROTECTION FOR STOCKS AND BONDS

This section is similar to that presented in Chapter 14 for passive commodity futures. As we discussed in Chapter 14, the greatest concern for any investor is downside risk. If equity and bond markets are becoming increasingly synchronized, international diversification may not offer the protection sought by investors. The ability to protect the value of an investment portfolio in hostile or turbulent markets is the key to the value of any macroeconomic diversification.

Within this framework, an asset class distinct from financial assets has the potential to diversify and protect an investment portfolio from hostile markets. We saw in Chapter 14 that commodity futures have the ability to diversify a stock-and-bond portfolio. They provide strategic diversification. We now face the question of whether skill-based strategies like managed futures can provide the same amount of downside protection as commodity futures.

Recall that in Exhibit 14.10 we presented the return distribution for a portfolio that was 60% the S&P 500 and 40% U.S. Treasury bonds. Our concern is the shaded part of the return distribution. This shows where the returns to the stock-and-bond portfolio were negative. That is, the shaded part of the distribution shows both the size and the frequency with which the combined return of 60% S&P 500 plus 40% U.S. Treasury bonds earned a negative return in a particular month. The average monthly return in the shaded part of the distribution was −2.03%. It is this part of the return distribution that an investor attempts to avoid or limit.

We attempt to protect against the downside of this distribution by making a 10% allocation to managed futures to our initial stock-and-bond portfolio. Therefore, the new portfolio is a blend of 55% S&P 500, 35% U.S. Treasury bonds, and 10% managed futures. If managed futures can protect against downside risk, we can conclude that it is a valuable addition to a stock-and-bond portfolio.

Once again, we use the MLMI as a benchmark to determine if CTAs can improve the downside protection over a passive trend following strategy. Exhibit 15.12 provides the results for the downside protection. We can see that in every stock/bond/managed futures portfolio the number of negative months with managed futures is less than in the 60/40 stock/bond portfolio. In addition, the average return of a negative month declines when managed futures are added to the stock-and-bond portfolio. Unfortunately, the average monthly return declines in every portfolio with managed futures except for the stock/bond/diversified managed futures portfolio. Again, free lunches are hard to come by. On the one hand, managed futures does provide some downside protection, but at a cost of reduced expected return. Furthermore, the downside protection of each managed futures strategy is no better than that for the MLMI.

There is an improvement in the Sharpe ratio for two managed futures strategies: currency and diversified. All of the other strategies either have the same or lower Sharpe ratio as the stock/bond portfolio. So the downside risk protection does not necessarily result in a better risk and return tradeoff. Compare this result to Exhibit 14.16 and the

EXHIBIT 15.12 Summary of Downside Protection for Managed Futures

Portfolio	Average Return	Standard Deviation	Skew	Kurtosis	Sharpe	Number of Neg. Months	Average Return Negative Month	Downside Risk Protection
60/40 S&P 500/U.S. Treasury	0.81%	2.64%	-0.16	0.33	0.16	66	-2.03%	N/A
55/35/10 S&P500/Bonds/Barclay CTA	0.79%	2.41%	-0.04	0.40	0.16	63	-1.90%	14.28%
55/35/10 S&P500/Bonds/Agriculture CTA	0.77%	2.43%	-0.21	0.31	0.15	65	-1.88%	11.78%
55/35/10 S&P500/Bonds/Currency CTA	0.80%	2.42%	-0.06	0.56	0.17	62	-1.93%	14.32%
55/35/10 S&P500/Bonds/Fin & Metal CTA	0.79%	2.38%	-0.04	0.33	0.16	62	-1.93%	14.32%
55/35/10 S&P 500/Bonds/Diversified CTA	0.81%	2.41%	0.00	0.38	0.17	63	-1.89%	14.91%
55/35/10 S&P500/Bonds/MLMI	0.79%	2.38%	-0.12	0.26	0.16	62	-1.89%	16.80%

addition of commodity futures to the portfolio. In Chapter 14 we showed how a passive commodity index (the GSCI and the DJ-AIG) could not only reduce the number of negative months, but also provide a better risk and return tradeoff than the 60/40 stock/bond portfolio.

The downside risk protection demonstrated by managed futures products is consistent with the research of Schneeweis, Spurgin, and Potter and Anson.[17] Specifically, they find that a combination of 50% S&P 500 stocks and 50% CTA managed futures outperforms a portfolio comprised of the S&P 500 plus protective put options. Unfortunately, our research indicates that only in limited circumstances do managed futures products offer financial benefits greater than that offered by a passive futures index.

CONCLUSION

In this chapter we examined the benefits of managed futures products. Prior empirical research has not resolved the issue of whether managed futures products can add value either as a standalone investment or as part of a diversified portfolio.

On a standalone basis, our review indicates that managed futures products mostly outperformed a naive trend following index represented by the MLMI. The MLMI is a transparent commodity futures index that mechanically applies a simple price trend following rule for buying or selling commodity futures. With the exception of agriculture CTA programs, we did find evidence to conclude that skill-based CTA trading can outperform this passive index of commodity futures.

In particular, the MLMI has a significant negative skew of –0.257. This demonstrates a large bias towards large downside returns. In contrast, the managed futures indexes all showed a positive skew. Similar to our discussion on hedge funds, the ability to shift the distribution of returns from a negative bias to positive bias is a demonstration of skill. The mechanical active strategy of the MLMI results in a negative skew, but the active trading of commodity trading advisors results in a positive skew to the distribution, providing the opportunity for upside potential. Unfortunately, the active managed futures trading strategies

---

[17] See Thomas Schneeweis, Richard Spurgin, and Mark Potter, "Managed Futures and Hedge Fund Investment for Downside Equity Risk Protection," *Derivatives Quarterly* (Fall 1996), pp. 62–72. See also Mark Anson, "Managing Downside Risk in Return Distributions Using Hedge Funds, Managed Futures and Commodity Futures," *The CTA Reader* (2004).

also had a higher volatility associated with their returns which resulted in most cases in a lower Sharpe ratio.

On a portfolio basis, the results were more encouraging. We found that managed futures products did provide downside risk protection that ranged from 11.78% to 16.80% over the sample period. However, CTA managed products did not outperform passive commodity futures indexes either on a Sharpe ratio basis or with respect to downside risk protection. This conclusion merely highlights the fact that managed futures products are alpha drivers, not beta drivers. Last, on a portfolio basis, we found that managed futures did not improve the efficient frontier when added to a stock-and-bond portfolio. This is distinctly different from what we observed with the commodity futures indexes. Again, the reason is the difference between beta drivers and alpha drivers. Commodity futures indexes introduce a new asset class into the stock-and-bond portfolio. This provides for greater diversification and an expansion of the efficient frontier. Managed futures, on the other hand, are active trading strategies, not a new asset class. Their goal is to assist in tactical asset allocation by adding value through skill-based investment programs. Diversification is not their purpose; excess return is.

Private Equity

CHAPTER 16

Introduction to Venture Capital

The private equity sector purchases the private stock or equity-linked securities of nonpublic companies that are expected to go public or provides the capital for public companies (or their divisions) that may wish to go private. The key component in either case is the private nature of the securities purchased. Private equity, by definition, is not publicly traded. Therefore, investments in private equity are illiquid. Investors in this marketplace must be prepared to invest for the long haul—investment horizons may be as long as five to 10 years.

"Private equity" is a generic term that encompasses four distinct strategies in the market for private investing. First, there is venture capital, the financing of startup companies. Second, there are leveraged buyouts (LBOs) where public companies repurchase all of their outstanding shares and turn themselves into private companies. Third, there is mezzanine financing, a hybrid of private debt and equity financing. Finally there is distressed debt investing. These are private equity investments in established (as opposed to startup) but troubled companies.

Private equity is as old as Columbus' journey to America. Queen Isabella of Spain sold her jewelry to finance Columbus' small fleet of ships in return for whatever spoils Columbus could find in the New World. The risks were great, but the potential rewards were even greater. This in a nutshell summarizes the private equity market: a large risk of failure but the potential for outstanding gains.

More generally, private equity provides the long-term equity base of a company that is not listed on any exchange and therefore cannot raise capital via the public stock market. Private equity provides the working capital that is used to help private companies grow and succeed. It is a long-term investment process that requires patient due diligence and hands on monitoring.

In this chapter, we focus on the best known of the private equity categories: venture capital. Venture capital is the supply of equity financing to startup companies that do not have a sufficient track record to attract investment capital from traditional sources (e.g., the public markets or lending institutions). Entrepreneurs that develop business plans require investment capital to implement those plans. However, these startup ventures often lack tangible assets that can be used as collateral for a loan. In addition, startup companies are unlikely to produce positive earnings for several years. Negative cash flows are another reason why banks and other lending institutions as well as the public stock market are unwilling to provide capital to support the business plan.

It is in this uncertain space where nascent companies are born that venture capitalists operate. Venture capitalists finance these high-risk, illiquid, and unproven ideas by purchasing senior equity stakes while the firms are still privately held. The ultimate goal is to make a buck. Venture capitalists are willing to underwrite new ventures with untested products and bear the risk of no liquidity only if they can expect a reasonable return for their efforts. Often venture capitalists set expected target rates of return of 33% or more to support the risks they bear. Successful startup companies funded by venture capital money include Cisco Systems, Cray Research, Microsoft, and Genentech.

We begin with a brief history of venture capital. We then consider the role of a venture capitalist in a startup company raising a venture capital fund. Next we review the heart of the venture capital industry— the business plan. We then review the current structure of the industry. This is followed by a review of the different stages of venture capital financing. We conclude with a case study of a startup company financed with venture capital.

THE HISTORY OF VENTURE CAPITAL

While the history of private equity can be traced back to the days of Columbus discovering the new world, the formal process of private equity investing can be traced back to the 1800s in the United Kingdom. In the 1800s, the developed nations of the world were undergoing a significant economic change. Previously, wealth had been defined in terms of the amount of real estate an individual owned. "Land barons" were aptly named.

However, starting in the 1800s, economic society began to transform itself from an agricultural one to an industrial one. Instead of ownership of land, ownership of goods and services became the new denominator of wealth. Wealthy land barons began to finance the companies of entrepreneurs by purchasing an equity ownership in the company. Private equity had come of age.

The first modern venture capital firm was American Research and Development. It was formed in 1946 as a publicly traded closed-end fund. Its investment objective was to finance companies in growth industries, at that time broadcasting, aerospace, and pharmaceuticals.

Over the next 12 years, a small number of venture capital firms (less than 20) were established. Most were structured as closed-end funds like American Research and Development. In 1958 two new developments were introduced into the venture capital industry.

First, Congress created *Small Business Investment Companies* (SBICs). SBICs are licensed and regulated by the Small Business Administration. These are government-backed but privately owned investment companies that provide both management assistance and venture financing for startup companies. These companies include Citicorp Venture Capital and Clinton Capital. SIBCs have provided financing to successful household names such as Apple Computer, Federal Express, and Intel Corporation. Today there are an estimated 300 SBICs in the United States, concentrated in states with high levels of entrepreneurial talent such as California, Massachusetts, New York, and Texas.[1]

The second development in 1958 was the formation of the first venture capital limited partnership, Draper, Gaither, and Anderson. Limited partnerships have become the standard tool for investing in venture capital by wealthy and institutional investors. Although imitators soon followed, limited partnerships accounted for a small number of the venture capital vehicles throughout the 1960s and 1970s. Furthermore, the annual flow of money into venture capital limited partnerships or closed end funds never exceeded a few hundred million dollars during this time period.[2]

A third important watershed in the development of the venture capital industry was a change in the "prudent person" standard in the rules governing the pension fund industry in the 1970s. Since 1974, corporate pension plans have been governed by the *Employee Retirement Income Security Act of 1974* (ERISA). ERISA was established to ensure proper investment guidelines for the mounting pension liabilities of corporate America.

---

[1] See W. Keith Schilit, "Structure of the Venture Capital Industry," *The Journal of Private Equity* (Spring 1998), pp. 60–67.
[2] See Paul Gompers and Josh Lerner, "The Use of Covenants: An Empirical Analysis of Venture Partnership Agreements," *Journal of Law and Economics* (October 1996), pp. 463–498.

Initially, ERISA guidelines prohibited pension funds from investing in venture capital funds because of their illiquid and high-risk status. In 1979, the Department of Labor (which oversees ERISA) issued a clarification of the prudent person rule to indicate that venture capital and other high-risk investments should not be considered on a standalone basis, but rather on a portfolio basis. In addition, the rule clarified that the prudent person test is based on an investment review process and not on the ultimate outcome of investment results. Therefore, as long as a pension fund investment fiduciary follows sufficient due diligence in considering the portfolio effects of investing in venture capital, the prudent person test is met. The change in the prudent person rule allowed pension funds for the first time to wholly endorse venture capital investing.

The 1980s saw yet another new development in the venture capital industry: the Gatekeeper. Although many pension funds and wealthy investors access the venture capital industry through investment funds or limited partnerships, few investors have devoted resources to evaluate and monitor these investments. Investors' lack of experience and expertise in venture capital led to the birth of investment advisers to fill this gap.

In the 1980s, investment advisers came to prominence to advise pension funds and wealthy investors on the benefits of venture capital investing. These gatekeepers got their name because venture capital funds and limited partnerships could no longer access pension fund investment staffs directly. Venture capitalists now had to go through the investment adviser to get a capital commitment from a pension fund. In turn, gatekeepers pooled the resources from their clients and became a dynamic force in the venture capital industry. By 1991, up to one-third of all pension fund commitments to venture capital and one-fifth of all venture money raised came through a gatekeeper.[3]

Venture capital financing increased steadily in the 1980s from about $1.5 billion in commitments in 1980 to over $5 billion in commitments in 1987. During this time, the number of active venture capital investment vehicles increased fourfold. However, the stock market crashes in 1987 and 1989 as well as the recession of 1990 to 1991 reduced the capital commitments to about $2.5 billion by 1991.

The 1990s saw the longest economic growth cycle ever experienced in the United States. Since the U.S. recession that ended in 1991, the economy has sustained strong growth with a minimum of inflation. This is the perfect environment for venture capital to blossom.

Exhibit 16.1 demonstrates the growth of investment capital committed to venture capital from 1990 through 2005. For the first half of

---

[3] Gompers and Lerner, "The Use of Covenants: An Empirical Analysis of Venture Partnership Agreements."

EXHIBIT 16.1 Venture Capital Investing, 1990–2005

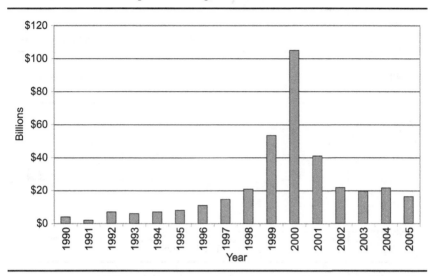

Source: Data obtained from Thomson Financial Venture Economics.

the decade (1990 to 1995), the annual commitments to venture capital generally ranged from $5 billion to $7 billion. However, starting in 1996, the venture capital industry experienced exponential growth. The average annual growth rate of venture capital commitments between 1995 and 2000 was 82%. From 1990 through 1999, investing in venture capital increased ninefold. The frenzy of venture capital investing peaked in year 2000 with over $100 billion committed to the venture capital industry in one year. This one year virtually equaled all of the venture capital that had been committed over the previous decade. However, with the bursting of the technology bubble in year 2000, the amount of capital committed to venture capital declined rapidly.

This growth was fueled by three factors: robust returns in the stock market in the United States, a strong initial public offering (IPO) market, and low inflation. These three factors allowed investors to simultaneously increase their risk tolerance and to extend their investment horizons. Increased risk tolerance allowed investors to bear the high risks of startup companies. Extended investment horizons allowed investors to accept long lock-up periods associated with venture capital investing.

Exhibit 16.2 demonstrates the returns to venture capital compared to the S&P 500 over a one-year, three-year, five-year, and 10-year investment horizon (1996 to 2005). We include the returns for late stage, early stage, and balanced venture capital funds. We can see that over a long-term horizon, the returns to venture capital dominate those of the S&P 500.

EXHIBIT 16.2   Returns to Venture Capital

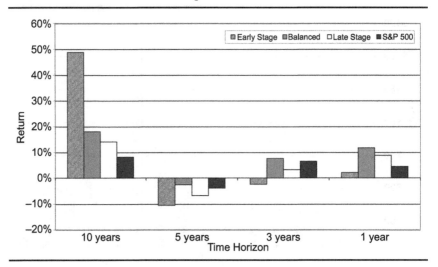

Source: Data obtained from National Venture Capital Association.

This should be expected because investors should be compensated for the risk of startup companies and the lack of liquidity of their holdings.

However, when we examine the 1-, 3-, and 5-year venture capital returns to the public stock market, the returns are mixed. There are three reasons for this. First, the technology bubble inflated the values of startup companies beyond a reasonable rate of return. The popping of this bubble had a much more significant impact on the returns to private equity investing than public stock market investing. Second, the 5-year return period includes the recession of 2001 to 2002. This period hurt all equity investments, but undermined the returns to venture capital in particular. Finally, the financial markets experienced a three-year bear market during 2000 to 2002. During this time period, every developed stock market around the world suffered annual double-digit declines. While this hurt public equity investing, it was even more devastating to the private equity market.

The old saying that "what is good for the goose is good for the gander" is particularly true for the public and private equity markets. When the public equity markets provide solid investment returns, the opportunity for venture capital investments to be harvested at excellent rates of return is even better. Conversely, a weak public stock market can be the kiss of death to venture capital returns.

Given all of the economic turmoil during 2000 to 2002, a more realistic appraisal of venture capital returns is the 10-year horizon. Over a full economic cycle, venture capital returns should be expected to earn a premium over the public stock market of 5% to 7%.[4] Over the 10-year cycle, for example, balanced and late-stage venture capital investments earned a premium over the S&P 500 of 10% and 6%, respectively.

The new millennium began with a bang, but by the end of its first full year of 2000, ended with a whimper. The NASDAQ stock market, the primary listing ground for private companies going public through IPOs, came crashing down to earth. Throughout the late 1990s, the valuations associated with companies listed on the NASDAQ became inflated compared to companies listed in the S&P 500 and the Dow Jones 30 Industrial Companies.

Exhibit 16.3 demonstrates the value of the NASDAQ composite index compared to the S&P 500 and the Dow Jones Industrials from the beginning of 1995 through the end of 2005.[5] The thick line on top of the graph represents the value of the NASDAQ, while the thin line in the middle is the S&P 500 and the dashed line at the bottom represents the Dow Jones 30 Industrials. As can be seen, the NASDAQ tracked closely the valuations of the S&P 500 and the Dow Jones until the beginning of 1999. Then valuations began to diverge with the NASDAQ soaring in value compared to the S&P 500 and the Dow Jones. This created a valu-

EXHIBIT 16.3 A Technology Bubble

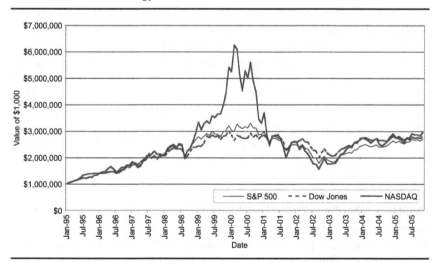

---

[4] See Keith Ambachtsheer, "How Should Pension Funds Managed Risk," *Journal of Applied Corporate Finance* (Summer 1998), pp. 1–6.
[5] To compare the values of these stock indexes, we measure the value of $1,000 invested in each index over the period January 1995 through December 2005.

ation "bubble" fueled by the belief that technology stocks would take over the world and create a new economic paradigm that defied basic principles of cash flows and valuation. However, the bubble in burst in 2000 when new technology companies failed to produce the earnings and revenue growth forecast by optimistic Wall Street analysts. By the beginning of 2001, these three stock indexes had converged back to similar values. As Exhibit 16.3 shows, the bubble quickly deflated and by 2001, the valuations of technology companies listed on the NASDAQ had converged back to similar valuations for more traditional companies comprising the Dow Jones 30 Industrial Stocks as well as for the S&P 500.

Going forward in the new decade of the 2000s, rational pricing has come back to the stock market as well as the venture capital market. The fund raising by venture capitalists is at the level of the mid-1990s.

THE ROLE OF A VENTURE CAPITALIST

Venture capitalists have two roles within the industry. Raising money from investors is just the first part. The second is to invest that capital with startup companies.

Venture capitalists are not passive investors. Once they invest in a company, they take an active role either in an advisory capacity or as a director on the board of the company. They monitor the progress of the company, implement incentive plans for the entrepreneurs and management, and establish financial goals for the company.

Besides providing management insight, venture capitalists usually have the right to hire and fire key managers, including the original entrepreneur. They also provide access to consultants, accountants, lawyers, investment bankers, and most importantly, other business that might purchase the startup company's product.

In this section we focus on the relationship between the venture capitalist and his investors. In the next section we consider the process by which a venture capitalist selects investments.

The Relationship of the Venture Capitalist to Her Investors

Before a venture capitalist can invest money with startup ventures, she must go through a period of fund raising with outside investors. Most venture capital funds are structured as limited partnerships, where the venture capitalist is the general partner and the investors are limited partners. Each venture capital fund first goes through a period of fund raising before it begins to invest the capital raised from the limited partners.

The venture capitalist, or her company, is the general partner of the venture capital fund. All other investors are limited partners. As the general partner, the venture capitalist has full operating authority to managed the fund as she pleases, subject to restrictions placed in the covenants of the fund's documents.

As the venture capital industry grew and matured through the 1980s and 1990s, sophisticated investors such as pension funds, endowments, foundations, and high-net-worth individuals began to demand contractual provisions be placed in the documents and subscription agreements that establish and govern a private equity fund. These covenants ensure that the venture capitalist sticks to her knitting and operates in the best interest of the limited partners who have invested in the venture capital fund.

These protective covenants can be broken down into three broad classes of investor protections: (1) covenants relating to the overall management of the fund; (2) covenants that relate to the activities of the general partners; and (3) covenants that determine what constitutes a permissible investment.[6]

Restrictions on the Management of the Venture Capital Fund

Typically, the most important covenant is the size of an investment by the venture capital fund in any one startup venture. This is typically expressed as a percentage of the capital committed to the venture capital fund. The purpose is to ensure that the venture capitalist does not bet the fund on any single investment. In any venture capital fund, there will be startup ventures that fail to generate a return. This is expected. By diversifying across several venture investments, this risk is mitigated.

Other covenants may include a restriction on the use of debt or leverage by the venture capitalist. Venture capital investments are risky enough without the venture capitalist gearing up the fund through borrowing.

In addition, there may be a restriction on coinvestments with prior or future funds controlled by the venture capitalist. If a venture capitalist has made a poor investment in a prior fund, the investors in the current fund do not want the venture capitalist to throw more good money after bad. Last, there is usually a covenant regarding the distribution of profits. It is optimal for investors to receive the profits as they accrue. Furthermore, distributed profits reduce the amount of committed capital in the venture fund which in turn reduces the fees paid to the venture capitalist. It is in the venture capitalist's economic interest to hold onto profits, while investors prefer to have them distributed as they accrue.

---

[6] See Josh Lerner, *Venture Capital and Private Equity* (New York: John Wiley & Sons, 2000).

Restrictions on the Activities of the General Partner

Primary among these is a limit on the amount of private investments the venture capitalist can make in any of the firms funded by the venture capital fund. If the venture capitalist makes private investments on her own is a select group of companies, these companies may receive more attention than the remaining portfolio of companies contained in the venture fund.

In addition, general partners are often limited in their ability to sell their general partnership interest in the venture fund to a third party. Such a sale would likely reduce the general partner's incentive to monitor and produce an effective exit strategy for the venture fund's portfolio companies.

Two other covenants related to keeping the venture capitalists' eye on the ball. The first is a restriction on the amount of future fund raising. Fund raising is time consuming and distracting—less time is spent managing the investments of the fund. Also, the limited partners typically demand that the general partner spend substantially all of his time on managing the investments of the fund—outside interests are limited or restricted.

Restrictions on the Type of Investments

Generally, these covenants serve to keep the venture capitalist focussed on investing in those companies, industries and transactions where she has the greatest experience. So, for instance, there may be restrictions or prohibitions on investing in leveraged buyouts, other venture capital funds, foreign securities, or companies and industries outside the realm of the venture capitalists' expertise.

Venture Capital Fees

Venture capitalists earn fees two ways: management fees and a percentage of the profits earned by the venture fund. Management fees can range anywhere from 1% to 3.5%, with most venture capital funds in the 2% to 2.5% range. Management fees are used to compensate the venture capitalist while she looks for attractive investment opportunities for the venture fund.

A key point is that the management fee is assessed on the amount of committed capital, not invested capital. Consider the following example: the venture capitalist raises $100 million in committed capital for her venture fund. The management fee 2.5%. To date, only $50 million dollars of the raised capital has been invested. The annual management fee that the venture capitalist collects is $2.5 million—2.5% × $100 million—even though not all of the capital has been invested. Investors pay the management fee on the amount of capital they have agreed to commit to the venture fund whether or not that capital has actually been invested.

Consider the implications of this fee arrangement. The venture capitalist collects a management fee from the moment that an investor signs a subscription agreement to invest capital in the venture fund—even though no capital has actually been contributed by the limited partners yet. Furthermore, the venture capitalist then has a call option to demand—according to the subscription agreement—that the investors contribute capital when the venture capitalist finds an appropriate investment for the fund. This is a great deal for the venture capitalist— she is paid a large fee to have a call option on the limited partners' capital. Not a bad business model. We will see later that this has some keen implications for leveraged buyout funds.

The second part of the remuneration for a venture capitalist is the profit sharing or incentive fees. This is really where the venture capitalist makes her money. Incentive fees provide the venture capitalist with a share of the profits generated by the venture fund. The typical incentive fee is 20% but the better known venture capital funds can charge up to 35%. That is, the best venture capitalists can claim 1/3 of the profits generated by the venture fund.

Similar to our discussion of hedge fund incentive fees in Chapter 10, the incentive fees for venture capital funds are a free option. If the venture capitalist generates profits for the venture fund, she can collect a share of these profits. If the venture fund loses money, the venture capitalist does not collect an incentive fee. This binary fee payout can be described as

$$\text{Payout on incentive fee} = \text{Max}[i \times \text{Profits}, 0] \qquad (16.1)$$

where

i = the percent of profit sharing by the venture capitalist, e.g., 20%

Profits = the profits generated by the venture fund

Equation (16.1) is the basic equation for the payout on a call option. Similar to our option pricing model in Chapter 10 for hedge fund incentive fees, this option has significant value to the venture capitalist. Furthermore, valued within an option context, venture capital profit sharing fees provide some interesting incentives to the venture capitalist.

For example, one way to increase the value of a call option is to increase the volatility of the underlying asset. This means that the venture capitalist is encouraged to make riskier investments with the pool of capital in the venture fund to maximize the value of his incentive fee. This increased risk may run counter to the desires of the limited partners to maintain a less risky profile. It is also fascinating to realize that this incentive fee is costless to the venture capitalist—he does not pay any price for the receipt of this option. Indeed, the venture capitalist gets paid a management fee in addition to this free call option on the profits of the venture fund. As we noted previously, this is not a bad business model for the venture capitalist.

Fortunately, there is a check and balance on incentive fees in the venture capital world. Most, if not all, venture capital limited partnership agreements include some restrictive covenants on when incentive fees may be paid to the venture capitalist. There are three primary covenants that are used.

First, most venture capital partnership agreements include a clawback provision. A clawback covenant allows the limited partners to clawback previously paid incentive fees to the venture capitalist if, at the end/liquidation of the venture fund, the limited partners are still out of pocket some costs or lost capital investment. This prevents the venture capitalist from making money if the limited partners do not earn a profit.

Second, there is often an escrow agreement where a portion of the venture capitalist incentive fees are held in a segregated escrow account until the fund is liquidated.

Again this ensures that the venture capitalist does not walk away with any profit unless the limited partners also earn a profit. If a profit is earned by every limited partner, the escrow proceeds are released to the venture capitalist.

Finally, there is often a prohibition on the distribution of profit sharing fees to the venture capitalist until all committed capital is paid back to the limited partners. In other words, the limited partners must first be paid back their invested capital before profits may be shared in the venture fund. Sometimes this covenant also includes that all management fees must also be recouped by the limited partners before the venture capitalist can collect his incentive fees.

Just as a side observation, it is interesting to note that these types of profit sharing covenants are not used in hedge fund limited partnership agreements.

THE BUSINESS PLAN

The venture capitalist has two constituencies: investors on the one hand, and startup portfolio companies on the other. In the prior section we discussed the relationship between the venture capitalist and her investors. In this section we discuss how a venture capitalist selects her investments for the venture fund.

The most important document upon which a venture capitalist will base her decision to invest in a startup company is the business plan. The business plan must be comprehensive, coherent, and internally consistent. It must clearly state the business strategy, identify the niche that the new company will fill, and describe the resources needed to fill that niche.

The business plan also reflects the startup management team's ability to develop and present an intelligent and strategic plan of action. The business plan not only describes the business opportunity but also gives the venture capitalist an insight to the viability of the management team.

Last, the business plan must be realistic. One part of every business plan is the assumptions about revenue growth, cash-burn rate, additional rounds of capital injection, and expected date of profitability and/or IPO status. The financial goals stated in the business plan must be achievable. Additionally, financial milestones identified in the business plan can become important conditions for the vesting of management equity, the release of deferred investment commitments, and the control of the board of directors.

In this section we review the key elements of a business plan for a startup venture. This is the heart and sole of the venture capital industry—it is where new ideas are born and capital is committed.

Executive Summary

The executive summary is the opening statement of any business plan. In this short synopsis, it must be clear what is the unique selling point of the startup venture. Is it a new product, distribution channel, manufacturing process, chip design, or consumer service? Whatever it is, it must be spelled out clearly for a nontechnical person to understand.[7]

The executive summary should quickly summarize the eight main parts of the business plan:

1. The market
2. The product/service
3. Intellectual property rights
4. the management team
5. Operations and prior operating history
6. Financial projections
7. Amount of financing

---

[7] See British Venture Capital Association, "A Guide to Private Equity," White paper, October 2004.

8. Exit opportunities

We next discuss briefly each part of the business plan.

The Market

The key issue here is whether there is a viable commercial opportunity for the startup venture. The first question is whether there is an existing market already. If the answer is yes, this is both good and bad. It is good because the commercial opportunity has already been demonstrated by someone else. It is bad because someone else has already developed a product or service to meet the existing demand.

This raises the issue of competition. Virtually every new product already has some competition at the outset. It is most unlikely that the product or service is so revolutionary such that there is no form of competition. Even if the startup venture is first to market, there must be an explanation on how this gap in the market is currently being filled with existing (but deficient) solutions.

An existing product makes a prima facie case for market demand, but then the startup venture must describe how its product/service improves upon the existing market solution. Furthermore, if there is an existing product, the startup venture should make a direct product comparison including price, quality, length of warranty, ease of use, product distribution, and target audience.

In addition to a review of the competition, the startup venture must describe its market plan. The marketing plan must include three elements: pricing, product distribution, and promotion.

Pricing is clear enough. If the product is first to market, it can command a price premium. Furthermore, in today's electronic markets, prices erode rapidly. The startup venture must describe its initial margins, but also how those margins will be affected as technology advances are made.

Product distribution is simply a way to describe how the startup venture will get its product to the market. Will it use wholesalers, retailers, the internet, or direct sales? Is a sales force needed? Is a 24-hour help desk required? Also, different distribution channels may require different pricing. For example, wholesalers will need price discounts to be able to make a profit when they sell to retailers. Conversely, the startup company may wish to offer a discount to those that order the product directly from the startup venture.

Finally, the startup venture must describe its promotion strategy. A discussion of trade shows, the Internet, mass media and tie-ins to other products should be described. The startup venture should indicate whether its product should be marketed to a targeted audience or whether it has mass appeal. The cost of promotional materials and events must also be evaluated as part of the business plan.

The Product or Service

A description of the product or service should be done along every dimension which establishes the startup venture's unique selling point. Furthermore, this discussion must be done in plain English without the psychobabble or jargon that normally creeps into the explanation of technology products.

In fact, the key part of this section of the business plan is to cement the unique selling point of the product or service. Is it new to the market, available at a lower price, constructed with better quality, constructed in a shorter timeframe, provided with better customer service, smaller in size, easier to operation, and so on? Each of these points can provide a competitive advantage upon which to build a new product or service.

One-shot, single products are a concern for a venture capitalist. The upside will be inevitably limited as competition is drawn into the market. Therefore, business plans that address a second generation of products are generally preferred.

Intellectual Property Rights

The third essential part of the business plan is a discussion of intellectual property rights. Looking forward a few pages in this chapter at Exhibit 16.5 provides a current view of the industries to which venture capital flowed in 2005. Most of these industries are technology related such as computer software, telecom, biotech, and semiconductors.

Most startups in the technology and other growth sectors base their business opportunity on the claim to proprietary technology. It is very important that a startup's claim and rights to that intellectual property be absolute. Any intellectual property owned by the company must be clearly and unequivocally assigned to the company by third parties (usually the entrepreneur and management team). A structure where the entrepreneur still owns the intellectual property but licenses it to the startup company are disfavored by venture capitalists because license agreements can expire or be terminated leaving the venture capitalist with a shell of a startup company.

Generally, before a venture capitalist invests with a startup company, it will conduct patent and trademark searches, seek the opinion of a patent counsel, and possibly ask third parties to confidentially evaluate the technology owned by the startup company.

Additionally, the venture capitalist may ask key employees to sign noncompetition agreements, where they agree not to start another company or join another company operating in the same sector as the startup for a reasonable period of time. Key employees may also be asked to sign nondisclosure agreements because protecting a startup company's proprietary technology is an essential element to success.

The Startup Management Team

Venture capitalists invest in ideas and people. Once the venture capitalist has reviewed the startup venture's unique selling point, she will turn to the management team. Ideally, the management team should have complementary skill sets: marketing, technology, finance and operations. Every management team has gaps. The business plan must carefully address how these gaps will be filled.

The venture capitalist will closely review the resumes of every member of the management team. Academic backgrounds, professional work history and references will all be checked. Most important to the venture capitalist will be the professional background of the management team. In particular, a management team that has successfully brought a previous startup company to the IPO stage will be viewed most favorably.

In general, a great management team with a good business plan is viewed more favorably than a good management team with a great business plan. The best business plan in the world can still fail from inability to execute. Thus a management team that has demonstrated a previous ability to follow and execute a business plan gets a greater chance of success than an unproven management team with a great business opportunity.

However, this is where a venture capitalist can add value. Recognizing a great business opportunity but a weak management team, the venture capitalist can bring his or her expertise to the startup company as well as bring in other, more seasoned management professionals. While this often creates some friction with the original entrepreneur, the ultimate goal is to make money. Egos often succumb when there is money to be made.

In addition to filling in the gaps of the management team, the venture capitalist will need to round out the board of directors of the startup venture. One seat on the board will be filled by a member of the venture capitalist's own team. However, other directors may be added to fill in some of the gaps found among the management team. These gaps might include distribution expertise. In addition, the venture capitalist may ask an executive from an established company to sit on the board of the startup to provide contacts within the industry when the startup is ready to look for a strategic buyer. In addition, a seasoned board member from a successful company can lend credibility to a startup venture when it decides to go public (see our case study on CacheFlow/Blue Coat at the end of this chapter).

Last, the management team will need a seasoned chief financial officer (CFO). This will be the person primarily responsible for bringing the startup company public. The CFO will work with the investment bankers to establish the price of the company's stock at the initial public offering. Since the IPO is often the exit strategy for the venture capitalist as well as some of the founders and key employees, it is critical that the CFO have IPO experience.

Operations and Prior Operating History

The operations section of the business plan discusses how the product will be built or the service delivered. This will include a discussion of production facilities, labor requirements, raw materials, tax incentives, regulatory approvals, and shipping.

In addition, if a prototype has not yet been developed, then the business plan must lay out a time line for its production as well as its cost. Cost of production must be discussed because this will feed into the gross margin discussion as part of the financial projections (discussed next).

Last, barriers to entry should be described. While there might be a higher cost of production at the outset, it will also prevent competition from entering the market later.

Venture capitalists are not always the first investors in a startup company. In fact, they may be the third source of financing for a company. Many startup companies begin by seeking capital from friends, family members, and business associates. Next they may seek a so called "angel investor": a wealthy private individual or an institution that invests capital with the company but does not take an active role in managing or directing the strategy of the company. Then come the venture capitalists.

As a result, a startup company may already have a prior history before presenting its business plan to a venture capitalist. At this stage, venture capitalists ensure that the startup company does not have any unusual history such as a prior bankruptcy or failure.

The venture capitalist will also closely review the equity stakes that have been previously provided to family, friends, business associates, and angel investors. These equity stakes should be clearly identified in the business plan and any unusual provisions must be discussed. Equity interests can include common stock, preferred stock, convertible securities, rights, warrants, and stock options. There must still be sufficient equity and upside potential for the venture capitalist to invest. Finally, all prior security issues must be properly documented and must comply with applicable securities laws.

The venture capitalist will also check the company's articles of incorporation to determine whether it is in good legal standing in the state of incorporation. Furthermore, the venture capitalist will examine the company's bylaws, and the minutes of any shareholder and board of directors meetings. The minutes of the meetings can indicate whether the company has a clear sense of direction or whether it is mired in indecision.

Financial Projections

In light of the discussion on operations and cost of projections, this information leads right into the financial projections. A comprehensive set of financial statements are required including income statement, balance sheet, and cash flow projections. These projections must be realistic but at the same time, entice the venture capitalist that there is a sufficient return to be earned to warrant the investment of capital.

First, the income statement must show in which year a breakeven point will be achieved. Most business plans show a profit being turned by the third year after initial financing. The income statement should include realistic sales forecasts, allowances for discounts, clear numbers for the cost of goods sold, and reasonable estimates of marketing and other overhead costs. Gross margins and net margins must meet the return requirements of the venture capitalist.

The balance sheet is important to determine at what point debt and other forms of financing should be added to the capital structure of the startup venture. Also, the balance sheet should reflect the receivables received from the sale of the product as well as reasonable assumptions about the timing and collection of those receivables.

Last the cash flow statement provides the venture capitalist with a realistic burn rate on the cash on hand. Initially, all firms require infusions of capital to fund their working capital. However, at some point of time, the startup venture must become self financing such that its operating and expansion needs can draw from the money raised from the sale of its products.

For all of these financial projections, different scenarios must be included. What happens if a new competitor comes to the market quickly or the economy experiences a period of recessionary growth? Generally, the forecasts should include a base case of sales growth, a pessimistic case, and an optimistic case.

Amount of Financing

This section of the business plan gets down to brass tacks: how much money is the startup venture requesting? This ties in neatly from the financial projections. As part of the assessment of cash flows, the startup company needs to estimate its burn rate. The *burn rate* is simply the rate at which the startup venture uses cash on a monthly basis. The amount of financing requested must be equal to the burn rate over the time horizon expected by the startup venture.

Exit Plan

Eventually, the venture capitalist must liquidate her investment in the startup company to realize a gain for herself and her investors. When a venture capitalist reviews a business plan she will keep in mind the timing and probability of an exit strategy.

An exit strategy is another way the venture capitalist can add value beyond providing startup financing. Venture capitalists often have many contacts with established operating companies. An established company may be willing to acquire the startup company for its technology as part of a strategic expansion of its product line. Alternatively, venture capitalists maintain close ties with investment bankers. These bankers will be necessary if the startup company decides to seek an IPO. In addition, a venture capitalist may ask other venture capitalists to invest in the startup company. This helps to spread the risk as well as provide additional sources of contacts with operating companies and investment bankers.

Venture capitalists almost always invest in the convertible preferred stock of the startup company. There may be several rounds (or series) of financing of preferred stock before a startup company goes public. Convertible preferred shares are the accepted manner of investment because these shares carry a priority over common stock in terms of dividends, voting rights, and liquidation preferences. Furthermore, venture capitalists have the option to convert their shares to common stock to enjoy the benefits of an IPO.

Other investment structures used by venture capitalists include convertible notes or debentures that provide for the conversion of the principal amount of the note or bond into either common or preferred shares at the option of the venture capitalist. Convertible notes and debentures may also be converted upon the occurrence of an event such as a merger, acquisition, or IPO. Venture capitalists may also be granted warrants to purchase the common equity of the startup company as well as stock rights in the event of an IPO.

Other exit strategies used by venture capitalists are redemption rights and put options. Usually, these strategies are used as part of a company reorganization. Redemption rights and put options are generally not favored because they do not provide as large a rate of return as an acquisition or IPO. These strategies are often used as a last resort when there are no other viable alternatives. Redemption rights and put options are usually negotiated at the time the venture capitalist makes an investment in the startup company (often called the *Registration Rights Agreement*).

Usually, venture capitalists require no less than the minimum return provided for in the liquidation preference of a preferred stock investment. Alternatively, the redemption rights or put option might be established by a common stock equivalent value that is usually determined by an investment banking appraisal. Last redemption rights or put option values may be based on a multiple of sales or earnings. Some redemption rights take the highest of all three valuation methods: the liquidation preference, the appraisal value, or the earnings/sales multiple.

In sum, there are many issues a venture capitalist must sort through before funding a startup company. These issues range from identifying the business opportunity to sorting through legal and regulatory issues. Along the way, the venture capital must assess the quality of the management team, prior capital infusions, status of proprietary technology, operating history (if any) of the company, and timing and likelihood of an exit strategy.

THE CURRENT STRUCTURE OF THE VENTURE CAPITAL INDUSTRY

The structure of the venture capital industry has changed dramatically over the past 20 years. We focus on three major changes: sources of venture capital financing, venture capital investment vehicles, and specialization within the industry.

Sources and Uses of Venture Capital Financing

The structure of the venture capital marketplace has changed considerably since 1985. What is most notable is the leading sources of venture capital financing. For example, over the period 1985 to 1990, the leading source of venture capital financing was pension funds. This came as a result of the revisions to the prudent person standard for pension fund investing in 1979. Over the 1985 to 1990 period, pension funds accounted for almost 70% of venture capital funding. Endowments and intermediaries, on the other hand, were a smaller source of venture capital funds. Also, in 1985 to 1990, government agencies accounted for about 11% of the total source of venture capital funds.[8]

---

[8] See Steven Lipin, "Venture Capitalists 'R' Us," The *Wall Street Journal* (February 22, 2000), p. C1.

By 2005, the landscape of venture capital financing had changed considerably. Pension funds account for only about 50% of the source of venture capital funds. Government agencies supplied almost no money to venture capital in 2005, squeezed out by private sources. The federal and state governments no longer need to support the venture capital industry. Virtually all money comes from institutional and other investors willing to take the risk of startup companies in return for sizeable gains.

To replace the decline of pension funds and government agencies, three new sources of venture capital funds have grown over the last 15 years: endowments and foundations, intermediaries, and individuals. Endowments, with their perpetual investment horizons, are natural investors for private equity. Also, as the wealth of the United States has grown, wealthy individuals have allocated a greater share of their wealth to venture capital investments. Last, intermediaries such as private equity fund of funds, hedge funds, cross over funds, and interval funds have entered the venture capital market. Exhibit 16.4 demonstrates the changing sources of venture capital financing in the United States.

Exhibit 16.5 demonstrates another trend in the venture capital industry, the surge of financing for Internet-related companies the use to which venture capital was put to use in 2005. Over $16 billion flowed into startup ventures. Exhibit 16.5 is the complement to Exhibit 16.4, it presents the uses of venture capital financing in 2005. Companies whose

EXHIBIT 16.4 Sources of Venture Capital Commitments

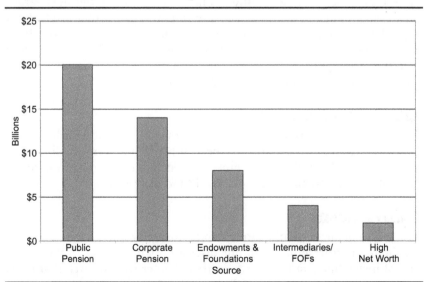

EXHIBIT 16.5   Uses of Venture Capital, 2005

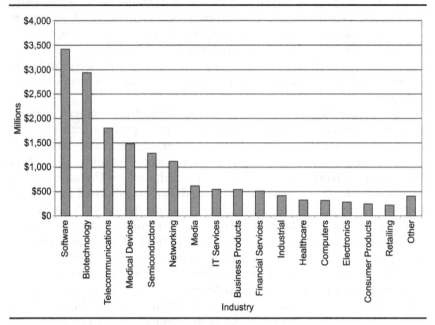

Source: Data obtained from PricewaterhouseCoopers/MoneyTree.

business opportunity depended solely on an Internet application received more than twice as much venture capital financing as the next largest category, communications. In fact, the four categories that are technology related (computers, semiconductors, computer software, and Internet) accounted for 60% of the use of venture capital financing in 1999. Not surprisingly, the bulk of venture capital flowed to the technology, biotech, media, medical devices, and telecom industries.

Venture Capital Investment Vehicles

As the interest for venture capital investments has increased, venture capitalists have responded with new vehicles for venture financing. These include limited partnerships, limited liability companies, corporate venture funds, and venture capital fund of funds.

Limited Partnerships

The predominant form of venture capital investing in the United States is the limited partnership. Recall our discussion with respect to the regulation of hedge funds in Chapter 8. In that chapter we indicated that hedge funds operated either as "3(c)(1)" or "3(c)(7)" funds to avoid registration as an investment company under the Investment Company Act of 1940. The same regulatory exemptions apply to venture capital funds.

As a limited partnership, all income and capital gains flow through the partnership to the limited partner investors. The partnership itself is not taxed. The appeal of the limited partnership vehicle has increased since 1996 with the "Check the Box" provision of the U.S. tax code.

Previously, limited partnerships had to meet several tests to determine if their predominant operating characteristics resembled more a partnership than a corporation. Such characteristics included, for instance, a limited term of existence. Failure to qualify as a limited partnership would mean double taxation for the investment fund—first, at the fund level and second, at the investor level.

This changed with the U.S. Internal Revenue Services decision to let entities simply decide their own tax status by checking a box on their annual tax form as to whether they wished to be taxed as a corporation or as a partnership. "Checking the box" greatly encouraged investment funds to establish themselves as a limited partnership.

Limited partnerships are generally formed with an expected life of 10 years with an option to extend the limited partnership for another one to five years. The limited partnership is managed by a general partner who has day to day responsibility for managing the venture capital fund's investments as well as general liability for any lawsuits that may be brought against the fund. Limited partners, as their name implies, have only a limited (investor) role in the partnership. They do not partake in the management of the fund and they do not bear any liability beyond their committed capital.

All partners in the fund will commit to a specific investment amount at the formation of the limited partnership. However, the limited partners do not contribute money to the fund until it is called down or "taken down" by the general partner. Usually, the general partner will give one to two months notice of when it intends to make additional capital calls on the limited partners. Capital calls are made when the general partner has found a startup company in which to invest. The general partner can make capital calls up to the amount of the limited partners' initial commitments.

An important element of limited partnership venture funds is that the general partner/venture capitalist has also committed investment capital to the fund. This assures the limited partners of an alignment of interests with the venture capitalist. Typically, limited partnership agreements specify a percentage or dollar amount of capital that the general partner must commit to the partnership.

Limited Liability Companies

Another financing vehicle in the venture capital industry is the limited liability company (LLC). Similar to a limited partnership, all items of net income or loss as well as capital gains are passed through to the shareholders in the LLC. Also, like a limited partnership, an LLC must adhere to the safe harbors of the Investment Company Act of 1940. In addition, LLCs usually have a life of 10 years with possible options to extend for another one to five years.

The managing director of an LLC acts like the general partner of a limited partnership. She has management responsibility for the LLC including the decision to invest in startup companies the committed capital of the LLC's shareholders. The managing director of the LLC might itself be another LLC or a corporation. The same is true for limited partnerships; the general partner need not be an individual, it can be a legal entity like a corporation.

In sum, LLCs and limited partnerships accomplish the same goal—the pooling of investor capital into a central fund from which to make venture capital investments. The choice is dependent upon the type of investor sought. If the venture capitalist wishes to raise funds from a large number of passive and relatively uninformed investors, the limited partnership vehicle is the preferred venue. However, if the venture capitalist intends to raise capital from a small group of knowledgeable investors, the LLC is preferred.

The reason is twofold. First, LLCs usually have more specific shareholder rights and privileges. These privileges are best utilized with a small group of well-informed investors. Second, an LLC structure provides shareholders with control over the sale of additional shares in the LLC to new shareholders. This provides the shareholders with more power with respect to the twin issues of increasing the LLC's pool of committed capital and from whom that capital will be committed.

Corporate Venture Capital Funds

With the explosive growth of technology companies in the late 1990s, many of these companies found themselves with large cash balances. Microsoft, for example, had current assets (cash, cash equivalents, and receivables) or over $48 billion, and generated a free cash flow of over $15 billion in 2005. Microsoft and other companies need to invest this cash to earn an appropriate rate of return for their investors.

A corporate venture capital fund is an ideal use for a portion of a company's cash. First, venture capital financing is consistent with Microsoft's own past; it was funded with venture capital over 20 years ago. Second, Microsoft can provide its own technological expertise to help a startup company. Last, the startup company can provide new technology and cost savings to Microsoft. In a way, financing startup companies allows Microsoft to "think outside of the box" without committing or diverting its own personnel to the task.

Corporate venture capital funds are typically formed only with the parent company's capital, outside investors are not allowed to join. In addition to Microsoft, other corporate venture funds include Xerox Venture Capital, Hewlett-Packard Co. Corporate Investments, Intel Capital, and Amoco Venture Capital. Investments in startup companies are a way for large public companies to supplement their research and development budgets. In addition to accessing to new technology, corporate venture capital funds also gain the ability to generate new products, identify new or diminishing industries, acquire a stake in a future potential competitor, derive attractive returns for excess cash balances, and learn the dynamics of a new marketplace.

Perhaps the best reason for corporate venture capital funds is to gain a window on new technology. Consider the case of Supercomputer Systems of Wisconsin. Steve Chen, the former CEO of Cray Research left Cray to start his own super computer company. Cray Research is a supercomputer company that was itself a spin-off from Control Data Corp., which in turn was an outgrowth of Sperry Corporation. When Mr. Chen founded his new company, IBM was one of his first investors even though IBM had shifted its focus from large mainframe computers to laptop computers, personal computers, and service contracts.[9]

Another example is Intel Capital, Intel Corporation's venture capital subsidiary. The goal of Intel Capital is to develop a strategic investment program that focuses on making equity investments and acquisitions to grow the Internet economy, including the infrastructure, content, and services in support of Intel's main business which is providing computer chips to power personal and laptop computers. To further this goal, Intel Capital has provided venture capital financing to companies like Peregrine Semiconductor Corp., a startup technology company that designs, manufactures and markets high-speed communications integrated circuits for the broadband fiber, wireless, and satellite communications markets.

Since its founding in 1991, Intel Capital has invested more than $4 billion in approximately 1,000 companies in more than 30 countries. Of this 1,000, 160 portfolio companies have been acquired and another 150 have gone public on exchanges around the world—a combined success rate of 31% for startup ventures.

---

[9] See Schilit, "Structure of the Venture Capital Industry."

EXHIBIT 16.6   Intel Capital's Venture Capital Program

Fund	Amount (millions)
Intel Communications Fund	$500
Intel Capital India Technology Fund	$250
Intel Digital Home Fund	$200
Intel Capital China Technology Fund	$200
Intel Capital Middle East and Turkey Fund	$50
Total	$1,200

Intel Capital's program is sufficiently mature now that Intel has five separate funds from which to seed startup ventures. These are presented in Exhibit 16.6.

There are, however, several potential pitfalls to a corporate venture capital program. These may include conflicting goals between the venture capital subsidiary and the corporate parent. In addition, the five- to 10-year investment horizon for most venture capital investments may be a longer horizon than the parent company's short-term profit requirements. Furthermore, a funded startup company may be unwilling to be acquired by the parent company. Still, the benefits from corporate venture capital programs appear to outweigh these potential problems. As of 2005, there were almost 100 corporate venture capital subsidiaries in the United States.

Another pitfall of corporate venture capital funds is the risk of loss. Just as every venture capitalist experiences losses in her portfolio of companies, so too will the corporate venture capitalist. This can translate into significant losses for the parent company.

Take the case of Dell Computers. Dell took a charge of $200 million in the second quarter of 2001 as a result of losses from Dell Ventures, the company's venture capital fund. Additionally, in June 2001, Dell reported that its investment portfolio has declined in value by more than $1 billion.[10]

Eventually, Dell decided to exit the venture capital business all together. It sold the remainder of its venture capital portfolio to Lake Street Capital, a San Francisco private equity firm, for $100 million in 2005.

Intel Corp. reported in year 2001 that its technology portfolio declined more than $7 billion in value. For example, in the second quarter of 2000, Intel reported a $2.1 billion gain from the sale of its venture

---

[10] See Joseph Menn, "Tech Giants Lose Big on Start-Up Ventures," *Los Angeles Times* (June 11, 2001).

capital investments. Gains from Intel's technology portfolio helped to keep its earnings growth intact. Conversely, in the second quarter of 2001, Intel reported only a $3 million gain from the sale of its investments from its venture capital subsidiary.[11]

However, where Dell did not succeed, Intel has recovered and has rebuilt its venture capital portfolio. In 2005, Intel had over $1 billion of venture capital investments on its financial statements.

Perhaps the most extreme case of nonperforming corporate venture capital investments is that of Comdisco Inc. Comdisco sought bankruptcy protection in July 2001 after making $3 billion in loans to startup companies that were unable to repay most of the money.[12] The company wrote off $100 million in loans made by its Comdisco Ventures unit, which leases computer equipment to startup companies. In addition, Comdisco also took a $206 million reserve against earnings from investments in those ventures.

Venture Capital Fund of Funds

A venture capital fund of funds is a venture pool of capital that, instead of investing directly in startup companies, invests in other venture capital funds. The venture capital fund of funds is a relatively new phenomenon in the venture capital industry. The general partner of a fund of funds does not select startup companies in which to invest. Instead, she selects the best venture capitalists with the expectation that they will find appropriate startup companies to fund.

A venture capital fund of funds offers several advantages to investors. First, the investor receives broad exposure to a diverse range of venture capitalists, and in turn, a wide range of startup investing. Second, the investor receives the expertise of the fund of funds manager in selecting the best venture capitalists with whom to invest money. Last, a fund of funds may have better access to popular, well-funded venture capitalists whose funds may be closed to individual investors. In return for these benefits, investors pay a management fee (and, in some cases, an incentive fee) to the fund of funds manager. The management fee can range from 0.5% to 2% of the net assets managed.

Fund of fund investing also offers benefits to the venture capitalists. First, the venture capitalist receives one large investment (from the venture fund of funds) instead of several small investments. This makes

---

[11] See Cesca Antonelli, "Chipmaker's Profit Plunges 94%; Intel Still Beats Analysts Forecasts," *Bloomberg News* (July 18, 2001); and Menn, "Tech Giants Lose Big on Start-Up Ventures."

[12] See Jeff St. Onge, "Comdisco Seeks Bankruptcy Protection from Creditors," *Bloomberg News* (July 16, 2001).

fund raising and investor administration more efficient. Second, the venture capitalist interfaces with an experienced fund of funds manager instead of several (potentially inexperienced) investors.

The Life Cycle of a Venture Capital Fund.

A venture capital fund is a long-term investment. Typically, investors' capital is locked up for a minimum of 10 years—the standard term of a venture capital limited partnership. During this long investment period, a venture capital fund will normally go through five stages of development.

The first stage is the fund raising stage where the venture capital firm raises capital from outside investors. Capital is committed—not collected. This is an important distinction noted above. Investors sign a legal agreement (typically a subscription) that legally binds them to make cash investments in the venture capital fund up to a certain amount. This is the committed, but not yet drawn, capital. The venture capital firm/general partner will also post a sizeable amount of committed capital.

Fundraising normally takes six months to a year. However, the more successful venture funds such as Kleiner, Perkins, Caufield and Byers typically fund raise in just two to three months.

The second stage consists of sourcing investments, reading business plans, preparing intense due diligence on startup companies and determining the unique selling point of each startup company. This period begins the moment the fund is closed to investors and normally takes up the first five years of the venture fund's existence.

During stage two, no profits are generated by the venture capital fund. In fact, quite the reverse, the venture capital fund generates losses because the venture capitalist continues to draw annual management fees (which can be up to 3.5% a year on the total committed capital). These fees generate a loss until the venture capitalist begins to extract value from the investments of the venture fund.

Stage three is the investment of capital. During this stage, the venture capitalist determines how much capital to commit to each startup company, at what level of financing, and in what form of investment (convertible preferred shares, convertible debentures, etc.). At this stage the venture capitalist will also present capital calls to the investors in her venture fund to draw on the capital of the limited partners. Note that no cash flow is generated yet, the venture fund is still in a deficit.

Stage four begins after the funds have been invested and lasts almost to the end of the term of the venture capital fund. During this time the venture capitalist works with the portfolio companies in which the venture capital fund has invested. The venture capitalist may help to improve the management team, establish distribution channels for the

EXHIBIT 16.7   The Life Cycle of a Venture Capital Fund

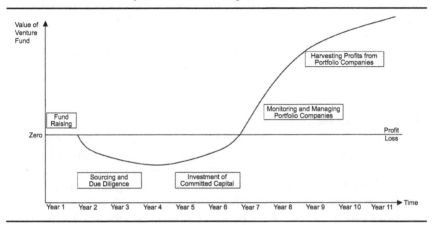

new product, refine the prototype product to generate the greatest sales, and generally position the startup company for an eventual public offering or sale to a strategic buyer. During this time period, the venture capitalist will begin to generate profits for the venture fund and its limited partner investors. These profits will initially offset the previously collected management fees until a positive net asset value is established for the venture fund.

The last stage of the venture capital fund is its windup and liquidation. At this point, all committed capital has been invested and now the venture capitalist is in the harvesting stage. Each portfolio company is either sold to a strategic buyer, brought to the public markets in an initial public offering, or liquidated through a Chapter 7 bankruptcy liquidation process. Profits are distributed to the limited partners and the general partner/venture capitalist now collects her incentive/profit sharing fees.

These stages of a venture capital firm lead to what is known as the "J Curve Effect." Exhibit 16.7 demonstrates the J Curve. We can see that during the early life of the venture capital fund, it generates negative revenues (losses) but eventually, profits are harvested from successful companies and these cash flows overcome the initial losses to generate a net profit for the fund. Clearly, given the initial losses that pile up during the first four to five years of a venture capital fund, this type of investing is only for patient, long-term investors.

Specialization within the Venture Capital Industry

Like any industry that grows and matures, expansion and maturity lead to specialization. The trend towards specialization in the venture capital industry exists on several levels: by industry, geography, stage of financing, and "special situations." Specialization is the natural byproduct of two factors. First, the enormous amount of capital flowing into venture capital funds has encouraged venture capitalists to distinguish themselves from other funds by narrowing their investment focus. Second, the development of many new technologies over the past decade has encouraged venture capitalists to specialize in order to invest most profitably.

Specialization by Industry

Specialization by entrepreneurs is another reason why venture capitalists have tailored their investment domain. Just as entrepreneurs have become more focused in their startup companies, venture capitalists have followed suit. The biotechnology industry is a good example.

The biotech industry was born on October 14, 1980, when the stock of Genentech, Inc. went public. On that day, the stock price went from $39 to $85 and a new industry was born. Today, Genentech is a Fortune 500 company with a market capitalization of $28 billion. Other successful biotech startups include Cetus Corp., Biogen, Inc., Amgen Corp., and Centacor, Inc.

The biotech paradigm has changed since the days of Genentech. Genentech was founded on the science of gene mapping and slicing to cure diseases. However, initially it did not have a specific product target. Instead, it was concerned with developing its gene mapping technology without a specific product to market.

Compare this situation to that of Applied Microbiology, Inc. of New York. It has focused on two products with the financial support of Merck and Pfizer, two large pharmaceuticals.[13] One of its products is an antibacterial agent to fight gum disease contained in a mouthwash to be marketed by Pfizer.

Specialized startup biotech firms have led to specialized venture capital firms. For example, Domain Associates of Princeton, New Jersey focuses on funding new technology in molecular engineering. However, specialization is not unique to the biotech industry. Other examples include Communication Ventures of Menlo Park, California. This venture firm provides financing primarily for startup companies in the telecommunications industry. Another example is American Health Capital Ventures of Brentwood, Tennessee that specializes in funding new health care companies.

---

[13] See W. Keith Schilit, "The Nature of Venture Capital Investments," *The Journal of Private Equity* (Winter 1997), pp. 59–75.

Specialization by Geography

With the boom in technology companies in Silicon Valley, Los Angeles, and Seattle, it is not surprising to find that many California-based venture capital firms concentrate their investments on the west coast of the United States. Not only are there plenty of investment opportunities in this region, it is also easier for the venture capital firms to monitor their investments locally. The same is true for other technology centers in New York, Boston, and Texas.

As another example, consider Marquette Ventures based in Chicago. This venture capital company invests primarily with startup companies in the Midwest. Although it has provided venture capital financing to companies outside of this region, its predominate investment pattern is with companies located in the midwestern states.[14] Similarly, the Massey Birch venture capital firm of Nashville, Tennessee has provided venture financing to a number of companies in its hometown of Nashville as well as other companies throughout the southeastern states.

Regional specialization has the advantage of easier monitoring of invested capital. Also, larger venture capital firms may overlook viable startup opportunities located in more remote sections of the United States. Regional venture capitalists step in to fill this niche.

The downside of regional specialization is twofold. First, regional concentration may not provide sufficient diversification to a venture capital portfolio. Second, a startup company in a less-exposed geographic region may have greater difficulty in attracting additional rounds of venture capital financing. This may limit the startup company's growth potential as well as exit opportunities for the regional venture capitalist.

Special Situation Venture Capital

In any industry, there are always failures. Not every startup company makes it to the IPO stage. However, this opens another specialized niche in the venture capital industry: the turnaround venture deal. Turnaround deals are as risky as seed financing because the startup company may be facing pressure from creditors. The turnaround venture capitalist exists because mainstream venture capitalists may not be sufficiently well-versed in restructuring a turnaround situation.

Consider the following example.[15] A startup company is owned 50% by early and midstage venture capitalists and 50% by the founder. Product delays and poor management have resulted in $10 million in corporate assets and $15 million in liabilities. The company has a negative net worth and is technically bankrupt.

---

[14] Schilit, "The Nature of Venture Capital Investments."

[15] A similar example is in Schilit, "The Nature of Venture Capital Investments."

The turnaround venture capitalist offers the founder/entrepreneur of the company $1 million for his 50% ownership plus a job as an executive of the company. The turnaround venture capitalist then offers the startup company's creditors 50 cents for every one dollar of claims. The total of $8.5 million might come from a $1 million dollar contribution from the turnaround venture capitalist and $7.5 million in bank loans secured by the $10 million in assets. Therefore, for $1 million the turnaround venture capitalist receives 50% of the startup company and restores it to a positive net worth.

The founder of the company is happy because he receives $1 million for a bankrupt company plus he remains as an executive. The other venture capitalists are also happy because now they will be dealing with another venture specialist plus the company has been restored to financial health. With some additional hard work the company may proceed on to an IPO. The creditors, however, will not be as pleased, but may make the deal anyway because 50 cents on the dollar may be more than they could expect to receive through a formal liquidation procedure.

An example of such a turnaround specialist is Reprise Capital Corp. of Garden City, New Jersey. In 1997, this company raised $25 million for turnaround venture capital deals.

In summary, the growth of the venture capital industry has created the need for venture capital specialists. The range of new business opportunities is now so diverse that it is simply not possible for a single venture capital firm to stay on top of all opportunities in all industries. Therefore, by necessity, venture capitalists have narrowed their investment domain to concentrate on certain niches within the startup universe. Specialization also leads to differentiation, which allows venture capitalists to distinguish themselves from other investment funds.

STAGE OF FINANCING

While some venture capital firms classify themselves by geography or industry, by far the most distinguishing characteristic of venture capital firms is the stage of financing. Some venture capitalists provide first stage, or "seed capital" while others wait to invest in companies that are further along in their development. Still other venture capital firms come in at the final round of financing before the IPO. A different level of due diligence is required at each level of financing because the startup venture has achieved another milestone on its way to success. In all, there are five discrete stages of venture capital financing: angel investing, seed capital, first stage capital, second state/expansion capital, and mezzanine financing. We discuss each of these separately below.

Angel Investing

Angel investors often come from "F & F": Friends and Family. (Sometimes, venture capitalists include a third "F" for Fools.) At this stage of the new venture, typically there is a lone entrepreneur who has just an idea—possibly sketched out at the kitchen table or in the garage. There is no formal business plan, no management team, no product, no market analysis—just an idea.

In addition to family and friends, angel investors can also be wealthy individuals who "dabble" in startup companies. This level of financing is typically done without a private placement memorandum or subscription agreement. It may be as informal as a "cocktail napkin" agreement. Yet without the Angel Investor, many ideas would wither on the vine before reaching more traditional venture capitalists.

At this stage of financing, the task of the entrepreneur is to begin the development of a prototype product or service. In addition, the entrepreneur begins the draft of his business plan, assesses the market potential, and may even begin to assemble some key management team members. No marketing or product testing is done at this stage.

The amount of financing at this stage is very small—$50,000 to $500,000. Any more than that would strain family, friends, and other angels. The funds are used primarily to flush out the concept to the point where an intelligent business plan can be constructed.

Seed Capital

Seed capital is the first stage where venture capital firms invest their capital. At this stage, a business plan is completed and presented to a venture capital firm. Some parts of the management team have been assembled at this point, a market analysis has been completed, and other points of the business plan as discussed previously in this chapter are addressed by the entrepreneur and his small team. Financing is provided to complete the product development and, possibly, to begin initial marketing of the prototype to potential customers. This phase of financing usually raises $1 to $5 million.

At this stage of financing, a prototype may have been developed and the testing of a product with customers may have begun. This is often referred to as "beta testing," and is the process where a prototype product is sent to potential customers free of charge to get their input into the viability, design, and user friendliness of the product.

Very little revenue has been generated at this stage, and the company is definitely not profitable. Venture capitalists invest in this stage based on their due diligence of the management team, their own market analysis of the demand for the product, the viability of getting the product to the market while there is still time and not another competitor, the additional management team members that will need to be added, and the likely timing for additional rounds of capital from the same venture capital firm for from other venture capital funds.

Examples of seed financing companies are Technology Venture Investors of Menlo Park, California, Advanced Technology Ventures of Boston, and Onsent, located in Silicon Valley.[16] Seed capital venture capitalists tend to be smaller firms because large venture capital firms cannot afford to spend the endless hours with an entrepreneur for a small investment, usually that may be no greater than $1 to $2 million.

Early Stage Venture Capital

At this point the startup company should have a viable product that has been beta tested. Alpha testing may have already begun. This is the testing of the second generation prototype with potential end users. Typically, a price is charged for the product or a fee for the service. Revenues are being generated and the product/service has now demonstrated commercial viability. Early stage venture capital financing is usually $2 million and more.

Early stage financing is typically used to build out the commercial scale manufacturing services. The product is no longer being produced out of the entrepreneur's garage or out of some vacant space above a grocery store. The company is now a going concern with an initial, if not complete management team. At this stage, there will be at least one venture capitalist sitting on the board of directors of the company.

The goal of the startup venture is to achieve market penetration with its product. Some of this will have already been accomplished with the beta and alpha testing of the product. However, additional marketing must now be completed. In addition, distribution channels should be identified by now and the product should be established in these channels. Reaching a breakeven point is the financial goal.

Late Stage/Expansion Venture Capital

At this point the startup company may have generated its first profitable quarter, or be just at the breakeven point. Commercial viability is now established. Cash flow management is critical at this stage, as the com-

---

[16] Schilit, "The Nature of Venture Capital Investments."

pany is not yet at the level where its cash flows can self sustain its own growth.

Last stage/expansion capital fills this void. This level of venture capital financing is used to help the startup company get through its cash crunch. The additional capital is used to tap into the distribution channels, establish call centers, expand the manufacturing facilities, and to attract the additional management and operational talent necessary to the make the startup company a longer-term success. Because this capital comes in to allow the company to expand, financing needs are typically greater than for seed and early stage. Amounts may be in the $5 million to $15 million range.

At this stage, the startup venture enjoys the growing pains of all successful companies. It may need additional working capital because it has focussed on product development and product sales, but now finds itself with a huge backload of accounts receivable from customers upon which it must now collect. Inevitably, startup companies are very good at getting the product out of the door but very poor at collecting receivables and turning sales into cold hard cash.

Again, this is where expansion capital can help. Late stage venture financing helps the successful startup get through its initial cash crunch. Eventually, the receivables will be collected and sufficient internal cash will be generated to make the startup company a self-sustaining force. Until then, one more round of financing may be needed.

Mezzanine Stage

Mezzanine venture capital is the last stage before a startup company goes public or is sold to a strategic buyer. At this point a second generation product may already be in production if not distribution. The management team is together and solid, and the company is working on managing its cash flow better. Manufacturing facilities are established, and the company may already be thinking about penetrating international markets. Amounts vary depending on how long the bridge financing is meant to last but generally is in the range of $5 to $15 million.

The financing at this stage is considered "bridge" or mezzanine financing to keep the company from running out of cash until the IPO or strategic sale. The startup company may still have a large inventory of uncollected accounts receivable that need to be financed in the short term. Profits are being recorded, but accounts receivable are growing at the same rate of sales.

Mezzanine financing may be in the form of convertible debt. In addition the company may have sufficient revenue and earning power that traditional bank debt may be added at this stage. This means that the startup company may have to clean up its balance sheet as well as its statement of cash flows. Commercial viability is more than just generating sales, it also requires turning accounts receivable into actual dollars.

The J Curve for a Startup Company

Exhibit 16.8 presents the J curve for a startup company. Similar to the J curve for a venture capital fund, the initial years of a startup company generate a loss. Money is spent turning an idea into a prototype product and from there beta testing the product with potential customers. Little or no revenue is generated during this time. It is not until the product goes into alpha testing that revenues may be generated and the startup becomes a viable concern.

Once a critical mass is generated—where sales are turned into profits and accounts receivable is turned into cash—then it becomes a matter of timing until the startup company achieves a public offering. Additional rounds of financing may be needed to get the company to its IPO nirvana. At this point commercial viability is established, but managing the cash crunch becomes critical.

A VENTURE CAPITAL CASE STUDY: CACHEFLOW INC./ BLUE COAT SYSTEMS

As an example of how different venture capital firms invest at different points of a startup company life cycle consider the example of Cache-

EXHIBIT 16.8 The Life Cycle of a Startup Company

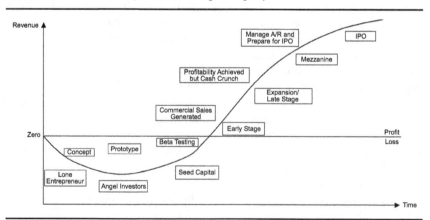

Flow Inc.[17] CacheFlow was founded in 1996 by Michael Malcolm, a renowned computer scientist and former professor at the University of Waterloo in Canada. Malcolm and his team quickly realized that the Internet is inherently slow. Therefore, CacheFlow was founded to produce the first Internet accelerator to speed up applications on the World Wide Web. CacheFlow was started to make network-caching equipment that would allow Internet pipeline to flow smoother and faster. Internet accelerators allow date to be stored and updated frequently at popular web sites so that users can get them quickly from a cache of data rather than from an original computer server.

CacheFlow started operations with $1 million in seed capital raised from a dozen angel investors in March 1996. From this initial angel investment, CacheFlow was quickly able to assemble a business plan and to seek more formal rounds of venture capital.

In October 1996, only six months after it was funded with angel capital, CacheFlow received its first venture capital infusion, selling 3.2 million shares of Series A convertible preferred stock at 87.5 cents per share ($2.8 million) to Benchmark Capital Partners for a 25% stake in the company. In December 1997, CacheFlow raised a middle round of venture capital financing from U.S. Ventures. U.S. Ventures paid $6 million for Series B preferred convertible preferred stock for 17% of the company. Next, in March 1999, CacheFlow received $8.7 million in late stage venture capital from Technology Crossover Ventures. This venture capital group paid $4.575 a share for Series C convertible preferred stock for 7% of the company. Finally, in November 1999, just before its initial public offering, CacheFlow sold 280,953 shares of Series D preferred stock at a price of $11.04 for $3.1 million.

This final sale was an important capstone for CacheFlow before going public. The sale was to one individual, Marc Andreessen, one of the original founders of Netscape, and a well-known Silicon Valley entrepreneur. He purchased all of the Series D convertible preferred

---

[17] For a great case history on a startup company, see Suzanne McGee, "Venture Capital 'R' Us, CacheFlow: The Life Cycle of a Venture-Capital Deal," *Wall Street Journal* (February 22, 2000), p. C1. See also "Corporate Profile for CacheFlow," *Business Wire, Inc.*, May 21, 1999; and Mike Strathdee, "Internet Equipment Company, Started by UW Professor, Goes Public," *Toronto Star Newspaper*, October 6, 1999; and Matt Krantz, "CacheFlow IPO Rockets 428%," *USA Today*, November 22, 1999; "CacheFlow Completes Strategic Transition to Web Security Business by Becoming Blue Coat," *Bloomberg News* (August 21, 2002); "Blue Coat Directors Approve one for five Reverse Stock Split," *Bloomberg News* (September 13, 2002); "Blue Coat Achieves #1 Market Share in New Security," *Bloomberg News* (July 8, 2003).

stock and also joined the CacheFlow board of directors. This provided a significant boost to CacheFlow's public offering.

CacheFlow recorded its first revenue in January 1998. Its products were initially sold to Internet service providers, and later, Fortune 500 companies seeking an improvement for their rapidly growing websites. At the time of its public offering, CacheFlow had an accumulated deficit of $26.2 million and had lost more than $6 million in it is most recent quarter on sales of only $3.6 million.

CacheFlow went public on November 18, 1999 at a price of $24 a share. Its stock price exploded on the first day of trading and closed at 126⅝ a share, a one day price increase of 102⅝ or 427%. Not bad for one day's work. The first day's closing price for CacheFlow gave it a market value approaching $3 billion. Based on the purchase prices for the different series of convertible preferred stock, by the end of the first day of trading, Series A holders had a return of over 14,000%, Series B stockholders had a gain of over 5,400%, and Series C stock holders had a gain of over 2,600%. Series D shareholders had a much smaller gain— only a 1,150% gain—but the holding period from purchase of Series D through the IPO was only two and a half weeks.

CacheFlow's stock price reached a peak of $165 at the end of November 1999. Since then, CacheFlow's fortunes have not fared as well. Cache-Flow's stock price declined by 51% in November 2000 when its revenue growth failed to please analysts and investors. In addition, CacheFlow announced in February 2001 that its third quarter revenues were only about $21 million, less than half of what analysts had projected. The company announced that it was restructuring to reduce costs and aggressively managing its headcount. By the end of 2001, its stock price had declined to pennies on the dollar. Exhibit 16.9 demonstrates the rise and fall of the fortunes of CacheFlow Inc. (on a split adjusted basis).

With its stock price trading below $1, CacheFlow had to reinvent itself. First, it changed its business model and product development. Instead of providing caching services to speed up the Internet, Cache-Flow found that its security applications were more valuable to customers. Consequently, CacheFlow changed its product delivery to being a strategic provider of security appliances that protect and control enterprise website infrastructures. CacheFlow developed security applications to combat the increased assault on website locations by hackers and other mischief makers. Instead of providing speed to the World Wide Web, it now provides Internet security.

Second, CacheFlow changed its name to reflect its new technology and business model. On August 21, 2002, CacheFlow renamed itself Blue Coat Systems, Inc. (NASDAQ: BCSI). The new name reflected a culmination of CacheFlow's strategic evolution to a security provider of the Internet.

EXHIBIT 16.9   Price History of CacheFlow/Blue Coat Systems[a]

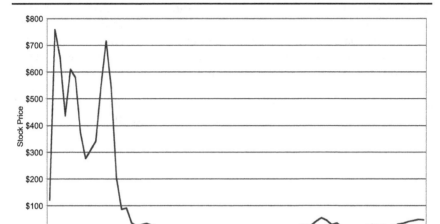

[a] Adjusted for the 1 for 5 reverse stock split.

Shortly after changing the name of the company, in September 2002, the board of directors implemented another change—a reverse stock split. The board approved a one-for-five reverse stock split that decreased the number of shares outstanding, and increased the share price of the company above $1.

The company is now a viable concern. Its net sales revenue for the calendar year ended April 30, 2005 was $96.2 million. In addition, its net income was $5.4 million. In addition, Blue Coat had a strong balance sheet in 2005 with $47.2 million in cash and cash equivalents and net working capital of $35.2 million.

CONCLUSION

The venture capital industry has grown tremendously over the past 50 years, but the fundamental concept remains unchanged: investing private capital with promising but untested business opportunities in order to reap long-term returns that offer a significant premium above the general stock market.

The long bull market of the 1990s combined with the greatest period of economic expansion in U.S. history helped to fuel extraordinary growth in the venture capital industry. However, a slow down in the technology sector as well as the U.S. and global economies have cooled the return expectations of venture capitalists and investors alike. As a result, commitments to venture capital funds declined significantly in years 2001 to 2005 compared to year 2000. Looking forward, venture capital will remain a popular and rewarding alternative equity investment strategy. However, the stellar returns earned in 1999 should not be expected to repeat any time in the near future. We caution that the returns to venture capital will be consistent with their risk profile and will not produce the large oversized gains that were witnessed in 1999 to 2000.

CHAPTER 17

Introduction to Leveraged Buyouts

L everaged buyouts are a way to take a company with publicly traded stock private, or a way to put a company in the hands of the current management (sometimes referred to *management buyouts* or *MBOs*). LBOs use the assets or cash flows of the company to secure debt financing either in bonds issued by the corporation or bank loans, to purchase the outstanding equity of the company. In either case, control of the company is concentrated in the hands of the LBO firm and management, and there is no public stock outstanding.

LBOs represent a mechanism to take advantage of a window of opportunity to increase the value of a corporation. Leverage buyouts can be a way to unlock hidden value or exploit existing but under-funded opportunities.

We begin this chapter with a brief history of the LBO market. Next we provide a theoretical example of how LBOs work. We then discuss how LBOs add value, providing short case histories of successful buyout transactions. As successful as LBO transactions have been, there are risks and we examine these risks in light of the large leverage ratios used to fund buyouts. We also examine the fee structures of LBO funds and other methods by which LBO funds make money. Last, we consider some of the corporate governance advantages of LBOs.

THE HISTORY OF LBOs

Although it was not until the 1970s that the investment value of LBOs became apparent, they began after World War II, when the Great Depression was still fresh in the minds of the investing public and Corporate America. In fact, at the bottom of the Depression, corporate bond defaults across all bonds (investment grade and noninvestment grade) hit a high of 13%. Consequently, debt was viewed negatively and was under utilized. Simultaneous with the limited use of debt was the development of the conglomerate—large companies with widely scattered business units across multiple industries. Management ranks began to grow with the advent of MBA programs and inefficiencies began to creep into these large conglomerates. As a result profitability began to slide.

In 1976, a new investment firm was created on Wall Street, Kohlberg Kravis Roberts & Co. (KKR).[1] The founders of KKR had previously worked at Bear Stearns and Company, and they helped to pioneer the LBO transaction as early as 1968. No firm has had a greater impact on the leveraged buyout market than KKR. Indeed, many of the transactions discussed in this chapter were originated by KKR.

KKR began with just $3 million of its own funds to invest, but soon raised enough capital from other investors to finance the buyout in 1977 of A.J. Industries, a small manufacturing conglomerate. The transaction was for $94 million and consisted of $62 million in bank debt and $32 million of KKR and investor equity. At that time, there were no investors willing to provide subordinated debt to finance an LBO transaction.

This changed with KKR's buyout of Houdaille Industries in 1979. This transaction was financed with 86% debt in the form of senior and subordinated notes. The Houdaille deal demonstrated to the market that for leveraged buyouts there were many investors willing to purchase the debt of an LBO in addition to providing the equity.

The 1980s witnessed the rise of another key element of LBOs: the junk bond. Junk bonds are subordinated debt typically with little in the way of collateral protection. These bonds are just one step above equity, often have a low credit rating, and trade similar to equity. Junk financing is popular because the bond terms can be flexible like private bank financing, but at the same time, appeal to a broader investor base.

Michael Milken became famous for developing Drexel Burnham Lambert's junk bond business. By the mid-1980s, Michael Milken was one of the most powerful men on Wall Street (even though he operated out of the Beverly Hills, CA office of Drexel Burnham Lambert). The deals that Michael Milken and KKR put together demonstrated that a company's cash flows and strength of management team were more creditworthy assets than traditional forms of collateral such as property, plant, and equipment.[2]

---

[1] Their offices are actually in midtown Manhattan.

[2] Michael Milken was subsequently arrested, indicted, and convicted of securities fraud for the role he played in financing several corporate takeovers in the 1980s. The subsequent securities scandal resulted in the demise of Drexel Burnham Lambert.

Fed by junk bond financing, LBO deals reached a crescendo in 1989 when KKR bought the giant food conglomerate RJR Nabisco Inc. for $31 billion in a deal that was documented in the book and movie titled *Barbarians at the Gate.*

In the 1990s, LBO transactions hit two walls. First, there was the U.S. recession of 1990 to 1991 which, while brief, pushed out credit spreads to unfriendly levels and this put a lid on junk bond financing for buyouts. By the end of 1991, 26 of 83 large LBOs completed between 1985 and 1989 had defaulted on their debt financing. Second, in 1998, the default by the Russian government on its treasury bonds once again sent credit spreads spiraling upwards. While in the 1980s, debt accounted for as much as 95% of some LBO deals, by the end of the 1990s, high debt loads of over 75% became unattractive.

The new millennium started much more quietly in the LBO market than in years past. After hitting a peak of over $100 billion in 2000, fund raising trailed off, slowed down by the recession of 2001 to 2002. Still annual fund raising remains around the $60 billion a year level. Exhibit 17.1 presents the growth of the LBO market from 1980 through 2004.

The sheer number of LBO firms seeking investor capital have spurred this growth. While in the 1970s only two firms dominated the

EXHIBIT 17.1   Leveraged Buyouts Committed Capital

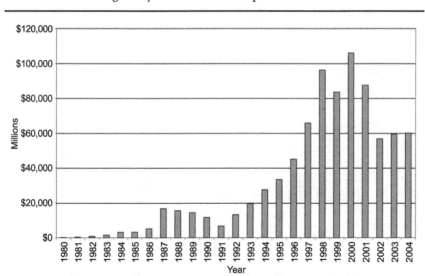

Source: Data obtained from Thomson Financial Venture Economics.

market, KKR and Forstmann Little & Co., there are now well over 1,000 LBO funds competing for money and companies. The growth of this market has led to mixed returns for investors. Exhibit 17.2 presents the 10-year, five-year, three-year, and one-year returns to leveraged buyouts compared to the S&P 500. The one-, three-, and five-year returns to leveraged buyouts do provide superior returns compared to the public stock market, but the 10-year returns are less compelling.

As can be seen, the returns earned by LBO investment pools have declined over the 1990s as too much money chased too few deals. The bursting of the technology bubble as well as the economic recession that followed put the brakes on LBO activity early in the new millennium. For example, in year 2000, the biggest LBO deal was Donaldson, Lufkin & Jeanrette Inc.'s $3.8 buyout of U.S. meat produce IBP Inc. (formerly known as Iowa Beef Processors), which eventually lost out to a higher bid from Tyson Foods. However, as the decade of the 2000s has progressed, large buyouts have come back into fashion demonstrated by the 2005 buyout of Hertz Corporation from Ford Motor Company by the Carlyle Group and Clayton Dublier & Rice for $15 billion.

Currently, the major challenge facing LBO firms is finding sufficient deals in which to invest their capital. The large pool of industrial conglomerates in the 1980s that were ripe to buyout, strip down, and then resell have disappeared. This was a ready-made pipeline for LBO trans-

EXHIBIT 17.2   Returns to Leveraged Buyouts

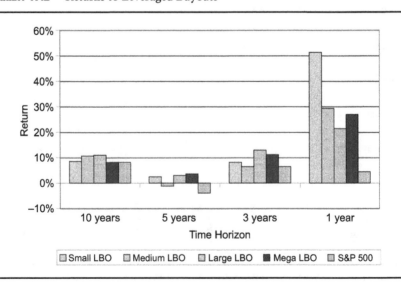

Source: Data obtained from Thomson Financial Venture Economics.

EXHIBIT 17.3   Equity Percentage in LBO Deals

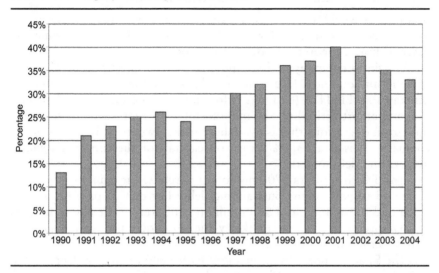

actions, but it has dried up as more and more companies specialize within their core competencies instead of diversifying into wayward industries. With so much money pouring into the LBO market, LBO investment firms have been forced to consider alternative investment vehicles for their investor capital.

Another byproduct of the flow of capital into LBO funds is the decline in the leverage ratio. In 1990, the average equity contributed to the buyout was about 13% of the bid price. However, by the end of the 1990s buyout funds were putting more equity into their deals. In 1999 it was 36%, and the amount of equity contributed to LBOs peaked in 2001 at 40%. Exhibit 17.3 demonstrates the larger equity component of LBO deals.

As the amount of leverage in each LBO deal declines, so does the potential return. Declining returns may stem the tide of investor capital flowing into LBO funds. However, the average amount of equity contributed to LBOs has slowly declined since its peak in 2001. A key contributor to the lower equity ratio has been the amount of very cheap financing available at very attractive rates in 2003 through 2005.

As we look from 2006 onward, we see LBO funds hitting a new stride. Mega funds in excess of $10 billion are becoming common with the largest fund being the 2006 close of Texas Pacific Group's most recent LBO fund at $14.25 billion. In seems likely that a $20 billion dollar fund is not far out of reach in the very near future.

A THEORETICAL EXAMPLE OF A LEVERAGED BUYOUT

In a perfect world, everyone makes money, and no one is unhappy. We will discuss some spectacular LBO failures below. In the meantime, we describe how a theoretical LBO should work.

Imagine a company that is capitalized with a market value of equity of $500 million and a face value of debt of $100 million. The company generates an EBITDA (earnings before interest and taxes plus depreciation and amortization) of $80 million. EBITDA represents the free cash flow from operations that is available for the owners and debtors of the company. This is a 13.3% return on capital for the company's shareholders and debtholders.

An LBO firm offers $700 million to purchase the equity of the company and to pay off the outstanding debt. The debt is paid off at face value of $100 million and $600 million is offered to the equity holders (a 20% premium over the market value) to entice them to tender their shares to the LBO offer.

The $700 million LBO is financed with $600 million in debt (with a 10% coupon rate) and $100 million in equity. The company must pay yearly debt service of $60 million to meet its interest payment obligations. After the LBO, the management of the company improves its operations, streamlines its expenses, and implements better asset utilization. The result is that the cash flow of the company improves from $80 million a year to $120 million a year.[3] By foregoing dividends and using the free cash flow to pay down the existing debt, the management of the company can own the company free and clear in about seven years.

This means that, after seven years, the LBO firm can claim the annual cash flow of $120 million completely for itself. Using a long-term growth rate of 2% per year and a discount rate of 12%, this cash flow is worth

$$\$120 \text{ million}/(0.12 - 0.02) = \$1.2 \text{ billion}$$

Therefore, the total return on the investment for the LBO transaction is

$$[\$1.2 \text{ billion}/\$100 \text{ million}]^{1/7} - 1 = 42.6\%$$

---

[3] Studies of LBOs indicate that corporate cash flows increase 96% from the year before the buyout to three years after the buyout. See Michael Jensen, "The Modern Industrial Revolution, Exit, and the Failure of Internal Control Systems," in Donald H. Chew, Jr. (ed.), *The New Corporate Finance*, 2nd ed. (New York: Irwin/McGraw-Hill, 1999).

The amount of 42.6% represents the annual compounded return for this investment. Notice the impact that leverage has on this transaction. The company is financed with a 6:1 debt to equity ratio. This is a very high leverage ratio for any company.

However, the cash flows generated by the company are used to pay down the debt to a point where the company is completely owned by the equity holders. The equity holders receive a very high return because the debt used to finance the transaction is locked in at a 10% coupon rate. This means that any operating efficiencies and capital gains generated from the business accrue to the benefit of the equity holders. This is a keen incentive for the equity holders to improve the operations of the company.

As the above example demonstrates, the returns to LBO transactions can be quite large, but the holding period may also be commensurately long. At the end of seven years, the management of the company can reap the $1.2 billion value through one of four methods:

1. The management can sell the company to a competitor or another company that wishes to expand into the industry.
2. Through an initial public offering. Consider the example of Gibson Greetings. This company was purchased from RCA for $81 million with all but $1 million financed by bank loans and real estate leasebacks. When Gibson Greetings went public, the 50% equity interest owned by the LBO firm was worth about $140 million, equal to a compound annual rate of return of over 200%.
3. Another LBO. The management of the company doubled its value from $600 million to $1.2 billion. They can now refinance the company in another LBO deal where debt is reintroduced into the company to compensate management for their equity stake. In fact, the existing management may even remain as the operators of the company with an existing stake in the second LBO transaction, providing them with the opportunity for a second go round of leveraged equity appreciation.
4. Straight refinancing. This is similar to method 3, where a company reintroduces debt into its balance sheet to pay out a large cash dividend to its equity owners.

Consider United Defense Industries Inc. This company is the main contractor on the U.S. Army's Bradley fighting vehicle and in the development of the Crusader field artillery system. The Carlyle Group, an LBO firm operating out of Washington D.C., purchased United Defense in 1997 from the FMC Corp and Harsco Corp. for $850 million with $173 million in equity and the rest in debt. By July 2001, United Defense had paid down its debt to $235 million. At that point, the Carlyle Group added more debt to United Defense's balance sheet by arranging for a loan of $850 million. Of the $850 million refinancing, The Carlyle Group used $400 million to pay a dividend to its investors which include pension funds, endowments, and wealthy individuals.

The Appeal of a Leveraged Buyout

Leverage buyouts have a number of appealing characteristics to corporate management and investors alike. From the perspective of corporate management, the benefits of a buyout are:

- The use of leverage whose interest payments are tax deductible.
- Less scrutiny from public equity investors.
- Freedom from a distracted corporate parent.
- The ability of the management of the company to become significant equity holders and to enjoy in the upside of building the business.

From the shareholders' side of the equation, they typically respond favorably to a leveraged buyout because the bid price for their shares is typically at a large premium compared to the market price. Consequently, they also share in a portion of the upside potential of the LBO when they tender their shares at a premium to initiate the buyout transaction.

More to the point leveraged buyout firms often target company's that have a depressed stock price. This is one of the leading criteria for an LBO target (which we will discuss in more detail below). Consequently, shareholders often welcome an LBO bid because it typically reflects superior pricing to what they can currently receive for their shares in the market place.

Financing a Leveraged Buyout

As our simple example demonstrated above, a leveraged buyout will be financed with a combination of debt and equity, with debt being the large majority of the financing. Generally, in every LBO deal, there are three tranches of financing: senior debt, mezzanine debt, and equity. Senior debt is typically bank financing along with credit/finance companies and insurance companies. Mezzanine debt is purchased by mezzanine debt funds (another form of private equity that we will discuss in the next chapter), insurance companies, and other institutional investors. Last is the equity tranche, which will be held by the LBO firm that has taken the company private, the management of the company, and some "equity kickers" from the mezzanine debt tranche. Exhibit 17.4 lays out the layers of LBO financing.

EXHIBIT 17.4 Tranche Financing for a Leveraged Buyout

Financing Tranche	Percentage of Transaction	Expected Return	Financing Parameters	Source of Funding
Senior debt	40% to 60%	4% to 5% over LIBOR	4- to 6-year payback 2× to 3× EBITDA	Commercial banks Finance companies Insurance companies
Mezzanine debt	20% to 30%	10% to 16% coupon 17% to 20% total return	5- to 7-year payback 1× to 2× EBITDA Equity Kickers to boost Total Return	Mezzanine debt funds Insurance companies Instutitional investors Investment banks
Equity	20% to 40%	25% to 40%	5- to 7-year exit	LBO firm Management of company Equity kickers for mezzanine debt

As an example of recent financing for a large buyout deal, Exhibit 17.5 details the financing for the $11.5 billion leveraged buyout of SunGard Data Systems in 2005. SunGard provides trade clearing and data processing for stock, option, and future exchanges. This transaction was financed with $6 billion in bank loans, $2 billion in mezzanine debt, and $3.5 billion of equity from several LBO firms. The 30% equity contribution of the LBO firms is a bit lower than the current average equity contribution, but SunGard's dominant position in the trade clearing business demonstrated strong cash flows to support a higher level of debt financing.

HOW LBOs CREATE VALUE

The theoretical example given in the previous section is a good starting point for describing an LBO transaction; but there is no standard format for a buyout, each company is different, and every LBO deal has different motivations. However, there are five general categories of LBOs that illuminate how these transactions can create value.

LBOs that Improve Operating Efficiency

A company may be bought out because it is shackled with a noncompetitive operating structure. For large public companies with widespread equity ownership, the separation of ownership and management can create agency problems with ineffective control mechanisms. Management may have little incentive to create value because it has a small stake in the company, and monitoring of management's actions by a diverse shareholder base is likely to be just as minimal.

Under these circumstances, management is likely to be compensated based on revenue growth. This may result in excess expansion and operating inefficiencies resulting from too much growth. These examples often occur in mature industries with stable cash flows. Consider the following case history.

Safeway Corporation

In 1986, KKR took Safeway, a grocery/supermarket chain, private at a cost of $4.8 billion. The transaction was financed with 86% debt financing. At the time Safeway had an expensive cost structure that was not competitive with the rest of the supermarket food industry. Its employees earned wages that were 33% above the industry average. In sum, Safeway had stores that were losing money, inefficient inventory controls, and other poor operating procedures. Safeway's managers were compensated based on revenue growth, not profitability.

EXHIBIT 17.5 Financing Tranches for the SunGard Data Systems Buyout

Financing Tranche	Dollar Amount	Percentage of Transaction	Financing Parameters	Source of Funding
Senior bank loans	$4 billion	34.80%	7-year term loan at LIBOR + 2.5%	5-bank consortium led by JP Morgan Chase
	$1 billion	8.70%	Bridge loan	
	$1 billion	8.70%	Revolving credit facility	
Total bank loans	$6 billion	52.20%		
Mezzanine debt	$1.6 billion	13.90%	7-year, fixed coupon at 9.125%	CDO funds
	$400 million	3.50%	Floating rate at LIBOR + 4.5%	Insurance companies
Total mezzanine debt	$2 billion	17.40%	Both offerings rated "junk" by S&P	Mezzanine debt funds
Equity	$3.5 billion	30.40%	Collects the benefits of any capital gains and residual cash flows	Club deal of 7 LBO firms
Total	$11.5 billion	100.00%		

Drastic measures were implemented: renegotiations with unions, employee layoffs, and store closings. For example, Safeway sold its poorest performing division in Salt Lake City to Borman's Supermarkets for $75 million, and sold all 121 stores in its Dallas division to different grocery chains. Within two years, all divisions lacking wage parity with Safeway's competitors had been divested. This resulted in a reduction of over 1,000 stores and a 40% reduction in employees.

In addition, regional managers were compensated not by how much they generated in sales (the prior incentive scheme), but instead, on how well their operations earned a return on the market value of capital employed. As a result, managers worked harder to keep costs in line, closed underperforming stores, and expanded the business only when it appeared profitable.

The freedom to cut costs and the necessity to meet high debt service forced the management of Safeway to think of profits first, and expansion second. It worked, and KKR eventually took public again the company after it had improved its operations and profitability. The LBO investors earned an annualized return of almost 43%.

Safeway is an example where value creation came not from entrepreneurial input, but rather from greater operating efficiencies. The grocery chain industry is a mature industry. New innovations are rare; it is a high volume, low margin business. Margin expansion comes not from brilliant insights into new strategies, but rather, from increasing operating efficiencies. As a result, Safeway is best categorized as an efficiency buyout.[4] Efficiency buyouts often result in a reduction in firm assets and revenue, but eventually, an increase in firm profits.

Such a buyout introduces more concentrated ownership and a better incentive scheme to mitigate agency problems. Management is given a stake in the company with an incentive scheme tied not to increasing revenues, but to increasing operating margins and equity value. In addition a high leverage ratio is used to ensure that management has little discretion to pursue inefficient projects. Last, the LBO firm replaces the diverse shareholder base and provides the active oversight that was lacking by the prior (widespread) equity owners.

Unlocking an Entrepreneurial Mindset

Another way an LBO can create value is by helping to free management to concentrate on innovations. Another frequent LBO strategy is the unwanted (or neglected) operating division. Often an operating division

---

[4] See Robert Hoskisson, Mike Wright, and Lowel W. Busenitz, "Firm Rebirth: Buyouts as Facilitators of Strategic Growth and Entrepreneurship," *The Academy of Management Executive* (February 2001).

of a conglomerate is chained to its parent company and does not have sufficient freedom to implement its business plan. An LBO can free the operating division as a new company, able to control its own destiny.

Duracell Corporation

Duracell was a division of Kraft Foods, a consumer products company, but its batteries were very different from the consumer foods (cookies, macaroni and cheese, etc.) primarily produced by Kraft. Duracell was too small and too different from its parent company to warrant much attention. The buyout of Duracell was led by its management in a MBO because they felt that they could increase the value of the company if they were freed from a bureaucratic parent company.

Duracell was taken private in 1988. The goal of management was not to sell assets and shrink the company (although it did consolidate its production by eliminating small plants). Instead, the company increased its budget for research and development, producing batteries that were not only longer lived, but also were more environmentally friendly. Additionally, management pursued an overseas expansion plan, to become a dominant supplier around the globe. Finally, management implemented an aggressive marketing and advertising campaign.

In short, once unshackled from a corporate parent, Duracell was free to pursue its expansion plans with the capital that it previously did not receive from its corporate parent. However, this capital was costly, and more than ever, the management of Duracell had to focus on cash flows and efficient use of existing assets—there was no corporate parent with deep pockets to bail it out.

In response to the pressure to manage its debt service and increase the value of equity, Duracell adopted the concept of *economic value added* (EVA). EVA is a method for evaluating projects and performance by including a charge against profits for the cost of capital that a company employs.[5] The capital charge under EVA measures the return that investors could expect to earn by investing their money in a portfolio of stocks with similar risk as the company.

The EVA approach to value creation has gained popular attention because it reflects economic reality rather than accounting conventions

---

[5] The formula for EVA is Net operating profits after tax − (Cost of capital) × (Total capital employed). See Al Ehrbar, *EVA: The Real Key to Creating Wealth* (New York: John Wiley & Sons, 1998). Many firms have adopted EVA as a way to measure their performance including Coca-Cola, Briggs & Stratton, and Boise Cascade. In addition, the California Public Employees' Retirement System (CalPERS) uses EVA in its annual review of corporate governance of corporations based in the United States.

such as earnings per share or return on equity. Accounting-based measures can be distorted by noncash charges, early revenue recognition, and other accounting conventions. This may lead to a temptation by management to manipulate accounting-based performance measures such as earnings per share. Conversely, EVA measures the opportunity cost of capital based on the risk undertaken to achieve a revenue stream. As a result, EVA redirects management's focus from accounting numbers to equity value creation.

Duracell was a success story. It managed to increase its cash flows from operations at an annual rate of 17% from 1989 through 1995. Eventually, KKR negotiated the sale of Duracell to the Gillette corporation, resulting in a compound annual return of 40%. Management's shares were valued in excess of $45 at the time compared to the price of $5 a share at the time of the buyout.[6]

Duracell is a prime example of an entrepreneurial LBO. Once freed from Kraft Foods, Duracell could implement new innovations such as mercury-free alkaline batteries. Not only was the production process cheaper, its new environmentally friendly batteries appealed to the public. Additionally, Duracell developed rechargeable nickel hydride batteries for use in laptop personal computers. And rather than build new production facilities as it had done previously, Duracell formed manufacturing joint ventures in Germany, Japan, India, and China. This helped Duracell to expand internationally while deploying its capital most efficiently under the principles of EVA.

It is important to note that in an entrepreneurial LBO, the leverage ratio cannot be as high as for an operating efficiency LBO. The reason is that there must be sufficient flexibility for the managers/entrepreneurs to pursue their new initiatives. Whereas in the Safeway example management's actions needed to be restricted, in the Duracell example management's actions needed to be indulged. A moderate amount of leverage is usually required (50% to 70%) which provides sufficient discipline, but still allows for innovative flexibility.

The Overstuffed Corporation

One of the mainstream targets of many LBO firms are conglomerates. Conglomerate corporations consist of many different operating divisions or subsidiaries, often in completely different industries. Wall Street

---

[6] For more details on the Safeway and Duracell buyouts, see George Baker and George David Smith, "Leveraged Management Buyouts at KKR: Historical Perspectives on Patient Equity, Debt Discipline and LBO Governance," in Rick Lake and Ronald Lake (eds.), *Private Equity and Venture Capital: A Practical Guide for Investors and Practitioners* (London: Euromoney Books, 2000).

analysts are often reluctant to follow or "cover" conglomerates because they do not fit neatly into any one industrial category. As a result, these companies can be misunderstood by the investing public and therefore undervalued. Consider the following case history.

Beatrice Foods

In yet another KKR deal, Beatrice Foods (a food-processing conglomerate) was bought out in an LBO in 1986 for $6.2 billion. This was a 45% premium over the company's market value one month earlier.

Over the next two years, the management of the company, with KKR's assistance, sold off $7 billion of assets, reaping an $800 million gain over the initial LBO price. This is a clear demonstration of how the market and Wall Street analysts can undervalue a company. The LBO transaction paid for itself in the asset sales alone. This is all the more impressive when we recall that when KKR purchased the company for $6.2 billion, this price was at a 45% premium to the company' current stock price. Beatrice Foods is an excellent example of an undervalued conglomerate.

As might be expected, sales for the streamlined company declined from $11.4 billion to $4.2 billion after the $7 billion of asset sales. Yet, profits increased from about $300 million to almost $1 billion. Finally, after the sale of assets, the total debt of Beatrice Foods rose only slightly from $300 million to $376 million. The annual compounded return on this transaction was in excess of 40%.

Beatrice Foods is similar in some respects to the Safeway example. In each case, entrepreneurial insight was not required. Instead, strong operating management was the key to a successful LBO. In Safeway's case, management's job was to eliminate inefficient and unprofitable divisions. Safeway sold off these divisions and made them someone else's problem.

Similarly, Beatrice Food's management also pared down its assets, not necessarily to improve operations, but instead, to give the company a better focus and identity. Beatrice was "overstuffed" in that it had too many products across too many markets, resulting in a lack of coverage by the investment community and a lack of understanding of its core value.

Last, what Safeway and Beatrice needed was strong monitoring by their shareholders. In their public form this was difficult to do for both companies because of their widespread shareholder base. However, in the LBO format, the equity of both companies was concentrated in the hands of the LBO fund. This resulted in close monitoring of their operations. What these companies needed was not more growth, but rather, a business plan that focussed on streamlining and improving core divisions.

Buy and Build Strategies

Another LBO value creation strategy involves combining several operating companies or divisions through additional buyouts. The LBO firm begins with one buyout and then acquires more companies and divisions that are strategically aligned with the initial LBO portfolio company. The strategy is that there will be synergies from combining several different companies into one. In some respects, this strategy is the reverse of that for conglomerates. Rather than strip a conglomerate down to its most profitable divisions, this strategy pursues a "buy and build" approach. This type of strategy is also known as a "leveraged build-up."

Berg Electronics

The buyout firms of Hicks, Muse, Tate & Furst and Mills & Partners jointly purchased Berg Electronics from the DuPont Corporation in 1993 for a purchase price of $335 million. At that time, DuPont's evaluation of Berg indicated that it generated about $18 million in profit on revenue of $380 million. Berg manufactured computer connectors as well as socket and cable assembly products for the telecommunications industry.

Berg Electronics was used as a platform for further leveraged transactions in the same industry. Over the next five years, Berg Electronics made eight acquisitions under the direction of Hicks, Muse and Mills & Partners including the acquisition of AT&T's connector business and Ericsson AB's connector division. By 1997, Berg had sales of $785 million and profits of over $180 million and employed 7,800 workers in 22 countries.

In early 1998, the buyout firms distributed shares in Berg to their investment partners and retained 20% of the firm for themselves. In August 1998, Framatome Connectors International, based in France and the third largest maker of electrical connectors, purchased Berg Electronics for $35 a share, for a total of $1.85 million, a 41% gain in purchase price before including the effects of leverage. Based on the initial equity contributed, the Berg Electronics transaction earned an estimated return in excess of 1,000%.[7]

LBO Turnaround Strategies

The U.S. economic recession of 2001 to 2002 highlighted another form of LBOs: the turnaround LBO. Unlike traditional buyout firms that look for successful, mature companies with low debt to equity ratios and stable management, turnaround LBO funds look for underperforming companies with excessive leverage and poor management. The targets

---

[7] See Hoskisson, Wright, and Busenitz, "Firm Rebirth: Buyouts as Facilitators of Strategic Growth and Entrepreneurship."

for turnaround LBO specialists come from two primary sources: (1) ailing companies on the brink of Chapter 11 bankruptcy and (2) underperforming companies in another LBO fund's portfolio.

One LBO firm that pursues such a strategy is Questor Management Co. This company was founded in 1995 and has specialized in turnaround and distressed investments of troubled companies in other LBO firm's portfolios.

Aegis Communications Group

Aegis Communications Group is a teleservices company that offers integrated marketing services including customer acquisition, customer care, high volume outbound database telemarketing, and marketing research. Aegis started as the result of a buy and build strategy but subsequently morphed into a turnaround strategy.

In December 1996, Thayer Capital Partners, through its buyout fund, Thayer Equity Investors III, purchased majority stakes in two teleservice companies, Edward Blank Associates and LEXI International Inc. In 1997, these two companies were combined with a third company in Thayer Capital's portfolio to build IQI, Inc. Thayer Capital then used IQI, Inc. as a merger partner with ATC Communications Group in July 1998 to form Aegis Communications Group. The plan was to build a national call center servicing company for other companies that wished to outsource their customer service lines for efficiency purposes. This was a classic buy-and-build strategy. After the merger, Thayer Capital became Aegis Communications' largest shareholder.

Unfortunately, the Aegis buy-and-build strategy was not a success story. From a high price of $19 in 1996, Aegis stock quickly dropped to $1 at the beginning of 1999. In August 1999, Thayer Capital brought in Questor to help revive the company. Aegis was suffering from high employee turnover, and an over leveraged balance sheet. Questor purchased $46.75 million in Series F senior voting convertible preferred stock in Aegis that was used to repay about $43 million in existing bank debt. As a result of its capital infusion, Questor was able to control approximately 47% of Aegis' voting stock.

Initially, Aegis' stock price increased to $1.875 a share in 2000, but then drifted to below $1 in 2001. In March 2001, Questor and Thayer Capital acquired the remaining outstanding shares of Aegis that they did not already at an offer price of $1 which was a 45% premium over the current price of 68 cents. The total cost was about $30 million (of which $10 million went back to other Thayer Capital funds).

However, Aegis fortunes continued to erode as it racked up losses of $19 million and $22 million in 2003 and 2004. Its stock price tumbled

EXHIBIT 17.6   Aegis Communications Price

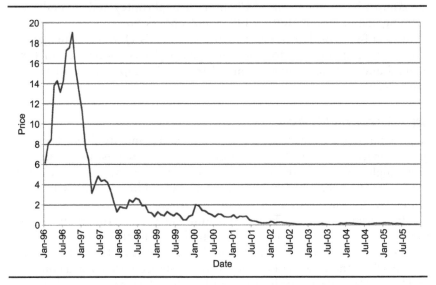

to pennies on the dollar, even trading below 1 cent a share in 2003. To try and salvage some portion of its value, Questor and Thayer Capital initially agreed to sell Aegis to AllServe Systems of England for $22.7 million in September 2003. This deal however, fell through.

However, Questor and Thayer were rescued by a second offer from Essar Group of India and Deutsche Bank who bid $28 million to acquire 80% of the equity of Aegis. Eventually, in 2005, Aegis converted a significant amount of its debt outstanding to common stock to satisfy three promissory notes held by another investor, World Focus. The approximately $100 million that Questor and Thayer had invested was wiped out. Exhibit 17.6 shows a price chart for Aegis.

LBO FUND STRUCTURES

In this section we discuss how LBO funds are structured as well as discuss their fees. While LBO funds are very similar to venture capital funds in design, they are much more creative in fee generation.

Fund Design

Almost all LBO funds are designed as limited partnerships. This is very similar to the way hedge funds and venture capital funds are established. In fact many LBO funds have the name "partners" in their title.

Every LBO fund is run by a general partner. The general partner is typically the LBO firm, and all investment discretion as well as day to day operations vest with the general partner. Limited partners, as their name applies, have a very limited role in the management of the LBO fund. For the most part, limited partners are passive investors who rely on the general partner to source, analyze, perform due diligence, and invest the committed capital of the fund.

Some LBO funds have advisory boards comprised of the general partner and a select group of limited partners. The duties of the advisory board are to advise the general partner on conflicts of issue that may arise as a result of acquiring a portfolio company or collecting fees, provide input as to when it might be judicious to seek independent valuations of the LBO fund's portfolio companies, and to discuss whether dividend payments for portfolio companies should be in cash or securities.

Similar to hedge funds and venture capital funds, LBO funds must be aware of the regulatory restrictions that apply to the offering of interests in their fund. To avoid being deemed an investment company, LBO funds take advantage of the 3(c)(1) and 3(c)(7) provisions of the Investment Company Act of 1940. These provisions were discussed at length in Chapter 8 with respect to hedge funds and are equally applicable to LBO funds.

Fees

If there was ever an investment structure that could have its cake and eat it too, it would be an LBO firm. LBO firms have any number of ways to make their money.

First, consider the annual management fees charged by LBO firms. These range from 1.25% to 3%. Consider the recent Blackstone Fund that raised $12 billion. The management fee on this fund is reported at around 2%. Two percent times $12 billion equals $240 million in annual management fees. And these fees are collected before any profits are recorded, indeed, even before any investments are made.

In addition, LBO firms share in the profits of the investment pool. These incentive fees usually range from 20% to 30%. Incentive fees are profit sharing fees. For instance, an incentive fee of 20% means that the LBO firm keeps one dollar out of every five earned on LBO transactions. Also, this incentive fee is a "free option" just as we discussed with respect to the incentive fees for venture capital funds and hedge funds.

LBO firms also may charge fees to the corporation that it is taken private of up to 1% of the total selling price for arranging and negotiating the transaction. As an example, KKR earned $75 million for arranging the buyout of RJR Nabisco, and $60 million for arranging the buyout of Safeway Stores. These transaction fees are divided up differently by LBO firm; there is no standard practice. Some LBO firms keep all of these fees for the LBO firm itself and do not share the transaction fees with their limited partner investors. Some LBO firms split the transaction fees with the percentage kept by the LBO firm ranging from 75% to 25%. Still other LBO firms include all of these fees as part of the profits to be split up between the general partner and the limited partners.

Not only do LBO firms earn fees for arranging deals, they can earn breakup fees if a deal craters. Consider the Donaldson, Lufkin & Jenrette LBO of IBP Inc. This $3.8 billion buyout deal, first announced in October, 2000 was subsequently topped by a $4.1 billion takeover bid from Smithfield Foods Inc. in November, 2000. This bid was in turn topped by a $4.3 billion takeover bid from Tyson Foods Inc. in December 2000. Despite losing out on the buyout of IBP, as part of the LBO deal terms, DLJ received a $66.5 million breakup fee from IBP because it was sold to another bidder.

In addition to earning fees for arranging the buyout of a company or for losing a buyout bid, LBO firms may also charge a divestiture fee for arranging the sale of a division of a private company after the buyout has been completed. Furthermore, an LBO firm may charge director's fees to a buyout company if managing partners of the LBO firm sit on the company's board of directors after the buyout has occurred. In fact there are any number of ways for an LBO firm to make money on a buyout transaction.

In summary, LBO firms are "Masters of the Universe" when it comes to fee structures. It is no wonder that they have become such popular and profitable investment vehicles.

The J Curve Effect

In our prior chapter on Venture Capital, we described the J curve effect for a venture capital fund. The same effect applies to leveraged buyout funds. LBO funds go through the same stages as a venture capital fund: fund raising, due diligence, investment, and harvesting of profits.

Recall from our discussion in Chapter 16, that initially, a private equity fund will provide negative returns in the early part of its life. This is because the LBO firm draws management fees from its investor limited partners to finance the sourcing of deals, to conduct due diligence of potential LBO candidates, and to monitor the portfolio companies once an investment is made. Therefore, in the early part of the LBO fund's life, the fund will generate a negative cash flow reflecting the cost of management fees. However, as the fund matures, and portfolio companies are sold to generate the fund's investment returns, it is expected that the investment profits should more than compensate for the initial management fees charged, and eventually, the private equity fund generates positive cash flows for its investors.

EXHIBIT 17.7   J Curve for Leveraged Buyout Firms—Cumulative IRRs by Vintage Year

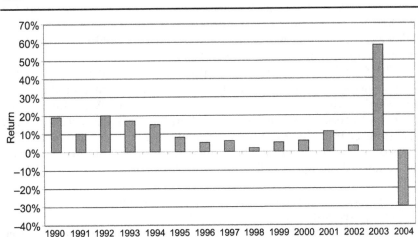

Source: Data obtained from Thomson Financial Venture Economics.

Exhibit 17.7 demonstrates the J curve effect from another angle. In this exhibit, we introduce the concept of "vintage year." Vintage year is a way to compare private equity funds based on their year of formation. For example, it would be unfair to compare an LBO fund in its first year of operations with an LBO fund it its eighth year of operations because in the former fund, it is just getting started with the sourcing of private equity deals and due diligence, while in the latter fund, it is in the profit harvesting stage. Therefore, to make an "apples to apples" comparison, it is only fair to compare a fund of one vintage year to other funds of the same vintage year—these funds have all left the starting gate at the same time.

Exhibit 17.7 shows the return by vintage year (year of formation). Notice that the most recent year shows the most negative returns. This is an application of the J curve effect. More recent vintage year funds are still in their sourcing, due diligence, investment, and monitoring phases. They tend to have lower rates of return because they have not had sufficient time to implement their business plan and harvest profits from their portfolio companies. The one exception is vintage year 2003 which shows remarkable returns by comparison to any year. An extremely robust stock market in 2003 (after a 3-year bear market) allowed LBO firms to exit firms quickly and profitably.

PROFILE OF AN LBO CANDIDATE

We now turn to how LBO firms find good buyout candidates. Or, another way to consider the question is: What makes a good LBO Candidate? In this section we examine the profile of a public company that has been bandied about as a potential candidate.

The Gap Inc., the largest specialty clothing retailer in the United States, was identified as a potential LBO candidate in a credit report published by the Bank of America in January 2006.[8] When looking for LBO candidates, buyout firms look at both financial characteristics and operating characteristics. Not surprisingly, the financial characteristics focus on cash flows and the ability to support large amounts of debt on the balance sheet. Specifically, LBO firms look for:

- A history of profitability with steady profit margins.
- Strong free cash flows to service additional debt levels.
- A balance sheet this is not already overburdened with a high debt level.
- A strong balance sheet with a large cash/current asset balance.
- A weak stock price.

Exhibits 17.8 and 17.9 demonstrate many of the financial characteristics that LBO firms look for. First, the operating and net margins for The Gap are 13% and 7%, respectively. Not overwhelming, but sufficient to generate interest from LBO firms. Furthermore, The Gap has been a consistent profit maker. In addition, its balance sheet is solid with 63% of its assets identified as current assets (assets which will mature in less than one year). This demonstrates excellent liquidity. Also, its debt equity ration is 51% debt/49% equity. This would allow The Gap to take on additional debt in a leveraged buyout. In addition, The Gap generates a significant free cash flow after interest and taxes. This shows the ability to support and service a higher debt ratio. Last the price per share of The Gap has languished as demonstrated in Exhibit 17.9, particularly during 2005 when The Gap shares declined approximately 17%.

On the operating side of the equation, LBO firms look for:

- A mature firm with a strong brand name and competitive market position.
- Products that are not subject to technological obsolescence.
- A diversified customer base that generates recurring revenues.

---

[8] Caroline Salas, "Banc of America says LBOs, Buybacks Perilous for Bonds," January 4, 2006.

EXHIBIT 17.8 The Gap Inc. Financial Statements

Income Statement	Millions	Balance Sheet	Millions
Net sales	16,267	Current assets	6,304
Less cost of goods sold	9,886	Noncurrent assets	3,676
Less selling & admin.	4,296	Other assets	368
Operating income	2,085	Total assets	10,048
Interest expense	167	Current liabilities	2,242
Nonoperating expenses	46	Noncurrent liabilities	2,870
Income tax	722	Total debt	5,112
Net income	1,150	Shareholders equity	4,936

Free Cash Flow	Millions
Starting cash	2,253
Operating cashflow	1,620
Investment cashflow	160
Cashflow for financing	−1,796
Cash paid for taxes	−891
Cash for interest	−168
Free cash flow	1,178

EXHIBIT 17.9 A Picture of a Potential LBO Candidate: The Gap, Inc.

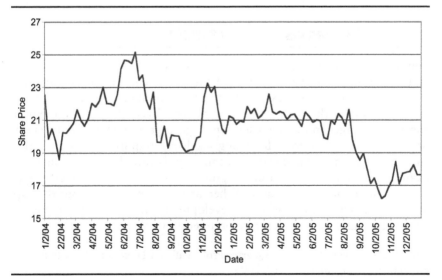

▦ A management team that might need some improvement to increase operating efficiency.

Considering The Gap, it is a mature retailer with a strong brand name— virtually every shopping mall in America has a Gap. Clothing products are not subject to technological obsolescence, although fashion trends can change rapidly. The Gap has a diversified customer base with Baby Gap, Kid's Gap and regular Gap stores so that literally from the cradle to at least middle age, there is a recurring customer base. In addition, given holiday's that require new clothes, different seasons of the year, back to school shopping, etc. The Gap easily has recurring revenues.

Last is the management team. During 2005, The Gap experienced significant turnover of its management ranks, as it replaced its Chief Design Officer and Head of Marketing during the Christmas holiday season. While significant turnover might scare off some LBO firms, others might be encouraged. Some LBO firms might consider this an opportunity to bringer greater design and operating efficiencies to The Gap to improve its meandering performance. In addition, The Gap has recently been criticized as a tired brand in its competition against other specialty retailers such as the Banana Republic and Abercrombie & Fitch.[9] Again, while this might discourage some LBO firms, it might also encourage others to take a great brand name and energize it with fresh management and ideas.

In summary, The Gap has many of the financial and operating criteria that make for an attractive LBO candidate. Stay tuned to your Bloomberg screens.

VENTURE CAPITAL VERSUS LEVERAGED BUYOUTS

Venture Capital and Leveraged Buyouts are two sides of the capital markets coin. While venture capital funds nascent, startup companies, leveraged buyouts target established mature companies. They operate at opposite ends of the life cycle of a company. Every corporation experiences three stages in its life: a startup stage, a growth stage, and a stable or mature stage. Different financing needs are required for these different stages and different product technology is found in each stage. For example, as a startup, venture capital is necessary to get a prototype product or service out the door. Whereas in a leveraged buyout the capital is necessary not for product development but to take the company private so that it can concentrate on operating efficiencies.

---

[9] See Andria Cheng, "Gap 3rd Quarter Profit Falls on Discounts, Cuts Forecast," *Bloomberg News*, November 17, 2005.

EXHIBIT 17.10 Venture Capital versus Leveraged Buyouts—Startup versus Mature

Company Characteristics	Startup	Mature
Market environment	Developing	Developed
Product demand	Undiscovered	Established
Customer base	Early adopter	Widespread acceptance
Management type	Entrepreneur	Seasoned
Management skills	Idea generation	Operations management
Revenues	Just beginning	Recurring & predictable
Capital consumption	Ravenous	Conservative
Competitive advantage	New technology	Distribution, marketing, production
Financing characteristics	Venture capital	Leveraged buyout
Target IRR	40% to 50%	20% to 30%
Shareholder position	Minority	Control of company
Board seats	One or two	All
Valuation	Compare to other companies	Discounted cash flow model
Use of debt	Non existent	Majority of financing
Investment strategy	Finance innovation	Improve operating efficiency
Time to exit	2 to 5 year	4 to 7 years
Exit options	IPO, acquistion	IPO, acquisition or recapitalization

A summary of the differences between startup companies and the venture capital they need compared to the companies targeted by LBO firms is presented in Exhibit 17.10.

In terms of company characteristics, startup companies generally have a new or innovative technology that can be exploited with the right amount of capital. The management of the company is typically idea driven rather than operations driven. There may not even be a proven revenue model yet and the capital consumption is high.

Conversely, with an LBO, there is an established product, if not, in fact, an established industry. The management of the company is driven not by idea generation but by operating efficiency. Revenues are established, recurring, and fairly predictable. Also, a mature company generally has self-sustaining cash flows that allows it to fund its growth internally.

It is also interesting to note the equity stake venture capitalists acquire versus that of leveraged buyout firms. A venture capital firm will typically acquire a significant, but minority position in the company. Control is not absolute. Conversely, in a leveraged buyout all of the equity is acquired and control is absolute. In addition, venture capitalist and LBO firms have different target internal rate of returns that they wish to achieve. While both are quite high, not surprisingly, venture capital target IRRs are higher. The reason is simple: There is more risk funding a nascent company with brand new technology than an established company with regular and predictable cash flows.

The last significant difference between venture capital and leveraged buyouts is the investment strategy. Venture capital finance new, but unproven technology. The technology may even be disruptive in that it is so radical that it defines a new industry like the Sony Walkman of the early 1980s or revolutionizes an existing industry like the Apple iPod in the early 2000s. Conversely, leveraged buyouts look to see where they can add operating efficiencies or expand product distribution. New technology or innovation is not the cornerstone of their investment philosophy. They take an existing product and re define it through better production processes, new marketing to a new audience, or an expansion of existing distribution channels. The product is established; LBO firms seek only to improve it.

RISKS OF LBOs

LBOs have less risk than venture capital deals for several reasons. First, the target corporation is already a seasoned company with public equity outstanding. Indeed, many LBO targets are mature companies with undervalued assets.

Second, the management of the company has an established track record. Therefore, assessment of the key employees is easier than a new team in a venture capital deal.

Third, the LBO target usually has established products or services and a history of earning profits. However, management of the company may not have the freedom to fully pursue their initiatives. An LBO transaction can provide this freedom.

Finally, the exit strategy of a new IPO in several years time is much more feasible than a venture capital deal because the company already had publicly traded stock outstanding. A prior history as a public company, demonstrable operating profits, and a proven management team make an IPO for a buyout firm much more feasible than an IPO for a startup venture.

The obvious risk of LBO transactions is the extreme leverage used. This will leave the company with a high debt to equity ratio and a very large debt service. The high leverage can provide large gains for the equity owners, but it also leaves the margin for error very small. If the company cannot generate enough cash flow to service the coupon and interest payments demanded of its bondholders, it may end up in bankruptcy, with little left over for its equity investors. "Leveraged Fallouts" are an inevitable fact of life in the LBO marketplace.

Consider the example of Robert Campeau's buyout of the department store chain Allied Stores in December 1986. Campeau bid $3.6 billion for the stores, a 36% premium over the common share price at that time. With such a high offer, shareholders quickly tendered their shares and the company became private. The deal was highly leveraged. Of the $3.6 billion, $3.3 billion was financed by callable senior and subordinated notes.

Upon completion of the LBO, Campeau quickly sold a large portion of Allied Stores' assets for $2.2 billion and paid down the outstanding debt. As a result, sales of Allied Stores declined from $4.2 billion in 1986 to $3.3 billion in 1988. In addition to asset sales, employment declined significantly from 62,000 employees in 1986 to 27,000 in 1988. As a result, the Allied Stores, which lost $50 million in 1986, turned a profit in 1988.

Unfortunately, the debt to equity ratio of Allied Stores remained high, and the company could not generate sufficient cash flow to meet its debt service. The chain filed for bankruptcy in 1990.

Another example of a retailing LBO is the management buyout of Macy's Department Stores in 1986. Unlike the Allied Stores example, the management of Macy's attempted to keep the company intact rather than sell off chunks of assets. Macy's was purchased for $3.5 billion, about a 20% premium over the existing stock price at that time. Over the next two years, sales increased from $4.7 billion to $5.7 billion as Macy's management pursued a course of expansion rather than contraction. Unfortunately, the cost of expansion as well as the high debt service turned Macy's from a profitable company to a money losing venture. By 1988, Macy's debt service was $570 million.[10] That is, its interest payments (not the face value of debt) totaled almost $600 million. By the end of 1991, Macy's had over $5.4 billion dollars of debt on its balance sheet. The large debt ratio plus the recession of 1991 forced Macy's into Chapter 11 bankruptcy protection in January 1992.

Although high debt levels eventually forced Allied Stores and Macy's into bankruptcy, there are several advantages to using large leverage ratios. First, high levels of debt financing allows equity investors with only a small amount of capital to realize large gains as debt

---

[10] See W. Keith Schilit, "The Nature of Venture Capital Investments," *The Journal of Private Equity* (Winter 1997), pp. 59–75.

levels are paid down. Second, a high debt level means a small equity level and this allows the management of a buyout company to purchase a significant equity stake in the company. This "carrot" provides for a proper alignment of management's interests with that of the LBO investment firm. Finally, high debt levels and debt service payments are a useful "stick" to keep management operating at peak levels of efficiency to ensure that the debt is paid down at timely intervals.

CORPORATE GOVERNANCE AND LBOs

One of the interesting byproducts of an LBO transaction is the development of strong corporate governance principles. Corporate governance is the process by which the managers of a corporation align their interests with the equity owners of the business (the shareholders). Corporate governance plays a key part in a successful LBO transaction. We briefly describe the corporate governance issue and then consider how LBOs address this problem.

Agency Costs and Firm Management

The objectives of senior management may be very different from that of a corporation's equity owners. For instance, management may be concerned with keeping their jobs, and presiding over a large empire. Conversely, shareholders want value creation. In a large company, equity ownership may be so widely dispersed that the owners of the company cannot make their objectives known to management, or even control management's natural tendencies. This raises the issue of agency costs. (We address the value added of corporate governance in Chapter 26.)

In a corporation, senior management is the agent for the shareholders. Shareholders, as the owners of the company, delegate day-to-day decision-making authority to management with the expectation (or hope) that management of the company will act in the best interests of the shareholders.[11] The separation of ownership and control of the corporation results in agency costs.

Agency costs come in three forms. First, there is the cost to properly align management's goals with that of shareholders. Alignment usually is achieved in the form of incentives for management that may include stock options, bonuses, and other performance-based compensation. Second, there is the cost of monitoring management. This may include auditing financial statements, shareholder review of management perquisites, and

---

[11] At CalPERS, we often refer to ourselves as "Shareowners" rather than "Shareholders."

independent reviews of management's compensation structure. Third, agency costs can include the erosion of shareholder value from management-led initiatives that are not in the best interests of value creation.

In a well-known study, Jensen and Meckling demonstrate that the agents of a company (management) will act in the best interests of the principals (shareholders) only if appropriate incentives are given to the agents and the agents are monitored. [12] This is where LBO firms come in.

LBO firms replace a disperse group of shareholders with a highly concentrated group of equity owners. The concentrated and private nature of the shareholders allows the management of the buyout firm to concentrate on maximizing cash flows, not earnings per share. Management no longer has to account to outside analysts or the media regarding its earnings growth. Furthermore, the management of the now private company is often given a significant equity stake in the company. This provides for an exact alignment of interests between the management/agents of the company and its principals/shareholders. As the company's fortunes increase, so will the personal fortunes of the management.

With a majority of the remaining equity of the once public/now private company concentrated in the hands of the LBO firm, the interaction between equity owners and management becomes particularly important. After a company is taken private, LBO firms maintain an active role in guiding and monitoring the management of the company. They are active, not passive shareholders. In addition, the LBO firm most often will establish incentive goals for the management of the company such as when the management may collect a bonus and for how much.

After a transaction is complete, an LBO firm remains in continuous contact with the management of the buyout firm. As the majority equity owner, the LBO firm has the right to monitor the progress of management, ask questions, and demand accountability. Often an LBO firm will ask for detailed monthly reports from either the CEO or CFO of the company so that the LBO firm can monitor the progress management has made towards implementing their business plan. A constant dialogue between the management of a company and its equity investors is the essence of corporate governance.

Establishing a New Business Plan

For a successful LBO, it is imperative that the management of the company and the LBO firm agree on the business plan for the company going forward. This is very different from how a public corporation

---

[12] See Michael Jensen and William Meckling, "Theory of the Firm: Managerial Behavior, Agency Costs and Ownership Structure," *The Journal of Financial Economics* (October 1976), pp. 305–60.

operates. Rarely does a public company submit its business plan to its shareholders for approval. The reason is twofold. First, the shareholder base is so disperse that it is impractical to seek shareholder approval. Second, most shareholders are not sufficiently knowledgeable that they can fully assess the business plan.

The corporate governance paradigm changes with an LBO company. As the supermajority shareholder of the private company (up to 80% to 90% of the equity may be owned by the LBO firm, the remainder with management), the LBO firm is able to provide clear and complete direction to its agents (the management of the company). Although the specific business plans vary from LBO company to company, there are three common goals.

First, the management of the company and the LBO firm must come up with a plan to unlock the intrinsic value of the company. This might mean shedding marginally profitable divisions or subsidiaries and concentrating on the company's core strength. It might mean cutting back on expansion plans to focus on improving the profitability of existing operations. It might mean streamlining operations by reducing the existing workforce and cutting back on overhead. In sum, there must be some economic rationale why the LBO makes sense.

Second, a plan to meet the existing debt service and to pay down debt must be implemented. This is a key control over the management of the company. If the debt cannot be paid down, there will be no appreciation of the equity of the company, and bankruptcy may result. Management is forced to focus on maximizing profits and utilizing assets most efficiently. It is not in management's best interests to be wasteful or to pursue empire-building if this means that their equity stake in the private company will depreciate.

Consequently, the management and the LBO firm must work together to develop the long-term value of the equity in the company. Since management of the company also has an equity stake, its interests are perfectly aligned with that of the LBO firm. LBO transactions take time to come to fruition, the average length of investment is between six and seven years. During this time, the value of the equity position must be increased and an exit strategy must be fulfilled. It is not enough to unlock the hidden value of a buyout company, both the management and the LBO firm must be able to cash in this value.

Ideally, LBO firms should not interfere with management's implementation of the business plan, but rather, should act as a sounding board or consultant for management's ideas. LBO firms can bring their prior experience to the management of a company as well as their access to investment bankers, lawyers, consultants, accountants, and other professionals.

Spillover of Corporate Governance to the Public Market

The principles of corporate governance that LBO firms apply to their private companies have three important benefits for the public market.

First, the strong governance principles that an LBO firm implements in its private firms should remain when those firms are taken public again. Proper management incentives and monitoring mechanisms have already been established. Even if the private company is sold to another corporation (possibly a public company), the robust corporate governance principles should have an impact on the acquiring company's bottom line.

Second, LBO transactions are a warning to management of public companies. If a company has a poor incentive scheme and minimal shareholder monitoring, it may be ripe for an LBO acquisition. Furthermore, there is no guarantee that the existing management of a public company will remain after the LBO transaction. The LBO firm will have the final say as to who remains and who departs. This threat may provide an incentive for the management of public companies to adopt strong corporate governance principles that increase shareholder value.

Finally, the incentive and monitoring schemes implemented by LBO firms for their portfolio companies provide guidance to management and shareholders alike. Management of public companies can view how new concepts such as EVA can increase shareholder value while providing for just performance compensation. In addition, the principle of enhancing shareholder wealth has now become firmly established in Corporate America. Empire building by corporate executives is no longer rewarded. Instead, executive management and shareholders alike focus on cash flows and share prices, not revenues and conglomerates. Shareholders can also observe the impact that the owners of a business can have on a company's performance if they can concentrate their power at a shareholder meeting. Shareholder power is an enormous tool and LBOs have used it most effectively.

The Dismantling of Conglomerates

We indicated earlier that conglomerates are popular targets for LBO firms, although there are very few left. As business schools churned out tens of thousands of MBA graduates in the 1960s, 1970s, and 1980s, diversification became all of the rage. "Don't put your eggs all in one basket," a lesson learned in business school, became a motto for many companies as they bought unrelated businesses in an attempt to diversify their operating risks.

Examples (in the 1980s) include Mobil Corporation's purchase of the retail store chain Montgomery Ward and Exxon Corporation's establishment of a personal computer division, Exxon Information Systems. Homogeneous, single-industry firms were discouraged, diversification was the new game in town.

Unfortunately, diversification at the corporate level is unnecessary and redundant. Investors could just as easily purchase shares of Mobil and Montgomery Ward if they wished to diversify their portfolio with oil and retailing stocks, or Exxon Corporation and Hewlett Packard if they wanted oil and personal computer exposure. In addition, corporations on a diversification binge had to pay large premiums to the market in expensive tender offers.

Ultimately, this led to depressed share prices of the conglomerate. The large premiums paid by the conglomerates represented corporate waste because there was no reason to pay a large premium for something shareholders could already do themselves, and at a cheaper price. As a result the share prices of conglomerates languished because there were no synergies to be gained by wanton diversification.

However, this is where LBOs added value. Not only did they buy out conglomerates by the bucket full, they paid top dollar, thereby returning to shareholders of the conglomerates some of the prior corporate waste from diversification. They also streamlined the conglomerate, spinning off unrelated divisions into pure plays. This added value for the LBO firm's investors as well as for the new shareholders of the pure-play spinoffs.

More than any other factor, LBO firms stopped the unnecessary diversification of large corporations. The pickings were just too easy for LBO firms, and eventually, conglomerates faded away to a corporate form of the past.

MERCHANT BANKING

As a final discussion we take a moment to briefly describe merchant banking. Merchant banking is a first cousin of leveraged buyouts. Sometimes, it is difficult to distinguish between the two.

Merchant banking is the practice of buying nonfinancial companies by financial institutions. Most investment banking companies and large money-center banks have merchant banking units. These units buy and sell nonfinancial companies for the profits that they can generate for the shareholders of the merchant bank. In some cases the merchant banking units establish limited partnerships similar to LBO funds. At that point there is very little distinction between a merchant banking fund and the LBO funds discussed above.

Consider the example of DLJ's attempted purchase of IBP, Inc. In October 2000, DLJ announced a $3.8 billion buyout of IBP. The terms included $750 million in equity, $1.65 billion in debt borrowing, and the assumption of $1.4 billion of IBP liabilities.

DLJ Merchant Banking Partners III contributed 55% of the equity for the transaction. This merchant banking fund was created with capital contributed by DLJ and its employees. DLJ Merchant Banking Partners III operated as a private LBO fund because only DLJ and its employees could invest in the fund; outside investors were excluded.

Merchant banking started as a way for Wall Street investment banks and Midtown money center banks to take a piece of the action that they helped to fund. If a bank loaned money to an LBO group to purchase a company, the merchant banking unit of the bank would invest some equity capital and get an equity participation in the deal. Soon the merchant banking units of investment banks established their own buyout funds and created their own deals.

While merchant banking is designed to earn profits for the investment bank, it also allows the bank to leverage its relationship with the buyout company into other money-generating businesses such as underwriting, loan origination, merger advice, and balance sheet recapitalization. All of these ancillary business translate into fee generation for the investment bank.

For instance, as part of the IBP buyout, DLJ arranged the debt financing for IBP consisting of three separate tranches: a $500 million in 5.5-year revolving credit, a $500 million 5.5-year term loan, and a $650 million seven-year term loan. DLJ eventually lost its buyout bid for IBP to Tyson Foods Inc. (which bid $4.3 billion for IBP). However, had the buyout been completed, DLJ would have collected significant fees for arranging the $1.65 billion credit facility. Nonetheless, DLJ's merchant banking unit still earned a $66.5 million breakup fee.

The risk of merchant banking is that an investment bank will continue to throw good money after bad to a company owned by its merchant banking unit. An example is Goldman Sachs' purchase of AMF Bowling Inc. Goldman led a $1.37 billion leveraged buyout of the bowling company in 1996 along with buyout firms Kelso & Co. and the Blackstone Group.[13]

Goldman Sachs subsequently brought AMF Bowling public again in November 1997 in an IPO that raised about $263 million at a share price of $19.50. After the IPO, Goldman Sachs remained the majority shareholder with about 54% of the company. A year later, in December 1998, Goldman Sachs paid almost $48 million for $343 million face

---

[13] See Gregg Wirth, "Bum Deals: As a Buyout Binge Looms, Will Wall Street Learn from its Merchant Banking Mistakes?" *Investors Dealers Digest* (February 12, 2001).

value of zero-coupon convertible debentures. At that time, AMF's share price had declined over 80% to the $4 to $5 range.[14]

From the time of its buyout, AMF went on a buying spree, increasing its bowling centers from about 300 to in 1996 to over 500 by 1998. Unfortunately, AMF expanded just at a time when customer demand for its bowling equipment, accessories, and bowling center packages declined. The leverage from the buyout and its acquisition binge quickly pushed AMF's total debt to over $1.2 billion. Eventually, AMF's debt burden combined with its operating losses became so large that AMF Bowling Worldwide, the main operating subsidiary of AMF Bowling Inc. filed for Chapter 11 bankruptcy in July 2001. It is estimated that the cost to Goldman through its equity and bond purchases was at least $400 million.[15]

CONCLUSION

Over the last 25 years, leveraged buyouts have become a mainstream investment product. Most institutional investors now commit some component of their portfolios to leveraged buyouts. Indeed, the primary investors in LBO funds are pension and endowment funds. The State of Oregon's $1 billion dollar commitment to KKR's Millennium Fund is a good indication of the institutional level of interest in buyouts.

Leveraged buyout funds rival venture capital funds in the amount of money committed for investment. Over the 15-year period of 1990–2004 the amount of capital committed to leveraged buyout funds has exceeded $600 billion.[16] There are two reasons for this swell of investment into buyout funds. First, LBOs are less risky than venture capital investments because they target established companies with existing profits. Second, LBO firms have been able to generate positive returns comparable to venture capital.

While short-term returns to LBO funds exceed that of the public stock markets, longer-term returns (10 years) do not indicate a significant premium. The short-term return premiums have worked to increase the appetite of investors for private equity funds, as $10 billion funds are becoming commonplace.

However, the LBO industry has begun to mature as an investment industry. The best indication of this are the Club Deals of private equity firms pooling their resources together as they get into bidding wars

---

[14] In July 1999 AMF repurchased approximately 45% of its outstanding debentures.
[15] See Wirth, "Bum Deals."
[16] As reported in *Venture Economics*. However, venture capital funds have accelerated the pace of their fund raising in 2004 and 2005.

against other clubs. Witness the recent buyout of Hertz Corporation by the Club of LBO partners Clayton, Dublier & Rice and The Carlyle Group and Merrill Lynch's private equity group. This club competed against another club that included the Blackstone Group, Texas Pacific Group, Bain Capital and Thomas H. Lee. We will have more to say about club deals when we discuss trends in private equity in a later chapter.

CHAPTER 18

Debt as Private Equity Part I: Mezzanine Debt

In this chapter we discuss a form of private equity that appear as debt on an issuer's balance sheet. Mezzanine debt is closely linked to the leveraged buyout market, and this strategy can result in a significant equity stake in a target company. In addition, like venture capital and LBOs, mezzanine debt provides an alternative investment strategy within the equity asset class.

It is important to recognize that mezzanine debt investing can be distinguished from traditional long-only investing. The reason is that this form of private equity attempts to capture investment returns from economic sources that are mostly independent of the economy's long-term macroeconomic growth. While the direction of the stock market and the health of the overall economy may have some influence on a company, it is more likely that the fortunes of the company will be determined by its capital structure.

OVERVIEW OF MEZZANINE DEBT

Mezzanine debt is often hard to classify because the distinction between debt and equity can blur at this level of financing. Oftentimes, mezzanine debt represents a hybrid, a combination of debt of equity. Mezzanine financing gets its name because it is inserted into a company's capital structure between the "floor" of equity and the "ceiling" of senior, secured debt. It is from the in between nature of this type of debt that mezzanine derives its name.

Mezzanine debt is a hybrid security that has features of both debt and equity. Typically, mezzanine financing is constructed as a intermediate term bond with some form of equity participation, or "kicker" thrown in as additional enticement to the investor. The equity portion provides the investor with an interest in the upside of the company while the debt component provides a level of high cash payments.

The most common form of mezzanine financing is an intermediate term note, typically unsecured, coupled with stock warrants to purchase the stock of the acquiring company. The coupon payments on the note may be in cash or as *payment-in-kind* (PIK). Payment in kind means that instead of paying cash on the mezzanine debt, the company distributes more notes to the investor. This increases the company's leverage as well as the investor's equity stake in the company (through the receipt of more warrants).

Mezzanine financing does not have to be in the form of debt, sometimes it is in the form of preferred stock. In such circumstances, the preferred stock generally has a set dividend payment as well as a conversion right into the common stock. The main point is that mezzanine finance provides the filler between the senior debt of the company and its bottom line common equity holders.

Exhibit 18.1 provides a general view of the capital structure of a company. This exhibit demonstrates that mezzanine financing can take several forms between senior debt and common equity. Therefore, the gap that mezzanine finance might provide can be quite large, and include several tranches of junior debt or preferred equity.

Mezzanine financing is not used to provide cash for the day-to-day operations of a company. Instead, it is used during transitional periods in a company's life. Frequently, a company is in a situation where its

EXHIBIT 18.1 Overview of Corporate Capital Structure

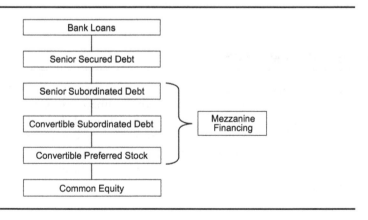

senior creditors (banks) are unwilling to provide any additional capital and the company does not wish to issue additional stock. Mezzanine financing can fill this void.

Mezzanine debt has become increasingly popular for two reasons. First, after the 2001–2002 recession in the U.S. economy, banks and other senior debt lenders became less aggressive about providing capital. Second, there are fewer lending institutions in the bank market. As a result of many mergers and consolidations in the banking sector, the number of participants in syndicated bank loans has declined from 110 lenders in 1998 to 43 by 2005.

Still, mezzanine financing is a niche market, operating between "story credits" and the junk bond market. Story credits are private debt issues that have a good "story" to sell them. Generally, these are senior secured financings with good credit and an interesting story to spin. However, not all firms have good credit or interesting stories. Mezzanine debt may be their best source of financing.

Mezzanine financing is often described as a "middle market" vehicle. This refers to companies that are not as large as those companies who have ready access to the financial markets and larger than companies that have a need for venture capital. Companies in this middle market category form the broad backbone of any economy, generally in the range of $200 million to $2 billion of market capitalization.

Some investors, such as insurance companies, view mezzanine as a traditional form of debt. Insurance companies are concerned with the preservation of capital, the consistency of cash flows, and the ability to make timely interest payments. Other investors, such as mezzanine limited partnerships, LBO firms, and commercial banks, focus on the capital appreciation, or equity component of mezzanine debt. Often these firms demand an equity "kicker" be attached to the mezzanine debt. This kicker is usually in the form of equity warrants to purchase stock at a discounted strike price.

Return Expectations for Mezzanine Financing

Mezzanine financing provides a greater risk profile to an investor than senior debt because of its unsecured status, lower credit priority, and equity kicker. Typically, the total return sought by investors in mezzanine financing is in the rage of 15% to 20%.

However, this return range is significantly below that for venture capital and leveraged buyouts. The reduced return reflects a lower risk profile compared to other forms of private equity. The reason is two-fold. First, mezzanine financing does not translate into control of the company compared to a leveraged buyout. Mezzanine financing is much more passive than that of an LBO. Second, mezzanine financing is appropriate for those companies that have a reliable cash flow. This is in contrast to venture capital where the startup company does not have sufficient cash flows to support debt.

The largest piece of the total return is the coupon rate on the mezzanine security; usually 10% to 16%. Furthermore, this coupon payment may be divided between cash payment and payment in kind. The reminder of the upside comes from the equity kicker—either warrants of some other equity conversion.

Exhibit 18.2 presents the returns to mezzanine financing funds over the last 16 years. As can be seen, the returns are quite variable, reflecting the higher risk associated with this type of investment. Although returns are mostly in the low to mid-teens, the returns can be as high as 30%.

However, overall this asset class did not live up to its return expectations. The average return over this period is only about 10%—significantly below the target returns for this asset class.

Mezzanine Debt and the J Curve

In Chapters 16 and 17 we discussed the J curve effect for private equity. Essentially, in the early years of a private equity fund, the fund experiences a negative return because it incurs management fees while invest-

EXHIBIT 18.2   Returns to Mezzanine Debt[a]

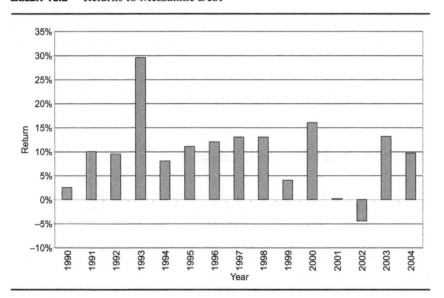

[a] Average = 9.81%, Std. Dev. = 7.79%, Sharpe = 0.64.

ing the fund's capital. It generally takes up to four to five years before the general partner for the private equity fund begins to harvest profits from its initial investments. Until then, the fund experiences a negative cash flow to pay for the assessed management fees.

However, with a mezzanine fund, the J curve effect is not a factor. One of the distinct advantages of mezzanine financing is its immediate cash on cash return. Mezzanine debt bears a coupon that requires twice yearly interest payments to investors. As a result, mezzanine financing funds can avoid the steep negative returns associated with venture capital or leveraged buyout funds.

Mezzanine Compared to Other Forms of Financing

Not only does mezzanine financing fill a gap in a company's capital structure, it also fills a gap in the capital markets. Increasingly, high-yield financing is not available to middle market companies. High-yield issues now tend to start at $400 million and up. The same is true for leveraged loans. Generally, it is large public companies that tap the high yield or leveraged loan market. Conversely, mezzanine financing generally seeks amounts below $400 million.

Mezzanine financing is highly negotiated, and can be tailored to any company's situation. The flipside is that the level of tailoring makes mezzanine debt illiquid. Any trading usually involves a lengthy negotiated process between the company that issued the mezzanine debt to buy back its securities or with a secondary private equity investor. In both cases, mezzanine debt is often sold at a large discount in the secondary market.

In Exhibit 18.3 we compare mezzanine debt to leveraged loans and high-yield debt. Notice that leveraged loans have the most strict debt covenants which leads to greater protection from default but also a lower return. Furthermore, leveraged loans do not contain any type of equity kicker, so they do not share in any upside of the company. A credit rating is also required before a bank will lend credit through a leveraged loan while this is not necessary for mezzanine debt. In addition, leveraged loans typically have a floating interest rate tied to LIBOR while mezzanine debt has a fixed coupon. Finally, mezzanine financing typically has some PIK provision with respect to its coupon payments while leveraged loans never have such a provision.

These are just some of the differences between leveraged loans and mezzanine debt. High-yield debt falls somewhere in between these two forms of financing. Exhibit 18.3 shows the differences between these three types of financing.

EXHIBIT 18.3 A Comparison of Leveraged Loans, Mezzanine Debt and High-Yield Bonds

	Leveraged Loans	High-Yield Bonds	Mezzanine Debt
Seniority	Most senior	Contractual and structural subordination	Lowest priority
Type of security	First lien on assets	Unsecured	Unsecured
Credit rating	Required	Required	Not required
Loan covenants	Extensive	Less Comprehensive	Minimal—typically related only to payment of coupons
Term	5 years	7 to 10 years	4 to 6 years
Amortization	Installments	Bullet Payment	Bullet payment
Coupon type	Cash/Floating	Cash/Fixed	Cash/PIK/Fixed
Coupon rate	LIBOR + 300 to 450	8% to 12%	10% to 16%
Prepayment penalty	Usually none	High—usually the company must pay a call premium	Moderate—sometimes equity conversion is forced
Equity kicker	None	Sometimes	Almost always—usually equity warrants
Recovery if default	60% to 100%	40% to 50%	20% to 30%
Liquidity	High	Low	Minimial

EXAMPLES OF MEZZANINE FINANCING

As noted above, mezzanine financing fills either a gap in a company's financial structure or a gap in the supply of capital in the financial markets. This makes mezzanine financing extremely flexible. The examples below demonstrate this flexibility. Note that while mezzanine financing is mostly the domain of smaller companies in the middle market, large companies are not excluded from its use, as the Hertz Company example demonstrates below.

Mezzanine Financing to Bridge a Gap in Time

Mezzanine financing has three general purposes. First, it can be financing used to bridge a gap in time. This might be a round of financing to get a private company to the IPO stage. In this case, mezzanine financing can either be subordinated debt convertible into equity, or preferred shares, convertible into common equity upon the completion of a successful IPO.

Examples of this time-gap financing include Extricity, Inc. a platform provider for business-to-business relationship management. In May 2000, Extricity raised $50 million in mezzanine financing from a broad group of corporate and financial investors. Within a matter of days after its mezzanine round, Extricity also filed a registration statement for an IPO, but subsequently withdrew its registration statement as the market for IPOs cooled off. However, the mezzanine round of financing was sufficient to get Extricity through the next 10 months until March 2001, when the company was purchased for $168 million by Peregrine Systems Inc., a business-software maker.

Similarly, the Internet company iComs, Inc. raised $20 million in mezzanine financing while awaiting its IPO window of opportunity. The mezzanine debt was structured as subordinated convertible debt plus warrants. This financing was later supplemented by a sale of 14% of the company to Lycos, Inc.

The above examples demonstrate a common use of mezzanine financing in an uncertain economy. The slowdown in the U.S. economy has led to a substantial decrease in IPOs. Initial public offerings declined 86% from the first quarter of 2000 to the first quarter of 2001. The delay in many IPOs drove private companies to seek a mezzanine round of financing, to bridge the time until the company can launch a successful IPO.

Mezzanine financing may also be used to fill a gap in time associated with project finance. Project finance focuses on the completion of a specific corporate project as opposed to general growth or production. For instance, a real estate developer needs to finance the construction of a new office building. Upon completion of the office building, the developer will be able to execute a first mortgage using the completed building as collateral for the loan. However, the bank is unwilling to bear the construction risk and will not provide the mortgage financing until the building is completed. In order to complete the construction process, the developer will seek mezzanine financing to bride the gap of time while the office building is under construction. Then the long-term financing will be received and the mezzanine debt retired.

An example is the $235 million high-yield issue for the construction of an 800 room Hilton Hotel Corporation hotel in Austin, Texas. The construction of this hotel had been delayed several times until financing was finalized in March 2001. U.S. Bancorp Piper Jaffray underwrote the financing for the project that consisted of $100 million in Series A senior debt and $135 million in Series B mezzanine debt. The senior bonds will mature in 2015, 2020, and 2030 and the mezzanine debt can be called sooner.

Another example of time-gap, or project, financing is that of RangeStar Wireless, a telecommunications company. In May 2000, this company announced the completion of a $25 million dollar round of mezzanine financing to complete the development of its Invisible Antenna project.

Mezzanine financing that is used to bridge a gap in time for project financing is usually deployed quickly. There may be less time in which to complete the deal, and due diligence may not be as rigorous. As a result, time-gap mezzanine financing bears more risk and will be priced accordingly, usually with a coupon rate of 12% to 14% with equity kickers that bring the total return up to the 20% to 30% range.[1] Alternatively, mezzanine debt used to finance another round of private capital before an IPO may have more time to complete the due diligence process, but will still be priced expensively commensurate with the considerable risk of a private company.

Mezzanine Financing to Bridge a Gap in the Capital Structure

A second and more common use of mezzanine financing is to bridge a gap in the capital structure of a company. In this case, mezzanine financing is used not because of time constraints but rather because of financing constraints between senior debt and equity. Mezzanine financing provides the layer of capital beyond what secured lenders are willing to provide while minimizing the dilution of a company's outstanding equity.

Mezzanine debt is used to fill the gap between senior debt represented by bank loans, mortgages and senior bonds, and equity. Consequently, mezzanine debt is junior, or subordinated, to the debt of the bank loans, and is typically the last component of debt to be retired.

Under this definition, mezzanine financing is used to fund acquisitions, corporate recapitalizations, or production growth. More generally, mezzanine financing is used whenever the equity component of a transaction is too low to attract senior lenders such as banks and insurance companies. Senior lenders may require a lower debt-to-equity ratio than the borrower is willing to provide. Most borrowers dislike reducing their equity share price through offerings that dilute equity ownership. Consider the following examples.

In 2000, the Indian Group Tata acquired the British organization Tetley Group. The financing package for the acquisition included £60 million of equity, £140 million of senior debt, a vendor loan of £20 million, and £50 million of mezzanine debt in the form of subordinated debt with warrants. Bank lenders were reluctant to loan funds until a mezzanine tranche of financing was in place.

---

[1] See Bailey S. Barnard, "Mezzanine Financing Demystified," *Mergers & Acquisitions Insights* (April 2000).

To highlight the niche nature of mezzanine financing, consider the case of Superior Candy Co., a 45-year old candy company that wanted to acquire a competitor of similar size. The Great Candy Co. agreed to be acquired by Superior for $12 million. Unfortunately, Superior Candy could only obtain $7.7 million from its senior lender. This transaction was too small to attract the attention of traditional Wall Street houses to finance an issue of junk bonds. Fortunately, Superior Candy completed the deal by obtaining the remaining capital from a mezzanine fund in return for issuing subordinated debt with warrants that gave the mezzanine investor less than 20% of the company.[2]

As a final example of how mezzanine financing can be used to plug a gap in a company's capital structure, consider the recapitalization of Elis Group. The company was originally bought out by the LBO firm BC Partners in 1997. In 2000, Goldman Sachs, BNP Paribas, and Credit Agricole Indosuez arranged the Eu1.13 billion refinancing of the buyout that was split into five tranches: a EUR 400 million seven-year term loan at 200 basis points over LIBOR, a EUR 50 million seven-year term loan at 250 basis points over LIBOR, a EUR 400 million eight-year term loan at 250 basis points over LIBOR, a EUR 50 million seven-year revolver, and a USD 130 million 10-year mezzanine tranche that was priced at 450 basis points over LIBOR. To demonstrate the flexibility of mezzanine financing, this layer of debt was priced in U.S. dollars to encourage U.S. mezzanine investors to participate.

To illustrate the equity-like nature of mezzanine financing, in a subsequent IPO of Elis Group stock, the mezzanine tranche was taken out before any of the senior EUR 1 billion senior debt. Simply stated, one form of equity (mezzanine) was replaced with another (common shares).

Mezzanine Financing to Bridge a Gap in an LBO

The third popular use of mezzanine debt is a tranche of financing in many LBO deals. For instance, LBO target companies may not have the ability to access the bond markets right away, particularly if the target company was an operating division of a larger entity. It may not have a separate financial history to satisfy SEC requirements for a public sale of its bonds. Consequently, a mezzanine tranche may be necessary to complete the financing of the buyout deal. Alternatively, a buyout candidate may not have enough physical assets to provide the necessary collateral in a buyout transaction. Finally, bank lenders may be hesitant to lend if there is not sufficient equity committed to the transaction. Mezzanine debt is often the solution to solve these LBO financing problems.

---

[2] Lawrence M. Levine, "Filling a Financing Shortfall with Mezzanine Capital," *Mergers & Acquisitions* (November–December 1998).

In Europe, mezzanine debt is an especially popular form of LBO financing because of the disclosure requirements associated with a bond offering. Most buyout firms choose the mezzanine financing route to bypass the bond markets and keep the company private. However, this usually means paying coupon rates of 17% to 18% in Europe plus providing equity kickers in the form of warrants.[3]

Consider the buyout of U.K. food group Rank Hovis McDougall. In early 2001, Rank Hovis McDougall was bought out by Doughty Hanson in a £1.139 billion LBO. The buyout included a 10-year mezzanine tranche of £245 million. JP Morgan Chase subsequently restructured the buyout financing to include £600 million of asset securitization, £300 million of senior debt, and £200 million of mezzanine financing.

The use of mezzanine financing to complete an LBO deal is not limited to European transactions. It is also popular in the United States. Consider the $750 million of CB Richard Ellis Services Inc., the largest commercial property broker in the United States. In February 2001, the company agreed to be bought out by an investor group led by Blum Capital Partners. The purchase price was financed with a combination of about 63% debt and the remainder, equity. Blum Capital received a commitment from Credit Suisse First Boston and DLJ Investment Funding Inc. for debt financing that included a $400 million tranche of senior debt and a $75 million tranche of mezzanine debt.

The mezzanine tranche often reflects a layer of quasi equity to banks in an LBO deal. Usually, the mezzanine tranche receives an equity kicker to solidify its status as "equity." Consider the leveraged buyout of Buffets Inc. by the private equity firm Caxton-Iseman Capital in July 2000. CSFB Mezzanine Club contributed $55 million in mezzanine debt in the form of senior subordinated notes plus warrants. Similarly, the buyout of Wilmar Industries, Inc. by Partheon Investors in June 2000 contained a $40 million mezzanine tranche in the form of subordinated notes plus warrants in addition to senior lending of $133 million. In each case, an equity kicker was added to the mezzanine tranche to reflect the equity-like nature of the financing.

As another recent example of mezzanine financing, consider the leveraged buyout of the Hertz Corporation. In 2005 a consortium of private equity firms including the Carlyle Group and Clayton Dubilier & Rice engineered a $15 billion leveraged buyout of Hertz from the Ford Motor Company. This was a highly competitive deal that pitted another consortium comprised of the Blackstone Group, T. H. Lee Partners and Texas Pacific Group against the winning bidders.

---

[3] See Mairin Burns, "High Yield is Back in Europe but Mezz Debt Lives On," *Buyouts* (February 5, 2001).

To finance this leveraged buyout, a full spectrum of leveraged loans, high-yield bonds and mezzanine debt was used. Given the brand recognition of Hertz, its global competitive position (number one in rental car sales), its stable cash flow, and the backing of two well-established private equity firms, banks and investors were keen to finance this deal. The buyout firms negotiated $3.85 billion of senior loans broken down into a $1.7 billion seven-year term loan, a $300 million delayed draw-term loan, a $250 million letter of credit facility, and a $1.6 billion asset based, revolving credit facility. These loans were priced in the range of 2.25% over LIBOR—an extremely competitive rate for Hertz and below the initial expectations of about 2.75% over LIBOR that had been expected. Next Hertz sold $1.8 billion of senior notes at a yield of 8.875% maturing in 2014, and 225 euro-worth of senior notes at 7.875% maturing in 2014. Hertz then sold $600 million of subordinated notes due in 2016 at a coupon rate of 10.5%. This last tranche of financing was the mezzanine tranche, with a coupon rate a bit below what mezzanine financing normally seeks, but given the strength of interest to purchase Hertz debt, not surprising. Initial expectations for Hertz's lower tranches of debt were expected to fetch a rate of 11.25%. Exhibit 18.4 shows the debt financing for the Hertz LBO.

EXHIBIT 18.4   Debt Financing for the Hertz Company LBO

USD 1.7 Billion seven-year term loan at LIBOR + 225

USD 300 million delayed draw-term loan at LIBOR + 225

USD 250 letter of credit at LIBOR + 225

USD 1.6 billion asset-based, revolving credit at LIBOR + 2%

USD 1.8 billion of eight-year senior notes at 8.875%

EUR 225 million of eight-year senior notes at 7.875%

USD 600 million of 10-year subordinated notes at 10.5%

Mezzanine Finance in Real Estate

Mezzanine financing is a popular vehicle in real estate financing. Again, mezzanine financing plugs the gap between the senior mortgage from a bank lender and the equity contributed by the owner of the real estate. Unlike mezzanine financing in a corporation, real estate mezzanine financing typically does not have an equity kicker.

In real estate, banks are generally not willing to lend more than 60% on a loan to value ratio. This leaves considerable room for mezzanine to fill the gap between the equity of the project and the senior bank mortgage.

As an example, in 2005 the owner of a 500,000 square-foot distribution center outside of Indianapolis needed about $15 million to build out the remaining space in its warehouse. The property was an essential parts distribution hub for the Ford Motor Company and needed to expand to handle the increased traffic through the distribution center.

Capital Source Finance based in Maryland structured a loan package that included $11.1 million senior secured loan, a $1.5 million mezzanine loan, and the owner of the distribution center kicked in $2.2 million. Overall, the combined senior and mezzanine loans provided investors with a yield of 10%.

INVESTORS IN MEZZANINE DEBT

In the section above, we reviewed the uses of mezzanine debt. In this section we review the investors in mezzanine debt. In addition, we consider the advantages of mezzanine financing to both the investor and the issuer.

Mezzanine Funds

Mezzanine funds must pay attention to the same securities laws as hedge funds, venture capital funds, and buyout funds. This means that mezzanine funds must ensure that they fall within either the 3(c)(1) or the 3(c)(7) exemptions of the Investment Company Act of 1940. These "safe harbor" provisions ensure that mezzanine funds do not have to adhere to the filing, disclosure, record keeping, and reporting requirements as do mutual funds.

There are two key distinctions between venture capital funds and mezzanine funds. The first is the return expectations. Mezzanine funds seek total rates of return in the 15% to 20% range. Compare this to LBO funds that seek returns in the mid-to-high twenties and venture capital funds that seek returns in excess of 30%. This puts mezzanine funds at the lower end of the private equity risk spectrum.

EXHIBIT 18.5   Risk-and-Return Spectrum for Private Equity

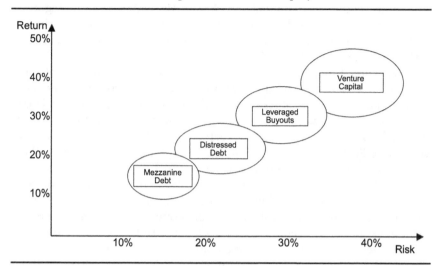

Exhibit 18.5 shows the risk and return spectrum for the four basic forms of private equity: venture capital, leveraged buyouts, distressed debt (discussed in the next chapter) and mezzanine financing. Mezzanine financing is the least risky of the private equity strategies. Part of this comes from the fact that mezzanine debt is not subject to J curve effect unlike venture capital or leveraged buyouts, and is not faced with a distressed situation like distressed debt.

For example, senior bank debt in a private equity transaction is usually priced at 200 to 250 basis points over LIBOR, while mezzanine financing usually bears a coupon rate of 400 to 600 basis points over LIBOR. In addition, mezzanine financing will contain some form of equity appreciation such as warrants or the ability to convert into common stock that raises the total return towards 20%.

Mezzanine financing is the most expensive form of debt because it is the last to be repaid. It ranks at the bottom of the creditor totem pole, just above equity. As a result, it is expected to earn a rate of return only slightly less than common equity. Exhibit 18.2 demonstrates that rates of return are quite favorable—generally in the 14% to 15% range—but have been as high as 30% in any given year. Given the highly leveraged nature of companies that use mezzanine debt, the return can, in fact, resemble that of equity returns.

Second, mezzanine funds are staffed with different expertise than a venture capital fund. Most venture capital funds have staff with heavy technology-related experience including former senior executives of software, semiconductor, and Internet companies. In contrast, mezzanine funds tend to have financial professionals, experienced in negotiating "equity kickers" to be added on to the mezzanine debt offering as well as trying to ensure the most favorable credit terms to get any shot at the assets on the balance sheet of the creditor.

Mezzanine funds have not attracted the flow of investor capital compared to venture capital funds or leveraged buyout funds. However, mezzanine funds have enjoyed steady growth throughout the 1990s. In 2003, the five largest mezzanine funds were DLJ Investment Partners at $1.6 billion, TCW/Crescent Mezzanine Partners III at $1.2 billion, Blackstone Mezzanine Partners at $1.1 billion, GS Mezzanine Partners at $1 billion and TCW/Crescent Mezzanine Partners II at $0.81 billion.[4] Note that the size of these funds is considerably smaller than the gargantuan ($10 billion plus) of leveraged buyout funds. This reflects that mezzanine financing is distinctly a middle market phenomenon and cannot support mega funds of the type commonly associated with leveraged buyouts.

Another reason why mezzanine financing has not attracted as much capital is that with a robust economy throughout most of the 1990s, mezzanine debt was not a necessary component of many transactions. Second, mezzanine financing tends to be small, generally in the $20 million to $300 million range. Mezzanine debt, while it yields greater returns than junk bonds, cannot compete with the returns earned by venture capitalists and leveraged buyout funds.

Mezzanine funds look for businesses that have a high potential for growth and earnings, but do not have a sufficient cash flow to receive full funding from banks or other senior creditors. Banks may be unwilling to lend because of a short operating history or a high debt to equity ratio. Mezzanine funds look for companies that, over the next four to seven years, can repay the mezzanine debt through a debt refinancing, an initial equity offering, or an acquisition.

Mezzanine funds are risk lenders. This means that in a liquidation of the company, mezzanine investors expect little or no recovery of their principal. Mezzanine debt is rarely secured. As the last rung of the financing ladder (see the Hertz example, above) it is often viewed as a form of equity by the more senior lenders. Consequently, mezzanine investors must assess investment opportunities outside of conventional banking parameters. Existing collateral and short-term cash flow are less of a consideration. Instead, mezzanine investors carefully review the management team and its business plan to assess the likelihood that future growth will be achieved by the issuing company. In sum, similar to stockholders, mezzanine debt investors assume the risk of the company's success or failure.

---

[4] "Mezzanine Debt—Another Level to Consider," *Bank of America* (August 2003).

Investors in mezzanine funds are generally pension funds, endowments, and foundations. These investors do not have the internal infrastructure or expertise to invest directly in the mezzanine market. Therefore, they enter this alternative investment strategy as limited partners through a mezzanine fund. Mezzanine funds also tend to reflect a similar fee structure as venture capital and LBO funds: a management fee in the 1% to 2% range and generally, a profit sharing fee of 20%.

Similar to hedge funds, venture capital funds and LBO funds, mezzanine funds are managed by a general partner who has full investment discretion. Many mezzanine funds are managed by merchant banks who have experience with gap financing or by mezzanine professionals who previously worked in the mezzanine departments of insurance companies and banks.

Other Mezzanine Lenders

Pension and endowment funds are not the only investors in mezzanine debt. The high coupon rates plus the chance for some upside potential also appeals to more conservative investors.

Insurance Companies

As previously noted, insurance companies are a major source of mezzanine financing. They are a natural provider of mezzanine debt because the duration of their liabilities (life insurance polices and annuities) are best matched with longer-term debt instruments.

These investors take more of a fixed income approach and place a high value on the scheduled repayment of principal. Insurance companies are more concerned with a higher coupon payment than with the total return represented by equity warrants. Therefore, insurance companies act more like traditional lenders than like equity investors. They provide mezzanine financing to higher quality credit names and emphasize the preservation versus appreciation of capital.

Traditional Senior Lenders

Interestingly, banks and other providers of senior secured debt often participate in mezzanine financing. This financing takes the form of "stretch" financing where a bank lends more money than it believes is prudent given existing assets. This excess advance of debt beyond the collateral value of a company's business assets is the "stretch" part of the financing, and is often called an "airball."[5]

---

[5] See Bailey Barnard, "Mezzanine Financing Demystified."

Stretch financing may be provided, for instance, when an LBO firm agrees to put up more equity for a buyout deal. Generally, the amount looked for is 30% or more equity in the LBO. In addition, the senior lender may ask for an equity kicker such as warrants to compensate it for stretching its financing beyond the assets available.

Traditional Venture Capital Firms

As the economy has softened, venture capital firms have looked for ways to maintain their stellar returns. Additionally, the large flows of capital into venture funds have created the need for venture capital funds to expand their investment horizons. As a result, there has been a greater interest in mezzanine financing.

Consider the example of Metrika Inc, a privately owned developer and manufacturer of quantitative medical devices. In April 2001, this company raised $26 million in mezzanine financing to scale up production and market Metrika's quantitative testing device of hemoglobin A1c, a measure of long-term glucose control for people with diabetes. The financing was led by Oak Hill Capital Partners, L.P., a private equity partnership founded by Robert M. Bass and Sutter Hill Ventures. Oak Hill Capital invests across a wide variety of private equity transactions. However, Sutter Hill Ventures is one of Silicon Valley's original venture capital firms. Founded in 1962, Sutter Hill Ventures generally provides venture capital financing for technology and health care based startup companies.

As the example above demonstrates, the lines between mezzanine financing and different forms of private equity can become blurred. With respect to pre-IPO companies, it is difficult to distinguish where venture capital ends and mezzanine financing begins. Also, as we noted above, mezzanine financing can be used as the last leg in the capital structure of a startup company before it goes public. This bridge financing allows the company to clean up its balance sheet before its IPO.

Advantages of Mezzanine Debt to the Investor

Mezzanine debt is a hybrid. It has debtlike components but usually provides for some form of equity appreciation. This appeals to investors who are more conservative but like to have some spice in their portfolios.

High Equity-Like Returns

The high returns to mezzanine debt compared to senior debt appeals to traditional fixed income investors who look for a little extra yield. Mezzanine debt typically has a coupon rate that is 200 to 300 basis points over that of senior secured debt (in the Hertz example it was 167.5 basis points above the senior bonds). Additionally, given an insurance company's long-term investment horizon, it may be less concerned with short-term earnings fluctuations.

Furthermore, mezzanine debt often has an equity kicker, typically in the form of warrants. These warrants may have a strike price as low as $0.01 per share. The amount of warrants included is inversely proportional to the coupon rate. The higher the coupon rate, the fewer the warrants that need to be issued.

Nonetheless, the investor receives both a high coupon payment plus participation in the upside of the company should it achieve its growth potential. The equity component can be significant, representing up to 5% to 20% of the outstanding equity of the company. For this reason, mezzanine debt is often viewed as an investment in the company as opposed to an unsecured lien on assets.

Priority of Payment
Although mezzanine debt is generally not secured by collateral, it still ranks higher than equity and other unsecured creditors. Therefore, mezzanine debt is senior to trade creditors.

Schedule of Repayment
Like senior secured debt, mezzanine debt usually has a repayment schedule. This schedule may not start for several years as senior debt is paid off, but it provides the certainty of when a return of capital is expected.

Instant Returns
Unlike other forms of private equity, mezzanine debt provides instant returns through the coupon payment on the debt. This provides investors with a high level of current return instead of waiting for returns along the J curve.

Board Representation
A subordinated lender generally expects to be considered an equity partner. In some cases, mezzanine lenders may request board observation rights. However, in other cases, the mezzanine lender may take a seat on the board of directors with full voting rights.

Restrictions on the Borrower
Although mezzanine debt is typically unsecured, it still may come with restrictions on the borrower. The mezzanine lender may have the right to approve or disapprove of additional debt, acquisitions made by the borrower, changes in the management team, and the payment of dividends.

Advantages to the Company/Borrower

Mezzanine debt is a tool for plugging holes in a company's business plan. It can be shaped and molded to meet the company's business needs. Its malleability appeals to corporate issuers.

Flexibility

There are no set terms to mezzanine financing. Subordinated debt comes in all shapes, maturities, and sizes. The structure of mezzanine debt can be as flexible as needed to accommodate the parties involved. For example, the repayment of principal is usually deferred for several years and can be tailored to fit the borrowers cash flow projections.

Semiequity

Mezzanine lenders focus on the total return of the investment over the life of the debt. Therefore, they are less concerned with collateral or short-term earnings fluctuations. In fact, subordinated unsecured debt resembles a senior class of equity, and most senior lenders consider a company to have strengthened its balance sheet by adding this layer of capital.

Lengthening of Maturity

The borrower can improve its cash flow by lengthening the maturity of the debt repayment associated with mezzanine financing. This is because the payback of the mezzanine debt is often delayed until the fifth or sixth year, and is usually paid with a bullet payment.

No Collateral

The borrower does not have to pledge any collateral for mezzanine debt.

Pay in Kind

As discussed previously, mezzanine debt coupons are often structured so that some form of the coupon is not required to be paid in cash but can be paid in kind. This means that the holder of the mezzanine debt receives additional issuances of debt as part of the coupon payment on the debt. This can provide the issuer of the mezzanine debt considerable flexibility if there is a crunch on the cash flows of the company.

Less Equity Dilution

The borrower has not immediately diluted the equity of its outstanding shares. True, mezzanine debt almost always comes with some form of equity kicker that will eventually dilute the number of outstanding common shares. However, this "kicker" may not kick in for several years, affording the company a chance to implement its business plan and improve its share price before it is subject to dilution. Additionally, the company can refinance the mezzanine debt at a later date with traditional bonds before the equity kickers kick in.

Cheaper than Common Equity

Even though senior lenders may consider mezzanine financing to be a form of equity, it does not carry all the risks of equity. Therefore, it does not need to yield the same total return as expected by shareholders.

Exhibit 18.6 shows a typical term sheet for a mezzanine debt offering.

Negotiations with Senior Creditors

The subordination of mezzanine debt is typically accomplished in an agreement with the company's existing creditors. The agreement is usually called an "intercreditor agreement." The intercreditor agreement may be negotiated separately between the senior creditors and the mezzanine investor, or it may be incorporated directly into the loan agreement between the mezzanine investor and the company. In either case,

EXHIBIT 18.6   Hypothetical Terms for a Mezzanine Debt Offering

Company	Company XYZ
Debt amount	$50 million
Security on debt	None
Interest rate	12% coupon with up to 4% of coupon as PIK
Maturity	6 years
Amortization	Six-year bullet
Subordination	Subordinated to bank loans and senior notes
Conversion rights	None
Warrants	10 warrants per $1,000 face value detachable and exercisable at $0.50
Exercise period	3 years from the date of issuance until maturity
Tag along rights	Holders of warrants have the right to participate in any sale of common stock by the issuer
Drag along rights	Company may require debt holders to sell their warrants in the sale of a controlling interest of the company
Board representation	None
Registration	None—sold as an exempt offering under Rule 144A of the Securities Act of 1933

this agreement places certain restrictions on both the senior creditor and the mezzanine investor.

Subordination

The subordination may be either a blanket subordination or a springing subordination.[6] A *blanket subordination* prevents any payment of principal or interest to the mezzanine investor until the senior debt is fully repaid. A *springing subordination* occurs when the mezzanine investor receives payments while the senior debt is outstanding. However, if a default occurs or a covenant is violated, the subordination "springs" up to stop all payments to the mezzanine investor until the default is cured or fully repaid.

Acceleration

The violation of any covenant may result in the senior debt lender accelerating the senior loan. This means that the senior lender can declare the senior debt due and payable immediately. This typically forces a default and allows the senior lender to enforce the collateral security.

Drawdown

The order of drawdown is important to senior lenders. Because senior lenders often view mezzanine capital as a form of equity financing, they will require that mezzanine debt be fully drawn before lending the senior debt.

Restrictions to Amending Credit Facility Documents

Intercreditor agreements usually restrict amendments to the credit facility so that the terms of the intercreditor agreement cannot be circumvented by new agreements between the individual lenders and the borrower.

Assignment

Senior lenders typically restrict the rights of the mezzanine investor to assign its interests to a third party. Generally, senior lenders will allow an assignment providing the assignee signs a new intercreditor agreement with the senior lender.

Insurance Proceeds

Mezzanine lenders typically want any insurance proceeds to be deployed to purchase new assets for the borrower and not to repay senior debt.

---

[6] See Chapman Tripp and Sheffield Young, "Mezzanine Finance: One Person's Ceiling is Another Person's Floor," *Finance Law Focus* (November 1998).

The reason is the equity-like nature of mezzanine financing. Mezzanine investors consider their debt to be a long-term investment in the company where a significant return component depends upon the operations of the company appreciating in value.

Takeout Provisions

A takeout provision allows the mezzanine investor to purchase the senior debt once it has been repaid to a certain level. This is one of the most important provisions in an intercreditor agreement and goes to the heart of mezzanine investing. By taking out the senior debt, the mezzanine investor becomes the most senior level of financing in the company, and in fact, can take control of the company. At this point, the mezzanine investor usually converts its debt into equity (either through convertible bonds or warrants) and becomes the largest shareholder of the company.

From the above discussion, it can be seen that intercreditor agreements are a matter of give and take between senior secured lenders and mezzanine investors. Mezzanine investors are willing to grant senior lenders certain provisions that protect the capital at risk of the senior lenders. In return, mezzanine investors have the ability to buyout the senior debt and then assert their equity rights in the company.

CONCLUSION

In this chapter, we identified a form of debt investing that is really a variation on private equity investing. Mezzanine financing is the epoxy of the financing world. It fits in where traditional debt and equity cannot. Like epoxy, mezzanine financing is thoroughly flexible. Its shape and size is dependent upon the specifics of the financing needed. In addition, mezzanine can strengthen a debtor company's balance sheet, providing the "glue" between debt and equity.

Borrowers like mezzanine capital because it provides an inexpensive way to raise money without immediately diluting the outstanding equity of the company. Investors, on the other hand, like the high yields offered by mezzanine debt plus the ability to share in some of the appreciated value of the debtor company. Both like the ability to tailor mezzanine financing to the needs of the borrower and the investment requirements of the lender. Like epoxy, mezzanine debt can be twisted into many different shapes and sizes.

The returns to mezzanine however, are decidedly mixed. Despite target return ranges of 15% to 20% and presence of equity kickers, the average mezzanine fund over the last 15 years only achieved a rate of return of 10%. This return exceeded U.S. treasury bonds but was less than the stock market—generally the target range for mezzanine debt.

CHAPTER 19

Debt as Private Equity Part II: Distressed Debt

D istressed debt investing is the practice of purchasing the debt of troubled companies. These companies may have already defaulted on their debt or may be on the brink of default. Additionally, distressed debt may be that of a company seeking bankruptcy protection. Now a company seeking protection from its creditors does not seem like a very tasty investment, but beneath the distress of the company investment opportunities exist. Like the other forms of private equity previously discussed, this form of investing requires a longer-term horizon and the ability to accept the lack of liquidity for a security where no trading market may exist.

Similar to mezzanine debt discussed in the previous chapter, the returns to distressed debt are less dependent upon the overall performance of the stock market. This is because the value of the debt of a distressed or bankrupt company is more likely to rise and fall with the fortunes of the individual company. In particular, the company's negotiations with its creditors will have a greater impact on the value of the company's debt than with the movement of the general economy.

The key to distressed debt investing is to recognize that the term "distressed" has two meanings. First, it means that the issuer of the debt is troubled—its liabilities may exceed its assets—or it may be unable to meet its debt service and interest payments as they become due. Therefore, distressed debt investing almost always means that some workout, turnaround, or bankruptcy solution must be implemented for the bonds to appreciate in value.

Second, "distressed" refers to the price of the bonds. Distressed debt often trades for pennies on the dollar. This affords a savvy investor the opportunity to make a killing if she can identify a company with a viable business plan but a short-term cash flow problem.

In this chapter we begin with a short discussion on the growth of the distressed debt marketplace. We then describe the nature of investors that seek value in distressed debt. Next we provide a brief overview of the bankruptcy process and how this can influence the value of distressed debt. Then we examine the different ways that distressed debt can be used to generate superior returns either through an equity stake in the company or through more opportunistic methods.

THE GROWTH OF THE DISTRESSED DEBT MARKET

Exhibit 19.1 presents the face value of all distressed portfolios from 1990 to 2003. As can be seen, the distressed market has doubled during this time period. Several factors influenced this growth.

First, many more types of commercial loans are available for resale. In addition to the traditional industrial loans that are routinely bought and sold, there are many new types of loan portfolios that include auto deficiencies; credit card paper; medical and healthcare receivables; personal loans; retail sales agreements; insurance premium deficiencies; and aviation, boat, and recreational vehicle loans.

Second, many more banks and other lenders are managing their assets from a global portfolio perspective as opposed to an account level basis. Proactive risk management techniques are being applied that prune or

EXHIBIT 19.1 Size of the Defaulted and Distressed Debt Market

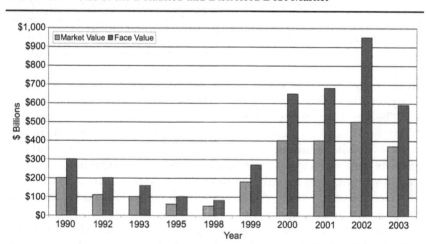

Source: Dr. Edward Altman, "Defaulted Bond & Bank Loan Markets and Outlook," GFA Seminar, NYU Stern School of Business, March 29, 2004.

"groom" the portfolio to achieve a desired risk and return balance. The result is that banks are selling nonperforming and subperforming loans in the market at attractive discounts to get them off their books.

Third, debt loads continue to grow and, with it, the level of lower quality debt is also increasing. Exhibit 19.2 shows the growth of low quality debt issuance over the period 1993 to 2005. Notice that during the U.S. recession of 2001 to 2002, the percentage of low quality debt decreased significantly, only to pick up during the growth years of 2003 to 2005.

This relationship is important to note because there has been an historical relationship between the issuance of high-yield bonds in one year and the incidence of bond defaults a few years later. During the recession of 1990 and 1991, default rates of corporate bonds were 10% each year. This lead to a tightening of credit standards by banks, rating agencies, and investors. Consequently, post the 1990–1991 recession, bond defaults declined significantly both due to an upbeat U.S. economy, but also because of tighter credit standards. However, bond issuance rose significantly in the late 1990s based on "irrational exuberance" resulting in an overabundance of low quality debt that quickly became distressed debt in 2001 to 2002. The reader can see now that a new generation of distressed debt is being incubated with the high level of low-quality debt issued. All that is needed is a slow down in economic growth to transform this low quality debt to distressed status.

EXHIBIT 19.2   Low Quality Debt as a Percentage of Total High-Yield Bonds

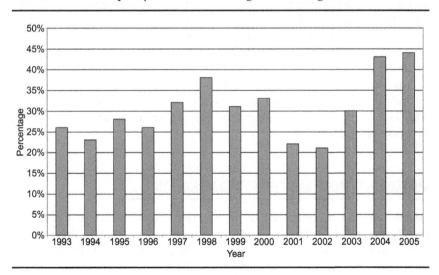

Data gathered from Standard and Poor's.

EXHIBIT 19.3   Annual Defaults of Investment Grade and Subinvestment Grade
Bonds

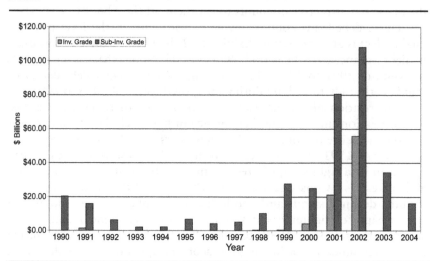

Source: Moody's Investors Service.

Fourth, the U.S. robust economy through most of the 1990s spawned thousand of new companies, not all of which were successful. This also added to the supply of distressed debt. These new companies were prime candidates for the distressed debt market during the recession of 2001 and 2002. However, it was not just subinvestment grade companies that officially became distressed credits during the last recession, many investment grade companies also experienced some form of distress of payment default. Exhibit 19.3 provides the annual amount of defaulted bonds for the period 1990 to 2004. Notice that during recessionary periods (1990 to 1991 and 2001 to 2002) distressed debt levels rise. This is a key point: Distressed debt players are most active during the low points in the economic cycle.

VULTURE INVESTORS AND HEDGE FUND MANAGERS

Distressed debt investors are often referred to as "vulture investors," or just "vultures" because they pick the bones of underperforming companies. They buy the debt of troubled companies including subordinated debt, junk bonds, bank loans, and obligations to suppliers. Their investment plan is to buy the distressed debt at a fraction of its face value and then seek improvement of the company.

Sometimes this debt is used as a way to gain an equity investment stake in the company as the vultures agree to forgive the debt they own in return for stock in the company. Other times, the vultures may help the troubled company to get on its feet, thus earning a significant return as the value of their distressed debt recovers in value. Still other times distressed debt buyers help impatient creditors to cut their losses and wipe a bad debt off their books. The vulture, in return, waits patiently for the company to correct itself and for the value of the distressed debt to recover.

There is no standard model for distressed debt investing, each distressed situation requires a unique approach and solution. As a result, distressed debt investing is mostly company selection. There is a low covariance with the general stock market.

The returns for distressed debt investing can be very rewarding. Distressed debt obligations generally trade at levels that yield a total return of 20% or higher. For example, during the last economic recession an estimated 15% to 20% of all leveraged bank debt loans traded at 80 cents on the dollar or less.[1]

Exhibit 19.4 presents the year-by-year returns to distressed investing over the period 1991 to 2005. As can be seen, these returns can exceed 70% in any given year. The average annual return over this time was 14%.

EXHIBIT 19.4   Returns to Distressed Debt[a]

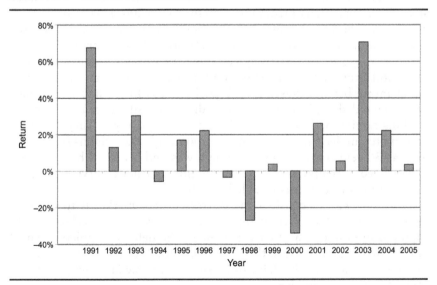

[a] Average = 13.98%, Std. Dev.= 28.72%, Sharpe = 0.32.

---

[1] See Riva D. Atlas, "Company in Trouble? They're Waiting," *New York Times* 21 January 2001.

DISTRESSED DEBT IS AN INEFFICIENT AND SEGMENTED MARKET

One reason that the distressed debt market is attractive to vulture and other investors is that it is an inefficient market. First, distressed debt is not publicly traded like stocks. Furthermore, most distressed bonds were issued in a private offering under Rule 144A of the Securities Act of 1933, which allows companies to sell their bonds directly to institutional investors instead of retail investors. These bonds lack liquidity from the outset, and what little liquidity exists dries up even more when the company becomes distressed. The lack of liquidity leads to bonds trading at steep discounts to their true value.

A second reason that the distressed debt market is inefficient is that it is a segmented market. Segmented markets occur when certain classes of investors "deselect" themselves from the market. For example, many pension funds are banned by their charters from investing in below investment grade debt. So when a company becomes distressed, the fund must sell the bonds regardless of their true value, often at depressed prices. Another form of segmentation occurs with banks. Banks are in the business of lending credit, not the tedious work out process of a bankruptcy situation. Consequently, they may sell their nonperforming loans at prices that offer a considerable discount to vulture investors who have greater experience at working out a plan of reorganization for a company. Finally, trade creditors are in the business of producing goods, not managing a distressed debt portfolio. They also may sell their claims at discount prices.

Take the example of Barney's clothing stores. This is one of the most successful brand names in retail clothing with shops that sell high-end merchandise beyond most people's pocketbook. In the late 1990s, Barney's expanded rapidly leading to a distressed situation in which the clothing retailer had overextended itself. Subsequently, Barney's filed for bankruptcy under Chapter 11. At that point, its trade claims sold for as little as 30 cents on the dollar. Barney's was and is a solid business that experienced a temporary distress situation. Barney's survived and its trade claims subsequently doubled in value.

Another way to consider the distressed debt market is to examine recovery rates. Once a company becomes distressed or declares bankruptcy it does not mean that the value of the debt is completely wiped out. In almost all instances, there is some amount of recovery value. Not the full face value of the debt, to be sure, but some amount is typically offered to the debt holder.

Exhibit 19.5 demonstrates the three-year cumulative default rate and recovery rates for both bonds and bank loans. Bank loans are typically senior to bond financing in a company's capital structure. This is reflected

EXHIBIT 19.5   Recovery Rates for Corporate Bonds and Bank Loans

Rating	Bonds			Loans		
	Default Rate	Recovery Rate	Loss Rate	Default Rate	Recovery Rate	Loss Rate
Baa	1.60%	37.40%	1.00%	1.60%	49.70%	8.00%
Ba	5.30%	15.40%	4.50%	10.00%	69.60%	3.10%
B	21.10%	23.30%	16.20%	24.30%	70.30%	7.20%
Caa to C	51.70%	22.30%	40.10%	59.30%	66.00%	20.20%

in the recovery rate for bank loans compared to corporate bonds—the recovery rate is generally twice as great for bank loans as corporate bonds.

DISTRESSED DEBT AND BANKRUPTCY

Distressed debt investing and the bankruptcy process are inextricably intertwined. Many distressed debt investors purchase the debt while the borrowing company is currently in the throes of bankruptcy. Other investors purchase the debt before a company enters into bankruptcy proceedings with the expectation of gaining control of the company. In either case a brief summary of Chapter 11 Bankruptcy is appropriate to understanding distressed debt investing.

Overview of Chapter 11

Chapter 11 of the U.S. Bankruptcy Code recognizes the corporation as a going concern.[2] It affords a troubled company protection from its creditors while the company attempts to work through its operational problems. Only the debtor company can file for protection under Chapter 11.

Generally, under a Chapter 11 bankruptcy, the debtor company proposes a plan of reorganization that describes how creditors and shareholders are to be treated under the new business plan. The claimants in each class of creditors are entitled to vote on the plan. If all impaired classes of security holders vote in favor of the plan, the bankruptcy court will conduct a confirmation hearing. If all requirements of the bankruptcy code are met, the plan is confirmed and a newly reorganized company will emerge from bankruptcy protection.

The process of Chapter 11 Bankruptcy is illustrated in Exhibit 19.6.

---

[2] See 11 U.S.C. sections 101 and sequence.

EXHIBIT 19.6   An Overview of the Chapter 11 Bankruptcy Process

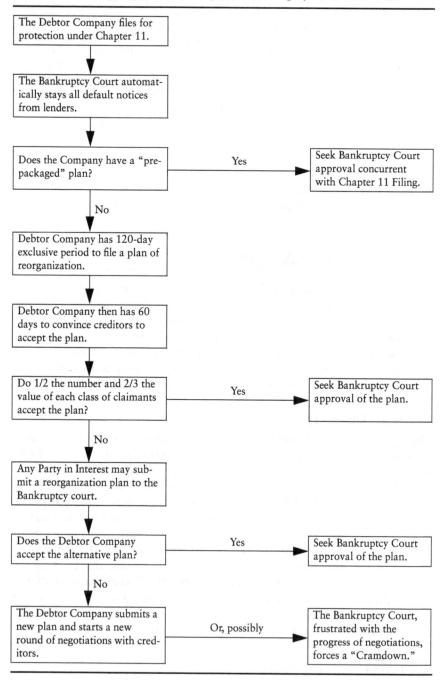

Classification of Claims

Under the bankruptcy code, a reorganization plan may place a claim in a particular class only if such claim is substantially similar to the other claims in that class. For instance, all issues of subordinated debt by a company would constitute one class of creditors under a bankruptcy plan. Similarly, all secured bank loans (usually the most senior of creditor claims) are usually grouped together as one class of creditors. Finally, at the bottom of the pile is common equity, the last class of claimants in a bankruptcy.

Plan of Reorganization

The debtor has an exclusive right to file a plan of reorganization within 120 days of seeking Chapter 11 bankruptcy protection.[3] If the debtor company files a plan during this 120-day window, it has another 60 days to lobby its creditors to accept the plan. During this time (120 days plus 60 days) no other party in interest may file a competing reorganization plan.[4]

After the exclusive period ends, any claimant may file a reorganization plan with the bankruptcy court. At this point the gloves come off and senior and subordinated creditors can petition the bankruptcy court to have their reorganization plan accepted.

This is the interesting part of a bankruptcy process and it can become very acrimonious. In the Federated/Macy's case discussed below, the negotiations became so intense that the bankruptcy court appointed Cyrus Vance, the former U.S. Secretary of State, to mediate the discussions.

A plan is accepted when all classes of claimants vote in favor of the plan. This is an important point because any one class of creditors can block a debtor's plan of reorganization.

Prepackaged Bankruptcy Filing

Sometimes a debtor company agrees in advance with its creditors on a plan of organization before it formerly files for protection under Chapter 11. Creditors usually agree to make concessions up front in return for equity in the reorganized company. The company then files with the bankruptcy court, submits its already negotiated plan of reorganization, and quickly emerges with a new structure. The discussion of Loews Cinemas later in this chapter is an example of a prepackaged Chapter 11 filing.

Voting within a Class

To constitute an acceptance of a plan of reorganization either (1) the class must be completely unimpaired by the plan (i.e., the class will be

---

[3] See 11 U.S. C., section 1121(b).

[4] However, the bankruptcy court may increase or reduce this exclusive period "for cause."

paid in full) or (2) one half in number and two-thirds in dollar amount of claims in the class must vote in favor of the reorganization plan.

All claims within a class must receive the same treatment. If the members of a class vote in favor of a reorganization less than unanimously, and any dissenting claimants in the class receive at least what they would have obtained in a Chapter 7 Liquidation plan, the dissenters are bound to receive the treatment under the reorganization plan. The reason is that the dissenters are no worse off than they would be under a liquidation of the company, and may be better off if the reorganized company is successful.

Blocking Position

A single creditor can block a plan of reorganization if it holds one-third of the dollar amount of any class of claimants. Recall, that acceptance of a plan is usually predicated on a vote of each class of security holders, which requires support of two-thirds of the dollar amount of the claims in each class of creditors. Therefore, a single investor can obtain a blocking position by purchasing one-third of the debt in any class. A blocking position will force the debtor company to negotiate with the blocking creditor.

The Cramdown

Under Section 1129(b) of the bankruptcy code, a reorganization plan may be confirmed over the objection of any impaired class that votes against it so long as the plan (1) does not unfairly discriminate against the member of that class, and (2) is fair and equitable with respect to the members of that class.[5] This provision of the bankruptcy court is called the *cramdown* because it empowers the bankruptcy court judge to confirm a plan of reorganization over the objections of an impaired class of security holders. (The plan is "crammed down" the throat of the objecting claimants.)

Cramdowns are usually an option of last resort if the debtor and creditors cannot come to agreement. Bankruptcy courts have considerable discretion to determine what constitutes "unfair discrimination" and "fair and equitable" treatment for members of a class. In practice cramdown reorganizations are rare. Eventually, the debtor and creditors come to some resolution.

Absolute Priority

A plan of reorganization must follow the rule of priority with respect to its security holders. Senior secured debtholders, typically bank loans,

---

[5] See 11 U.S.C., section 1129(b)(1).

must be satisfied first. The company's bondholders come next. These may be split between senior and subordinated bondholders. The company's shareholders get whatever remains. As the company pie is split up it is usually the case that senior secured debt is made whole and that subordinated debt receives some payment less than its face value with the remainder of its obligation is transformed into equity in the reorganized company. Finally, the original equity holders often receive nothing. Their equity is replaced by that converted from the subordinated debt.

It may seem unfair that the original equity holders are wiped out, but this is the residual risk that is born by every shareholder in every company. As the U.S. Supreme Court has stated, "one of the painful facts of bankruptcy is that the interests of shareholders become subordinated to the interests of creditors."[6]

Also, throughout the bankruptcy process, the debtor company's outstanding debt may be freely bought and sold. This allows distressed debt investors the opportunity to purchase undervalued debt securities with the anticipation that the debtor company will implement a successful reorganization.

The ability in the bankruptcy process to wipe out the ownership of existing shareholders and to transform the debt of senior and subordinated creditors into the company's new equity class is a key factor in distressed debt investing. The examples below demonstrate how distressed debt investors may gain control of a company through Chapter 11 Bankruptcy proceedings.

Chapter 7 Bankruptcy.

If a plan of reorganization cannot be accepted by the creditors for the company, the company may liquidate its assets. This is a Chapter 7 bankruptcy process. Under Chapter 7, the company is no longer considered a going concern. Chapter 7 results in a liquidation of the company's assets for the benefit of its debt holders. Essentially it shuts down its operations and parcels out its assets to its creditors.

DISTRESSED DEBT INVESTMENT STRATEGIES

There are three broad categories of investing in distressed debt securities. The first approach is an active approach with an intent to obtain control of the company. In this strategy, the investors intend to assume an active role in the management and direction of the company. These

---

[6] See Commodity Futures Trading Commission v. Weintraub, 471 U.S. 343, at 355 (1985).

investors typically purchase distressed debt to gain control through a blocking position in the bankruptcy process with a subsequent conversion into the equity of the reorganized company. Often, these investors purchase the more junior debt that is most likely to be converted into the equity of the reorganized company—these are sometimes called "fulcrum securities."

This strategy will also seek seats on the board of directors, and even, the chairmanship of the board. This is the most risky and time intensive of the distressed investment strategies. Returns are expected in the 20% to 25% range, consistent with those for leveraged buyouts—where control of a company is also sought.

The second general category of distressed debt investing seeks to plan an active role in the bankruptcy and reorganization process but stops short of taking control of the company. Here the principals may be willing to swap their debt for equity or for another form of restructured debt. Again an equity conversion is not required because control of the company is not sought. These investors participate actively in the creditors' committee to ensure the most beneficial outcome for their of debt. They may accept equity kickers such as warrants with their restructured debt. Their return target is in the 15% to 20% range—very similar to mezzanine debt investors.

There are passive or opportunistic investors. They often do not take an active role in the reorganization and rarely seek to convert their debt into equity. These investors buy debt securities that no one else wants. These investors might be the purest of the vulture investors because they have no goal other than to pick at the scraps that other investors wish to leave behind. These vultures receive their "scraps" from several sources:

- Banks and other financial institutions that do not have the time or inclination to participate in the bankruptcy reorganization.
- High yield mutual funds that are restricted in their ability to hold distressed securities—there may be limits as to the amount of distressed securities that they can hold in their portfolios.
- Investors that invested in high-yield bonds for their high coupon payments, but do not want to convert a high cash yield into an equity position in the company.

Exhibit 19.7 provides an overview of these strategies. In the following sections, we examine specific examples of distressed debt investment strategies both active and passive.

EXHIBIT 19.7   Distressed Debt Investment Strategies

Active, Seeking Control	Active, Not Seeking Control	Passive
Often seeks one-third of a class of debt to block and control the Chapter 11 bankruptcy process. Control of the company is expressly sought through an equity for debt conversion. Control is also sought through board seats and even the chairmanship. Investors play a direct role in restrucruting both the capital structure of the company as well as its business plan. Additional equity infusions might be made after the equity for debt conversion. Exit timeframe is two to four years Return expectation is 20% to 25%	May seek one-third of a debt class to obtain a blocking position. Will take an active role in the restructuring process. Will be an active participant in the creditors's committee. Typically, will not seek control but may be willing to accept an equity for debt conversion. If not a full conversion, may seek equity kickers. Exit timeframe is 1 to 3 years. Return expectation is 15% to 20%	Goal is to purchase debt securites that are undervalued and trading significantly below their face value. Various strategies may include credit arbitrage among different levels of seniority or fire sale purchases. Buy securities from more risk averse investors who cannot commit the time required for a bankruptcy reorganization. Holding period is up to one year. Return Expecation is 12% to 15%.

Using Distressed Debt to Recycle Private Equity

LBO firms are a great source for distressed debt. "Leveraged fallouts" occur frequently, leaving large amounts of distressed debt in their wake. However, this provides an opportunity for distressed debt buyers to jump in, purchase cheaply nonperforming bank loans and subordinated debt, eliminate the prior private equity investors, and assert their own private equity ownership.

Consider Regal Cinemas Inc., the largest U.S. theater chain. Regal was originally taken private in 1998 in a combined effort of Hicks, Muse, Tate & Furst and KKR. The two buyout firms each put up about $500 million in equity to purchase the firm for $1.5 billion. Over the next two years, Regal added $1.2 billion to its balance sheet in bank debt and subordinated notes.

Unfortunately, over capacity of movie theaters, a slowing U.S. economy, and fewer blockbuster movies resulted in a loss of $167 million for Regal in the first nine months of 2000. In December 2000, bank lenders refused to let the company pay interest to its subordinated bondholders because it would violate loan covenants. Regal's debt officially became distressed.

In stepped distressed debt buyers Philip Anschutz and Oaktree Capital Management. Together, they purchased 82% of Regal's outstanding bank debt and 95% of its subordinated debt paying 70 to 75 cents on the dollar. In September 2001, Regal announced a prepackaged bankruptcy plan where holders of Regal's bank debt would receive all of the equity in the reorganized company. In effect, Anschutz and Oaktree Capital replaced the private equity ownership of KKR and Hicks, Muse in Regal Cinemas with their own private equity stake. In fact, in May 2001, KKR had already written off its $492 million investment in Regal Cinemas. However, for Philip Anschutz and Oaktree, their prospects improved. Regal Cinemas went public in May 2002. Fourteen percent of the company was sold for $342 million, for a total market value of the company of $2.5 billion—significantly more than what Philip Anschutz and Oaktree paid for the distressed debt.

Distressed Buyouts

Even as leveraged buyout firms create distress situations, they also actively invest in this arena. After all, bankruptcy court and creditor workouts provide opportunities to purchase undervalued assets. Often, creditors are sufficiently worried about receiving any recovery that they bail out of their positions when possible, opening up the door for buyout firms to scoop up assets on the cheap. This is another form of active control in the distressed area. Consider the following example.

Vlasic Foods International Inc., the maker of Vlasic pickles[7] and Swanson and Hungry Man frozen dinners, filed for Chapter 11 bankruptcy in early 2001, listing $458 million in assets and $649 million in debts, including almost $200 million in outstanding junk bonds. Vlasic was originally purchased by Campbell Soups in 1978. Twenty years later, Campbell Soup spun out Vlasic to a group of senior managers. A group of 22 banks lent Vlasic $560 million to pay Campbell as part of the split off. Vlasic incurred additional debt over the next two years to finance its operations.

In June 2001, the U.S. Bankruptcy Court in Delaware agreed to a cash bid by Hicks, Muse, Tate & Furst of $370 million for the assets of Vlasic. Following the strict priority of bankruptcy proceedings, the $370 million was first used to pay secured creditors in full. The remainder, about $70 million, was used to pay unsecured creditors approximately 35 to 40 cents on the dollar. Existing equity shareholders received no payment; their value was wiped out by the bankruptcy.

---

[7] Remember the TV commercials with the cartoon stork that talked like Groucho Marx?

Consider the advantages to Hicks, Muse of the Vlasic deal. First, the buyout firm acquires for $370 million, assets that have a book value of $458 million. This does not take into account the productive ability of those assets to generate a market value in excess of their book value.

Second, Hicks, Muse acquired several well-known brand names. In fact, the A.J. Heinz & Co. had initially bid $195 million for Vlasic's pickle and barbecue sauce divisions while the company was in bankruptcy. It is possible that Hicks, Muse could negotiate a better deal with Heinz or another packaged food company for the sale of those assets.

Third, Hicks, Muse acquired the company free and clear of any outstanding debt. This was all wiped out through the bankruptcy proceedings. This allows for the opportunity to refinance the company with new debt while keeping the company out of bankruptcy proceedings.

Last, all shareholder equity was wiped out in the bankruptcy proceedings. Hicks, Muse became the sole owner of Vlasic Foods. Once purchased, Hicks, Muse pursued the same business plan that it used for many buyouts: streamline operations, sell unrelated business units to generate cash, provide stronger management, and promote Vlasic's well-known brand names.

Compare this example of Hicks, Muse to the one previous with respect to Regal Cinemas. LBO firms can be both suppliers and acquirers of distressed assets. It might be fair to say that "what goes around, comes around." Better yet, private equity firms specialize in seeking undervalued companies. However, not every private equity deal succeeds, and these underperforming companies, through distressed debt, can become another source of private equity investing.

Shortly after the Vlasic acquisition by Hicks Muse, the name of the company was changed to Pinnacle Foods Corp. Hicks Muse sold Pinnacle to JP Morgan Partners (the private equity arm of JP Morgan) in 2003 for $485 million for a gain of $115 million, or 31% over two years time.

Converting Distressed Debt to Private Equity in a Pre-Packaged Bankruptcy

In February 2001, Loews Cineplex Entertainment Corp., the largest publicly traded U.S. movie theater chain, and one of the largest movie theater chains in the world, filed for Chapter 11 Bankruptcy. At the same time, it signed a letter of intent with Oaktree Capital Management, LLC and the Onex Corporation to sell Loews Cineplex and its subsidiaries to the investor group. This was a "prepackaged" bankruptcy where the debtor agrees in advance to a plan of reorganization before formerly filing for Chapter 11 Bankruptcy.

The letter agreement proposed that Onex and Oaktree convert their distressed debt holdings of about $250 million of senior secured bank debt and $180 million of unsecured company bonds into 88% of the equity of the reorganized company. Unsecured creditors, including subordinated debtholders, would receive the other 12% of equity.[8] All existing equity interests would be wiped out by the reorganization. Last, the remaining holders of bank debt would receive new term loans as part of the bankruptcy process equal in recovery to about 98% of the face amount of current debt.

In this prepackaged example, Onex and Oaktree became the majority equity owners of Loews by purchasing its bank and subordinated debt. Furthermore, their bank debt was converted to a private equity stake because all public shares of Loews were wiped out through the bankruptcy proceedings. Loews two largest shareholders, Sony Corporation (40% equity ownership) and Vivendi Universal SA (26%) lost their complete equity stake in Loews. In effect, the bankruptcy proceeding transformed Loews from a public company to a private one.

Loews was subsequently sold to another group of private equity investors including Bain Capital, The Carlyle Group and Spectrum Equity Partners in June 2004. The sale price was $1.5 billion of which 88%—$1.32 billion—went to Onex and Oaktree. Based on their original investment of $430 million, this was a profit of $890 million for an IRR of 45%.

Using Distressed Debt for a Takeover

As a good example of how a corporation can use distressed debt to take control of another company, consider the merger of Federated Department Stores and R.H. Macy & Co. Federated was able to gain control of Macy's with an initial investment in distressed debt of only $109 million.

Federated itself was a victim of the leveraged fallouts of the late 1980s and early 1990s. Federated was taken private in an LBO by Robert Campeau in 1988, the same gentleman that took Allied Department Stores private in 1986. Campeau's vision was to create a huge retailing empire anchored by two separate retailing chains: Allied and Federated. Unfortunately, the high debt burden of both buyouts forced both companies into Chapter 11 bankruptcy in January 1990.

Federated Department Stores emerged from bankruptcy in February 1992 after creditors agreed to swap $4.8 billion in claims for equity in the reorganized company. This helped to reduce Federated's debt from $8.3 billion to $3.5 billion, and reduced its interest payments from $606 million to $259 million. The connection to Robert Campeau was

---

[8] Oaktree Capital also owned about 60% of Loews' senior subordinated notes.

severed. In an ironic twist of fate, Federated emerged from bankruptcy just nine days after Macy's filed for Chapter 11 bankruptcy protection. Macy's was another victim of a leveraged fallout.

Soon after the Macy's bankruptcy filing, Federated made overtures to acquire its long-time rival. This was another twist of fate because Macy's had bid against Robert Campeau in 1988 for control of Federated. Macy's rebuffed Federated's inquiries because it believe that the company could be better served if it remained independent.[9]

With Macy's mired in negotiations with its senior creditors regarding a plan of reorganization and a takeover out of the question (there was no equity to takeover), Federated decided to become one of Macy's creditors. In January 1994, Federated purchased one half of Macy's most senior secured debt from Macy's largest creditor: the Prudential Insurance Co. of America. Prudential held a senior loan of $832.5 million that was secured by 70 of Macy's best stores. With accrued interest, the total of the distressed debt was $1 billion, representing one-sixth of Macy's total debt.[10]

Federated paid $109.3 million for one half of this loan with a promissory note to pay the remainder in three years. In addition, Federated received an option from Prudential to purchase the remaining half of Prudential's senior loan within three years. Overnight, Federated became Macy's largest and most senior creditor.

Given its new standing as a senior secured creditor, Federated received standing from the bankruptcy court to (1) challenge Macy's plan of reorganization (Federated now had a blocking position within the senior secured class of creditors); (2) propose a competing plan to the bankruptcy court; and (3) obtain nonpublic financial information regarding Macy's business prospects.

Federated proposed converting its bank debt into equity and assuming Macy's existing liabilities. Macy's continued to resist. Specifically, Macy director Laurence A. Tisch teamed up with counsel for bondholders holding $1.2 billion in subordinated debt and demanded a reorganization plan valued at least $4 billion.[11] Meanwhile Federated received support from Fidelity Management & Research Co. which signed a "lock-up letter" stating that it would only support a plan that gave the banks full recovery in return for the banks support of Federated's

---

[9] See Richard Siklos, "Macy's Holiday Revival," *The Financial Post* (December 24, 1994), pp. 46–47.

[10] See "Federated Buys Large Share of Macy Debt," *Facts on File World News Digest* (January 6, 1994).

[11] See Karen Donovan, "Macy Merger Squeezes out Weil Gotshal; Bankruptcy Judge Approves Federated's Takeover Plan," *The National Law Journal* (December 19, 1994).

plan.[12] The lock-up letter worked and Federated was able to merge the two companies in December 1994 when it agreed to convert its senior loan to equity and to assume $4.1 billion in outstanding Macy's debts.[13]

Distressed Debt as an Undervalued Security

Distressed debt is not always an entrée into private equity; it can simply be an investment in an undervalued security. In this instance, distressed debt investors are less concerned with an equity stake in the troubled company. Instead, they expect to benefit if the company can implement a successful turnaround strategy.

Consider the bankruptcy of Montgomery Ward & Co. in July 1997. Montgomery Ward was the first mail-order merchant in 1872 (Sears was second) and became a successful and savvy mass merchandiser throughout most of the 1900s.[14] However, it failed to ride the wave of the post-World War II economic boom and was eventually eclipsed by other large retailers such as Sears and J.C. Penney's.

As a result, Montgomery Ward went through several owners in the 1970s and 1980s including Marcor Inc., Mobil Oil Corporation, and a senior management buyout. Despite its varied ownership, Montgomery Ward could not turn itself around. Its lack of brandname goods, dingy stores, and out-of-date image kept customers away and led to its July 1997 Chapter 11 bankruptcy filing.[15]

Montgomery Ward's bankruptcy provided an opportunity for distressed investors, vendors, and bank lenders alike. By October 1997, Ward's unsecured debt was trading around 35 cents on the dollar. At that price, distress debt investors such as the Third Avenue Value Fund, bought $17 million of Ward's debt from its vendors.[16] In addition, secured lender New York Life accepted an unsolicited bid from Merrill Lynch & Co. for its entire senior Montgomery Ward debt of $40 million. Nationwide Insurance Cos. also sold $31.5 million of its secured debt.

---

[12] Id.

[13] There was significant legal maneuvering before the deal was completed including the appointment of Cyrus R. Vance, the former U.S. Secretary of State, to mediate the discussions between Macy's, Federated, and other outstanding creditors.

[14] In fact, it was a Montgomery Ward copywriter who invented the character and illustrated poem "Rudolph the Red-Nosed Reindeer" for Santa Claus to give to children in Montgomery Ward department stores. Rudolph was an instant hit and helped to draw large crowds to Montgomery Ward stores.

[15] See Jef Feeley, "Wards Emerges From Bankruptcy Court to Clouded Future," *Bloomberg News* (August 2, 1999).

[16] See Rekha Balu, "Debt Traders Capitalize on Vendor Uncertainty; Buying, Selling Ward's Stakes could Affect Proceedings," *Crain's Chicago Business* (October 6, 1997).

From a distressed investor's point of view the Montgomery Ward's bankruptcy provided a good opportunity because GE Capital Inc. already owned more than 50% of Ward's. Additionally, it was one of its largest creditors having provided $1 billion in financing for the retailer's previous reorganization plan. It seemed reasonable to believe that GE Capital would provide additional relief to get the company out of bankruptcy. In fact, GE Capital did step up to the plate and paid $650 million for the remainder of the company (plus its Signature Group direct marketing arm) as well as wiping clean the $1 billion in debt. Montgomery Ward emerged from bankruptcy in August 1999.

However, GE Capital did not step up as much as some distressed debt investors had hoped. Secured creditors were paid in full, but unsecured creditors received only 26 to 28 cents on the dollar. Those distressed debt investors who purchased senior claims at a discount profited nicely. However, those who purchased vendor claims (unsecured debt) lost money.

As an unfortunate postscript, Montgomery Ward still could not make a go of it and filed for bankruptcy again in December 2000. This time there was no reorganization. The company went out of business.

However, the name "Wards" lives on. Through the bankruptcy liquidation process, a Chicago based multi-title retail mailer, Direct Marketing Services Inc., acquired the marketing rights to use the Montgomery Wards name in June 2004 and resurrected the Montgomery Wards catalog in September 2004. Although there are no longer any Montgomery Ward stores, the name lives on through on-line retailing.

Distressed Debt in a Fire Sale

In American parlance, a "fire sale" is a liquidation of inventory at prices far below their normal value. The term comes from the fact that after a devastating fire to a business, what inventory remains is sold at distressed prices. This is the best example of distressed debt as an opportunistic investment strategy.

An excellent example of a fire sale is Refco, Inc. In October of 2005, a spectacular fraud was uncovered at Refco, Inc., a leading broker in the futures industry. It was revealed that Refco's Chief Executive Officer, Phillip Bennett had allegedly hidden from investors a $430 million receivable that he owed to Refco and that Refco's 2002–2005 financial statements could not be relied upon. He was subsequently indicted by a grand jury in New York for violating U.S. securities laws.[17]

---

[17] See "Former Refco CEO Phillip Bennett Indicted for Securities Fraud," *Bloomberg News*, November 11, 2005.

EXHIBIT 19.8   Stock Price of Refco from IPO to Bankruptcy

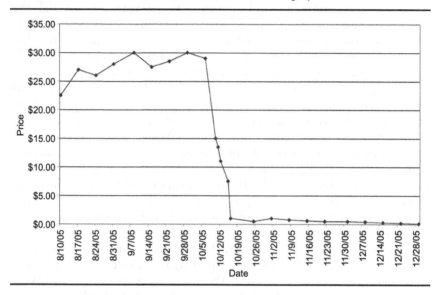

What is fascinating about Refco is that this was a private equity deal to begin with. The large buyout firm Thomas H. Lee had purchased a large private equity stake in Refco and subsequently had taken the company public in an initial public offering in August of 2005. Refco stock was sold at $22 a share in a $670 million IPO. Only two short months later, the fraud was uncovered and Refco's stock price spiralled down. Exhibit 19.8 shows the rapid decline of Refco's common stock price.

Refco quickly entered into bankruptcy liquidation proceedings under Chapter 7 of the Bankruptcy Code to pay off its creditors. At the time of its bankruptcy filing, Refco had one bond issue outstanding, 9% notes due 2012. Vulture investors quickly swooped down on these bonds.

Before the discovery of the fraud, the Refco bonds were well received by the market and were trading at close to 110 with a yield of 7%. Once the fraud was discovered, these bonds dropped as precipitously as Refco's stock price, falling from 110 down to 40 (40 cents on the dollar), a drop of 63% of value in the first few days of Refco's fraud revelation. However, these were senior securities and therefore had considerably more protection than stockholders or other unsecured creditors. Investors who sold these bonds did so in a panicked fire sale— willing to part with them at severely depressed prices But distressed and vulture investors made out like bandits. Exhibit 19.9 shows the steep decline of the Refco bonds along with a strong recovery in market value. After the initial fire sale, Refco bonds doubled in value from 40 to 80.

EXHIBIT 19.9   Price of Refco 9% Bond due 2012

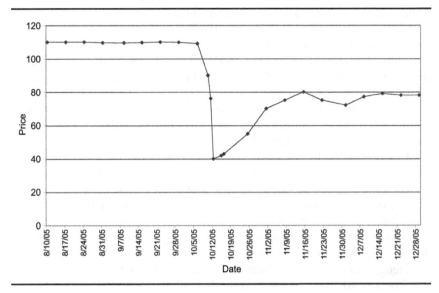

The key to this vignette is that distressed debt investing must take advantage of opportunities. The Refco fire sale took place quickly with traditional investors bailing out of Refco's bonds without a rational analysis of their value in the bankruptcy liquidation. Also, traditional investors were not ready for the rigors of the bankruptcy process, and so they sold their bonds for whatever they could get for them.

This example of distressed debt investing also demonstrates another useful principle about this market: there is always something left for creditors in a bankruptcy. Compare Exhibit 19.8 with 19.9. Exhibit 19.8 shows that the price of Refco's stock declined precipitously once the fraud was uncovered, and it never recovered. Effectively, Refco's stock is worth zero. This highlights that the equity owners of the company really do bear the final losses associated with the company— Refco's shareholders had their investment wiped out.

Conversely, Exhibit 19.9 shows the value of Refco's bonds. While the bond prices declined just as steeply as Refco's stock price upon the discovery of the fraud, their value subsequently recovered. And while the bond prices did not reach their prefraud valuations, there was still 80 cents on the dollar worth of value left. A much better situation than losing everything as a stockholder. This is the added value of debt: creditors come first, equityholders come last.

Distressed Debt Arbitrage

If there is any way to skin an arbitrage, hedge fund managers will think of it. While this is not a private equity form of investing, it is a form of equity arbitrage best suited for hedge fund managers.

The arbitrage is constructed as follows. A hedge fund manager purchases distressed debt which she believes is undervalued. At the same time, she shorts the company's underlying stock. The idea is that if the bonds are going to decline in value, the company's stock price will decline even more dramatically because equity holders have only a residual claim behind debtholders.

Conversely, if the company's prospects improve, both the distressed debt and equity will appreciate significantly. The difference then will be between the coupon payment on the debt versus dividends paid on the stock. Since a company coming out of a workout or turnaround situation almost always conserves its cash and does not pay cash stock dividends, the hedge fund manager should earn large interest payments on the debt compared to the equity.

Hedge fund managers might very well be called active/passive managers. The key to their dual nature is that while the hedge fund manager actively trades the securities of the distressed company, she has no interest in an active role in the future direction of the company. Hedge fund managers typically do not participate in the restructuring of the company. Their goal is to make a play on the relative value of the distressed companies securities. Their holding period is typically six months to one year—much less than the time period needed to exert control and influence.

Risks of Distressed Debt Investing

There are two main risks associated with distressed debt investing. First, business risk still applies. Just because distressed debt investors can purchase the debt of a company on the cheap does not mean it cannot go lower. This is the greatest risk to distressed debt investing, a troubled company may be worthless and unable to pay off its creditors. While creditors often convert their debt into equity, the company may not be viable as a going concern. If the company cannot develop a successful plan of reorganization, it will only continue its spiral downwards.

It may seem strange, but creditworthiness does not apply. The reason is that the debt is already distressed because the company may already be in default and its debt thoroughly discounted. Consequently, failure to pay interest and debt service has already occurred.

Instead, vulture investors consider the business risks of the company. They are concerned not with the short-term payment of interest and debt service, but rather, the ability of the company to execute a viable business plan. From this perspective, it can be said that distressed debt investors are truly equity investors. They view the purchase of distressed debt as an investment in the company as opposed to a lending facility.

Consider the case of Iridium LLC, a satellite-telephone system with $1.5 billion in high-yield debt. Motorola Inc. started Iridium in 1997, and owned 18% of the company. Iridium launched a network of 66 satellites to build a global telephone network. After Iridium went public in 1997, its market capitalization reached almost $11 billion.

However, Iridium's business plan eventually fell apart as it failed to attract enough customers to make the business viable. Iridium's phones were too bulky, about the size of a brick, much larger than the small, pocket-sized cellular phones to which consumers had become accustomed. In addition, service was unreliable, the satellite phones worked poorly in buildings and cars. Instead of the 600,000 subscribers that Iridium had projected, it could only muster 20,000.

As a consequence, Iridium could not meet the interest payments on $800 million of senior bank debt. Still, in May 1999, distressed debt investors jumped to buy Iridium's 14% subordinated notes for 26 cents on the dollar when it appeared that Iridium would be able to restructure its senior bank loans. However, the restructuring failed, and with over $3 billion in debt Iridium filed for Chapter 11 bankruptcy in August 1999.

At the time of its bankruptcy, Iridium's subordinated notes were trading at 14.5 cents on the dollar. Unfortunately, Iridium's financial woes continued as the company sank further and further into losses and debt. By March 2000, Iridium's subordinated bonds were trading at 2 to 3 cents on the dollar. Iridium was finally put out of its misery in November 2000 when the bankruptcy court liquidated the company for a paltry $25 million. Its bonds were worthless.

The second main risk is the lack of liquidity. The distressed debt arena is a fragmented market, dominated by a few players. Trading out of a distressed debt position may mean selling at a significant discount to the book value of the debt. For example, at the time of the Loews bankruptcy filing, its senior subordinated notes were trading at an offer of 15, but with a bid of 10, a gap of 5 cents or $50 dollars for every $1000 face value bond.

In addition, purchasers of distressed debt must have long-term investment horizons. Workout and turnaround situations do not happen overnight. It may be several years before a troubled company can correct its course and appreciate in value.

CONCLUSION

In this chapter we showed how distressed debt investing is really another form of private equity. Indeed, many LBO firms invest in the distressed debt of companies with an eye towards controlling the equity of the reorganized company. Also, failed LBOs are a significant source for the distressed debt market.

Distressed debt rarely occurs because of some spectacular event that renders a company's products worthless overnight. Usually, a company's financial condition deteriorates over a period of time due to inefficient management or excessive leverage. The management of a company that was once established in the marketplace may become tired or rigid, unable or unwilling to cope with new market dynamics. As a result the company fails to execute its business plan or worse yet, tries to implement an obsolete business plan. Conversely, some companies engage in aggressive expansion plans that lead to an excessive use of leverage. This leaves the company operating on a fine edge with respect to cash flows. Should the cash flows decline, an overleveraged company can quickly run afoul of being unable to pay its debts as they become due. This leads to a distressed situation.

This is where private equity managers earn their bread and butter. Revitalizing a company and implementing new business plans are their specialty. The adept distressed investor is able to spot these tired companies, identify their weaknesses, and bring a fresh approach to the table. By purchasing the debt of the company, the distressed debt investor creates a seat for herself at the table with the ability to turn the company around.

CHAPTER 20

The Economics of Private Equity

The prior four chapters have been descriptive in nature. In Chapter 16 we provided a narrative overview of the venture capital market. Similar descriptions were provided for leveraged buyouts, mezzanine debt, and distressed debt investing. In this chapter, we consider the risks and returns associated with private equity investing.

Consistent with our prior analysis of hedge funds and commodities, we begin with an examination of how these classes of private equity have performed relative to the broader stock market. We also review the distribution of returns associated with the different classes of private equity and consider private equity within a portfolio context.

THE PERFORMANCE OF PRIVATE EQUITY

In this section we compare the performance of each class of private equity to that of the S&P 500. Our purpose is simply to determine how private equity returns compared to public equity returns over the period 1991 to 2005.

Venture Capital

Venture capitalists seek to earn a long-term rate of return in excess of 5% above that of the public stock market. This risk premium provides compensation for three main risks. First, there is the business risk of a startup company. Although many startups successfully make it to the IPO stage, many more fail to succeed. A venture capitalist must earn a sufficient return to compensate her for bearing the risk of corporate failure. Although public companies can also fail (see our distressed examples in Chapter 19), venture capital is unique in that the investor takes

501

on the business risk before a company has the ability to fully implement its business plan.

Second, there is the lack of liquidity. There is no public market for trading venture capital interests. What secondary trading exists is limited to other private equity investors.

This is a fragmented market with inefficiencies. The tailored nature of a venture capitalists portfolio will not suit all buyers all of the time. Consequently, the sale of an interest in a venture capital fund is not an easy task. Furthermore, another venture capital firm may not have the time or ability to perform as thorough a due diligence as the initial investing firm. The common solution is to discount heavily another venture capitalists' portfolio in a secondary transaction.

Third, there is the lack of diversification associated with a venture capital portfolio. The capital asset pricing model (CAPM) teaches us that the only risk that investors should be compensated for is the risk of the general stock market, or systematic risk. Unsystematic, or company specific risk can be diversified away. However, the CAPM is predicated upon security interests being freely transferable. This is not possible in the venture capital marketplace. The lack of liquidity prohibits transferability. Consequently, company specific risk must be rewarded.

Also, the CAPM requires diversification. Yet, as we discussed in Chapter 16, venture capital firms have become more specialized. This specialization developed as a result of the intensive knowledge base needed to invest in the technology, telecom, and biotech industries. Specialization is also determined by the stage of investment in the life cycle of a startup company. Unfortunately, specialization leads to concentrated portfolios, the very anathema of the CAPM.

Specialization might be the most important development in the venture capital world. Not only does specialization help private equity managers invest more efficiently, it allows them to earn a higher return over the market. Another way to state this observation is that specialization may lead to a higher long-term risk premium over a market benchmark to reflect the increased risk associated with concentrated portfolios.

In light of these risks, we examine the returns to venture capital compared to the S&P 500 stock index, our proxy for the market return. We include all stages of venture capital (seed, early, and late) in our analysis. In Exhibit 20.1, we graph the value of $1,000 invested at the beginning of 1991 through the end of year 2005. This 16-year period should be sufficient to reveal any long-term risk premium earned by venture capitalists.[1]

---

[1] For venture capital, LBOs and mezzanine debt, we use data from the Venture Economics database. This information presents the average returns from reporting investment firms. For distressed debt, we use data from Hedge Fund Research, Inc.

EXHIBIT 20.1   Value of an Investment in Venture Capital

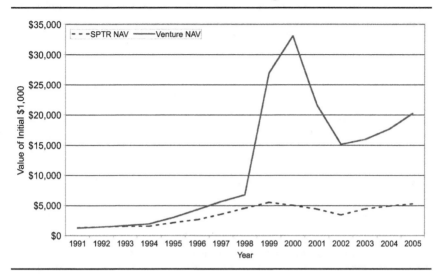

Not surprising, venture capital returns exceed those for the general stock market. For most of the 1990s, venture capital earned a steady excess return over the S&P 500. However, beginning in 1998, venture capital returns skyrocket compared to the S&P 500. This insanity culminated in a return to the average venture capital fund of 298% in 1999.

Clearly, this was an unusual time, when many technology stocks traded beyond any bounds of rationality. During this time, many newly minted Wall Street analysts outdid themselves with outrageous forecasts of performance and almost criminally deficient stock price projections. We demonstrated in Chapter 16 how this technology bubble burst with the NASDAQ composite first soaring above the S&P 500 and the Dow Jones Industrial Average, and then crashing back down to earth.

It is clear now that many startup companies were thoroughly overvalued.

It should be noted that venture capital returns are dependent upon a healthy public stock market. A three-year bear market during 2000 to 2002 resulted in depressed public stock prices and discouraged IPOs for startup companies. A strong public securities market supports the IPO market—the major exit strategy of most venture capitalists.

When the stock market weakened in 2001 and 2002, venture capital returns came tumbling down to earth. Still venture capital has provided a healthy risk premium over the public markets during this time period.

EXHIBIT 20.2   Investment in Different Stages of Venture Capital

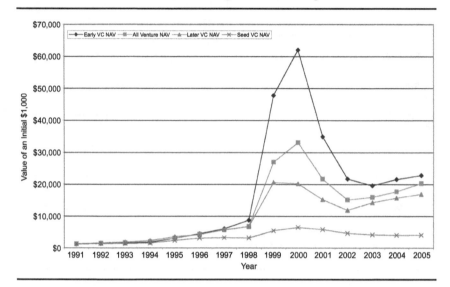

In Exhibit 20.2, we break down the returns to the venture capital industry by the stage of venture investing: seed, early, and late stage venture funds. We also include the return to all venture funds as a comparison.

First, note that the returns to the different stages of venture capital investing are similar through 1998. Then the outlier year of 1999 occurred where the returns to early stage venture capital funds earned an amazing 446% in one year. However, these oversized returns (even for venture capital) quickly reversed with three years of negative returns. As 2005 closed out, the returns to the different stages of venture capital are once again, roughly equivalent.

The one exception is seed venture capital. This stage of investing earned smaller returns that late stage of early stage venture capital funds. This is interesting because, presumably, seed capital venture funds are at greatest risk because of they are typically the first investors in any startup company. Nonetheless, seed capital venture funds did not participate as extensively in the outrageous returns of 1999 or the subsequent crash of the returns to venture capital funds in 2000 to 2002.

Leveraged Buyouts

Like venture capital firms, leverage buyout firms also concentrate on company selection as opposed to market risk. However, leveraged buyout funds have less risk than venture capital funds for two reasons.

First, leverage buyouts take private public companies that are considerably beyond their IPO stage (or they buy out established operating divisions of public companies). The business risk associated with startup companies does not exist. Typically, buyouts target successful but undervalued companies. These companies generally have long-term operating histories, generate a positive cash flow, and have established brand names and identities with consumers.

Second, LBO firms tend to be less specialized than venture capitalists. While LBO firms may concentrate in one sector from time to time, they tend to be more eclectic in their choices for targets. LBO target companies can range from movie theaters to grocery stores.[2] Therefore, although they maintain smaller portfolios than traditional long-only managers, they tend to have greater diversification than their venture capital counterparts.

Consequently, we expect to see returns less than that for venture capital, but possibly, more than that earned by the broader stock market. In Exhibit 20.3 we present the value of a $1,000 investment in an average LBO fund as tracked by Venture Economics versus that for the S&P 500 over the time period 1991 to 2005.

EXHIBIT 20.3   Value of an Investment in Leveraged Buyouts

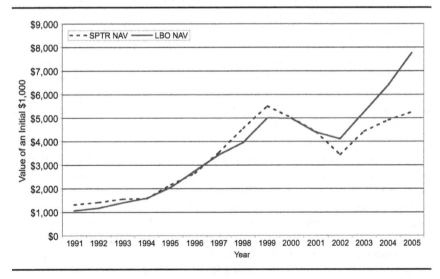

[2] For instance, at the time that KKR was writing down its investment in Regal Cinemas, it was racking up large gains from its investment in Randall's Food Markets, Inc.

EXHIBIT 20.4   Value of an Investment in Different LBO Sizes

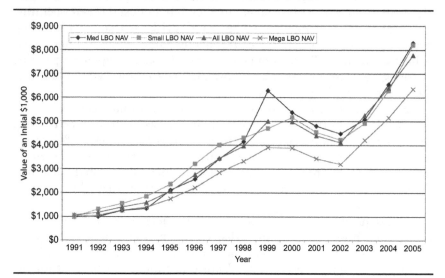

We see that LBO firms in fact earn a lower return than venture capital firms. In fact, the return to all LBO funds follow that of the stock market until 2002 when their outperformance compared to the public stock market becomes apparent. Over the long period LBO funds do outperform the public market. However, with respect to the S&P 500, the returns over the 11-year period are about even. While LBO firms earned a premium to the S&P 500 in the first half of the 1990s, the stock market outperformed LBO funds in the second half until the decline in the market in year 2000. In the end, over the period 1990 to 2000, the S&P 500 and the average LBO firm provided an investor with just about the same total return.

In Exhibit 20.4 we examine the different types of LBO funds. LBO funds distinguish themselves by the the size of the companies that they take private. Generally, they classify themselves as investing in small companies ($100 million to $500 million in sales revenue), midcapitalization ranges ($500 million in sales to $2 billion), and large LBO firms ($2 billion in revenues and larger). In Exhibit 20.4 we also include the returns to all LBO funds as a benchmark for a comparison.

Exhibit 20.4 shows that the LBO funds tend to track closely together throughout this period with small LBOs and medium-size LBOs earning consistently higher returns than large LBO deals. The likely culprit for lower returns in large LBO deals is due to the fact that most large deals are conducted in an auction process. Most large buyouts use an investment banker to attract the highest bid. This auction process leads to a more efficient market with less return potential. Conversely, small and midsize LBOs tend to be engaged in a one on one basis with the company going private. Auctions are more an exception and less the rule with smaller LBOs than for the larger deals. This makes the market less efficient and, as a result, the returns to small and medium-size LBOs demonstrate a return premium over mega-LBO funds.

Note also that there is much less variation among the different classes of LBO funds compared to the different classes of venture capital funds. Exhibit 20.2 demonstrates much greater variation among the types of venture funds compared to the LBO funds displayed in Exhibit 20.4. The conclusion is that type of LBO fund is much less a critical decision factor in an investor's portfolio than the type of venture capital fund selected.

Mezzanine Debt

Recall our discussion of mezzanine debt in Chapter 18. Mezzanine financing is a hybrid. It has debtlike components such as coupon payments and a fixed maturity date, but at the same time, it also provides for equity appreciation, usually in the form of warrants or an equity conversion factor. Consequently, we expect it to perform less than the equity investments of venture capital or LBO firms. In addition, given its debt component, we expect it to perform less than the S&P 500. However, the high fixed coupon associated with mezzanine debt should provide steady returns, with much less volatility than the stock market.

Exhibit 20.5 confirms our expectations. Mezzanine debt performed about the same as the S&P 500 during the first half of the 1990s. During this time, the large coupon payments on mezzanine debt plus some equity appreciation provided returns that were slightly less than the U.S. equity market. In addition, its returns are steady and much less variable than the stock market, demonstrating the advantage of its debt component.

Mezzanine debt's under performance compared to the S&P 500 should not be viewed negatively because mezzanine financing is designed to under perform the stock market. This may seem like an odd statement, but it's true. Because of its debt component, an investor has some downside protection. If the company's fortunes decline and the stock price with it, the investor will at least have the principal repayment and large coupon payments to reward her. This downside protection is most evident during the bear stock market years of 2000 to 2002. The investor has some protection on the downside, but in return must sacrifice some appreciation on the upside. In addition, mezzanine debt ranks higher than a company's equity in the seniority of a company's equity structure. Consequently, it should not earn returns superior to the public equity market because it has less risk than common stock.

EXHIBIT 20.5   Value of an Investment in Mezzanine Debt

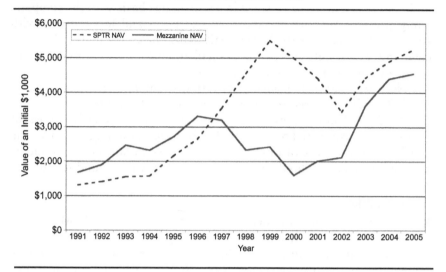

Distressed Debt

Distressed debt investors are usually equity investors in debt's clothing. Most of the time, the vultures are looking to swoop in, purchase cheap debt securities, convert them to stock, turn around the company, and reap the rewards of appreciation. So, they are less concerned with coupon payments, debt service, or repayment schedules. They are in it for the equity that can be squeezed out of distressed debt situations.

The risks they bear are large; as we discussed in the previous chapter, "distressed" means companies in trouble. Similar to venture capital, there is a large business risk associated with distressed debt investing. The management of the troubled company must arrest the company's decline and turn it around. Typically, management can stop a company's decline by seeking Chapter 11 Bankruptcy protection. However, the harder part is coming up with a plan of reorganization that will reward senior and unsecured creditors. If successful, distressed debt investors can reap a bonanza. Thus, distressed debt investors are exposed to event risk, either the event that the company will declare bankruptcy or that the company will not be able to emerge from bankruptcy protection.

Like LBO and venture capital funds, distressed debt investors also tend to run concentrated portfolios of companies. However, distressed debt investors tend to invest across industries as opposed to concentrating in a single industry. This may lead to better diversification than venture capital funds.

EXHIBIT 20.6   Value of an Investment in Distressed Debt

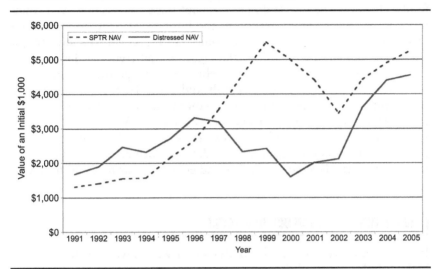

Within the risk spectrum, distressed debt investors fall in between mezzanine debt and LBO firms. Like LBO firms, distressed debt investors purchase securities of companies that have an established operating history. In most cases these companies are way past their IPO stage. However, unlike LBO firms that target successful but stagnant companies, distressed investing targets troubled companies. These companies have progressed past stagnation, and may already be in bankruptcy proceedings.

Like venture capital and LBO funds, distressed debt investors assume considerable business risk. However, distressed debt investing is less risky than venture capital or LBOs because debt holders stand in line at a higher seniority than equity investors in an LBO. The company's current problems might be due to poor execution of an existing business plan, an obsolete business plan, or simply poor cash management. These problems can be fixed whereas a startup company with a product that does not sell cannot.

Exhibit 20.6. presents the value of distressed debt investing compared to the S&P 500. As can be seen, distressed debt investors were rewarded for accepting the extra business risk of investing in troubled companies. Additionally, distressed debt investors earned returns that were greater than mezzanine debt but less than LBO firms and venture capital firms. Unfortunately, the returns are a bit disappointing. While distressed debt outperformed the stock market during the early and mid-1990s, it has underperformed the stock since then. Given the company specific risk undertaken as well as the risk of company distress, we would expect to see results that are more in line with the stock market, although less than LBO funds. However, the results do not bear out these conclusions. As a result, investors should carefully scrutinize the business plan of distressed debt investment funds. There should be some return premium for investing in troubled companies, but Exhibit 20.6 presents a different conclusion.

We also note that distressed debt investors performed poorly in 1998 when the Russian bond default and Long-Term Capital Management sent shock waves through the credit markets. This forced investors to flee to safety in U.S. Treasury securities and AAA-rated bonds. The heightened scrutiny of credit risk adversely impacted the returns to distressed debt. In addition, distressed debt performed poorly during the downturn of the U.S. stock market and economy during 2000 to 2001.

PRIVATE EQUITY RETURN DISTRIBUTIONS

In this section we perform the analysis that was previously deployed for hedge funds, commodities, and managed futures. Through the process of graphing the returns to private equity we try to understand the nature of the risks associated with this form of investing.

In previous chapters we introduced the concepts of skewness and kurtosis. These are statistical measures that help to describe the distribution of returns earned from an investment in an asset class.

Recall that skewness and kurtosis are defined by the third and fourth moments of the distribution, respectively. A normal (bell-shaped) distribution has no skewness because it is a symmetrical distribution. The values of kurtosis in the following exhibits are measured relative to a normal, bell-shaped distribution. A positive value for kurtosis indicates a distribution with "fatter" than normal tails, (a condition called leptokurtosis) while a negative value indicates a distribution with "thinner" than normal tails (platykurtosis).

Normal distributions can be defined by the first two moments of the distribution—the mean and the variance. Therefore, for a normal distribution, a Sharpe ratio is an appropriate measure for risk and return. However, if higher moments of the distribution are present, a Sharpe ratio may not capture the complete risk and return tradeoff.[3] This is why we plot the return distribution to observe if it exhibits nonnormal properties that might not be captured by a Sharpe ratio analysis.

---

[3] For a detailed examination of symmetric performance measures and asymmetric return distributions, see Mark Anson, "Symmetric Performance Measures and Asymmetric Trading Strategies: A Cautionary Example," *Journal of Alternative Investments* (Summer 2002), pp. 81–85.

We take the data contained in the Venture Economics database, and recalibrate them to plot a frequency distribution of the returns associated with venture capital, LBOs, and mezzanine debt. This data is presented on a quarterly basis. For distressed debt investing, we use the return information in the HFRI database. The HFRI data is presented on a monthly basis. The following exhibits provide a graphical depiction of the range and likelihood of returns associated with private equity investing. We calculate the mean, standard deviation, skew, and kurtosis associated with each strategy.

As benchmarks for our analysis we use the data from Exhibit 6.2 with respect to the S&P 500 and the Salomon Brothers Cash Pay High Yield Index. Exhibit 6.2 shows that the skew for the public stock market is –0.63, while the value of kurtosis is 0.58. Therefore, the public stock market has a slight bias to the downside, but little exposure to larger outlier events (fat tails). Conversely, for high-yield bonds, the skew is more negative at –0.81 with a large value of kurtosis of 4.16. This demonstrates a larger bias to the downside with large/fat tails. Specifically, the condition of a negative skew and a large value of kurtosis exposes a return distribution to considerable downside risk.

The distribution of returns to high-yield bonds demonstrated a significant downside tail. This "fat" tail reflects the event risk of downgrades, defaults, and bankruptcies. As we explained in Chapter 6, credit risk is simply another way to describe event risk.

A negative skew indicates that the mean of the distribution is to the left of (less than) the median of the distribution. This means that there are more frequent large return observations to the left of the distribution (negative returns) and there are more small and midrange positive return observations to the right of the distribution. In other words, large negative outlying returns occur more frequently than large positive outlying returns, indicating a bias to the downside.

A positive skew indicates the reverse of a negative skew. It indicates that the mean of the distribution is to the right of the median and that there are more frequent large positive returns than there are large negative returns. A positive skew demonstrates a bias to the upside.

Venture Capital

Exhibit 20.7 presents the frequency distribution for the quarterly returns to venture capital over the last 20 years. The first thing that might strike the reader is how "flat" the distribution is. That is, there is no large concentration of return mass—it is spread out throughout the distribution. This is further emphasized by the large quarterly value of standard deviation; 11%. Simply put, an investor in venture capital should expect a wide variation of returns. This investment class is not for the weak-

EXHIBIT 20.7   Frequency Distribution for Venture Capital[a]

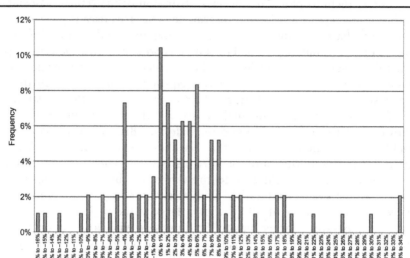

[a] Average = 4.13%, Std. Dev. = 11.00%, Skew = 2.76, Kurtosis = 14.89, Sharpe = 0.27.

hearted. Second, it is clear that venture capital investments generate a return pattern with large positive values for both skewness and kurtosis. The implication is that there are more large positive returns than negative returns associated with venture capital investing (the large positive skew). In addition, the large positive value of kurtosis (leptokurtosis) indicates that there are many more large outliers associated with venture capital returns than associated with a normal distribution.

The large value of positive kurtosis (14.89) for venture capital is partly influenced by the recent history of the venture capital market. A total return of over 200% in 1999 was indeed an outlier, unlikely to repeat any time in the near or distant future. These large positive returns helped to generate the large tails associated with the venture capital distribution.

The second reason for the large outlier returns is the very nature of venture capital investing. When a company does well it can be a "20 bagger" or better, generating tremendous returns for its venture capital investors.[4] Unfortunately, many startup companies go bust and the venture capitalist loses her investment.

---

[4] The terminology "20 bagger" comes from Peter Lynch, the former manager of the Fidelity Magellan Fund. He often referred to a stock in baseball terms. Therefore, a "two-bagger" was a stock that doubled your money, a three-bagger tripled your money, and so on. A 20-bagger indicates a company that appreciates in value twentyfold compared to the cost of the venture capital investment.

This return pattern is ideal for posting a large positive skew with a large positive value of kurtosis. If a company goes bust, the most a venture capitalist can lose is the money she invested. However, if the company is successful, the gains can be extraordinary. This return pattern is similar to a call option. The venture capitalist has a simple binary choice with respect to every business plan: invest or do not invest. Investing in a startup company is similar to the purchase of a call option. The price of the option is the capital that the venture capitalist invests in the startup company. If the company fails, the venture capitalist forfeits her option premium—the capital invested. However, if the startup company is successful, the venture capitalist shares in all of the upside—much like a call option.

Venture capital returns have a positive skew of 2.76 compared to a negative skew for the S&P 500 of 0.63 over the same time period. This demonstrates that the concentrated company selection of venture capitalists was able to avoid the negatively skewed pattern of the broader stock market returns. This is a demonstration of company selection skill. In sum, a large positive skew combined with a large value of kurtosis translated into large positive returns for venture capital investors.

Leveraged Buyouts

Exhibit 20.8 presents the frequency distribution for LBOs. Interestingly, the return pattern to LBOs shows a much more symmetrical distribution of

EXHIBIT 20.8   Frequency Distribution for LBOs[a]

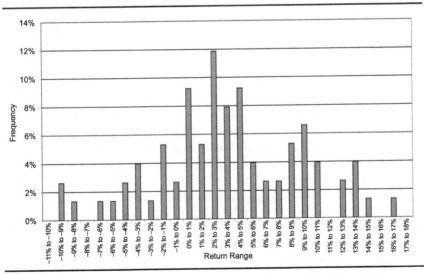

[a] Average = 3.49%, Std. Dev. = 5.66%, Skew = –0.03, Kurtosis = –0.076, Sharpe = 0.4.

returns than that for venture capital. The values for skew and kurtosis are close to zero indicating a normal or symmetrical distribution of returns.

LBO firms have far less business risk than venture capital firms. LBO firms target successful, established but undervalued companies while venture capitalists work with new and unproven companies. These firms have operating management in place, an established product and brand name, an operating history, and stable balance sheets. LBO firms then implement a better business plan that generates a larger cash flow, and add leverage to boost the returns to equity.

As a result, the return pattern to LBOs resembles more that of the public stock market than venture capital. There is almost no skew and almost no kurtosis. The returns to LBO funds, in fact, demonstrate a remarkably symmetrical return pattern. Large downside returns occur with the same frequency of large positive returns. Overall, LBO firms generate an average quarterly return of 3.5% with a volatility that is much lower than that for venture capital at 5.66%. This return pattern results in a higher Sharpe ratio for LBOs of 0.40 compared to 0.27 for venture capital. Bottom line, LBO funds provide a better risk return tradeoff than for venture capital funds.

Last, it is interesting to note that the return distribution for LBO funds has a negative value of kurtosis. Although, small, this demonstrates that a condition where the tails of the distribution are thinner than that for a normal distribution. Simply, LBO funds do not demonstrate an exposure to outlier events as do venture capital funds. Those investors looking for less risk in their portfolios would be more attracted to LBO funds instead of venture capital funds.

Mezzanine Debt

Given its status as a hybrid, part debt and part equity, we would expect to see lower returns than for venture capital and LBOs, but also lower volatility of returns. Both cases are observed—mezzanine debt earns less than venture capital and LBOs, but there is also less risk. Interestingly, the Sharpe ratio for mezzanine debt and LBO funds are the same at 0.40 reflecting an equivalent tradeoff between return and volatility.

With respect to skew and kurtosis, we observe a negative skew and a positive value of kurtosis. This is similar to the negative skew and positive value of kurtosis for high-yield bonds. However, junk bonds have a much larger negative skew and value of kurtosis indicating a larger downside fat tail than mezzanine debt. This is reflective of the credit/event risk associated with high-yield bonds. From this analysis, we can conclude that mezzanine debt has much less exposure to event risk than high-yield bonds. This is due to the fact that mezzanine funds share in

EXHIBIT 20.9   Frequency Distribution for Mezzanine Financing[a]

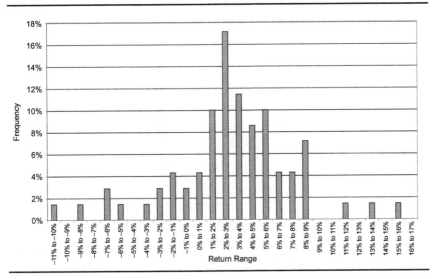

[a] Average = 3.00%, Std. Dev. = 4.50%, Skew = –0.32, Kurtosis = 1.62, Sharpe = 0.4.

the upside of the company through some form of equity kicker. This provides a level of diversification away from mezzanine debt's exposure to credit events.

Distressed Debt

Although distressed debt is a way to convert outstanding debt into equity, the investor must bear the event risk that the company will cease to function. As we discussed in the prior chapter, distressed companies may already be in Chapter 11 bankruptcy proceedings. However, Chapter 11 bankruptcy protection is not a panacea, the company could end up liquidating similar to the Montgomery Ward and Iridium examples in Chapter 19.

Consequently, credit risk still exists. From Chapter 6 we know that event risk translates into a negative skew value with a large value of kurtosis. Exhibit 20.10 demonstrates a negative skew of –0.63 and a large value of kurtosis of 7.05. These values are in excess of that found for high-yield bonds.

Our conclusion is that distressed debt investing, while producing very favorable returns over the period 1990 to 2005, still exposed investors to considerable event risk. This risk was on par with that observed for high-yield bonds. Therefore, investors in distressed debt should expect to bear the event risk associated with troubled companies—that

EXHIBIT 20.10   Frequency Distribution for Distressed Debt[a]

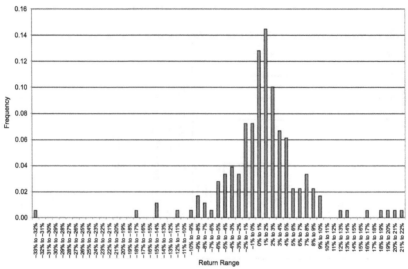

[a] Average = 1.11%, Std. Dev. = 6.05%, Skew = –0.63, Kurtosis = 7.05, Sharpe = 0.12.

is, that the company will cease its operations. Given the larger downside tail risk that distressed debt investing incurs, an investor should ask, is it worth it? The answer is yes. The average monthly return for distressed debt of 1.11% is greater than that for high-yield bonds of 0.68%.

Correlation of Private Equity Returns

The above analysis considered each class of private equity in isolation. In this section we consider how the different classes of private equity work with each other. In other words we check to see if the different classes do indeed provide different return patterns that are less correlated with each other, or whether the returns to the different classes are clustered with each other.

Exhibit 20.11 provides a correlation matrix with the four classes of private equity as well as large-capitalization stocks (S&P 500), small-cap stocks (Russell 2000), high-yield bonds, and U.S. Treasury bonds. The results are revealing. First, the different classes of private equity investing have low correlations with each other. This indicates that each class of private equity can be a useful addition to a diversified portfolio of stocks and bonds because the returns to the different private equity classes do not "double up" on one another.

EXHIBIT 20.11 Correlation Analysis for Private Equity Classes with Stocks and Bonds

	S&P 500	RU 2000	10-Yr. T-bond	High Yield	Venture	LBO	Mezzanine	Distressed
S&P 500	1.00							
RU 2000	0.75	1.00						
10-yr. T-bond	0.14	0.04	1.00					
High yield	0.63	0.89	0.31	1.00				
Venture	0.34	0.23	−0.40	−0.14	1.00			
LBO	0.76	0.52	−0.21	0.30	0.43	1.00		
Mezzanine	0.39	0.35	0.20	0.32	−0.05	0.44	1.00	
Distressed	0.30	0.76	−0.02	0.85	−0.12	0.15	0.05	1.00

Second, it can be seen from Exhibit 20.11, that the returns to private equity have low correlations with traditional asset classes. Notably, three of the four classes of private equity are negatively correlated with the returns to U.S. Treasury bonds. In addition, the classes of private equity have a low correlation with large-cap and small-cap stocks; the one exception is LBO fund returns which have a correlation with the S&P 500 of 0.76. Otherwise, it appears that private equity is a very good diversifier for a traditional portfolio of stocks and bonds.

PRIVATE EQUITY WITHIN A DIVERSIFIED PORTFOLIO

The popularity of private equity investments has led to many studies on the value of investing in these vehicles.[5] Exhibit 20.11 indicates that the different classes of private equity have a low correlation with the traditional asset classes of Treasury bonds and public equity. We examine these potential benefits in the rest of this section.

---

[5] See, Alon Brav and Paul Gompers. "Myth or Reality? The Long-Run Underperformance of Initial Public Offerings: Evidence from Venture and Non-Venture Capital-Backed Companies," *The Journal of Finance* (December 1997), pp. 1791–1821; Paul Gompers and Josh Lerner, "Money Chasing Deals? The Impact of Fund Inflows on the Valuation of Private Equity Investments," *The Journal of Financial Economics* (2000), pp. 281–325; Paul Gompers and Josh Lerner, "The Challenge of Performance Assessment," in Rick Lake and Ronald Lake (eds.), *Private Equity and Venture Capital* (London: Euromoney Books, 2000); and Paul Gompers, "Grandstanding in the Venture Capital Industry," *The Journal of Financial Economics* (1996), pp. 131–156.

There are, however, concerns about the returns to private equity. First, Gompers and Lerner conclude that inflows to private equity funds have a substantial impact on the pricing of private equity investments.[6] The implication is that there is too much money chasing too few deals, and that the positive valuations associated with private equity investments may be due to new capital inflows instead of real economic value.

Second, Gompers demonstrates that young venture capital firms bring private companies to the public market earlier than older venture capital firms in order to establish a positive reputation.[7] He concludes that this type of signaling causes real wealth losses in the form of underpriced IPOs and lower-valued equity stakes, and that this loss is borne by the limited partners in the venture fund.

Despite these potential caveats, empirical research indicates that private equity has favorable risk and return characteristics. We examine these properties within a portfolio framework.

Building a Diversified Portfolio with Private Equity

We now examine the ability of private equity to expand the investment opportunity set. Following the same analysis we performed for commodity futures and managed futures, we first build the efficient frontier using stocks and bonds. We then blend in a 10% allocation to each class of private equity. Our results are presented in Exhibits 20.12 to 20.15.

We begin by examining the addition of venture capital to a traditional portfolio of stocks and bonds. Exhibit 20.12 demonstrates a considerable improvement in the efficient frontier. The addition of venture capital to stocks and bonds leads to a significant, positive shift in the efficient frontier.

We find similar results for leveraged buyouts, mezzanine finance, and distressed debt. However, the diversification benefits diminish with distressed debt; this is consistent with distressed debt's downside tail. Still, distressed debt does provide for an expanded efficient frontier along with the other classes of private equity.

In the opening chapter of this book we maintained that private equity is not really a different asset class but just one point along the equity investment spectrum. However, the results in Exhibits 20.12 to 20.15 demonstrate that the diversification properties of private equity compared to public equity and bonds provide a source of returns that can be viewed both for their excess returns as well as diversification properties.

---

[6] See Gompers and Lerner, "Money Chasing Deals?"
[7] See Gompers, "Grandstanding in the Venture Capital Industry."

EXHIBIT 20.12   Efficient Frontier with Venture Capital

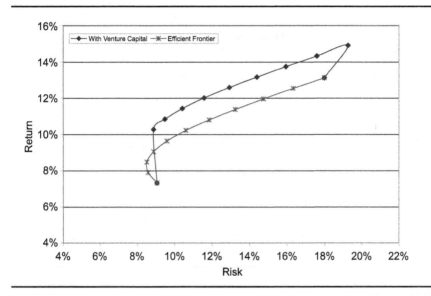

EXHIBIT 20.13   Efficient Frontier with LBOs

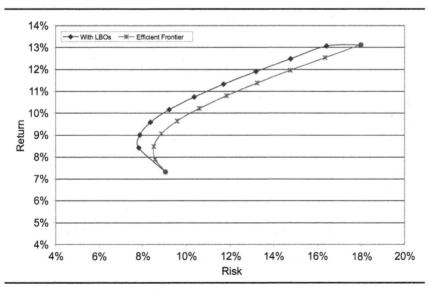

EXHIBIT 20.14   Efficient Frontier with Mezzanine

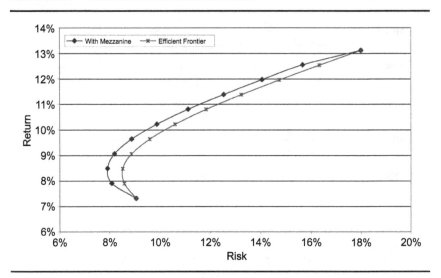

EXHIBIT 20.15   Efficient Frontier with Distressed Debt

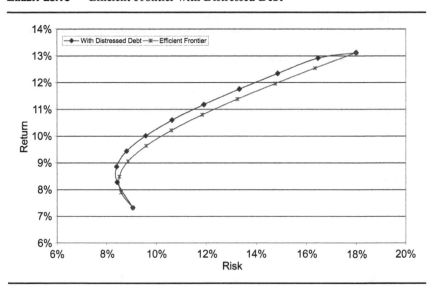

CONCLUSION

This chapter was concerned with the economics of private equity. Initially, we observed that venture capital and leveraged buyouts earned risk premiums in excess of that of the public stock market while mezzanine finance and distressed debt underperformed compared to public equity. We did observe that the Sharpe ratios for venture capital, leveraged buyouts and mezzanine debt exceeded that of the public stock market while distressed debt had a lower Sharpe ratio.

We found that the return distributions for the four classes of private equity were very different. Venture capital for example, presented a large positive skew with a large positive value of kurtosis, indicating a large fat tail to the upside. This is consistent with our description of venture capital as a call option on the success of a startup company. Essentially, venture capital is exposed to positive event risk. Conversely, distressed debt displayed a large negative skew value along with a large value of kurtosis, indicating a fat downside tail. This is consistent with an asset class that is exposed to negative event risk: the risk of defaults and bankruptcies. Leveraged buyouts and mezzanine debt displayed much more symmetrical returns.

In our examination of private equity in a portfolio context, we found that private equity was an effective diversifying agent. Specifically, we found that each class of private equity provided an expanded efficient frontier when added to a portfolio of stocks and bonds. The conclusion is that private equity is a valuable addition to a diversified stock portfolio.

CHAPTER 21

Performance Measurement for Private Equity

The prior chapters on private equity have demonstrated the tremendous growth for private equity investing. The commitment to private equity has become a significant part of the investment portfolio for both retail and institutional investors. However, very little has been produced regarding the pricing and benchmarking of private equity returns.

The private equity market is an example of a market where information is difficult to acquire. In the public equity markets, researchers often assume that the markets are efficient; that is, that there are no asymmetries of information among market participants. This assumption does not hold in the private equity market.

The problem becomes particularly acute in performance measurement. The benchmark chosen to measure the performance of a private equity manager is a key factor in assessment and allocation of capital to that manager. Additionally performance assessment is important for determining bonuses at endowments, pension funds, and foundations that are measured by the performance of their private equity portfolios.

In this chapter, we present a method for measuring private equity performance relative to market indexes. We begin by describing the problem of measuring private equity performance. We then examine the returns to private equity compared to several stock-and-bond indexes to find an appropriate benchmark. This allows us to measure the excess risk-adjusted return earned by private equity managers. Last, we examine whether private equity portfolios are susceptible to stale or managed pricing, and attempt to determine which is the culprit.

THE PROBLEM

Part of the problem of performance measurement in the private equity arena is the structure of the marketplace. There are four main participants: issuers, intermediaries, investors, and information processors. The issuers generally share the trait of being locked out of the public markets. Private equity is generally one of the most expensive forms of capital financing. Issuers of private equity are usually new and emerging firms that cannot raise money in the public markets or public firms going private that need massive amounts of private financing.

The private nature of the securities offered requires intensive research to determine if they are priced fairly. There is no "semistrong" form of market efficiency where security prices reflect all available public information.[1] These instruments are also closely held, so liquidity may not exist. Consider the case of CacheFlow Inc./Blue Coat, a startup Internet company mentioned in Chapter 16. Each series of preferred stock offered by this company was purchased by only one or two investors. There was virtually no market for CacheFlow's securities outside of the venture capitalists that purchased the securities in the first place.

Consequently, private equity securities are thinly traded if at all. Without a market for trading these securities, their value is often set by appraisal instead of an objective market price. The labor-intensive nature of valuing these securities makes the private equity arena a particularly inefficient market for pricing.

The pricing of private equity securities is further confounded by the intermediaries in this market. Approximately 80% of the capital committed to private equity is managed by intermediaries, limited partnerships that collect pools of investment capital. Each limited partnership is managed by a general partner, the private equity specialist.

The third group in the private equity arena is the investors, typically institutions and high-net-worth individuals. These investors commit their capital to an intermediary because they often lack the staff or expertise to make private equity investments directly. Typically, the general partner of the intermediary has broad discretion to invest the money as it sees fit.

---

[1] The theory of efficient capital markets states that there are three forms of efficiency: weak, semistrong, and strong. Weak market efficiency states that security prices reflect all past information. Semistrong market efficiency states that security prices reflect all past and current publicly available information. Strong market efficiency states that security prices reflect all information, both private and public. It is generally believed that the public equity markets are semistrong efficient; that is, the prices of publicly traded securities reflect all past and current public information regarding the underlying issuer.

The general partner of a private equity limited partnership has broad discretion not only to make investments, but also to determine their "fair value." Without publicly traded prices to determine fair value, most intermediaries have considerable flexibility to mark the value of the partnership's investment portfolio. Furthermore, the general partner's incentive or profit sharing fees is dependent upon how the value of the partnership's portfolio changes. This has led one researcher to claim that many limited partnerships pursue "marketing supportive accounting," where the general partner is slow to mark down its portfolio positions to a reasonable estimate of fair value.[2]

Many general partners of private equity limited partnerships are reluctant to market their portfolio positions up or down until there is an objective market event that allows for repricing. This could be an additional round of private equity financing, an IPO, or a secondary trade of some of the securities in the over-the-counter market. However, an additional transaction may not happen for another six months or even for another year.

Companies that receive investment capital from private equity partnerships often remain privately held for many years after the investment has been made. These companies have no observable market price to present an objective value. Marking to market portfolio investments may not be possible. Consequently, many private equity firms maintain a conservative estimate of the value of their investments by keeping them at book value. Yet this may not reflect either the growth or decline of value of the private equity portfolio.

Private equity limited partnerships hold various combinations of illiquid exchange-traded securities as well as privately issued, over-the-counter securities. The illiquid nature of these securities can lead to nonsynchronous price changes given the movement of the overall stock market. For example, even publicly traded securities in the small-capitalization range of the stock market do not trade on a continuous basis and, therefore, the stock prices for small-cap companies may not reflect their true value because they lag the pricing of the stock market as a whole.

The capital asset pricing model (CAPM) teaches us that the price of a security can be related to the amount of exposure it has to market risk. Market risk is the only risk that should be compensated because firm-specific risk can be diversified away through a portfolio approach to investing. However, the CAPM assumes that all securities are freely transferable, and this is not the case with private equity securities.

---

[2] See Andrew Weisman, "The Dangers of Historical Hedge Fund Data," Working paper, Nikko Securities International, 2000.

In the vernacular of investment management, private equity valuations suffer from "stale pricing." Stale pricing is the condition that the book value of private equity investments may not be "fresh" in the sense that the price of private equity securities may not reflect current market value. Under the CAPM, fresh prices may be obtained monthly, weekly, and even daily, by observing how security prices react to concurrent movements in the broader stock market.

However, the stale pricing of illiquid securities will not necessarily react concurrently with a broad market index. This is what is meant by "stale pricing"—that private equity prices may lag the price movements of a readily observable public securities benchmark. If this is the case, stale pricing can reduce estimates of volatility and correlation to broad-based securities indexes.

Alternatively, it might be the case that private equity valuations suffer not from stale pricing, but from "managed pricing." Private equity managers have virtually complete discretion to mark the value of their portfolios. Consequently, they might "manage" their portfolio valuations, by pricing illiquid securities when it is convenient and profitable to do so. Managed pricing may also lead to a lag time between observable public market valuations and those in a private equity portfolio.

We note in brief, that the proliferation of the fourth category of participants in the private equity market, information processors, has grown in an attempt to address these problems. Information processors come in the form of agents, consultants, gatekeepers, and advisers. They exist to reduce the problems of information asymmetry that are common to the private equity marketplace. Part of their respective jobs is to try to filter through the performance results of the limited partnership private equity funds to determine how stale the pricing might be.

There are two other potential problems with pricing private equity portfolios. First, one researcher has indicated that the flow of funds into venture capital limited partnerships may create an environment where too much money is chasing too few deals resulting in inflated private equity valuations.[3] However, this problem is not peculiar to the private equity market; it exists in the public equity markets, too. For instance, see Exhibit 16.3 in Chapter 16, which demonstrates the "too much money" phenomenon with respect to the prices of publicly traded securities in the NASDAQ market.

Second, private equity limited partnerships that are in the process of fund raising tend to be aggressive in the pricing of their portfolios.

---

[3] See Paul Gompers and Josh Lerner, "Money Chasing Deals? The Impact of Fund Inflows on the Valuation of Private Equity Investments," *The Journal of Financial Economics* 55 (2000), pp. 281–325.

These funds may neglect to mark down portfolio values that are underwater and may value still private companies above cost.[4] This problem is peculiar to the private equity industry, and it may contribute to the managed pricing problem. In our next section, we discuss some possible solutions to these problems.

PRIOR EFFORTS TO MEASURE PRIVATE EQUITY PERFORMANCE

Some progress has been made to resolve the problems identified so far. Industry groups have been formed to address the problem of stale or managed pricing. Efforts have been made to mark-to-market private equity portfolios. Both of these methods have merit.

For example, the Institutional Limited Partners Association, the not-for-profit industry group that represents the interests of institutional investors in private equity partnerships, has attempted to establish reporting standards.[5] In addition, the British Venture Capital Association has introduced a set of valuation standards that its members must follow.[6] Nonetheless, these attempts to establish standard valuation practices still provide considerable flexibility to the private equity fund managers. For example, there is no clear distinction between early and late stage financing or the private equity firms that pursue these strategies. All in all, considerable discretion remains with the general partners of private equity funds to determine the valuations of their portfolios.

Furthermore, the established guidelines generally emphasize the principle of *conservatism*. That is, private equity portfolios should not be marked to market until an observable event (such as a new round of financing) that provides an objective valuation point. While these procedures might make the returns across different private equity funds more comparable, they make it more difficult to compare the returns to private equity to other asset classes. This means that private equity funds can demonstrate that they have outperformed their peers in the private equity marketplace, but they may not be able to demonstrate that they

---

[4] See Paul Gompers, "Grandstanding in the Venture Capital Industry," *The Journal of Financial Economics* 42 (1996), pp. 136–156.
[5] See Institutional Limited Partners Association, "Proposal for a Standard Industry-Wide System for Measuring Interim Performance of Venture Capital Partnerships" (May 1990).
[6] See British Venture Capital Association, "Guidelines for the Valuation and Disclosure of Venture Capital Portfolios" (1993).

have outperformed the broader equity or (in the case of mezzanine or distressed debt) bond markets.

Another tenet of the principle of conservatism is to mark portfolio values down quickly and up slowly. That is, losses should be recognized as soon as they can be reasonably estimated. Conversely, gains should be recognized less quickly, only when they are assured.

Another solution to the problem of stale or managed prices is to mark to market each investment in a private equity portfolio on a periodic basis. This proposal does not wait until there is an observable and objective event such as an IPO. Instead, it reevaluates all holdings in the portfolio on a periodic basis (typically, quarterly) in an attempt to determine fair value.

This proposed solution is very time intensive, but it can produce reasonable results. Gompers and Lerner apply this approach to examine the returns from a single private equity group, the E.M. Warburg, Pincus & Co. private equity portfolio.[7] First, they use a single period CAPM regression model where the returns to the Warburg Pincus portfolio are measured against the returns to the public stock market. A single-period model simply means that the current returns to the Warburg Pincus portfolio were regressed against the current returns to the publicly traded stock market.

In a CAPM regression model, the idea is to determine what amount of variation in the dependent variable (the Warburg Pincus private equity portfolio) that is determined by the variation in the independent variable (the stock market return). The important measure of performance is the constant term, or intercept, in the regression equation. This term represents the excess return earned by the private equity portfolio over and above that of the general stock market return. In other words, when the effects of the stock market have been controlled for, the residual return represented by the intercept determines whether the market-adjusted return earned by private equity is superior to or inferior to the performance of the broad stock market.

In their first regression, Gompers and Lerner find that the intercept is equal to 2.68% per quarter. This indicates that private equity can earn an excess return of 2.68% per quarter on a risk-adjusted basis.[8] They also find an R^2 of 0.28.

---

[7] See Paul Gompers and Josh Lerner, "The Challenge of Performance Assessment," *The Journal of Private Equity* (Winter 1997), pp. 5–12.

[8] However, it does not appear that Gompers and Lerner subtracted the cash rate of return from the excess return. If not, a Treasury bill return should be subtracted from the excess return to determine the true size of the private equity manager's alpha. Also, Gompers and Lerner do not distinguish between different types of private equity such as venture capital, leveraged buyouts, and so on.

In their second regression, they use the same single-period CAPM model, but they mark to market the private equity portfolio of Warburg Pincus. Mark to market is accomplished by taking every company in the Warburg Pincus portfolio and assigning it to a three-digit Securities Industry Classification. For each industry, Gompers and Lerner calculated an equal-weighted industry index from the public market values of firms in the same industry. They then adjust the portfolio investments by the change of value of the matched industry public market index.

They find the explanatory power of the single period CAPM regression increases when private equity investments are marked to market. The R-square of the new equation increased to 0.492. Also the intercept term declined to 1.97%. That is, once the private equity portfolio is marked to market, the excess return earned on the risk-adjusted portfolio declines by 71 basis points.

A FRAMEWORK FOR MEASURING PRIVATE EQUITY PERFORMANCE

In this section we propose two methods by which to measure private equity performance. First, we describe how to adjust private equity investments for their exposure to market risk. We then consider several different benchmarks for each class of private equity.

Adjusting Private Equity Returns for Market Exposure

In Chapters 16 through 19 we discussed the various forms of private equity and gave some indication of their higher risk profile. The reasons are now obvious: long holding periods, new companies subject to the whims of the economy, the lack of a well-developed secondary trading market, and nascent business plans that take time to come to fruition.

Given the large exposure to market risk that private equity investments provide, it is reasonable to ask if private equity funds are adding any value beyond the returns they receive from their market exposure. Essentially, private equity managers provide a package of returns that contains four essential ingredients: (1) the return earned for exposure to market risk; (2) a return premium for a portfolio that is less liquid and, therefore, subject to stale pricing; (3) the private equity manager's active skill; and (4) leverage applied to that skill.[9]

The problem most investors face is separating the return due to market exposure from that earned from the private equity manager's

---

[9] A similar claim can be made for those hedge funds that are exposed to market exposure such as those demonstrated in Exhibit 6.2 in Chapter 6.

skill. The solution most often pursued is to regress the historical returns from private equity investments on the concurrent returns of a broad based market index such as the NASDAQ or the Russell 1000. A broad market index is used as a proxy for market risk. In this regression analysis, the return to the private equity investment is the dependent variable, and the return to the market index is the independent variable. The regression equation typically takes the form of

$$R_{i,t}(\text{PE}) = \alpha + \beta R_{m,t} + \varepsilon_{i,t} \tag{21.1}$$

where

$R_{i,t}(\text{PE})$ is the return to private equity investments at time t.
$R_{m,t}$ is the return on a broad-based market index at time t.
β is a measure of the systematic exposure of private equity returns to the broad-based market index.
$\varepsilon_{i,t}$ is a residual term which measures the variation of private equity returns that are not explained by movements in the broad-based market index or the private equity manager's skill.
α is the return due to the private equity manager's skill.

This is a simple one-factor (the broad market return) regression model.[10] Equation (21.1) can be turned around to produce:

$$R_{i,t}(\text{PE}) - \beta R_{m,t} = \alpha + \varepsilon_{i,t} \tag{21.2}$$

Equation (21.2) is the risk-adjusted formula for private equity returns. It says that if we subtract the amount of exposure to the broad-based market index from the returns to private equity, what should be left is the excess return earned by the private equity manager. Equation (21.2) disentangles market returns from private equity returns to determine a measure of manager skill.

Equation (21.2) can be further refined by subtracting the return earned from investing in U.S. Treasury bills from the left hand side of the equation. If a private equity manager cannot find any viable investments, she should at least earn a rate of return equal to U.S. Treasury bills because this is the safest short-term investment available. There-

---

[10] This is similar to the model used by Gompers and Lerner. They also use the three-factor Fama-French model which includes a factor for market risk, size, and book value. They find similar results to the one factor model. That is, the explanatory power of the three-factor regression equation increases if private equity investments are marked to market. See Gompers and Lerner, "The Challenge of Performance Assessment."

fore, a private equity manager must earn a risk-adjusted return in excess of Treasury bills to demonstrate active skill, or alpha. Equation (21.2) can be expressed as

$$[R_{i,t}(\text{PE}) - \text{Tbill}] - \beta[R_{m,t} - \text{Tbill}] = \alpha + \varepsilon_{i,t} \qquad (21.3)$$

where

$[R_{i,t}(\text{PE}) - \text{Tbill}]$ represents the net of fees return earned by private equity in excess of a cash rate of return.

$[R_{m,t} - \text{Tbill}]$ represents the return on the market index in excess of the cash rate of return.

α is the risk-adjusted excess return earned by the private equity manager.

ε is an indication of residual effects that are not explained by the data; it indicates random noise in the data.

Equation (21.3) can be used as a performance measure for private equity. First, the term β (beta) is a measure of the systematic risk of the private equity portfolio in relation to the market index. It is a measure of risk in relation to the broader stock or bond market. A value of beta greater than one indicates a private equity portfolio that has greater sensitivity to the movements of the overall stock or bond market than a diversified basket of stocks or bonds. Conversely, a beta value less than one indicates a portfolio that has less sensitivity to the movements of the overall stock or bond market.

The term α (alpha) is the intercept of the equation and it measures the return earned by the private equity portfolio after taking into account the effects of the broad stock or bond market and the current cash rate of return. The intercept represents the excess risk-adjusted return earned by the private equity manager over and above that for the market return and a cash return. It measures the return received due to the private equity manager's skill.

Notice that equation (21.3) contains two residual terms, alpha and epsilon (ε). Epsilon represents random noise in the data. In other words it is not attributed to manager skill. So how do we know whether the residual term is alpha or epsilon? This is where statistics come into play. If the residual term is statistically significant, then this is a demonstration of a consistent economic effect, that is, alpha or manager skill. However, if the residual term is not statistically significant, then this is an indication of only random noise—ε—and not manager skill.

Private Equity Benchmarks

One of the problems with measuring private equity performance is determining the appropriate benchmark to use. For instance, in Chapter 16, we described how the returns to venture capital are closely linked to the over-the-counter stock market. Therefore, a natural starting point for venture capital would be to select the NASDAQ as an appropriate benchmark. We also include the Russell 1000, Russell 2000, and the S&P 500 as potential benchmarks.

In Chapter 17 we demonstrated how leveraged buyouts often take private established companies that suffer from some form of inefficiency. The nature of these mature companies would suggest that a stock market index with larger capitalized stocks might be a more appropriate benchmark for LBOs. The Russell 1000 or S&P 500 might be good suggestions. In addition, we include the NASDAQ and Russell 2000 indexes in case there are any small-capitalization stock effects.

For mezzanine debt, the choice is less clear. This is because mezzanine is a hybrid product with components of debt and equity. Therefore, we use both debt and equity indexes to determine which has the greatest explanatory power for this class of private equity. First, recall our discussion in Chapter 18 that mezzanine financing is a middle market phenomenon. Therefore, we choose small to mid cap stock indexes to measure the systematic risk of mezzanine finance. We also use a high-yield bond index to capture the greater risk profile that mezzanine debt has compared to investment grade bonds or bank loans. Last, we use a hybrid index to measure the systematic risk of mezzanine debt—the Salomon Brothers Convertible Bond index. Convertible bonds are hybrids themselves, containing elements of both debt and equity and are similar to mezzanine financing.

Then there is distressed debt. Once again distressed debt can have a hybrid nature. It is the debt of a troubled company. Therefore, it could be treated as a high-yield bond investment. Alternatively, distressed debt is often converted to equity as part of the workout solution for the troubled company. It may fluctuate in value similar to the equity stock market. Consequently, we also include both debt and equity benchmarks for distressed debt.

We start with the Russell 1000 and Russell 2000. The reason that we use both a large-cap and a small-cap stock index is that distressed companies come in all sizes. Distressed debt need not be issued by small-cap companies and, in fact, in our discussion of distressed debt, we provided examples of large-cap companies that were part of this alternative asset class. We also include the Salomon Brothers Cash Pay High Yield index to capture the risky nature of distressed debt as well as a convertible bond index.

ANALYSIS OF PRIVATE EQUITY BENCHMARKS

To find an appropriate benchmark for each category of private equity, we examine a simple one period, one factor, regression model. We then expand these regressions to determine if there is managed or stale pricing associated with private equity investments.

For venture capital, LBOs, and mezzanine debt, we use data from *Venture Economics*. This database represents the returns earned from private equity limited partnerships that voluntarily report their returns to *Venture Economics*. For distressed debt, we use data from *Hedge Fund Research Inc.* (HFRI). Similarly, the data from HFRI contains return information voluntarily reported by fund managers who have total control over the prices that they report. The voluntary nature of this reporting is an important point that we will touch on in our conclusion to this chapter.

Simple One Period/One Factor Regression Results

In this section we use equation (21.3) as our regression model to determine the amount of excess return associated with private equity. Exhibit 21.1 presents the regression results for venture capital. We regress the quarterly returns to venture capital as the dependent variable against the returns for the NASDAQ, Russell 1000, Russell 2000, and S&P 500. The returns are quarterly over the period 1985 to 2005.

In all cases the beta coefficient is statistically significant at the 1% level. In other words, we can state that, with 99% confidence, the beta coefficients in each regression equation is significant in explaining the variability of the returns to venture capital. The alpha, or intercept, however, is not significant in each equation. It is either weakly significant at the 5% or 10% level, or not statistically significant, in the case of the S&P 500. Since alpha is used to measure the skill of the venture capital manager, there is some question as to the level of skill that venture capitalists add beyond that of the stock market return.

For instance, with respect to venture capital returns regressed on the NASDAQ, the beta coefficient equals 0.48 and the alpha (or intercept)

EXHIBIT 21.1 Single-Period Regression Analysis for Venture Capital

Market Index	Alpha	*t*-Statistic	Beta	*t*-Statistic	R-Square
Russell 1000	1.88%	1.76	0.61	4.68	21%
Russell 2000	2.12%	1.97	0.42	4.19	18%
S&P 500	1.60%	1.46	0.59	4.41	19%
NASDAQ	1.69%	1.78	0.48	6.98	37%

coefficient equals 1.69%. The beta is a measure of the covariance of the returns to venture capital with those of the NASDAQ. A beta less than one indicates that the returns to venture capital are less sensitive compared to the movement of the NASDAQ stock market than a diversified basket of stocks. A beta greater than one indicates that the returns to venture capital are more sensitive to the movements of the NASDAQ stock market than a diversified basket of stocks. For all four regression equations, the beta values ranged from 0.41 with respect to the Russell 2000 to 0.61 for the Russell 1000. In each case, the returns to venture capital demonstrate less sensitivity compared to the movements of the broader stock market.

The intercept value of 1.69% with respect to the NASDAQ regression indicates that, on average, the returns to venture capital generated a risk-adjusted return in excess of a cash rate of return of 1.69% per quarter or about 6.8% per year. The ability to generate risk-adjusted returns that are almost 7% greater than a cash rate of return is a clear demonstration of manager skill. The risk-adjusted return for the other three market indexes is even greater; for example, the quarterly alpha compared to the Russell 2000 is 2.12% or about 8.5% a year.

Also, we note that the simple one period regression model of equation (21.3) generated reasonable R-square measures. R-square measures the amount of variability in the dependent variable (venture capital returns) that is explained by the independent variable (the market indexes). For example, R-square measures were 18% for the Russell 2000 to 37% for the NASDAQ.

The statistically significant results presented in Exhibit 21.1 demonstrate that a considerable portion of the returns to venture capital is dependent upon the performance of the broad stock market. This makes sense. A strong stock market provides for a healthy IPO market which, in turn, translates into good venture capital performance.

Exhibit 21.2 presents the results for the one period regression equations for LBOs. Again we use quarterly return data. The beta coefficients for each index range from 0.22 for the NASDAQ to 0.42 for the

EXHIBIT 21.2 Single-Period Regression Analysis for Leveraged Buyouts

Market Index	Alpha	t-Statistic	Beta	t-Statistic	R-Square
Russell 1000	1.80%	3.51	0.42	6.77	38%
Russell 2000	1.95%	3.59	0.28	5.59	29%
S&P 500	1.55%	2.97	0.42	6.71	37%
NASDAQ	1.88%	3.49	0.22	5.80	30%

two large-cap stock indexes. The R-square measure is reasonably strong also, ranging from 29% for the NASDAQ to 38% and 37% for the two large-cap stock indexes.

In general, the size of the beta coefficients in Exhibit 21.2 are lower than that for venture capital in Exhibit 21.1. This indicates that LBO funds are less dependent upon the returns to the broad stock market. Their returns are based more on the unique characteristics of individual companies. We might conclude that LBO funds generate return patterns that are exposed more to company specific risk than systematic market risk. Last, we note that the large-cap stock indexes—the Russell 1000 and the S&P 500—have greater explanatory power (higher R-squares) than the small-cap indexes. This reflects that leveraged buyouts are more a factor for larger companies than smaller companies.

In each case the value of the intercept is statistically significant at the 1% level (in fact the t-statistics for the alpha coefficient are almost identical in the four equations). The risk-adjusted returns in excess of cash range from 1.55% per quarter for the S&P 500 to 1.95% for the Russell 2000. This indicates annual risk adjusted rates of return in excess of a Treasury bill cash rate of about 6% to 8%.

Exhibit 21.3 presents the regression results for mezzanine debt. Reflecting mezzanine debt's dual nature as debt and equity, we find much less explanatory power from the market indexes. R-square measures are low, in the range of 1.5% to 15%. Clearly, mezzanine financing is a category of securities that defies easy description.

We find that the beta coefficient for mezzanine debt with respect to each index is smaller compared to the beta coefficients observed for venture capital and leveraged buyouts. This also indicates lower explanatory power of the market indexes to describe the return pattern of mezzanine debt. The betas however, are statistically significant, except for the Salomon high-yield index—which is surprising given the riskier nature of mezzanine debt.

However, the risk-adjusted excess return is statistically significant in each equation. The alpha coefficient ranges from 1.58% for the NASDAQ

EXHIBIT 21.3 Single-Period Regression Analysis for Mezzanine Financing

Market Index	Alpha	t-Statistic	Beta	t-Statistic	R-Square
Russell 2000	1.64%	3.14	0.11	2.17	6.30%
NASDAQ	1.58%	3.09	0.10	2.74	9.70%
Salomon Cash Pay	1.71%	2.96	0.14	1.00	1.50%
Salomon Convertibles	1.87%	3.66	0.25	3.14	15.40%

to 1.87% for the convertible bond index, about 6% to 7% a year. This is what we would expect. Consistent with our discussions in Chapter 18, we would expect mezzanine debt to earn a lower excess return compared to venture capital or LBOs to reflect its lower risk.

The low R-squares associated with the regression equations for mezzanine debt indicate that it is a good portfolio diversification tool. The reason is that the returns to mezzanine debt are less influenced by the general movements in either the stock or bond market.

Recall from our discussion in Chapter 18 that mezzanine debt is a form of "gap financing." It is used to plug a gap in time, capital structure, or LBO financing. Gaps in business plans occur regardless of the movements of the stock or bond markets. Consequently, there is less reason to expect mezzanine debt to be correlated with broad market indexes.

In Exhibit 21.4, we finally present the regression results for distressed debt. In each case, the beta is statistically significant, for both equity and debt indexes. The beta ranges from 0.25 for the Russell 1000 to 0.68 for the Salomon high-yield index. All of the beta coefficients are significant at the 1% level. Distressed debt demonstrates a hybrid nature between debt and equity more so than mezzanine debt.

Furthermore, the R-square reaches a high of 44% based on the Russell 2000. The greater variability explained by the Russell 2000 might reflect the fact that distressed debt companies tend to be established companies that have run into financial trouble. These are companies significantly past their IPO stage. However, the R-square for the Salomon Brothers Cash Pay High Yield index produces an R-square of 43%—just about equivalent. The closely similar R-square values demonstrate the hybrid nature of distressed debt—it displays characteristics of both debt and equity.

The quarterly alpha coefficient ranged from 1.68% with respect to the high-yield index to 2.2% for the Russell 1000. This indicates that the average annual risk-adjusted return in excess of a cash return is about 7% to 9% per year. This is somewhat consistent with our prior example in Chapter 18 that distressed debt has a higher risk profile than mezzanine debt (see Exhibit 18.5).

EXHIBIT 21.4   Single-Period Regression Analysis for Distressed Debt

Market Index	Alpha	*t*-Statistic	Beta	*t*-Statistic	R-Square
Russell 1000	2.20%	4.65	0.25	4.29	23%
Russell 2000	2.07%	5.17	0.26	6.91	44%
Salomon Cash Pay HY	1.68%	4.01	0.68	6.74	43%
Salomon Convertibles	1.71%	3.91	0.41	6.05	40%

In Chapter 19 we indicated that distressed debt investors are dealing with companies that have a great risk of survival. However, distressed debt investing is not as risky as venture capital because the target company usually has a long operating history with identifiable products. Therefore, the investment risk is less than venture capital. In addition, distressed debt, cash flow, and assets have a less risky position than leveraged buyouts. This may seem a bit strange at first, but consider that distressed debt does not mean unsecured debt. Distressed debt is generally secured by some physical asset in the event of liquidation. Therefore, distressed debt players are guaranteed some downside protection based on the assets of the company. Consistent with this analysis, we find distressed debt managers produce an excess return slightly less than that for venture capital and leveraged buyouts.

A Multiperiod Analysis of Private Equity Returns

We discussed above that the returns to private equity investing may lag that of the public securities markets. This means that examining private equity returns based on contemporaneous market returns may not fully reveal the extent to which private equity returns depend upon the returns to the broad stock or bond market. Therefore, the simple one-period regression models we performed above may not provide accurate estimates of the systematic risk of private equity returns as measured by β or the risk-adjusted excess return as measured by α, the regression intercept.

In fact, the estimates of beta may be biased downwards while the estimates of alpha may be biased upwards because private equity pricing may not occur contemporaneously with changes in the public securities markets. This lack of nonsynchronous pricing might then be embedded in the alpha intercept. This would inflate the alpha coefficient to a greater extent that we might observe if we could capture these lagged pricing effects. In other words, what we label skill by the private equity manager as measured by the alpha intercept in the single-period regressions might, in fact, reflect lagged pricing effects instead of real skill. This problem also occurs with respect to small, public firms where the trading of their securities is limited.

To solve the problem of stale or lagged pricing, equation (21.1) can be expanded to include multiperiod pricing effects:[11]

$$R_{i,t}(\text{PE}) = \alpha + \beta_0 R_{m,t} + \beta_1 R_{m,t-1} + \beta_2 R_{m,t-2} + \beta_3 R_{m,t-3} + \ldots + \varepsilon_{i,t} \quad (21.4)$$

---

[11] This method has been applied successfully to hedge funds. See Clifford Asness, Robert Krail, and John Liew, "Do Hedge Funds Hedge?" *The Journal of Portfolio Management* (Fall 2001), pp. 6–19.

Equation (21.4) is an equation where the returns to private equity in period t are regressed against the contemporaneous returns to the market as well as the lagged returns to the market from prior periods $t - 1$, $t - 2$, $t - 3$, and so forth. Equation (21.4) is a "multiperiod" extension of regression equation (21.1).

If the returns to private equity are due to either stale or managed pricing, we should see a significant influence from prior market returns. That is, stale or managed pricing may result in a delay between the time that changes in the value of the public securities market are observed and the time when these changes in value are reflected in the returns to private equity portfolios. By including prior market returns in our regression equation, we can observe the nonsynchronous or delayed market effects on private equity returns.

In equation (21.4), the summed beta of $\beta_0 + \beta_1 + \beta_2 + \beta_3 + ...$, provides a more accurate measure of how the returns to private equity covary with the public securities market. The reason we can do this is that beta coefficients are linearly additive. In other words, by summing the regression coefficients for both contemporaneous and lagged market effects we should be able to obtain a better measure of the systematic risk associated with private equity. In addition, by taking into account both contemporaneous and lagged stock/bond market effects, we should also obtain a better estimate of alpha, the measure of the private equity manager's skill.

With respect to equation (21.4), we can perform the same transformations to achieve the same risk-adjusted return (in excess of a cash rate) demonstrated in equation (21.3). Equation (21.5) presents this transformation:

$$[R_{i,t}(\text{PE}) - \text{Tbill}] - \beta_0[R_{m,t} - \text{Tbill}] - \beta_1[R_{m,t-1} - \text{Tbill}]$$
$$- \beta_2[R_{m,t-2} - \text{Tbill}] - \beta_3[R_{m,t-3} - \text{Tbill}] = \alpha + \varepsilon_{i,t} \qquad (21.5)$$

We regress the returns to private equity on the contemporaneous market return as well as the market return for the prior three quarters. In this way, we can observe the full impact of the public securities markets on the returns to private equity.[12] We note that the Treasury bill returns in equation (21.5) must also be lagged to coincide with the lagged stock or bond market returns.

Exhibit 21.5 presents the results for venture capital. Once again, we regress the current returns to venture capital against the current return to the public stock market as well as the return to the public stock market for the prior three quarters. With respect to the NASDAQ stock

---

[12] We also went further than one year in our lagged variables but found no measurable increase in explanatory power.

EXHIBIT 21.5 Multiperiod Regression Analysis for Venture Capital

Market Index	Alpha	t-Statistic	Beta(0)	t-Statistic	Beta(−1)	t-Statistic	Beta(−2)	t-Statistic	Beta(−3)	t-Statistic	R-Square
Russell 1000	0.89%	0.81	0.62	4.93	0.22	1.76	0.31	2.48	0.220	1.75	31%
Russell 2000	1.52%	1.31	0.47	4.48	0.16	1.48	0.22	2.03	0.080	0.82	23%
S&P 500	0.18%	0.16	0.60	4.61	0.22	1.67	0.31	2.42	0.230	1.8	29%
NASDAQ	0.48%	0.55	0.48	8.15	0.21	3.62	0.22	3.76	0.175	2.96	57%

market, the results are illuminating. Each beta coefficient is significant at the 1% level. This means that the returns to the NASDAQ stock market for both the current quarter as well as the prior three quarters are all statistically significant in explaining the current returns to venture capital. This is a strong demonstration of stale or managed pricing. Similar results are demonstrated for the other stock indexes.

Furthermore, the R-square measure increases in each regression equation in Exhibit 5. For example, the R-square for NASDAQ is now 57%—a significant level of explanatory power. Clearly, using four quarters of stock market returns are important to describe the returns venture capital.

The summed betas in Exhibit 21.5 demonstrate a much higher covariance with the market returns than that presented in Exhibit 21.1. For example, the summed betas in Exhibit 21.5 with respect to the NASDAQ equal 1.085 compared to 0.48 for the single-period model displayed in Exhibit 21.1. Simply put, when we allow for stale or managed pricing, we find that the returns to VC have a much greater exposure to the returns to the public securities markets. Similar results are found for each of the lagged stock market indexes presented in Exhibit 21.5.

Finally, we find that alpha (the intercept term) declines significantly when we account for lagged market returns. For example, the alpha term in Exhibit 21.5 with respect to the NASDAQ stock market is 0.48% per quarter (about 2% per year) compared to 1.69% (about 6.8% per year) presented in Exhibit 21.1. Therefore, this measure of the private equity manager's skill declines by 4.8% a year when we account for lagged market returns. This indicates that a considerable amount of manager skill observed from quarter to quarter can be explained by prior market returns. In fact, the alpha intercept with respect to the NASDAQ index is no longer statistically significant. So we must conclude that the residual amount is really *epsilon*. This means that when lagged market returns are included, any residual return is just a matter of random chance—not skill.

Exhibit 21.6 presents the results for LBO returns. We find that there is also a lagged effect for LBO returns although not as pronounced as for venture capital. The market return observed in the prior two quarters are significant in explaining the returns to LBO portfolios in the current quarter. The R-square measures for each stock market index increase, demonstrating the ability of prior returns to explain the current returns to leveraged buyouts. However, the alpha intercepts still remain statistically significant. Apparently, lagged stock market pricing does not explain away the skill factor of leveraged buyout managers as it does for venture capital managers. We can conclude that the excess return generated by LBO fund managers is reasonably robust to contemporaneous and lagged stock market returns.

EXHIBIT 21.6 Multiperiod Regression Analysis for Leveraged Buyouts

Market Index	Alpha	t-Statistic	Beta(0)	t-Statistic	Beta(−1)	t-Statistic	Beta(−2)	t-Statistic	Beta(−3)	t-Statistic	R-Square
Russell 1000	1.18%	2.26	0.43	6.86	0.100	1.58	0.100	1.66	0.083	1.38	43%
Russell 2000	1.25%	2.25	0.32	6.18	0.110	2.21	0.090	1.72	0.067	1.35	36%
S&P 500	0.80%	1.44	0.43	6.71	0.081	1.29	0.100	1.56	0.090	1.49	42%
NASDAQ	1.20%	2.24	0.23	6.11	0.084	2.30	0.074	2.02	0.030	0.83	40%

Exhibit 21.7 presents the lagged regression results for mezzanine debt. Lagged market returns have less of an impact on the returns to mezzanine debt. Similar to leveraged buyouts, the returns to mezzanine debt are explained by lagged market returns, but not as much as venture capital. The R-square measure increases for each index, although mezzanine debt still displays the greatest amount of variability in returns that cannot be explained by stock or bond indexes.

We also observe that the alpha intercepts remain statistically significant with respect to each stock or bond index. While the alpha intercepts decline from the prior single period regressions, they still remain statistically significant at the 1% level. This indicates that a considerable amount of manager skill remains even when we consider lagged pricing effects for mezzanine debt.

Exhibit 21.8 presents the results for lagged market returns and distressed debt. We find that the contemporaneous β_0 and one period logged $\beta(-1)$ to be statistically significant for each market index. In particular, we find that the lagged values of the Russell 2000 have significant explanatory power for the returns to distressed debt. The first two betas, β_0 and β_1, are both significant at the 1% level, and the contemporaneous and lagged market returns explain 54% (the R-square measure) of the returns to distressed debt. Curiously, lagged betas $\beta(-2)$ and $\beta(-3)$ show negative coefficients—indicating a reverse pricing trend the greater the lagged stock or bond index return. These results are puzzling, but not statistically significant such that we can draw conclusions. That is, prior negative stock returns lead to positive current returns for the distressed debt and vice versa. They may simple reflect the anticyclical nature of distressed debt managers—they are most active at the low points of the business cycle and most dormant when the economy is robust.

Last, the alpha coefficient in each equation decline slightly, but not to the same extent of venture capital or leveraged buyouts. Furthermore, the alpha coefficients all remain statistically significant at the 1% level. This reflects that quite a bit of the skill generated by distressed debt managers is genuine—it cannot be explained by prior stock or bond market returns.

Exhibit 21.9 summarizes our results; comparing the single period regression equations to the multiperiod equations. We compare the single period beta coefficients for each component of private equity and each market index to that for the summed beta in the lagged regressions. It is apparent that when prior market returns are included in the regression equation, the impact of the market returns is much greater in explaining the variability of returns to private equity.

EXHIBIT 21.7 Multiperiod Regression Analysis for Mezzanine Financing

Market Index	Alpha	t-Statistic	Beta(0)	t-Statistic	Beta(-1)	t-Statistic	Beta(-2)	t-Statistic	Beta(-3)	t-Statistic	R-Square
Russell 2000	1.46%	2.52	0.130	2.37	0.073	1.31	0.024	0.45	0.021	0.39	9.10%
NASDAQ	1.30%	2.38	0.100	2.65	0.077	2.07	0.017	0.46	0.043	1.17	17.30%
Salomon Cash Pay	1.65%	2.67	0.065	0.43	0.180	1.18	-0.120	-0.81	0.190	1.30	6.20%
Salomon Convertible	1.60%	2.78	0.240	1.85	0.080	0.96	0.053	0.64	0.090	1.09	20.00%

EXHIBIT 21.8 Multiperiod Regression Analysis for Distressed Debt

Market Index	Alpha	t-Statistic	Beta(0)	t-Statistic	Beta(-1)	t-Statistic	Beta(-2)	t-Statistic	Beta(-3)	t-Statistic	R-Square
Russell 1000	2.19%	4.55	0.27	4.53	0.140	2.39	-0.075	-1.29	-0.110	-1.95	33%
Russell 2000	1.81%	4.38	0.30	7.56	0.130	3.49	-0.020	-0.50	-0.040	-1.17	54%
Salomon Cash Pay HY	1.32%	2.83	0.65	5.71	0.260	2.39	0.002	0.01	-0.020	-0.20	48%
Salomon Convertibles	1.51%	3.59	0.41	6.78	0.135	2.24	-0.0200	-0.33	-0.064	-1.05	51%

EXHIBIT 21.9 Comparison of Single-Period versus Multiperiod Regression Analysis

Venture Capital	Single-Period Beta	Multiperiod Beta β(0) + β(−1) + β(−2) + β(−3)	Change in Beta	Single-Period Alpha	Multiperiod Alpha	Change in Alpha	Improvement in R-Square
Russell 1000	0.61	1.370	0.760	1.88%	0.89%	−0.99%	10%
Russell 2000	0.42	0.930	0.510	2.12%	1.52%	−0.60%	5%
S&P 500	0.59	1.360	0.770	1.60%	0.18%	−1.42%	10%
NASDAQ	0.48	1.085	0.605	1.69%	0.48%	−1.21%	20%
Leveraged Buyouts							
Russell 1000	0.42	0.713	0.293	1.80%	1.18%	−0.62%	5%
Russell 2000	0.28	0.587	0.307	1.95%	1.25%	−0.70%	7%
S&P 500	0.42	0.701	0.281	1.55%	0.80%	−0.75%	5%
NASDAQ	0.22	0.418	0.198	1.88%	1.20%	−0.68%	10%
Mezzanine Finance							
Russell 2000	0.11	0.248	0.138	1.64%	1.46%	−0.18%	2.80%
NASDAQ	0.10	0.237	0.137	1.58%	1.30%	−0.28%	7.60%
Salmon Cash Pay HY	0.14	0.315	0.175	1.71%	1.65%	−0.06%	4.70%
Salomon Convertibles	0.25	0.463	0.213	1.87%	1.60%	−0.27%	4.60%
Distressed Debt							
Russell 1000	0.25	0.225	−0.025	2.20%	2.19%	−0.01%	10%
Russell 2000	0.26	0.370	0.110	2.07%	1.81%	−0.26%	10%
Salmon Cash Pay HY	0.68	0.892	0.212	1.68%	1.32%	−0.36%	5%
Salomon Convertibles	0.41	0.461	0.051	1.71%	1.51%	−0.20%	11%

Furthermore, as the explanatory power of the lagged market returns increases, the alpha, or excess return declines. In every category of private equity and for every market index, the excess return in the multiperiod regression is less than that observed in the single-period regressions. Consequently, part of a private equity manager's excess return that is reported in the current quarter of performance is a reflection of prior market returns earned in previous quarters instead of genuine manager skill.

STALE VERSUS MANAGED PRICING: A SNAPSHOT OF PRIVATE EQUITY MANAGER BEHAVIOR

Summarizing our results so far, we have found that lagged market returns have a significant impact in explaining the returns reported by venture capital funds, distressed debt funds and LBO funds. These results indicate that private equity portfolios reflect changes in the prices of marketable securities over a period of time up to one year. In other words, there is nonsynchronous (lagged) pricing between private equity portfolios and stock-and-bond market returns.

We now come to the crux of our final issue: Are these nonsynchronous private equity returns due to stale pricing or managed pricing? This raises interesting behavioral issues for private equity managers. Managed pricing indicates a level of behavior that we try to capture as this part of the chapter. The noncontemporaneous impact of market returns on private equity portfolios could be due to the structure of the private equity market. That is, illiquid securities which are marked to market only when there are observable, but infrequent events (such as an IPO, new round of financing, etc.). This would result in stale prices where private equity portfolios are "refreshed" with a time delay compared to the public securities markets.

Under the scenario of stale pricing, there should be no difference in how private equity portfolios are marked in up versus down markets. That is, we should see equivalent values for alpha intercepts and lagged beta coefficients during times when the securities markets are doing well as when the securities markets are doing poorly. Equivalent alphas and betas in up versus down markets would indicate that there is no bias in the pricing of private equity portfolios—the values of the portfolios are priced equally whatever the direction of the financial markets may be.

Alternatively, the lagged impact of market returns on private equity portfolios could be due to private equity managers who actively manage the pricing of their portfolios. It is possible that private equity fund managers mark the value of their portfolios up or down when it is most favorable to do so. Keep in mind that private equity managers have almost unfettered ability to mark the prices of their investments up or down. There is no standard for the pricing of private equity portfolios. Under this explanation, we would not see equivalent values of alphas or betas in up versus down markets—the values would be different, indicating a bias to marking to market the portfolio depending on whether the stock-and-bond markets were increasing or decreasing. In other words, we might be able to reveal private equity behavior at work.

Based on the nature of profit-sharing fees earned by private equity fund managers, they might be reluctant to mark down their portfolios and quick to mark up their investment portfolios. This is particularly true during periods of fund raising for new funds by the private equity managers. In other words, if managed pricing is the source of these lagged effects, then private equity managers may be more aggressive in marking up their portfolios when the public securities market is performing well, but less aggressive in marking down their portfolios when the public securities market is performing poorly. It is in their economic interest to pursue this form of managed pricing.

Under these circumstances, when the public stock-and-bond markets are performing well, we would expect private equity managers to be quick to mark *up* the value of their portfolios. Lagged market returns would then have a smaller impact (and the lagged betas would be smaller in value). However, when the public stock-and-bond markets are performing poorly, we would expect private equity managers to smooth out the downside impact on their portfolios. In other words, private equity managers may be slower to mark *down* their portfolios. Lagged market returns would then have a larger impact in explaining the returns to private equity (and the lagged beta coefficients would be larger).

The above theory assumes that private equity managers are unscrupulous and actively manage their portfolio values to enhance their profit sharing fees instead of benefiting their investors.[13] There is a converse to this hypothesis. Alternatively, investors might effectively monitor private equity managers through annual audits and advisory committees. Under these circumstances, private equity managers may not be able to manage the pricing of their investment portfolios to their advantage.

If private equity managers are monitored effectively by investors, then it is more likely that they will be quick to mark down the value of their portfolios in down markets and slow to mark up the value of their portfolios in up markets. This is the Rule of Conservatism discussed earlier in this chapter. This will lead to the lagged market returns having a greater impact in up markets than in down markets.

---

[13] There is some evidence to support the selfish behavior of venture capital firms. See Gompers, "Grandstanding in the Venture Capital Industry."

Another consideration is the risk to reputation. Private equity manages who have a positive track record with investors will be less likely to pursue managed pricing to their benefit because it may harm their reputation with investors. To protect their reputation, these scrupulous managers would then be quick to mark down their portfolio values (small lagged effect) and slow to mark up their portfolios (large lagged effect).

To summarize, if private equity managers manage the pricing of their portfolios to their advantage, we would expect the lagged betas to have a greater impact in down markets. Conversely, if private equity managers are properly monitored, or do not wish to risk the damage to their reputation, then we would expect the lagged betas to have a greater impact in up markets. This introduces a behavioral element into our analysis, which has not been previously examined.

Finally, if managed pricing is not prevalent, then the performance of the lagged betas should be symmetrical. That is, there should be minimal difference in the lagged beta coefficients between up and down markets. In addition, there should be no difference in the value of the alpha intercept; it should be the same in up versus down markets. In this case the culprit for the significance of lagged market returns would be stale pricing.

To address the issue of managed pricing, we simply run the multiperiod regressions of equation (21.5) with dummy variables.[14] A dummy variable is a way to split the world into two distinct states. In state one, the stock or bond market performs well. In state two, the stock or bond market performs poorly. Dummy variables are often referred to as binary variables because they describe only two states of the world (up/down, bad/good, perform well/perform poorly, Cubs win/Cubs lose, etc.). Dummy variables are often multiplied against the independent variables in the regression equation to capture this binary view of the world. Our new equation looks like this:

$$
\begin{aligned}
R_{i,t}(\text{PE}) - \text{Tbill} = {} & \alpha + D \times \beta_0 [R_{m,t} - \text{Tbill}] + D \times [\beta_1 (R_{m,t-1} - \text{Tbill})] \\
& + D \times [\beta_2 (R_{m,t-2} - \text{Tbill})] \qquad\qquad (21.6) \\
& + D \times [\beta_3 (R_{m,t-3} - \text{Tbill})] + \varepsilon_{i,t}
\end{aligned}
$$

To conduct this analysis, we run equation (21.6) twice. In the first analysis, we set the dummy variable (D) equal to 1 when the stock markets perform well, and 0 when the market performs poorly. We then calculate the size of the lagged betas. In the second analysis, we set the dummy variable equal to 1 when the stock markets perform poorly and

---

[14] For an application of this technique to hedge funds, see Asness, Krail, and Liew, "Do Hedge Funds Hedge?"

0 when the markets perform well. Again we calculate the sum of the lagged betas. By performing this procedure we can observe the values for the lagged betas in up markets versus those in down markets. If the nonsynchronous pricing in private equity portfolios is due to managed pricing, we would expect to see asymmetry in the values of the lagged betas between up and down markets. Similarly, we would see different values for X in up U.S. down markets.

To simplify this analysis, we consider only those regression equations from Exhibits 21.5 through 21.8 that demonstrated the greatest lagged effect. For venture capital returns, the R-square measure was highest for the NASDAQ. For LBO funds we use the Russell 1000; for mezzanine finance we use the NASDAQ; and for distressed debt we use the Russell 2000.

Our results are presented in Exhibit 21.10. For each category of private equity, we divide this exhibit into two states of the world: Up markets and down markets. We present each beta coefficient associated with lagged market returns as well its t-statistic. We also present the R-square measure for both up market and down market regression equations.

For venture capital, Exhibit 21.10 demonstrates an asymmetry in lagged pricing. Specifically, all of the beta coefficients (lagged and contemporaneous) in up markets are large and are all significant at either the 1% or 2.5% level. In addition, the R-square measure remains large at 50%.

Conversely, with respect to down markets, only the first beta coefficient (β_0) is significant at the 1% level. None of the lagged beta coefficients are statistically significant at either the 1% or 5% level. Furthermore, the R-square measure is low, at 24%.

The above results demonstrate managed pricing by venture capital managers. The size and significance of the lagged beta coefficients in up markets and the lack of significance of any lagged beta coefficient in down markets indicates that venture capital managers apply the rule of conservatism. They are slow to incorporate positive stock market returns into their portfolios, preferring to wait until they are assured of earning these returns. Conversely, when the stock market performs poorly, venture capital managers are quick to incorporate these negative returns into their private equity portfolios. What is also interesting is the size and sign of the alpha intercept. In up markets, the alpha is now negative at –2.59% and is statistically significant at the 1% level. This demonstrates that not only do venture capital managers show no skill in up markets, the alpha is negative, indicating that the activities of venture capital managers in up markets is a drag on performance. Conversely, the alpha intercept in down markets is now very large at 5.4%—almost 22% annually!

Now is it really the case that the venture capitalist's skill can vary by this much in up versus down markets? The answer is no—what this reflects more is the behavior of the venture capitalist in pricing his portfolio than distinct changes in his skill level.

EXHIBIT 21.10 Multiperiod Regression Analysis in Up versus Down Markets

Market Index	Alpha	t-Statistic	Beta(0)	t-Statistic	Beta(-1)	t-Statistic	Beta(-2)	t-Statistic	Beta(-3)	t-Statistic	R-Square
Venture Capital											
NASDAQ Up Market	-2.59%	-2.34	0.73	7.07	0.300	3.71	0.280	3.34	0.2200	2.120	50%
NASDAQ Down Market	5.40%	4.31	0.64	4.65	-0.010	-0.06	0.100	0.85	0.0600	0.590	24%
Leverage Buyouts											
Russell 1000 Up Market	-0.38%	-0.52	0.53	4.13	0.093	1.78	0.180	2.18	0.2600	2.370	30%
Russell 1000 Down Market	3.62%	6.02	0.64	6.06	-0.050	-0.32	-0.030	-0.27	0.0002	0.002	34%
Mezzanine Debt											
NASDAQ Up Market	0.49%	0.76	0.18	3.10	0.140	2.89	0.020	0.43	0.0040	0.083	21%
NASDAQ Down Market	2.29%	3.53	0.11	1.57	-0.009	-0.14	0.002	0.04	0.0370	0.510	5%
Distressed Debt											
Russell 2000 Up Market	0.82%	1.36	0.35	4.99	0.154	2.86	0.046	0.82	-0.0290	-0.460	35%
Russell 2000 Down Market	3.96%	7.86	0.47	5.66	0.021	0.24	-0.130	-1.91	-0.0590	-0.880	40%

The results for LBOs are similar. The beta coefficients in up markets are all statistically significant while in down markets only $\beta(0)$ is statistically significant. Also, similar to venture capital, the alpha intercept in up markets in negative, while in down markets it is positive. Again these results demonstrate that leveraged buyout fund managers engage in managed pricing. LBO funds also apply the rule of conservatism.

Mezzanine debt also shows evidence of managed pricing. The beta coefficients for $\beta(0)$ and $\beta(-1)$ are statistically significant in up markets while only $\beta(0)$ is statistically significant in down markets. Notice also that the alpha intercept is much more positive in down markets than in up markets. The R-Square value is much greater in up markets—indicating mezzanine debt managers manage the pricing of their portfolios much more in up markets than in down.

Finally, distressed debt displays some competing results. The lagged betas are significant in both up and down markets but with different effects. $\beta(-1)$ is statistically positive in up markets, but insignificant in down markets. Conversely, $\beta(-2)$ is significantly negative in down markets, but insignificant in up markets. It is difficult to draw clear conclusions from the differences in pricing other than there are clearly different pricing effects in up versus down markets. This also demonstrates managed pricing because the pricing effects are not symmetrical between up and down markets. However, consistent with other forms of private equity, the alpha intercept in up markets is much weaker than the alpha intercept in down markets. Clearly, private equity managers prefer to claim skill in more difficult markets than in good markets.

CONCLUSION

In reviewing appropriate benchmarks for private equity, we found that the NASDAQ is a suitable performance measure for venture capital, particularly when lagged market returns are included in measuring venture capital returns. It is clear that the over the counter stock market—where most initial public offerings for new companies are listed—is a significant factor in explaining the returns to venture capital. For leveraged buyouts, the large-cap Russell 1000 stock index proved to be a useful benchmark when allowing for lagged market returns. This reflects the more mature nature of the companies targeted for leveraged buyouts—generally, they are more established and have a larger market capitalization.

Mezzanine debt was the most difficult to categorize. Using stock, high yield, and convertible bond indexes, the best R-square measure we could produce was 20% in Exhibit 21.7. Mezzanine debt is clearly a hybrid security that is not closely related to stock or bond market indexes. This indicates a good opportunity to diversify a traditional stock-and-bond portfolio.

Distressed debt demonstrated both equity, high yield, and hybrid properties as the Russell 2000 stock index, the Salomon Brothers Cash Pay High-Yield Bond Index, and the Salomon Brothers Convertible Bond Index were significant in explaining the returns to distressed debt. Each provided an R-square in Exhibit 21.8 around 50%—a significant amount of explanatory power. We also found alpha erosion when we included lagged market returns in each category of private equity. In fact for venture capital, lagged market returns completely eroded the skill of the venture capital manager to an insignificant level.

Finally, there is considerable evidence of managed pricing in private equity portfolios. We observed asymmetric pricing with respect to lagged market variables in every category of private equity. Specifically, we saw greater strength in the lagged beta coefficients in up markets compared to down markets. Surprisingly, when stock-and-bond markets performed poorly, we found that private equity managers were quick to mark down the value of their portfolios and slow to mark up their portfolios when the stock-and-bond markets performed well. This is contrary to private equity managers' incentive schemes, but consistent with proper monitoring by investors and the risk to reputation that might be suffered by improper pricing.

To be blunt, human nature being what it is, it does not take much imagination to consider that some managers might mark to market their portfolios more quickly in up markets to capture larger incentive fees (and slower in down markets to forestall the loss of incentive fees).[15] It is in their economic interest to do so.

Yet it appears that private equity investors manage to monitor private equity managers effectively such that human nature does not affect the valuation of the underlying private equity portfolios. Most private equity fund managers agree to an annual outside audit by an auditing firm chosen by the investors in the fund. Additionally, most private equity fund managers conduct quarterly portfolio reviews with their investors. As a result, it is difficult for private equity managers to manage the pricing of

---

[15] In fact, Gompers has documented the human nature aspect of nascent venture capital managers bringing startup companies to the public markets earlier that might otherwise be prudent in order to establish a reputation in the private equity marketplace. See Gompers, "Grandstanding in the Venture Capital Industry." Therefore, there may be a difference between new private equity managers who wish to establish a reputation and established private equity managers who wish to protect their reputation. The former may be more aggressive in pricing their portfolios while our results indicate that the latter tend to be more conservative in pricing their portfolios.

their investment portfolios to their advantage. Inevitably, they would be caught either by their investors or by the outside auditors.

An additional explanation for private equity managers may be the requirements of GAAP accounting. Under GAAP, the Rule of Conservatism is applied in the idea of "Lower of Cost or Market." That is under GAAP, securities should be reported at the more conservative value between cost or current market value. This conservative approach to valuing securities would also contribute to the behavior of marking down portfolios quickly and marking up portfolios slowly.

We note that the data used for the analysis in this chapter was voluntarily reported to the databases we used by private equity managers. This may indicate a form of self-selection bias. Possibly, those managers who voluntarily report their return information to databases have a reputation to protect. As a result, the return information reported to the private equity databases may come only from those scrupulous managers who do not manage the pricing of the private equity investment portfolios to their advantage. In other words, this universe of data may unintentionally exclude return information from private equity managers who do not apply the same scruples to portfolio pricing as those managers who voluntarily report their return information.

CHAPTER **22**

Trends in Private Equity

There have been a number of recent changes in the private equity market at the beginning of the new millennium. First, with respect to LBOs, what was previously thought to be a segmented, inefficient marketplace has turned into an efficient, auction-driven asset class. This has resulted in many secondary sales of private equity portfolios. Second, the efficiency of the LBO market has forced private equity investors to look to new forms of private equity investments such as leveraged loans and PIPES. We review the growth of the LBO industry and observe some interesting trends. We also consider some of the more esoteric parts of the private equity market and draw some conclusions.

INDUSTRY GROWTH AND MATURATION

It may seem unusual to think of it in this way, but the private equity marketplace is a growth industry along the lines of healthcare, biotech, and semiconductors. Exhibit 22.1 displays the growth of this industry since 1991. From 1991 to 2000, the commitments to private equity funds increased twentyfold. The primary driver was the fact that private equity went from being a "cutting edge" investment for institutional investors to a core holding in any long-term investor's portfolio. Pension funds now include an average allocation to private equity equal to 5%, while endowments and foundations go as high as 15%. Although commitments to private equity slowed down after the busting of the technology bubble and the three-year bear market, commitments have regained their momentum in 2004 and 2005. This large inflow of investment capital into private equity funds has brought new opportunities and challenges for private equity managers.

EXHIBIT 22.1 Commitments to Private Equity Funds

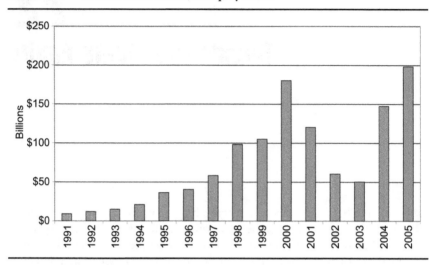

An Auction Market

Whenever such a large sum of capital enters an investment market, inefficiencies begin to erode. This has led to two new developments in the private equity market. The first is an auction market environment.

In the past, private equity deals were sourced by a single private equity firm without any competitive bidding from other private equity firms. The traditional model of private equity was one where a single private equity firm approached a standalone public company about going private, or approached a parent company with respect to spinning off a subsidiary. In this model, the lone private equity firm would work with the executive management of the public company (or parent company) to develop a financing plan for taking the public company or a subsidiary private. This process might take months or years to bring a deal to fruition, and the private equity firm worked on building its relationship with the senior management of the company.

The rules have now changed. Single-sourced deals are a thing of the past. Now, when a parent company decides to sell a subsidiary in a leveraged buyout format, it almost always hires an investment banker to establish a bidding process among several private equity firms. Each private equity firm is pitted against other private equity firms in a bidding contest where the highest bidder wins—but the private equity investor loses because there is less upside to extract from each private deal.

The auction process reflects the maturation of the private equity industry. It is part of the natural evolution of any industry that as more capital is attracted to that industry, inevitably, competition follows. More competition means erosion of returns on invested capital. In fact, an auction market is one definition of an efficient market.

The large inflow of capital into private equity deals resulted in private equity firms and investors seeking better returns outside the United States. However, this brought the same competitive environment to the European private equity market place. Exhibit 22.2 provides a sampling of the competition for private equity deals in Europe. This demonstrates anecdotally that the European private equity market has also achieved auction status.

Ironically, in some cases, auctions in the private equity market place can be *less* efficient than a single-sourced deal. In a private equity auction, a private equity firm has less time to review the target company's financial statements and operations. In an auction, the bidding process compresses time—the opposite of a single-sourced deal where a private equity firm works with the executive management of a company over a long period before taking the company private. The shorter timeframe associated with an auction simply means that there is less time for a private equity firm to conduct a thorough due diligence. Finally, in an auction market, the private equity firm may meet with senior management only two or three times. Contrast this with a single-sourced deal where the private equity firm meets extensively with the senior management before taking the company private.

Club Deals

A recent development in the private equity market, particularly as it relates to LBO firms, is the club deal. In the past, LBO firms worked on exclusive deals; one on one with the acquired company. However, the large inflow of capital into the private equity market has forced LBO firms to work together in "clubs." Of the 845 deals completed in 2005, 125 of them were club deals where one or more LBO firms worked together to share costs, present a business plan, and contribute capital to the deal.

EXHIBIT 22.2   Competition in for Buyout Deals in Europe

Transaction	Comment
Groupo Coin invites 12 buyout firms to bid for a majority stake	Second largest department store chain in Italy.
Saga Ltd.'s $1.8 billion sale attracts over 10 bidders	U.K.-based insurance and vacation planning group is put up for sale.
Unwins Wine draws interest from more than 50 potential bidders	An operator of 387 wine and liquor stores in United Kingdom.

Interesting, while club deals are new to the LBO world, venture capital firms have worked together for years. Witness the example of Cache-Flow/BlueCoat Inc. in Chapter 16. Each stage of this startup company was financed by a different venture capital firm. Venture capital firms long ago learned that bringing in different levels of expertise into a startup venture can add to the long-term prospects of the company.

Club deals have the advantage of limiting the auction process so that a company may be acquired at a more attractive price. In addition, club deals bring in diverse skill sets that can enhance the overall profitability of the target company. Also club deals help to spread the risk particularly for large private equity deals. Witness the recent club deal for the Hertz Rent-a-car Company where the $15 billion buyout wash shared between Clayton Dubilier & Rice, The Carlyle Group, and Merrill Lunch Global Private Equity. Similarly, the purchase of SunGard Data Systems for $11.3 billion was an even larger club deal with Silver Lake Partners, Blackstone Group, Texas Pacific Group, Thomas H. Lee Partners, KKR, and Providence Equity Partners. Exhibit 22.3 describes some recent club deals in 2005. Note that club deals are now just as common in Europe as in the United States.

EXHIBIT 22.3   Private Equity Club Deals in 2005 and 2006

Deal	Size	Club Members
Hertz Company	USD 15 billion	Clayton Dubilier & Rice The Carlyle Group Merrill Lynch Global Private Equity
SunGard Data Systems	USD 11.3 billion	Silver Lake Partners Blackstone Group Texas Pacific Group Thomas H. Lee Partners KKR Providence Equity Partners
Toys 'R' Us	USD 8.8 billion	Bain Capital Vornado Realty Trust
GMAC	USD 8.8 billion	KKR Goldman Sachs Capital Partners Five Mile Capital Partners
VNU NV	EUR 7.5 billion	KKR Blackstone Group AlpInvest Partners Nv The Carlyle Group Hellman & Friedman Thomas H. Lee Partners

The argument against club deals is that it might reflect a lack of opportunities in the market for the amount of capital that the LBO firms have to put to work. This is the old argument of too much money chasing too few deals. In addition, there is the concern that too many cooks in the corporate kitchen can spoil the dinner. In a club deal, it is less clear who will take the lead in the business plan, which private equity firm will sit on the Board of the private company, who will be responsible for monitoring performance, and who will negotiate with outside lenders to provide the debt financing for the LBO. Club deals, lastly, may reflect a private equity firm that has no real deal flow other than talking to other private equity firms.

THE SECONDARY PRIVATE EQUITY MARKET

Another example of an efficient market is a market with secondary trading. In the public stock market, secondary trading takes place on an exchange—for example, the New York Stock Exchange, the NASDAQ, the London Stock Exchange, or the Deutsche Bourse. Secondary trading is an indication of investor interest and provides liquidity to the market. In the past, there was no secondary market for private equity, but now that has changed at both the private equity firm level as well as the investor level.

Secondary Buyouts

Another demonstration of the increased efficiency of the private equity market place is the secondary buyout model. Increasingly, private equity firms are selling to one another as an exit strategy. Private equity firms, flush with capital commitments from investors are now looking at competitor private equity firms a source of deals or as an exit strategy.

Rather than find new deals, private equity firms are looking at existing private deals—another potential symptom of too much capital in the private equity industry. This is in contrast to the traditional exit strategies of a public offering, recapitalization, or sale of the private company to a strategic buyer (a corporation in the same or related industry).

Initially, secondary buyouts were rare. Private equity firms were reluctant to sell a portfolio company to another private equity firms in a buyout-to-buyout deal. There was a stigma of failure associated with not being able to take a company public or sell it to a strategic partner.

Now the market for buyout-to-buyout deals is robust. In 2003, there were $18 billion of private-to-private deals, and $40 billion in 2004. The buyout-to-buyout market has been particularly strong in Europe where more than 40% of the buyouts completed in 2005 were buyout-to-buyout deals. Exhibit 22.4 shows the growth of the secondary market in Europe.

EXHIBIT 22.4   Growth of Secondary Buyouts in Europe

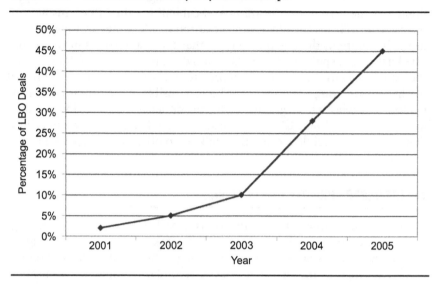

As an example of a buyout-to-buyout deal, consider the case history of Jostens Inc. Jostens, a maker of high school and college class rings and yearbooks, was initially taken private by the Investcorp of Bahrain for $227 million in May 2000. Investcorp subsequently sold Jostens in 2003 to CSFB Private Equity in a private-to-private deal worth $500 million. This translates to a 30% internal rate of return for Investcorp of Bahrain.

Jostens was not done yet. CSFB had previously acquired Von Hoffman Corp. and Arcade Marketing, two other specialty printers for its private equity portfolio. For Von Hoffman, CSFB paid $106 million in equity, while for Arcade Marketing, CSFB paid $90 million. CSFB then sold all three printing companies to Kohlberg, Kravis & Roberts for $2.2 billion in July 2004. This represented an IRR for CSFB of approximately 20% to 25%.

Now, it was KKR's turn. KKR merged the three printing companies together to form a new company called Visant. Furthermore, in anticipation of a later public offering, Visant filed an annual 10-K report with the SEC where it reported 2005 sales of $1.5 billion and total EBITDA of $293 million. Using the Gordon constant growth model with an estimated cost of capital of 12% and an estimated growth rate of 2%, a conservative value for Visant is

$$\$293 \text{ million} \div [12\% - 2\%] = \$2.93 \text{ billion}$$

This represents an almost $800 million gain on an investment of $2.2 billion for a return of over 36% to KKR and its investors. Exhibit 22.5 summarizes the buyout-to-buyout-to-buyout for Jostens.

EXHIBIT 22.5   A Case Study of a Secondary Buyout to Buyout

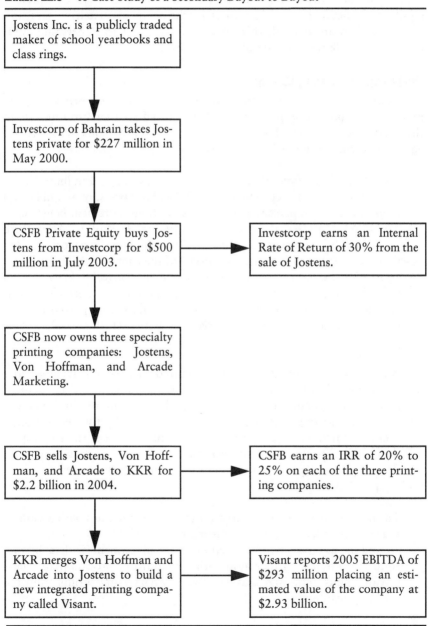

There is, however, one large problem with private-to-private deals. Along the way, at each sale point, incentive fees are earned. Consequently, part of the value associated with an operating company is pulled out by each private equity firm along the private-to-private food chain. Another way to look at the issue is that each private-to-private equity sale incurs transaction costs in the form of incentive fees and each time fees are earned, this erodes the value of the operating company just a little more to the ultimate investor.

The Investor Secondary Market

In a similar vein more investors are rationalizing their private equity investments and selling portions of their limited partnership interests in the secondary market. There are three primary reasons why private equity investors may need to sell part of their portfolio:

- *To raise cash for funding requirements*. For example, 3 million Americans are expected to retire by 2012. This will put pressure on public and corporate pension plans to generate cash to fund retirement benefits.
- *There may be strategic shifts in institutional portfolios*. After three years of a bear market (2000 to 2002) many large investors decided that they needed to trim the risk profile of their investment portfolios.
- *Institutional investors need to rebalance their portfolios from time to time*. This is a form of active portfolio management where allocations to asset classes sometimes are decreased, resulting in a partial liquidation of an asset class. Without a secondary market, this would not be possible.

A key risk, however, is that once a limited partner sells its stake in a private equity fund in a secondary market transaction, it is most unlikely that the general partner of the fund will invite the limited partner to join in future private equity funds sponsored by the general partner. General partners, as a general rule, do not like to see their investors sell their limited partnership interests to outside third parties.

From a buyer's perspective, there are several advantages to a secondary purchase:

- The investor gains exposure to a portfolio of companies with a vintage year that is different from his existing portfolio.
- Secondary interests typically represent an investment with a private equity firm that is farther along in the investment process than a new private equity fund and may be closer to harvesting profits from the private portfolio.

■ Purchasing the secondary interest of a limited partner who wishes to exit a private equity fund may be a way for another investor to gain access to future funds offered by the general partner.

Exhibit 22.6 indicates the growth in secondary funds. Secondary fund raising slowed down temporarily during the bear market years of 2000 to 2002, but has since recovered. The largest secondary fund to date is Coller Capital's $2.6 billion secondary fund which closed in 2002. In January 2004, this fund purchased the private equity portfolio of Abbey National PLC for $1.33 billion.

Another development in the secondary market is "primary secondaries." These are secondary sales not to a limited partnership or other specialized secondary fund, but instead, directly to an institutional investor. These primary secondaries have to main goals. The first is to establish a relationship with the general partner—either the LBO or venture capital firm—whose interests are being sold so as to gain further access to investment vehicles offered by the general partner. Second, the purchase of outstanding secondary interests can reduce the J curve effect by purchasing secondary interests of a fund that has already invested its capital and is now in the profit harvesting stage.

It should be noted that private equity secondary sales are still developing. Therefore, there will be a discount price to the net asset value of the fund interests being sold. This is necessary to entice the secondary

EXHIBIT 22.6   Secondary Private Equity Funds

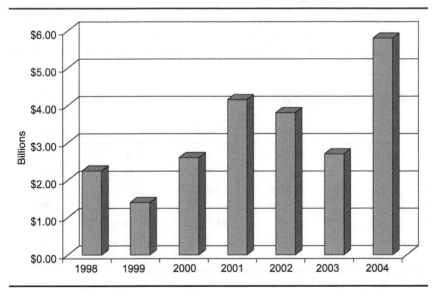

buyer. The discount is larger depending on the vintage year offered for sale. The closer the vintage year of the fund to the sale date the larger the discount because the shorter time period means that the private equity fund has had less time to generate profits for investors.

Impact on Returns

With the private equity market becoming more efficient and driven by an auction process with a growing secondary market, returns are expected to suffer. Traditionally, private equity firms aimed for hurdle rates in excess of 20%. However, the competitive nature of this market has trimmed these return forecasts down to 20% or less.

Exhibit 22.7 presents the one-, three-, five-, and 10-year returns earned by buyout firms through 2005. The S&P 500 is added a benchmark. Most private equity firms expect to earn a premium of 400 to 500 basis points above the public markets to compensate investors for the lack of liquidity and the concentrated portfolios of private equity firms. While the one year results are excellent, the three-year results are just on par with the public stock market. The results for five and ten years are more favorable and do demonstrate a return premium for LBO funds. Still the results are mixed. LBO funds, in particular, flush with cash, will need to find new ways to put this investment capital to work.

NEW TRENDS IN PRIVATE EQUITY

To maintain performance, private equity firms have turned to other avenues to gather assets and generate returns. At the same time, private equity firms now receive competition for deals from some unexpected sources.

EXHIBIT 22.7 Leveraged Buyout Performance

	1 year	3 year	5 year	10 year
Small funds	48.00%	9.00%	2.40%	26.30%
Medium funds	34.00%	8.60%	0.20%	17.90%
Large funds	25.00%	15.60%	1.80%	12.80%
Mega funds	33.00%	15.80%	3.90%	11.10%
All Buyout Funds	32.50%	14.70%	3.10%	13.30%
S&P 500	10.00%	14.70%	−3.10%	11.20%

Source: Data obtained from Thomson Venture Economics.

Business Development Companies

2004 saw the private equity firms take advantage of the mutual fund laws to start *business development companies* (BDCs) as a way to raise and invest new funds. This essentially is a way to bring private equity investing to the retail market.

BDCs were created by the Small Business Investment Incentive Act of 1980—an amendment to the Investment Company Act of 1940, which is the group of laws that regulate mutual funds in the United States. BDCs are a special type of closed end mutual fund that were established to encourage investments in small private businesses. Closed end mutual funds are retail investment funds where the investor cannot redeem her shares by selling them back to the mutual fund management company. Instead, closed end mutual funds have their shares traded on a stock exchange; most closed end mutual funds have their shares listed on the New York Stock Exchange or NASDAQ.

Despite their good intentions, BDCs were underutilized and gathered dust for more than twenty years until private equity firms dusted off these little used funds and filed registration statements with the Securities and Exchange Commission to offer such funds. Exhibit 22.8 lists several recent BDC filings with the SEC, with total dollars expected to be raised at almost $7 billion.

These private equity BDCs share a number of common elements.

- They all state that the BDC will invest in mezzanine debt: unsecured senior and junior debt, convertible bonds and preferred stock, and debtor-in-possession financing.
- The fee structure of each of the funds listed in Exhibit 22.8 is a 2% management fee and a 20% incentive fee.
- They plan to contribute the mezzanine layer of financing needed for other private equity deals.

Interestingly, the one successful BDC that has completed its registration statement with the SEC and sold public shares in the fund is the Apollo Investment Corp., which raised almost $1 billion in its public offering. Much of the investment capital with AIC is invested in the mezzanine debt associated with leveraged buyout deals of other private equity firms such as Thomas H. Lee (United Industries), KKR (Sealy Mattress), and Abry Partners (Language Line).

The biggest benefit to private equity firms is that a BDC provides the private equity firm with a permanent base of captured investment capital that will never be redeemed. This provides an extremely profitable net present value from the management fees applied against this permanent investor capital. For example, the Apollo BDC raised $1 bil-

EXHIBIT 22.8   Recent BDC Filings

Name of BDC	Manager of Fund	IPO Amount (millions)	Target Investments
Apollo Investment Corporation	Apollo Investment Group	$930	Long-term sub. debt and senior secured loans
Blackridge Investment Corporation	Blackstone Group	$850	Mezzanine, senior secured bank loans
KKR BDC Inc.	Kolhberg, Kravis, Roberts	$750	Secured and unsecured senior and junior debt
BlackRock Kelso Capital	BlackRock/Kelso & Co.	$750	Long-term sub. debt and senior secured loans
Triarc Deerfield	Indepenent Manager	$750	Mezzanine, senior secured bank loans
Porticoes Investment Management	Indepenent Manager	$575	Long-term sub. debt and senior secured loans
Gleacher Investment Corp.	Eric Gleacher	$500	Mezzanine and senior debt
THL Investment Capital Corp.	Thomas H. Lee Partners	$500	Long-term sub. debt and senior secured loans
Evercore Investment Corporation	Evercore Group	$460	High yield, distressed debt, bridge loans
Ares Capital Corporation	Ares Capital Management	$450	1st and 2nd lien senior loans and mezzanine
Gores Investment Corporation	Gores Technology Group	$250	Senior debt, mezzanine and debtor-in-possession
Marathon Capital Finance	Marathon Asset Man.	$200	Mezzanine, senior secured bank loans
Total in millions		$6,965	

lion and charges a 2% management fee. If we assume that the cost of capital to the BDC is equal to 15%, then the present value to the private equity firm from accrual of the BDC's management fees is

$$[2\% \times \$500 \text{ million}] \div 15\% = \$133,333,333$$

This amount reflects the present value of the BDC *before* the collection of any profit sharing fees—at 20%. It also assumes that the BDC does not appreciate (or depreciate) in value. Furthermore, unlike a traditional private equity fund, the incentive fees can be collected before there is a return of investor capital, and there are no clawbacks. Exhibit 22.9 shows the value of the AIC shares since public offering in 2004.

The economic benefits to the private equity firm are apparent, but what about the benefits and risks to the investor? The benefits include:

- Gaining access to mezzanine debt market.
- Having liquidity in tradable shares
- The ability to earn returns significantly in excess of traditional bonds.

The risks include:

- The BDC shares may trade at a discount to the initial public offering. However, Exhibit 22.9 shows that the shares of AIC have risen from an initial offering price of $15 to $18.

EXHIBIT 22.9 Apollo Investment Corporation Share Price

- The fee structure is expensive compared to other closed end mutual funds.
- The BDC may lack experience investing in mezzanine debt.

Regarding the lack of experience with respect to mezzanine debt investing, below is the language taken from another BDC prospectus regarding the BDC's expertise in mezzanine debt investing:

> The Investment Advisor will be led by [Blank] who has [Blank] years of experience in the investment industry, together with a team of [Blank] professionals that will be dedicated full-time to the operation of the Investment Advisor.

In summary, many private equity firms were quick to file prospectuses to launch their own BDC, but only the AIC has been successfully launched.

Hedge Funds and Private Equity

Hedge funds have begun to compete with private equity firms in the purchase of corporate assets. A recent case is the bidding competition for Texas Genco in its sale by its parent company, CenterPoint Energy. The bidding war for this energy generation company pitted Seneca Capital, Caxton Associates and Cerberus Capital Management—three hedge funds—against the private equity firms of KKR, Texas Pacific Group, Hellman and Friedman and The Blackstone Group. Fascinating to see not only a club deal of private equity firms joining together for these assets, but competing against a club of hedge funds—the most secretive and competitive of investment vehicles. The private equity consortium eventually won the auction for the assets, but this is an indication of things to come.

This creates the third new strategy for private equity—if you cannot beat hedge funds, join them. For example, Texas Pacific Group, the large U.S.-based private equity firm announced in 2005 it planned to start a new hedge fund called TPG-Axon Capital, and that it plans to raise up to $3 billion. This is on top of TPG's 2006 $12 billion buyout fund. The Blackstone Group already has a successful fixed income arbitrage hedge fund called Blackstone Bridge as well as a $9 billion hedge fund of funds business. Bain Capital, another well-known private equity manager, has run the Brookside Capital hedge fund for several years with almost $4 billion of assets under management.

The attraction of hedge funds to private equity firms is easy to see. The advantages compared to the typical deal terms of a private equity firm are many:

- Hedge funds are another source of fund raising and fee generation. Fund raising for hedge funds were estimated at $125 billion in 2005.
- Hedge fund incentive fees are front-loaded.
- Hedge fund incentive fees are based on changes in net asset value, not realized profits like private equity funds.
- Hedge fund incentive fees are collected on a regular basis, either quarterly or semiannually.
- Investor capital does not need to be first returned first to collect incentive fees.
- Management fees do not need to be recouped before incentive fees are paid.
- Hedge funds have no provisions for the claw back of management or incentive fees.

In summary, the deal terms for a hedge fund are much more favorable than that for private equity funds. Another consideration is that hedge funds have lower hurdle rates than private equity funds. Most private equity funds target returns in the 20% range, while hedge funds aim to beat a cash index plus some premium (e.g., LIBOR + 6%). This provides hedge funds with a competitive advantage against private equity firms when bidding for operating assets. Lower hurdler rates allow hedge funds to bid more aggressively than private equity firms.

The Growth of Leveraged Loans

Another asset class that private equity firms have moved into is leveraged loans—the market for syndicated bank loans to noninvestment grade borrowers. Loans made by banks to corporations can be divided into two general classes: those made to companies with investment grade credit ratings and leveraged loans. A leveraged loan is made to a corporate borrower that is "leveraged"—that is, a company that is not investment grade, often due to excess leverage on its balance sheet. Generally, a loan is considered leveraged if:

- The company has outstanding debt that is rated below BBB– by S&P or lower than Baa by Moody's.
- The loan bears a coupon that is in excess of 150 basis points over LIBOR.
- The loan has a second lien interest after other senior secured loans— the second lien loan market is often used synonymously with the leveraged loan market.

In many respects, leveraged loans are similar to high-yield debt/junk bonds in terms of credit rating and corporate profile. In fact, many non-investment grade corporations have both high-yield bonds and leveraged loans outstanding. Since private equity firms are used to dealing with banks and other fixed income investors to finance their buyouts, leveraged loans provide a natural extension of their financing business.

This is apparent when considered in light of the secondary trading of leveraged loans. Exhibit 22.10 demonstrates the growth of the secondary trading of leveraged loans. Institutional investors have an increasing focus on active total return management. This has led to an increase in the secondary trading for leveraged loans as an absolute return product. As a result, the rate of issuance of leveraged loans has surpassed that of high-yield financing. This is an important development because banks were once reluctant to lend to below investment grade companies, but this has changed. With the entry of institutional investors into this space—through private equity vehicles—leveraged loans have become an accepted form of investing. And who better to invest in leveraged loans than LBO firms that for years have sought high yield financing for their buyout targets for years.

Leveraged loans were helped in their secondary trading once they became rated by recognized rating agencies. For example, Moody's Investor Service began to assign credit ratings to bank loans in 1995. Moody's recognized the growing importance of institutional loan investors, and the increase in active management practiced by commercial

EXHIBIT 22.10 Secondary Trading of Leveraged Loans

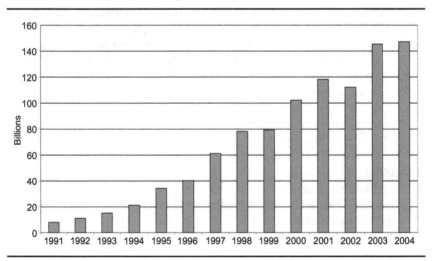

banks in managing their credit exposure. Today, Moody's rates over $800 billion of bank loans. The distribution of Moody's ratings on U.S. bank loans is definitely skewed towards the leveraged loan market. Exhibit 22.11 shows the distribution of bank loan ratings provided by Moody's. Approximately 78% of the rated bank loans fall into the sub investment grade categories (Ba, B and Caa—C rated categories).

All of this has contributed to the growth of the leveraged loan market compared to the high-yield bond market. This is demonstrated in Exhibit 22.12. Note the significant decline in both leveraged loans and high-yield bonds during the recession of 2001–2002. Not surprisingly, during times of economic turmoil, both banks and the financial markets are unwilling to invest in less than stellar credit risks.

Last, we look at the investors in leveraged loans as of the end of 2004. Exhibit 22.13 provides a description of the investors in the leveraged loan markets. Much of the interest in leveraged loans has come from *collateralized loan obligations* (CLO) funds. These are special purpose vehicles that purchase bank loans from banks, and repackaged them in asset-backed securities known as CLOs. We will discuss these vehicles in our chapters on credit derivatives. However, CLO structures are not alone, many private equity firms have increased their activity in this area because leveraged bank loans provide high yields, stability of returns, and seniority of credit claim in the event of default.

Notice that banks (U.S., Asian, Canadian, and European) account for only 28% of the leveraged loan market. Going back to the 1990s,

EXHIBIT 22.11   Distribution of Bank Loan Ratings

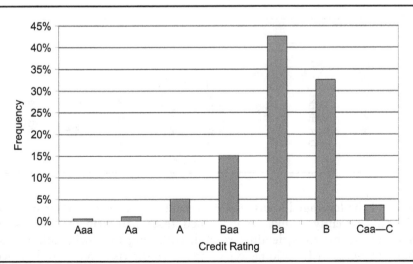

EXHIBIT 22.12 Leveraged Loans Compared to High-Yield Bonds

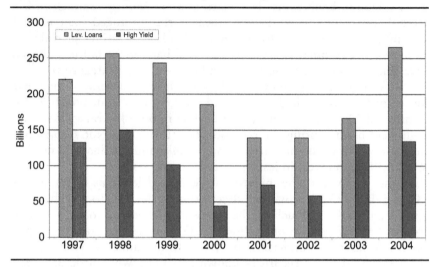

EXHIBIT 22.13 Investors in the Leveraged Loan Market

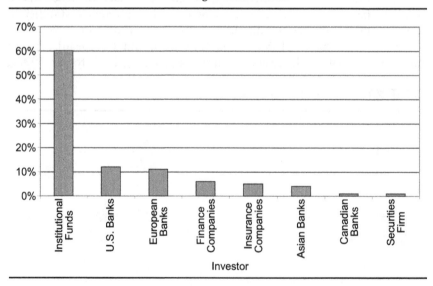

most of the leveraged loans issued by banks were held on their balance sheets. Currently, banks have learned that their primary skill is in assessing credit risks, lending capital, collecting loan origination fees, but not necessarily holding on to those credit risks on their balance sheets. Consequently a large portion of leveraged loans made each year (over 70%) are sold in the secondary market to investors who are much better at assessing the investment risk of holding on to a leverage loan for three to five years.

Stated differently, large commercial banks have changed their business model from a traditional lender where the bank loan is kept on their balance sheet to an originator and distributor of debt. Commercial banks are in the fee generation business, not the asset management business. Origination and distribution of bank loans allow banks to both collect fees as well as manage their credit risk. In short, commercial banks capitalize on their strengths—lending money and collecting loan fees. The subsequent management of the asset (the leveraged loans) is increasingly left up to institutional investors.

PRIVATE INVESTMENT IN PUBLIC ENTITIES (PIPES)

PIPE transactions are privately issued equity or equity-linked securities that are done outside of a public offering. Typically, these securities are exempt from registration under Regulation D of the Securities Act of 1933. These transactions are undertaken by companies that already have common stock that is publicly traded. PIPE issuers can be anything from small companies listed in the over-the-counter market to NYSE listed companies.

PIPEs form a cross-over strategy between venture capital and LBOs. While many PIPE transactions involve small, nascent corporations of the type that interest venture capitalists, other PIPE transactions involve established public companies—the domain of the LBO market. Thus venture capitalists and leveraged buyout firms might find themselves side by side on a PIPE deal because it has elements of startup capital along with private financing for more established companies. The PIPE boom rode the stock market of the 1990s. The PIPE market peaked in year 2000 at $24 billion before the dot-com bubble burst. Since then the market has grown back to slightly less than its former peak. Exhibit 22.14 shows the growth of this market over since it began in 1995.

Most PIPE transactions are designed for small capital infusions—in the range of $10 million to $50 million. However, some PIPE transactions are in excess of $200 million. Clearly, smaller PIPE transactions appeal to venture capitalists who take much smaller bets on companies, while the larger PIPEs appeal to LBO firms who have a much greater quantity of capital to invest. An example would be the Level 3 $800 million PIPE offering of convertible securities in 2005.

EXHIBIT 22.14   The PIPEs Market

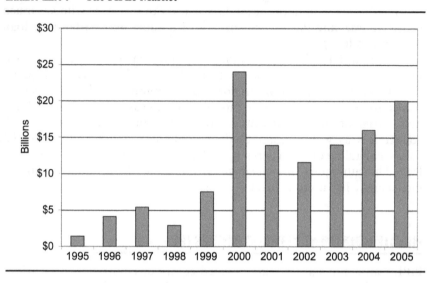

The advantage for a company is that it can quickly raise capital without the need for a lengthy registration process. Initially, they were used by small growing companies that were strapped for cash and for whom the initial public offering did not raise sufficient capital for their operations. However, larger companies view PIPES as a quicker and cheaper process for raising capital quickly, especially from a friendly investor. Furthermore, the management of the company does not need to be distracted with a prolonged "road show" that typically precedes every public offering of stock. Management can remain focused on the operations of the business while receiving an equity infusion that strengthens the balance sheet.

The advantage for the investor is that it can acquire a block of stock at a discount to the public market price. This is particularly appealing for private equity firms that have large chunks of cash to commit to companies. In addition, the issuer of the PIPE usually commits to registering the equity securities with the SEC within the next six months. This feature is particularly appealing for private equity firms: they get to purchase cheap equity with a ready made exit strategy—a public registration in six months time.

PIPES fall into two broad categories: traditional and structured. Traditional PIPES are straightforward private purchases of common equity and preferred stock with a fixed conversion into common shares. Traditional PIPEs have a single conversion price, fixed at a premium to the current market price of the outstanding public stock, which is maintained throughout the life of the PIPE.

Conversely, structured PIPES include the more exotic investments such as floating rate convertible preferred stock, convertible resets, and common stock resets. These PIPEs have a floating conversion price which can change depending upon the price of the publicly traded common stock. This can lead to the financial situation of a "toxic PIPE" or a "death spiral."

Under a structured PIPE, if the stock price of the issuer declines in value, the PIPE investor receives a greater number of shares to convert into, or the conversion price declines commensurately with the outstanding stock price. This can lead to a situation that is potentially poisonous to the company's financial health. A toxic PIPE works as follows:

- A company goes public before it has a chance to fully establish its business strategy.
- The company quickly burns through its IPO cash and needs more capital to continue its growth.
- With an unstable balance sheet and uncertain cash flows, the public stock market is closed to further public offerings of common stock.
- Private equity investors agree to provide more capital in return for PIPEs that can be converted into stock at a floating conversion rate and at a discount to the common stock price.
- Either the private equity investors short the stock of the company, or the company's fortunes decline.
- The downward pressure on the company's common stock price triggers larger and larger conversion ratios for the PIPE investors resulting in greater and greater dilution of the common stock of the company.
- The company must reduce the conversion ratio for the PIPEs into common stock at lower and lower prices which continues to drive down the common stock price resulting in an even lower conversion ratio for the PIPEs.
- The PIPE investors either sell their converted shares, or take control of the company through their lopsided conversion ratio for the company's common stock.

While this scenario sounds improbable, more than one PIPE transaction has led to poisonous results for a company. Consider the case of Log On America. Log On America, Inc. was a provider of high-speed Internet access. In February 2000, Log On issued $15 million of convertible preferred shares to Promethean Asset Management LLC of New York, Citadel Limited Partnership of Chicago, and Marshall Capital Management Inc., a unit of Credit Suisse First Boston. The preferred shares were structured so that they were convertible into more shares of common stock if the price of Log On's common shares fell. The lower the price of Log On's common share price, the greater the conversion ratio for the preferred shares.

Shortly after the PIPE transaction, Log On's stock price fell significantly. In a lawsuit filed in the U.S. District Court in New York City in August 2000, Log On alleged that three investment firms drove down its stock price through short sales of the company's stock so that they could convert preferred shares they held into more common shares. According to the lawsuit, the decline in Log On's stock was sufficient to result in the conversion of the preferred stock into 8 million shares of common stock, equal to roughly 50% of the company's equity. The lawsuit contended that the firms planned to acquire enough shares to take control of the company. Unfortunately for Log On, a federal judge did not agree and the lawsuit was dismissed in December of 2001.

However, Log On's problems did not stop there. Shortly thereafter, Log On's common shareholders filed a class action lawsuit alleging, among other things, that the company issued materially false and misleading information regarding the revenues of the company and its expected profitability. Unfortunately, Log On could not executed its business plan and filed for Chapter 11 bankruptcy protection in July 2002. Log On was subsequently liquidated in 2003. Exhibit 22.15 presents the stock price history of Log On.

EXHIBIT 22.15   A PIPE Gone Bad: Log On America

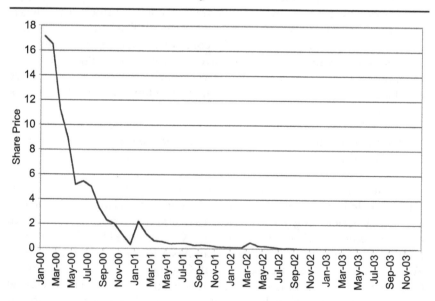

Not all PIPE transactions result in such drastic declines of a company. For example, in 2003, Apax Partners purchased a $250 million PIPE from the Phillips–Van Heusen Corporation. The PIPE infusion was used by Phillips–Van Heusen to acquire Calvin Klein Inc. for $430 million in a successful merger.

Still the abusive practices associated with some PIPEs was sufficient enough for the SEC to step in and begin to enforce unethical behavior associated with PIPE transactions. Today, although floating conversion rate PIPEs still exist, almost all have a floor value beyond which the floating conversion rate is capped. This prevents the death spiral and eliminates the toxicity of prior PIPE transactions.

CONCLUSION

The competitive environment for private equity firms has changed significantly. What was once an inefficient, almost secretive, deal-driven market where private relationships were the primary source of deal flow has now turned into an efficient auction driven market where relationships between private equity firms and executive management of an operating company have little time to develop.

This has forced private equity firms to seek new sources of revenues and businesses. While it is advantageous to seek out new sources of business and returns, there are several risks involved. Particularly troubling is the cross over between hedge funds and private equity. On the one hand, hedge fund managers are now bidding for operating assets in open competition with private equity firms. The current size of the hedge fund industry is estimated in the $1.5 trillion range. If just 10% of these assets—$150 billion—competed with private equity firms for deals, there would be an even larger inflow of funds than that presented in Exhibit 22.1. This means more money would be chasing the same number of deals.

Business development companies are a potential growth vehicle for private equity firms, particularly LBO firms. The benefits are many: captive assets that produce a long-term annuity of management fees, no redemption rights, and the ability to start charging incentive fees right away. Still only one BDC has been successfully launched to date. The hype over BDCs seems to have died as quickly as it began.

Finally, PIPE deals are another way for private equity firms to spread their over abundance of capital around. These transactions appeal both to venture capital and LBO firms and are another form of a cross over strategy. However, the SEC has turned a stern eye towards

PIPE transactions because of the toxicity of certain PIPE transactions that drove companies out of business. Since its peak in year 2000, the PIPE market has recovered but with greater protection for corporate issuers of PIPEs.

Credit Derivatives

CHAPTER 23

Introduction to Credit Derivatives

C redit derivatives are financial instruments that are designed to transfer the credit exposure of an underlying asset or issuer between two or more parties. They are individually negotiated financial contracts, which may take the form of options, swaps, forwards or credit linked notes where the payoffs are linked to, or derived from, the credit characteristics of the referenced asset or issuer. With credit derivatives, a financial manager can either acquire or hedge credit risk.

Many asset managers have portfolios that are very sensitive to changes in the spread between riskless and risky assets and credit derivatives are an efficient way to hedge this exposure. Conversely, other asset managers may use credit derivatives to target specific exposures as a way to enhance portfolio returns. In each case, the ability to transfer credit risk and return provides a new tool for portfolio managers to improve performance.

Credit derivatives, therefore, appeal to financial managers who invest in high-yield bonds, bank loans, or other credit dependent assets. The possibility of default is a significant risk for asset managers, and one that can be effectively hedged by shifting the credit exposure.

In their simplest form, credit derivatives may be nothing more than the purchase of credit protection. The ability to isolate credit risk and manage it independently of underlying bond positions is the key benefit of credit derivatives. Prior to the introduction of credit derivatives, the only way to manage credit exposure was to buy and sell the underlying assets. Because of transaction costs and tax issues, this was an inefficient way to hedge or gain exposure.

Credit derivatives therefore represent a natural extension of the financial markets in order to unbundle the risk-and-return buckets associated with a particular financial asset such as credit risk. They offer an important method for investment managers to hedge their exposure to credit risk because they permit the transfer of the exposure from one party to another. Credit derivatives allow for an efficient exchange of credit exposure in return for credit protection.

Before we can discuss credit derivatives we must first review the underlying risk which these financial instruments transfer and hedge. We begin this chapter with a discussion of credit risk. We then review the credit risks inherent in four important financial markets: high-yield bonds, leveraged bank loans, and sovereign emerging market debt, and distressed debt. Each of these markets is especially attuned to the nature and amount of credit risk undertaken with each investment. Furthermore, as we shall see in the next chapter, these four credit markets comprise the main collateral that underlie the collateralized debt obligation market. We also provide several examples of how credit derivatives may be used in these markets—and a thorough review of credit default swaps—the primary growth engine of the credit derivative market.

THE THREE SOURCES OF CREDIT RISK

A fixed income debt instrument represents a basket of risks. There is the risk from changes in interest rates (duration and convexity risk), the risk that the issuer will refinance the debt issue (call risk), and last, the risk of defaults, downgrades, and widening credit spreads (credit risk). The total return from a fixed income investment such as a corporate bond is the compensation for assuming all of these risks. Depending upon the rating on the underlying debt instrument, the return from credit risk can be a significant part of a bond's total return.

There are three important types of credit risk: default risk, downgrade risk, and credit spread risk. *Default risk* is the risk that the issuer of a bond or the debtor on a loan will not repay the outstanding debt in full. Default risk can be complete in that no amount of the bond or loan will be repaid, or it can be partial in that some portion of the original debt will be recovered. *Downgrade risk* is the risk that a national rating agency will lower its credit rating for an issuer based on perceived earnings capacity. *Credit spread risk* is the risk that the spread over a reference riskless rate will increase for an outstanding debt obligation. Credit spread risk and downgrade risk differ in that the latter pertains to a specific, formal credit review by an independent agency while the former is the financial markets' reaction to perceived credit deterioration.

A debtor is deemed to be in default when it fails to make a payment on its outstanding obligations. This can be as simple as the failure to make one scheduled coupon payment on an outstanding bond, or one interest payment on an outstanding loan. A bond or loan that has failed to make a scheduled payment is considered to be in default and the price of the asset declines accordingly.

In the following three exhibits we examine the three forms of credit risk. First, Exhibit 23.1 plots the default rates over the last 25 years for Baa rated bonds—the lowest level of investment grade bonds—versus single B rated high-yield bonds, as tracked by the Moody's rating agency. As Exhibit 23.1 indicates, default risk is a significant risk for high-yield bonds, but a small risk for investment grade bonds.

Exhibit 23.2 demonstrates the second source of credit risk: the risk of a credit downgrade. This happens when a *nationally recognized statistical rating organization* (NRSRO) reduces the credit rating on the outstanding debt of an issuer. The credit rating agencies call this "rating migration."

EXHIBIT 23.1   Default Rates for Investment Grade and High-Yield Bonds

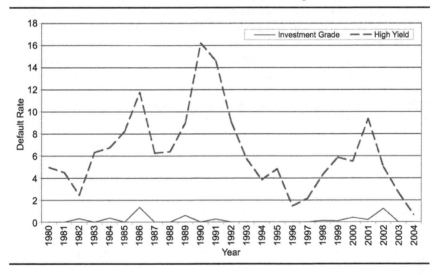

EXHIBIT 23.2   Demonstration of Ratings Migration for Investment Grade and High-Yield Bonds

	Aaa	Aa	A	Baa	Ba	B	Caa-C	Default	WR
Baa rated (investment grade)	0.05%	0.32%	4.68%	80.69%	5.46%	0.82%	0.15%	0.30%	7.53%
Single B rated (high yield)	0%	0.06%	0.20%	0.75%	6.55%	71.09%	5.74%	4.32%	11.30%

Rating migration can be both positive and negative. An increase in credit rating demonstrates an improvement in the financial health of a company and investors normally react by bidding up the price of the company's related debt. Conversely, a downward rating migration indicates a deteriorating financial condition and results in lower bond prices. We plot the rating migration from Moody's rating matrix over the history of 1920 to 2004. We focus on investment grade, Baa rated, and high yield, B rated, bonds.

Exhibit 23.2 demonstrates that rating migrations can cut both ways. For example, looking at Baa rated bonds, we can see that the long-term average annual positive migration from Baa rated to single A rated is 4.68% while the long run average negative rating migration to Ba is 5.46%. Similarly for single B rated bonds, the long run average positive migration to Ba is 6.55% while a negative ratings migration to Caa through C rated is 5.74%. Note also, that for single B rated bonds, there is a long run average migration to default status of 4.32% annually.

Finally, in Exhibit 23.3, we graph the credit spread for single B rated bonds and Baa rated bonds compared to U.S. Treasury bonds. U.S. Treasury bonds are regarded as default free. Therefore, the credit spread for all other bonds are compared to U.S. Treasury bonds. In Exhibit 23.3, the top solid line represents the credit spread for high-yield bonds while the bottom dashed line represents investment grade bonds.

EXHIBIT 23.3 Credit Spreads over U.S. Treasury Bonds

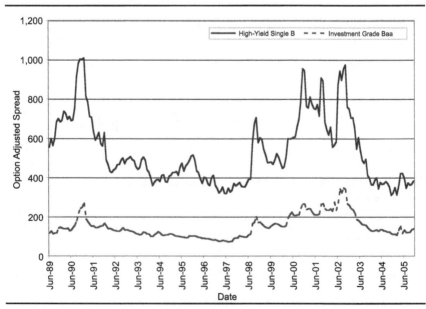

Regardless of whether a company is in more or less danger of defaulting on its bonds, there are points in time when investors in the credit markets perceive high-yield bonds to be more credit risky than other times. This is reflected in rising credit spreads. Exhibit 23.3 plots the credit spread for high-yield bonds over the period 1989 to 2005.

Notice, for instance, that in 1998, when the economy was reasonably robust, there was a credit crisis when the Russian government defaulted on a series of outstanding bonds. Regardless of the prospects for corporations to repay their bond obligations on time, the credit markets suddenly became "more risky" and credit spreads increased accordingly. Rising credit spreads lead to lower high-yield bond values and lost value for investors. The reader can also observe that during periods of economic recession, credit spreads for high-yield bonds and investment grade bonds tend to widen, but the widening process for high-yield bonds is dramatic.

Credit risk is influenced by both macroeconomic events and company specific events. For instance, credit risk typically increases during recessions or slowdowns in the economy. In an economic contraction, revenues and earnings decline across a broad swath of industries, reducing the interest coverage with respect to loans and outstanding bonds for many companies caught in the slowdown. This is demonstrated clearly in Exhibit 23.3 with respect to the U.S. recession of 2001 to 2002. Additionally, credit risk can be affected by liquidity crisis when investors seek the haven of liquid U.S. government securities. This last example is most readily demonstrated during the late summer of 1998 when the twin crisis of the Russian Bond default and the bailout of Long-Term Capital Management sent shock waves through the credit markets. Liquidity temporarily dried up for credit risky investments and there was a flight to safety for U.S. Treasury bonds.

Company specific events are unrelated to the business cycle and impact a single company at a time. These events could be due to a deteriorating client base, an obsolete business plan, noncompetitive products, outstanding litigation, or for any other reason that shrinks the revenues and earnings of a particular company.

There are two common methods of measuring credit risk. The first is a company's credit rating. NRSROs categorize corporations according to their credit risk. These firms include Standard & Poor's, Moody's Investors Services, and Fitch Ratings. Credit ratings are assigned on the basis of a variety of factors including a company's financial statements and an assessment of management.

Second, credit risk can be measured by the credit risk premium. This is the difference between the yield on a credit risky asset and that of a comparable default-free U.S. Treasury security. The premium is the compensation that investors must be paid to hold the credit risky asset.

As a company's credit quality deteriorates, a larger credit risk premium will be demanded to compensate investors for the risk of default.

In fact, the non-U.S. Treasury fixed income market is often referred to as the "spread product" market. This is because all other fixed income products, such as bank loans, high-yield bonds, investment grade corporate bonds, or emerging market debt, trade at a credit spread relative to U.S. Treasury securities. Hence the term "spread products."

The Effect of Credit Risk

Several parties are affected by credit risk. First, bond issuers and corporate borrowers are affected because their ability and the expense of borrowing money, either from the capital markets or from banks, depends upon their credit rating. A higher credit rating means not only cheaper financing, it also means a broader pool of capital from which to borrow. Many pension funds, endowments, mutual funds, and high-net-worth investors have limits on the amount of high-yield investments they may make. Therefore, a smaller pool of investors exist to purchase high-yield debt, and this increases the cost to borrowers.

Investors are also affected by credit risk. The credit rating at the time of purchase of a bond or making of a commercial loan determines the coupon that either the investor or the bank will receive. However, should the credit rating deteriorate after the investment is made, the value of the underlying bond or loan will also deteriorate.

Most commercial loans pay floating rates, depending upon the movement of an underlying risk-free rate (a comparable U.S. Treasury rate). Banks are less exposed to interest rate risk. However, the credit risk premium is usually set at the time the loan is made. If the credit premium subsequently increases, the bank will not be fully compensated for the credit risk it bears.

Traditional Methods of Managing Credit Risk

Credit risk has been traditionally managed by underwriting standards, diversification, and asset sales.[1] Consider a bank that is analyzing a corporate client for a bank loan. The bank will first consider the company's financial position, its revenue growth, earnings potential, interest coverage, and operating leverage. Next the bank will consider the corporation's balance sheet, its ratio of debt to equity and short-term liabilities to long-term liabilities. Then the bank will review the industry in which

---

[1] See Robert Neal, "Credit Derivatives: New Financial Instruments for Controlling Credit Risk," *Economic Review* (Federal Reserve Bank of Kansas City), Second Quarter 1996.

the company operates. It will consider competitive pressures, consolidation, new products, and growth prospects. The bank will then set a limit on the amount it will loan and will consider the loan amount against the bank's total limit for the industry in which the company operates.

Diversification is the second traditional method of managing credit risk. Banks build loan portfolios consisting of commercial loans across several different industries. This reduces the likelihood that all of the loans will suffer defaults at the same time. It is simply an application of "don't put all of your loans in one basket."

Finally, banks have sold their loan portfolios to reduce their exposure to certain industries or clients. While effective, this method can be difficult to implement. The reason is that banks build custom loan portfolios that match the particular balance sheet composite for the bank as well as its target audience of commercial borrowers. A loan portfolio for one bank will not perfectly suit another bank. Therefore, the sale of a loan portfolio usually entails a considerable discount.

However, this issue has largely been eliminated over the past decade with the increase in collateralized debt obligations. These are notes that are securitized by a pool of bank loans. The loans are packaged together, and new securities are issued to outside investors. We discuss these securities at length in Chapter 24.

CREDIT RISKY INVESTMENTS

In a sense, every bond that is not a U.S. Treasury bond is considered a credit risky investment. However, in this section, we will consider four types of fixed income investments that are considered at the farther region of the credit risky spectrum: high-yield bonds, leveraged loans, distressed debt, and emerging market bonds. In addition, it is these categories of credit risky investments that form the primary collateral for collateralized debt obligations (CDOs) which we will discuss in the next chapter.

To provide a brief introduction into the risk and return characteristics of these four classes of credit risky investments, we include Exhibits 23.4 and 23.5. Exhibit 23.4 provides the average return, standard deviation, and Sharpe ratio for these four investments over the period 1991 to 2005. We also include the S&P 500 and 10-year U.S. Treasury bonds for comparison. Notice, for instance, that leveraged loans and emerging market bonds have a very favorable risk and return tradeoff compared to both the U.S. stock market and U.S. Treasury bonds.

EXHIBIT 23.4   Expected Returns, Standard Deviations, and Sharpe Ratios

	S&P 500	10-Year U.S. Treasury	High-Yield Bonds	Distressed Debt	Leveraged Loans	Emerging Markets
Average	12.00%	7.45%	9.47%	13.98%	6.71%	11.76%
Std. Dev.	17.88%	8.77%	12.23%	28.72%	3.02%	15.32%
Sharpe	0.40	0.30	0.38	0.32	0.63	0.45

EXHIBIT 23.5   Correlation Matrix

	S&P 500	10-Year UST	High Yield	Distressed	Leveraged Loans	Emerging Market
S&P 500	1.00					
10-Year UST	0.12	1.00				
High Yield	0.66	0.27	1.00			
Distressed	0.30	−0.02	0.85	1.00		
Lev. Loans	0.59	−0.08	0.65	0.39	1.00	
Emerging Mkt.	0.33	0.14	0.49	0.48	0.10	1.00

Exhibit 23.5 presents a correlation matrix for these four credit investments. Notice that these asset classes have a very low correlation with the U.S. stock market, and almost no correlation with the U.S. Treasury bond market. In fact, distressed debt and leveraged loans have a slightly negative correlation with Treasury bonds. The key takeaway from Exhibit 23.5 is that credit risk provides a different risk and return exposure from stock market risk (the S&P 500) or interest rate risk (U.S. Treasury bonds). Therefore, these credit risky investments provide an opportunity to diversify a portfolio of traditional stocks and bonds.

High-Yield Bonds

The high-yield bond market has become a large economic force in the capital markets. The term "high yield" generally means those bonds that have a large credit risk premium compared to a comparable risk-free bond. High-yield bonds are generally considered to be those bonds that lack an investment grade credit rating. This includes securities that are rated lower than BBB by Standard & Poor's and less than Baa by Moody's Investor Services.

The high-yield bond market is subject to considerable credit risk. Consider Exhibit 23.6. This is the distribution of monthly returns for high-yield bonds over the period 1990 to 2005. As we have previously discussed in other chapters, credit risky assets have a negative skew and

EXHIBIT 23.6 Frequency Distribution for High-Yield Bonds[a]

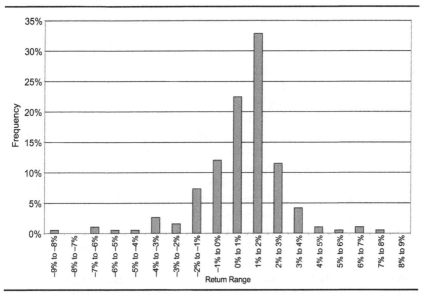

[a] Average = 0.75%, Std. Dev. = 2.05%, Skew = –0.81, Kurtosis = 4.16, Sharpe = 0.17.

a large value of leptokurtosis. This leads to condition generally called "fat tails"—where the probability mass of the return distribution is concentrated in outlier events. These two statistics indicate that high-yield bonds are subject to considerable downside exposure. That is, high-yield bonds have a large, negative, fat tail. This risk is translated in the form of defaults, downgrades, or increased credit spreads.

Exhibit 23.7 plots the Salomon Smith Barney/Citigroup High Yield Cash Pay index over the time period 1990 to 2005. We can see that high-yield bonds have generally increased in value over this time period. However, note that the value of high-yield bonds plateaued during the 1998 to 2002. This was a period marked by the popping of the technology bubble, an economic recession, and numerous corporate accounting scandals that roiled the market. Also note, from Exhibit 23.4 that high-yield bonds have an expected return and volatility somewhere in between U.S. stocks and Treasury bonds. Just about what we would expect for bonds that contain default risk but also, stand in line ahead of equity holders in the event of default.

Leveraged Bank Loans

The leveraged loan market is typically defined as bank loans that are made to companies that have a credit rating below investment grade, or loans that are priced at LIBOR + 150 basis points or more. Similar to high-yield bonds, bank loans are subject to the risk that the borrower will pay down the loan faster than expected or refinance the loan (call risk) as well as the risk of default, downgrade, and increased credit spread.

The corporate bank loan market typically consists of syndicated loans to large and midsized corporations. They are floating rate instruments, often priced in relation to LIBOR. Corporate loans may be either *revolving credits* (known as *revolvers*) that are legally committed lines of credit, or term loans that are fully funded commitments with fixed amortization schedules. Term loans tend to be concentrated in the lower credit rated corporations because revolvers usually serve as backstops for commercial paper programs of fiscally sound companies.

Term bank loans are repriced periodically. Because of their floating interest rate nature, they have reduced market risk resulting from fluctuating interest rates. Consequently, credit risk takes on greater importance in determining a commercial loan's total return.

The leveraged loan market rivals that of the high-yield bond market. Institutional investor in the bank loan market has grown rapidly from 1996 to 2005. Previously, leveraged loans were primarily the purview of the banks that lent the money to corporate borrows. However, increasingly, institutional investors have entered this market as a means of seeking consistent yield in their fixed income portfolios. Exhibit 23.8 demonstrates this growth.

EXHIBIT 23.7   Salomon Brothers High-Yield Cash Pay Index

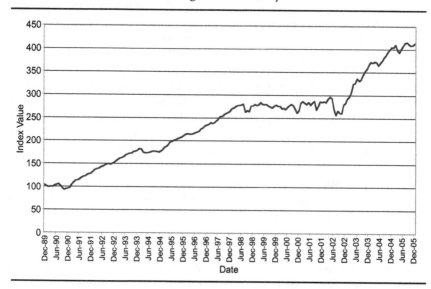

EXHIBIT 23.8   Participation of Institutional Investors in Leveraged Loans

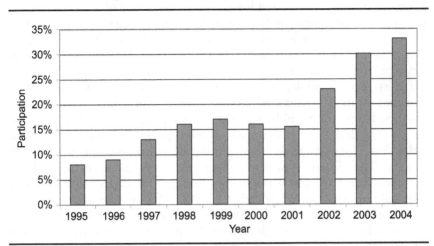

This growth has been fueled by several factors. First, over the past several years, the bank loan market and the high-yield bond market have begun to converge. This is due partly to the relaxing of commercial banking regulations which has allowed many banks to increase their product offerings, including high-yield bonds. Contemporaneously, investment banks and brokerage firms have established loan trading and syndication desks to compete with those of commercial banks.

In addition to banks and brokerage firms, insurance companies have become increasingly involved in the bank loan business as demonstrated by the Citicorp/Travelers Insurance merger. As regulatory barriers continue to fall, there will be fewer distinctions between commercial banks, brokerage firms, and insurance companies. Integration of these three branches of financial service firms has led to a greater expansion of the leveraged loan market.

A third reason is the acceptance of bank loans as a form of investment by institutional investors. Pension funds, endowment funds, mutual funds, and high-net-worth individuals have all entered the market for bank loan investing. Institutional investors seek bank loans because they meet their need for higher spreads and match up well against their liabilities. The entrance of the rating organizations into the bank loan market makes it easier for investors to classify bank loans by investment grade versus leveraged status. For example, as of the end of 2003, the total volume of rated bank loans by Moody's was $633 billion of which approximately half were leveraged loans.

The entrance of institutional investors has led to a change in the structure of many syndicated loans. Where the tenor of a bank loan was previously in the two- to four-year range, longer-term loans are being arranged to meet the longer investment horizons of institutional investors. Often a syndicated loan will be offered with different tranches constructed not by differences in credit ratings but by differences in maturity. For example, Allied Waste's recent loan facility had three tranches. Tranche A was a $2.25 billion term loan with a five-year tenor, Tranche B was for $1 billion maturing in six years, and Tranche C was for $1.25 billion with a maturity of seven years. The tranches of these "alphabet" loans have different pricing despite having the same credit quality. The different pricing reflects the different maturities of the tranches. The A tranche was usually priced in the range of LIBOR + 150, with subsequent tranches priced at LIBOR + 250 and up.

Investors are further enticed to the bank loan market by the securitization of bank loans through collateralized loan obligations. These obligations are in a format that investors already understand: the asset-backed security. We discuss collateralized loan obligations in more detail in the next chapter.

Finally, a new and more efficient capital market has emerged for bank loans. Many commercial banks have realized that their strength is best displayed in reviewing the creditworthiness of borrowers and originating new loans, but not necessarily holding those loans on their balance sheet. Consistent with the development of the collateralized loan obligation market, banks can now repackage these loans and sell them to other investors. In this way banks can better manage their risk capital and generate higher returns on equity.

Exhibit 23.9 and 23.10 provide a graphical review of the leveraged loan market. Despite their status of noninvestment grade, leverage loans display very consistent returns. Notice that the distribution of returns is much "tighter" than for high-yield bonds. That is, there are fewer outlier returns; much of the probability mass of the leveraged loan return distribution is concentrated in the 1% to 2% range. Still, with a negative skew value of −1.08 and a value of kurtosis of 3.24, leveraged loans demonstrate the same downside, fat tail as high-yield bonds.

Exhibit 23.10 shows the consistent growth of the leveraged loan index. Although leveraged loans are at risk to the occasional large downside event, they tend to earn consistent returns. This was demonstrated in Exhibit 23.9 where 86% of the probability mass is concentrated in the 1% to 2% range. This credit risky asset class offers the most consistent returns of the four credit risk categories examined.

EXHIBIT 23.9   Frequency Distribution for Leveraged Loans[a]

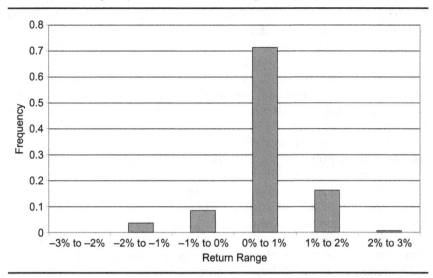

[a] Average = 0.54%, Std. Dev. = 0.64%, Skew = −1.08, Kurtosis = 3.24, Sharpe = 0.22.

EXHIBIT 23.10   CSFB Leveraged Loan Index

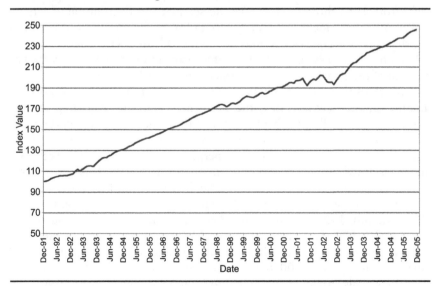

Emerging Market Debt

Credit risk is not unique to the domestic U.S. financial markets. When investing in the sovereign debt of a foreign country, an investor must consider two crucial risks. One is political risk—the risk that even though the central government of the foreign country has the financial ability to pay its debts as they come due, for political reasons (e.g., revolution, new government regime, trade sanctions), the sovereign entity decides to forfeit (default) payment. The second type of risk is credit risk—the same old inability to pay one's debts as they become due.

A sovereign government relies on two forms of cash flows to finance its government programs and to pay its debts: taxes and revenues from state-owned enterprises. Taxes can come from personal income taxes, corporate taxes, import duties, and other excise taxes. State-owned enterprises can be oil companies, telephone companies, national airlines and railroads, and other manufacturing enterprises.

In times of economic turmoil such as a recession, cash flows from state-owned enterprises decline along with the general malaise of the economy. Additionally, tax revenues decline as corporations earn less money, as unemployment rises, and as personal incomes decline. Lastly, with a declining foreign currency value, imports decline, reducing revenue from import taxes.

Exhibit 23.11 provides the return distribution for emerging market debt from 1993 through 2005. We can see that this distribution of returns has a long downside tail. This negative tail of probability mass is even fatter than that for high-yield bonds or leveraged loans. With a skew value of –2.15 and a kurtosis value of 11.45, this distribution of returns has the fattest tail of the bunch. There is a distinct bias towards large negative returns.

Much of this downside bias, however, can be traced to two events. As Exhibit 23.12 demonstrates, the performance of the emerging market bonds was generally positive for most of this time period. However, there were two periods of notable decline. The first was in October 1997, when the "Asian Contagion" hurt the emerging markets. In this month, the index declined by 10.5%. Second, in August 1998, the Russian government defaulted on its bonds, sending the index down by 27.4%.

For example, consider the Russian government 10% bond due in 2007. In July 1997 when this bond was issued, its credit spread over a comparable U.S. Treasury bond was 3.50%. However, by the time the Russian government defaulted on its bonds, the credit spread had increased to 53% (5,300 basis points) over comparable U.S. Treasury securities. This spread widening led to billions of dollars of losses as Russian bonds traded for just pennies on the dollar.[2]

---

[2] See "Financial Firms Lose $8 Billion so Far," *Wall Street Journal* (September 3, 1998), p. A2.

EXHIBIT 23.11 Frequency Distribution for Emerging Market Debt[a]

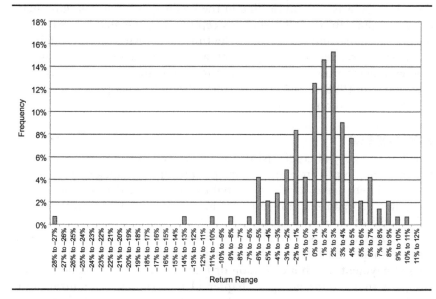

[a] Average = 0.98%, Std. Dev. = 4.43%, Skew = –2.15, Kurtosis = 11.45, Sharpe = 0.13.

EXHIBIT 23.12 JP Morgan EMBI Index

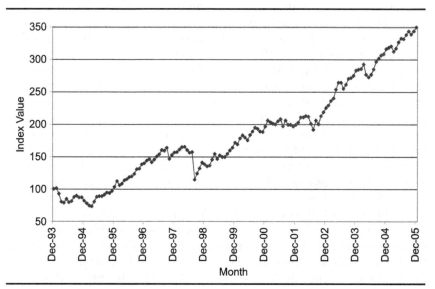

Once again, we note that credit risk is not all one sided. Even though there was a rapid decline in the credit quality of emerging market sovereign debt in 1997, such a steep retreat presented opportunities for credit quality improvement at the time of the Russian Bond default, the market recovered quickly. After a nasty 27% decline in August, emerging market bonds surged 20% for the remainder of 1998. From its low point in 1998 to the end of 2005, the index has posted a gain of 318%, for an average annual return of 18%.

Distressed Debt

Our last category of credit risky investments was previously discussed in the chapters on private equity. Some private equity managers play in the distressed debt arena for the potential to convert the debt into an equity stake in a reorganized company. In this section, we focus on the credit risk profile of distressed debt.

Distressed debt is generally considered debt that is impaired in some way or shape. This can be debt that is already in default through the missed payment of a bond coupon or loan interest; it can be bonds of a company that is undergoing a Chapter 11 bankruptcy reorganization; it can be the debt of a company that has good growth prospects but severe cash flow problems; or finally, it can be the debt of a company with a very low credit rating and a high probability of bankruptcy filing. Loans and bonds that meet the profile of one of these scenarios all are fair game for the distressed debt players.

Exhibit 23.13 displays the distribution of monthly returns for distressed debt from 1990 to 2005. Notice how spread out the returns are—from –33% to +22%. Distressed debt has by far the greatest dispersion of the credit risky investments. This is evidenced by its high monthly standard deviation of returns of 6.05%. In fact, Exhibit 23.13 demonstrates that distressed debt has a higher annual volatility than even U.S. stocks—28.7% versus 17.9%. Clearly, this is not an asset class for the faint of heart. In addition, distressed debt demonstrates the same large negative downside tail as other credit risky investments. With a skew of –0.63 and a kurtosis of 7.05, the return distribution for distressed debt also suffers from large negative fat tails.

Exhibit 23.14 plots the Salomon Smith Barney/Citigroup distressed debt index. This index clearly shows the greatest volatility. Notice the downward spike in 1998. From August through October 1998, during the Russian bond default and Long-Term Capital Management crisis, distressed debt bonds declined 35% in value. Also, in June of 2005, the distressed debt market took another significant hit when the bonds of General Motors were downgraded to junk debt status. About $196 bil-

EXHIBIT 23.13   Frequency Distribution for Distressed Debt[a]

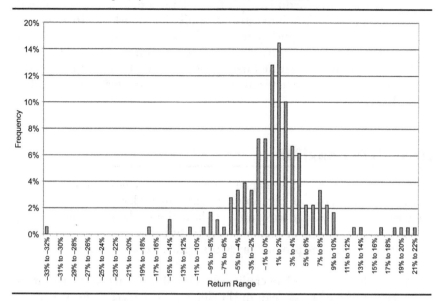

[a] Average = 1.11%, Std. Dev. = 6.05%, Skew= –0.63, Kurtosis = 7.05, Sharpe = 0.12.

EXHIBIT 23.14   Salomon Brothers Bankruptcy Index

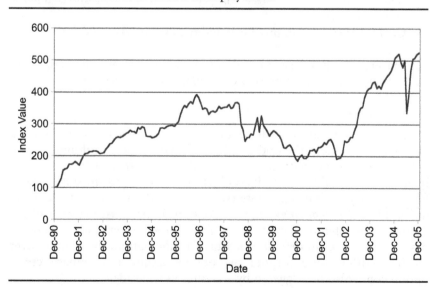

lion of General Motors debt was cut to BB from BBB by Standard and Poor's. Such a dramatic downgrade for so large a debt issuer sent shockwaves throughout the subinvestment grade debt market. However, the distressed debt market quickly recovered after GM, surging almost 37% in the following two months. The takeaways from Exhibits 23.13 and 23.14 is simply that distressed debt (not surprisingly) is subject to considerable credit risk, particularly events like the downgrading of GM or bond defaults.

CREDIT OPTION DERIVATIVES

In the prior sections of this chapter we provided a demonstration of credit risk and it importance in determining asset value. Here we review one of the basic credit derivative structures: credit options. These instruments may be used for transferring or accumulating credit exposure.

Credit derivatives provide investors with several advantages.

- Credit derivatives isolate credit risk. This allows a more efficient management of credit risk than the buying and selling credit risky assets to increase or decrease an investor's credit exposure.
- Credit derivatives transfer credit risk. Again this may be a more efficient way to gain or reduce credit exposure than buying and selling the underlying assets.
- Credit derivatives can provide liquidity to the market in times of credit stress.
- Through the purchase and sale of underlying credit collateral, credit derivatives provide more rigorous and transparent pricing.

Credit Put Option

In its simplest form, a credit option can be a binary option. With a binary credit option, the option seller will pay out a sum if and when a default event occurs with respect to a referenced credit (e.g., the underlying issuer is unable to pay its obligations as they become due). Therefore, a binary option represents two states of the world: default or no default. It is the clearest example of credit protection. At maturity of the option, if the referenced credit has defaulted the option holder receives a payout. If there is no default at maturity of the option, the option buyer receives nothing and forgoes the option premium. A binary credit option could also be triggered by a ratings downgrade.

A European binary credit option pays out a sum only at maturity if the referenced credit is in default. An American binary option can be exercised at any time during its life. Consequently, if an American binary credit option is in the money (a default event has occurred), it will be exercised immediately because delaying exercise will reduce the present value of the fixed payment.

Consider an American credit put option that pays the holder of the option the difference between the strike price and market value of the bond if a high-yield bond is in default.[3] If the bond is not in default, the pay off to the put option is zero. This option may be described as

$$P[B(t)] = \begin{cases} X - B(t) \text{ if the bond is in default} \\ 0 \text{ otherwise} \end{cases}$$

where

X = the strike price of the put option
$B(t)$ = the market value of the bond at default[4]

This type of credit derivative protects the investor only after default has occurred. The bond may have declined in price before the issuing company declares a default.

Instead of waiting for an actual default to occur, the strike price of the option can be set to a minimum net worth of the underlying issuer below which default is probable. For instance, if the firm value of the referenced credit (Assets − Liabilities) falls to \$100 million, then the binary credit option will be in the money.

Alternatively, a binary credit put options may be based on credit ratings as the threshold or trigger. For instance, in January 1998 bondholders forced the International Finance Corporation of Thailand (IFCT) to redeem \$500 million in bonds several years before their maturity. The bond issue contained a provision that allowed investors to put the bonds back to the issuer at face value should the sovereign credit rating of Thailand fall below investment grade.

---

[3] Typically, the market price of the bond is fixed at some period of time after the default such as one month from the default date. Also, the condition of default must be specified. This could be a failure to make a timely payment of interest or principal or it may be triggered by a Chapter 11 bankruptcy filing.

[4] Mathematical formulae have been developed to determine the value of credit options. These equations can be quite complicated. Generally, they fall into two types of pricing methodologies: structural versus term structure. For more information regarding credit option pricing formulae, see Mark J. P. Anson, Frank J. Fabozzi,, Moorad Choudhry, and Ren-Raw Chen, *Credit Derivatives: Instruments, Pricing, and Applications* (Hoboken, NJ: John Wiley & Sons, 2004).

EXHIBIT 23.15   Binary Credit Put Option on IFCT Bonds

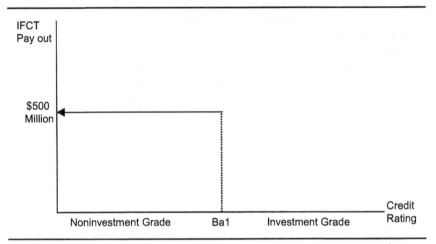

This binary credit put option may be expressed as

$$P[V(t); \$500 \text{ million}] = \begin{cases} \$500 \text{ million} - V(t); \text{ if credit rating is below} \\ \qquad\qquad\qquad\qquad \text{investment grade} \\ \$0; \text{ if credit rating is above investment grade} \end{cases}$$

Exhibit 23.15 demonstrates the payout to the credit put option on the IFCT bonds.

Credit Call Options

In addition to the binary put option described above, the IFCT bonds also provided that investors would receive an additional 50 basis points of coupon income should the credit rating of Thailand decline by two notches. Furthermore, investors would receive 25 basis points of coupon income for every subsequent decline in credit rating thereafter. These call options were in effect until a below investment grade credit rating was reached. Then the bonds were putable as described above.

The ability to earn additional yield as the credit rating of Thailand declined is the same as a series of binary call options. These options may be expressed as

$$C[CR(t); ICR] = \begin{cases} \$2,500,000; \text{ if } CR(t) \text{ is two grades below } ICR \\ \$0; \text{ if } CR(t) \text{ is not two grades below } ICR \end{cases}$$

where $CR(t)$ is the current credit rating for Thailand at time t, ICR is the initial credit rating of Thailand at the issuance of the bonds, and $\$2,500,000 = 0.005 \times \$500,000,000$.

The payout function for these binary credit call options are displayed in Exhibit 23.16. The bonds suffered three credit downgrades before they hit the noninvestment grade level and became putable.

The reader may question why the IFCT would issue bonds with attached binary credit options. The reason is one of cost. Options are not free. By attaching credit options to its bonds, the IFCT was in fact selling these options to its investors in return for paying a lower coupon rate. Through the "sale" of these credit options, the IFCT was able to initially lower its funding costs by 100 basis points. Unfortunately, the credit rating of Thailand deteriorated, resulting, ultimately, in a greater expense to IFCT.

Credit-Linked Notes

Credit-linked notes (CLNs) are bonds issued with an imbedded credit option. Typically, these notes can be issued with reference to a single corporation, or a basket of credit risks. The holder of the CLN is paid a coupon and the par value of the note at maturity if there is no default on the underlying referenced corporation or basket of credits. However, if there is some default, downgrade, or other adverse credit event, the holder of the CLN will receive either a lower coupon payment or only a partial redemption of the CLN principal value.

EXHIBIT 23.16   Binary Credit Call Options on IFCT Bonds[a]

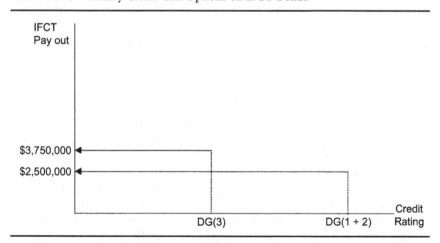

[a] DG(1 + 2) indicates the first two credit downgrades.
  DG(3) indicates the third downgrade.

Why would an investor purchase a CLN? The reason is simple. By agreeing to bear some of the credit risk associated with a corporation or basket of other credits, the holder of the CLN will receive a higher coupon on the CLN. In effect the holder of the CLN has sold some credit insurance to the issuer of the note. If a credit event occurs, the CLN holder must forego some of his coupon or principal value to make the seller of the note whole. If there is no credit event, the holder of the CLN collects an insurance premium in the form of a higher coupon rate. The investor in the CLN is, in fact, selling credit protection in return for a higher yield on the CLN.

CLNs appeal to investors who wish to take on more credit risk but are either wary of standalone credit derivatives such as swaps and options, or who may be limited in their ability to access credit derivatives directly. In contrast a CLN is just that—a coupon paying note. This is an on-balance sheet debt instrument that any investor can purchase. Furthermore, they can be tailored to achieve the specific credit risk profile that the CLN holder wishes to target.

Total Return Credit Swap

A total return swap transfers all of the economic exposure of a referenced asset or a referenced basket of assets to the credit swap buyer. A total return credit swap includes all cash flows from the referenced asset as well as any capital appreciation or depreciation of those assets.

If the total return payer owns the underlying referenced assets, it has transferred its economic exposure to the total return receiver in return for a payment usually tied to LIBOR. Effectively, the total return payer has a neutral position with respect to the underlying credit risky asset that will earn LIBOR plus a spread. However, the total return payer has only transferred the economic exposure of the referenced assets to the total return buyer, it has not transferred the physical ownership of the assets. The total return payer must continue to finance the underlying assets at its marginal cost of borrowing or the opportunity cost of investing elsewhere the capital tied up by the referenced assets.

Exhibit 23.17 displays a total return credit swap. Assume the credit seller borrows money from the capital markets at LIBOR. It uses the borrowed cash to purchase the credit risky asset, and receives the total return from the asset. The credit seller then enters into a swap agreement with the credit buyer where the buyer will receive the total return from the credit risky asset in return for paying to the credit seller LIBOR + spread.

From the credit seller's perspective, all cash flows net out to the spread over LIBOR. Therefore, the credit seller's profit is equal to the spread times the dollar value of the credit swap. From the credit buyer's perspective, it receives the total return on a credit risky asset without

EXHIBIT 23.17   Total Return Credit Swap

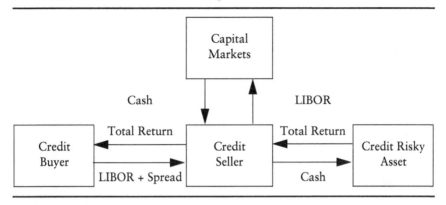

having to use its own capital to purchase the asset. These types of swaps are often known as "renting a balance sheet" because the referenced asset remains on the seller's balance sheet at the seller's cost of funds.[5]

CREDIT DEFAULT SWAPS

By far the most important development in the credit derivative market is the *credit default swap* (CDS). This credit derivative is primarily responsible for the amazing growth of the credit derivative market. Exhibit 23.18 demonstrates the explosive growth of this market over the past seven years. Notice that the notional amount of these contracts is now measured in the trillions of dollars.

A key component fueling this expansion is the growth of the synthetic collateralized debt obligations (CDOs). Synthetic CDOs use CDS to gain exposure to credit risk. We will discuss CDOs extensively in the next chapter.

There is a key difference between a total return credit swap and a CDS. In a CDS, there is a contingent payment only following a credit event. Conversely, for a total return credit swap, payments are made to reflect changes in the market value of the credit risky asset.

A credit default swap is similar to the binary put options discussed above in that its primary purpose is to hedge the credit exposure to a referenced asset or issuer. In this sense, credit default swaps operate in a

---

[5] Another form of credit derivative is a credit forward contract. These contracts act like one-period total return credit swaps. For more detail, see Mark Anson, *Credit Derivatives*.

EXHIBIT 23.18   Growth of the Credit Derivative Market

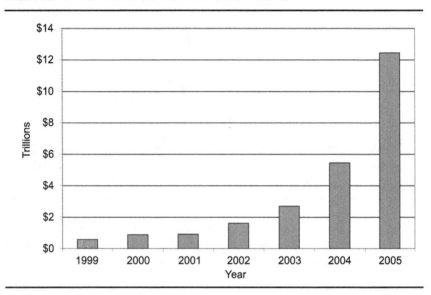

similar fashion to a standby letter of credit. A credit default swap is the simplest form of credit insurance. It is simply a bilateral contract where the credit protection buyer pays a periodic fee (or insurance premium) to the credit protection seller in exchange for a contingent payment if a credit event occurs with respect to an underlying credit risky asset. A CDS may be negotiated on any one of the credit risky investments discussed at the beginning of this chapter.

There are two types of credit default swaps. The first type and, by far, the predominant CDS is a bilateral contract where the credit protection buyer pays a periodic premium on a predetermined amount (the notional amount) in exchange for a contingent payment from the credit protection seller to reimburse the buyer for any losses suffered from a specified credit event.

Exhibit 23.19 demonstrates the predominant form of a credit default swap. In Exhibit 23.19, the credit risk of the underlying risky asset is transferred from the credit protection buyer to the credit protection seller.

A variation on the credit default swap is for the owner of the credit risky asset to pass on the total return of the asset to the credit protection seller in return for a certain payment. The credit protection buyer gives up the uncertain returns of the credit risky asset in return for certain payments from the credit protection seller. The credit protection seller

EXHIBIT 23.19   Credit Default Swap with Transfer of Default Risk

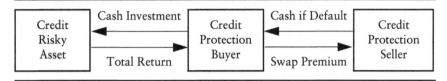

EXHIBIT 23.20   Credit Default Swap with Transfer of Total Return

now receives both the upside and the downside of the return associated with the credit risky asset. Exhibit 23.20 demonstrates this swap.

Large banks are the natural dealers for credit default swaps because it is consistent with their letter of credit business; and, not surprisingly, banks are the largest players in this market. Banks may sell credit default swaps as a natural extension of their credit lending business. Alternatively, a bank may use a credit default swap to hedge the credit exposure that exists on its balance sheet. For example, a bank may wish to reduce its exposure to a particular corporate borrower, or an industry that is geared for difficult times. The bank can reduce its exposure to its customer credit risk in most cases without the knowledge or consent of the bank's primary borrowers.

Credit default swaps are very flexible. For instance, a credit default swap may state in the contract the exact amount of insurance payment in the event of a credit event. Alternatively, a credit default swap may be structured so that the amount of the swap payment by the credit protection seller is determined after the credit event. Usually, this is determined by the market value of the referenced asset after the credit event has occurred.

The Mechanics of a Total Return Swap

The CDS market is contract driven. By this, I mean, each CDS is a privately negotiated transaction between the credit protection buyer and seller. Fortunately, the International Swaps and Derivatives Association—the primary industry body for derivatives documentation—has established standardized terms for CDS. In this section we provide some detail on the standard ISDA agreement.

CDS Spread

The premium to be paid by the credit protection buyer is often called the spread and it is quoted in basis points per annum on the notional value of the CDS. CDS spreads are not credit yield spreads in the manner of Exhibit 23.3, but rather prices quotes for buying credit insurance. Typically, the price of insurance is paid quarterly by the protection buyer.

Contract Size and Maturing

ISDA does not impose any limits on size or length of term of a CDS; this is up to the negotiation of the parties involved. Most CDS fall in the range of $20 million to $100 million with a tenor of three to five years.

Trigger Events

This is the heart of every CDS transaction. Trigger events determine when the credit protection seller must make a payment to the credit protection buyer. As you might imagine both sides to a CDS negotiate these terms intensely. The credit protection buyer wishes to have the trigger events defined as broadly as possible, while the credit protection seller wants to have these events construed as narrowly as possible.

ISDA provides for six kinds of trigger events, but the parties to a CDS can add more; although the six events identified by ISDA cover virtually all types of credit events. The six credit events are:

- *Bankruptcy.* This pretty much says it all regarding a company's inability to pay its debt.
- *Failure to pay.* While a company my not be in bankruptcy yet, it may not be able to meet its debt obligations as they come due.
- *Restructuring.* Any form of debt restructuring that is disadvantageous to the credit protection buyer. "Restructuring" is a fuzzy term and ISDA attempts to clarify this part of the standard contract by offering four options for the parties to consider.
- *Obligation acceleration.* All bond and loan covenants contain provisions that accelerate the repayment of the loan or bond if the credit quality of the borrower begins to deteriorate. This could be any number of events such as a failure to pay or a bankruptcy (which ISDA covers independently), or a ratings downgrade.
- *Obligation default.* Any failure to meet a condition in the bond or loan covenant that would put the borrower in breach of the covenant. This could be something like the failure to maintain a sufficient current ratio, or a minimum interest earnings coverage ratio.

■ *Repudiation/moratorium.* This is most frequently associated with sovereign or emerging market debt. This is simply a refusal by the sovereign government to repay its debt as it comes due or even an outright rejection of its debt obligations.

Settlement

If a credit event occurs, settlement can be made either with a cash payment or with a physical settlement. In a cash settlement, the credit protection seller makes the credit protection buyer whole by transferring to her an amount of cash to make up for the lost value of the underlying credit risky bond.

Cash settlement does not occur as frequently as one might expect because it is difficult to get a good market quote for a distressed asset. Therefore, most CDS use physical settlement upon the occurrence of a credit event. Under physical settlement, the credit protection seller purchases at par value the impaired loan or bond from the credit protection buyer. The credit risky asset is physically transferred to the credit protection seller's balance sheet, and now she has the incentive to get as much in recovery value as possible form the impaired asset.

Delivery

Within certain limits, the credit protection buyer has a choice of assets that she can deliver for physical settlement. This raises the issue of which is "cheapest to deliver." In general, the credit protection seller can deliver the following:

■ Direct obligations of the referenced entity such as corporate bonds or bank loans.
■ Obligations of a subsidiary of the referenced entity if the subsidiary is at least 50% or more owned by the referenced entity (this is sometimes called "qualifying affiliate guarantees").
■ Obligations of a third party that the referenced entity may have guaranteed—known as "qualifying guarantees."

Keep in mind that although ISDA provides standard terms, the parties to a CDS can negotiate any and all terms plus throw in a few of their own if they wish. The main point is that the standardization of CDS terms has provided the infrastructure for the huge growth of the credit derivative markets as demonstrated in Exhibit 23.18.

Risks of Credit Swaps

While credit derivatives offer investors alternative strategies to access credit risky assets, they come with specialized risks. These risks apply equally to credit options as well as credit swaps.

First, there is operational risk. Operational risk is the risk that traders or portfolio managers could imprudently use credit swaps. Since these are off-balance sheet contractual agreements, excessive credit exposures can be achieved without appearing on an investor's balance sheet. Without proper accounting systems and other backoffice operations, an investor may not be fully cognizant of the total credit risk exposure.

Second, there is counterparty risk. CDS are individually negotiated, private transactions. They are illiquid investments with a very limited secondary market. Furthermore, the legal documentation associated with a CDS may prevent one party from selling their share of the CDS without the other party's consent. This creates the risk that the counterparty to a swap agreement will default on its obligations. It is ironic that a credit protection buyer, for example, can introduce a new form of credit risk into her portfolio (counterparty credit risk) from the purchase of a credit default swap. For a credit protection buyer to suffer a loss two things must happen: (1) There must be a credit event on the underlying credit risky asset; and (2) the credit protection seller must default on its obligations to the credit protection buyer.

Another source of risk is liquidity risk. Currently, there are no exchange-traded credit derivatives. Instead, they are traded over the counter as customized contractual agreements between two parties. The very nature of this customization makes credit derivatives illiquid. Credit derivatives will not suit all parties in the financial markets, and a party to a custom tailored credit derivative contract may not be able to obtain the "fair value" of the contract if he tries to sell his position.

Last, there is pricing risk. As the derivative markets have matured, the mathematical models used to price derivative contracts have become increasingly complex. These models are dependent upon assumptions regarding underlying economic parameters. Consequently, the pricing of credit derivatives is sensitive to the assumptions of the models.

Credit derivatives join together the world of traditional guarantees with financial derivatives. Financial guarantee pricing models traditionally were based on credit ratings and historical default and ratings migration rates. Conversely, the sophisticated nature of the derivatives market uses mathematical models instead of historical information to price the derivative instruments. The key point for the reader is to understand that history and math do not always work in harmony.

CONCLUSION

This chapter was designed to be a brief introduction to credit risk and new derivative products that may be used to access credit risky assets. Credit derivatives provide new tools for banks, insurance companies, and institutional investors to buy, sell, diversify, and trade units of credit risk. In addition, credit derivatives allow investors to achieve favorable yields to match their outstanding liabilities.

Chief among the new credit derivatives is the Credit Default Swap. According to ISDA, these instruments account for more than half the growth of the credit derivative market. Not only are they used for credit risk management as demonstrated in this chapter, they form the foundation for much of the growth of the CDO market described in the next chapter.

In our next chapter we introduce the collateralized debt obligation market. This market would not be as successful and large without the initial development of the credit derivative market. Wall Street and investors have embraced these alternative strategies to access credit return.

CHAPTER 24

Collateralized Debt Obligations

Collateralized debt obligations (CDOs) are a form of asset-backed security (ABS) where a pool of fixed income instruments are repackaged into highly rated securities. These structures were born in the late 1980s as banks began to repackage high-yield bonds that they held on their balance sheet that were not the type of liquid assets that banks demand. These securities were called *collateralized bond obligations* (CBOs), and they were backed by a portfolio of senior or subordinated bonds issued by a variety of corporate or sovereign issuers. CBOs are just another form of a debt instrument that is backed not by the credit of a single issuer, but instead, is supported by the credit of many different issuers. Following on the heels of CBOs banks began to realize that they had other assets on their balance sheet—leveraged loans—that could be repackaged into a collateral pool and sold to investors. Hence collateralized loan obligations (CLOs) were born in the early 1990s.

From these two streams of asset-backed securities, CDOs were born. A CDO is simply a security that is backed by a portfolio of bonds and loans together. In fact, the term "CDO" is often used broadly to refer to any CLO or CBO structure. In its simplest form, a CDO is a trust or special purpose vehicle that purchases loans and bonds from banks, insurance companies, corporate issuers, and other sellers, and then issues new securities to investors where the new securities are collateralized by the bonds and loans contained in the trust.

In this chapter, we provide an introduction to the CDO marketplace. We describe the various uses for CDOs as well as the risks and benefits. We also provide some examples of recent CDO structures. Then we consider how CDO structures may be combined with other forms of alternative investment strategies such as private equity and hedge funds.

GENERAL STRUCTURE OF CDOs

As just explained, the term CDOs can be used to broadly refer to any collateralized bond obligation or collateralized loan obligation. These two categories describe a large portion of the CDO marketplace. However, there are also investment vehicles that combine both bonds and loans into a single asset-backed pool. These structures are best referred to as collateralized debt obligations because the underlying pool of collateral contains both bonds and loans. Therefore, the term CDO may also refer to a hybrid asset-backed structure where the supporting collateral is a combination of debt instruments including bank loans, high-yield corporate bonds, emerging market sovereign debt, and even other CDO securities.

Size of the Market for CBOs and CLOs

The first CDO was created in 1987 by bankers at the now defunct Drexel Burnham Lambert for a savings and loan association called Imperial Savings Association. The transaction size was $100 million. From this simple beginning, the CDO market has grown to hundreds of billions of dollars.

Exhibit 24.1 shows the growth of the CDO market. As can be seen, CDO issuance grew rapidly throughout the second half of the 1990s and hit a peak in year 2000 before retrenching during the short U.S. recession of 2001 to 2002. However, CDO issuance rebounded in 2003 through 2005. CDO issuance is expected to exceed $150 billion in 2006.

EXHIBIT 24.1   Growth of the CDO Market

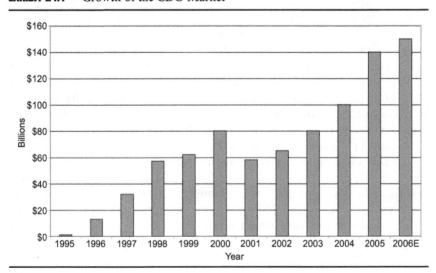

Why the Growth of CDOs?

CDOs are all about repackaging and transferring credit risk. The collateral underlying a CDO can be high-yield bonds, leveraged loans, distressed debt, emerging market bonds, or real estate mortgages. The ability to pool together bonds, loans or mortgages of different sizes and credit qualities to form a diversified pool of credit risky assets and then to sell investment grade notes that participate in this pool is a powerful financial tool for investors, banks, asset managers, and brokerage houses.

Most investors are under invested in credit. Yet, as demonstrated in the prior chapter, credit risky assets have a low correlation with the U.S. stock market and U.S. Treasury bond market. This offers the opportunity for excellent diversification through credit exposure.

CDOs provide investors with convenient access to a ready-made diversified pool of credit risky assets. This is more efficient than if the investor had to construct a credit risky portfolio on its own. Furthermore, CDOs allow the investor to pick and choose among the different classes of credit risky assets: high-yield bonds, bank loans, emerging market debt and so forth. There are CDO vehicles for every type and kind of credit risky bond, loan, and mortgage out there.

Better still, CDOs issue multiple classes of securities against the credit risky collateral pool, with each class or tranche of CDO security having a different level of seniority and credit rating. This process is called "credit tranching," and it allows an investor to even more finely tune her desired level of credit exposure. The investor chooses the risk attachment point to the underlying credit risky collateral pool.

For banks, CDOs allow the bank to manage credit risks of its balance sheet of loans. Asset managers, of course, collect asset management fees for managing the CDO structure—there would be no incentive for asset managers to construct CDOs otherwise. Brokerage firms, finally, collect underwriting fees for selling CDO tranches to clients.

Overview of the CDO Marketplace Balance Sheet versus Arbitrage CDOs

The asset-backed nature of CDO securities may be used to effect two main types of transactions: *balance sheet CDOs* and *arbitrage CDOs*. Banks and insurance companies are the primary sources of balance sheet CDOs. They use these structures to manage the assets on their balance sheet. Frequently, balance sheet CDOs tend to be in the form of collateralized loan obligation structures.

There are several goals of a balance sheet CDO.

■ A bank or insurance company might wish to reduce its credit exposure to a particular client or industry. It transfers this risk to the CDO.

■ The bank or insurance company might wish to reduce its regulatory capital charges. Selling a portion of its loan or bond portfolio to a CDO can free up regulatory capital required to support those credit risky assets.

■ The bank or insurance company may need a capital infusion.

Although CLO structures were invented in the late 1980s, it was not until the ROSE Funding No. 1 CLO in November 1996 that the value of CLOs to manage balance sheet risk became apparent. In that transaction National Westminister Bank sold $5 billion of high quality commercial bank loans to the ROSE CLO. This sale represented 15% to 20% of Nat West's total loan book (about 2,000 corporate loans). The transaction not only provided new funding to Nat West, it also released up to $400 million of regulatory capital.[1]

Since the Nat West transaction, banks have realized that they can use the asset-backed securities market to manage their balance sheets. This is a vast improvement over the traditional way for a bank to manage its credit exposure: using its lending policies to cut back on its lending exposure in one industry while increasing its loan exposure in a different industry. The dramatic increase in technology and financial engineering in the 1990s allows banks to manage their credit risks more finely. In today's financial markets, many banks have concluded that their expertise lies in analyzing credit risk and originating loans to match that risk, but not necessarily in holding the loans on their balance sheet.[2]

In contrast to banks, money managers are the main suppliers of arbitrage CDOs. Initially, most arbitrage CDOs were in the form of a CBO structure because money managers tended to have more experience managing high-yield bonds than leveraged loans. However, arbitrage CDOs have expanded dramatically, and now contain bonds, mortgages, commercial loans, and even investments in other CDO structures. The ultimate goal is to make a profit instead of managing balance sheet risk.

Furthermore, within these two broad categories are several subcategories that further segment the CDO marketplace. For instance, balance sheet CDOs can be either *cash funded* or can be *synthetically constructed* through the use of credit derivatives. Similarly, arbitrage CDOs can be funded with cash or through the use of credit derivatives.

Exhibit 24.2 presents an overview of the different segments of the CDO market. We present examples of each segment in our continuing discussions.

---

[1] See Charles Smithson and Gregory Hayt, "Tools for Reshaping Credit Portfolios: Managing Credit Risk," *RMA Journal* (May 2001).

[2] See Kenneth E. Kohler, "Collateralized Loan Obligations: A Powerful New Portfolio Management Tool for Banks," *Securitization Conduit* 1 (Summer 1998), pp. 5–19.

EXHIBIT 24.2 Overview of Collateralized Debt Obligations

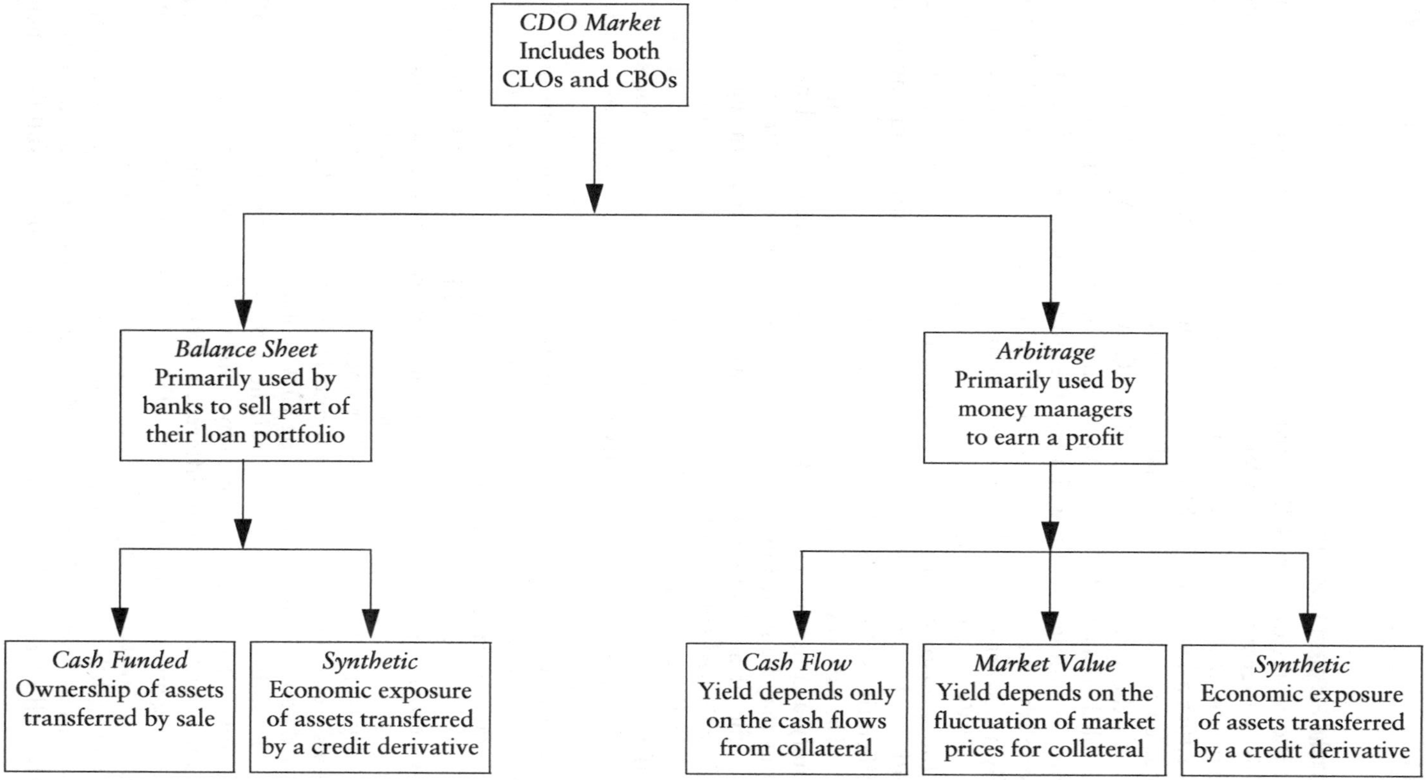

CDO Market
Includes both
CLOs and CBOs

Balance Sheet
Primarily used by
banks to sell part of
their loan portfolio

Arbitrage
Primarily used by
money managers
to earn a profit

Cash Funded
Ownership of assets
transferred by sale

Synthetic
Economic exposure
of assets transferred
by a credit derivative

Cash Flow
Yield depends only
on the cash flows
from collateral

Market Value
Yield depends on the
fluctuation of market
prices for collateral

Synthetic
Economic exposure
of assets transferred
by a credit derivative

Special Purpose Vehicles

At the center of every CDO structure is a special purpose vehicle (SPV). This is a term to describe a legal entity that is established to accomplish a specific transaction such as a CDO structure. SPVs are usually set up as either a Delaware or Massachusetts business trust or as a special purpose corporation (SPC), usually Delaware based.

In the case of a balance sheet CDO, the SPV will most often be established as a CLO trust. The selling bank will be the sponsor for the trust, meaning that it will bear the administrative and legal costs of establishing the trust. In the case of an arbitrage CDO, the SPV is usually a CBO trust and the sponsoring entity is typically a money manager.

SPVs are often referred to as "bankruptcy remote." This means that if the sponsoring bank or money manager goes bankrupt, the CDO trust will not be affected. The trust assets remain secure from any financial difficulties suffered by the sponsoring entity.

The SPV owns the collateral placed in the trust, and issues notes and equity against the collateral it owns. These collateralized debt obligations may be issued in different classes of securities or "tranches." Each tranche of a CDO structure may have its own credit rating. The most subordinated tranche of the CDO is usually called the equity tranche.

At the core of every SPV is the slicing and dicing of credit risk into different classes or tranches of securities. The SPV issues notes differentiated by their level of seniority in the SPV structure. Typically, there are three main tranches to every CDO: senior, mezzanine, and equity. The nomenclature of the CDO market parses these tranches out more finely into: super senior tranche, senior tranche, senior mezzanine tranche, mezzanine tranche, and the equity tranche.

Typically, every tranche of notes issued by the CDO SPV receives an investment grade rating by a nationally recognized statistical rating organization (NRSRO) with the exception of the equity tranche. The equity tranche is the "first loss" tranche. It is the last to receive any cash flows from the CDO collateral and is the first tranche on the hook for any defaults or lost value of the CDO collateral.

Usually the super senior tranche is the largest tranche (up to 85% of the total SPV notes), followed by tranches of less seniority. Each class or tranche of SPV notes has different rights and priorities concerning payments generated by the CDO collateral. The seniority of the tranches form a "waterfall" by which it is dictated how the proceeds from the CDO cashflows (both coupon receipts and liquidation sales) will first be used to meet the obligations owed to the most senior tranche of the SPV. After all of the claims of the super senior tranche are fulfilled, then the

EXHIBIT 24.3   A Basic CDO Structure and Waterfall

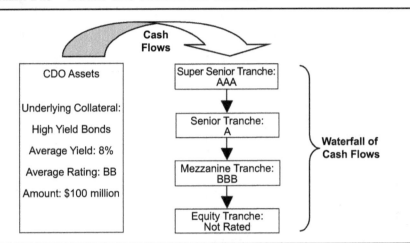

CDO cashflows are used to meet the obligations of the senior tranche, and so forth. Exhibit 24.3 demonstrates the waterfall structure.

These securities are issued privately to institutional investors and high-net-worth individuals. The collateral held by the SPV produces cash flows that are used to pay interest and dividends on the notes and equity issued by the SPV. The majority of principal on the securities issued by the SPV is paid at the end of the life of the SPV, usually from final principal pay-offs or the sale of the SPV assets.

BALANCE SHEET CDO STRUCTURES

Balance sheet CDO structures are typically constructed as collateralized loan obligations. Following Exhibit 24.2, we consider two examples of balance sheet CDO structures: cash funded and synthetic. We diagram how these structures work and discuss the benefits to a bank or other lending institution from sponsoring a CLO structure.

Cash Funded Balance Sheet CDO

In a balance sheet CDO, the seller of the assets is usually a bank that seeks to remove a portion of its loan portfolio from its balance sheet. The bank constructs a CLO special purpose vehicle to dispose of its balance sheet assets into the CLO structure. Exhibit 24.4 demonstrates this type of CLO structure.

EXHIBIT 24.4 Structure of a Balance Sheet CLO

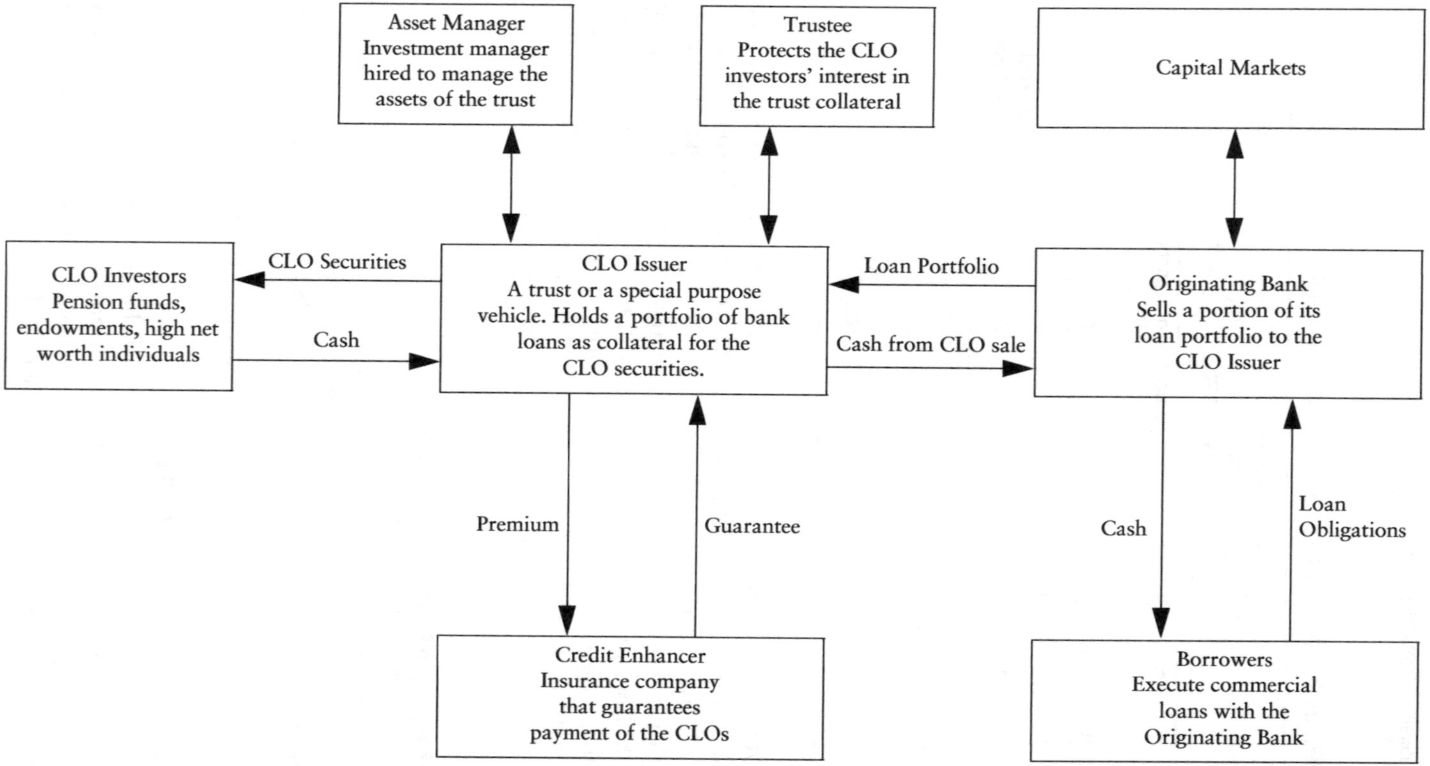

Capital Markets

Originating Bank
Sells a portion of its
loan portfolio to the
CLO Issuer

Borrowers
Execute commercial
loans with the
Originating Bank

Loan Obligations

Cash

Trustee
Protects the CLO
investors' interest in
the trust collateral

Loan Portfolio

Cash from CLO sale

Asset Manager
Investment manager
hired to manage the
assets of the trust

CLO Issuer
A trust or a special purpose
vehicle. Holds a portfolio of bank
loans as collateral for the
CLO securities.

Credit Enhancer
Insurance company
that guarantees
payment of the CLOs

Guarantee

Premium

CLO Securities

Cash

CLO Investors
Pension funds,
endowments, high net
worth individuals

Notice that there are several players in a CLO structure. First, the bank receives funding from the capital markets. Then the bank loans money to a commercial borrower. In return for lending cash, the bank receives a secured loan obligation from the borrower. The bank then pools several of these loans (it can be as many as several hundred) and sells the pool of loans to the CLO trust in return for cash. The CLO trust in turn issues securities to outside investors in the form of debt securities. These debt securities represent a claim on the pool of commercial loans contained in the CLO trust. The CLO trust uses the cash received from the sale of the CLO securities to pay the bank for the purchase of the commercial loans. This is called a cash-funded balance sheet CDO structure because there is an actual sale and transfer of the bank's loan portfolio to the CLO trust.

CLO trusts usually have a professional asset manager to manage the assets contained in the trust. This can be the selling bank where the bank is hired under a separate agreement to manage the portfolio of loans that it sold to the CLO trust. Also, the CLO trust will have a trustee whose job it is to protect the security interests of the CLO investors in the trust's assets. Usually, this is not the bank or an affiliate because of conflict of interest provisions. Last, the CLO trust may purchase a credit enhancement from an outside insurance provider. The credit enhancement guarantees from a third-party timely payment of interest and principal on the CLO securities up to a specified amount, and ensures that they will receive an investment grade credit rating.

Many bank CLOs are self-liquidating. All interest and principal payments from the commercial loans are passed through to the CLO investors. Other balance sheet CLOs provide for the reinvestment of loan payments into additional commercial loans to be purchased by the CLO trust. After the initial reinvestment period, the CLO trust enters into an amortization period when the loan proceeds are used to pay down the principal of the outstanding CLO tranches.

Synthetic Balance Sheet CDO

Synthetic balance sheet CDOs differ from the cash funded variety in several important ways. First, cash-funded CDOs are constructed with an actual sale and transfer of the loans or assets to the CDO trust. Ownership of the assets is transferred from the bank's balance sheet to that of the CDO trust. In a synthetic CDO, however, the sponsoring bank or other institution transfers the total return profile of a designated basket of loans or other assets via a credit derivative transaction, usually a credit default swap or a credit return swap. Therefore, the bank transfers its risk profile associated with its assets, but not the legal ownership of assets.

Second, in a cash flow CDO, the proceeds received from the sale of the CDO securities are used to purchase the collateral for the CDO trust. The cash flows from the collateral held by the CDO trust are then used to pay the returns on the CDO securities. Conversely, the cash proceeds from a synthetic balance sheet CDO are usually invested in U.S. Treasury securities. The interest received from these securities is used to fund the swap payments to the bank.

Third, a synthetic balance sheet CDO can use leverage. The use of leverage can boost the returns received by the CDO investors, thereby increasing the attractiveness of the CDO securities.

Finally, a synthetic balance sheet CDO is less burdensome in transferring assets. Certain commercial loans may require borrower notification and consent before being transferred to the CDO trust. This can take time and increases the administration costs.

Exhibit 24.5 demonstrates a synthetic balance sheet CDO. Assume that a bank establishes a SPV in the form of a trust for a balance sheet CLO. The bank wishes to reduce its exposure to a basket of loans on its balance sheet.[3]

The CLO trust issues medium term notes to investors that the trust records on its balance sheet as a liability and the investors record on their balance sheets as a privately issued 144A security.[4] The proceeds from the sale of the CLO securities are used to purchase U.S. Treasury securities with the same maturity as the CLO securities. The CLO securities receive an investment-grade credit rating because they are backed by default-free U.S. Treasury securities.

Next the SPV enters into a total return swap with the bank where the SPV will pay to the bank LIBOR + 100 basis points in return for receiving the total return on the referenced basket of bank loans. The total return from the bank loans includes both interest payments plus any appreciation or depreciation of the loan value. The SPV in turn passes through to the CLO security holders the total return from the loan portfolio.

Notice that the CLO security holders are insulated from the derivative transaction with the bank. The CLO trust acts as a middleman or buffer between the CLO security holders and the bank so that the CLO investors do not have to enter a swap directly with the bank. This could be problematic for certain pension funds or endowment funds that do not have the authority to negotiate swap agreements.

---

[3] We omitted the asset manager and trustee from this exhibit to make the diagram less cluttered. These two entities are still used, but are not crucial to our example.

[4] These private securities are typically offered in the form of SEC Rule 144A. Under this rule, the securities do not need to be registered with the SEC via a registration statement, but may be sold only to qualified institutional buyers.

EXHIBIT 24.5 Synthetic Balance Sheet CLO

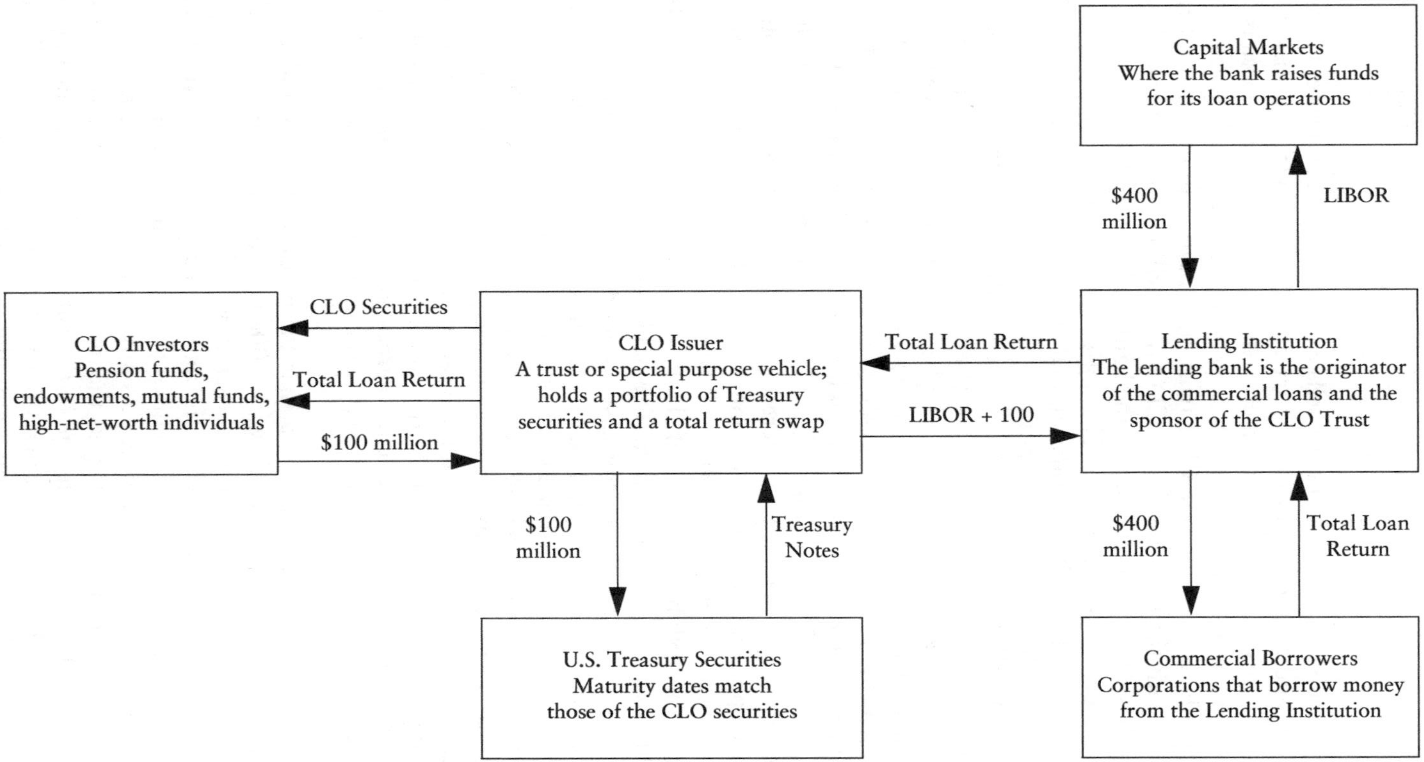

Capital Markets
Where the bank raises funds for its loan operations

Lending Institution
The lending bank is the originator of the commercial loans and the sponsor of the CLO Trust

Commercial Borrowers
Corporations that borrow money from the Lending Institution

LIBOR

$400 million

Total Loan Return

$400 million

Total Loan Return

LIBOR + 100

CLO Issuer
A trust or special purpose vehicle; holds a portfolio of Treasury securities and a total return swap

Treasury Notes

$100 million

U.S. Treasury Securities
Maturity dates match those of the CLO securities

CLO Securities

Total Loan Return

$100 million

CLO Investors
Pension funds, endowments, mutual funds, high-net-worth individuals

Assume that the CLO trust sells $100 million of securities to institutional and high-net-worth investors and that the trust securities mature in four years. The CLO trust uses the $100 million to purchase U.S. Treasury notes that mature in four years and accrue interest at 6% annually. In addition, the CLO trust enters into a four-year total return swap with the bank where the CLO trust will pay to the bank LIBOR + 100 basis points annually, and the bank will pay the CLO trust the total return on its loan portfolio. The notional value of the swap transaction is $400 million. The average annual interest rate earned on the bank loans is LIBOR + 250 basis points.

In Exhibit 24.5, the notional value of the total return swap does not equal the face value of CLO trust securities sold. This is a demonstration of the leverage that can be applied in a synthetic balance sheet CLO compared to the cash funded CLO discussed earlier. Under the swap agreement, the CLO trust agrees to pay the bank LIBOR + 100 on a notional value of $400 million, while receiving from the bank the total return on a $400 million basket of loans. The total return on the loan basket equals the average interest payment of LIBOR + 250, plus any price appreciation or depreciation associated with the bank loans.

Take a moment to review all of the cash flows for the bank displayed in Exhibit 24.5. All of the cash flows net out to a single fee of 100 basis points for the bank. The bank receives $400 million from the capital markets and uses this cash to build a commercial loan portfolio. The bank pays for its funding at straight LIBOR. From the commercial loans, the bank receives LIBOR + 250 in interest payments plus any appreciation or depreciation in the value of the loans (together the interest payments plus any change in loan value equals the Total Loan Return). The bank passes on the interest payments and any appreciation or depreciation to the CLO trust under the terms of the total return swap agreement. The CLO trust agrees to pay the bank LIBOR + 100 which covers the banks funding costs at LIBOR plus adds 100 basis points.

Exhibit 24.6 demonstrates that all of these inflows and outflows cancel out leaving the bank with 100 basis points times the notional value of the swap, or an annual cash flow of $4 million.

The CLO investors receive the return on all of the CLO trust's assets and contractual agreements. This includes the net income on the swap agreement of 150 basis points plus any increase or decrease in the value of the basket of bank loans plus the interest earned on the U.S. Treasury securities. If there is no change in the value of the loans, then at maturity of the CLO securities, investors will receive the four-year Treasury rate plus 150 basis points on a notional value of $400 million.

EXHIBIT 24.6   Net Gain or Loss for the Synthetic Balance Sheet CLO

	Cash Inflow	Cash Outflow	Net Gain/Loss
Raise $400 million from capital markets	$400,000,000		
Loan $400 million to commercial borrowers		$400,000,000	
Net Gain or Loss			0
Receive interest on bank loans	LIBOR + 250		
Pay bank loan interest to the CLO Trust		LIBOR + 250	
Net Gain or Loss			0
Receive loan appreciation or depreciation	Change in Loan		
Pay loan appreciation/depreciation to the CLO Trust		Change in Loan	
Net Gain or Loss			0
Receive swap payments from the CLO Trust	LIBOR + 100		
Pay interest on borrowings from capital markets		LIBOR	
Net Gain or Loss			100 basis points

This highlights the use of leverage in the synthetic balance sheet CLO. Investors in the CLO trust committed only $100 million of capital but received 150 basis points of income on $400 million of bank loan exposure. This is equivalent to earning 600 basis points on $100 million. Plus the investors in the CLO trust receive the return earned on the four-year U.S. Treasury notes. Therefore, investors in the CLO trust receive a rate of return that is 600 basis points greater than a comparable Treasury note. The ability to add 600 basis points of credit spread return on an investment grade security far exceeds the return that an investor could earn if it purchased the loans outright from the bank.

If this sounds like a great deal for the investors, it is even a better deal for the bank. Not only does the bank reduce its risk exposure to a basket of bank loans, it also frees up regulatory capital associated with these risky assets because it has transferred the risk (but not the assets) to the CLO trust. On top of this risk reduction, the bank receives a swap fee of $4 million per year. In other words, through a synthetic balance sheet CLO, the bank is paid to reduce its risks. The bank gets its cake and eats it too.

The $100 million of U.S. Treasury securities serves as collateral for the CLO trust's side of the total return swap with the sponsoring bank. If the basket of referenced loans declines in value, the Treasury securities will pay for this decline. For this reason, the CLO trust's position is often referred to as the "first loss position." This means that the first $100 million of loss on the basket of bank loans will be absorbed by the CLO trust. The remaining $300 million "second loss position" is retained by the bank because it still owns the basket of loans. Therefore, the bank can receive regulatory capital relief only for the first loss position of $100 million.

In practice, the CLO trust is constructed so that if the first loss position is fully drawn upon, the trust will liquidate. The trust will pay out any remaining accrued interest to the holders of the trust certificates and then close its operations. The CLO securities will be rendered worthless.

Credit Default Swaps and CDO Trusts

Initially, most synthetic balance sheet CDOs used a total return swap to transfer the credit risk exposure from the bank to the CDO Trust. However, now most synthetic balance sheet CDOs are constructed with a credit default swap (CDS).

Exhibit 24.7 shows a synthetic balance sheet CDO using a CDS. The key difference is in the payments between the bank and the CDO Trust. Under the terms of the CDS, the bank now makes periodic payments to the CDO trust. These payments reflect the insurance premium that the bank must pay as the credit protection buyer. In effect, the CDO trust sells credit insurance to the bank for which the bank must make periodic

EXHIBIT 24.7   Synthetic Balance Sheet CDO with a Credit Default Swap

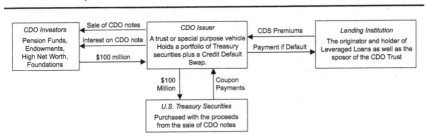

payments—the CDO trust is the credit protection seller. Compare this to Exhibit 24.5 where it was the CLO trust that made periodic payments (LIBOR + 100) to the bank. The CDO trust, in turn, combines the periodic payments from the bank with the interest proceeds from the U.S. Treasury securities to make payments to the CDO note holders.

In return for receiving periodic insurance premiums from the bank, the CDO trust now bears the risk of loss on the referenced bank loans that remain on the bank's balance sheet. The CDS requires the CDO trust to make payments to the bank upon any condition of default. Conditions of default are spelled out in the swap agreement between the bank and the CDO trust (these conditions were described in detail in the prior chapter).

Synthetic CDOs are often called "correlation products" because the CDS contract references the default of more than one bank loan or obligor. Investors in the CDO buy correlation risk. This is the joint default risk between several obligors. The job of the CDO manager is to structure the CDS so that the correlation risk is minimized. That is, the CDO manager does not want all defaults to occur at the same time.

The key point of this section is that the transfer of credit risk from the bank to the CDO trust through a synthetic balance sheet transaction is done primarily with CDS. This has helped fuel the growth of the credit derivative market.

Benefits to Banks from CLOs

Although there is a growing demand from investors for CLO structures, banks are equally motivated to build CLO trust structures. Risk reduction as indicated above is just one of several benefits to banks from CLOs.

Reducing Risk-Based/Regulatory Capital

Reducing risk-based/regulatory capital is the single most important motivation for a bank to form a CLO trust. Under the 1988 Basle Accord adopted by the G-10 group of industrialized nations, banks in these nations are required to maintain risk-based capital equal to 8% of the outstanding balance of commercial loans.[5] The 8% regulatory capital charge required for commercial loans is the highest percentage of capital required to be held against any asset type.

Using a CLO trust to securitize and sell a portfolio of commercial loans can free up regulatory capital that must be committed to support the loan portfolio. Consider a bank with a $500 million loan portfolio that it wishes to sell. It must hold risk-based capital equal to 8% × $500 million = $40 million to support these loans. The bank sponsors a CLO trust where the trust purchases the $500 million loan portfolio from the bank and finds outside investors to purchase all of the CLO securities. The bank no longer has any exposure to the basket of commercial loans and now has freed $40 million of regulatory capital that it can use in other parts of its balance sheet.

Unfortunately, sometimes the equity tranche of the CLO trust is unappealing to outside investors and cannot be sold. Under this circumstance, the sponsoring bank may have to retain an equity or "first loss" position in the CLO trust. If this is the case, the regulatory capital standards require the bank to maintain risk-based capital equal to its "first loss" position. For example, if the sponsoring bank had to retain a $10 million equity piece in the CLO trust to attract other investors, it must take a one-for-one regulatory capital charge for this first loss position. This means that only $40 million − $10 million = $30 million of regulatory capital will be freed by the CLO trust.

Increasing Loan Capacity

In our regulatory capital example above, not only does the bank free up $40 million of regulatory capital, it also receives cash proceeds from the sale of its loans to the CLO trust. The funds generated by the loan securitization can be used to originate additional commercial loans at either better rates or better credit quality or it can be used to purchase different assets for the bank's balance sheet. Either way, the bank has generated a large cash inflow that it can use to strengthen its balance sheet.

Improving ROE and ROA Measures

With its cash in hand, the bank can reduce its overall balance sheet by paying down its liabilities. In fact, if the bank can reduce its overall capital base and at the same time increase the proportion of higher yielding assets, it will increase its return on equity (ROE) and return on assets (ROA).

---

[5] For a more detailed discussion on the Basle Accord and it impact on regulatory capital, see Mark Anson, *Credit Derivatives* (New Hope, PA: Frank J. Fabozzi Associates, 1999).

Continuing with our example from above. Assume that the bank's cost of funds is LIBOR and that the $500 million portfolio of loans earns on average LIBOR + 100 basis points. Therefore, the bank earns $5 million per year on this loan portfolio. The required regulatory capital is $40 million for a ROE of $5 million ÷ $40 million = 12.5%.

The bank uses the $500 million received from the sale to the CLO trust to loan out in the residential mortgage market. The bank receives loan income of LIBOR + 0.75% on the residential mortgages. However, the regulatory capital required to support residential mortgages is one half of that for commercial loans, or $20 million. The bank's return on equity is now: $3.75 million ÷ $20 million = 18.75%.

Reducing Credit Concentrations

The selling bank may be at the limit of its credit exposure to one industry or group of borrowers. It may find this industry profitable in terms of commercial loans, but cannot increase its exposure. By selling part of its loan portfolio, it has produced more "dry powder" to lend to that borrower or industry.

In addition to reducing credit concentrations, CDOs can help a bank manage its overall credit exposure to the leveraged loan market. Exhibit 24.8 shows the level of global loan defaults over the period 1996 to 2004 as followed by Moody's. As can be seen, during times of economic slowdown, like the U.S. recession of 2001 to 2002, loan defaults increase.

EXHIBIT 24.8   Global Loan Defaults

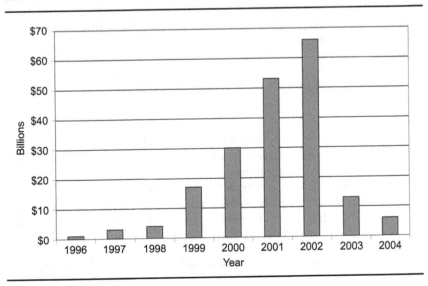

Therefore, when a bank expects a slowdown in the economic cycle of growth, CDO products can help it manage its credit risk.

Preserving Customer Relations

A bank is often in the uncomfortable position of accepting more exposure to a bank client that it wishes. In order to maintain its relationship with its borrowers, the bank can reduce its exposure to the client by selling a portion of the bank's loan portfolio pertaining to the client to the CLO trust. In a CLO, the portfolio manager for the trust is often the bank so that the borrowing client need not even know that its loan has been sold to the CLO trust.

Competitive Positioning

There is a large investor base of pension funds, endowments, mutual funds, insurance companies, and high-net-worth individuals that seek to invest in bank loans.[6] In the last chapter we showed that institutional investor participation in bank loans now exceeds 30%. Simply, bank loans have come of age not just as a lending tool for banks and corporate borrowers, but as a mainstream investment for those that seek greater yield.

CLO trusts are the natural format for achieving this exposure. Furthermore, large banks desiring to position themselves in this increasingly competitive marketplace may wish to establish a program of CLO trusts in order to attract and maintain qualified investors for the CLO securities.

Credit Enhancements

Most CLO structures contain some form of credit enhancement to ensure that the CLO securities sold to investors will receive an investment grade rating. These enhancements can be internal or external. Generally, credit enhancements are made at the expense of lower coupon rates paid on the CLO securities. While we discuss credit enhancements with respect to CLO trusts, these provisions are equally applicable to all CDO structures.

Subordination

Subordination is the most common form of credit enhancement in a CDO transaction and it flows from the structure of the CLO trust. This in an internal credit enhancement.

For instance, CLO trusts typically issue several class or tranches of securities. The lower level, or subordinated tranches, provide credit support for the higher rated tranches. As we discussed previously, the equity tranche in a CLO trust provides the "first loss" position with

---

[6] See Smithson and Hayt, "Tools for Reshaping Credit Portfolios; Managing Credit Risk."

respect to a basket of loans. This tranche provides credit enhancement for every class of CLO securities above it.[7]

Junior tranches of a CDO are rated lower than the senior tranches but in return receive a higher interest rate commensurate with their subordinated status and therefore greater credit risk. The payment structure of a CDO can vary, but it is usually is one of three forms: sequential pay, fast pay/slow pay, or pro rata.

In a sequential-pay CDO, the senior tranches must be paid in full before any principal is paid to the junior tranches. In a fast pay/slow pay CDO, the senior tranches are paid down faster than the junior tranches. Last, in a pro rata payment, the senior and junior tranches are paid down at the same rate. Most CDO structures go with a sequential-pay format.

This payment structure is often referred to as the "waterfall." As interest and principal payments are received from the underlying collateral, they flow down the waterfall, first to the senior tranches of the CLO trust and then to the lower rated tranches. Subordinated tranches must wait for sufficient interest and principal payments to flow down the tranche structure before they can receive a payment. The concept of the waterfall is demonstrated in Exhibit 24.3.

Overcollateralization

Overcollateralization results from the senior/junior nature of tranches in a CDO. For example, consider a CDO trust with a market value of collateral trust assets of $100. The CDO trust issues two tranches. Tranche A is the senior tranche and consists of $80 million of securities. Tranche B consists of $20 million of subordinated securities and is paid after the senior tranche is paid in full. The level of overcollateralization for the senior tranche is $100/$80 = 125%. The funds used to purchase the excess collateral come from the subordinated tranche; tranche B provides the overcollateralization to tranche A. Overcollateralization is an internal credit enhancement.

Spread Enhancement

Another internal enhancement can be excess spread of the loans contained in the CLO trust compared to the interest promised on the CLO

---

[7] Most CLO structures are "delinked." That is, there is no link with the selling bank, the CLO trust holds ownership over the loan assets. In this case the credit rating of the bank does not affect the CLO trust. In some cases, however, the CLO trust remains linked with the selling bank. In this case, the bank sells the risk to the CLO trust via a credit-linked note or a credit swap so that the CLO trust must depend upon the creditworthiness of the selling bank to collect on the trust's assets.

securities. The excess spread may arise because the assets of the CLO trust are of lower credit quality than the CLO securities and therefore yield a higher interest rate than that paid on the CLO securities. A higher yield on the trust assets may also result from a different term structure. This excess spread may be used to cover any losses associated with the CLO trust loan portfolio. If there are no losses on the loan portfolio, the excess spread accrues to the equity tranche of the CLO trust.

Cash Collateral or Reserve Account

Excess cash is held in highly rated instruments such as U.S. Treasury securities or high-grade commercial paper that provide security to the debt holder of the CLO trust. Cash reserves are often used in the initial phase of a cash flow transaction. During this phase, cash proceeds received by the trust from the sale of its securities are used to purchase the underlying collateral and the reserve account. Cash reserves are not the most efficient form of credit support because they generally earn a lower rate of return than that required to fund the CLO securities. Therefore, there is a clear tradeoff: A higher cash reserve account means greater credit support but at the expense of lower interest payments on the CLO securities.

External Credit Enhancement

An external credit enhancement is provided by an outside third party in the form of insurance against defaults in the loan portfolio. This insurance may be a straightforward insurance contract, the sale of a put option, or the negotiation of a credit default swap to protect the downside from any loan losses. The effect is to transfer the credit risks associated with the CLO trust collateral from the holders of the CLO trust securities to the insurance company.

ARBITRAGE CDOs

An arbitrage CDO seeks to make a profit. The profit is earned by selling CLO/CBO securities to outside investors at a price that is higher than that paid for the assets placed into the CLO/CBO structure. Most often an arbitrage CDO consists of bonds purchased on the open market. These bonds are then placed into the CDO trust and the manager of the trust sells new securities (the CBOs) to new investors. An arbitrage profit is earned if the CDO trust can sell its securities at a lower yield than the yield received on the bond collateral contained in the trust.

Exhibit 24.9 presents the structure for a CBO trust. Many of the same players that were introduced in Exhibit 24.4 are used in the formation of a CBO trust. The difference is that the seller of the assets to the trust is usually not a bank, but an investment management firm interested in making money through the CBO structure. In Exhibit 24.9, the seller of the bonds will earn a profit from the CBO trust if the "Cash from CBO Sale" exceeds the cash paid for the original bonds.

The key to understanding arbitrage CDOs is that they are driven by profit making considerations. First, there is the arbitrage or excess spread income that can be earned. We will show a demonstration of this in a moment. In addition, asset managers—the primary sponsors of arbitrage CDOs—earn a management fee for managing the assets of the CDO trust. In the asset management business, the game is all about accumulating assets under management, and a CDO trust is simply another way to apply an asset management fee to another pool of assets.

Cash Flow Arbitrage CDO

In a cash flow arbitrage CDO, the repayment of the CDO securities are dependent upon cash flows from the underlying pool of bonds and loans. These structures typically invest in high-yield bonds but can also invest in bank loans, investment grade corporate debt, mortgages, emerging market bonds, and any other credit risky security.

In a cash flow CDO, the trust holds the bonds and receives the debt service (principal and interest payments). The CDO trust securities are sold to match the payment schedules of the bonds held as collateral by the trust. As the collateral pays down, the CDO trust pays down its securities.

In some cases, the cash flow arbitrage CDO is *static*. This means that the collateral held by the CDO trust does not change, it remains static throughout the life of the trust. There is no active buying or selling of securities once the CDO trust is established.

However, most arbitrage CDOs are actively managed. This means that after the initial CDO portfolio is constructed, the manager of the CDO trust can buy and sell bonds that meet the CDO trust's criteria to enhance the yield to the CDO investors and reduce the risk of loss through default.

Cash flow arbitrage CDO trusts are dependent upon default and recovery rates. For example, assume that a CDO trust has two tranches or classes of securities. Tranche A is the senior class and represents $100 million in CDO securities. Class B is the subordinated, or equity class, and is $50 million of securities. Underlying the CDO trust is $150 million of high-yield bonds that pay income to the trust of LIBOR + 4%.

EXHIBIT 24.9 Structure of an Arbitrage CDO/CBO

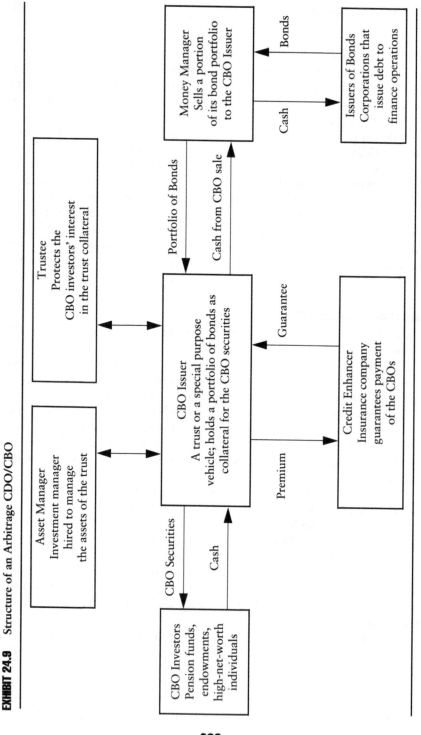

The senior tranche is promised payments of principal plus LIBOR + 1%, the subordinate tranche receives whatever is left after the senior tranche is fully paid. For simplicity, we assume that the CDO trust is organized for one year with a bullet payment at the end of one year and that LIBOR is equal to 5%.

We demonstrate several scenarios: no default of high-yield bonds, a 1% default rate, 2% default rate, and so on up to a 5% default rate. The historical recovery rate for defaulted high-yield debt is about 40%. Therefore if 5% of the bonds default, the CDO trust would expect to recover $5\% \times 40\% = 2\%$, resulting in a net loss of 3%.[8]

Under the no-default scenario, at maturity of the CDO trust, the subordinated equity tranche of the CDO trust will receive

$150 million $\times$ (1+[LIBOR + 4%]) − $100 million $\times$ (1+[LIBOR + 1%])
= $57.5 million

On an original investment of $50 million, this is a return of 15%.

Under the next scenario, 1%, or $1.5 million of the high-yield bonds held by the CDO trust, default. With a recovery rate of 40%, this is a net loss of $0.9 million that must be absorbed by equity tranche. Under this loss scenario, the equity tranche will receive

$148.5 million $\times$ (1 + [LIBOR + 4%]) + $0.6 million
− $100 million $\times$ (1 + [LIBOR + 1%]) = $56.465 million

On an original investment of $50 million, this is a return of 12.93%

These scenarios can be used to generate a yield table of the equity tranche for this CDO structure. Exhibit 24.10 provides a graph of the default rate and the resulting yield to maturity for the equity tranche. As can be seen, the return to the equity tranche declines quickly as the default rate rises. At a default rate of 5%, the return to the equity tranche is less than 5%.

The important point to this example is that the return on investment for both tranches depends only on the cash flows received by the CDO trust. The critical factors associated with these cash flows are the default rate for the high-yield bonds held by the CDO trust and the recovery rate on those bonds once they default.

At no time does the market value of the high-yield bonds affect the return to the CDO investors. Although the prices of the high-yield

---

[8] We also assume that recovery on any defaulted bond is made by the maturity of the CDO trust. In practice, recovery can take several years, stretching out the payments to the equity tranche of the CDO. Last, we assume that all accrued income is lost on defaulted debt, and that any recovery pertains only to the face value of the debt.

EXHIBIT 24.10 Projected Return for Equity in a Cash Flow Arbitrage CDO

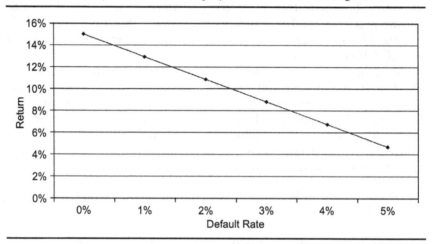

bonds may fluctuate up and down, this does not affect the returns to the CDO security holders as long as the underlying collateral pays its coupons and principal at maturity.

Market Value Arbitrage CDO

With these CDO structures, the return earned by investors is linked to the market value of the underlying collateral contained in the CDO trust. These structures are used when the maturity of the collateral assets purchased by the trust does not match precisely the maturity of the CDO securities. This is usually the case.

Consider the example of a CDO trust that buys high-yield bonds. It is unlikely that the trust can sell securities that perfectly mimic the maturity of the high-yield bonds held as collateral. Therefore, the cash flows associated with a market value arbitrage CDO come from not only the interest payments received on the collateral bonds, but also from the sale of these bonds to make the principal payments on the CDO securities. Therefore, the yield on the CDO securities is dependent upon the market value of the high-yield bonds at the time of resale.

Given the dependency on market prices, market value arbitrage CDOs use the total rate of return as a measure of performance. The total rate of return takes into account the interest received from the high-yield bonds as well as their appreciation or depreciation in value.

Let us use the same example as above for the cash flow CDO structure. There are two tranches, a $100 million tranche paying LIBOR + 1% and an equity tranche. The CDO trust lasts for one year, and at the end of one year both tranches of securities receive a bullet payment. The difference is that at the end of one year, the CDO trust must sell its underlying high-yield bond portfolio to fund the redemption of the CDO trust securities.

Under this scenario, we assume not that there are defaults, but instead that the high-yield bond portfolio has suffered a decline in value of 0% to 5%. Under the 0% decline in value scenario, the return to the equity tranche in a market value CDO will be the same as under the cash flow example, 15%.

Under a decline of value of 1%, the return to the equity tranche will equal:

$$\$150 \text{ million} \times (1 + [\text{LIBOR} + 4\%]) - \$100 \text{ million}$$
$$\times (1 + [\text{LIBOR} + 1\%]) - \$1.5 \text{ million} = \$56 \text{ million}$$

This equals a total return of $56 million ÷ $50 million = 12%.

In Exhibit 24.11 we provide a graph similar to Exhibit 24.10 that plots the return to the equity tranche versus the decline in value of the high-yield bond portfolio. As we can see, a decline in market value results in a more precipitous decline (compared to a cash flow arbitrage CDO) in the return to the equity tranche of this CDO trust. The reason is that there is no opportunity for the trust collateral to recover the lost value. The high-yield bonds must be sold to fund the redemptions of the CDO securities. This decline in value is locked in at the time of the liquidation of the trust.

EXHIBIT 24.11 Expected Return for the Equity Tranche of a Market Value CDO

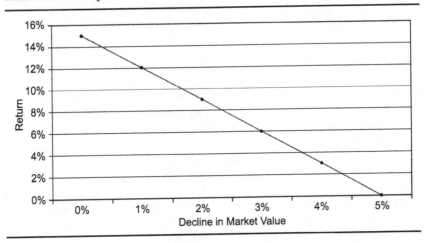

Practically, a market value CDO trust will also experience defaults just like cash flow CDO trusts. When this occurs, the market value trust must take into account defaults and recovery rates as well as changes in market value. In fact it is likely that as default rates increase, the market value of the bond portfolio will decrease. These complementary effects can erode the return to the equity tranche even faster than indicated in Exhibits 24.10 and 24.11.

Synthetic Arbitrage CDOs

Synthetic arbitrage CDOs simulate the risk transference similar to a cash sale of assets without any change in the legal ownership of the assets. The risk is transferred by a credit default swap or a total return credit swap.

Synthetic arbitrage CDOs are used by asset management companies, insurance companies, and other investment shops with the intent of exploiting a mismatch between the yield of underlying securities and the lower cost of servicing the CDO securities. These structures are less administratively burdensome when compared to cash-funded structures particularly when attempting to transfer only a portion of a credit risk.

Synthetic CDO trusts can also be used to provide economic exposure to high-yield assets that may be relatively scarce and difficult to acquire in the cash market. Last, synthetic CDO trusts can employ leverage. In Exhibit 24.5 we demonstrated a synthetic balance sheet CLO where the leverage ratio was 4 to 1.

The mechanics of a synthetic arbitrage CDO are similar to those demonstrated in Exhibit 24.5. The CDO trust enters into a swap agreement on a reference portfolio of fixed income securities. The portfolio may be fully funded or only partially funded at the time of the swap agreement (there is often a "ramping up" period when credit risky assets are selected for the reference portfolio). Under the swap agreement, the CDO trust will pay LIBOR plus a spread to the sponsoring money manager, and in return, receive the total return on the reference portfolio. The total return includes interest received from the securities in the reference portfolio as well as any price appreciation or depreciation. The reference portfolio is funded on the balance sheet of the sponsoring institution.

One key difference of a synthetic arbitrage CDO compared to a cash flow CDO is that the swap payments are made periodically, usually on a quarterly basis. Therefore, the underlying collateral must be marked to market each quarter to determine the total return on the credit swap. This exposes the CDO securities holder to market risk similar to a market value arbitrage CLO trust discussed above.

Profiting from an Arbitrage CDO Trust

We have mentioned several times that the motivation for an arbitrage CDO trust is to earn a profit. We provide an example of how this is done.

Assume a money manager establishes an arbitrage CDO to invest in high-yield bonds. The trust will have a life of three years and raises $500 million by selling three tranches of securities. The security tranches issued by the trust are divided by credit rating. In Tranche A, debt with the highest priority is issued against the highest credit quality bonds in the trust collateral. This senior debt tends to have a lower return and volatility than that of the composite bond portfolio return and volatility.

The second or mezzanine tranche is securitized with the average credit quality bond in the pool and the subordination of the equity tranche. Here the credit rating of Tranche B may not be any greater than that of the average high-yield bond owned by the CDO trust, but this tranche still has the advantage of a diversified pool of bonds and the seniority to the last CDO tranche. The final tranche is subordinated to the two other CDO tranches and is securitized with the lowest credit quality bonds in the trust portfolio. For this tranche, the risk is the highest, but the bonds securing it are also the highest yielding. The equity tranche also collects any residual income generated by the CDO collateral.

Exhibit 24.12 provides a more detailed example of this arbitrage CDO trust. Consider a money manager that has a portfolio of high-yield bonds with credit ratings of the underlying issuers equal to BB. The bonds pay an average coupon of 9%, have a face value of $500 million, and a current market value of $450 million. The money manager sells these bonds to the trust for a fee of 20 basis points ($900,000). In addition, the money manager charges an annual management fee of 50

EXHIBIT 24.12   An Arbitrage CDO Structure

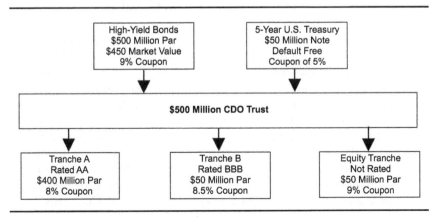

basis points for managing the face value of the Trust's assets: 50 basis points × $500 million = $2,500,000. Last there is a fee for the Trustee to oversee the indenture clauses of the CDO notes. This fee is $500,000.

Additionally, the CDO trust buys a $50 million three-year U.S. Treasury note at an annual coupon of 5%. The Treasury note will be used to provide credit protection to Tranche A and allow for a AA credit rating. The $50 million is the difference between the $500 million of notes sold by the CDO trust and the purchase price of the high-yield bonds of $450 million.

Tranche A has a $400 million face value, a coupon of 8% and is rated AAA. This tranche gets the highest credit rating possible because it is partly principal protected by the three-year Treasury note and by the subordination of the other two tranches. However, the Tranche A investors receive a higher coupon than U.S Treasuries because they have a claim on a portion of the passthrough return earned from the high-yield bond portfolio.

The second tranche has a face value of $50 million, a stated coupon of 8.5%, and is rated BBB. This tranche has a higher rating than the underlying bonds because it has first loss protection through the equity tranche. However, the first loss protection only covers the first $50 million worth of defaulted bonds. After that, Tranche B will lose dollar for dollar of defaulted bonds in the CDO collateral pool. Therefore, this tranche does not have the same principal protection as Tranche A, and consequently receives a lower credit rating but a higher coupon payment.

Tranche C is the equity tranche. It does not get paid until Tranches A and B receive their payments. Consequently, this tranche bears all of the residual risk of the CDO trust just as stockholders bear all of the residual risk in a corporation. This tranche has a face value of $50 million, a stated coupon of 9.00%, and is not rated. Effectively, this class has the same risk as the high-yield bonds in the collateral pool, or a BB credit rating.

Where does the trust get the money to pay for the money manager's annual fee of $2.5 million? It receives the money from the spread between the coupons collected from the CDO collateral pool of high-yield bonds and three-year Treasury note and the coupon payments it must pay out to the CDO note holders. Note that the stated coupon on each tranche is less than (or equal to) the average interest coupon on the high-yield bonds. The difference between the interest income earned on the high-yield bonds and that paid to the CDO security holders is spread income to the CDO trust. The trust uses this spread income to pay the management fee. Any residual income left over accrues to the Tranche C security holders—the equity investors in the CDO trust.

It is often the case that the money manager will retain a portion of the equity in the CDO tranche. The manager purchases the equity tranche for two reasons. The first is to reap the excess spread income received from the CDO trust. The money manager can profit from the arbitrage it creates between the CDO collateral income and the coupon payments on the CDO notes. The second is to attract other investors who may not wish to bear the subordinated risk of the equity tranche.

The spread income that can be earned in a CBO trust is demonstrated in Exhibit 24.13. Together, the Treasury note and the high-yield bonds generate $47,500,000 in annual income. The three CBO tranches and annual management and trustee fees, however, only require $43,750,000 of annual cash payments. The difference of $3,750,000 is the spread earned by selling CDO securities at a lower yield than earned by the high-yield bond portfolios. This residual income accrues to the equity tranche and results from the arbitrage between the receipt of income from the high-yield bonds and the payments required to the CDO note holders.

In summary, there are three ways to make a profit from an arbitrage CDO. First, the money manager can earn a transaction fee for selling its high-yield portfolio to the CDO trust. Second, the money manager, as an equity investor in the CDO trust, can earn the spread or arbitrage income from the CDO trust between the CDO collateral income and the payouts on the CDO notes. Last, the CDO sponsor usually is also the manager of the CDO trust and can earn management fees for its money management expertise.

EXHIBIT 24.13   Cash Flows for an Arbitrage CDO

Inflows		
	9% on $500 million high-yield bonds	$45,000,000
	5% on $50 million U.S. Treasury note	$2,500,000
Total		$47,500,000
Outflows		
	8% on $400 million Tranche A notes	$32,000,000
	8.5% on $50 million Tranche B notes	$4,250,000
	9% on $50 million equity tranche	$4,500,000
	Annual management fee	$2,500,000
	Annual trustee fee	$500,000
Total		$43,750,000
	Net annual CDO trust income	$3,750,000

CDO LIFE CYCLE

In most arbitrage CDOs there is a three-period life cycle. First, there is the ramp up period during which the CDO trust uses the proceeds from the CDO note sale to acquire the initial collateral pool. The CDOs trust documents will govern what type of assets may be purchased.

The second phase is normally called the revolving period, during which the manager of the CDO trust actively manages the collateral pool for the CDO, buying and selling securities and reinvesting the excess cash flows received from the CDO collateral pool.

The last phase is the amortization period. During this phase, the manager for the CDO stops reinvesting excess cash flows and begins to wind down the CDO by repaying the CDO debt securities. As the CDO collateral matures, the manager uses these proceeds to redeem the CDO's outstanding notes.

AN EXAMPLE OF A CDO STRUCTURE

As the discussion above indicated, CDOs can come in all shapes and sizes. Frequently, these investment vehicles have several classes of securities outstanding and can invest in several different types of collateral. We provide an example of recent CDO, below. We provide two examples below.

The Highgate ABS CDO, Ltd. is a newly sponsored CDO with a closing date of December 2005. Its sponsor and manager is Vanderbilt Capital Advisors, a registered investment adviser under the Investment Advisers Act of 1940 with more than $7 billion in fixed income assets under management.

The tranches of the CDO were sold by the Royal Bank of Canada Capital Markets and were rated by Moody's Investors services. Exhibit 24.14 shows the structure of the credit tranches for the Highgate CDO. Class A-1 is the super senior tranche, Class A-2 is the senior tranche, Class B is the senior mezzanine tranche, Classes C & D are the mezzanine tranches, and last, the preference shares is the equity tranche which is not rated.

Underlying these CDO tranches is a pool of collateral that includes residential mortgage backed securities, commercial mortgage backed securities, notes from other CDO trusts, and synthetic securities. Exhibit 24.15 describes the underlying collateral of this pool.

Exhibit 24.16 provides the weighted average rating for the CDO collateral. The weighted average collateral rating is often a covenant specified as part of the CDO trust indenture. This ensures that the average rating of the underlying collateral does not fall below a certain credit rating. This protects the CDO note holders.

EXHIBIT 24.14 Highgate ABS CDO, Ltd.

Credit Tranche	Amount	Percent	Rating
Class A-1 notes	$601,200,000	80%	Aaa
Class A-2 notes	$71,918,000	9.57%	Aaa
Class B notes	$50,201,000	6.68%	Aa2
Class C notes	$9,018,000	1.20%	A2
Class D notes	$8,642,000	1.15%	Baa2
Equity tranche	$10,521,000	1.40%	No rating
Total	$751,500,000		

EXHIBIT 24.15 Highgate ABS CDO Underlying Collateral

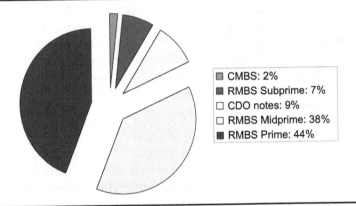

CMBS: 2%
RMBS Subprime: 7%
CDO notes: 9%
RMBS Midprime: 38%
RMBS Prime: 44%

EXHIBIT 24.16 Weighted Average Credit Rating for the Highgate ABS CDO, Ltd.

Collateral Rating	Assign Credit Ranking	Percent of Collateral Pool	Weighted Average Rating
Aaa	1	34.02%	0.3402
Aa1	2	6.67%	0.1334
Aa2	3	27.05%	0.8115
Aa3	4	8.62%	0.3448
A1	5	4.13%	0.2065
A2	6	14.22%	0.8532
A3	7	5.29%	0.3703
Weighted average ranking			3.0599
Equals a weighted average credit rating			Aa2

Exhibit 24.16 shows that the average credit rating is Aa2. This is the same rating as the Class B or super mezzanine notes. Notice how the financial engineering of the CDO works in this example. Fully 80% of the notes issued by the Highgate CDO receive Moody's highest credit rating of Aaa even though the weighted average credit rating of the underlying collateral equals that only of the super mezzanine B tranche notes. By repackaging credit risk, CDOs can neatly carve up the risk spectrum to provide investment opportunities at all levels of credit exposure.

NEW DEVELOPMENTS IN CDOS

There have been many new recent developments in the CDO market place such as extending the CDO structure to distressed debt, hedge funds, commodity exposure, private equity CDOs, single-tranche CDOs, unfunded CDO tranches, and even CDOs on top of CDOs. We take a brief look at all of these new fangled CDO ideas. In our discussion of distressed debt investing in Chapter 16, we noted how default rates have increased in the United States during the time period 2000 to 2001. This increase in default rates has led to an increased interest in distressed debt-backed CDOs.

As second new development has been the extension of CDOs to hedge funds. This comes as a result of the tremendous amount of capital pouring into the hedge fund market. Finally, CDOs have been applied to private equity investments. These three new developments demonstrate how barriers are being broken between different segments of the alternative investment market.

Distressed Debt CDOs

A recent development in the CDO market is a distressed debt CDO. As its name implies, the primary collateral component is distressed debt. Distressed debt included both securities for which the issuer is in default of the bond payments, and nondefaulted securities that trade in distressed ranges in anticipation of a future default by the issuing entity. Distressed debt securities are generally defined as those loans or subordinated debt that trade at a coupon rate 10% or greater compared to a U.S. Treasury rate or are in some sort of distress such as default, bankruptcy, cash flow crisis, and the like. In Chapter 23 we referred to the group of credit risky assets as "spread products." Distressed debt may be referred to as "big spread products."

Distressed debt CDOs usually have a combination of defaulted securities, distressed, but unimpaired securities, and nondistressed securities. The CDO manager will use historical default rates and estimated recovery amounts as well as the timing of default and recovery for distressed assets and nondistressed assets. In addition, for securities already in default, the CDO manager may use simulation models to determine how historical recovery patterns may change in times of additional market stress or lack of liquidity.

The appeal of the CDO structure is the ability to provide a series of tranches of collateralized securities that can have an investment grade credit rating even though the underlying collateral in the CDO is mostly distressed debt. Investors are then able to sample the distressed debt market more effectively by choosing a distressed debt CDO tranche that matches their level of risk aversion. The CDO securities can receive a higher investment rating than the underlying distressed collateral through one or several of the credit enhancements described above.

To date, the main suppliers of assets for distressed debt CDOs have been banks. Banks use these CDOs to manage the credit exposure on their balance sheets. Assets for a CDO are purchased at market value. When a bank sells a distressed loan or bond to a distressed debt CDO it will usually receive a loss because it issued the loan or purchased the bond at par value. It was after the issuance of the loan or bond purchase that the asset became distressed resulting in a decline in market value.

Still banks are willing to provide the collateral to distressed debt CDOs for several reasons. First, it stops the deterioration of value on the bank's balance sheet. Any further decline in value of the distressed loan will be at the expense of the CDO and the holders of the CDO's equity tranches.

Second, by removing distressed loans from its balance sheet, the bank reduces its nonperforming asset ratio. This allows it to obtain regulatory capital relief from its relevant banking authority, and this regulatory capital can be used for other bank business.[9]

Consider the Patriarch Partners distressed loan CDO. In January 2001, Patriarch purchased a portfolio of $1.35 billion of troubled loans from FleetBoston Financial Corp representing about 10% of FleetBoston's troubled loan portfolio. The purchase price was $1 billion, a 26% discount from the face value of the loans. The trust collateral consisted of 188 commercial loans from 91 borrowers.[10]

---

[9] The amount of regulatory capital that banks are required to maintain is determined by the Basle Committee on Banking Regulations and Supervisory Practices, which established global regulatory capital standards for industrialized nations. See Anson, *Credit Derivatives.*

[10] See Mark Pittman, "Patriarch Purchase of Fleet Loans a Bet on Collecting on Bad Debts," *Bloomberg News* (January 11, 2001).

EXHIBIT 24.17   Patriarch CLO Trust of Distressed Bank Loans

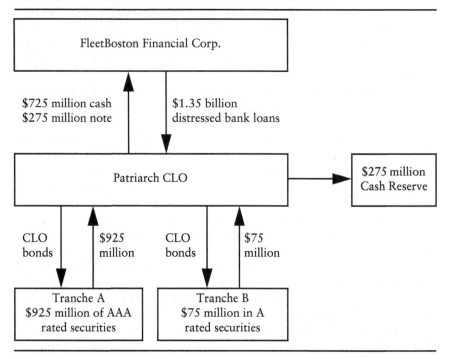

To finance the purchase of the loans, Patriarch Partners sold $925 million in AAA rated bonds and $75 million of A rated bonds. To receive an investment grade credit rating for its CDO bonds, Patriarch had to establish a credit enhancement. It established a large reserve account of about $275 million. Patriarch was able to establish this reserve account because of the $1 billion it paid to FleetBoston, $725 was in cash and $275 million was in the form of a zero-coupon note. Therefore, Patriarch had $275 million from the sale of the trust securities that it could allocate to the reserve account. This CDO structure is presented in Exhibit 24.17.

From Patriarch's perspective, if it can successfully collect on all of the troubled loans, it stands to collect considerable income from the excess spread between the loan collateral and the interest paid on the trust securities. For instance, the AAA rate CDO tranche was priced at an interest rate of about LIBOR + 50 basis points, considerably less than that received from the commercial loans.

From FleetBoston's perspective, it could sell the loans without taking a complete write-off. In addition, FleetBoston was able to reduce its loan-loss reserves by $75 million by removing the troubled loans from its balance sheet. FleetBoston can also profit because the value of the

$275 million zero-coupon bonds are tied to the amount collected from the troubled loans.[11]

Hedge Fund CDOs

In March 2001, Ferrell Capital Management began marketing CDO securities that were backed by investments in hedge funds. The Ferrell CDO is backed primarily by the AIG International Relative Value Fund, which is the underlying asset via a $200 million investment. The hedge fund invests in commodity arbitrage, currency arbitrage, and merger arbitrage in both the United States and Europe. This is a significant growing area for CDO structures and we devote the following chapter to a complete discussion of what are now called "Collateralized Fund Obligations."

Collateralized Commodity Obligation

In December 2004, Barclays Capital launched the first Collateralized Commodity Obligation (CCO). The product was rated by Standard and Poors and is structured similarly to synthetic arbitrage CDO.

The key difference is that instead of referencing a pool of credit risky assets via a swap, the underlying assets of the CCO are Commodities Trigger Swaps (CTS). CTS are similar to CDS in that there are trigger events that require a payment by one swap holder to another. These trigger events are based on underlying commodity buckets hitting different price hurdles.

The Apollo CCO references a diversified pool of CTS including precious metals, base metals and energy commodities. The payment of the CCO note principal and coupons is dependent upon a short averaging period immediately prior to the five-year maturing of the CCO.

The trigger events in the CTS cut both ways. If commodity prices have increased over the five-year period of the CCO, the CCO note holders will be rewarded—the trigger events will be positive. However, if commodity prices decline, the CCO note holders will receive less than par value on their notes. Exhibit 24.18 demonstrates the new CCO.

Private Equity CDO

Another intersection in the alternative investment marketplace is that of CDOs and private equity. In July 2001, JP Morgan Partners and Prime Edge sponsored a new CDO trust that raised EUR 150 million (about USD 128 million at that time) by selling CDO securities that are collateralized by investments in private equity funds.[12] Furthermore, Standard &

---

[11] Pittman, "Patriarch Purchase of Fleet Loans a Bet on Collecting on Bad Debts."

[12] See Dan Primack, "Prime Edge and JP Morgan Partners Put Private Equity into Debt," *Private Equity Week* (June 11, 2001).

EXHIBIT 24.18   Synthetic Arbitrage CCO with a Commodity Trigger Swap

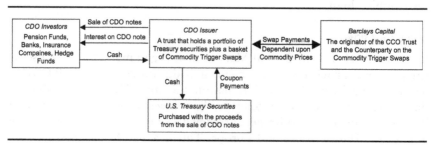

Poor's issued an investment-grade credit rating for the CDO securities in what was the first stand-alone credit rating for a private equity vehicle.

The EUR 150 million was invested in a diversified pool of 35 pre-approved European private equity fund managers. The CDO trust issued three tranches of securities. Tranche A carried a AA rating (with an insurance guarantee from Allianz Risk Transfer) and had a term of 12 years and raised EUR 72 million. Tranche B was rated BBB, also had a term of 12 years, and raised EUR 33 million. The equity or subordinated tranche of EUR 45 million was unrated.

Single-Tranche CDOs

Single-tranche CDOs provide a very targeted structure of credit risk exposure. In a single-tranche CDO, the sponsor sells only one tranche from the capital structure of a CDO. Consider Exhibit 24.14. This showed several tranches that were associated with the Highgate CDO.

In a single-tranche CDO, the sponsor could sell just one of these tranches, and potentially keep the rest for its balance sheet. A single-tranche CDO uses a CDS just like a normal synthetic CDO. The main difference is that in a single-tranche CDO, only a specific slice of the portfolio risk is transferred to the investors rather than the entire portfolio risk.

Single-tranche CDOs allow for even more customization for an investor such as collateral composition, maturity of the single-tranche note, weighted average credit rating, and so on. As a result, single-tranche CDOs are the most finely tuned of any structure. For this reason, single-tranche CDOs are sometimes referred to as "bespoke CDOs" or "CDOs on demand."

There are two main advantages to an investor from a single-tranche CDO. The first has already been alluded to—investors have considerably more control over the terms of a single-tranche CDO than the typical multitranche CDO. Second, there is no waterfall in a single-tranche CDO. All cash flows flow to the investor.

Unfunded CDOs

Another new development of CDOs is the *unfunded tranche*. This can only apply in a synthetic CDO where the credit exposure is gained via a CDS. In an unfunded CDO, an investor that "buys" the unfunded tranche does not pay a purchase price. Instead, the CDO notes for the unfunded class represent purely a CDS where the investor receives payments as a credit protection seller and must pay the CDO issuer (as the protection buyer) if the underlying CDO portfolio suffers credit losses.

Exhibit 24.19 demonstrates an unfunded CDO structure. Class A is the unfunded tranche of the CDO. The remaining classes pay cash for the CDO securities in their tranche and follow the normal waterfall of seniority and payments.

Typically, the unfunded tranche writes a CDS on the entire portfolio of the CDO collateral. Class A holders make no principal investment but receive periodic payments from the CDO trust for protecting the CDO trust from risk of loss on the CDO collateral portfolio.

The unfunded tranche is typically the super senior tranche in the CDO structure. This may seem odd, but the structure works like this.

The unfunded Class A tranche is like an insurance policy on a $500 million credit risky portfolio with a $100 million deductible. Before the Class A tranche investors are required to make payments to the CDO trust for credit losses, the losses on the CDO portfolio must first exceed the $100 million associated with the junior tranches. Until that point, no payments are due from the unfunded tranche. This provides the Class A tranche investors with a reasonably certain ability to collect their payments from the CDO trust without making payments themselves.

EXHIBIT 24.19 An Unfunded CDO Tranche Structure

Tranche	Type	Amount	Percent of Deal	Subordination	Ratings
Class A notes	Super Senior	$400,000,000	80%	20%	Not rated
Class B notes	Senior	$50,000,000	10%	10%	AAA
Class C notes	Mezzanine	$25,000,000	5%	5%	A
Class D notes	Equity	$25,000,000	5%	0%	Not rated
		$500,000,000			

CDO Squared

Some CDOs invest in the notes and tranches of other CDO structures. That is, the collateral pool of a CDO might itself contain notes from another CDO. In fact, if the reader could please check back with Exhibit 24.15, she will see that 9% of the Highgate ABS CDO collateral pool contained CDO notes from other CDO structures.

CDO structures that invest primarily in the notes from other CDOs are called *CDO squared* and are often referred to by the mathematical expression CDO to the second power.

Such layering of CDO deals must be done with caution because their are two levels of assumptions that go into the valuation models for these compound deals. First, there is the model and underlying assumptions for the first CDO structure, and then there is a second layer of models and assumptions once the CDO note is purchased by the second CDO trust. This can compound the model risk associated with CDO structures.

RISKS OF CDOs

There are considerable risks associated with CDO trusts. We provide a short discussion in this section, but the list is by no means comprehensive. For instance, if hedge funds begin to offer CDOs all the economic risks of the CDO must be considered as well as the risks peculiar to hedge fund management.

Default Risk of the Underlying Collateral

Default risk is the single greatest risk associated with an investment in a CDO structure. The lower down the totem pole of tranches the investor acquires, the greater the risk.

One example of the risks associated with CDOs is provided by the American Express Company.[13] As a result of its investments in CDOs, it was forced to take a more than $1 billion pretax charge for losses associated with these investments.

The investments were made by the company's money management unit, American Express Financial Advisors (AEFA). In the late 1990s, AEFA decided to increase the high-yield bond portion of its portfolio to 12% of a pool of assets AEFA managed for the parent company, and to

---

[13] See Paul Beckett, Mitchell Pacelle, and Tom Lauricella, "How American Express Got in Over its Head with Risky Securities," *Wall Street Journal*, 27 July 2001, p. A1.

include in its high-yield bond portfolio CDO investments. AEFA purchased CDO securities in about 60 different trusts, and in some cases, bought the lower rated or equity tranches of the CDO.[14]

Unfortunately, with high-yield default rates increasing significantly from prior years, the riskier tranches of CDO structures began to default, resulting in large losses. American Express initially reported a loss from these investments of $182 million in April 2001. In July, the company announced an additional $826 million charge from its investments in CDOs. Of this amount, $403 million was due to problems related to the investment grade tranches of CDOs it owned, and the remainder from losses and planned sales of high-yield bonds and lower-grade CDO tranches.[15]

The experience of American Express also illustrates another risk with CDO investing. Investors all too often rely on the reports generated by the CDO manager to determine the value of the collateral in the CDO.

To its credit, once the problem came to light, American Express performed its own analysis of the credit risk associated with the CDO collateral. In its analysis, American Express used an estimate that default rates would continue in the 8% to 9% range and stay constant for the next 18 months. This assumption led to the significant charges associated with its CDO portfolio. These estimates were more conservative than the more optimistic estimates generated by the CDO managers. Also American Express analyzed the credit risk associated with about 8,500 bonds underlying the CDO trusts in which it had invested.[16]

The lesson is that in times of stress, CDO managers may be slower or reluctant to write down or write off the investments contained in the CDO trust. The investor may need to perform its own analysis to determine the extent of the damage.

Another example of CDO default risk is the example of CalPine Corp. Calpine is the second largest energy producer in California. In December 2005, its credit rating was cut by Moody's to Caa—low-rated junk status. Only a few short weeks later, CalPine declared bankruptcy.

At the time of its bankrupcty, Calpine had $17 billion of debt outstanding. More than half of this debt was contained in CDO trusts. Moody's Investor Services identified 467 CDOs that had Calpine debt in

---

[14] Beckett, Pacelle, and Lauricella, "How American Express Got in Over its Head with Risky Securities."

[15] Beckett, Pacelle, and Lauricella, "How American Express Got in Over its Head with Risky Securities."

[16] Beckett, Pacelle, and Lauricella, "How American Express Got in Over its Head with Risky Securities."

their CDO trust. The proportion of affected portfolios ranged from 0.2% to a whopping 23%, with a median exposure of 1.4%. Clearly, with more than 400 CDO trusts having exposure to Calpine, its bankruptcy will have a significant impact on the value of CDO notes held by investors.

Downgrade Risk

Downgrade risk refers to a reduction in credit rating of the CDO trust securities themselves (and not the underlying collateral). Prior to 2001 no AAA rated CDO tranche had ever been downgraded. However, with the general slowdown of the U.S. economy and the increase in default rates, downgrades were inevitable. In July 2001, Standard & Poor's downgraded, six AAA rated CDO tranches because of losses associated with the underlying trust collateral. While a downgrade will not hurt an investor if she holds her CDO trust security to maturity and receives full payments, it might harm her in the interim if she decides to sell her securities.

Now S&P or Moody's credit rating transitions for CDOs both up and down are common. In 2005, S&P upgraded the credit rating for 125 CDO tranches while it downgrade 102. Moody's upgraded 49 CDO tranches while downgrading 89. Clearly, with the growth of the CDO marketplace, NRSROs have become much more vigilant in monitoring the credit riskiness of CDO tranches.[17]

CDO Default Rates

The three-year bear market from 2000 to 2002, the recession of 2001 to 2002 and the corporate accounting scandals of 2002 all contributed to rocky times in the credit markets. CDOs did not go unscathed.

Moody's Investor Services reviewed 2,719 U.S. CDO tranches from 1993 through 2003 and found that 262 of these tranches (9.6%) had become impaired. *Impairment* is defined primarily as tranches that have suffered payment defaults that have remained uncured. The total dollar amount of impaired tranches was $7.9 billion out of a total $247.1 billion of CDO tranches that Moody's had rated, for a 3.2% impairment rate.[18]

Exhibit 24.20 shows the dollar amount of CDO tranche impairment. Not surprisingly, the largest dollar amount and number of CDO tranches that became impaired occurred in 2002—the last year of a three year bear market, the end of the 2001 to 2002 recession, and the year of the corporate accounting scandals.

---

[17] See Brian McManus, "Year-End Surveillance Review for 2005 and Outlook for 2006," Wachovia Securities, December 19, 2005.

[18] See Moody's Special Comment, "Default and Loss Rates of U.S. CDOs: 1993–2003," March 2005.

EXHIBIT 24.20   CDO Tranche Impairment

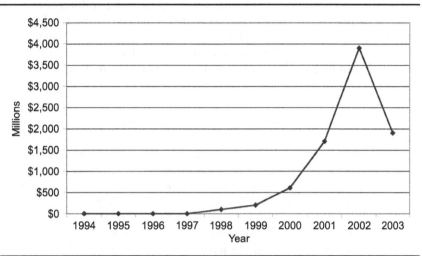

Differences in Periodicity

It may be that the frequency with which payments are received on the underlying collateral does not coincide with the frequency with which payments must be made on the CDO securities. This risk can be compounded when payments on different assets are received with different frequencies.

For instance, consider a CDO collateralized by both high-yield bonds and commercial loans. High-yield bonds pay interest semiannually while commercial loans typically pay interest quarterly. If the trust's assets (the underlying bond and loan collateral) pay interest more frequently than the trust securities, then the transaction may be subject to negative carry (the trust has to hold the interest payments received from the collateral securities in low interest bearing accounts and wait for the payment date on its securities). Alternatively, if the trust assets pay interest less frequently than the securities issued by the trust, the trust may be faced an interest deficiency (the trust must find some way to fund the interest payments due on its securities).

This problem is often solved through the use of a swap agreement with an outside party, where the trust swaps the payments on the underlying collateral in return for interest payments that are synchronized with that of the trust securities.

Difference in Payment Dates

A risk due to the difference in payment dates arises from a mismatch between the dates on which payments are received on the underlying trust collateral, and the dates on which the trust securities must be paid. For example, consider a CBO trust whose underlying collateral consists entirely of high-yield bonds that pay semiannual interest each July and January. Unfortunately, the CDO trust securities pay semiannual interest in March and October. Similar to the problem of periodicity, this mismatch can be cured in a swap with an outside counterparty.

Basis Risk

Basis risk occurs when the index used for the determination of interest earned on the CDO trust collateral is different from the index used to calculate the interest to be paid on the CDO trust securities. For instance, the interest paid on most bank loans is calculated on a LIBOR plus a spread, but other assets may be based on a certificate of deposit rate in the United States. The combination of these assets in a single CDO trust will result in different bases used to determine the interest payments on the CDO trust securities. One way to counter this problem is to issue one or more tranches with a fixed interest rate. This way the underlying index will not affect the required payment to the CDO securities. However, this may lead to spread compression risk.

Spread Compression

Spread compression risk arises when credit spreads decline or compress over time, reducing interest rate receipts from the underlying collateral. Arbitrage CDOs based on high-yield bonds and commercial loans are susceptible to this risk.

For example, suppose a CDO trust is based on a portfolio of leveraged loans earning LIBOR + 200. The trust issues securities that, in the aggregate, pay an average of LIBOR + 100. Over the life of the trust, some of the commercial loans mature and must be replaced with new collateral for the CDO trust. However, in the interim, credit spreads have declined so that the same credit quality loan is now priced at LIBOR + 100. The CDO trust has now lost its arbitrage, and furthermore, there is no excess spread to cushion any defaults that may occur with the new loans.

Yield Curve Risk

CDO trust portfolios with assets across a spectrum of maturity ranges will be impacted by changes in the yield curve represented by shifts in the curve, its shape, and its steepness.

For example, falling interest rates may result in a reduction of the positive spread between the CDO trust assets and its securities. This will have the similar impact as the spread compression described earlier if the trust securities have a fixed coupon rate instead of a floating coupon rate. In addition, high yielding collateral may be called away in the case of high-yield bonds, or prepaid in the case of commercial loans and replaced with lower yielding collateral. This will erode the arbitrage of the CDO trust.

The slope of the yield curve will also impact the profitability of an arbitrage CDO. For example, throughout most of the 1990s, the U.S. yield curve was upward sloping. Consequently, there has been a negative carry between holding cash reserve accounts and the higher interest that must be paid on long-term CDO trust securities.

WARF versus WAS

Every CDO active manager must balance the *weighted average rating factor* (WARF) of the underlying collateral pool with the *weighted average spread* (WAS) over LIBOR. WARF measures the average credit rating of the underlying collateral contained in the CDO trust. All CDO indentures contain covenants as to the average credit rating of the collateral pool. The flip side is that CDO indentures often have a weighted average spread over LIBOR that they are required to maintain. So there is a tradeoff: The CDO active manager can reduce the WARF to get more yield, or increase the credit worthiness of the CDO collateral pool (raise the level of WARF) only at the expense of yield.

For example, during 2005, with a reasonably strong U.S. economy, credit spreads remained low and leverage loan prices experienced price compression as credit spreads were reduced. As a result, many active CDO managers began to look at second lien loans as a way to boost the WAS over LIBOR. Unfortunately, second lien loans are subprime loans and can dramatically reduce the WARF. In fact, most of the second lien loans issued in 2005 were rated single B minus or lower—low even on the junk debt scale.

Notice that this can lead to competing incentives among the tranche classes of the CDO. For example, for the super senior and senior classes, their yields are driven strictly by maintaining collateral of good credit quality so that they do not experience and credit losses on their notes. However, for the equity tranche, there might be an incentive to lower the WARF and raise the WAS because any extra or arbitrage income spread accrues to the equity tranche. Bottom line, for higher-rated tranches of a CDO, be wary of the CDO manager lowering WARF to raise the WAS.

CONCLUSION

This chapter was designed to introduce the reader to the basics of the collateralized debt obligation market. This is a huge market, with issuance now over $150 billion per year, and with new entrants every day.

The CDO market has also witnessed the intersection of other alternative investment strategies, including private equity, hedge funds, and distressed debt. Although commercial loans and high-yield bonds are the most popular form of assets for a CDO, just about any type of underlying asset can be used to collateralize a CDO trust. For instance, commodity trigger swaps are now appropriate for a CDO trust structure. In addition, the first CDO trust backed by equity default swaps was introduced in 2004.

In sum, the expanse of the CDO marketplace is limited only by the imagination of money managers, banks, and investment bankers to bundle new assets into trust structures. The limiting factor is getting the rating agencies to review and issue an investment-grade credit rating for the tranches of the CDO trust securities. To that end, the rating agencies must be able to develop a coherent method for analyzing the underlying collateral. Without investment grade credit ratings, CDOs will not be able to sell their securities.

CHAPTER 25

Collateralized Fund Obligations: Intersection of Credit Derivative Market and Hedge Fund World

Collateralized fund obligations (CFOs) are the latest extension in credit securities. They are the intersection of the hedge fund world and the credit derivative market. These are privately-issued, structured bonds that are backed by a pool of hedge fund investments. In short, they are an extension of the asset backed securities (ABS) market to the hedge fund world.

CFO bonds are based on the same idea as structured debt backed by pools of bonds, bank loans or other debt instruments. CFOs are another form of asset backed security. Similar to other collateralized obligations, CFO bonds are issued by a trust fund or a special purpose vehicle (SPV) that then invests the sale proceeds in a pool of hedge funds that support the payment of coupons and principal on the outstanding bonds.

A BRIEF REVIEW OF COLLATERALIZED OBLIGATIONS

Collateralized obligations (COs) are a form of ABS where a pool of assets are blended together and then repackaged into highly rated securities. ABS have been used to repackage everything from car loans to credit card receipts. In the prior chapter we covered collateralized loan obligations, collateralized bank obligations, and collateralized debt obligations. We provide a brief review in this chapter—exact details and examples can be found in the prior chapter.

Banks began to use asset-backed structures in the late 1980s as a way to repackage bank loans that were not easily transferable into securities that could be bought and sold. These securities were called *collateralized loan obligations* (CLOs), and they were backed by a portfolio of secured or unsecured bank loans made by a variety of commercial borrowers. CLOs now account for approximately one third of the new leveraged loan volume.

In the early 1990s a new variation of this structure was created, collateralized bond obligations (CBOs). A CBO is a security that is backed by a portfolio of senior or subordinated bonds issued by a variety of corporate or sovereign issuers. CBOs are just another form of a debt instrument that is backed not by the credit of a single issuer, but instead, is supported by the credit of many different issuers. CBOs account for over half of the new high-yield bond issuance.

CLOs and CBOs later evolved into *collateralized debt obligations* (CDOs) where the primary security is backed by a combination of both bank loans and bonds. The asset-backed nature of collateralized securities may be used to effect two main types of transactions: balance sheet collateralized obligations and arbitrage collateralized obligations.

Banks and insurance companies are the primary sources of balance sheet COs. They use these structures to manage their commercial loan investments listed on their balance sheet. The goal of a balance sheet CO is typically to reduce regulatory capital requirements. By selling a portion of their loan portfolios, banks and insurance companies can free up regulatory capital required to support those loans. Therefore, balance sheet COs tend to be in the form of CLO structures.

In contrast to balance sheet COs, money managers are the main suppliers of arbitrage COs. The ultimate goal of an arbitrage CO is to make a profit instead of managing balance sheet risk. All CFO structures are arbitrage deals.

At the center of every CO structure is a *special purpose vehicle* (SPV). This is a term to describe a legal entity that is established to accomplish a specific transaction such as a CDO structure. SPVs are usually set up as either a Delaware or Massachusetts business trust or as a special purpose corporation, usually Delaware based.

In the case of a balance sheet CO, the SPV will generally be established as a CLO trust. The selling bank will be the sponsor for the trust, meaning that it will bear the administrative and legal costs of establishing the trust. In the case of an arbitrage CO, the sponsoring entity is typically a money manager.

SPVs are often referred to as "bankruptcy remote." This means that if the sponsoring bank or money manager goes bankrupt, the CO trust will not be affected. The trust assets remain secure from any financial difficulties suffered by the sponsoring entity.

The SPV owns the collateral placed in the trust, and issues notes and equity against the collateral it owns. The collateralized obligations may be issued in different classes of securities or "tranches." Each tranche of a CO structure may have its own credit rating. The most subordinated tranche of the CO is usually called the equity tranche.

These securities are issued privately to institutional investors and high-net-worth individuals. The collateral held by the SPV produces cash flows that are used to pay interest and dividends on the bonds issued by the SPV. The majority of principal on the securities issued by the SPV is paid at the end of the life of the SPV, usually from final principal payments after the sale of the SPV assets.

AN EXAMPLE OF A COLLATERALIZED FUND OBLIGATION

With this background in place, we now move forward to discuss collateralized fund obligations (CFOs). In May 2002, the first two CFO structures came to the market. One was a $550 million CFO structure offered by Man Group Plc. The second was a $250 offering for the Diversified Strategies CFO. This offering was brought to the market by Investcorp Management Services Ltd. of Bahrain. It contained several tranches of both dollar- and euro-denominated, floating rate notes that were rated investment grade by Standard and Poor's.

Exhibit 25.1 displays the Diversified Strategies CFO. Five tranches of structured notes were issued, each with five-year bullet maturities. The first four tranches have semi annual interest payments tied to LIBOR.[1] The equity tranche receives a maximum annual coupon of 5% contingent upon the performance of the portfolio of hedge funds.[2] The equity tranche also receives any residual appreciated value associated with the DSF II fund of funds.

The CFO notes were issued by Diversified Strategies CFO, a *société anonyme* incorporated in Luxembourg. Diversified Strategies took the cash flow received from the sale of the CFO bonds and invested the proceeds in redeemable shares issued by Diversified Strategies Fund II, a hedge fund of funds. In turn, DSF II invested the proceeds received from

---

[1] To protect itself against unusually high floating rates, Diversified Strategies CFO was required to enter into an interest rate cap agreement to hedge this risk.

[2] The equity tranche receives its contingent payment only after the performance of the hedge fund portfolio has appreciated such that the NAV of the portfolio is 150% of the outstanding principal balance of the senior CFO bonds.

EXHIBIT 25.1 Structure of the Diversified Strategies CFO

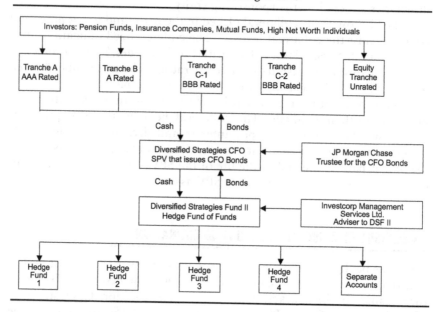

the sale of its shares in individual hedge funds and separately managed accounts. The redeemable shares in DSF II form the primary collateral for the Diversified Strategies CFO.

JP Morgan Chase serves as trustee to the Diversified Strategies CFO while Investcorp Management Services is the advisor to DSF II.[3] As Trustee, JP Morgan Chase is responsible for notifying Investcorp Management Services when the next coupon payment will be due on the CFO bonds and when the trustee will redeem its shares in DSF II. Investcorp Management Services must then given notices to the individual hedge fund managers or the separate accounts so as to have sufficient cash to redeem the shares put to DSF II by the trustee.

Exhibit 25.2 shows the tranche structure for the Diversified Strategies CFO. The weighted average cost of Tranches A through C-2 is 105 basis points over LIBOR. The equity tranche receives a contingent coupon and whatever residual return is accrued after the first four tranches receive their payments.

One reason why the first four tranches were able to obtain an investment grade rating was because of the large equity contribution. The

---

[3] Investcorp Management Services also serves as the collateral manager to Diversified Strategies CFO to the extent this SPV holds cash or short-term notes in addition to the redeemable shares issued by the DSF II Fund.

EXHIBIT 25.2   Diversified Strategies CFO

Tranche	Rating (S&P)	Amount (millions)	Interest Rate
A	AAA	USD 125.00	LIBOR + 60
B	A	USD 32.50	LIBOR + 160
C-1	BBB	USD 10.00	LIBOR + 250
C-2	BBB	EUR 16.20	LIBOR + 250
Equity	unrated	USD 66.30	5%
		USD 250.00	

This material is reproduced with the permission of Standard & Poor's, a division of The McGraw-Hill Companies, Inc. See Juan Carlos Martorell, Sandra Johnson-Harris, and Christopher Howley, "Presale: Diversified Strategies CFO S.A." Standard & Poor's, April 4, 2002.

equity tranche of the CFO structure comprises 26.5% of the capital structure of the SPV. The equity tranche is considered *overcollateralization* in that this tranche provides subordination to classes A through C-2 of the CFO bonds. Stated more simply, the equity tranche is used as the first-loss tranche. Should the hedge fund of funds decline in net asset value, this tranche serves as the buffer to protect the senior CFO bond tranches.

The rating methodology used by Standard & Poor's took into account the long-term return expectations of the fund of funds as well as the probability of realizing an adequate level of return to meet the debt service requirement of the CFO bonds.[4] S&P was able to rate the CFO transaction through simulation analysis of the expected net asset value of the hedge fund of fund investments and by using hedge fund indexes as proxies for expected returns by hedge fund strategy.[5]

In order to increase the probability of meeting the projected returns needed to redeem the CFO bonds, the hedge fund of funds was subject to a number of diversification requirements including:[6]

- The number of hedge fund managers in the fund of funds.
- The concentration with any one hedge fund manager.
- The concentration within any one hedge fund strategy.
- A minimum number of hedge fund strategies.
- Liquidation and redemption rules for the hedge fund managers.

---

[4] See Juan Carlos Martorell, Sandra Johnson-Harris and Christopher Howley, "Presale: Diversified Strategies CFO S.A.," Standard & Poor's, 4 April 2002.
[5] See Standard & Poor's, "Ratings Assigned to Diversified Strategies CFO's Notes in Structured Hedge Fund of Funds Deal," 28 June 2002.
[6] See Martorell et al, 4 April 2002.

EXHIBIT 25.3   Diversification by Hedge Fund Strategy

Hedge Fund Strategy	Maximum Allocation by % of NAV
Distressed debt	12%
Risk arbitrage	30%
Convertible arbitrage	30%
Equity market neutral	30%
Relative value	20%
U.S. equity L/S	20%
International equity L/S	20%
Macro discretionary	15%
Macro systematic	15%
Portfolio insurance	15%
Multistrategy	15%

This table is reproduced with the permission of Standard & Poor's, a division of The McGraw-Hill Companies, Inc. See Juan Carlos Martorell, Sandra Johnson-Harris, and Christopher Howley, "Presale: Diversified Strategies CFO S.A." Standard & Poor's, April 4, 2002.

EXHIBIT 25.4   Diversification by Investment Vehicle

Category of Diversification	Limit
Minimum number of investment vehicles	25
Minimum number of managers	20
Single investment vehicle limit	9%
Single manager limit	12%
Maximum number of vehicles with an allocation greater than 6%	8
10 largest investment vehicles as a percent of NAV	50%
Minimum percent of assets in managed accounts	20%

This material is reproduced with the permission of Standard & Poor's, a division of The McGraw-Hill Companies, Inc. See Juan Carlos Martorell, Sandra Johnson-Harris, and Christopher Howley, "Presale: Diversified Strategies CFO S.A." Standard & Poor's, April 4, 2002.

Exhibit 25.3 sets the maximum allocation by hedge fund strategy. As this exhibit indicates, the DSF II fund is well diversified across 11 hedge fund strategies. This diversification is an important benefit that we will discuss further.

Exhibit 25.4 sets the diversification by investment vehicles. The allocation and diversification requirements are reviewed at the end of each month.

In addition to diversification and allocation requirements, the Diversified Strategies CFO also had to meet certain liquidity requirements. The hedge fund of funds must maintain at least 20% of its total assets in separate managed accounts at all times. Separate accounts are much easier to liquidate than investments in hedge funds because most hedge funds allow liquidations only at appointed times (such as quarterly or semiannually), while a separate managed account can be liquidated at any time. If the 20% liquidity threshold is breached, then Investcorp will be required to immediately liquidate sufficient investments from the separate accounts and convert them to cash or cash like instruments that mature before the next coupon payment on the CFO bonds.

To protect the senior tranches of the CFO bonds, an event of default is set at the point where the NAV of the fund of funds portfolio falls below the total principal amount of the outstanding senior (rated) CFO bonds. At this point, the "first loss" capital associated with the equity tranche will be exhausted. If such an event occurs, the Trustee will liquidate the entire collateral (it will put its redeemable shares back to the DSF II fund of funds) and will use the proceeds pay the principal on the senior notes.

BENEFITS OF CFOs

CFO structures offer benefits to both hedge fund managers and investors. In an arbitrage CFO the investment management company profits two ways. First, it earns management and incentive fees for advising the SPV and the master fund of funds. Second, the investment manager usually retains a large portion of the equity tranche of the CFO. It then pockets the difference between the interest paid on the CFO bonds and the returns earned from the hedge fund of funds (the arbitrage return).

There are additional reasons why the CFO market is appealing to hedge fund managers and investors alike. First, hedge fund managers are often plagued by "hot money"—money pulled from hedge funds by investors during a period of market volatility, or a period of underperformance. Sudden redemptions of hedge fund interests can hurt the hedge fund manager's performance as well as erode the value of the fund to the remaining investors. To some extent hedge fund managers have corrected this problem through "lock-ups"—a period of time after initial investment before an investor can withdraw its money (hedge fund managers have learned this trick from their private equity brothers and sisters).

Hedge fund managers look for "sticky money"—investment funds that are difficult to withdraw. In addition to lock-ups, securitization can also create sticky money. Even though investors can trade in and out of the CFO notes like any other bond, the capital committed to the master hedge fund of funds (DSF II) through the CFO offering will stay with the master fund until the maturity of the CFO bonds. This allows a fund of funds manager the flexibility to invest in those hedge funds that invest in less liquid instruments. CFOs also offer hedge fund managers a new source of investment funds as well as a way to diversify their source of funding.

From an investor's perspective, pension funds, insurance companies, mutual funds, and trust departments of banks can receive exposure to hedge funds through these asset-backed securities when they might not otherwise be allowed in their investment charter to invest directly in hedge funds. These bonds have a stated coupon, a fixed maturity, and provide greater liquidity than limited partnership interests in individual hedge funds.

Many pension funds, mutual funds, and insurance companies either do not have an allocation to hedge funds or are restricted in the types of assets in which they may invest. For instance, most life insurance companies invest 90% to 95% of the insurance premiums collected in fixed income securities to provide a low-risk ability to pay policy benefits. They cannot tap into the hedge fund market through direct investments or even through a fund of funds manager. However, life insurance companies usually are allowed to purchase private label bonds—bonds issued in a private offering under Regulation 144a of the Securities Act of 1933. Consequently, the fixed income structure of a CFO bond allows the insurance company to add hedge fund exposure to its portfolio.

Another advantage of CFOs is that they are less likely to be hit by a ratings downgrade compared to a traditional collateralized debt obligation (CDO) structure that is backed by corporate debt. For example, in the last year of the three year bear market (2000 to 2002), Standard and Poor's initiated more than 90 downgrades of CDO bonds. Forty of these were lowered from investment grade to noninvestment grade. The downgrades associated with CDO bonds were more than one fourth of all asset-backed securities that were downgraded during the 2002.

The large number of CDO downgrades reflected the general economic malaise of the U.S. economy. Traditional CDO structures are backed by corporate bonds and bank loans and these business organizations suffered credit erosion during the period of economic recession in 2001 to 2002. In contrast, hedge returns are dependent upon the investment skill of the hedge fund manager and not the strength of the economy. Therefore, CFO bonds offer diversification from traditional CDO structures.

Another advantage of CFO bonds is less risk than CDO bonds. As an asset class, CDO bonds can have greater volatility than traditional fixed income securities for several reasons. CDO bonds are backed by

EXHIBIT 25.5   Correlation Matrix of Returns

	FOF	Lev. Loans	High Yield
FOF	1.00		
Leveraged loans	0.35	1.00	
High yield	0.43	0.65	1.00

smaller and more concentrated pools of collateral, they have greater exposure to event risk (corporate downgrades, defaults, and bankruptcies), and generally have a large exposure to high-yield bonds. In contrast, CFO bonds are backed by investments in many different hedge fund strategies, which in turn invest in a multitude of underlying securities. This provides greater diversification than a CDO structure backed by a concentrated pool of high-yield bonds or corporate loans.

Finally, the bearish sentiment of the financial markets was exacerbated in 2002 and 2003 by numerous examples of accounting failures and corporate malfeasance. These scandals added an additional risk premium to corporate securities that reduced the value of outstanding CDO bonds backed by high-yield bonds or bank loans. Conversely, CFO bonds were not affected by corporate accounting scandals because their value was tied to the skill of the hedge fund managers.

These points can all be summarized in Exhibit 25.5 that measures the correlation of returns between hedge fund of funds, high-yield bonds, and leveraged loans. These are the three primary collateral classes that underlie CFOs, CBOs, and CLOs. We measure the returns for the past 10 years. From Exhibit 25.5 it is clear that the returns to hedge fund of funds have a very low correlation with the returns earned from leveraged loans, 0.35. Hedge fund of funds also have a low correlation with the returns to high-yield bonds of 0.43. The correlation of hedge fund of funds with either leveraged loans or high-yield bonds is lower than the correlation of returns between high-yield bonds and leveraged loans, the primary collateral for CDO bonds. Therefore, CFO bonds have the potential to offer greater diversification when combined with other asset-backed structures.

RISKS OF COLLATERALIZED FUND OBLIGATIONS

The risks associated with CFOs flows primarily from the underlying collateral that supports the CFO bonds. This is the hedge fund of funds. As Exhibit 25.3 indicates, for example, the Diversified Strategies CFO bonds are supported by investments in 11 different hedge fund strategies. This pool of hedge fund strategies provides a diversified fund of funds of investment to support the CFO bonds.

To better assess the risks of CFO investing, we analyze the distribution of returns associated with hedge fund of fund returns. Similar to our procedure in prior chapters, we plot a frequency distribution of the monthly returns for hedge fund of funds for the period 1991 to 2005. Monthly returns are chosen because most investors monitor their portfolio returns on a month to month basis. Although different hedge fund strategies can generate substantially different return distributions (see Chapter 6) we focus on the return pattern to hedge fund of funds because the collateral underlying CFO bonds is a diversified pool of hedge funds. This diversification of hedge fund strategies should reduce the dispersion of returns between different strategies.

Exhibit 25.6 presents the frequency distribution for hedge fund of funds. The mean monthly return is 0.80%, or about 9.6% per year. Hedge fund of funds also have a positive Sharpe ratio, demonstrating out performance over a cash benchmark. However, the returns to hedge funds also display a positive value for kurtosis of 4.34.

Kurtosis is a term used to describe the general condition that the probability mass associated with the tails for a return distribution is different from that of a normal distribution. Kurtosis is a way of measuring

EXHIBIT 25.6   Frequency Distribution for Fund of Funds[a]

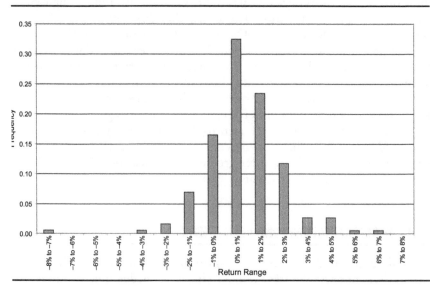

[a] Average = 0.80%, Std. Dev. = 1.60%, Skew = –0.24, Kurtosis = 4.34, Sharpe = 0.25.

outlier events. A positive value of kurtosis is known as *leptokurtosis*, and this describes a distribution of returns that has significant mass concentrated in outlier events—returns that deviate far from the average return. Generally, investors prefer a return distribution with low values of kurtosis. That is, investors prefer an asset return pattern to be concentrated around the mean of the distribution with fewer outlier events.

The hedge fund of funds return distribution also has a small negative skew value of –0.24. The *skew* of the distribution measures the symmetry of the distribution of returns. Again this value is measured relative to a normal distribution. A normal distribution has no skew, it is perfectly symmetrical. A negative skew indicates that the mean of the distribution of returns is to the left of (less than) the median of the distribution. This indicates that large negative outlying returns occur more frequently than large positive outlying returns, indicating a bias to the downside. The negative skew and the large value of kurtosis indicates a bias towards large negative returns. This demonstrates a "fat tail" effect—that there is a greater concentration of probability mass in the left hand tail of the return distribution for hedge fund of funds, indicating exposure to large negative outlier returns.

Consequently, we conclude that hedge fund of funds cannot be fully described by a Sharpe ratio (which is based on the mean and variance) analysis. Hedge fund of funds have considerable exposure to outlier events. Therefore, investors in CFO bonds can expect the underlying collateral (hedge fund of funds) to have on occasion large changes in its net asset value, with a bias towards large negative changes.

For comparison, we include in Exhibits 25.7 and 25.8, the frequency distribution for high-yield bonds and leveraged loans, the primary underlying collateral for CBO and CLO structures. High-yield bond returns have a similar exposure as hedge fund of funds to large outlier events with a kurtosis equal to 4.16, but have a larger negative skew value of –0.81. Therefore, high-yield bonds demonstrate a significant downside tail risk. This "fat" tail reflects the exposure to event risk of downgrades, defaults, and bankruptcies associated with credit risky assets. In addition, the downside tail for high-yield bonds is "fatter" than that for hedge fund of funds.

Leveraged loans demonstrate a very similar return patter to hedge fund of funds and high-yield bonds. Leveraged loans have a negative skew of –1.08 and a value of kurtosis of 3.24, again indicating a bias to the downside. While the tail for leveraged loans may not be as fat as that for FOF or high-yield bonds—leveraged loans have the smallest value of kurtosis—leveraged loans also has the largest negative skew—indicating a greater bias towards negative returns than either high-yield bonds or FOF. However, we do note that leveraged loans have the smallest value of standard deviation—0.64%—and a Sharpe ratio on par with hedge fund of funds.

EXHIBIT 25.7 Frequency Distribution for High-Yield Bonds[a]

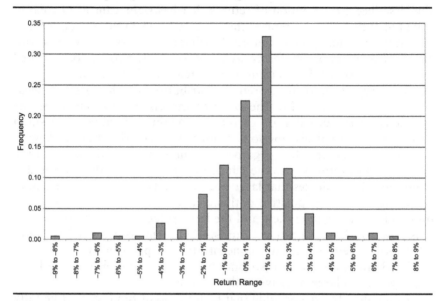

[a] Average = 0.75%, Std. Dev. = 2.05%, Skew = –0.81, Kurtosis = 4.16, Sharpe = 0.17.

EXHIBIT 25.8 Frequency Distribution for Leveraged Loans[a]

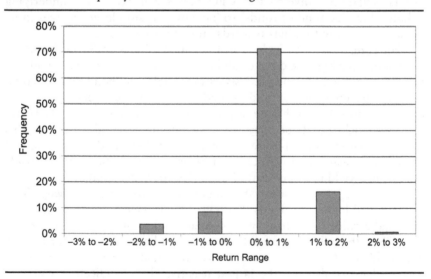

[a] Average = 0.54%, Std. Dev. = 0.64%, Skew = –1.08, Kurtosis = 3.24, Sharpe = 0.22.

Even though hedge fund of funds, high-yield bonds and leveraged loans have similar return patterns, we must remember that these return patterns are not parallel to one another. We know this because as we demonstrated in Exhibit 25.5, the correlation between the returns to high-yield bonds and hedge fund of funds is only 0.43, and between leveraged loans and fund of funds is only 0.35. Therefore, CFO structures should provide good diversification benefits versus CBO structures or CLO structures.

COLLATERALIZED COMMODITY OBLIGATIONS

Not to be outdone by hedge funds and CFOs, commodity investors have gotten into the game of asset-backed securities. In December 2005, Barclays Capital, the investment bank of Barclays PLC, launched the first *collateralized commodity obligation* (CCO)—the first rated credit instrument that provides fixed income investors with access to the commodities asset class.

These bonds are rated by Standard and Poor's where the underlying assets are *commodity trigger swaps* (CTS). CTS have "trigger events" analogous to credit events under credit default swaps. These events are determined by commodity price levels where the payment of the principal of the CCO is dependent on the prices of a basket of commodities over an averaging period immediately prior to the maturity of the CCO bonds. In essence, an investor in a CCO bond receives exposure to a static portfolio of CTS.

In a CDS, a payment is triggered if there is a credit default event such as a bankruptcy, reduced credit rating, or failure to pay. Using the same derivatives technology as a CDS, a CTS will result in a payment if a commodity price (or basket of commodities prices) falls below a preset trigger price. The loss for a CTS is determined only at maturity of the CCO notes. This means that a decline in commodity prices prior to the averaging period cannot cancel out or knock out a tranche of the CCO structure. This also means that the coupon payments on the CCO will be protected through the maturity of the CCO note. While the coupon payments are protected, the principal is not. If a trigger event occurs under the CTS, the maturity value of the CCO note will be less than its face value.

In order to receive a credit rating from Standard and Poor's, the commodity exposure is subject to construction rules to ensure a broadly diversified basket of commodities. This minimizes the likelihood of a trigger event and maximizes the likelihood of the payout of par value of the CCO notes at maturity.

EXHIBIT 25.9 Barclays' Collateralized Commodity Obligation

Portfolio Construction Rules to Earn an Investment Grade Credit Rating

1. Loss profile of CTS are determined using historical observations.
2. A diversified basket of 16 commodities including industrial metals, precious metals, and energy commodities. Agriculture and livestock may be added to the CTS at a later date.
3. Commodities cannot be included in the CTS basket if their one year moving average is greater than 150% of their five-year moving average. This reduces the likelihood of selling protection against commodity price spikes.
4. Each price trigger must differ by at least 5% from triggers in the same commodity. This reduces the chances of multiple triggers occurring at the same time in one commodity.

As in other CDO and CFO structures, the lowest-rated tranche of the CCO notes is considered the equity tranche and bears the first loss should commodity prices fall below the trigger levels. The first trigger on any CTS is set at 65% of the current spot price. This means that prices would need to fall by over 35% over the term of the CCO notes before the equity tranche investors to be impaired. As investors move up the capital structure of the CCO tranches, the decline in commodity prices would have to be significant before their capital is impaired. Exhibit 25.9 summarizes the main requirements of the CCO notes to receive an investment grade credit rating from Standard and Poor's.

CONCLUSION

Collateralized fund obligations are a bridge between the credit derivative market and the hedge fund industry. CFOs are a new way to attract, and even more important, retain investor capital. They provide hedge fund managers with a stable base of investment capital.

From an investor's perspective, CFOs offer exposure to hedge fund managers for institutional investors that might not otherwise be able to invest directly in hedge funds. CFO bonds also offer diversification with respect to other asset-backed securities such as CBO and CLO bonds.

Finally, the returns to hedge fund of funds have a risk profile that demonstrates significant exposure to outlier events. While the distribution of returns associated with the collateral underlying CFO bonds is similar to the underlying collateral for CBO and CLO structures, the returns streams are not parallel. Hedge fund of funds have a very low correlation with high-yield bonds and leveraged loans. This provides the opportunity for good diversification.

Corporate Governance

CHAPTER 26

Corporate Governance as an Alternative Investment Strategy

In our chapter on leveraged buyouts, we discussed how they have a positive impact on the corporate governance of target companies. Most public companies have widespread equity ownership. Shareholders tend to be scattered about the investor universe. As a result, monitoring the management of the company may not be easy. A single shareholder may be able to raise only a small voice. The advantage rests with management not with shareholders.

This advantage shifts with a leveraged buyout. LBOs introduce a more concentrated ownership structure. In effect, the leveraged buyout firm replaces the diverse shareholder base and provides a measure of active oversight that was lacking with a fragmented equity ownership structure. Leveraged buyout firms pursue an active corporate governance program where the managers of the company are held accountable for their actions by the equity owners.

It is clear from the returns earned by LBO firms, that solid corporate governance initiatives can add value and enhance the wealth of shareholders. However, corporate governance need not be limited to leveraged buyout firms. Any shareholder can be an active owner. In fact, corporate governance is often referred to as *shareholder activism*. We use both terms interchangeably in this chapter.

It may seem odd to discuss corporate governance in the context of alternative assets. Yet shareholder activism is certainly not a mainstream investment strategy. In fact, there are three reasons why corporate governance should be classified as an alternative equity investment strategy.

First, this strategy actively engages the executive management of public companies with the purpose of strengthening the companies' internal controls and financial performance. In this respect, corporate governance programs are very similar to private equity investment portfolios. Second, corporate governance programs target the internal controls of public companies independent of the current state of the equity market. Therefore, shareholder activism can provide a positive return stream that has less than perfect correlation with equity market returns. Finally, corporate governance programs tend to have small, concentrated investment portfolios, similar to private equity and hedge funds. Therefore, corporate governance fulfills the characteristics of an alternative investment strategy, the same as private equity or hedge fund portfolios.

We begin this chapter by discussing the nature of agency problems and the lack of corporate control. Next we discuss equity index investing and the role it plays in corporate governance. We then provide a brief introduction to corporate governance programs. We also review prior empirical studies regarding the benefits of shareholder activism. Then we provide some empirical results from the California Public Employees' Retirement System's (CalPERS) corporate governance program.

AGENCY PROBLEMS AND THE LACK OF CORPORATE CONTROL

Shareholders are the ultimate decision makers for any public company. After all, they own the company and can choose to do with it what they will. However, it is not practical for shareholders to make every day to day decision concerning the operations of the company. Consequently, shareholders delegate this authority to the managers of the company. The managers as agents are supposed to act in the best interests of their principals—the shareholders. However, problems may arise when the agents do not act in the best interest of their principals.

Agency Theory and Problems

In their seminal paper, Jensen and Meckling postulated agency problems in the management of public corporations.[1] An agency problem can arise when managers of public companies pursue their own economic self-interest instead of maximizing shareholder wealth. For instance, managers may work less vigorously on behalf of the shareholders, pursuing instead luxurious offices, corporate power, higher salaries and bonuses, and other perquisites of their employment. In essence, managers are human beings and are prone to pursue their own agendas instead of those for shareholders.

---

[1] See Michael Jensen and William Meckling, "Theory of the Firm: Managerial Behavior, Agency Costs and Ownership Structure," *Journal of Financial Economics* (October 1976), pp. 305–360.

This problem is particularly acute in large public companies where the shareholders are widely dispersed. In this circumstance, there may not be sufficient incentives for individual owners to expend their financial or reputational resources to monitor the behavior of managers.

There are three solutions to the agency problem. The first is to ensure that managers have as significant ownership stake in the company as the shareholders. The goal of increasing shareholder wealth is then perfectly consistent with increasing the agent's wealth. Notice that in leveraged buyouts, for example, the management of the company always has a significant equity stake in the business.

If the managers of the company do not have a significant ownership stake in the company, then compensation schemes must be adjusted to align the agents' self-interest with that of the shareholders. Specifically, compensating managers based on objective performance that increases shareholder wealth such as share price performance will provide consistency of shareholder and manager goals. This concept is known simply as pay for performance and it requires transparent compensation metrics where the management of the company are rewarded when shareholders are rewarded.

A corporate monitoring system can alleviate the agency problem as well as the need for large equity stakes by managers or incentive schemes that align economic interests. Corporate internal controls can provide effective monitoring of management's performance and behavior which ensure that shareholders' best interests are fulfilled. A significant element of the corporate monitoring function should be performed by a public company's Board of Directors. The Directors of the company represent the shareholders and therefore, must monitor and hold accountable the actions and performance of executive management.

The twin problems of human behavior and the inability to monitor effectively can lead to a breakdown in corporate internal control systems. We next consider how some of these controls breakdown and how they may be corrected.

Failure of Internal Corporate Control Systems

In the early 1990s there was a change in many boardrooms across corporate America. Many CEOs were removed by their board of directors. These companies included American Express, General Motors, Chrysler, IBM, Kodak and Westinghouse. These highly publicized departures were examples where internal corporate controls worked, even if they were a bit late. Unfortunately, all too often, the board of directors takes vital action only after the company is in a severe financial mess. Then the bankruptcy court or a takeover by another company is the frequent solution.

Corporate control systems are the responsibility of a company's board of directors. Directors are elected by the shareholders and have the final responsibility for the activities of the firm. It is the board's job to hire and fire the CEO, to establish appropriate compensation schemes, and to ensure appropriate controls are in place so that shareholders' interests are best served. The board of directors has access to confidential corporate information and the power to provide effective oversight of the company's managers.

There are several control points that can lead to a more efficient allocation of a corporation's resources and ensure shareholder wealth maximization. Unfortunately, all too frequently these control points fail to function properly.

Board Agenda

Although the CEO of every corporation must answer to the board of directors, it is most often the case that the agenda for every board meeting is set by the CEO rather than the directors themselves. This is often out of necessity because the CEO is the person most knowledgeable about the company's business affairs. However, this allows the CEO to control the amount of information as well as the content that is fed to the board of directors. Directors can operate effectively only when they have complete information.

Furthermore, some directors may not have sufficient financial or industry expertise to interpret the information provided by the CEO. Even if the information provided by the CEO is concise, pertinent, and well-organized, the director may have only limited time to digest the information and make an intelligent decision. Unfortunately, some board agenda items may be too complicated to arrive at the right decision within the limited timeframe of a one-day board meeting.

Board Composition

Another unfortunate fact of corporate America is that the CEO has considerable input into who will sit on his or her board of directors. Cronyism is not out of the question. Board members who have a current or prior affiliation with the CEO are often selected, raising questions of objectivity.

Few boards of directors use recruiting agencies to find appropriate candidates for board vacancies. Frequently, board vacancies are filled by word of mouth, personal networks, or informal referrals, instead of a rigorous and objective search. A good solution is for the company to establish and update annually the criteria for selecting candidates for nomination to the board of directors.

Even then there may be a lack of cohesiveness among board members. A board of directors is a group of individuals working towards a common goal. Yet, most board members have businesses and professions to run outside of the corporate boardroom. They are busy people that have only a limited time to interact. Under these circumstances it is not unusual that directors might be inhibited from speaking their minds and providing useful insight.

All too frequently, many board members are also managers (insiders) of the corporation. Insiders acting as board members present a conflict of interest because one of the functions of the board is to review the performance and compensation of the corporation's managers. Ideally, a board of directors should have only one insider sit on the board: the CEO.

Equity Alignment

Jensen and Meckling indicate that one of the best ways to resolve the agency problems is to have managers own a significant stake in the company. Furthermore, this ownership stake must be sufficiently large to have an impact on the manager's wealth.[2]

Yet, many CEOs and directors have small equity stakes in the companies they manager and direct. In a study of the equity holdings of CEOs of the 1,000 largest corporations in the United States, the median holding was 0.2% of the company's outstanding equity.[3]

Another issue is the amount of equity held by directors. Frequently, these holdings are small or nonexistent. Equity ownership of the underlying company is rarely a condition of board membership. This problem can be solved by compensating directors, in part, in the form of stock and stock options. While a few companies have adopted this compensation scheme, equity participation by board members continues to be small.

Board Size

The saying "Nothing gets done by committee" can apply to a board of directors as well. The larger the board size, the less likely it is to take concerted action. With a large board of directors, a consensus must be reached. Not only does this take time, but it can also result in mild rather than decisive action.

While there is no ideal board size, smaller is better, generally less than 10 board members is preferred. Larger boards are easier for the CEO to control because it is often the case that when searching for a

---

[2] Id.

[3] See Michael Jensen, "The Modern Industrial Revolution, Exit, and the Failure of Internal Control Systems," in Donald H. Chew, Jr. (ed.), *The New Corporate Finance*, 2d ed. (New York: Irwin/McGraw-Hill, 1999).

consensus, a large board will look to the CEO for guidance. This defeats the independent oversight by the board of directors.

Large corporate boards can be made effective through the use of committees. In particular, a corporate board of directors should have an audit committee, a nominating committee, and a compensation committee. Each of these committees should consist only of independent directors (it would not make sense to have a compensation committee populated by corporate insiders).

Joint CEO/Chairman Role

Perhaps the single largest breakdown with respect to internal corporate control mechanisms is the combination of the CEO's title with that of the Chairman of the Board. In both roles the joint CEO/Chairman has total control of the corporation. Not only does the joint CEO/Chairman have control over the corporation's day to day operations, but also over the board of directors that oversees managers for the corporation.

There is simply too great a conflict of interest with respect to the joint CEO/Chairman because it is too easy for that individual to act in his or her self-interest instead of those of the company's shareholders. Without the leadership of an independent director it is difficult for the board of directors to perform its critical oversight function.

In summary, corporate governance often does not work in the United States as it should. Agency problems, human nature, large and unwieldy boards of directors, and CEO power and control contribute to this breakdown. The failure of corporations to act in the best interests of shareholders can lead to a diminution of shareholder value. This provides an opportunity for shareholder activism to enhance returns. In short, corporate governance is an alternative investment strategy for equity portfolios.

EQUITY INDEX INVESTING

Equity index investing is a proxy for investing in an asset class. It is an efficient way to gain economic exposure to the publicly traded equity markets. The chosen index is assumed to represent the risk-and-return properties of an asset class to which the investor wishes to obtain exposure.

In the United States, the public equity market is so large that a number of different indexes have been constructed to capture different parts of the stock market. For example, the S&P 500 is designed to track the largest capitalized stocks in the United States. Conversely, the Russell 1000 and 2000 are designed to track large-, mid-, and small-cap stocks. Last, the Wilshire 5000 is designed to capture the full public equity market in the United States. The size and growth of equity index investing has distinct implications for corporate governance programs.

A large equity index will represent the actively traded securities within a public stock market. The index represents the total of all active management decisions regarding those public companies because an investor is buying into the ideas of all active management in that asset class.[4] While the decisions of active equity managers cannot be observed, the impact those decisions have on equity prices can be observed. As a result, index investing means tracking not only the actions of the best investment managers in the equity marketplace, it also means tracking the mediocre and just plain bad equity managers. Similarly, equity index investing means tracking not only the good performing companies, but also, the mediocre.

Index investing is often referred to as "passive" investing. However, an investor does not need to be a passive index investor. It is possible to enjoy the benefits of efficient equity asset class exposure while attempting to improve the overall risk and return profile of the asset class. This is the goal of shareholder activism.

The Size of the Equity Index Market

Equity index investing is a popular strategy with both institutional and retail investors. The size of this market is huge. Exhibit 26.1 presents

EXHIBIT 26.1   Top Index Managers

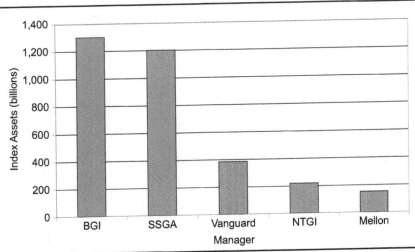

the amount of index assets managed by the five largest providers of index management. The total is almost $3 trillion dollars. The industry total for all index providers is over $4 trillion dollars. In the United States, about 18% of tax-exempt institutional equity assets are indexed, and foreign equities represent about 25% of the equity index assets.[5]

Finally, Exhibit 26.2 demonstrates that index investing is a growth industry. From 2001 through 2005, this industry has almost doubled, with an annual growth rate of 16%.

The sheer size of the equity index market makes it fertile ground for corporate governance programs. This is especially true among institutional investors who have sufficient resources to apply a corporate governance program. Institutional investors have a distinct advantage due to their size. Institutional ownership (pension funds, endowments, money management firms, and family offices) of the U.S. equity market has more than doubled over the past 25 years. Exhibit 26.3 demonstrates the growth of institutional ownership.

The size of the institutional market means that large institutions trade primarily among themselves in an effort to manage risk and enhance returns. Concerted action on the part of institutional investors can have an impact on the performance of public companies. Therefore, corporate governance can have an impact not only on targeted companies, but also the broader stock market. The lessons made public and learned by one corporation can influence the performance of other public corporations.

EXHIBIT 26.2   Growth of Indexed Assets

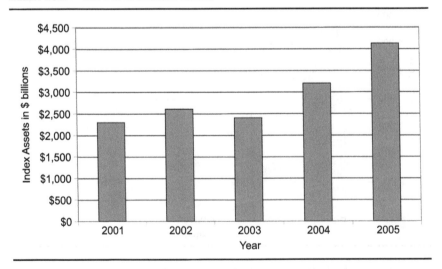

---

[5] Id.

EXHIBIT 26.3   Institutional Equity Ownership

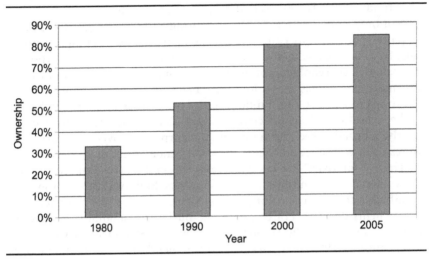

An Example

Consider the following example. An institutional investor holds 1% of XYZ company stock in its passive index fund worth $100 million. The management of the company has pursued "empire-building" strategies that are costly but do nothing to increase shareholder wealth. As a result, the company has declined in value by 5% each year for the last three years. Yet the management of the company seems content to build their empire despite the lost value to shareholders.

Unfortunately, the institutional investor cannot sell the stock because it must pursue a buy and hold strategy in its index fund. Passive index investing imposes a significant constraint on an investor: the inability to sell an underperforming stock. Index investors achieve a breadth of equity exposure cheaply and efficiently. However, they must accept the poor financial performance of those underachieving companies that are contained in their chosen index.

If the management of XYZ company continues to pursue its strategy, the institutional investor can expect to lose next year another 5% or $5 million from its investment. Under these circumstances, the institutional investor would be better off if it pursued a program of corporate governance with XYZ company. In fact, the institutional investor has an incentive to spend up to $5 million to stop management's empire building strategy.

Shareholder activism need not be limited to a single company. A reasonable strategy to pursue is a course of action aimed at improving the overall performance of public companies contained in the investor's index fund. This is the essence of corporate governance.

Not only can an active shareholder bring about a change in a specific company, that company can serve as an example to other public corporations. By effecting changes in the behavior and management of corporate agents, active shareholders can improve the financial performance. Moreover, more companies may alter their behavior and management practices to avoid conflict and public scrutiny from other investors. Publicity can be a useful and an effective tool for shareholder activism. Consequently, a broad based and highly public corporate governance program can result in widespread benefits for a large index fund investment.

These "spillover" effects can boost the performance of the overall equity asset class in addition to specific stocks. Spillover effects, however, are difficult to measure. Nonetheless, there is anecdotal evidence that these benefits do exist. For example, the Business Roundtable (an association of CEOs of public companies) released a Statement of Corporate Governance in 1997 that lists their recommendations on best practices regarding corporate governance. Several of the recommended practices were key issues among shareholder proposals throughout the 1990s.[6]

Pension funds and other institutional index investors have a fiduciary duty of care to manage their plan assets prudently. While there is no distinct fiduciary duty to monitor investments, this duty is often subsumed as part of the concept of a prudent investor. The duty to monitor investments is particularly important with respect to indexed investments.

A BRIEF REVIEW OF CORPORATE GOVERNANCE PROGRAMS

Corporate governance programs are another way of describing shareholder activism. Over the past decade, institutional investors have begun to flex their muscles with respect to underperforming corporations. Specifically, these investors have engaged the management of poor performing companies in proxy proposals, direct discussions with executive management, and direct negotiations on corporate goals and vision. The goal of shareholder activism is perfectly selfish: to enhance shareholder wealth.

Informed shareholders no longer rely on the discipline of the financial markets to correct corporate performance. In the 1980s, many academics and economists argued that poor performing companies would be subject to takeovers and acquisitions. This corrective action of the finan-

---

[6] See Diane Del Guercio and Jennifer Hawkins, "The Motivation and Impact of Pension Fund Activism," *The Journal of Financial Economics* 52, no. 3 (June 1999), pp. 293–340.

cial markets was expected to provide the proper incentives to managers to take corrective action before they lost their jobs through a merger.

However, the era of highly leveraged buyouts and takeovers came to an end with the takeover of RJR Nabisco. This buyout marked both the peak and the end of the junk bond financing of the 1980s. Afterward, the burden of corporate control fell to the shareholders of public companies.

A Definition of Corporate Governance

In a nutshell, corporate governance may be described as the prudent and active use of shareholder rights to increase shareholder wealth. Shareholders must act like owners and continue to exercise their ownership rights in a public company. Over 70 years ago, Graham and Dodd first commented:[7]

> The choice of a common stock is a single act, its ownership is a continuing process. Certainly, there is just as much reason to exercise care and judgment in being a shareholder as in becoming one.

Corporate governance is then shareholder activities intended to monitor and influence corporate management.

All companies experience inevitable periods of stock price appreciation and depreciation as profitability increases and wanes. These periods will occur whether or not a corporation practices good principles of governance. However, accountable governance may mean the difference between prolonged periods of underperformance and responding quickly to a new course of corporate action.

Shareowner vs. Shareholder

Once upon a time, physical assets defined an individual's net worth. Land Barons were aptly named as the ownership of real estate was the most significant asset an individual could own.

However, over time, our economic society changed from an agricultural one to an industrial one. With this transformation, a new denominator of wealth was born: the ownership interest in the production of goods and services. This wealth was embodied in the ownership of corporate entities.

Initially, voting rights of public companies followed common law—the law developed by courts through their judicial decisions. This com-

---

[7] Benjamin Graham and David Dodd, *Security Analysis*, 1st ed. (New York: McGraw-Hill, 1934).

mon law followed a per capital rule of one vote per person. This law was derived from the old tradition of British partnerships where each partner had an equal vote.

Yet the rule of one vote per person did not work well with respect to raising capital for public companies. Shareholders were unwilling to commit more capital without getting a greater say in the management of the company. Eventually, the individual states had to step in and establish new statutes and laws governing shareholder rights. This law was based on the rule of One Share equals One Vote. Still it was not until 1926 that the New York Stock Exchange adopted a one vote per share rule.

During this time bank and trust companies became the custodians for wealth accumulation. Initially, they held land deeds, mortgages, jewelry and bullion for their clients. However, as the industrial age progressed, they became "Holders of Shares" for their wealthy clients. It is from this service that the term Shareholder was born.

In 1990 a new term was established for equity owners in public companies: Shareowner.[8] This term was originally coined by the California Public Employees' Retirement System and has now been adopted by the CFA Institute—that professional body which grants the CFA Charter through a rigorous program to investment professionals. Shareownership embodies two important principles. First, it reminds all interested parties—executive management, directors, creditors—who is the ultimate owner of the company. Second, with the acknowledgement of share ownership comes the obligation to continue to exercise ownership rights in a public company in a prudent and productive manner.

SEC Rule 14a-8

Rule 14a-8 under the Securities and Exchange Commission Act of 1934 is the Shareholder Proposal Rule. Under this rule, shareholders may submit proposals to a public company for inclusion in that company's proxy materials. Shareholder proposals are brief statements requesting certain action by the management of a public company. In effect, the shareholder/principal formally requests that the agents/managers follow a course of action for the shareholder's/principal's benefit.

These proposals are included on the company's proxy statement at the expense of the company (the company has to print and distribute the proxy statements) along with management's response to the proposal and management's voting recommendation. Once added to the company's proxy statement, the shareholder proposal must be presented at

---

[8] See Robert Carlson, Charles Valdes, and Mark Anson, "Share Ownership: The Foundation of Corporate Governance," *The Journal of Investment Compliance* (Spring 2004), pp. 54–61.

the annual shareholders' meeting of the public company. In between the proxy mailing date and the annual meeting, managers and dissident shareholders may contact other shareholders to gather support for their proposals. The proposal is voted on by shareholders at the annual meeting for the company, along with other issues such as the election of directors. In sum, the proxy process provides active shareholders with a convenient format for presenting their ideas regarding the company's corporate governance.

Even if a shareholder proposal passes by the requisite majority, the management of the company does not have to implement the requested action. A passed shareholder proposal is not binding on the corporation unless the corporation's bylaws make such proposals binding on the management of the company. Nonetheless, the passing of a shareholder proposal is a strong indication to management of the course of action it should pursue to please the owners of the company (if they value their jobs).

Del Guercio and Hawkins examine shareholder proposals submitted by large institutional investors over the period 1987 to 1993.[9] They find that the most prevalent proposals request confidential voting by shareholders, rescinding of poison pills and other antitakeover provisions, and independence of the board of directors. These proposals are designed to strengthen the corporate controls and financial performance.

The proxy process was made easier for active investors in 1992 when the SEC passed new rules that allowed shareholders to communicate more directly with one another. Prior to 1992, the only way for shareholders to communicate with each other without running afoul of the SEC rules regarding shareholder groups was through the proxy process. However, in 1992, the SEC relaxed the restrictions in its proxy rules with respect to disclosure of communications among shareholders.

The new rules significantly lowered the costs of corporate governance programs. Institutional investors could now pursue less formal governance programs that direct proxy proposals. Private communications with management as well as other shareholders became more common. However, the threat of a shareholder proposal in a public proxy statement remains a serious threat.

Prior Research on Corporate Governance Programs

Although corporate governance investment programs are a relatively new phenomenon, considerable research has examined their financial impact. The ultimate goal of corporate governance is to increase share-

---

[9] See Del Guercio and Hawkins, "The Motivation and Impact of Pension Fund Activism."

holder wealth. However, prior studies are divided as to whether corporate governance programs add value.

For example, Wahal finds an insignificant stock price reaction over a seven-day event period around the proxy mailing dates for a sample of 211 shareholder proposals.[10] However, in a subsample of CalPERS-targeted companies, significant positive stock returns were observed, indicating that CalPERS is a positive influence on firm performance.

Del Guercio and Hawkins also find no significant stock price effect from shareholder proposals at the proxy date or in the three years following the targeting of companies.[11] However, they do find that shareholder proposals are followed by significant additional corporate governance activity and broad corporate change such as asset sales and restructuring. Furthermore, they find that firms targeted by CalPERS or subject to a proposal on antitakeover issues are significantly more likely to receive a takeover bid.

Karpoff, Malatesta, and Walking find no significant stock price reaction to shareholder proxy proposals and no operating performance improvement over one to three years following the shareholder proposal.[12] Gillan and Starks find that shareholder proposals sponsored by institutional investors receive considerable support from other investors, and have a small but measurable negative impact on stock prices.[13] Forjan finds that there is a negative stock price reaction when shareholder proposals are submitted to management.[14] However, in a subsample of shareholder proposals that succeed, the stock price reaction is positive.

Smith finds that CalPERS has been successful in changing the corporate governance structure in almost 75% of the cases studied.[15] For those shareholder proposals submitted by CalPERS that are successful, he finds a significant positive stock price reaction. For those proposals that are unsuccessful, the share price reaction is negative. Smith con-

---

[10] S. Wahal, "Pension Fund Activism and Firm Performance," *The Journal of Financial and Quantitative Analysis* 31 (1996), pp. 1–23.

[11] See Del Guercio and Hawkins, "The Motivation and Impact of Pension Fund Activism."

[12] See Johathan Karpoff, Paul Malatesta, and Ralph Walking, "Corporate Governance and Shareholder Initiatives: Empirical Evidence," *The Journal of Financial Economics* 42, no. 3 (November 1996), pp. 365–395.

[13] See Stuart Gillan and Laura Starks, "Corporate Governance Proposals and Shareholder Activism: The Role of Institutional Investors," *The Journal of Financial Economics* 57, no. 2 (2000), pp. 275–305.

[14] James Forjan, "The Wealth Effects of Shareholder Sponsored Proposals," *Review of Financial Economics* 8, no. 1 (January 1999), pp. 61–72.

[15] Michael Smith, "Shareholder Activism by Institutional Investors: Evidence from CalPERS," *The Journal of Finance* 51 (1996), pp. 227–252.

cludes that CalPERS is successful in monitoring managers and increasing shareholder wealth.

Similarly, Nesbitt studies the wealth effects associated with CalPERS corporate governance program.[16] He finds, over the period 1987 to 1992, that companies that are contacted by CalPERS by letter experience positive long-term performance in excess of the S&P 500. Specifically, Nesbitt finds significant stock price performance in excess of the S&P 500 for a sample of companies contacted by CalPERS.

In summary, the empirical evidence regarding the economic impact of shareholder proposals is unsettled. Some studies show no increase in shareholder wealth from the submission of shareholder proposals, some studies show a negative impact on shareholder wealth, and some studies show a positive impact on shareholder wealth. In the next section we consider a different form of shareholder activism, and its impact on shareholder wealth.

EXAMINING THE BENEFITS OF A CORPORATE GOVERNANCE PROGRAM

The empirical studies cited above provide mixed evidence concerning the value added from corporate governance programs. However, most of these studies examine only brief time periods associated with corporate governance programs. Furthermore, shareholder proposals are only one tactic that may be used in corporate governance programs.

In this section we analyze the value added with respect to the CalPERS' corporate governance program over the time period 1992 to 2004, a period of sufficient time and macroeconomic diversity to provide a realistic look at the constructive nature of a corporate governance program. In addition, rather than examining shareholder proposals, we consider the economic impact of the publication of CalPERS' Focus List of public companies.

CalPERS' Focus List

Since 1992, CalPERS has focussed its attention on companies considered by several measures to be "poor" financial performers. By centering its attention and resources in this way, CalPERS believes that it can demonstrate to those who might question the value of corporate governance, specific and tangible economic results.[17]

---

[16] Stephen Nesbitt, "Long-Term Rewards from Shareholder Activism: A Study of the "CalPERS" Effect," *The Journal of Applied Corporate Finance* (Winter 1994), pp. 75–80.

[17] See The California Public Employees' Retirement System, "Corporate Governance Core Principles and Guidelines," April 13, 1998.

The CalPERS' Focus List was first born in 1992 when CalPERS publicly identified 10 large public corporations in a published list. CalPERS announced that these companies were poor performers, and therefore, should bear the public scrutiny associated with their under performance. Furthermore, CalPERS stated that it would continue to monitor closely the performance of these companies and would consider shareholder proposals and other actions necessary to improve the financial performance of companies placed on the Focus List.

In fact, CalPERS takes an active role with those companies placed on its Focus List. This activity begins several months before the Focus List is released. CalPERS begins the process in the spring of every year by screening a universe of approximately 1,600 public companies across all industries and levels of market capitalization. Over the course of two to three months CalPERS reduces this universe to a list of 20 to 25 companies that it believes demonstrate poor financial performance as well as poor corporate governance principles. These companies become candidates for CalPERS' Focus List.

CalPERS contacts potential corporate candidates in late summer or early autumn of each year. Over the course of the next four to six months, CalPERS meets directly with the executive management and directors of candidate companies to discuss its concerns and to provide management with an opportunity to make a case for exclusion from the Focus List.

Sometimes, potential candidates react immediately to CalPERS initial contact by initiating share buybacks, or by implementing new internal controls in the hopes that a positive short-term boost to their share price might persuade CalPERS to exclude them from the Focus List. These changes are made in response to the concerns expressed by CalPERS as a large institutional investor and to forestall inclusion on the Focus List.

The final Focus List is usually published in spring of the year following initial contact. Some potential candidates are excluded because they agree to make changes to their control procedures or have already implemented them. The remaining candidates that do make the Focus List are included because of lack of progress or responsiveness to CalPERS' shareholder concerns. Focus List graduates are based on three criteria: return on capital, corporate governance principles, and performance versus an industry peer group.

Return on capital is measured using the principles of Economic Value Added (EVA). We discussed EVA briefly with respect to the case history for the Duracell Corporation in our discussion of private equity. Briefly, EVA is a method for evaluating projects and performance by including a charge against profits for the cost of capital that a company employs.[18] Capital charges under EVA measure the return that investors could expect to earn by investing their money in a portfolio of stocks with similar risk as the company.

The EVA approach to value creation reflects economic reality because EVA measures the opportunity cost of capital based on the risk undertaken to achieve a revenue stream. This is in contrast to accounting ratios such as earnings per share or return on equity that can be distorted by noncash charges, early revenue recognition, and capitalized expenses. These accounting conventions are applied at the discretion of management and may lead to a temptation by management to manipulate accounting-based performance measures such as earnings per share. The beauty of EVA is that it redirects management's focus from accounting numbers to equity value creation.

Industry performance is relatively straightforward. CalPERS' measures a company's stock price performance relative to its peers for a five-year period. Those companies that have large underperformance are eligible for the Focus List.

Lastly, CalPERS' considers a company's corporate governance principles. Issues such as staggered/classified boards of directors, lack of independent directors, a combined CEO/Chairman of the Board, and poison pills are just some of the key issues that makes a company eligible for the list.

All in all, eligible candidates for CalPERS' Focus List must demonstrate poor financial performance and poor corporate governance principles. As mentioned above, sooner or later all companies experience a period of underperformance. However, it is those companies that have poor corporate governance principles that are more likely to experience a prolonged (even fatal) period of underperformance.

A Test of CalPERS' Focus List

CalPERS' has published its Focus List each year since 1992. Although the list originally included 12 companies, in recent years, the list has not been fixed at any specific number to allow the CalPERS' investment staff the flexibility to include only the most egregious candidates.

We examine the stock price reaction of all companies included on the Focus List over the 13-year period from 1992 to 2004. The sample size of companies is 112. The study period is rich in economic detail including two periods of Federal Reserve tightening of interest rates (1992 to 1993, and 1999 to 2000) as well as three periods of Federal Reserve easing (1994, 1997 to 1998, and 2001 to 2003). In addition there was the

---

[18] The formula for EVA is: Net operating profits after tax − (Cost of capital) × (Total capital employed).

"Tequila Crisis" of 1994 to 1995, the Asian Contagion of 1997 to 1998, the bursting of the technology bubble in 2000, the recession of 2001 and 2002, and a three year equity bear market in 2000 to 2002.

The key purpose is to determine whether the Focus List is an effective way to increase shareholder wealth. If corporate underperformance is the result of lack of effort or poor decision making that can be corrected through public scrutiny or improved corporate controls, then inclusion on the Focus List might be expected to reinvigorate the company to improve its effort and financial performance. At the very least, inclusion on the Focus List should arrest the declining fortunes of those companies that are targeted. Examining a company's stock price performance before inclusion on the Focus List, at the time of announcement of the Focus List, and after inclusion on the Focus List might provide some evidence of the economic value of corporate governance programs.

To test the impact of the Focus List, we use a methodology known as an event study.[19] We avoid a prolong discussion of the econometrics necessary to produce an event study. The key point to understand is that an event study measures the *excess returns* associated with an announcement. Excess returns are defined as the returns earned over and above a risk-adjusted rate of return for the company being examined. In other words, a positive excess return indicates a "bonus" to investors—a return premium greater than they would expect or demand to compensate them for risk of holding the stock of a company.[20]

We examine five periods of performance associated with companies that appear on CalPERS' focus list. The first two periods are the three to six months leading up to the date of publication of CalPERS' annual list and the three-month period prior to the announcement of the Focus List. As noted above, one of the criteria for Focus List inclusion is poor stock price performance. Consequently, we might expect to see negative stock price performance leading up to the announcement date. Conversely, there might be a concerted effort by companies to improve their stock price performance in an attempt to avoid inclusion in the Focus List. This could lead to positive stock price performance leading up to the publication of the Focus List.

---

[19] For details on event studies, see Mark Anson, "Financial Market Dislocations and Hedge Fund Returns," *Journal of Alternative Assets* 5, no. 3 (2002), pp. 78–88.

[20] The empirical results presented in this section have been published in two financial journals. See Mark Anson, Ted White, and Ho Ho, "The Shareholder Wealth Effects of CalPERS' Focus List," *Journal of Empirical Finance* 15 (2003), pp. 102–111; and Mark Anson, Ted White and Ho Ho, "Good Governance Works: More Evidence from CalPERS," *Journal of Asset Management* 5 (2004), pp. 149–156.

There could also be competing economic effects at the time of publication by CalPERS of its Focus List. On the one hand, there might be a negative stock price impact as investors react unfavorably to the identification of by CalPERS of poorly governed companies. Yet many investors may view inclusion on CalPERS' Focus List a positive development because of CalPERS' underlying commitment to work with those companies to improve their corporate controls and stock price performance. Indeed, the empirical results prove this to be the case.

Finally, we examine the performance of companies after the publication date of the Focus List. We examine three time periods: the first three months after the publication of the Focus List, six months after the publication, and one year after the publication. Here, the results should be unequivocal. If there is value to CalPERS' corporate governance program, we should see a positive stock price performance after the publication date of the Focus List.

The economic results of CalPERS' Focus List program are contained in Exhibit 26.4. Exhibit 26.4 which presents the full sample of the Focus List companies over the past 13 years. We observe significant, positive, excess stock price performance after the release of the Focus List. The excess returns over the three-month, six-month, and one-year period or are economically and statistically significant. For example, for the total Focus List sample, the one-year *average* excess return is over 59%. Again, these are excess returns—returns over and above a risk adjusted rate of return that investors would normally demand to hold equity in a risky company. This is a remarkable result. The 59% represents a return premium not previously available to investors. We also observe positive excess returns before the release of the Focus List and at the time the list is published, but these returns are statistically insignificant. Still this is an indication that companies begin to show improved performance leading up to the publication of the Focus List. In summary, soon after the Focus List is received, the corporations contained in the list experience significant positive price effects to their share prices. Furthermore, this positive price impact does not erode in subsequent periods. In summary, significant, lasting economic value is added through the CalPERS' Focus List.

EXHIBIT 26.4   Cumulative Excess Returns for CalPERS' Focus List

	$t-180$ days to $t-90$	$t-90$ days to Announcement	Announcement to $t+90$ days	Announcement to $t+180$	Announcement to $t+365$
Mean CER	−0.18%	6.20%	12.93%	29.40%	59.40%
T Statistic	−0.04	1.46	3.03	4.21	4.91

EXHIBIT 26.5   Cumulative Excess Returns for Small- versus Large-Cap Stocks

	$t - 180$ days to $t - 90$	$t - 90$ days to Announcement	Announcement to $t + 90$ days	Announcement to $t + 180$	Announcement to $t + 365$
Large-Cap Stocks					
Mean CER	2.53%	7.91%	20.15%	35.50%	68.04%
T-statistic	0.4	1.24	3.15	3.39	3.75
Small-Cap Stocks					
Mean CER	−3.81%	2.93%	11.79%	13.70%	38.28%
T-statistic	−0.66	0.51	2.03	1.44	2.33

The results of this analysis differ from that of Caton, Goh, and Donaldson.[21] They study the financial performance of companies contained in the Focus List released by the Council of Institutional Investors and find significant negative excess returns associated with the release date of the list.[22] One difference may the purpose of the Council's Focus List versus that of CalPERS'. The Focus List produced by the Council serves exclusively as identification. It is intended to unmask companies with poor corporate governance, but the Council normally does not make any attempt to improve the companies' governance practices. Conversely, CalPERS' goal is not only to identify those corporations that have poor performance and governance, but also to work with those companies to improve their governance procedures and financial performance. As a result, investors may react more favorably to companies contained on CalPERS' Focus List compared to that of the Council's.

Exhibit 26.5 provides another snap shop of the positive excess returns associated with CalPERS' Focus List. In this exhibit, we divide the CalPERS' Focus List sample into large-cap stocks (those included in the S&P 500 stock index) and small-cap stocks. We can see that the

---

[21] See Gary L. Caton, Jeremy Goh, and Jeffrey Donaldson, "The Effectiveness of Institutional Activism," *Financial Analysts Journal* 57, no. 4 (July/August 2001), pp. 21–26. Also, the methodology used in this chapter was different than Caton *et al.* We formed portfolio of companies to account for the clustering of event dates while Caton *et al.* test individual companies. Testing individual companies assumes that there is no correlation among the excess returns. The lack of correlation may be violated when companies share the same event date (such as the release of a list of companies at the same time).

[22] The Council of Institutional Investors is an industry association or more than 120 large U.S. pension funds, both public and private.

impact for CalPERS' Focus List is much greater for large-cap stocks than small-cap stocks—68% versus 38%.

This is another demonstration of corporate governance at work. Large, Fortune 500 companies typically have the most disperse share-owner base. These companies typically have hundreds of millions of shares outstanding with no one shareowner owning a significant percentage. With such a scattered shareowner base, it is difficult to monitor the actions of the executives of large corporations.

However, it is clear that when CalPERS' steps into the fray to improve the governance of large-cap companies, the stock market reacts very favorably. Investors now have a champion that will protect their interests. The impact is less for small-cap stocks because the ownership is often more concentrated with one or two shareowners owning significant stakes and therefore able to monitor the actions of executive management more effectively. Still the CalPERS' effect produces a 38% one-year excess return—nothing to sneeze at.

Similar results have been found for other governance investment programs. A recent study conducted by the London Business School on the Hermes Pensions Management Focus Fund found similar excess return performance. Using a sample of 67 corporate engagement strategies of the Hermes Focus Funds with public corporations in the United Kingdom, excess returns of 4.5% were observed around the engagement date. These returns are both economically and statistically significant.[23]

Governance Style Investing

While CalPERS' Focus List is one demonstration of the value added through proactive shareownership, another form of economic investing has developed over the past eight years: governance funds. Corporate governance funds are limited partnerships much like hedge funds. The difference is that governance fund managers pursue an active engagement strategy with the companies in which they invest. This is a long only strategy in public companies where the goal is to improve the governance metrics of the public company in the expectation that better accountability, transparency, and alignment of economic incentives will lead to improved shareowner wealth.

In 2000, the CalPERS Investment Staff presented a business plan to the CalPERS Board of Trustees with the goal of investing capital with governance style investors. Since then several billion U.S. dollars have been committed to the program. Exhibit 26.6 presents the performance

---

[23] See, Marco Becht, Julian Franks, Colin Mayer and Stefano Rossi, *Returns to Shareholder Activism: A Clinical Study*, Working paper of the London Business School, February 2006.

EXHIBIT 26.6   CalPERS Corporate Governance Program versus the S&P 500

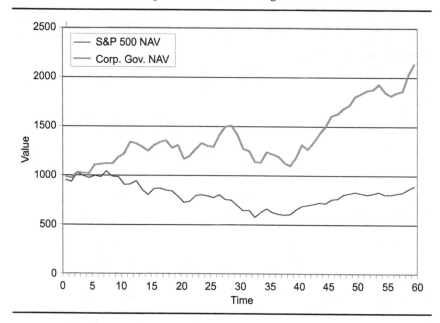

results for this program. The gray line at the top of the chart is the returns to CalPERS' governance program and the thin line at the bottom of the chart represents the S&P 500 stock index. As can be seen, this program has outperformed the U.S. stock market by a significant amount over the past five years. Over this time period, which included a three-year bear market in stocks, CalPERS' governance investments earned a compound annual rate of 16.9% versus −2.3% for the S&P 500—another demonstration of significant value added from corporate governance.

Of even more interest is the scatter plot in Exhibit 26.7. This Exhibit plots the returns to CalPERS' governance investing program versus the returns to the S&P 500. There is no discernible pattern to this graph which is all the more evident by the beta and R-square measures for the governance program versus the S&P 500, −0.087 and 0.01, respectively. Simply, there is no correlation between CalPERS' governance investing program and the stock market. This conclusion is all the more interesting when you consider the fact that CalPERS' governance investing program is designed to invest in public companies. The result is an investment program that outperforms the stock market while not being correlated with the stock market—a combination worthy of any alternative investment strategy.

EXHIBIT 26.7   CalPERS' Corporate Governance Program: Correlation with the Stock Market

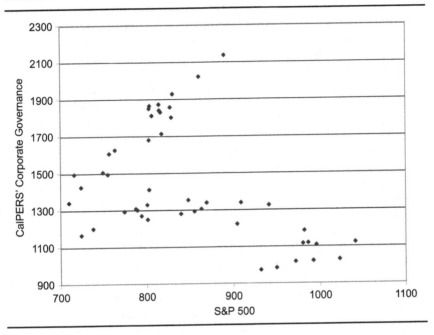

CONCLUSION

Corporate governance pays. This chapter demonstrated two ways that shareowners can add value through corporate governance. First, CalPERS Focus List provides significant, positive economic value added while producing portfolios of companies that have a low correlation with the broad stock market. Second, CalPERS program of investing with fund managers that pursue a governance form of investing also provided a significant return premium versus the U.S. stock market. Despite the economic benefits that can be derived from corporate governance, these programs are not implemented by institutional investors to the same extent as other alternative investment strategies. The reasons are several.

First, there is the risk of legal liabilities for investors that pursue confrontational discussions with corporate executives. Shareholder proposals may lead to costly and time consuming proxy battles should a corporate target decide to fight back against the principles of corporate governance.

Second, there is the "free rider" problem. When a large institutional investor pursues a successful plan of corporate governance, all shareholders benefit. Those shareholders who contribute nothing to the corporate governance initiative receive just as much benefit as the institutional investor who actively pursued the governance plan of action. Therefore, an investor who decides to implement a corporate governance program must realize in advance that many will benefit from its actions while it will bear all of the costs.[24]

Third, many institutional investors do not have either the staff or the expertise to pursue corporate governance initiatives. Institutions such as CalPERS, Hermes Pensions Management, and TIAA-CREF are rare in that they have dedicated corporate governance units within their investment departments.

Fourth, many institutions have a passive investment approach through index funds. These investors may not believe that lost value in an index fund is a sufficient economic incentive to risk their reputation as well as their financial resources on such public and active investment strategies.

Yet, the cost of corporate governance programs is small relative to the size of an investor's assets. For instance, Romano indicates that the annual cost to CalPERS of its corporate governance program is 0.002% (0.2 basis points) of CalPERS' domestic investments.[25] Del Guercio and Hawkins find that pension funds that pursue a corporate governance program spend less than one-half of a basis point per year.[26] In fact, Del Guercio and Hawkins conclude that if the California State Teachers Retirement System were to improve stock prices only 0.5% at its target firms, it could increase its portfolio by $2 million. The implication is that there is an even greater incentive at larger institutional investors to initiate a corporate governance program.

Furthermore, an institutional investor need not apply corporate governance alone. There are many other investors that share the same goal. For instance, the Council of Institutional Investors was founded in 1987 to address the similar concerns for large investors. One objective of the Council is to establish goals and guidelines for the effective governance of publicly traded corporations. To this end, the Council believes that all publicly traded companies and their shareholders and other con-

---

[24] CalPERS acknowledges the free rider issue. However, CalPERS realizes that it is a leader in investment management, and it is willing to assume a leadership role in corporate governance. Given the size of CalPERS' portfolio, it might be said that corporate governance is not only CalPERS' duty, but also its destiny.

[25] See Roberta Romano, "Less is More: Making Institutional Investor Activism a Valuable Mechanism of Corporate Governance," *Yale Journal of Regulation*, Summer 2001.

[26] See Del Guercio and Hawkins, "The Motivation and Impact of Pension Fund Activism."

stituencies benefit from written, disclosed governance procedures and policies.[27]

In addition to the economic benefits cited above from governance-style investing, a new frame of mind has entered the investment community: share ownership. As originally coined by CalPERS and now adopted by the CFA institute, shareowners have become more aware of their continuing ownership rights in public companies. These rights have value and can maximized through a thoughtful governance program.

In conclusion, corporate governance is an alternative investment strategy for institutional investors. Furthermore, this strategy is particularly useful for equity index investors. Index investors must accept the good companies with the mediocre. However, corporate governance can improve the efficiency of the total asset class, providing wealth benefits to index investors. Finally, the data presented in this chapter with respect to the CalPERS' governance program demonstrate that this alternative strategy can enhance investment returns.

---

[27] More information on the Council of Institutional Investors may be found at www.cii.org.

Index

3(c)(1) funds, 400–401
3(c)(7) funds, 400–401
20 bagger, 512
55/35/10 S&P500/bonds/EAFE, return distribution, 349
55/35/10 stocks/bonds/CRB, return distribution, 348
55/35/10 stocks/bonds/DJ-AIG, return distribution, 347
55/35/10 stocks/bonds/GSCI, return distribution, 346
55/35/10 stocks/bonds/MLMI, return distribution, 348
60/40 stock portfolio, monthly return (expectation), 349, 351
60/40 stocks/bonds, returns distributions, 345
144A securities, 33

Abernathy, Jerome, 186
Absolute priority, 486–487
Absolute return, 23
  products, 91–95
  strategies, 20
Acceleration, 474
Account representative, designation, 122
Accredited investor, definition, 207
Ackermann, Carl, 74, 183, 184
Active risk, 119
Agarwal, Vikas, 77
Agency
  costs, 446–447
  problems, 670–674
  theory/problems, 670–671
Agricultural commodities, managed futures (usage), 363–364

Alpha
  coefficient, 542
  range, 536
  decrease, 540
  demonstration, 531
  intercepts, 542
Alpha drivers, 15
  beta drivers, separation, 19–23
  categories, 20–21
  generation, 26–27
  review, 368–371
Alpha-only strategies, 23
Alternative assets
  class, definition, 3
  importance, 15
  overview, 12–13
  pursuit, information advantage (availability), 27–28
Altman, Edward, 478
Ambachtsheer, Keith P., 385, 675
Amenc, Noel, 79
American credit put option, 597
American Express Financial Advisors (AEFA), 646–647
AMF, public return, 451–452
Angel investing, 4411
Anjilvel, Satish, 74, 77
Ankrim, Ernest, 313
Annual returns, market stress, 312
Anson, Mark J.P., 16, 20, 76, 192, 197, 225, 244, 246, 313, 314, 341, 510, 597, 601, 624, 680, 686
Antonelli, Cesca, 405
Arbitrage, profits, 293–294
Arbitrage CBO, structure, 630

Arbitrage CDOs, 611, 628–637
  active management, 629
  cash flows, 637
  structure, 630, 635
  trust, profit, 635–637
Asian Contagion, 317, 592, 688
Asness, Clifford, 22, 537, 547
Asset allocation, 7–12, 229
  hedge fund indexes, usage, 244–248
  illustration, 247
  rethinking, 23–26
Asset classes, 7–8
  risk premiums, trading strategy risk premiums (contrast), 11–12
Asset-backed securities (ABSs), 609, 653
  downgrade, 660
  example, 639
Assets
  beta, 89
  economic input usage, 5
  location, trading strategy (contrast), 11
  management list, 115
  value, store, 5–6
Asset-weighted index, equal weighted index (contrast), 242–243
Atlas, Riva D., 481
Average return, volatility (relationship), 335–338

Backfilling process, 183
Baker, George, 432
Balance sheet CDOs, 611
  cash funding, 612

695

Balance sheet CDOs (*Cont.*)
goals, 611–612
structures, 615–628
synthetic construction, 612
Balu, Rekha, 494
Bank loans
direct obligations, 605
ratings, distribution, 569
recovery rates, 483
Bankruptcy, 604
claims, classification, 485
protection, emergence, 508
remote, 614
Barclay Agriculture CTAs,
return distribution, 364
Barclay CCO, 666
Barclay CTA Index, 362–363
return distribution, 362
Barclay CTA managed futures
indexes, usage, 361
Barclay Currency CTAs, return
distribution, 365
Barclay Diversified CTAs,
return distribution, 367
Barclay Financial and Metal
CTAs, return distribu-
tion, 366
Barnard, Bailey S., 462, 469
Barry, Ross, 183
Basis risk, 650
Basle Committee on Banking
Regulations and Super-
visory Practices, 641
Beatric Foods, LBO, 433
Becht, Maro, 689
Beckett, Paul, 646, 647
Beginning net asset value
(BNAV), 252–254
Bell curve, scrunching, 140
Benchmark risk, 33
Beta, 17
absence, 157
coefficients, 548
correlation coefficients,
relationship, 280
statistical significance,
533, 540
expansion risk, 194–195
level, 534
value, 531
Beta drivers, 15

performance, linearity, 18–
19
review, 368–371
Big spread products, 640
Binary credit put options,
597–598
Black, Fisher, 253
Black boxes, 62
Black-Scholes option pric-
ing model, applica-
tion, 254–255
Blanket subordination, 474
Blocking position, 486
Blume, Marshall, 141
Board of Directors, 671
agenda, 672
competition, 672–673
size, 673–674
Bodie, Zvi, 279, 313
Boeing, risk, 298
Bonds
average returns, 335
efficient frontier, 339
managed futures, downside
risk protection, 371–374
returns, volatility, 336
substitutes, 91
Born, Brooksley, 222
Boudreau, Bryan, 73, 77
Boykin, James, 7
Brav, Alon, 517
Bridge financing, 414
British Venture Capital Asso-
ciation, 391, 527
Broker-dealers, conduct, 210
Brorsen, B. Wade, 358
Brown, Stephen J., 73, 75,
77, 80, 98, 182, 183,
230, 231
Bullet payment, usage, 631
Burns, Mairin, 464
Busenitz, Lowel W., 430, 434
Business cycle, 309
Business development compa-
nies (BDCs), 563–566
fee structure, expense, 566
filings, 564
share value, 565
Business plan
establishment, 447–448
usage, 390–398

value, addition, 397
Business Roundtable, 678
Buy and build strategies, 434
Buyout deals (Europe), com-
petition, 555
Buyout-to-buyout deal, exam-
ple, 558

Cacheflow Inc./Blue Coat Systems
price history, 417
venture capital case study,
414–417
Caglayan, Mustafa Onur, 79
California Public Employees
Retirement System
(CalPERS), 94
3 and 30, response, 266
corporate government pro-
gram
S&P500, contrast, 690
stock market correlation,
691
focus list, 583–685
cumulative excess returns,
687
test, 685–688
money, raising (response),
265–266
targeted companies, 682
Call risk, 580
Capital
assets, 4–5
commitment, 406
depreciation, 100
structure (gap), mezzanine
financing (bridge), 462–
463
Capital Asset Pricing Model
(CAPM), 41
diversification requirement,
502
lessons, 525–526
Capital structure arbitrage, 46
Carlson, Robert, 680
Cash amount (75%), 266–267
Cash collateral, 628
Cash flow arbitrage CDO,
629–632
projected return, 632

Cash funded balance sheet CDO, 612, 615–617
Cash settlement, 605
Cash-burn rate, 391
Caton, Gary L., 688
Caxton Corporation, 225
Chapter 7 bankruptcy, 487, 496
process, overview, 484
Chapter 11 bankruptcy, 483–487
protection, 493
reorganization, 594
Chartered Financial Analyst (CFA) designation, 268–269
Cheapest to deliver, 605
Chen, Ren-Raw, 597
Cheng, Andria, 442
Chew, Jr., Donald H., 673
Chicago Board of Trade (CBOT), 289, 355
financial futures contracts, introduction, 356
Chicago Board Options Exchange (CBOE), 242
Chicago Mercantile Exchange (CME), 289, 355
currency futures, introduction, 356
Choudhry, Moorad, 597
Clark, David, 39
Class voting, 485–486
Clawback arrangements, 124
Clow, Robert, 231
Collateral yield, impact, 317–318
Collateralized bond obligations (CBOs), 609, 654
market, size, 610
structure, 628
Collateralized commodity obligation (CCO), 643, 665–666
Collateralized debt obligations (CDOs), 585, 601, 609
collateral, 614
default rates, 648
developments, 640–646
growth, reasons, 611

life cycle, 638
market, growth, 610
marketplace balance sheet, arbitrage CDOs (contrast), 611–613
overview, 613
risks, 646–651
squared, 646
structure, 610–615, 660
example, 638–640
tranche impairment, 649
trust, 636
maturity, 631
spread income, excess, 637
Collateralized fund obligations (CFOs), 653
benefits, 659–661
example, 655–659
risks, 661–665
structure, 656
Collateralized loan obligations (CLOs), 569, 654
benefits, 623–626
delinking, 627
market, size, 610
structures, 617, 628
invention, 612
Collateralized obligations (COs), review, 653–655
Collins, Daniel, 231, 361
COMEX, 355
Commodities
average returns, 335
buckets, 643
business cycle, relationship, 306–310
downside protection, summary, 350
exposure, 279–288
indexes, 321–332
components, comparison, 320–321
introduction, 277
markets, economics, 296–302
pools, 353
prices
financial asset prices, comparison, 302–303
GSCI proxy, 307
returns, 310

volatility, 336
swaps, forward contracts (relationship), 283–284
value, percentage, 295
Commodities Trigger Swaps (CTSs), 643
Commodity Exchange Act (CEA), 219–222
flowchart/rules, 223
Section 1.3(cc), 220
Section 4.5, 221
Section 4.7, 221
Section 4.13, 221
Section 6, 222
Commodity futures, 294–296
arbitrage, 296
asset class, empirical evidence, 313–314
contracts, 282–283
defensive investment, 343–351
economic rationale, 305–312
economic summary, 333–338
efficient investment frontier, relationship, 338–343
indexes, 315–321
comparison, 330–332
description, 315–316
return, source, 316–321
investment, 305
portfolio context, 333
Commodity Futures Trading Commission (CFTC), 108, 219–222, 224
CPO/CTA registration, 354
regulations, 288–289
Commodity Pool Operator (CPO), 108, 219–222, 316, 353
Commodity Research Bureau (CRB)
Commodity Index, 327–328
returns distribution, 328
Commodity trading advisor (CTA), 219, 316, 354
Commodity-based equity, 314
Commodity-linked notes, 284–288, 321
Competitive positioning, 626

Complexity risk premium, 12
Component weightings, 325
Concentrated portfolios, 21
Conglomerate corporations
  dismantling, 449–450
  size, problems, 432–433
Conservatism, principle, 527,
  552
Constrained investing, unconstrained investing (contrast), 10–11
Contango
  futures market, 299
  market, 298
Convenience yield, 296
Convergence trading hedge
  funds, 35, 51–66
  impact, 153–162
Convertible arbitrage, 35,
  154–156
Convertible bond
  arbitrage, 55–59
  economic drivers, 173
Convexity risk, 580
Corporate bonds
  direct obligation, 605
  recovery rates, 483
Corporate capital structure,
  overview, 456
Corporate control, absence,
  670–674
Corporate governance
  alternative investment strategy, 669
  definition, 679
  LBOs, relationship, 446–450
  programs
    benefits, examination,
    683–691
    research, 681–683
    review, 678–679
  spillover, 448
Corporate restructuring, short
  volatility (relationship),
  196
Corporate restructuring hedge
  funds, 34, 45–51
  usage, 149–153
Corporate venture capital funds,
  402–405
  formation, 403

Correlation coefficients, 278
Correlation matrix, 586
Correlation products, 623
Council of Economic Advisers,
  222
Council of Institutional Investors, 688
Counterparty risk, 119
Covenants, usage, 387
Cox, John, 254
Cramdowns, 486
Credit call options, 598–599
Credit concentrations, reduc-
  tion, 625–626
Credit default swaps (CDSs),
  601–606
  bilateral contract, 602
  CDO trusts, relationship,
  622–623
  contract size/maturation, 604
  default risk transfer, 603
  delivery, 605
  spread, 604
  trigger events, 604–605
Credit derivatives
  advantages, 596
  introduction, 579
  market
    hedge funds, intersection,
    653
    increase, 602
    transaction, 617
Credit enhancements, 626–628
Credit event, occurrence, 605
Credit facility documents, amendment restrictions, 474
Credit option derivatives, 596–
  601
Credit put options, 596–598
Credit risk
  impact, 584
  management, methods, 584–
  585
  sources, 580–585
Credit risky investments, 140,
  585–596
Credit spread risk, 580
Credit swaps, risks, 606
Credit tranching, 611
Credit-linked notes (CLNs),
  599–600

Cross-market/overlay, 23
Crowded shorts, noninvest-
  ment, 267–268
Crowley, Paul, 98
Crude oil futures
  backwardated market, 301
  Contango market, 300
  roll yield, calculation, 319
  term structure, 328
Crude oil prices, instability,
  299
CSFB Leveraged Loan Index,
  591
Cummings, Jack, 7
Cummins, Chip, 36
Currencies, 292–294
Customer relations, preser-
  vation, 626

Data risk, 180–184
Davies, Ryan, 197
Death spiral, 573
Debt
  loads, increase, 479
  private equity, equivalence,
  455, 477
  tilt, 23
Default risk, 580
Defaulted debt market, size,
  478
Default-free U.S. Treasury secu-
  rities, 583–584, 616
Del Guercio, Diane, 678, 681,
  682
Delta, 170
Descriptive statistics, 200
Deutsch, Karin, 328
Deutsche Bourse, 557
Dickson, Henry, 15
Disaster planning, usage, 122
Distressed bank loans, CLO
  trust, 642
Distressed buyouts, 490–491
Distressed debt, 477
  arbitrage, 498
  bankruptcy, relationship,
  483–487
  CDOs, 640–643
  fire sale, 495–497
  frequency distributions, 515–
  516, 595

Distressed debt (*Cont.*)
 investment
  risk, 498–499
  strategies, 487–499
  value, 508
 market
  increase, 478–480
  inefficiency/segmenta-
   tion, 482–483
  size, 478
 multiperiod regression analysis, 543
 performance, 508–510
 returns, 481
 riskiness, 594–596
 security, undervaluation,
  494–495
 single-period regression analysis, 536
Distressed debt-backed CDOs,
 640
Distressed loans, removal, 641
Distressed securities, 45–47
 hedge fund managers, 149–
  150
Diversification rules, 325–326
Diversified portfolio
 building, private equity
  (usage), 518
 private equity, inclusion,
  517–520
Diversified trading strategy,
 managed futures (usage),
  366–367
Dodd, David, 679
Donaldson, Jeffrey, 688
Donovan, Karen, 493
Double taxation, minimiza-
 tion, 105
Dow Jones Industrials Stock
 Index, 291
Dow Jones-AIG Commod-
 ity Index (DJ-AIGCI),
 325–327
 Commodity Index Weight,
  326
 comparison, problems, 351
 liquidity weighting, 331
 returns
  calculation, 326
  distribution, 327

Downgrade risk, 580, 648
Downside risk, 344
 exposure, 349
Drawdowns, 116, 474
Druckenmiller, Stanley, 171
Due diligence, checklist/execu-
 tive summary, 128–134
Duracell Corporation, MBO,
 431–432
Dusak, K., 279

Early stage venture capital, 412
Earnings before interest and
 taxes plus deprecia-
 tion and amortiza-
 tion (EBITDA), 424
Economic value added (EVA),
 431, 449
 formula, 685
 principles, 684–685
EDGAR filings, 48
Edwards, Franklin, 73, 79,
 183, 358
Efficient asset classes, inefficient asset classes (contrast), 9–10
Efficient capital markets, theory, 524
Efficient frontier. *See* Bonds;
 Stocks
 Barclay Agriculture CTAs,
  inclusion, 369
 Barclay CTA Index, inclusion, 368
 Barclay Currency CTAs,
  inclusion, 369
 Barclay Diversified, inclusion, 370
 Barclay Fin and Metal,
  inclusion, 370
 CRB, inclusion, 342
 distressed debt, inclusion,
  519
 DJ-AIG, inclusion, 341
 GSCI, inclusion, 340
 LBOs, inclusion, 518
 mezzanine, inclusion, 519
 MLMI, inclusion, 343
 venture capital, inclusion, 518
el Bied, Sina, 79
Elton, Edwin, 87, 357, 359

Emerging market debt, 592–
 594
 frequency distribution, 593
Employee Retirement Income
 Security of 1974 (ERISA),
 381–382
Ending net asset value (ENAV),
 252–254
Energy trading desks, 296
Entities, tax status decision,
 401
Entrepreneurial mindset,
 unlocking, 430–432
Epsilon, representation, 531
Equity
 alignment, 674
 floor, 455
 hedge, 34
 kickers, 457, 468
 market timers, 162–163
 status, 464
 tilt, 23
Equity index
 investing, 674–676
 market, size, 675–677
Equity long/short hedge funds,
 40–42, 162–163
 subindexes, 239
 usage, 145–147
Equity long/short investor,
 advertisement, 266–267
Equity market-neutral hedge
 funds, statistical arbi-
 trage hedge funds (rela-
 tionship), 157–158
Erb, Claude, 343
Euroland, birth, 344
Europe Australia and Far
 East (EAFE) index, 85
European binary credit option,
 596–597
Event risk, 191–202, 515
 exposure, 310–312
Event-driven hedge funds, 51
 investing pattern, 152–153
Event-driven strategies, 45
Excess returns, measurement,
 686
Exchange for physicals, 290
Executive summary, usage,
 391–392

Exit plan/strategy, usage, 397

External credit enhancement, 628

ExxonMobil invested capital, usage, 297

Ezra, D. Don, 675

Fabozzi, Frank J., 597

Fair value, determination, 525

Fama, Eugene, 141

Fat tail, usage, 145, 663

Federal Reserve Bank of New York, 222

Feeley, Jef, 494

Financial assets, arbitrage, 290

Financial futures, 289–292

Financial markets, hedge funds (impact), 79–80

Financial projections, importance, 396

Financial Times Stock Index (FTSE)

index, 306

negative correlation, 307

prices, dollar conversion, 278

Financials markets, managed futures (usage), 365–366

Financing. *See* Bridge financing; Mezzanine financing

amount, determination, 396–397

stage, 410–414

tranches, 429

FINEX, 289

Fire sale, 495

Firms, management, 446–447

First loss position, 622, 626–627

First loss tranche, 614

Fixed income arbitrage, 35, 52–55

hedge funds, 154

Food for Oil program, 312

Foreign currency, 292–294

Forjan, James, 682

Forstmann Little & Co., 422

Franks, Julian, 689

Free option, 437

issue, 251

Friends and family (F&F), investors, 411

Froot, Kenneth, 305, 314

Fund of funds (FOF), 35

frequency distribution, 162, 662

index, 238

manager, 167

Funding requirements, cash (raising), 560

Fung, William, 74, 80, 84, 92, 136, 137, 166, 172, 181, 182, 184

Futures commission merchant (FCM), 220

Futures contract, purchase, 287

Futures margin, cash deposit, 306

Futures prices, spot prices (relationship), 288–296

Gap, Inc. (LBO candidate), 441–442

Gelbtuch, Howard, 7

General partners, 560

activities, restrictions, 388

Generalized Autoregressive Conditional Heteroscedasticity (GARCH) models, 66

Generally accepted accounting principles (GAAP), 552

Gibson, Roger, 313

Gillan, Stuart, 682

Global loan defaults, 625

Global macro hedge funds, 35, 67–68

frequency distribution, 160–161

Goetzmann, William N., 73, 75, 77, 80, 98, 182, 183, 230, 231, 254

Goh, Jeremy, 688

Goldman, Sachs & Co. and Financial Risk Management Ltd., 72, 74, 76, 101

Goldman Sachs & Co., 309

Goldman Sachs Commodity Index (GSCI)

benchmark, 322–325

Commodity Group Weights, 323

construction, 323

examination, 285–288

Excess Return Index, 320–321

liquidity weighting, 331

physical weights, 323–324

return distributions, 324

Total Return Index, 320–321

usage, 311–312

Gompers, Paul, 381, 382, 517, 518, 526–528, 546, 551

Governance style investing, 689–691

Government agencies, decline (replacement), 399

Government National Mortgage Association (GNMA) mortgage-backed certificates, financial futures contract (introduction), 356

Graham, Benjamin, 679

Greenspan, Alan, 222

Greer, Robert, 4, 309, 313, 330

Grinold, Richard, 244

Gross domestic product (GDP), 43

Group of Five hedge funds, 225–226

Gruber, Martin, 87, 357, 359

Halpern, Philip, 307

Harvey, Campbell, 343

Hawkins, Jennifer, 678, 681, 682

Hayt, Gregory, 612, 627

Headline risk, 199–202

Hedge fund incentive fees, 251–252

data/results, 255–263

option theory, relationship, 252–255

performance statistics, 255

structure, explanation, 266

Hedge fund indexes, 236–244

construction, issues, 230–236

data biases, 232–233

diversification, 243–244

managed futures, inclusion, 238

performance, 238–240

Hedge fund indexes (*Cont.*)
 stock indexes, correlation,
  240–242
 illustration, 241
 summary, 237
 turnover, 238
Hedge fund investments
 markets, 110–111
 program, establishment, 71
 strategies, 80–95
  documentation, 111
 styles, 110
 types, 123
Hedge fund managers, 480–
  481
 administrative review, 121–
  122
 advisory committee, impact,
  126
 benchmark, establishment,
  112–113
 capacity, 114–115
 civil/criminal actions, 121
 clients, 127
 competitive advantage, 113
 due diligence, 97
  questions, 98–104
 employee turnover, 121–122
 fees, 123–124
 inattention, 272
 intelligence
  impact, 271–272
  reasons, 102–104
 investment
  objective, 99–100
  process, 100–102
  strategy, 110–115
 legal review, 123–126
 leverage, limitation, 120
 minimum net worth/earn-
  ing power require-
  ment, imposition, 141
 organization, 106–107
 ownership, 107
 performance review, 115–118
 portfolio position, 113–114
 references
  checklists, 134
  checks, 126–127
  registrations, 108
  regulatory actions, 121

 risk exposure, 165
 risk officer, selection, 120–
  121
 statistical data, 116–117
Hedge fund of funds (Hedge
  FOF), 68–69
 hedge fund strategies, 161–
  162
 return distribution, 663
 usage, 84–91
Hedge Fund Research Inc.
  (HFRI)
 convertible arbitrage, 259–
  260
 databases, usage, 256
 data/results, 255–263
 equity hedge, 257–258
 merger arbitrage, 261–262
Hedge fund strategies, 40–69
 diversification, 658
 equity understanding, 270–
  271
 risks, 139
Hedge funds
 administration, checklist, 133
 attorneys, payment/training,
  203
 benchmarks, 229
 categories, 34–35
 CDOs, 643
 counting, 216
 data, biases, 185, 234
 excess returns, 193
 fees, 236–238
 history, 36–39
 industry, growth, 38–39
 insurance risk, display, 163–
  166
 introduction, 31–34
 investability, 235–236
 Investment Advisers Act
  of 1940 regulations,
  217–219
 investment potential, 229–
  230
  comparison, 269
 legal review, checklist, 133–
  134
 management list, 115
 market exposure, 529

 market risk, display, 145–
  149, 162–163
 organization, 105–106
 performance
  data, checklist, 130–131
  persistence, 76–79
  withdrawals, impact, 117
  pricing, issues, 117–118
  private equity, relationship,
   566–567
  quotes (Top Ten), 265
  registration, benefits, 218
  regulation, 203
  return distributions, 135,
   141–162
  returns, serial correlation, 78
  risk, 169
   checklist, 132–133
   review, 118–121
  strategic review, checklist, 129–130
  structural review, 104–109
  studies, review, 136–141
  style, usage, 192
  subscription amount, 125–126
  universe, size, 230–232
Henker, Thomas, 84, 172, 243
Hensel, Chris, 313
Hertz Corporation, buyout,
  422, 464
 debt financing, 465
High-net-worth individuals, contractual provisions, 387
High-yield assets, economic
  exposure, 634
High-yield bonds, 586–587
 credit spread, 583
 default rates, 581
 downside tail, 663
 frequency distribution, 587,
  664
 interest payments, 649
 low quality debt, percentage, 479
 market value, 632
 pool, concentration, 661
 ratings migration, demonstration, 581
High-yield financing, 568
High-yield investments, 584
Hill, Joanne, 23, 26

Ho, Ho, 197, 686
Horvitz, Jeffery, 8
Hoskisson, Robert, 430, 434
Hot money, 659
Howley, Christopher, 657, 658
Hsieh, David, 74, 80, 84, 92, 136, 137, 166, 172, 181, 182, 184
Hurricane Katrina, impact, 299
Hurricane Rita, impact, 122

Ibbotson, Roger G., 73, 75, 77, 80, 182, 230, 231, 254
IBP buyout, 450–451
Idiosyncratic process risks, elimination, 102
IFCT bonds
   binary credit call options, 599
   binary credit put option, 598
Index managers, ranking, 675
Indexed assets, growth, 676
Individual managed accounts, 353
Inflation
   change, stocks/bonds/commodities (correlation), 308
   correlation, 334
   managed futures, correlation, 360
   protection, 333–335
   rate, stocks/bonds/commodities (correlation), 307
   stocks/bonds/commodities, correlation, 337
Ingersoll, Jr., Jonathan, 254
Initial margin, 282
Initial public offerings (IPOs), 383, 410, 528, 545
   benefits, 397–398
   delay, problems, 461
   discouragement, 503
Institutional equity ownership, 677
Institutional investors
   cutting-edge investments, 553
   investment reasons, 588–590
   portfolio rebalance, 560

securities, private issuance, 615
stocks, sale (problems), 677
Institutional Limited Partners Association, 527
Institutional portfolios, strategic shifts, 560
Insurance
   companies, mezzanine lenders, 468
   premium, 154
   proceeds, 474–475
Intellectual property rights, discussion, 393–394
Interest rate parity theorem, 293
Internal corporate control systems, failure, 671–674
International Derivatives and Swaps Association (ISDA), 604
   agreement, 603
International Monetary Market, 356
International stocks, downside protection, 347–348
Investable commodity futures indexes, 342
Investcorp Management Services, 656
Investment adviser
   definition, 215
   registration, issues, 218–219
Investment Advisers Act of 1940, 215–219
   flowchart, 219
   Rule 203 (b)(3)-2, 217–218
   Section 203 (b)(3), 216
   Section 203A (1), 215–216
   Section 205, 251
Investment Company Act of 1940, 212–215, 400–401
   3(c)(1)/3(c)(7) exemptions, 466
   amendment, 563
   flowchart, 214
   review, 214–215
   Section 3(c)(1), 212
   Section 3(c)(7), 212–213
   impact, 213–214
Investment grade bonds
   default rates, 581

ratings migration, demonstration, 581
Investments. *See* Hedge fund investments
   discovery, inability, 266–267
   ideas, source, 114
   program, hedge funds (inclusion question), 71–76
   securities, 111–112
   tangible nature, 305
   types, restrictions, 388
   vehicle, diversification, 658
Investor secondary market, 560–562
Investors, venture capitalist (relationship), 386–387
Irrational exuberance, 479
Irwin, Scott, 358, 359
Ix, Raymond, 328

J Curve Effect, 407, 438–439
Jacobs, Bruce, 60
Jaeger, Lars, 12
Jaffe, Austin, 7
Jensen, Greg, 22
Jensen, Michael, 424, 447, 670, 673
Johnson-Harris, Sandra, 657, 658
Joint CEO/chairman role, 674
Jones, Alfred W., 98
Jorion, Philippe, 37, 166, 190, 244
JP Morgan EMBI Index, 593

Kahn, Ronald, 244
Kansas City Board of Trade, 355
Kaplan, Paul, 313
Karpoff, Jonathan, 682
Kat, Harry, 79, 197
Kicker, inclusion, 456
Kingdon Capital Management, LLC, 225
Kohlberg Kravis Roberts & Co. (KKR), 420–422
Kohler, Kenneth E., 612
Koksal, Meric, 23, 26
Krail, Robert, 537, 547
Krantz, Matt, 415
Krukemyer, Terry, 358

Kurtosis, 140
  definition, 510
  incorporation, 199
  negative value, 144
  value, 147, 150, 156, 513

Lagged betas, 547
Lake, Rick/Ronald, 432
Lamm, Jr., R. McFall, 91
Land barons, 6, 380–381
Large-cap stock indexes, 535
Late stage/expansion venture
  capital, 412–413
Lauricella, Tom, 646, 647
Learned, Michelle, 244
Lease rates, 295
Leptokurtosis, 140
Lerner, Josh, 381, 382, 387,
  517, 518, 526, 528
Leveraged bank loans, 587–
  591
Leveraged buyouts (LBOs), 379
  appeal, 426
  benchmarks, 532
  candidate, profile, 440–442
  capital, commitment, 421
  company, corporate gover-
    nance paradigm (change),
    448
  equity percentage, 423
  example, 424–428
  fees, 437–438
  financing, 426, 428
    tracking, 427
  firms, J curve, 439
  frequency distribution, 513–
    514
  gap, mezzanine financing
    (bridge), 463–466
  history, 419–423
  introduction, 419
  investment value, 505
    size, impact, 506
  multiperiod   regression
    analysis, 541
  performance, 504–507, 562
  returns, 540
  risks, 444–446
  single-period   regression
    analysis, 534

turnaround strategies, 434–
  436
  arbitrage, 294
  markets, managed futures
    (usage), 364–365
  value creation process, 428–
    436
Leveraged buyouts (LBOs) funds
  design, 436–437
  structures, 436–439
  types, examination, 506
Leveraged fallouts, 445, 489
Leveraged loans
  frequency distribution, 591,
    664
  high-yield bonds, compar-
    ison, 570
  increase, 567–571
  institutional investors, par-
    ticipation, 589
  market, investor involve-
    ment, 570
  mezzanine debt/high-yield
    bonds, comparison, 460
  secondary trading, 568
Levine, Lawrence M., 463
Levitt, Arthur, 222
Levy, Kenneth, 60
Lhabitant, Francois-Serge, 34,
  244
Liang, Bing, 73, 98, 137,
  172, 181, 182, 231
Liew, Jimmy, 73, 183
Liew, John, 537, 547
Limited liability companies,
  402
Limited partnerships, 400–401
  establishment, 450
  interests, 660
  venture funds, 401
Lipin, Steven, 398
Liquidation bias, 233
Liquidity, absence, 499
Lo, Andrew, 181
Loan capacity, increase, 624
Lock-up periods, 659
  usage, 124–125
London Interbank Offered
  Rate (LIBOR), 463–
  465, 651
  basis points, level, 656

calculation, 625, 631
connection, 600
earning, 650
interest payment, 620
payment, 616, 632–633
range, 590
usage, 467, 567
London Metals Exchange
  (LME), 325
London Stock Exchange, 307,
  557
Long-only constraint, 82
Long-only investing, inexpe-
  rience, 268–269
Long-rate GDP measurement,
  309
Long-Term Capital Manage-
  ment (LTCM), 36–38,
  510
  crisis, 38, 191–192
  leverage, perspective, 223–
    224
  rescue, 222
  working paper, 166
Long-term ERP, measure-
  ment, 15
Long-term investment horizon, 471
Loomis, Carol, 36
Low-liquidity strategies, 23
Lu, Sa, 197
Lummer, Scott, 313
Lynch, Peter, 512

Ma, Cindy, 359
MacKmin, David, 7
Maginn, John, 244
Maintenance margin, 283
Malatesta, Paul, 682
Malkiel, Burton, 182
Managed futures, 353
  downside protection, sum-
    mary, 373
  empirical research, 357–360
  history, 354–357
  investment potential, 269
  portfolio context, 367–371
  return distributions, 360–
    367
Managed pricing, 526

Management buyouts (MBOs),
422
MAR, 239
MAR/CISDM, performance,
238
Marginal utility, increase, 245
Market
lease rate, 277
risk, 17
segmentation, 20–21
timers, 43–44
timing, 40
frequency distribution, 149
volatility, 659
Market direction hedge funds,
34, 40–45
Market risk hedge funds, 162–
163
Market value arbitrage CDO,
632–634
Market value CDO, equity
tranche (expected return),
633
Market-neutral hedge funds,
60–61
long/short market behavior,
157
Market-timing hedge funds,
148–149
Markowitz, Harry, 7
Marquette Ventures, 409
Martellini, Lionel, 79
Martorelli, Juan Carlos, 657,
658
Master trust, 269–270
account, 106
Mayer, Colin, 689
McCarthy, David, 358, 359
McEnally, Richard, 74, 183,
184
McGee, Suzanne, 415
McManus, Brian, 648
Mean-variance portfolio, 199
Meckling, William, 447, 670
Menn, Joseph, 404
Merchant banking, 450–452
Merger arbitrage, 48–50, 166
frequency distribution, 152
hedge funds, 150–152
Metals markets, managed
futures (usage), 365–366

Mezzanine debt
board representation, 471
borrower restrictions, 471
collateral, absence, 472
common equity, cost reduction, 473
company/borrower
advantages, 472–473
earnings/risk, comparison,
514–515
equity dilution, reduction,
472–473
financing comparison, 459–
460
flexibility, 472
high equity-like returns, 470–
471
instant returns, 471
investment value, 508
investor advantages, 470–471
investors, 466–475
J curve, impact, 458–459
managed pricing, evidence,
550
market, access, 565
maturity, lengthening, 472
offering, terms, 473
overview, 455–460
pay in kind, 472
payment priority, 471
performance, 507–508
popularity, 464
repayment schedule, 471
returns, 458
semiequity, 472
Mezzanine financing, 414–
415, 456, 532
examples, 460–466
expense, 467
frequency distributions, 515
multiperiod regression
analysis, 543
return expectations, 457–458
single-period regression analysis, 535
Mezzanine funds, 466–469
investors, 469
risk lenders, 468
Mezzanine lenders, 469–470
Mezzanine stage, 413–414
Mezzanine tranche, 635

Middle market
phenomenon, 468
vehicle, 457
Milgrim, Michael, 7
Milken, Michael, 420
Miller, Merton, 4
Modern portfolio theory
(MPT), 84
Modigliani, Franco, 4
Moix, Pierre-Yves, 245
Moody's Investor Services,
586–587, 648
Moore Capital Management,
Inc., 225
Moran, Matt, 242
Mortgage-backed securities
(MBSs), 54–55
Mount Lucas Management
Index (MLMI), 328–330
benchmark, usage, 361–
362, 372
composition, 329
passive futures index, 361
returns distribution, 330
strategy, average return,
362
MSCI EAFE index, 306, 307
exception, 308
Multimoment optimization,
196–199
illustration, 201
Multimoment portfolio, con-
struction, 199
Multiperiod pricing effects,
537–538
Mutual funds, unit sales, 205

Naik, Narayan, 77
Naive trading strategy, 367
NASDAQ, 557
100 Index, 291
composite index, 503
comparison, 385
index, 530, 533
regression, 534
R-square measure, 548
shares, listing, 563
stock market, 540
National Association of Securities Dealers (NASD),
authority, 210

National Futures Association (NFA), 108
National Securities Markets Improvement Act of 1996, 32
Nationally recognized statistical rating organization (NRSRO), 581, 583, 614
Natural resources companies, 280–282
Neal, Robert, 584
Nesbitt, Stephen, 683
Net asset value (NAV), 254, 659
New York Board of Trade, 355
New York Coffee, Sugar, and Cocoa Exchange (merger), 355
New York Cotton Exchange, 289
  merger, 355
New York Mercantile Exchange (NYMEX), 355
New York Stock Exchange, 557
  one vote per share rule, adoption, 680
  shares, listing, 563
  trading, initiation, 313
Nguyen, Peter, 278
Nicholas, Joseph G., 34
Niederhoffer, Victor, 189
  trading strategy, 190
Nikkei 225 Stock Index, 291
No-default scenario, 631
Nonlinear return distributions, 21
Nonsynchronous pricing, absence, 537
Non-U.S. Treasury fixed income market, 584
Normal backwardation (backwardation), Contango (contrast), 296–302

Obligation acceleration/default, 604
Office of the Comptroller of the Currency (OCC), 222
Office of Thrift Supervision (OTS), 222

One-factor regression model, 530
  results, 533–537
One-period regression results, 533–537
OPEC agreements, impact, 311
Operating efficiency, LBO impact, 428–430
Operations/operating history, importance, 395–396
Opportunistic hedge funds, 35
  investing, 81–83
  managers, 159–160
  strategies, 67–69
Opportunistic investors, 488
Option-adjusted spread (OAS), 55
Outside service providers, 108–109
Overcollateralization, 627, 657
Over-the-counter (OTC) derivatives, 224
Over-the-counter (OTC) market, company listing, 571

Pacelle, Mitchell, 226, 646, 647
Park, James, 77, 84, 98, 102, 172, 183, 231, 243, 358
Participation bias, 233
Passive investing, 675
Passive investors, 488
Passive trading strategy, 367
Payment dates, difference, 649–650
Payment failure, 604
Payment-in-kind (PIK), 456
  provision, inclusion, 459
Peer group (outperforming), failure risk, 27
Pension funds, decline (replacement), 399
Performance, measurement risk, 184–190
Performance-based compensation, 446
Periodicity, differences, 649
Peskin, Michael, 73, 77
Peters, Carl C., 359
Petsch, Melanie, 345
Pittman, Mark, 641, 643

Platykurtosis, 140
Polynomial goal programming, 197–199
Portable alpha, 88–91
Portfolios. *See* Concentrated portfolios
  frequency distribution, 346
  NAV, 655
  returns, 199
  selection, Multiple Objective Approach, 197
  tilt, 23
Potter, Mark, 359, 374
Prepackaged bankruptcy filing, 485
President's Working Group on Financial Markets, The, 36, 37
  impact, 222–225
Primack, Dan, 643
Primary secondaries, 561
Private adviser exemption, 217
Private commodity pools, 353, 354
Private equity, 379
  auction market, 554–555
  benchmarks, 532
  analysis, 533–545
  CDO, 643–644
  club deals, 555–557
  distressed debt conversion, prepackaged bankruptcy (usage), 491–492
  economics, 501
  funds, commitments, 554
  industry growth/maturation, 553–557
  manager behavior, 545–550
  market, problems, 384–385
  recycling, distressed debt (usage), 489–490
  risk-and-return spectrum, 467
  trends, 553, 562–571
Private equity performance, 501–510
  measurement, 523
  efforts, 527–529
  framework, 529–532
  problem, 524–527
Private equity returns
  correlation, 516–517

Private equity returns (*Cont.*)
distributions, 510–517
market exposure adjust-
ments, 529–531
multiperiod analysis, 537–
545
risk-adjusted formula, 530
Private investment in public
entities (PIPEs), 571–575
market, 572
Private-to-private deals, 557
Process risk, 102, 169–172
Product, description, 393
Profit-sharing fees, 546
Public commodity pools, 353–
354
Purcell, David, 98

Qualified Eligible Participant
(QEP), 221–222
Qualified purchasers, 32
introduction, 213
Qualifying affiliate guaran-
tees, 605
Qualifying guarantees, 605

Ramping up period, 634
Rating migrations, 581–582
Ravenscraft, David, 74, 183,
184
Rawls III, S. Warte, 284
Real assets, pattern, 309
Real estate, 6–7
mezzanine finance, usage, 466
qualification, 305
Realized risk premiums, 16
Redemption calls, 194
Redemptions, usage, 124–125
Registration statements, Secu-
rities Act of 1933 delin-
eation, 205
Regression equations, 530
multiperiod extension, 538
Regression models, 62
Regulation D, 206–210, 571
Regulatory capital, reduction,
623–624
Reinhard, Charles, 15
Relative value arbitrage, 63–66
short volatility strategies,
158–159

Relative value managers, 64
Rendleman, Richard, 254
Rentzler, Joel, 87, 357, 359
Reorganization plan, 485
Reprise Capital Corp., 410
Repudiation/moratorium, 605
Reserve account, 628
Restructuring, 604
Return on assets (ROA) measures,
improvement, 624–625
Return on equity (ROE) mea-
sures, improvement, 624–
625
Returns
correlation matrix, 661
private equity, impact, 562
Reuters/Jefferies CRB Futures
Price Index, 327–328
Revenue growth, assumptions,
391
Revolving credits (revolvers),
588
Ring, Alfred, 7
Ringgit, crash, 80
Risk
arbitrage, 45
budgeting, 85–88
mapping/measurement,
172–175
preferences, 253
Risk management, 118–120,
135, 169
implications, 162–167
risk, 177–180
Risk-based capital
maintenance, 624
reduction, 623–624
Risk-free arbitrage, preven-
tion, 89
Risk-free discount rate, 253
Risk-neutral valuation prop-
erty, inference, 253
RJR Nabisco Inc., purchase,
421
Road show, prolongation, 572
Roll yield, impact, 318–320
Rosansky, Victor, 279
Ross, Stephen, 254
Rossi, Stefano, 689
Rotenberg, Jason, 22
R-square measure, 535–536

Rubin, Robert, 222
Rubinstein, Martin, 254
Rule 10b-5, 211
Rule 501, 206–208
Rule 506, 206–208
Russell 1000 Index, 291, 530,
532, 533
Russell 2000 Index, 306, 533
Russell Investment Group, 23,
75
Russian government/bond
default, 53, 67, 592

Safe harbor provisions, 466
Salas, Caroline, 440
Salomon Brothers Bankruptcy
Index, 595
Salomon Brothers High-Yield
Cash Pay Index, 588
Salomon Smith Barney High
Yield Cash Pay Index,
306
Satyanarayan, Sudhakar, 314
Savanayana, Uttama, 358
Schilit, W. Keith, 381, 403,
409, 412, 445
Schneeweis, Thomas, 72, 73,
77, 137, 358, 359, 374
Scholes, Myron, 253
Second tranche, 635
face value, 626
Secondary buyout to buyout,
case study, 559
Secondary buyouts, 557–560
growth (Europe), 558
Secondary private equity funds,
561
Secondary private equity mar-
ket, 557–562
Securities
initial sale, 1933 Act (Sec-
tion 5a), 204–206
shorting, difference, 268–
269
Securities Act of 1933, 203–
210
flowchart, 209
hedge fund manager inter-
pretation, 208
Section 2(a)(1), 204
Section 4(2), 206, 207

Securities Act of 1933 (*Cont.*)
Section 5(a), 204–206
Section 17, 208–210, 211
Securities and Exchange Commission Act of 1934, 680
Securities and Exchange Commission (SEC), 31
authority, 224
delegation, 210
registration statement, filing, 353–354, 563
Rule 14a-8, 680–681
Rule 144A, 616
Securities Exchange Act of 1934, 210–211
Section 12(g)(1)(A)&(B), 214
Seed capital, 411–412
Segal, David, 190
Selection biase, contrary argument, 232
Semi-strong efficient market, 9
Senior creditors, negotiations, 473–475
Senior lenders, mezzanine lenders, 469–470
Senior secured debt, ceiling, 455
Senior tranches, payment, 627
Service
description, 393
providers, 126–127
Shareholder Proposal Rule, 680
Shareholders
decision-making authority, delegation, 446
replacement, LBO firm (impact), 447
Shareowner, shareholder (contrast), 679–680
Sharpe, William, 7, 74, 136, 172, 244
Sharpe ratio, 586
achievement, 181
improvement, 372–374
usage, 663
Shearmur, Malcolm, 231
Short put option, payoff, 165
Short rebate, negotiation, 57
Short selling, 40

frequency distribution, 148
Short selling hedge funds, 44–45, 162–163
Short volatility
basis, 186
investment strategy, 189
risk, 119, 195–196
Short-selling hedge funds, performance, 147–148
Siegel, Laurence, 313
Siklos, Richard, 493
Silberstein, Kurt, 197
Single-period regression analysis, multiperiod regression analysis (comparison), 544
Single-sourced deals, 554
Single-tranche CDOs, 644–645
Sinquefield, Rex, 343
Sirmans, C.F., 7
Skew, negative/positive values, 144
Skew measurement, 663
Skewness, 140
definition, 510
incorporation, 199
Skill-based investing, 145
access, 353
popularity, 344
Small Business Investment Company (SBIC), creation, 381
Small Business Investment Incentive Act of 1980, 563
Small-cap stocks, large-cap stocks contrast (cumulative excess returns), 688
Smith, Clifford, 254
Smith, George David, 432
Smith, Michael, 682
Smithson, Charles, 284, 612, 626
Soros, George, 171
Special purpose corporations (SPCs), 614
Special purpose vehicles (SPVs), 614, 653–655
Specialized startup biotech firms, 408
Spillover effects, 678

Spot prices
impact, 316–317
Spread compression, 650
Spread enhancement, 627–628
Spread product
market, 584
Spread products, 640
Springing subordination, 474
Spurgin, Richard, 72, 137, 358, 359, 374
St. Onge, Jeff, 405
Stale pricing, 526
managed pricing, contrast, 545–550
Standard & Poor's 500 (S&P500)
index, 291, 532–533
monthly returns, 179
stocks
comparison, 89
index, 502
underperformance, 19
value, 90
VaR calculation, 179
Standard & Poor's rating methodology, 657
Starks, Laura, 682
Startup company
J curve, 414
lifecycle, 414
Startup management team, usage, 394–395
Startup venture, market potential, 392–393
Statistical arbitrage (stat arb), 110
Statistical arbitrage (stat arb) hedge fund, 35, 62–63
Statistical tests, 200
Staum, Jeremy, 77, 84, 102, 172, 243
Stock indexes, arbitrage, 292
Stocks
average return, 335
efficient frontier, 339
managed futures, downside risk protection, 371–374
returns, volatility, 336
Storage costs, 295
Story credits, 457

Strategic allocations, tactical allocations (contrast), 8–9
Strategic asset allocation (SAA), tactical asset allocation (contrast), 17–19
Strategic review, 110–115
Strategy definition, 233–235
Strathdee, Mike, 415
Strongin, Steve, 345
Structured note
    GSCI call option, inclusion, 286
    GSCI futures contract, inclusion, 287
Style drift, 233–235
Subordination, 474, 626–627
Summed beta, 538, 540
Super asset classes, 4–7
Survivorship bias, 182
Swensen, David, 3
Syndicated loan, offering, 590
Synthetic arbitrage CCO, CTS (inclusion), 644
Synthetic arbitrage CDOs, 634, 643
Synthetic balance sheet CDO, 612, 617–622
    CDS, inclusion, 623
Synthetic balance sheet CLO
    net gain/loss, 621
    structure, 617

Takeout provisions, 475
Takeover, distressed debt (usage), 492–494
Tass database, usage, 231
Technology, bubble, 385
Tequila Crisis, 688
Time (gap), mezzanine financing (bridge), 460–462
Total return credit swap, 600–601
Total return swap
    mechanics, 603–605
    notional value, 620
Toxic PIPE, 573
Tradable shares, liquidity, 565
Transparency risk, 175–177
Tripp, Chapman, 474

Tudor Investment Corporation, 225
Tuna funds, 239, 240
Tuttle, Donald, 244

Underlying collateral, default risk, 646–648
Underlying commodity, purchase, 279–280
Unfunded CDOs, 645
    tranche structure, 645
United States/France, tax treaty, 105
Up/down markets, multiperiod regression analysis, 549
Urias, Michael, 73, 77
U.S. Treasury bills (T-bills)
    return, subtraction, 528
    usage, 306
U.S. Treasury bonds, credit spreads, 582
Utility maximization equation, solution, 246

Valdes, Charles, 680
Value at Risk (VaR), 177–180
    calculations, additivity, 180
Van Hedge, 239
Vance, Cyrus R., 494
Varangis, Panos, 314
Variation margin, 282–283
Venture capital
    case study, 414–417
    commitments, sources, 399
    comparison, 536
    fees, 388–390
    financing
        increase, 382–383
        sources/uses, 398–400
    firms, 470
    FOF, 405–406
    frequency distribution, 511–513
    fund, life cycle, 406–407
    history, 380–386
    industry
        geography, specialization, 409
        specialization, 407–410

    structure, 398–410
    introduction, 379
    investing (1990-2005), 383
    investment
        stages, 504
        value, 503
        vehicles, 400–406
    LBOs, contrast, 442–444
    multiperiod regression analysis, 539
    performance, 501–504
    returns, 384
    single-period regression, 533
    special situations, 409–410
    uses, 400

Venture capitalist
    remuneration, 389
    role, 386–390
Venture Economics database, data (usage), 502
Vintage year, concept, 439
Viskanta, Tadas, 343
Volatility event, 186
Vulture investors, 480–481

Wahal, S., 682
Walking, Ralph, 682
Ward, Barry, 359
Warsager, Randy, 307
Warwick Ben, 359
Waterfall
    formation, 614
    structure, 615
Weighted average rating factor (WARF), weighted average spread (WAS) contrast, 651
Weisman, Andrew, 186, 525
White, Ted, 686
Wirth, Greg, 451, 452
Wright, Mike, 430, 434

Yield curve risk, 650–651
Young, Sheffield, 474

Zero-risk premium, 15
Zero-sum game, 269
Zulauf, Carl, 358, 359